Characteristics of Emotional and Behavioral Disorders of Children and Youth

ELEVENTH EDITION

Characteristics of Emotional and Behavioral Disorders of Children and Youth

James M. Kauffman
University of Virginia

Timothy J. Landrum
University of Louisville

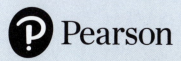

330 Hudson Street, NY, NY 10013

Director and Portfolio Manager: Kevin Davis
Content Producer: Janelle Rogers
Development Editor: Linda Bishop
Media Project Manager: Lauren Carlson
Portfolio Management Assistant: Anne McAlpine
Executive Field Marketing Manager: Krista Clark
Executive Product Marketing Manager: Christopher Barry
Procurement Specialist: Carol Melville
Full Service Project Management: Thistle Hill Publishing Services, LLC
Cover Designer: Carie Keller
Cover Image: Getty Images
Composition: Cenveo® Publisher Services

Credits and acknowledgments borrowed from other sources and reproduced, with permission, in this textbook appear on the appropriate page within the text.

Every effort has been made to provide accurate and current Internet information in this book. However, the Internet and information posted on it are constantly changing, so it is inevitable that some of the Internet addresses listed in this textbook will change.

Library of Congress Cataloging-in-Publication Data

Kauffman, James M., author. | Landrum, Timothy J., author.
Characteristics of emotional and behavioral disorders of children and
    youth / James M. Kauffman, University of Virginia, Timothy J. Landrum,
    University of Louisville.
Eleventh edition. | New York, NY : Pearson, [2018] | Includes
    bibliographical references and index.
LCCN 2017007939| ISBN 9780134449906 (hardcover) | ISBN
    0134449908 (hardcover)
LCSH: Behavior disorders in children. | Emotional problems of
    children.
Classification: LCC RJ506.B44 K38 2018 | DDC 618.92/89—dc23
LC record available at https://lccn.loc.gov/2017007939

1   17

ISBN-10: 0-13-444990-8
ISBN-13: 978-0-13-444990-6

BRIEF CONTENTS

CONTENTS

PART 3   Types of Disordered Behavior   149

8   Attention and Activity Disorders   151

9   Conduct Disorder   171

PREFACE

Like its earlier editions, this book is an introductory text about special education for children and youth with emotional or behavioral disorders (EBD). We use the acronym EBD throughout the book. EBD may be either singular or plural as we use it (we do not often refer to EBDs). The children and youth to whom we refer are identified in federal laws and regulations as having **emotional disturbance** (ED). We prefer EBD because it has become the dominant current term in the field in spite of federal language.

Because EBD is commonly observed in children and youth in all special education categories, the book will also be of value in courses dealing with the characteristics of intellectual and developmental disability (formerly called mental retardation), learning disabilities, or students in cross-categorical special education. Students in school psychology, educational psychology, or abnormal child psychology may also find the book useful.

Several comments are necessary to clarify our intentions in revising this book. First, developmental processes are important in our understanding of the problem of EBD. We have tried to integrate the most relevant parts of the vast and scattered literature on child development and show their relevance to understanding the children and youth who have these disorders. In struggling with this task, we have attempted not only to summarize what is known about why disorders occur but also to suggest how emotional and behavioral development can be influenced for the better, particularly by educators. Second, in concentrating primarily on research and theory grounded in reliable empirical data, we have revealed our bias toward social learning principles. We believe that if we examine the literature with a willingness to be swayed by empirical evidence rather than ideology, then a social learning bias is understandable. Third, this book is not, by any stretch of the imagination, a comprehensive treatment of the subject. An introductory book must leave much unsaid and many loose ends that need tying up. Unquestionably, the easiest thing about preparing this book was to let it fall short of saying everything, with the hope that readers will pursue the information in the works cited in the references and other reliable sources of information.

We have tried to address the interests and concerns of teachers and of students preparing to become teachers. Consequently, we have briefly described many interventions, particularly in the chapters in Part 3. However, we emphasize that the descriptions are cursory. This text does not provide the details of educational methods and behavioral interventions that are necessary for competent implementation by teachers. This is not *primarily* a methods or a how-to-do-it book.

NEW TO THIS EDITION

Our primary goal for this edition remains the same as for previous editions: to describe current research-based understandings of EBD in children and youth. This includes descriptions of the various ways that EBD may manifest, and an examination of historical trends and current best practice in the identification and professional response to EBD. Again, while this is not primarily a methods text, we also discuss research and resources that we hope prove helpful to professionals who work with children and youth with EBD and their families. Some of the significant changes we have made in the eleventh edition include:

First Time Offering as a Pearson Interactive eText

This is the first edition of *Characteristics of Emotional and Behavioral Disorders of Children and Youth* designed as an interactive eText. Digital features include an online glossary, point-of-use videos, and end-of-chapter assessments.

- *Videos.* Many chapters identify two to three videos that illustrate stories of students and their families, demonstrate classroom teaching and assessment practices, or provide a glimpse into the work and lives of professionals who support children and youth with emotional and behavioral disorders. Clicking on play button icons ▶ will launch the videos.

- *Self-Assessments*. Each chapter opens with a list of *learning outcomes* informing the reader of specific, results-oriented objectives to guide his or her study. Assessing mastery of these objectives is possible by clicking on the checkmark icon ✓ at the ends of chapters and taking the self-assessment quizzes.

New Content and Expanded Coverage

- Many new or updated citations are referenced in this edition including updated research findings that further support ideas and recommendations presented in various chapters. Please note that we have updated citations and information on many topics, but we have retained many citations of earlier, now classic research studies because newer findings have not refuted them.

- Several chapters have been reorganized and reordered to allow for a more logical and coherent presentation. For example, we have combined discussion of overt and covert forms of antisocial behavior into a single chapter on conduct disorder (Chapter 9). We also moved the discussion of our perspective on some basic assumptions we think teachers and others might find useful for teaching and working with children and youth with EBD to Chapter 1 (this was previously our closing chapter). We hope this provides greater context for the chapters that follow.

- The discussion of conceptual models has moved from Chapter 5 to Chapter 1, as we believe it is helpful and important for individuals to think about their own conceptual orientation to what EBD *is* as they consider the nature, causes, and appropriate responses to EBD that are discussed in subsequent chapters.

- Personal reflections in the chapters in Parts 1, 2, and 4 that do not directly involve instruction have been eliminated.

- The lengthy chapter on assessment presented in previous editions has been divided into two chapters to highlight the different purposes of assessment.

This edition is slightly shorter than the tenth. We have accomplished this reduction in overall length by striving to be comprehensive yet concise in coverage of topics, and reorganizing chapters and discussion. Most importantly, our text still urges readers to engage in self-questioning while reading. We hope this will make the reading more engaging and help students focus on important information without limiting the scope of the questions they might ask themselves or others.

ORGANIZATION OF THE TEXT

The organization of this book differs noticeably from that of most other texts. Our emphasis is on a clear description of EBD and an interpretation of research on the factors implicated in their development. We did not organize this book around theoretical models or psychiatric classifications but around basic concepts: 1) a personal statement or beginning point for teaching youngsters with EBD, along with the nature, extent, and history of the problem and conceptual approaches to it; 2) major causal factors; 3) the many facets of disordered emotions and behavior; and 4) assessment. We hope this organization encourages students to become not just good teachers but critical thinkers and problem solvers.

Part 1 begins with our perspective on where teachers of students with EBD need to start—the basic assumptions they need for their work. We also introduce the major conceptual models scholars have used to guide thinking about EBD, and we offer a description of the conceptual model that underlies the orientation of this book. Chapter 2 introduces major concepts related to definition and prevalence of EBD and historical antecedents of contemporary special education for children and youth with EBD. Chapter 3 traces the development of the field—how it grew from the disciplines of psychology, psychiatry, and public education—and summarizes major current trends.

Part 2 examines the origins of disordered behavior, with attention to the implications of causal factors for special educators. Chapter 4 discusses biological factors, Chapter 5 cultural factors, Chapter 6 the role of the family, and Chapter 7 the influence of the school. Each chapter integrates current research findings that may help us understand why children and youth acquire EBD and what preventive actions might be taken.

Types of disorders are discussed in Part 3, Chapters 8 through 13. The six chapters are organized around major behavioral dimensions derived from factor analyses of behavioral ratings by teachers and parents. Although no categorical scheme produces unambiguous groupings of all disorders, the chapters are devoted to the behavioral dimensions emerging most consistently from empirical research. Each chapter emphasizes issues germane to special education, including definitions and interventions.

Part 4 deals with procedures and problems in assessing EBD in more detail. Chapter 14 reviews the problems associated with screening student populations for risk of EBD, as well as evaluation procedures used to determine whether students are eligible for special education. Chapter 15 discusses assessment for instructional purposes and concludes with a discussion of the difficulty of assessment for the purpose of classifying disorders in ways that allow parents, educators, and other professionals to talk about EBD with a common language and understanding of the nature of the disorder.

INSTRUCTOR'S SUPPLEMENT

Instructor's Manual with Test Items

Each chapter in the Instructor's Manual contains the following: chapter focus questions, a list of key terms, test questions, learning activities, and case-based activities. Instructors can check students' basic understanding of topics by reviewing their responses in the online quizzes of the eText but use the different questions in the Instructor's Test Bank to create mid-term or final assessments.

ACKNOWLEDGMENTS

Any shortcomings of this book are our responsibility alone, but its worth has been enhanced substantially by others who have assisted us in a variety of ways. We are especially grateful to education editors Ann and Kevin Davis, Linda Bishop, and others at Pearson Education who provided guidance and technical services for this revision. We thank the reviewers of the tenth edition, who offered advance suggestions for the eleventh edition. The perceptive suggestions of Doug Carothers, Florida Gulf Coast University; Julienne Cuccio-Slichko, State University of New York at Albany; Louis Lanunziata, University of North Carolina at Wilmington; Holly Menzies, California State University, Los Angeles; and Carl R. Smith, Iowa State University resulted in substantial improvements in our work. We are also grateful to the contributors of the Personal Reflections in Part 2 for their willingness to share their knowledge and views on important questions about teaching students with various kinds of EBD. Many users of the book, both students and instructors, have given us helpful feedback over the years. We encourage those who are willing to share their comments on the book to write or call us with their suggestions.

J. M. K.
Charlottesville, VA

T. J. L.
Louisville, KY

PART 1 Point of Departure

INTRODUCTION

This book is about children and youth most people don't like. They're youngsters whose behavior arouses negative feelings in most of us and makes us want to respond with our own negative behavior or get away from them as fast as we can. In fact, the typical reaction of others, regardless of their age, is to get angry, give up, or simply withdraw to avoid unnecessary conflicts. These kids aren't usually described in sanitized language. They're more likely than most students to be described with disgust and foul language.

So, why would anyone want to teach these students? Makes you wonder! Thank goodness some people do. They care about these children and youth enough to want to work with them. They see these students' potential and want to teach them well.

These children and youth don't learn acceptable behavior unless somebody helps them. Part of the reason they don't learn without help is because of other people's reactions. These kids typically end up not only displeasing others but also making their own situations worse. They don't have many opportunities to learn or to redeem themselves in the eyes of their well-behaved peers, their parents, or their teachers because other individuals don't want to interact with them.

Emotional and behavioral problems of all types are interrelated, and few of the youngsters we're describing have just one kind of difficulty. They tend to have multiple problems. They have a real talent for getting under other people's skin, and they're skilled at lots of different ways of doing it. Some of the children and youth we're talking about are socially withdrawn, but most of them are too aggressive and have a history of being "in your face." Typically, they experience academic failure in addition to social rejection or alienation. They aren't usually popular or leaders of their peers—unless it's their antisocial peers, and then usually they're popular with their fellow misfits *because* of their antisocial behavior. Some of them are bullies, and some of them are popular *because* of their bullying. Some of them make friends initially but don't know how to keep friends.

Most of the children and youth with emotional or behavioral disorders (EBD—an abbreviation we use throughout the remainder of this book) are boys. However, an increasing percentage of them are girls.

Many of the youngsters we're considering *can* be identified in the primary grades or even before they start school, but most of them aren't. Most aren't identified for special education until they've exhibited very serious behavioral and academic problems in school for quite a while—usually for several years. Often, their problems are labeled something else for years before their EBD is recognized as such. For example, they might be called hyperactive or be said to have attention deficit–hyperactivity disorder (ADHD) before they're considered to have EBD.

Most adults choose to avoid these children and youth as much as possible because their behavior is so persistently irritating to authority figures

ENHANCEDetext
Video Connections 1.1
Watch the video "Behavior Disorders" about Nick, a student identified with EBD. Note that Nick is generally engaged in classwork and seems to have at least adequate academic skills; he just "gets in trouble" a lot.

ENHANCEDetext
Video Connections 1.2
In this video, "Schizophrenic Kids,"
you'll see kids with a very serious
disorder: childhood schizophrenia.
As Dr. Mark De Antonio of UCLA
notes in the video, these are rare
cases, but think about the level of
services and support a child and
family would need to deal with this
disorder. (https://www.youtube
.com/watch?v=PVHNGZ0Omx0)

that they seem to be asking for trouble and punishment. They're usually failures even in their own eyes. They don't get much gratification from life, and they repeatedly fall short of their aspirations. They just don't seem to understand what they need to do to get what they want *except* by acting in ways that drive other people crazy. They have disabilities, which means that their options in important aspects of daily living are highly restricted. Their behavior costs them many opportunities for gratifying social interaction and self-fulfillment.

A lot of people seem to assume that these are youngsters who should be referred to psychologists, psychiatrists, social workers, or professionals trained in mental health. Such referral may be desirable, but that's not what this book is about. What we educators have to ask about students with EBD are questions like these:

- How do we know one when we see one?
- What can teachers do to help them?
- What basic assumptions should we have about teaching and managing them?
- What teaching and management strategies are most likely to be successful?
- What should special education teachers expect as outcomes of their own work?

Thinking about EBD requires asking many questions about the way people think and behave. Imagination is required. That is, you must ask yourself questions and try out various answers—a kind of fantasy. One of the most effective strategies for learning about any topic is to make yourself try to answer the questions you ask. Once you begin asking questions, you're likely to find that the answers aren't as simple as they seemed at first.

Much of our thinking about our professional work is an internal dialogue. We imagine ourselves being asked questions about things we're supposed to know or expected to learn about. But many of the questions we can ask ourselves have no definitive answers. In some cases, we just have to say, "I don't know." Sometimes we have to be satisfied with educated guesses or personal opinions.

We begin the first chapter by summarizing some of the major ways scholars have explained both strange and commonplace behavior. These ideas guide us when we ask what basic concepts can help us most in working with students who exhibit unacceptable behavior. The way we think about things—how we go about analyzing problems and testing solutions—will have a profound effect on what we do with students. Then we give you *our* basic assumptions or concepts. However, we want you to understand that ours isn't the only way of looking at things. We just think it's the most useful one for us, at least.

Our purpose in the first chapter is to sketch out some basic assumptions and to say what we think are the most basic assumptions we need in educating children and youth with EBD. We briefly summarize four conceptual models and then a social-cognitive framework that provides the basis for our views about teaching and a view of interrelationships among causes, types of behavior, assessment, and intervention that we want you to keep in mind as you read the rest of the chapters. To the extent that our suggestions are useful, you will understand our views of good teaching as you read the rest of the chapters.

We suggest that you begin thinking about teaching students with EBD by examining expectations—not just expectations of students but also of your expectations of yourself as a teacher. Within the context of expectations, teachers must try to make sense of causal factors and their possible role in them. Professional educators also have an obligation to accomplish these tasks:

- Define and measure each student's behavior precisely enough to monitor progress and communicate that progress clearly to others.
- Design appropriate and corrective experiences for students.
- Communicate effectively with students about their behavior.
- Teach students self-control through modeling and direct instruction.
- Teach students to respect and value cultural differences.
- Focus on instruction, which is the most important business of special education.
- Remember that students are people, in many ways like us.

We offer a synopsis of our views on teaching in the first chapter because we feel it's important that every educator have a clear idea about what teachers can and should do to help students with EBD. Teaching students with EBD isn't the kind of work someone can do thoughtlessly or blindly. We don't mean to suggest that when you've thought things through you'll stop questioning yourself and others. Although we've written a statement revealing something of our own orientation to teaching, we don't consider it final or immutable. It's necessarily tentative, open to revision as we learn more about teaching and about students with special problems. In fact, we hope that reading this book will launch you on an adventure of self-questioning. We also hope you'll question the insight of our comments in the light of what you've experienced firsthand and what you've read, not only in this book but in many other sources as well. Ultimately, our hope is that you'll work toward articulating your own views on teaching particularly challenging students and that your self-questioning adventure will never stop.

As you'll see in Chapter 2, we have a very difficult problem right off the bat. Just what is EBD, anyway? As fundamental as this question might seem, we're immediately faced with an ambiguous answer and continuing controversy. And with that question still unanswered, we're faced with more questions: What's the percentage of students with EBD we might expect to find in most schools? Why should we care? As you may already have asked yourself, how can we accurately measure the extent of a problem we can't define precisely? Reading Chapter 2 should help you formulate questions about what might be required to meet the needs of students with EBD if there are as many such students as we estimate there are.

As we indicate in Chapter 3, the beginning of the field is difficult to describe precisely, partly because it's buried in the beginnings of related professions. If finding the roots of the field is difficult, predicting where it's going is even more so. We hope reading Chapter 3 will prompt you to ask many questions when you read about "new" or present-day developments: Have we heard this before? Who had this idea, and how did it work out? If this is a "recycled" idea, what's different about the way it's being presented today? Using our best logic and the facts we do have, what do we think would be the result of implementing this idea?

The questions we've posed for chapters in Part 1 are basic. But basic questions are often among the most difficult to answer. Their seeming simplicity is deceptive. Complete and satisfactory answers to them have eluded the sharpest minds for generations. As you begin reading this book, we hope you'll be curious about how researchers and teachers have tried to address these questions. And we hope you'll get excited about the questions you might ask yourself or others. Asking good questions and being reasonably skeptical of answers is part of what science is all about, in education as well as in any other field.

1 BEGINNING POINT: BASIC ASSUMPTIONS

VARIOUS WAYS OF THINKING ABOUT THE PROBLEM AND OUR IDEAS ABOUT GOOD TEACHING

Gagliar Images/Shutterstock

After reading this chapter, you should be able to:

1.1 Explain how thinking about behavior problems is linked to intervention strategies.

1.2 Briefly describe the most obvious strengths and weaknesses of four conceptual models: biological, psychoeducational, behavioral, and ecological.

1.3 Describe how you would choose a conceptual model.

1.4 Describe the major features of an integrated, social-cognitive model.

1.5 Understand the role of an effective teacher of students with EBD with regard to each of these: expectations; causes of behavior; definition, measurement, and assessment; work, play, love, and fun; direct, honest communication; self control; cultural differences; instruction; and thoughts about actual people.

1.6 Explain how causal factors, types of behavior, assessment, and intervention are interrelated in discussions of EBD.

THINKING ABOUT THE PROBLEM

People in every culture have ideas about what causes disturbing human behavior. They try to link presumed causes to procedures that they assume will eliminate, control, or prevent such behavior. We find several conceptual themes in the causes and remedies that have been suggested over the centuries. These themes have remained remarkably consistent for thousands of years. Contemporary ideas are only elaborations and extensions of their ancient counterparts. For purposes of explaining and controlling behavior, people have been seen as spiritual beings, biological organisms, individuals who are rational and emotional, and products of their environments (see Cook & Ruhaak, 2014 for introductory comments on causes).

It doesn't take professional training to see that nearly all aspects of young people's lives are fraught with potential for psychological problems. However, training in the social sciences may make people particularly aware of the multitude of possible causes of problems. Educators have always struggled with explaining human behavior—both troublesome and desirable behavior. Today we recognize so many possible causes that sorting through all of them is difficult.

For example, teachers now recognize that children and youth feel stress in everyday life and that school experiences can be particularly stressful. Recognizing that children and youth face stress, however, doesn't do much to help us understand the causes of disordered emotions or behavior or what to do about them. For most of us, some stress is good. It's one thing to recognize stress, but it's quite another thing to articulate a coherent view of how stress affects human development and to determine what kinds of stress are most debilitating. To offer another example, it's one thing to note that self-concept is an important aspect of emotional and behavioral development, but it's quite another to understand how self-esteem fits into the web of other influences on behavior.

To have more than a superficial understanding of EBD, we need a complex set of organizing principles—a *conceptual model*, or framework, for organizing and making sense of the vast array of ideas and information about causes and cures. Any simple explanation of human behavior will have its day in the popular imagination, but all such oversimplifications have a common fate: they become today's cliché and tomorrow's jest. That is, at first they're something everybody seems to say and know and accept as obvious, but later they're seen as jokes. One example from a long time ago illustrates how an oversimplified idea became a cliché and then a joke. Somebody in the early nineteenth century came up with the idea that masturbation caused insanity (see Sachs, 1905). Soon, masturbatory insanity became a cliché. (Most people thought, "Oh, yeah, the kid's gone insane because he masturbated.") Now most people see that idea as a joke—a truly preposterous notion (see Hare, 1962). An oversimplification that became popular in more recent years is that EBD is caused by stress and that finding ways to cope with stress is critical to mental health. Another oversimplification is that EBD just reflects low self-esteem.

Now, think about the difference between an oversimplification and a more complicated explanation in the case of youth violence, one of the hottest issues in the early twenty-first century. Many popular and professional journals and books tell us that violence has no single cause and no single cure; that we must integrate what we know about biological, psychological, sociological, and all other verifiable influences on behavior if we're to understand the causes of violence and address the problem effectively. This isn't simplistic. However, some articles in the popular press focus on particular explanations of violence, and sometimes they slip into oversimplification, or someone's interpretation of them does. Evolutionary psychologists study the interplay of behavior, neurochemicals, and the individual's environment—how each affects the other and how behavior has been shaped through genetic processes during human evolution. Glib statements about evolutionary psychology can be seriously misleading and be broadened to explain nearly every human emotional or behavioral problem. There's also the notion that violence is caused by lack of opportunity, but that notion by itself is an oversimplification. Opportunity is, in fact, important, but the causes of violence are more complicated than that.

BRIEF DESCRIPTIONS OF FOUR CONCEPTUAL MODELS

Alternative conceptual models of behavior (sometimes called *schools of psychology*) offer different explanations of human behavior and suggest how to change it. We present brief descriptions of the basic assumptions of four conceptual models. Keep three cautions in mind as you read:

- These descriptions are cursory, and much additional reading is required to obtain a full understanding of each model.
- The descriptions are purposely unidimensional and do not reflect the multiple perspectives that competent practitioners typically bring to bear.
- Models other than those we describe have been proposed, but we do not discuss them because so little reliable evidence supports them (e.g., the Freudian psychodynamic model and the religious view that serious behavior problems are the result of demon possession).

Our descriptions here are purposeful oversimplifications intended to highlight how conceptual models differ. Each of these models has advocates and critics. Some conceptual models are being strengthened through the gradual accumulation of scientific evidence (see Kauffman & Landrum, 2006 for a more complete description of various conceptual models; see Walker & Gresham, 2014 for evidence-based practices).

A particular model we describe might be more relevant to certain disorders than to others. For example, a **biological model** may be more relevant to schizophrenia than to conduct disorder.

Biological Model

Human behavior involves neurophysiological mechanisms. That is, a person can't perceive, think, or act without a central nervous system. One conceptual model begins with one or both of two hypotheses:

1. EBD is caused by physiological flaws.
2. EBD can be controlled through physiological interventions, such as medications.

Some writers suggest that disorders such as hyperactivity, depression, or hyperaggression are manifestations of genetic factors, brain dysfunction, brain structure, food additives, biochemical imbalance, and so on. Some suggest that EBD of most types is responsive to or most easily ameliorated by drugs, neurosurgery, or exercise or other body-based treatment. Accordingly, recognition of the underlying biological problem is assumed to be critical. However, successful treatment may or may not be aimed at resolving the physiological flaw. In many cases, we know of no way to repair or ameliorate the brain damage, genetic process, or metabolic disorder that is believed to cause the disorder. Consequently, we must be satisfied with understanding the physiological cause of the disorder and doing the best we can with treatment that involves changing the social environment.

Some management strategies are based on hypotheses about physiological processes but don't address known physiological disorders. For example, students may be given drugs to help control hyperactivity or schizophrenia, even though the physiological causes of their disorders haven't been established. Besides medications, interventions associated with a biogenic approach include diet, exercise, surgery, biofeedback, and alteration of environmental factors that exacerbate the physiological problem (see Forness, Freeman, & Paparella, 2006; Forness & Kavale, 2001; Forness, Walker, & Kavale, 2003; Konopasek & Forness, 2014; Kutcher, 2002).

Medical model has often been used as a derogatory term. It has been used to refer to special education in which medical diagnoses and psychiatric interventions are seen as more important than education. The term is sometimes still used to condemn special education for imitating medicine in any way. However, modern medicine is based on science, and "medical model" can be interpreted to mean simply a model of scientific inquiry and practice. Furthermore, biology, including the study of genetics, has important implications for understanding the causes and treatment of EBD (Cooper, 2014; Grigorenko, 2014; Mattison, 2014). Although special education is sometimes criticized as following a medical model, it is really patterned much more on law than on medicine (see Kauffman, 2007a).

Forness and Kavale (2001) proposed a *new* medical model. The new medical model refers to adopting a scientific approach to education and more closely approximating the methods of contemporary medical practice, especially medications. It isn't meant to replace but to supplement the behavioral model. The intention is to integrate behavior management and medicine, which are both based on scientific principles (see Forness et al., 2006; Konopasek & Forness, 2014).

The new medical model is worth considering in more detail. When it comes to the work of teachers, however, biological experiments can have relatively few implications for classroom practice. Teachers don't choose or alter students' genes, perform surgery, prescribe drugs, control diet, or do physical therapy. Teachers do, however, have enormous power over the social environment of the classroom as well as a significant measure of control over how they think about behavioral and emotional problems and how they act. And all of these can be done scientifically, in the best model of modern medicine. Furthermore, teachers should be aware of what medicine, particularly psychiatry, has to offer and be familiar with psychiatric terminology (Mattison, 2014).

Psychoeducational Model

The **psychoeducational model** shows concern for unconscious motivations and underlying conflicts, yet also stresses the realistic demands of everyday functioning in school, home, and community. A basic assumption of the psychoeducational model is that teachers must understand unconscious motivations if they are to deal most effectively with academic failure and misbehavior. This doesn't mean that they must focus on resolving unconscious conflicts. It means focusing on how to help the student acquire self-control through reflection and plan-ning and taking social contexts, culture, and other environmental conditions into account (see Learoyd-Smith & Daniels, 2014; O'Brennan, Furlong, O'Malley, & Jones, 2014).

Intervention based on a psychoeducational model sometimes includes therapeutic dis-cussions, or *life-space interviews*, later renamed *life-space crisis intervention*, to help youngsters understand that what they are doing is a problem, recognize their motivations, observe the consequences of their actions, and plan alternative responses to use in similar future circum-stances. Emphasis is on the youngster gaining insight that will result in behavioral change, not on changing behavior directly (see Long, Wood, & Fecser, 2001).

Ecological Model

An **ecological model** is based on concepts in ecological psychology and community psychol-ogy. In its early years, the approach also drew on the model of European *educateurs*, who work with youngsters in their homes and communities as well as their schools. The student is considered an individual enmeshed in a complex social system, both a giver and a receiver in social transactions with other students and adults in a variety of roles and settings. Emphasis is on the study of the child's entire social system, and intervention is directed, ideally, toward all facets of the student's milieu. Interventions used in ecological programs have tended to emphasize behavioral and social learning concepts and the ways in which they can be used to alter an entire social system (see Cantrell & Cantrell, 2007).

In the 1980s and 1990s, the melding of ecological concepts and social learning or behav-ioral theory was described as *ecobehavioral analysis*. An eco-behavioral analysis is an attempt to identify and use naturally occurring, functional events more skillfully and consistently to improve instruction and behavior management. If naturally occurring strategies, such as peer tutoring, can be validated as effective and applied consistently, then supportive, habilitative social systems might be built or strengthened with less reliance on artificial interventions that tend to be more costly, intrusive, temporary, and unreliable.

Behavioral Model

Two major assumptions underlie a **behavioral model**:

1. The essence of the problem is the behavior itself—what a person does.
2. Behavior is a function of environmental events—things that happen just before (**antecedents**) or right after (**consequences**) what someone does.

Nearly any maladaptive behavior is viewed as an inappropriate learned response to given circumstances; therefore, intervention should consist of rearranging antecedent events and consequences to teach more adaptive behavior. A behavioral model derives from the work of behavioral psychologists. With its emphasis on precise definition and reliable measurement, careful control of the variables thought to maintain or change behavior, and establishment of replicable cause–effect relationships, it represents a natural science approach. Interven-tions based on a behavioral model consist of choosing target responses, measuring their cur-rent level, analyzing probable controlling environmental events, and changing antecedent or consequent events until reliable changes are produced in the target behaviors (see Alberto &

Troutman, 2012; Kazdin, 2008; Kerr & Nelson, 2010; Kauffman, Pullen, Mostert, & Trent, 2011; Walker & Gresham, 2014; Walker, Ramsey, & Gresham, 2004).

CHOOSING MODELS

The challenge we face is choosing or constructing a defensible theory and using it consistently to evaluate alternative conceptual models. More simply, the challenge is to decide what's believable and what isn't and what's helpful and what isn't in understanding human behavior.

The conceptual models we have presented in brief weren't invented yesterday. They all have very old historical roots and many years of refinement, as well as present-day proponents (see Kauffman & Landrum, 2006). In our opinion, what is often referred to as social-cognitive theory provides the most believable and helpful way of looking at human behavior, including what is known as EBD. We describe that model after we make comparisons of the four models we have described so far, and in some sense it is an integration of these four models. We believe the social-cognitive model is also consistent with our opinions about good teaching and with a science of education.

Table 1.1 is our assessment of the main strengths and weaknesses of each of the four models we've described to this point.

We see several distinct options for dealing with conceptual models. First, we could adopt a single model as an unvarying theme, a template by which to judge all hypotheses and research findings. Although this option has the advantages of consistency and clarity, it is disconcerting to many careful thinkers because it assumes that everything important is defined in a particular way. Second, we could be nonevaluative. That is, we could assume that all concepts deserve the same attention and respect. This option has immediate appeal because it acknowledges that every model has both strengths and weaknesses, and it allows us to try to be unbiased. But this approach has many drawbacks. It assumes that we have no sound reasons for discriminating among ideas for particular purposes. It fosters the attitude that behavior

Table 1.1   Primary Strengths and Weaknesses of Four Conceptual Models

Model	Primary Strength	Primary Weakness
Biological	Based on reliable information about physiological processes	Teachers are not directly involved in altering physiological processes
Psychoeducational	Considers internal motivations for behavior that are often overlooked	Is supported by comparatively little empirical research
Ecological	Considers how behavior fits in its social context	Often requires control of multiple aspects of the environment
Behavioral	Based on learning and teaching, the primary focus in the classroom	Examines only observable behavior

management and education, like religion and political ideology, are better left to personal belief than to scientific scrutiny. And it leads inevitably to accepting bad ideas as having legitimacy and to witless self-contradiction. Finally, it supports fads based on little more than a bold assertion that something is true or works. Such fads are a serious impediment to progress in education (Anastasiou & Kauffman, 2011; Kauffman, 1999d, 2010c, 2011; 2014b; Kauffman & Sasso, 2006a; Kauffman, Ward, & Badar, 2016; Mostert, Kavale, & Kauffman, 2008; Sasso, 2001; Silvestri & Heward, 2016).

A third option, and the one we chose for this book, is to focus on hypotheses that can be supported or refuted by replicable and public empirical data whenever possible and careful critical thinking—ideas that lend themselves to investigation by the methods of science (see Cook, Landrum, Tankersley, & Kauffman, 2003; Crockett, 2001; Forness, 2005; Kauffman, 2011, 2014c; Kauffman & Landrum, 2006; Landrum, 2015; Landrum & Tankersley, 2004; Sasso, 2007 for elaboration). The result of this choice is that most or all of our discussion is consistent with a social-cognitive model, and useful concepts from other models are discussed as they are related to social learning.

Our choice for this book does not mean we believe there is only one way of knowing anything. However, we do believe that some ways of knowing are better than others for certain purposes. For educators who work with troubled children and youth, we believe the natural science tradition provides the firmest foundation for competent professional practice. The most useful knowledge is derived from experiments that can be repeated and that consistently produce similar results—in short, information obtained from investigations conducted according to well-established rules of scientific inquiry.

Not every problem can be approached through scientific experiment, and in such cases one must rely on logical analysis. But to the extent that reliable, quantitative, experimental evidence is available or can be obtained, we believe educators should make it the basis for their practice. Furthermore, the most useful scientific information for teachers is derived from controlled experiments that reveal how the social environment can be arranged to change behavior for the better and how individuals can be taught self-control.

A common misunderstanding of science is that it produces certainties. True, scientific research can bring us confidence in certain findings and produce findings that *seem* certain because they occur so predictably based on scientific evidence. However, science is tentative, in that its claims are *always* open to abandonment or revision, based on data obtained by the scientific method (Brooks, 2014; Kauffman, 2011, 2014c; Sasso, 2001, 2007). Science thrives on the unknown, the uncertain. In the social sciences, including special education, scientific findings are more likely to be tentative than in the physical sciences.

AN INTEGRATED, SOCIAL-COGNITIVE MODEL

The education of children and youth with EBD isn't now governed by a consistent philosophy or conceptual model that's linked to instructional methodology. Although slavish devotion to a single conceptual model isn't desirable, and diverse theories can be the basis for productive debate, our field would be advanced by a more integrated, less haphazard conceptual approach.

In practice, few professionals adhere rigidly to a single conceptual model. Most realize that multiple perspectives are needed for competent practice. Yet there's a limit in the degree to which anyone can be eclectic (picking and choosing concepts and strategies from various ideas) without being simple-minded and self-contradictory. Some conceptual models aren't complementary; they suggest radically different and incompatible approaches to a problem. Acceptance of one set of assumptions about human behavior sometimes implies rejection of another. We believe that a **social-cognitive model** provides the necessary integration of models that is needed.

As we use the term in this book, *social-cognitive* takes various other models into consideration and includes the developmental features of behavior. That is, we recognize that behavior must be evaluated in the context of normal development. There is continuity across developmental stages in the type of behavior that's adaptive or maladaptive, yet the same behavior may have different meanings at different ages. For example, a pronounced lack of age-appropriate social skills may be maladaptive at all developmental stages, but the particular behaviors that indicate social retardation may differ considerably, depending on the child's age and social circumstances (see Learoyd-Smith & Daniels, 2014; Strand, Barnes-Holmes, & Barnes-Holmes, 2003; Sugai & Lewis, 2004).

Social-cognitive theory is an attempt to explain human behavior from a natural science perspective by integrating what we know about behavioral psychology, physiology, the effects of the environment, and the role of cognition (thinking and feeling). Scientific research indicates indisputably that the consequences of our behavior—environmental responses created by our actions—affect the way we are likely to behave in the future. But behavioral research alone probably can't explain the subtleties and complexities of human conduct. Social-cognitive theory emphasizes **personal agency**: the ability of humans to use symbols for communication, to anticipate future events, to learn from observation or vicarious experience, to evaluate and regulate themselves, and to be reflectively self-conscious. Personal agency or social context adds a needed dimension to a behavioral analysis and provides a more complete explanation of human behavior (see Bandura & Locke, 2003; Malone, 2003).

We could provide many examples of the kind of research we believe fits into the social-cognitive model, but we are cautious in doing so for several reasons: First, many published research studies are not explicit about the conceptual model(s) on which they are based; second, the authors of articles we mention might not see their research as a good example; and third, some examples rely to a much greater extent than others on direct observation and measurement of behavior, more clearly exemplifying natural science applied to EBD. Nevertheless, we offer as examples the study by Feil et al. (2014) of a home-school intervention for preschoolers, the research review by Bruhn, McDaniel, and Kreigh (2015) of self-monitoring, and the study by Gumpel, Wiesenthal, and Söderberg (2015) of the relationship of several internal states (narcissism, perceived social status, and social cognition) to aggression.

GOOD TEACHING

We now describe the basic assumptions we have about teaching students with EBD. These assumptions are behind the suggestions we make for dealing with difficult students in the classroom. To a large extent, our primary concern is based on the best evidence we have for good instructional practices based on scientific evidence and logical thinking about the evidence (see Engelmann & Carnine, 2011; Hattie, Masters, & Birch, 2015; Hattie & Yates, 2013; Hirsch, Lloyd, & Kennedy, 2014; Kauffman, 2010c, 2011, 2015a; Lemov, 2014; Pullen & Hallahan, 2015).

Our statements about good teaching are based on a social-cognitive conceptual model. That is, we try to be scientific in the best sense of the word: to base what we say on both data obtained through the best research we can find and on careful, rational thinking about that evidence on various issues. We do not present the details of effective instruction here but try to explain how we suggest dealing with the job of teaching students who have EBD.

We use common language to describe what we think good teaching means. We use common language rather than theoretical, abstract terms—direct statements in which we are blunt about our views on what's important. In this section, we set the tone for the rest of the book.

Expectations

Setting appropriate expectations is not only important but also surprisingly difficult—if we take expectations seriously. What we expect of our students and ourselves is a critical factor in our choice of educational strategies. In part, our expectations determine what we and our students achieve. Furthermore, our expectations greatly influence how we evaluate what we and our students accomplish.

Unfortunately, the early twenty-first century may be remembered as an era of hollow slogans and trite pronouncements regarding educators' expectations. "All children can learn," for example, may be recalled as a particularly popular but banal phrase that was seldom followed by important questions regarding what all children can learn, at what rate, to what degree of proficiency, with what allocation of resources, or for what purpose. Likewise, holding "the same high expectations for all students" may be remembered as a gross oversimplification that ignores the need to recognize students' individual differences (Kauffman, 2010c, 2011; Kauffman & Badar, 2014a; Kauffman & Konold, 2007; Kauffman & Lloyd, 2017; Kauffman, Pullen, Mostert, & Trent, 2011).

Getting expectations just right for individual students, so they're challenging but not too high, requires extraordinary skill. It depends on accurate assessment—knowledge of test results and past performance, to be sure, but the kind of sensitivity to students that isn't just numbers and percentages. Expectations for students in special education are often too low, but just making them really high for the sake of saying that you have high expectations isn't very smart or helpful either. Either way, what's high for one person or group isn't necessarily high for another. And the student for whom expectations are set has to believe that he or she can reach them or they become just another reason to hate school.

Setting appropriate expectations for others, whether they're our students or our colleagues, and setting expectations for ourselves as teachers requires considerable reflection on what we know about teaching and learning. When it comes to students, we need to take into consideration the nature of each student's problems, our own limitations and biases, and the realities of statistical distributions (e.g., distributions *always* have averages, quartiles, etc., certain realities that no one should ignore; see Kauffman, 2015a; Kauffman & Lloyd, 2017). Let's hope that the coming years bring a more serious and reflective attitude toward what we should anticipate from ourselves and others, not just unthinking chatter about high expectations.

Educators are sometimes impulsive in setting their expectations for students, neglecting the questions that might help them establish a constructive and realistic foundation for teaching and its evaluation. The special educator working with students who have EBD must begin with the same questions that every teacher must ask before designing a behavior management plan:

- Could this problem be a result of inappropriate curriculum or teaching strategies?
- What do I demand and prohibit—and what should I?
- Why do certain behaviors bother me, and what should I do about them?
- Is the behavior I'm concerned about developmentally significant?
- Should I focus on a behavioral excess or a deficiency?
- Will resolution of this problem solve any others?
- How do I indicate my expectations?

Reflection demands much additional self-questioning to arrive at academic and behavioral expectations that don't sell the student short, set the student up for failure, or impose unacceptable personal or cultural biases (Kauffman et al., 2011).

Teachers are sometimes acculturated during their training or by others in the school system to expect too little or too much of themselves and other adults who live and work with children. The primary objective of some teachers seems to be survival or self-serving behavior, with little apparent concern for their role in improving the achievement and social behavior of their students or improving their own teaching skill. They accept little responsibility for their students' failure, seeking only to "put in their time" as teachers. They typically get what they expect and leave the world no better than they found it.

Other teachers see themselves as martyrs or saviors, sacrificing nearly all other personal desires for the sake of their students. Their students' failure becomes their personal failure, and they seem to be after a cure that will make their students "normal." They seldom get what they want, and they tend to leave education—often prematurely—embittered by their own human failure.

Predictably, those who expect too little of themselves tend to excuse the abuse, neglect, and incompetence of other adults. Those who expect too much of themselves are often disparaging of others who are unable or unwilling to measure up to their extraordinary personal standards. Self-understanding is a prerequisite for teaching children with EBD (Richardson & Shupe, 2003). Finding a level of expectation for oneself and others that facilitates personal growth, fosters hope and persistence in the face of failure, and allows one to develop supportive relationships with parents and other teachers is no small accomplishment. These are particularly daunting tasks for the many teachers who lack adequate training in teaching students with EBD.

Teachers' expectations of themselves as well as of the children they teach are often shaped by their culture, particularly the way teachers and teaching are viewed by others. Nobel Prize–winning novelist Mahfouz wrote about events in the life of an Egyptian family (Mahfouz, 2001). His story takes place a long time ago (about 1930), but the attitudes of the parents are similar to the attitudes of many today. The father tells his son Kamal, who wants to become a teacher, that teaching is not respected by anyone. Kamal's father goes on to describe a teaching career as worthless, a waste of time, not worthy of respect, and he suggests that none of the teachers Kamal has had deserves even to be called a human being. True, some teachers are inhumane. However, the wife of the patriarch, Kamal's mother, offers a different perspective on being a teacher. She does not understand why anyone would disparage the worthy profession of teaching, partly because she seems to understand the profoundly good effects a skilled teacher has on the lives of students.

Many teachers are shocked by the contempt some parents and other professionals show for them. Such contempt can shake teachers' confidence in their expectations for students and for themselves. However, some people understand the power of teaching and respect teachers. It's important to focus attention on the insights of people like Kamal's mother.

Part of the reason people have denigrated teaching is that they have failed to understand the special skills it requires. Many educators, including too many teacher educators, have not recognized that good teaching is a science that can be taught and learned, that it demands thoughtful practice and acquiring specific practical skills, just as do playing sports, playing musical instruments, singing, becoming a medical practitioner, or becoming really good at anything. A good teacher of youngsters with EBD must expect to continue learning and applying those teaching skills with very difficult learners as long as she or he is in the profession.

Causes of Behavior

The causes of EBD are almost always unknown. Causal factors may *contribute* to a disorder— not be the single cause. Contributing factors may be *predisposing* or *precipitating*. Both predisposing and precipitating factors increase the probability that a disorder will occur under given circumstances. Precipitating factors may trigger a maladaptive response, given a set of predisposing factors (see Cook & Ruhaak, 2014).

Vulnerability and resilience are important to understand, too (see Gerber, 2014). Vulnerability means that an individual is highly likely to develop EBD, given a set of predisposing and precipitating causal factors. Resilience means that an individual experiencing the same predisposing and precipitating factors is unlikely to or does not develop a disorder.

Teachers need to identify the contributing factors that may help account for their student's current emotional or behavioral status. We know that a variety of biological factors are important, but experience—including the experience a teacher can provide for a student in school—is at least as important as biology *and* it is a factor the teacher can do something about. The well-known interaction of nature and nurture in behavioral development is becoming ever stronger as the years pass and scientific research accumulates. The teacher's job is to focus on nurture.

The primary focus of the special educator must be on the contributing factors that the teacher can alter (see Hattie & Yates, 2013; Kauffman, 2011; Kauffman et al., 2011; Pullen, 2004). Factors over which a teacher has no control may be relevant to a teacher's first interactions with a child or youth, but a special education teacher typically has to start working with pupils *after* they already have EBD. A special education teacher has two primary responsibilities: First, to make sure to do no further disservice to the student; and second, to exert whatever control is possible over the student's *present* environment. This means that the classroom and school must foster more appropriate behavior in spite of unalterable past circumstances and what happens outside of school.

Certainly teachers may sometimes influence what happens outside the classroom, perhaps by working with parents to improve the home environment or using community resources for the child's benefit. But talk of influence beyond the classroom, including such high-sounding phrases as *ecological management* and *wraparound services*, is patent nonsense until the teacher has demonstrated that he or she can make the *classroom* environment conducive to improved behavior (see Engelmann & Carnine, 2011; Heward, 2003; Snider, 2006).

We're not saying that collaboration of school personnel with families and communities is unimportant. Yet we have to recognize that many teachers work under conditions in which administrators and consultants don't facilitate home–school or community–school ties. Teachers are often left on their own, and the individual contributions they can make outside the school are secondary to what they do in their classrooms.

Special educators must assume that behavior is predictable and controllable. No one can change the past, and the teacher alone can't alter many of the contributing factors operating in the present. So, a teacher must have faith that the proper classroom environment alone *can* make a difference in the student's life, even if nothing else can be changed. True, we must also hope that more than the classroom environment can be changed, and we must work toward that end. But we can't escape our responsibility for implementing best practices in the classroom or atone for our failures by pointing the finger at other factors such as the structure of education or the lack of comprehensive, integrated, collaborative services (cf. Kauffman, Nelson, Simpson, & Mock, 2017; Landrum, 2017).

Some people seem to suggest that not much can be done to influence children in school unless virtually everything in the child's life is changed. Children's culture is said to be an "emergent system" in which no particular intervention is going to make much difference or have a consistent, persistent effect (see Brooks, 2011). A mistaken assumption is that the causes of problem behavior are so complex and interactive that we cannot expect to do very much to help children unless we do many things together. With this assumption, the prospects for children are often quite gloomy. Teachers who work with difficult children whose disadvantages are many must not give up because they can change so little. To use a metaphor, we must light the candle we can, even though we know that it doesn't dispel all the darkness in our students' lives.

Definition, Measurement, and Assessment of Behavior

Teachers must have the primary role in determining students' eligibility for special education and deciding how children and youth will be served. They have to use assessment information to decide what they're going to teach. Their tolerance for and knowledge of individual students' behavior in their classrooms must become the ultimate criteria for deciding whether a student needs special help and, if so, what that student needs to learn and where that student can be educated most appropriately (Kauffman & Badar, 2014b, 2016; Kauffman, Mock, Tankersley, & Landrum, 2008; Kauffman, Anastasiou et al., 2016; Kauffman et al., 2015; Rozalski, Miller, & Stewart, 2017; Zigmond, 2015).

The problems of defining and classifying youngsters' disorders does not, fortunately, preclude useful measurement of behavior. The teacher can define and measure precisely the behaviors that result in conflict with others and are self-defeating. Indeed, the teacher who can't or won't pinpoint and measure the relevant behaviors of the students he or she is teaching is probably not going to be very effective.

Students with EBD need help primarily because they have behavioral excesses or deficiencies. Failure to define precisely and measure these behavioral excesses and deficiencies is a serious mistake. It's like the malpractice of a nurse who decides not to measure vital signs (heart rate, respiration rate, temperature, and blood pressure). Excuses that an incompetent nurse might give for failing to measure vital signs might be that he or she is too busy with other aspects of patient care, that subjective estimates of vital signs are enough, that vital signs are only superficial estimates of the patient's health, or that vital signs don't reveal the nature of the underlying pathology.

Special educators must change both academic and social behavior for the better, and they have to show that they have done so. Measurement doesn't have to be sophisticated to be extremely important, but it's indispensable in assessing needs and progress (Heward, 2003; Silvestri & Heward, 2016; Kauffman, 2011; Shinn, 2014). Failure to define and measure behavior change as accurately as possible is *indefensible*.

The technology of behavioral and academic measurement is readily available to teachers and has been for decades (e.g., Alberto & Troutman, 2012; Shinn, 2014). Students can be taught how to measure some of their own behavior, which gives them an additional opportunity to take more control of their own lives.

We're not suggesting that every behavior of every student should be measured or that the teacher should become preoccupied with measurement to the exclusion of other crucial concerns. Teaching is much more than measurement. A mechanical approach to teaching that excludes affective concerns is no more justifiable than an approach that neglects cognitive and behavioral goals. But if the student's most important behavioral and academic problems and achievements aren't measured and recorded, then it will be almost impossible for the teacher to communicate anything really important about the student's progress.

It's not sufficient for teachers to make subjective estimates like "She's a lot better this week" without any objective data on the student's behavioral change. Admittedly, some qualitative or emotional aspects of pupils' behavior and teachers' methods can't be measured directly, and these things might be important. We don't mean to imply that we should just ignore everything that can't be measured. *But it is unconscionable for a teacher of students with EBD not to observe exactly what a student does or doesn't do that's a problem and measure the social and academic behavior as objectively and precisely as possible.*

Without direct measurement of behavior, the teacher risks being misled by subjective impressions of the student's responses. Without such measurement, the teacher might also misperceive the effects of instruction on academic and social skills. It's reasonable to expect that the teacher will show objective and precise evidence of pupils' behavioral change and academic learning, as well as describe the quality of his or her relationship to students in more subjective and affective terms.

The purpose of measurement, whether it's standardized testing or informal testing, and even when it's direct observation and measurement, is to assess just what the student does and needs. Good assessment is ultimately useful in teaching. It tells the teacher of a student with EBD what the student knows and can do and what that student needs to learn.

The importance of measurement of both academic and social behavior has been demonstrated so clearly and frequently that we have to wonder why some teachers don't measure their pupils' behavior. Measurement has been neglected for at least the following reasons:

- Some special educators and teacher educators still have the idea that measurement of behavior doesn't matter much because behavior is a superficial aspect of psychopathology; the real problems are deep inside, unobservable and therefore not directly measurable.

Video Example

from

YouTube

▶

ENHANCEDetext
Video Connections 1.3
The video "Defining Behavior" provides a brief overview of the importance of precisely (operationally) defining behavior. Notice that these definitions lead directly to the means by which teachers would record the occurrence of behavior and monitor the effects of instruction or intervention. (https://www.youtube.com/watch?v=WtjyYZw20Rk)

- Parents sometimes accept less-than-adequate evidence of a teacher's ability.
- Some teachers don't understand the value of direct measurement of behavior or might not have training in how to do it well.
- Behavioral change sometimes occurs without measurement, which might lead someone to the false conclusion that measurement isn't important.
- Some teachers are incompetent or lazy.

Work, Play, Love, and Fun

Children and youth with EBD often don't do productive work or know how to play, give and receive love, and have fun. Yet these four experiences—work, play, love, and fun—are close to the essence of a satisfying and meaningful human life. Education of these students requires a curriculum that brings these essential experiences into sharp focus. This doesn't imply that we need a curriculum to teach these experiences directly; in fact, someone who wants to teach a youngster how to work, play, love, or have fun must have a curriculum with a content of useful specific skills, but the skills themselves don't constitute essential life experiences. The antics of many "fun seekers" and the desperate "play" of some professional athletes illustrate how hard it is to experience fun and play just by trying. Relations among events—the structure of experience as well as events themselves—teach a person to work, play, love, and enjoy. Yes, enjoying work—having fun doing it—is important, but we also realize that something's wrong with a person who has fun *only* while working or *only* while playing.

The teacher has to structure or order the environment for the pupil so that work is accomplished, play is recreational, love is felt, and fun is enjoyed—by the student and by the teacher. The teacher doesn't provide structure and order by allowing the student complete freedom to choose what to do. Youngsters with EBD have difficulty because they made unfortunate choices about what to do. The teacher must make value judgments about what a student should learn. A long time ago, a leading scholar in the education of youngsters with EBD noted how important it is for students to learn to read, write, spell, and do arithmetic. Students simply must have these academic skills, but it's also good for them to learn to hit a ball with a bat, catch a ball, play a guitar, scull a canoe, travel by bus across town, and so on (Hobbs, 1974). The teacher must have confidence in his or her own judgment about what's good for the youngster to learn and how the student should behave. Without such confidence, a teacher simply can't provide the necessary structure for learning.

We don't mean that the teacher always and only should decide what skills the pupil learns. The point isn't to make students mindlessly conform to behavioral standards but to require a reasonable standard of conduct and learning that will give them more personal choices and greater fulfillment in a free society.

In addition to the value judgments and difficult decisions a teacher must make about what to teach, questions remain about instruction. Two fundamental principles guide the organization of effective instruction: Choosing tasks that are appropriate for the pupil (tasks that are at the right level and at which the student can usually succeed) and arranging appropriate consequences for performance (see Kame'enui, 2015; Kauffman et al., 2011; Pullen & Hallahan, 2015; Scruggs & Mastropieri, 2015). We don't learn to work, play, love, and have fun through failure but through success and mastery. We don't learn pride, dignity, self-worth, and other attributes of good mental health by having our wishes immediately gratified but by struggling to overcome difficulties, meeting requirements, and finding that our own efforts will achieve desired goals.

We can't depend on our students to learn by some magical, mysterious, internally guided process; their learning will be ensured only by a skillful and sensitive adult who makes the expectations for their behavior appropriately difficult and meeting those expectations rewarding. Again, Hobbs (1974) had the right idea many years ago: the appropriate level of expectation—challenging but not overwhelming. The good teacher chooses tasks that are manageable for individuals and then gradually allows youngsters to set their own goals as they become attuned to their true capabilities and desires. The good teacher recognizes that a task that is very difficult for one student may be easy for another (or for herself/himself).

Ample evidence indicates that the order in which events are structured has a profound influence on students' learning—specifically, that making highly preferred events (play) contingent or dependent on less-preferred events (work) improves the individual's work performance (cf. Kerr & Nelson, 2010; Sprague, Jolivette, & Nelson, 2014; Walker, Ramsey, & Gresham, 2004). The expectation that someone will work before they play (or get paid) is a fundamental principle. An environment in which rewards and privileges (beyond those that are everyone's right) are gratis is stultifying. Earning your way, on the other hand, builds self-esteem. Way back in the last century, Esther Rothman (1970), who worked with disturbed and delinquent girls in New York City, commented on the value of work and pay. Pay, she noted, didn't necessarily mean money. For some students, special privileges, material items other than money, or doing things that are meaningful to the student might constitute the reward (see Kauffman, Pullen et al., 2011; Landrum & Kauffman, 2006; Rhode, Jenson, & Reavis, 2010). Meaningful reward for accomplishment is a time-honored means of teaching and encouraging students to do their best, notwithstanding the ignorance of those who consider rewards inherently demeaning (e.g., Kohn, 1993). Properly used rewards for performance have not been found to decrease intrinsic motivation (see McGinnis, Friman, & Carlyon, 1999). The fundamental principle underlying a token economy is payment of a fair wage for work. Rothman (1970) noted that one of the usual outcomes of work is also pride in oneself.

We won't be so presumptuous as to try to define *play*, *love*, or *fun*; a definition of *work*—purposeful and necessary expenditure of effort to achieve a desired goal—is enough. But we do note that for the emotionally healthy individual, work, play, love, and fun are inextricably intertwined, and for someone with EBD, they seem unrelated or unattainable. When a youngster's emotions and behavior have become disordered, the most effective strategy for restoring what some have called a vital balance or zest, joy, and deep fulfillment is to provide appropriate work and consistent consequences for performance. Play, love, and fun are likely to follow the experience of accomplishing a valued task and earning a reward by our own labor. To work is to build a sound basis for self-esteem. This includes academic work as well as other kinds. And eventually, skillful performance itself becomes a rewarding experience.

Direct, Honest Communication

Some advocates of a structured approach and some behavior-modification enthusiasts seem to imply that consistent consequences for behavior alone will be enough to bring about the necessary changes in students' behavior. But teaching is more than just providing a structured relationship among events. How we listen and talk to students changes their perceptions and their responses to other environmental events (Kauffman, Pullen et al., 2011; Lemov, 2014). In describing the consequences of behavior, for example, the teacher can emphasize either the positive or the negative. A teacher might say, "You may not use the internet until your math is finished." Another teacher might phrase it, "You may use the internet as soon as you finish your math." Both teachers have described the response–consequence relationship, and both statements are equally correct, but the second draws attention to the positive consequences of appropriate performance and the first to the negative results of nonperformance. Each statement may affect the student differently. Nonverbal communication is also important and should be consistent with what a teacher says. To be therapeutic, teachers must listen, talk, and act in ways that communicate respect, caring, and confidence, both in themselves and in their students.

It doesn't follow that teachers must always communicate approval or positive regard for a student's behavior. In fact, teachers must communicate disapproval with great clarity. We can't expect youngsters to learn appropriate behavior if we respond to all their behavior with approval or indifference. Candor, including honest appraisal of inappropriate behavior, will serve a teacher well. Consistent follow-through with positive and negative consequences for desirable and undesirable behavior, combined with extremely clear communication of expectations, will be successful in managing many or most behavioral problems.

Communication is a two-way affair, and teachers won't be successful unless they learn to listen with understanding, watch students' behavior carefully, and interpret accurately the relationship between children's verbal and nonverbal behavior. Youngsters who don't believe they're being listened to will go to the extreme to make themselves understood, often getting into additional trouble.

Directness in talking to children and youth facilitates communication. Many teachers and parents tend to be tentative, noncommittal, and confusing in their conversations with youngsters, often out of fear of rejecting or being rejected or perhaps because of the misguided notion that to help youngsters who have EBD, you must never tell them directly what to do (O'Leary, 1995). Youngsters don't usually profit from having to guess about adults' wishes or intentions. In fact, some of them will improve their behavior almost immediately if the teacher merely states clearly, forthrightly, and unequivocally how they are to behave. For the most part, good teaching is teacher-controlled, not student-controlled (see Heward, 2003; Kauffman, 2010c, 2011; Snider, 2006). And good teaching also includes making things really clear, including both academic and behavioral problems. Good teaching takes the ambiguity out of problems (Engelmann & Carnine, 2011).

Students with EBD are sure to test the teacher's honesty. Honesty is more than candor in expressing opinions and reporting facts accurately. Students want to know whether teachers are as good as their word. Teachers who make idle threats or fail to deliver positive and negative consequences as promised will surely run afoul of their students.

Self-Control

Overwhelming evidence shows that children learn a lot by watching the way other people behave (Kauffman, Pullen et al., 2011; Kerr & Nelson, 2010). Teachers whose own behavior isn't very good may corrupt rather than help students, regardless of their finesse with other teaching strategies. To be blunt, teaching students with EBD isn't an appropriate job for people who are social misfits or psychologically unstable. Imitating the teacher should lead to behavioral improvement, not to maladaptive conduct.

These statements shouldn't be taken to mean that the teacher has to be perfect. The expectation of perfection is itself maladaptive. Expecting perfection is a problem that the teacher will need to help some students with EBD overcome. Being able to accept imperfections in oneself and others and to cope constructively with one's own and others' failures are among the emotional and behavioral characteristics that the teacher must demonstrate.

About half a century ago, Hobbs (1966) summed up the kind of model a teacher should provide, and it remains a guiding ideal. The teacher should be a decent adult, well trained, able to give and receive affection, able to relax and experience joy, be firm but not abusive, have a sense of the usefulness of the day, and be a person of hope and quiet confidence that youngsters with EBD can be helped.

A teacher of students with EBD should be a model of self-control. Not only should the teacher model self-control, but he or she should also teach it through direct instruction. After all, appropriate self-guidance is inherent in the concept of individual rights, and loss of control characterizes disordered behavior. We don't mean that students should always be allowed to behave as they will without interference or that the teacher should never require a pupil to behave.

Students should be allowed to choose for themselves how to behave, except when they choose behavior that clearly isn't in their best interests or violates the rights of others. The teacher's role should be to structure the classroom environment so that students are aware of their options, can exercise choice in as many areas of behavior as possible, and are tutored in and rewarded for appropriate decisions. Students should be taught cognitive-behavior techniques, such as self-instruction, rehearsal, and guided practice, to make them as self-sufficient as possible in controlling their own behavior. External control may be required at first to humanize a pupil, but the task of truly humanistic education isn't finished until control is internalized by the student to the greatest extent possible (Bruhn, McDaniel, & Kreigh, 2015; Kauffman, Bantz, & McCullough, 2002; Kauffman, Pullen et al., 2011).

Cultural Differences

Teachers' understanding of cultural differences is critical for the success of students in general education (Ispa-Landa, 2015). Our assumption is that the same applies to special education. A good teacher is sensitive to cultural differences.

Sensitivity to cultural differences—multicultural sensitivity—is often *mis*interpreted to mean education adjusted according to students' skin color, gender, ancestry, religion, and so on (see Anastasiou, Kauffman, & Michail, 2016). The assumption is that education is more appropriate or effective when the teacher takes into account some group characteristic, particularly for a group that has been oppressed or marginalized by the larger society, rather than some more relevant cultural characteristic of the individual.

Oppression and marginalization of subcultural groups is a major problem in all parts of the world, including the United States of America (see Patterson & Fosse, 2015). The problem isn't peculiar to any continent, nation, color, creed, or institution. It's a human problem, and one that teachers encounter regardless of their color, gender, or location (see Anastasiou, 2017; Anastasiou, Gardner, & Michail, 2011; Anastasiou & Keller, 2017; Hallahan et al., 2015; Kauffman, Conroy, Gardner, & Oswald, 2008).

Cross-cultural understanding and multicultural education have received substantial attention in both general and special education in recent years. However, education that's culturally sensitive or responsive is seldom defined in ways that allow teachers or classroom observers to define just what a teacher should do to be sensitive or responsive to different cultures (Kauffman, 2011; Kauffman, Conroy et al., 2008). Moreover, cultural sensitivity and other important multicultural features of instruction are often described from a constructivist perspective that is both vague and based on students' group identities rather than individual characteristics (Anastasiou & Kauffman, 2012; Kauffman, 2015c; Kauffman & Badar, 2014a).

Group identity (by whatever characteristic, including disability) is the bedrock of racism, sexism, and other forms of unfair discrimination. The unfairness of discrimination is based on the idea that access, privilege, education, guilt, responsibility, and other forms of social judgment should be based on group identity rather than the individual. In fact, it defines the group characteristic (whether related to color, gender, religion, or other group identity) as merit itself. In effect, it's the assumption that if you belong to X group (defined by color, heritage, religion, or gender, for example), then we know Y (ability, preference, behavior, and so on) is true of you. It's stereotyping—the assumption that one of an individual's characteristics determines another, when in fact it doesn't. Separating individual from group characteristics and understanding that disability must be treated differently from other forms of diversity is essential for achieving social justice (Anastasiou et al., 2016; Kauffman & Landrum, 2009).

There is no substitute in avoiding stereotyping and respecting cultural differences for talking to individual students and their families to find out about them *as individuals* within the framework of science (Kauffman, Conroy et al., 2008). Of course, individuals may claim that science itself represents a cultural bias, but that is simply a canard for reasons explained in detail elsewhere (e.g., Anastasiou & Kauffman, 2011, 2013; Kauffman, 2011; Kauffman & Sasso, 2006b; Mostert, Kavale, & Kauffman, 2008; Sasso, 2007).

In education, insensitivity to individuality includes a focus on group identity. For example, a teacher might respond to a student as if his or her group identity were a sound basis for decisions about curriculum, instruction, or behavior management. But this is neither legally acceptable in special education nor the basis for a just society. In special education, it isn't legally permissible to determine such things as curriculum, instruction, or placement based simply on a student's group characteristic, such as the determination that a student is in a particular diagnostic group or has a particular cultural identity. Rather, special education must be based, by law, on a student's *individual* needs (Bateman, 2017; Bateman & Linden, 2012; Huefner, 2006; Kauffman, 2015c; Yell, Crockett, Shriner, & Rozalski, 2017).

Cultural sensitivity of any kind—whether it involves disability or a group characteristic such as color, gender, or religion—demands attention to the *individual*. The shame of education is too often that it is culturally insensitive because it doesn't demand the use of effective academic instruction and effective behavioral interventions. Evidence-based practices are often shunned, and faulty notions are embraced, even though effective, evidence-based practices are readily available (see Landrum, 1997; Morris & Mather, 2008; Walker & Gresham, 2014). Sometimes, unfortunately, reliable evidence is rejected because it's assumed to have been tainted by the group identity of the researcher (e.g., evidence is rejected because of the color or gender or other group identity of the person who provided it). However, the failure to use effective practices for instruction and behavior management ensures cultural insensitivity, regardless of any other good intention.

Instruction: The Business of Special Education

One of the most important lessons we have learned during the past several decades as educators of students with EBD is that academic instruction must not be ignored or even made secondary. The observation that the education of these students too often relegates academic instruction to a secondary concern and focuses on control or containment of misbehavior is a serious indictment that must not be allowed to characterize our work (Kauffman, 2010a; Kauffman & Landrum, 2007; Lane & Menzies, 2010).

We must refocus all of special education on instruction (Bateman, Lloyd, Tankersely, & Brown, 2015; Kauffman, 2014b, 2015a; Kauffman & Badar, 2014a, 2014b; Zigmond, 2015). For teachers of students with EBD, instruction is particularly important for two reasons. First, academic achievement is so fundamental to emotional and social adjustment that it's foolish not to make it a capstone of educational intervention. Enhancing their academic achievement is the single most reliable way of improving students' self-appraisal and social competence. Second, managing or modifying students' behavior is best approached, at least by teachers, as an instructional problem (Kauffman, 2010a, 2014b; Kauffman et al., 2011; Walker et al., 2004). This means placing more emphasis on the antecedents of problems—the settings or contexts in which behavioral problems predictably occur. It means thinking of social or emotional problems much as one would think of problems in teaching reading or math or any other academic subject. It means paying very careful attention to specifying precisely the behavior that is expected, modifying the contexts in which misbehavior happens, and rehearsing and prompting expected behavior. Strong reinforcement for desirable behavior is important, but it will be maximally effective only if the other instructional components are well implemented. We realize that some students won't respond as expected to instruction that is effective for most students (Kavale, Kauffman, Bachmeier, & LeFever, 2008; Shinn, 2014). Nevertheless, good instruction is the first requirement for effective behavior management.

Thoughts about Actual People

It's one thing to think of EBD in the abstract, but quite another thing to observe the reality (see Putnam, 2015). It's one thing to observe disorders happening in other peoples' lives, but quite another thing when they become a part of our own life. Too often, we forget to consider the lives of the parents and families as well as the lives of the teachers and students involved. We forget to consider what it's like to have a disorder and what it's like to have and be responsible for parenting or teaching a child or youth with a disorder (see Earley, 2006; Suhay, 2007; Warner, 2010). We forget that above all, we are dealing with real people who, like us, need love, attention, understanding, and support as well as correction or improvement. As Dr. Jill Jakulski, the principal of a special school serving middle school students with EBD, has said, as a teacher you've got to actually *like* the students you teach and be able to like and work with them regardless of what they said or did the day before. That's hard, and not everybody can do it.

We suggest that you consider an example in the accompanying case book—the case of John, as written by his mother. ADHD is both a common problem and a difficulty accompanying a variety of other disabilities. In fact, it's often a diagnosis or label that precedes "emotional disturbance" or "emotional/behavioral disorder." This case is much longer and more complex than those in the rest of the case book. In this sense, it's more realistic, because EBD isn't a simple matter with a simple solution. John is a case that asks us to think about all the chapters in this book and what they mean for John, his mother, his family, and his teachers.

INTERRELATIONSHIPS AMONG CAUSES, TYPES OF BEHAVIOR, ASSESSMENT, AND INTERVENTION

Given a social-cognitive model for conceptualizing human behavior, what's the best way to structure a coherent discussion of the characteristics of the EBD of children and youth? As Bandura (1986) noted, it's impossible to study all interactions at once. Trying to examine all causal factors simultaneously paralyzes scientific study because the task is overwhelmingly complex. We must study behavior, its assessment, its causes, and its effects in simpler, more manageable segments. This is true whether we're conducting research or summarizing and interpreting it.

Figure 1.1 is a diagram of how things are interrelated. The two overlapping circles indicate that assessment and intervention are overlapping, that in a few instances you might find an activity that's totally one or the other but that in most cases assessment and intervention go together. In the language of set theory, assessment and intervention are intersecting sets. You also see that we have listed several types of disorders and four major groups of causal factors,

Figure 1.1   Interrelationships among Causes, Types of Behavior, Assessment, and Intervention

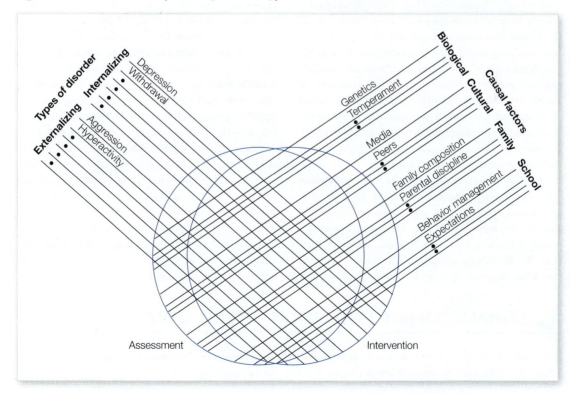

and the dots indicate that there are additional things we did not list in all of the categories. You can follow the lines through the overlapping circles. For example, we might choose to analyze a particular segment of the diagram, such as the assessment of genetic factors in depression. That is, the lines for genetic factors and depression meet. But, if you follow the genetics line, you see it intersects not only the line for depression but all the lines for all the other types of disorders, too. And if you follow the line for aggression, you see that it intersects with the lines for all of the causal factors. The diagram is intended to show how we can never completely separate the particular problem we're analyzing from all other problems and that both assessment and intervention are usually involved. For example, if we're studying the assessment of genetic factors in depression, then we can't totally ignore the assessment of temperament as a causal factor and the design of interventions involving peers and parents. Although we sometimes focus on one particular topic, we must be aware of how that topic is connected to others as well.

Our primary focus in the following sections of this book will first be on causal factors (Part 2), then on types of disorders (Part 3), and finally on assessment (Part 4). But, even as we attend to a particular topic or factor, we have to keep the others in mind.

SUMMARY

Beliefs about the nature of human beings determine what explanations we seek for behavior and the strategies we use in approaching EBD. Throughout history, people have been conceptualized as spiritual beings, biological organisms, rational and feeling individuals, and products of their environments. Biological, psychoeducational, ecological, and behavioral models all have particular advantages and disadvantages. A model derived from scientific experiments in social learning and self-control provides the most defensible basis for professional practice. A social-cognitive approach that involves thinking and feeling as well as behavior is consistent with this book.

Getting expectations just right is an important part of teaching. Expectations apply to both students and teachers, and it's important that they not be too high or too low. The most important causes for teachers to keep in mind are those they can do something about, which means focusing on what happens in school. Other causal factors

may be important, but the teacher usually can't do much about them. Teachers must define, measure, and assess students' behavior. In fact, competent teaching practice requires direct observation and measurement of behavior, both social and academic. Teachers must teach students how work, play, love, and fun are all important and are interrelated. This involves learning that play generally follows work, that work itself can be highly rewarding and fun, and that giving and receiving loving care is gratifying. Direct, honest communication with students is critical. Teachers should also provide good models of self-control. Cultural diversity adds value to life, and teachers should teach the acceptance of cultural diversity while teaching needed academic skills. Teachers must remember that the most important business of special education is effective instruction, keeping in mind that the students and families with whom we work as special educators are real people who need loving care as well as help.

✔ ENHANCEDetext END-OF-CHAPTER 1 QUIZ

Click on the checkmark icon to access an end-of-chapter quiz. Answer the questions to gauge your understanding of chapter concepts and better prepare you for case discussions.

CASES FOR DISCUSSION (See case book for additional cases.)

Where Do You Start with One Like This?

Derrick Yates

Derrick is a twelve-year-old placed in a class of high-average and gifted fifth graders, although his academic skills are at about third-grade level. He has been known as a terror, as unmanageable, by every teacher he has had in his school career. He is large for his age and is described as a "scary kid" with crooked, bucked teeth, a chilling laugh, and an odd look in his eyes. Because of his disruptive behavior, he has been allowed to attend school for only half days for protracted periods. The school's teacher assistance team has recommended that he be evaluated for possible special education services.

At home, Derrick's behavior is also highly problematic, threatening, and intimidating. His mother and father are divorced, and Derrick lives with his mother and younger sister and brother. He is enraged about the divorce and blames his mother for the family's breakup. The school social worker reports that Derrick killed the family dog with a butcher knife—beheaded and dismembered the dog and scattered the parts in the yard. His mother has had locks installed on the kitchen drawers for fear that Derrick would use knives and other kitchen utensils to harm her or his siblings. She has also had double locks installed on her bedroom door and lets the two younger children sleep with her for fear of Derrick. She reports that in a fit of rage stemming from her not asking him to talk with his father (who had called regarding child support) on the phone, Derrick one night assaulted her bedroom door with a butcher knife. Derrick's mother is at her wit's end, terrified of him and not able to get help from social services or mental health services.

Derrick's teacher this year is an experienced special educator who asked for reassignment to a general education classroom. Although she is well aware of Derrick's history, she has agreed to take Derrick in her class until the evaluation for special education is completed. Derrick knows that teachers and other students are afraid of him. He says that he likes to do mean things and glories in his bad reputation. However, for the first few days of this school year, his teacher has kept her cool, seemed unafraid of him, and observed no serious misbehavior. One day he approached her with this question: "You don't know about me, do you?"

Source: This case was rewritten from Kauffman, Pullen, Mostert, and Trent (2011).

Questions About the Case

1. What conceptual model offers the best understanding of the cause(s) of Derrick's behavior?

2. How would you describe the most important things to consider (using a social-cognitive model) in the case of Derrick, and how are these things interrelated?

3. Were you to design an intervention strategy for working with Derrick, where would you begin, and why?

4. What concepts would you draw on in deciding how best to respond to Derrick's question to his teacher?

What Should We Do with Buddy?

Buddy

I teach regular sixth grade. Buddy is one of the most unpleasant students I've met in my ten years of teaching. He's unpleasant physically and psychologically. He's always dirty and smelly, and the language he uses is hostile, mean, and unacceptable in polite society. Most of the time he makes other kids, as well as adults, want to get away from him as fast as possible and stay away from him as much as possible. I suppose you could describe this as just plain obnoxious. Amazingly, though, he's really a nice kid sometimes. But, generally, it's hard to imagine a more repulsive twelve-year-old than Buddy, so it's no wonder he's nobody's buddy in spite of his name.

I mean, just think about what he's like. He picks his nose until it bleeds and then wipes the blood and mucus on his papers. That's enough to gross out most people. But he also picks his ears and wipes the wax on his papers. He picks his acne and wipes the blood and pus on his papers. He spits on his papers and smears the saliva over his answers to try to erase them that way. Now, this kind of thing doesn't just gross out teachers; it grosses out other kids in the class.

But then there are things that drive me crazy as a teacher, like what he does with his papers. When he does use an eraser, he makes holes in his paper by rubbing too hard. He'll often write his answer at the wrong place on a paper and then circle it and draw an arrow to another wrong place. He frequently writes four-letter words and draws lewd pictures and swastikas on his papers. He punches holes in his papers, tears them, wads them up, tapes them together, rips them apart again, and re-tapes them. All the while, he mutters curses—he can't do the damned work because it was too babyish or too hard or too stupid or too crazy and "what kind of a stupid goddamned bastard am I to give him such crap?" Sure, other kids in my class often hear worse, but this kind of language isn't really acceptable to them in my class, and it's definitely not acceptable to me.

Buddy often makes himself the bane of everyone's existence. He teases and bullies smaller children unmercifully. He baits teachers and threatens other adults. Cleanliness and pleasantness just aren't his thing. The other day he referred to his former teacher as a "fuckstick." I'm pretty near the end of my patience with him.

I've talked to other teachers about Buddy and to my principal. Nobody seems to know what to do. His problems seem to be getting worse, but not suddenly so; he seems to be a lot like he was when he was six. His parents see him as just being a kid, not as being a problem. Also, because Buddy can be really nice, he's obviously got the potential to behave that way all the time. So when I bring up some of the things he does with other teachers, they say, "Well, yeah, but Buddy can be a really sweet kid, and I think people just need to take a deep breath and say, 'Ok, that's just the way he is.'"

Questions About the Case

1. How is a student like Buddy likely to fare in general education over the long haul? How should a general education teacher handle a student like Buddy?

2. Do you think Buddy has a disability? If not, why not? If so, why? Do you think he has an emotional or behavioral disorder?

3. Do you think Buddy needs special education? Why, or why not? If so, where do you think he should be served, and what do you think he needs?

4. If you were Buddy's teacher in either general or special education, what would you do to try to help him learn better behavior?

2 WHAT WE'RE ABOUT: THE PROBLEM AND ITS SIZE

DEFINITION AND PREVALENCE

Creative Images/Shutterstock

After reading this chapter, you should be able to:

2.1 List common terms used to describe the students we are talking about in this book.

2.2 Explain why EBD should be considered a disability.

2.3 State reasons that explain why defining EBD is so difficult.

2.4 Explain why identifying students with EBD requires arbitrary decisions.

2.5 Defend the position that 2 percent of the student population is a conservative estimate of prevalence.

2.6 State the approximate percentage of the public school population that is now receiving special education in the federal category *emotionally disturbed*.

Granted, we want to teach students with EBD as well as we can. We stated some of our basic assumptions in the last chapter, but we also have to turn our attention to details of just what we're referring to. We start this chapter with consideration of what to call the students to whom we're referring—the label we use and how we define their disability. Then we consider how many of them we might find—that is, what percentage of the general school population has what we consider EBD.

COMMON TERMINOLOGY

The terminology of the field is unsettled, if not confusing. And, of course, it's really hard to define something precisely when there are lots of different words to name it. So, before getting to the problem of definition, we need to consider just what terms or labels have been used or proposed for the students we're discussing.

Emotionally disturbed is the label currently used in federal special education legislation and regulations. However, **behaviorally disordered** is preferred by some professionals because they consider it a more accurate descriptor of the children and youth we're referring to. To many people, *behaviorally disordered* seems to be a less stigmatizing label than *emotionally disturbed*. Yet in the professional literature and in the laws and regulations of various states, many additional terms refer to the same population. For the most part, these terms combine one of the terms in Table 2.1, column A, with another from column B. Thus, in one state, the label may be *emotionally handicapped* or *emotionally impaired*, whereas in another it may be *behaviorally impaired*. Occasionally, combinations of two words from column A appear with one from column B: *socially and emotionally maladjusted, socially and emotionally disturbed, personally and socially maladjusted*, and so on. The point is that the terminology of the field is confused— sometimes as confused as the children and youth to whom we apply the labels. The issue of labeling is controversial, and we discuss it more later.

Confusing combinations of terms may eventually give way to a commonly accepted label for this category. The term *emotional or behavioral disorders* was adopted in the late 1980s by the National Mental Health and Special Education Coalition, a group formed in 1987 to foster collaboration among various professional and advocacy organizations (Forness, 1988a; Forness & Knitzer, 1992). By 1991, more than thirty professional and advocacy organizations were members of this coalition. The terminology *children and youth with emotional or behavioral disorders* has become more accepted. We consider the matter of whether to use the conjunction *or* or

Table 2.1   Combinations of Terms

Column A	Column B
Emotionally	Disturbed
Behaviorally	Disordered
Socially	Maladjusted
Personally	Handicapped
	Conflicted
	Impaired
	Challenged

and trivial. The mental health and special education coalition chose *emotional or behavioral disorders* over other possible labels simply to indicate that the children and youth to whom it refers may exhibit disorders of emotions or behavior—or both. It is a more clearly inclusive term than are many others. Unfortunately, it's not yet the term used in federal laws and regulations.

DEFINITION

When you meet children or youth who have disorders of the type we're discussing, they're likely to etch pictures in your memory that aren't easily erased. Nevertheless, these youngsters' disabilities are hard to define. We can have an intuitive grasp of what EBD is, but the definition of such a disorder—the construction of guidelines that foster valid and reliable judgments about who does and doesn't have it—is anything but simple (Mundschenk & Simpson, 2014).

A good definition is important because these children and youth have disabilities that won't be addressed unless their problems are seen for what they are—disabilities. Recall that in the introduction to Part 1 we mentioned that these students have limited options in important aspects of daily living. Compared to other students, they have limited options because their behavior is so problematic. Their behavior is inconsistent with their social–interpersonal environments and costs them lots of opportunities for gratifying social interaction and self-fulfillment.

One reason it's so difficult to write a reliable definition is that EBD isn't a thing that exists outside a social context. It's a label assigned according to cultural rules. This doesn't mean that the disorders don't exist or that they're just a figment of our imaginations or peculiar to our cultures, but it does mean that the social context is important.

A common objection to recognizing and defining EBD, as well as some of the other categories of special education, is that the categories are just social constructs. However, the fact that something is a social construct—something defined by societal rules and, therefore, open to redefinition or new understanding—doesn't make it insubstantial, unimportant, or indefensible. It's wise to remember that all of the following things are social constructs, too: justice, poverty, ethics, childhood, adolescence, love, culture, and family. We could give lots of other examples. Our point is simply this: EBD is a social construct, but so are many of the things we hold dear in a benevolent society. Even if EBD is said to be a social construct, it shouldn't be assumed to be merely a figment of imagination, dispensable, unwise, or uncivil (see Anastasiou & Kauffman, 2011, 2012; Mostert, Kavale, & Kauffman, 2008).

Science is our best tool for figuring things out (Kauffman, 2011, 2014c; Kauffman & Sasso, 2006a, 2006b). We want to find out as much about behavior and emotions as we can, primarily by using scientific methods to study them. However, the objective methods of natural science sometimes play a secondary role in designating behavior as deviant. EBD is whatever behavior a culture's chosen authority figures designate as intolerable. Typically, it's behavior that's perceived to threaten the stability, security, or values of a normal society. This doesn't mean that the identification of EBD is indefensible, just that it must be seen as a human social process.

Defining EBD is unavoidably subjective, at least in part. We can be objective and precise in measuring specific responses of individuals, and we can be painstakingly explicit in stating social norms, cultural rules, or community expectations for behavior. But we ultimately must realize that norms, rules, and expectations, and the appraisal of the extent to which particular individuals deviate from them, require subjective judgment. The problem of definition is made all the more difficult by differences in the following, and we discuss each of them in turn in more detail:

- Different conceptual models
- Different purposes of definition
- Complexities in measuring emotions and behaviors
- The range and variability of normal and deviant behavior
- The use of developmental norms and sociocultural expectations as comparisons—ecology
- Relationships to other exceptionalities
- The transience of many problems during human development
- The disadvantages inherent in labeling deviance

Different Conceptual Models

Lots of different conceptual models have been described in great detail. Each conceptual model includes a set of assumptions about why children behave as they do and what must be done to correct disorders. Not surprisingly, a definition based on the tenets of one conceptual model does little but baffle or disappoint those who hold the assumptions of a different model. Writing a definition to which everyone can subscribe, regardless of the person's conceptual persuasion, may be impossible. An additional problem is that many concepts about EBD are merely adaptations for children of conceptual models of adult psychopathology and don't consider the developmental differences of youngsters at various ages (see Kauffman & Brigham, 2009). Suffice it to say here that people who disagree about what EBD is in the abstract are apt to disagree also on a practical definition. It's important to note also that in discussions about the prevention of EBD—a positive goal that virtually everyone says is a good idea—those who disagree on a definition are likely to disagree also on what should be prevented and how to best prevent it (see Kauffman, 2014a).

Different Purposes of Definitions

Definitions serve the purposes of the people who use them. Courts, schools, clinics, and families rely on different criteria for definition. They don't necessarily deny the value of definitions for purposes other than their own, but they tend to give particular credence to definitions that are specific to what they do. For example, courts give greatest attention to law-violating behavior, schools focus primarily on academic failure, clinics use reasons for referral, and families and communities concentrate on behavior that violates their rules or strains their tolerance. Formulating a single definition that's useful to everybody who is responsible for youngsters' conduct is very difficult.

Our concern is with definitions that serve the purposes of education. Our focus is on school-related issues. We usually refer to the children and youth in question as students, and a definition of EBD that includes references to school will be most meaningful to us.

State and local education agencies use definitions that are quite varied and often include in their definitions statements regarding the supposed causes of EBD. States' regulations often cite biological or family factors as probable causes. They may also include requirements for certification that a youngster has a disorder or specify who may legitimately classify the child or youth.

State regulations may include exclusions, such as a statement that the disorders can't be caused by mental retardation or serious health impairments. State and local definitions vary so much that a student might be identified as having a disorder in one state or school district but not in another. Part of the problem is that there is wiggle room to be found in almost any definition.

Clearly, definitions can be seen as problematic if a student changes from "normal" to "disturbed" merely by moving across a boundary. The problem isn't a matter only of two people disagreeing about whether a particular behavior is being exhibited; it's in different policies about what a particular behavior means or requires.

States and localities may be moving slowly toward aligning their definitions with the definition used in federal regulations. However, great variability remains in terminology and definitions from one place to another. Moreover, the current federal definition itself presents serious problems, as we will see.

Complexities in Measuring Emotions and Behaviors

No tests measure personality, adjustment, anxiety, or other relevant psychological constructs precisely enough to define EBD. That is, we can't define EBD simply by a test score. Tests may help us understand a youngster's behavior, but the tests' reliability and validity aren't adequate for definition of EBD.

Tests assumed to measure internal states or personality constructs that can't be observed directly—projective tests—are especially questionable. Direct observation and measurement of behavior reduce reliance on indirect measurement, but these newer assessment techniques haven't resolved the problem of definition. It may be more useful for a teacher to know how frequently a student hits classmates or sasses adults than it is to know the student's responses to psychometric tests. However, there's no consensus among teachers or psychologists that a certain frequency of a particular behavior indicates EBD. Local norms for certain behavior problems may be useful in screening, but these local norms don't provide the basis for a definition either.

To compare students for purposes of classification, behavior must be measured under specified environmental conditions. This standard is required because behavior usually varies with social context. That is, we know that students behave differently under different circumstances. But even if environmental conditions are specified and students' behaviors are measured directly and reliably under those specified conditions, we still aren't likely to have a satisfactory definition. Even given a single set of circumstances, disordered and adaptive behaviors are defined by more than how often they occur.

The problem of measurement here is analogous to that in the fields of vision and hearing. Central visual acuity and pure-tone auditory thresholds can be measured precisely under carefully controlled conditions, but these measures don't indicate very well how efficiently a person sees or hears in the everyday environment. For example, two people with the same level of hearing on a test may function quite differently—one as hearing (using oral language almost exclusively) and the other as deaf (relying mostly on manual communication). Visual and auditory efficiency must be assessed by observing how the individual adapts to the changing demands of the environment for seeing and hearing. Behavioral adaptation must also be judged according to how well a person meets demands, which often change subtly. This judgment requires experienced "clinical" appraisal, which includes precise measurement but also knowledge of cultural and circumstantial influences on behavior.

Range and Variability of Normal and Deviant Behavior

A wide range of behavior may be considered normal. The difference between normal and disordered behavior is usually one of degree rather than kind, and there isn't a sharp line between the two. Most children and youth do nearly everything those with EBD do, but they do these things under different conditions, at a different age, or at a different rate. Crying, throwing temper tantrums, fighting, whining, spitting, urinating, screaming, and so on are behaviors that can be expected of all youngsters. Only the situations in which children and youth with EBD perform these acts or the intensity and rate at which they do them set them apart.

Longitudinal studies and surveys of youngsters' and parents' perceptions of problem behavior show clearly that a large number of children and youth who are considered normal show disturbing behaviors such as tantrums, destructiveness, fearfulness, and hyperactivity to some degree and at some time during their development. Most students are considered to have a behavior problem at some time by one of their teachers.

There is also great variability in deviant behavior. Deviant acts can range from physical assault on others to extreme withdrawal. An individual may exhibit behavior that alternates between extremes, and the degree of deviance may change markedly over time or with changes in the environment. Most classifications of human behavior aren't mutually exclusive—a person can have more than one kind of problem. It's extremely difficult to write a definition that includes all the different types and degrees of disorder.

Developmental Norms and Sociocultural Expectations: Ecology

Some of the behaviors that children and youth with disabilities exhibit are recognized as abnormal in nearly every cultural group and all social strata. Muteness, serious self-injury, eating feces, and murder are examples of behavior problems that are found in all or nearly all cultures and all or nearly all subgroups. Behaviors like these are discrepancies from nearly universal developmental norms. However, children and youth are sometimes considered deviant simply because their behavior violates standards specific to their particular culture or the social institutions in their environment, such as their school. Academic achievement, various types of aggression, sexual behavior, language patterns, and so on will be judged deviant or normal depending on the standards of an ethnic group, religion, family, school, and so on.

A given act or pattern of behavior may be considered disordered or deviant in one situation or context but not in another simply because of differences in people's expectations. That is, EBD is usually defined by social or cultural expectations, not by truly universal developmental norms. Failing to read by age seven, hitting others, taking others' belongings, and swearing, for example, are evaluated according to the standards of the child's community or group affiliation. However, extreme aggression, covert antisocial behavior, and socialization to the norms of deviant peers may not only violate social expectations specific to a culture but also may create developmental risk in nearly any culture (Kauffman & Brigham, 2009; Kauffman et al., 2011; Kazdin, 2001, 2008; Walker et al., 2004).

In many cases, EBD originates in or is made worse by social interactions. Many disorders are learned through modeling, reinforcement, extinction, and punishment—learning processes that shape and maintain much of everyone's behavior, both normal and deviant. Adults and other youngsters may accidentally arrange conditions that cause and support undesirable, inappropriate behavior. Ironically, the same adults who unwittingly shape inappropriate behavior may then initiate action to have the child or youth labeled as having EBD. The child or youth might behave quite differently if these adults changed their own behavior in relation to the youngster's or if he or she were placed in a different social environment. The problem in these cases is partly, and sometimes mostly, in the behavior of caretakers or peers.

We might be tempted to conclude that the child or youth with EBD isn't to blame for the way others react. But youngsters' behavior influences their parents, their teachers, their peers, and others who interact with them. Researchers have realized for many years that children *teach* their parents, teachers, and peers how to behave toward them as surely as they are taught by these others. Therefore, it isn't appropriate to ascribe fault exclusively to either the youngster with EBD or to others in the environment. Teaching and learning are interactive processes in which teacher and learner frequently, and often subtly, exchange roles. When a youngster has difficulty with teachers, peers, or parents, it's as important to consider their responses to the behavior as it is to evaluate the youngster's reactions to others.

An ecological perspective takes into account the interrelationships between the child or youth and various aspects of the environment. EBD isn't simply a youngster's inappropriate actions, but undesirable interactions and transactions between the youngster and other people. For example, a child's temper tantrums in school could indeed be a problem. An ecological perspective demands that the behavior of the child's teachers, peers, and parents—their expectations, demands, and reactions to the child's tantrums and other behavior, as well as the child's social goals and strategies—be taken into consideration in dealing with the problem.

Relationships to other Exceptionalities

Defining EBD to exclude other disabilities completely is unrealistic. Decades ago, Hallahan and Kauffman (1977) pointed out that there are many similarities among students with mild mental retardation (now usually called *intellectual disability*), learning disabilities, and emotional disturbance (now often called *EBD*). Considerable literature shows EBD in individuals with intellectual disability (mental retardation) or other disabilities (Blackorby, Knokey, Wagner, Levine, Schiller, & Sumi, 2007; Lee, Moss, Friedlander, Donnelly, & Horner, 2003; Matson & Laud, 2007; Sturmey, 2007). It's often difficult not only to distinguish among students with pervasive developmental disorders such as severe autism and intellectual disability, but in some cases it may also be difficult to distinguish very young children with severe EBD from those who are deaf, blind, or have cerebral palsy or traumatic brain injury. In fact, EBD probably occurs most frequently in combination with other disabilities.

Transience of Many Emotional and Behavioral Problems

EBD is often transitory, and the problems of those with EBD can be on-again-off-again. The idea that they're constant, 24/7 phenomena is a common but very serious misunderstanding. A youngster might exhibit EBD at one stage of development but not at another (Forness, Freeman, Paparella, Kauffman, & Walker, 2012; Hallahan et al., 2015; Kauffman & Brigham, 2009) or at one time but not another (Kauffman, Mock, & Simpson, 2007).

Behavioral problems exhibited by many young children are likely to disappear within a few years unless the problems are severe or include high levels of hostile aggression and destructiveness. Nevertheless, high levels of problem behavior in young children often do persist and become worse if not treated (Briggs-Gowan, Carter, Bosson-Heenan, Guyer, & Horwitz, 2006; Dunlap et al., 2006). Definitions must take into account age-specific and developmentally normal problems that don't persist over a long period of time.

Disadvantages in Labeling Deviance

Once a student's problem has been labeled, changing the label may be very difficult or impossible. This seems to be true regardless of the conceptual foundation of the definition with which the label is associated or the semantics of the label. Assigning any label is dangerous because the label is likely to stigmatize the youngster and can significantly alter the youngster's opportunities for education, employment, and socialization.

Still, we cannot talk about things, including disabilities such as EBD, without using labels (words) to describe them. Our definitions should be couched in language that will minimize damage to students when they are identified as members of a particular deviant group, but reducing stigma depends on changing social attitudes toward what we label, not on changing the label referring to undesirable characteristics (see Kauffman, 2014a, 2014b, 2015b; Kauffman & Badar, 2013; Kauffman & Hallahan, 2005b; Kauffman, Mock, Tankersley, & Landrum, 2008).

IMPORTANCE OF DEFINITION

The issue of definition may not appear at first thought to be major. If a student has EBD when adult authorities say so, then why not concern ourselves with the more important issue of effective intervention and leave the question of definition to those who enjoy arguing about words? Serious reflection leads us ultimately to conclude that definition is too important to leave to chance or whim.

The definition we accept reflects how we conceptualize the problem and therefore what intervention strategies we consider appropriate. A definition succinctly communicates a conceptual framework that has direct implications for practitioners. Medical definitions imply the need for medical treatment, educational definitions imply the need for educational solutions, and so on. Furthermore, a definition specifies the population to be served and thereby has a profound effect on *who* receives intervention, as well as *how* he or she will be served. It follows that if a definition specifies a population, then it will provide the basis for estimates of prevalence. Finally, decisions of legislative bodies, of government executives, and of school administrators concerning allocation of funds and training and employment of personnel are guided by the implications of working definitions. Vague and inappropriate definitions contribute to confused and inadequate legislation, foggy administrative policies, nonfunctional teacher training, and ineffective intervention. Definition is a crucial as well as a difficult problem, and it behooves special educators to construct the soundest possible definition that recognizes these students' disabilities in school.

A case in point is the current federal definition, which has been widely criticized for a variety of reasons as inadequate or inappropriate. The federal definition seems to indicate that a student must be failing academically to be classified as emotionally disturbed for special education purposes. This feature of the definition may result in denial of services to a large number of students with serious EBD but with academic skills judged adequate for their grade placement. Furthermore, the exclusion of children considered socially maladjusted but not emotionally disturbed may keep students with conduct disorders out of special education. So, we now look at just what that federal definition is.

Current Federal Definition

Only the definition written by Eli Bower long ago has had a significant influence on public policy at the national level (Bower, 1981). The current federal definition derives from Bower's research in the 1950s involving thousands of students in California. Although Bower's definition is a logical interpretation of his findings, the twisted version that was adopted by the U.S. Department of Education has been criticized for a long time as illogical (see Bower, 1982; Council for Children with Behavioral Disorders Executive Committee, 1987; Forness & Knitzer, 1992). To understand the issues involved here, you first have to understand Bower's definition and then compare it to the federal version, point by point.

In a classic treatise on definition and identification, Bower defined emotionally handicapped (ED or EBD) students as those exhibiting "to a marked extent and over a period of time" one or more of five characteristics (1981, pp. 115–116):

1. An inability to learn that cannot be explained by intellectual, sensory, or health factors

2. An inability to build or maintain satisfactory interpersonal relationships with peers and teachers

3. Inappropriate types of behavior or feelings under normal conditions

4. A general, pervasive mood of unhappiness or depression

5. A tendency to develop physical symptoms, pains, or fears associated with personal or school problems.

According to Bower, the first of these characteristics, problems in learning, is possibly the most significant school-related aspect of ED (or EBD). He goes on to explain that another important feature of his definition is the inclusion of the degree or level of severity of the problem.

Bower's definition has many good points, particularly its specification of five characteristic types of behavior. Still, it doesn't easily enable anyone to determine that a particular child or youth has or doesn't have EBD. There's much latitude in terms such as *to a marked extent* and *over a period of time*. There's also a need for subjective judgment about each of the five characteristics. Consider the problems in answering these questions:

- Just what is an inability to learn? Is it a one-year lag in achievement? Six months? Two years? Does it include the inability to learn appropriate social behavior, or only academic skills?
- How do you establish that an apparent inability to learn isn't explainable by intellectual or health factors? Do health factors include mental health factors?
- Exactly what are satisfactory interpersonal relationships with peers?
- What is inappropriate behavior, and what are normal conditions?
- When is unhappiness pervasive?

Bower's definition has had a tremendous influence on public policy, primarily because it's included, with a few but significant changes, in the rules and regulations governing implementation of Public Law 94–142 (now the *Individuals with Disabilities Education Improvement Act*—IDEA 2004). The federal definition of *emotionally disturbed* follows (with the most significant differences between it and Bower's definition indicated by italics):

4. Emotional disturbance is defined as follows:

    (i)   The term means a condition exhibiting one or more of the following characteristics over a *long* period of time and to a marked degree *that adversely affects a child's educational performance:*

        (A)   An inability to learn that cannot be explained by intellectual, sensory, or health factors.
        (B)   An inability to build or maintain satisfactory interpersonal relationships with peers and teachers.
        (C)   Inappropriate types of behavior or feelings under normal circumstances.
        (D)   A general pervasive mood of unhappiness or depression.
        (E)   A tendency to develop physical symptoms or fears associated with personal or school problems.

    (ii) *The term includes schizophrenia. The term does not apply to children who are socially maladjusted, unless it is determined that they have an emotional disturbance.*

Bower's terminology, *emotionally handicapped*, was changed to *emotionally disturbed*. That is perhaps insignificant. However, as the italics show, the federal rules and regulations contain three statements not found in Bower's original definition. These added statements do not make the definition clearer. They come close to making it nonsense. *That adversely affects educational performance* is particularly puzzling. Maybe it means that the regulation is concerned only with educational matters. But it's redundant with characteristic A, "An inability to learn," if educational performance is considered to mean only academic achievement. Furthermore, any student is extremely unlikely to exhibit one or more of the five characteristics listed "to a marked degree" and "over a long period of time" without adverse effects on academic progress. But what should we conclude about a student who exhibits, for example, characteristic D, "a general, pervasive mood of unhappiness or depression," and is academically on grade level or advanced for his or her age and grade? If educational performance is interpreted to mean just academic achievement, then the student would seem to be excluded. However, if educational performance is interpreted to include personal and social satisfaction in the school setting, then the clause is superfluous.

Even greater confusion is created by item ii regarding schizophrenia and social maladjustment. Any youngster with schizophrenia would clearly be included under the original definition—will exhibit one or more of the five characteristics listed (especially B or C, or both) to a marked extent an over a long period of time. Therefore, the addendum is unnecessary. The final addendum regarding social maladjustment is incomprehensible. No one can be socially maladjusted by any credible interpretation of that term without exhibiting one or more of the five characteristics (especially B, C, or both). Neither logic nor research supports the discrimination between

Video Example from YouTube

ENHANCEDetext
Video Connections 2.1
Watch the video "Issues in Identification, Evaluation, & Eligibility in the Category of EBD" (part 1). Note the elements of the federal definition of emotional disturbance the speaker discusses, particularly the examples of vague terminology used in that definition. (https://www.youtube.com/watch?v=7BQy3l6oJ3c)

social maladjustment and emotional disturbance (Bower, 1982; Cline, 1990; Costenbader & Buntaine, 1999; Landrum, 2017; Walker et al., 2004). Because of the limitations we have discussed, many professionals are very unhappy with the current definition and hope that it will soon be replaced.

Perspectives on Definition

In the early part of the twentieth century, psychiatric perspectives on definition tended to be accepted with little question by school personnel. Bower's work in California public schools in the 1950s and 1960s and the growth of special education programs for students with emotional or behavioral disorders led to definitions that were more closely related to students' behavior in the classroom (see Mundschenk & Simpson, 2014; Walker, Yell, & Murray, 2014). Most professionals recognize that a given definition is never adequate for all purposes. Knitzer (1982) wrote long ago that it's hard to use the usual terms to talk about youngsters who need mental health services without losing sight of the fact that they're unique individuals who are experiencing a lot of pain. This is still true.

Ironically, the current federal definition may be contributing to the underservice of students with emotional or behavioral disorders (see Forness et al., 2012; Kauffman et al., 2007, 2009). The additions to Bower's definition allow so many interpretations that students who need services can be easily excluded, either because they aren't failing academically or because they're said to be socially maladjusted but not emotionally disturbed or because they're said to be merely culturally different and misunderstood. Legal arguments continue over issues like whether a student must be academically delayed and whether delinquency involves emotional disturbance.

The definition of EBD remains partly subjective, even though several relevant characteristics of a student's behavior can be described clearly. Definition isn't completely objective for the same reasons that happiness and depression aren't. This doesn't mean that the search for a more objective definition should be abandoned or that it's impossible to improve the definition. For the definition to be most useful to educators, however, the subjective judgments that go into identifying students must include those of the teachers who work with them. In decisions made by groups of professionals, the teacher, not the psychologist, social worker, or psychiatrist, should be viewed as the most important "imperfect test" in determining whether a student needs help in school (see Gerber, 2005; Gerber & Semmel, 1984). However, using teachers' judgments puts great responsibility on teachers for making ethical decisions. It's a responsibility teachers can't avoid (Kauffman, Badar, & Wiley, in press).

An Emerging Alternative Definition

An alternative definition has been emerging for decades. Sometimes, changes are a very long time in coming. We believe it's important not to give up on the idea of changing the definition.

Although professionals agree on a substitute definition, they haven't been able so far (as of 2017) to persuade the U.S. Congress to adopt a new one. The National Mental Health and Special Education Coalition, which we mentioned earlier, created a working group assigned to propose a new definition. The working group represented more than a dozen different professional associations and advocacy groups, ensuring that the proposed definition would initially have a strong base of support. The definition proposed in the 1980s reads as follows:

I. The term *emotional* or *behavioral disorder* means a disability characterized by emotional or behavioral responses in school programs so different from appropriate age, cultural, or ethnic norms that they adversely affect educational performance, including academic, social, vocational, or personal skills, and which:

    (a)   is more than a temporary, expected response to stressful events in the environment;

    (b)   is consistently exhibited in two different settings, at least one of which is school related; and

    (c)   persists despite individualized interventions within the education program, unless, in the judgment of the team, the child's or youth's history indicates that such interventions would not be effective.

Emotional or behavioral disorders can co-exist with other disabilities.

II. This category may include children or youth with schizophrenic disorders, affective disorders, anxiety disorders, or other sustained disturbances of conduct or adjustment when they adversely affect educational performance in accordance with section I. (Forness & Knitzer, 1992, p. 13)

This definition obviously doesn't solve all the problems in identifying and serving children and youth with EBD. Nevertheless, the coalition and many of its member organizations believe it is a significant improvement because:

1. It uses terminology that reflects current professional preferences and concern for minimizing stigma.

2. It includes both disorders of emotions and disorders of behavior.

3. It is school-centered but acknowledges that disorders exhibited outside the school setting are also important.

4. It is sensitive to ethnic and cultural differences.

5. It does not include minor or transient problems or ordinary responses to stress.

6. It acknowledges the importance of prereferral interventions but does not require slavish implementation of them in extreme cases.

7. It acknowledges that children and youth can have multiple disabilities.

8. It includes the full range of emotional or behavioral disorders of concern to mental health and special education professionals without arbitrary exclusions. (Forness & Knitzer, 1992)

A major problem of the current federal definition is its exclusion of many antisocial children and youth who need special education and related mental health services. Yes, they are very irritating to their teachers and often to many other people as well. More importantly, they are among those with the worst prognosis for long-term success in life; they are youngsters with disabilities and need to be recognized as such.

The Coalition and many of the more than thirty professional and advocacy groups have formally endorsed the proposed definition and are working toward its incorporation into federal laws and regulations. Those who support the definition hope it will eventually become the standard adopted by the states as well. Meanwhile, we're stuck with the definition used in federal law and its regulations. You might also consider some examples of youngsters with EBD.

These examples illustrate just how hard it is to write a definition that includes all of them and all other examples we might give.

Examples of Disorders

Let's consider some examples of what it is we're trying to define. Children and youth can cause negative feelings and reactions in others in many different ways. As we will see in several of the following chapters, disordered emotions or behaviors may be described according to two primary dimensions: *externalizing* (aggressive, acting-out behavior) and *internalizing* (social withdrawal). The cases we describe here and in the accompanying case book illustrate the range in types of EBD and the variety of factors that can cause children and youth to become disabled. Compare the cases we describe to anything you might encounter in the media and you'll understand that we're talking about persistent human problems. That is, they're as old as human societies, but they're also as contemporary as today's news.

When you're thinking of the problem of writing a definition, remember that these problems appear in young children as well as adolescents, so the general definition can't be tied to age. They're exhibited by individuals who've grown up in privileged homes with caring parents as well as by those who've been neglected and abused and/or reared in poverty, so the general definition has to include all kinds of circumstances. They're often accompanied by lower-than-average intelligence but sometimes by intellectual brilliance, so the definition has to accommodate individuals regardless of how bright they are. They may be characterized by externalizing (acting out) or internalizing (withdrawn) behavior or alternation between the two, and they may be described from the perspective of an observer or of the self, so the definition can't include just one of those dimensions of behavior. In thinking about the following cases, remember the extreme variety of types of problems that a general definition of emotional or behavioral disorder has to cover.

Roger

Roger is twelve years old. He's now in seventh grade. He already has an extensive record of problems in his school, his family, and his neighborhood. He doesn't seem to get along well with anyone, and he has his own view of what happens when he's around. He might be seen by his classmates and teachers as giving someone "the finger," for example, but then he explains that he was just scratching his head or scratching his face. He tries to exonerate himself by saying that he didn't do anything wrong, it's just that other people have "dirty minds." He may tear up his book, but then maintain that he was just trying to put it back together because it was falling apart. He might call another student a bad name, but justify his actions by saying that the other student called him a bad name first and he was just responding in kind.

In short, Roger never takes responsibility for starting any negative interaction or for doing something inappropriate. Every teacher he's had since the first grade has noted that he exhibits problem behavior. Even so, he's never been evaluated for special education because his parents haven't asked for his evaluation, and the teachers and school administrators see him as just a "royal pain in the behind," as one of his teachers wrote. His parents separated—apparently after years of considerable hostility toward each other—when Roger was ten. He's an only child, and the speculation

Roger (continued)

of teachers and other professionals (e.g., school psychologists, social workers) who have had any contact with his parents is that his behavior problems are in large measure a result of his parents' conflicts.

Betsy

Betsy has had problems throughout school. She started exhibiting behavior teachers said was bizarre when she was in the first grade, but it got worse as she got older. At first, her teachers thought she was just a strange little girl. But they got really concerned when, by fourth grade, she was really "out of it." She seemed very easily distracted and hyperactive and was taking Ritalin. At first, people thought she had attention deficit–hyperactivity disorder (ADHD). And then the bottom dropped out of her academic skills. That is, she seemed to be going backward instead of making expected progress academically. She started having what appeared to be hallucinations, hearing voices and muttering to herself. Her behavior became so "weird" in the fourth grade that a psychiatrist diagnosed her as having childhood schizophrenia (a rare condition) and recommended that she be placed in a psychiatric hospital. These things were scary to Betsy herself, not just to other people. She was frightened both by the hallucinations, which seemed so real to her, and by her hospitalization.

She seemed to have a sense that something was wrong, but she couldn't stop hearing the voices and taking them seriously. The hospital was at first a frightening place to her because it was new, but it became a comforting place because her hallucinations started going away and she had lots of attention and routine.

In the psychiatric hospital, she took prescribed anti-psychotic medicine. She went to school in the psychiatric hospital, too, to try to keep up with her schoolwork. Three years later, she had improved so much and was making such dramatic educational progress that she was out of the psychiatric hospital and back in her regular neighborhood school. She was in the seventh grade when she returned to her public school, right where she should have been according to her age.

Betsy now seems to be doing fine, but she's still taking medication to control her hallucinations. And, of course, she and everyone else wonder whether this is just temporary or it's a permanent change.

Tom

Tom is eleven and in fifth grade. He has an IQ in the bright normal range. He doesn't have any physical disabilities or language problems. He didn't have any particular academic difficulties until fourth grade, when his grades suddenly began to go down. This year he's getting mostly Ds and Fs.

Tom didn't impress his teachers as being a problem in school until last year. But every teacher who's dealt with him in the past eighteen months has commented on his frequent misbehavior. He's difficult for teachers to manage because he frequently talks out, teases other kids, has temper tantrums, and gets out of his seat and wanders around the classroom. He's usually defiant and argues a lot with his peers and adults. His teachers see him as getting worse. His belligerence is so bad that he recently got into several fights in and around school, including one in which the other child was injured and required medical attention. Two weeks ago he was caught shoplifting a bag of candy from the local drugstore. Ratings by his teachers on a problem checklist indicate that his behavior is a problem more often than that of 90 percent of his classmates.

Tom doesn't have any really close friends, but other boys whose conduct is sort of like his tolerate him sometimes or even say they like him. He and his two older brothers live with his mother and stepfather, who provide little supervision or control. His parents have never shown any interest in his school progress or lack of it, and they've refused to recognize that he has any real problems. They don't see his fights or shoplifting as a big deal.

Tom's teachers are very concerned about him for several reasons. He doesn't complete most of his academic work, and he's failing in most subjects. He disrupts the class frequently by hitting or taunting other students or mumbling complaints about the teacher or his assignments. He spends a lot of his time in class drawing "tattoos" on his arms with felt-tip pens. Most of these have some sort of violent theme. No teacher has been able to establish a close relationship with him or produce significant improvement in his behavior.

Few people would disagree with the conclusion that Betsy has some sort of EBD. Partly, this is because her behavior was so unusual and involved hallucinations. Partly it is because a psychiatrist diagnosed her as having schizophrenia, a well-known mental illness. But Roger and Tom, although much more typical of youngsters with EBD, are the kinds of students people often disagree about. Their cases don't seem as clear-cut, and some people will argue that they should be seen as emotionally disturbed according to the federal definition, and others will argue that they shouldn't be. They're the kinds of students who make us wonder about where we should draw the line and for what reasons, what we should see as just being a pain in the rear and what we should see as EBD. Do they or do they not fit the definition? Should we or should we not count them as emotionally disturbed?

Given the difficulty and ongoing controversy about how to define EBD, it shouldn't be surprising that obtaining accurate information on how many children and youth experience such disorders is also a persistent challenge. We turn our attention now to the problem of determining the prevalence of EBD and the accompanying difficulties this challenge presents for schools.

PREVALENCE

Nearly all children and youth at some time, in some social context, could be said to exhibit EBD, regardless of how we define it. But classifying nearly all children and youth as disabled by these isolated, transitory, or minor problems would be silly. Indeed, suggestions that at any given time 20 percent or more of children and youth have serious psychological problems understandably create public disbelief and professional skepticism. A typical reaction is that bleeding hearts are making much ado about the normal pains of growing up, bemoaning the usual slings and arrows that people must suffer as part of their daily lives.

However, we face a worse problem. The general public and administrators tend to dismiss teachers' reports of problems as minor and unreliable. Teachers do sometimes mistake their own ineptitude in teaching and managing behavior for the EBD of students, and they do sometimes show undue concern for relatively trivial misbehavior. Nevertheless, skeptics use these facts to discount most or all teachers' opinions. If we want to argue convincingly for special services, then we must present the strongest possible case that the emotional and behavioral problems we're concerned about are unusual, debilitating, and not the result of teachers' inadequacies.

How frequently do students' emotional or behavioral problems clearly stand out from the usual difficulties of childhood and youth and seriously limit their options for social and personal development despite adequate teachers? The answer can't be entirely objective. Addressing the question requires that we establish arbitrary criteria. These criteria may be quite objective, but choosing them requires subjective judgment. Consider similar questions: How heavy (or thin or tall or short) must a person of a given age be to qualify as exceptional for medical purposes? How little income must a person have to be considered poor for purposes of public assistance? How different from the average in intelligence and social adaptation must a student be to qualify as having an intellectual disability (or giftedness) for special education purposes? In each case, we can "make" more people deviant—obese, poor, intellectually disabled, or EBD, for example—simply by changing an arbitrary definition (Kauffman & Hallahan, 2005b; Kauffman & Lloyd, 2017). Physicians, economists, social workers, psychologists, or educators may make their case for a given criterion, and their arguments may be convincing to legislators or others who make public policy or establish standards for judgment. The standards and policy are merely a matter of consensus, and they can be changed at will.

The number or percentage of children and youth who are judged to have EBD, then, is a matter of choice. Disordered emotion or behavior isn't a "thing," an objective entity that can be detached from the observer and social context. Emotional or behavioral disorder—like poverty or love or justice—is a social reality that we construct on the basis of our judgment as to what's tolerable and what's desirable in our society. Our task as professionals is to struggle with issues of prevalence, to make the most intelligent and caring choices we can about the lives of children and youth. We must seek to identify those students—and only those—for whom the risks associated with identification (such as social stigma) are outweighed by the advantages (effective intervention). This isn't easy. Although we can and must make difficult judgments about the risks and advantages entailed in identification, we can seldom be absolutely certain that our judgment of the individual case is correct.

Try to decide whether the students described earlier (Roger, Betsy, and Tom) and those described in the accompanying case book should be counted as having EBD. All of the descriptions are brief, and you probably believe you should have more information before making judgments. You should, in fact, have more information. Anyone should, and anyone would probably be unprofessional in making a judgment based solely on the sketchy information given in these cases. Still, at some point we have to decide who does or doesn't have EBD.

The Meanings of *Prevalence* and *Incidence*

Prevalence refers to the total number of individuals with X disorder in a given population. The prevalence of a disorder can be calculated for a given point in time (*point prevalence*) or over a given period of time, usually school years or a lifetime (*cumulative prevalence*)

ENHANCEDetext
Video Connections 2.2
In the video "Issues in Identification, Evaluation, & Eligibility in the Category of EBD" (part 2), you see a discussion about the estimated prevalence of EBD in school-aged children versus the actual percentage of children served under the federal category of emotional disturbance. (https://www.youtube.com/watch?v=IbLfGc5RoAY).

(see Forness et al., 2012). Prevalence is often expressed as a percentage of the population; the total number of cases is divided by the total number of individuals in the population. Thus, if 40 students out of a total student population of 2,000 in a school or school district are identified at a given time as having EBD, then the point prevalence is 2 percent.

Incidence refers to the rate of *inception*—the number of *new* cases of X disorder in a given population. *Cases* can refer to individuals or to episodes of the disorder (which means that an individual might be counted more than once during the incidence period if he or she exhibits the disorder, subsequently does not exhibit the disorder or goes into remission, and then exhibits the disorder again). Incidence, like prevalence, may be expressed as a percentage of the population, but this can be misleading when episodes rather than individuals are counted. Incidence addresses the question: How often does this disorder occur? Prevalence addresses the question: How many individuals are affected?

For special education purposes, prevalence has usually had more meaning than incidence. Teachers and school administrators have most often been concerned with knowing or estimating the number or percent of students who have EBD or some other disability in any given school year.

Why Should We Care about Prevalence?

Prevalence and incidence estimates might seem to have little meaning for classroom teachers. When your responsibility is to teach a certain number of difficult children, what difference does it make whether 2 percent, 5 percent, or 10 percent of the school's students have EBD? That's somebody else's problem!

However, for those who plan and administer special education programs at a district-wide, state-wide, or nation-wide level, prevalence and incidence are extremely important. Prevalence estimates and incidence rates are the basis for making budget requests, hiring staff, planning in-service programs, and so on. Frequently, school boards or school administrators decide to cut budgets or allocate additional funds because the percentage of children served by a program is more or less than that of neighboring school districts or state or national averages. Thus, although prevalence may seem irrelevant or purely academic to classroom teachers, it can ultimately affect their working conditions.

Making Prevalence Estimates

Estimates of the prevalence of EBD have varied from about 0.5 percent or less of the school population to 20 percent or more. It's easy to see why estimates have been varied and confused, regardless of whether point prevalence or cumulative prevalence is estimated. First, it's difficult, if not impossible, to count something that has no precise definition. Even when a definition is chosen, counting cases is difficult. Research clearly shows that identification rates are in part a consequence of the diagnostic criteria (e.g., Cluett et al., 1998). Even using a standard written definition, people seem to carry their own private definitions in their heads; they differ greatly in how they match the written definition to students' behavior

(Kauffman et al., 2007). Second, different ways of estimating the number of students with EBD can be used. Differences in methodology can produce drastically different results. Third, social policy and economic factors can be more powerful than methodology.

False Positives and False Negatives

Prevalence and incidence are usually estimated from a sample of the population in question because it isn't feasible to count every case in an entire state or nation or even in a large school district. Good estimates are based on standard screening procedures applied to a carefully selected sample. The methodological problems are similar to those of conducting a poll or making a projection during an election. Different numbers will tend to be obtained depending on how the sample is selected and what questions are asked.

In either estimating or identifying students as having EBD (or anything else), mistakes are inevitable. Some mistakes will be *false negatives* (students who should be but were not identified) and *false positives* (students who have been identified but should not have been). Put another way, we can say the mistakes could be:

False negatives—overlooked or missed
False positives—wrongly identified

Preference for false negatives and the fear of false positives are often sufficient to stop prevention, although false negatives occur far more often than false positives and should give us more concern. Consider this more carefully. If we believe the U.S. surgeon general's report on children's mental health (U.S. Department of Health and Human Services, 2001) and many prevalence studies, then we have to conclude that false negatives (children overlooked who should have been identified) far outnumber false positives (children falsely identified; see Forness et al., 2012; Kauffman et al., 2007, 2009; Warner, 2010). The reality seems to be, at least in mental health, that the problem is not overidentification but missing actual cases—false negatives. It seems to us very likely that the same mistake of not identifying true cases of EBD is a large problem in special education. When one looks at the data, is seems obvious that only a small proportion of youngsters whose EBD is clear are receiving psychiatric treatment. When effective interventions were rare, this was not such a big deal, but now it is. Especially unfortunate is the fact that psychiatric problems typically start early in life, and the risk for psychiatric disorders goes up for children who experience adversities or manifest EBD in their early years. So early intervention is clearly important, but the reality is that most early problems are ignored (see Costello, Egger, & Angold, 2005).

Economic Realities

At any given time, 2 percent is a very modest estimate (very probably an underestimate) of the school population whose EBD deserves special education. We have very good reason to believe that the percentage of the child population needing mental health services is much higher, and this is likely also an indication of the percentage needing special education for EBD (see Costello et al., 2005; Forness et al., 2012; Kessler, Berglund, Demler, Jin & Walters, 2005;

Video Example from YouTube

ENHANCEDetext
Video Connections 2.3
Part 3 of the video "Issues in Identification, Evaluation, & Eligibility in the Category of EBD" provides a discussion of who gets identified as having EBD—with an emphasis on the notion of false positives (students who are identified with EBD but really do not have a disorder) and false negatives (students who have true emotional or behavioral disorders but are not identified with EBD). (https://www.youtube.com/watch?v=8_xnTJcTtmE)

U.S. Department of Health and Human Services, 2001; Walker et al., 2004; Wang, Berglund, Olfson, Pincus, Wells, & Kessler, 2005). However, reports from the U.S. Department of Education indicate that less than 1 percent of the school population receives special education in the "emotionally disturbed" category. In short, the percentage served is much lower than the percentage estimated to need services, and this is true for all ethnic or racial groups.

The definition of *emotional disturbance* is sufficiently vague and subjective so that just about any student can be included or excluded as long as inclusion or exclusion serves a useful purpose. School systems and states find it useful to deny that students have EBD to stay within their budgets. Official nonidentification is a convenient way for many school officials to avoid the hassles, risks, and costs of expanded services. In addition, many professionals find it easy to rationalize nonidentification of students, often with reference to their gender, culture, age, family, or socioeconomic status.

Reasonable Estimates and Percentage Served

The most relevant question is this: What is a reasonable estimate of the percentage of students whose behavior is so persistently troublesome that special education is desirable? Reasonable estimates based on decades of population surveys are *at least* 3 percent to 6 percent of the student population (see Forness et al., 2012; Kessler, Berglund et al., 2005; Perou et al., 2013; U.S. Department of Health and Human Services, 2001; Wang, Berglund et al., 2005; Wang, Lane, Olfson Pincus, Wells, & Kessler, 2005).

In one nationally representative survey, nearly half (46 percent) of adults were found to have experienced a diagnosable mental disorder at some point in their lifetime (Kessler, Chiu, Demler, & Walters, 2005). Moreover, the mean age of onset for both anxiety disorders (experienced at some point by 29 percent of respondents) and impulse control disorders (experienced by 25 percent of respondents) was eleven years. At the beginning of the twenty-first century, the U.S. surgeon general released a report indicating that at least 5 percent of children and youth have seriously impairing mental health needs and that only about one in five of those with such needs receives any mental health services (U.S. Department of Health and Human Services, 2001). Another survey of children in the United States found that in any given year 13 to 20 percent could be expected to have a mental disorder and that the prevalence of such disorders has been increasing (Perou et al., 2013). This study and others have been criticized, and prevalence of severe disorders are said to have dropped and may be in the 10 to 13 percent range (Olfson, Druss, & Marcus, 2015). However, we may safely assume that at least half of the children and youth with serious mental health needs should be identified for special education and that 2.5 percent is a conservative estimate—*at least* 2.5 times the percentage of the school population receiving special education in the category "emotionally disturbed" in 2016 (and, very likely, in any subsequent year).

Several findings are consistent across a variety of studies spanning nearly half a century. First, most children and youth exhibit seriously troublesome behavior at some time during their development. Second, way more than 2 percent of school-aged youngsters are considered by teachers and other adults—consistently and over a period of years—to exhibit disordered behavior and to fit the federal definition of *emotionally disturbed*. Students now in programs for students with EBD, as well as those not identified but showing similar characteristics, have serious academic and social difficulties that they are not likely to overcome without intervention.

FACTORS AFFECTING PREVALENCE

Assume for the moment that we can agree about the definition of children and youth who should be identified as having EBD. What are some other factors that might increase or decrease the prevalence of these disorders?

Presumed Link Between Causes and Prevalence

At this point, it is sufficient to note that a variety of biological, family, school, and cultural conditions might make EBD occur more frequently, and we might therefore expect EBD to be more prevalent in some communities and schools and groups of students than in others. Nevertheless, those factors that might be expected to affect prevalence don't explain the extreme range of rates of service—differences that vary by a factor of four, from 0.05 percent of the school population in one state to more than 2 percent in another. So, besides risk factors, such as poverty, unemployment, malnutrition, dangerous communities, and the like, that might account for some variations in prevalence, other factors may be at work.

EBD isn't identified at the same rate across age groups, partly because of the nature of these disorders and the way our society responds to them. Relatively few are identified in the early grades; most are identified at age twelve to fourteen, and there's a steady increase in identification from early ages to middle teen years. We might speculate that the age trends for students with EBD are related to the increasing social difficulties youngsters face as they enter adolescence, which is a stressful period for all youth. Students with learning disabilities and intellectual disabilities may tend to have more obvious academic difficulties early in their school careers. Those with intellectual disabilities show steady and persistent school difficulties through adolescence, and some of those with learning disabilities begin to find a resolution of their difficulties by early adolescence. Students with EBD, however, often are identified later, often after years of struggle and after receiving other diagnostic labels.

Reluctance to Identify EBD

The problems of children with EBD tend to be overlooked or neglected for as long as possible—until they become so painfully obvious and intolerable to adults that something has to be done (see Warner, 2010). Although some estimates suggest that the majority of people who experience mental health needs eventually make contact with the service system, delays between the onset of their disorders and initial contact are often staggering—six to eight years for mood disorders and as long as twenty years or more for anxiety disorders (Wang, Berglund et al., 2005). By the time these children obtain services, they are older, and their problems are more severe than those identified in other categories (see Earley, 2006). Adults tend to respond to them by being more demanding and punitive. This may account, in part, for the fact that students with EBD leave school at higher rates and are placed more frequently in more restrictive settings than are students in other disability categories.

Disproportionality

EBD isn't identified in the same proportion across all ethnic groups. African American students are about 1.5 times more likely than Caucasian students to be identified based on raw

ENHANCEDetext
Video Connections 2.4
In part 4 of the video "Issues in Identification, Evaluation, & Eligibility in the Category of EBD" the speaker provides a brief overview of data on disproportionality, talks about some factors that might contribute to disproportionality, and describes things teachers might do to address these factors. (https://www.youtube.com/watch?v=lu_6kOYjktg)

percentage comparisons (i.e., based on comparison of percentage of the general population to percentage of students receiving special education) (National Research Council, 2002; Osher et al., 2004; Oswald, Coutinho, Best, & Singh, 1999; Skiba, Middleberg, & McClain, 2014). However, using the same raw percentage comparisons, students of Hispanic or Asian-Pacific Island ethnic groups are considerably less likely than are Caucasian students to be identified as emotionally disturbed. Males are much more likely to be identified as emotionally disturbed than are females (Oswald, Best, Coutinho, & Nagle, 2003). Although such patterns of disproportionality have been known for decades, they persist.

Disproportionality in identification is a serious matter and could be the result of a variety of factors, including bias in assessment. Moreover, there is pronounced variation from state to state in the degree of various ethnic groups' disproportionality. Research now suggests that comparisons of raw percentages are misleading. When comparisons are made to children with similar characteristics in achievement and behavior, African American and other minority children appear to be *under*-identified (Anastasiou, Morgan, Farkas, & Wiley, 2017; Kauffman & Anastasiou, in press; Morgan, Farkas, Cook, Strassfeld, Hillemeier, Pun, & Schussler, 2016). The causes remain unconfirmed but seem likely to be due to institutionalized racism that disproportionately denies services to children who are exposed disproportionately to risk factors for emotional and behavioral problems.

One might note that the percentage of no ethnic or gender group identified as emotionally disturbed exceeds the estimated prevalence of EBD among children and youth. However, the combined issues of prevalence and ethnic disproportionality clearly suggest that although all ethnic groups are underserved, some ethnic groups are more underserved than others. More specifically, false negatives seem clearly to be more of a problem than false positives among all ethnic groups, and false negatives appear to be a greater problem among ethnic groups that are *not* African Americans (Kauffman et al., 2007, 2009).

Social Policy and Economic Factors

Social policy and economic realities have effectively precluded the public schools' identification of 2 percent or more of the school-aged population as having EBD. Consider the economic realities. Way back in the 1970s, nearly a billion more dollars per year would have been needed from the federal government, plus nearly 1.4 billion more dollars from state and local sources, to serve 2 percent of the students in public schools (Grosenick & Huntze, 1979). These figures didn't include funds for training personnel or allowances for inflation. Today, services for 2 percent of the public school population would require many billions more dollars per year from federal sources alone than is currently budgeted. It seems highly unlikely that federal or state legislatures or local schools will make the required amounts of money available for training personnel and operating programs to serve this many students. Conservative political views also apparently are associated with lower than usual rates of identification of emotional and behavioral disorders (Wiley, Brigham, Kauffman, & Bogan, 2013; Wiley, Kauffman, & Plageman, 2015; Wiley &

Siperstein, 2011). Unfortunately, an ostensible concern for lowering immediate costs by simply not identifying EBD that exists (which also denies services to children who need them) may actually have the effect of increasing the long-term cost of responding to social deviancy when individuals with mental illnesses end up in jails or are unemployable (Kendziora, 2004).

Faced with a shortage of adequately trained personnel and insurmountable budget problems, what can we expect of school officials? They can't risk litigation and loss of the federal funds they do have by identifying students they can't serve. It's reasonable to expect that they will identify as many students as they can find resources to serve. The tragedy is that social policy (federal law) mandates the impossible and that the public—and a growing number of professionals—are likely to change their perceptions to match economic realities. The social policy mandate changes the question, at least for those who manage budgets, from "How many students with EBD are there in our schools?" to "How many can we afford to serve?" To save face and try to abide by the law, it's tempting to conclude that there are, indeed, precisely as many students with EBD as the schools are able to serve. Particularly in times of budget problems, it's tempting to make the case that we're actually misidentifying many students and should reduce the number of those who receive special education.

Pressures *not* to identify students as having EBD are powerful. These pressures have existed for a long time (Dunlap et al., 2006; Kauffman, 1999c, 2004, 2005, 2014a; Peacock Hill Working Group, 1991; see also Gage et al., 2010). We don't seem to be nearing the day when special education and related services will be provided for most of the 3 percent of the child population that Morse (1985) considered very seriously impaired.

Distaste for identifying students as exceptional and for providing special programs outside the regular class, even on a part-time basis, has led to efforts to merge or restructure special and general education, known since the 1990s as the *full inclusion movement* (see Kauffman & Hallahan, 2005a, 2005b; Mock & Kauffman, 2002; Zigmond, 2015; Zigmond & Kloo, 2017; Zigmond, Kloo, & Volonino, 2009). Proponents of full inclusion argue that most students now considered disabled are either not disabled at all or have mild disabilities. Because their disabilities are not real or are very mild, we can expect regular classroom teachers to deal with them effectively with little additional training or assistance. This viewpoint, even if it is well intentioned, suppresses the recognition of EBD and other disabilities for which special education and related services are appropriate. Thus, the trend appears to be toward identification of only those students whose behavior offends or disturbs others most egregiously—those with the most severe disorders (Forness et al., 2012).

Way back in the 1980s, a meeting of experts resulted in the following conclusions regarding underservice of students with EBD, then called "*seriously* emotionally disturbed," or SED, by special education (National Mental Health Association, 1986):

> A majority of SED (seriously emotionally disturbed) children are never identified as such and consequently do not receive the services they need. The reasons for this under identification are many:
>
> • There is concern about the stigma of labeling a child as "severely emotionally disturbed."

- No clear definition of SED eligibility exists in the law; therefore, states have had to operationalize a definition, resulting in a tremendous disparity among states.
- A lack of uniformity in identification procedures exists in states and localities.
- Because of funding constraints, states may set limits on the number of SED children they will identify.
- Children may not be identified, not only because of limited funding, but also because few or no appropriate services may be available in their community or because communities lack confidence in their ability to develop appropriate services due to lack of funding or because this is a difficult population to serve.
- A lack of clarity among clinicians in the mental health field on definitions and diagnoses compounds the difficulty educators have in making an assessment that a child is severely emotionally disturbed.
- The law explicitly excludes children who are "socially maladjusted," yet the distinctions between socially maladjusted and severely emotionally disturbed are confusing and meaningless. This confusion in labeling can result in some children not being identified or served.
- There is a tendency to identify children who present significant behavioral problems, and to overlook those who do not act out. In some communities, this, in part, results in an overrepresentation of black males identified as SED and an under-identification of females of all races who may not be labeled as troublesome.
- There are limited outreach efforts by schools and education systems to parents and professionals in the community to identify SED youth.
- There are also differences for SED children, compared to other populations with handicaps, in the degree of their handicap. SED children tend to be more disturbed before they are identified; those with mild or moderate disturbances may never be identified. (p. 5)

Nothing has changed in the intervening decades that makes these statements inaccurate. In fact, as the need for services for more children and youth with EBD has grown, American society's response has been to trim funding for social programs, including special education, that provide services to those in need (see Gage et al., 2010).

PREVALENCE AND INCIDENCE OF SPECIFIC DISORDERS

So far we've considered EBD in the general case. But because there are many types of disorders, it's possible to estimate the prevalence of some specific problems. Unfortunately, many of the same difficulties of estimation we have discussed for the general case also arise when considering more specific disorders. Nevertheless, some publications include prevalence or mental health service data for some of the subtypes of EBD (e.g., Wang, Berglund et al., 2005; Wang, Lane et al., 2005).

The classification of EBD is almost as problematic as the general definition. In addition, the methodology of estimation is at least as varied for many specific disorders as for the general case. Consequently, estimates of prevalence and incidence of specific disorders vary and are confusing. Whenever possible, we provide prevalence estimates in chapters dealing with specific disorders.

SUMMARY

The term in federal law remains *emotional disturbance*, although many would like to see the terminology change to *emotional or behavioral disorders* (EBD). Children and youth with EBD are disabled by behaviors that are discordant with their social–interpersonal environments. The definition of these disorders is a difficult matter complicated by differences in conceptual models, differences in the purposes of various social agencies, problems in measuring social–interpersonal behavior, variability in normal behavior, confusing relationships among EBD and other exceptionalities, the transience of many childhood disorders, and the effects of pejorative labels. No definition can be made completely objective. No definition has been universally accepted. The most common definition used in educational contexts is the one proposed originally by Bower and incorporated into the federal rules and regulations for IDEA. This definition specifies marked and persistent characteristics having to do with the following:

1. School learning problems
2. Unsatisfactory interpersonal relationships
3. Inappropriate behavior and feelings
4. Pervasive unhappiness or depression
5. Physical symptoms or fears associated with school or personal problems.

Inclusion and exclusion clauses of questionable meaning have been appended to these characteristics in the federal definition. Although improvements in definition are possible, and more objective criteria for identification are being developed, teachers' responsibility for judging students' behavior cannot be avoided.

An alternative definition has been proposed by the National Mental Health and Special Education Coalition using the term *emotional or behavioral disorder*. The proposed definition has been endorsed by many organizational members of the coalition who hope to incorporate the alternative definition into federal laws and regulations. Major points of the proposed definition are:

1. Emotional or behavioral responses in school
2. Difference from age, cultural, or ethnic norms

3. Adverse effect on educational performance (academic, social, vocational, or personal)
4. Responses to stress that are more than temporary or expected
5. Consistent problem in two different settings, including school
6. Persistent disorder despite individualized interventions
7. Possibility of coexistence with other disabilities
8. Full range of disorders of emotions or behavior

Nearly all children and youth exhibit behavior that is problematic at some time, as emotional and behavioral problems are a part of normal development. Prevalence figures must be accompanied by convincing arguments that members of the identified population are in need of special services because their problems are highly unusual and debilitating, and not the result of teacher inadequacy. Establishing criteria for identification, however, requires arbitrary judgment regarding what degree of difference is tolerable, as well as a judgment about the relative risks of identification and nonidentification.

Prevalence refers to the number or percentage of individuals exhibiting a disorder at or during a given time. *Incidence* refers to the number of new cases of a disorder occurring during a given interval. Prevalence has been of greatest interest to special educators. Prevalence may seem irrelevant to the everyday work of the teacher, but it is an important issue for those who plan and administer programs, with consequent implications for the teacher's working conditions.

Prevalence estimates are made difficult by the lack of a standard definition, methodological problems, and social policy and economic factors. If no standard definition is accepted, then it is difficult to count cases.

Reasonable estimates based on the best available research are that at least 3 percent to 6 percent of the school-aged population is in need of special education and related services because of EBD. Although the percentage of students served by special education is less than 1 percent, it doesn't seem likely that dramatic increases in the percentage will occur in the foreseeable future. Economic factors and other constraints, such as the full inclusion movement and other pressures toward nonidentification, appear likely to limit future estimates of prevalence. Ethnic disproportionality in identification is a serious and as yet unexplained problem. No ethnic group receives special education or other mental health services at or above the percentage suggested by prevalence studies.

✔ ENHANCEDetext **END-OF-CHAPTER 2 QUIZ**

Click on the checkmark icon to access an end-of-chapter quiz. Answer the questions to gauge your understanding of chapter concepts and better prepare you for case discussions.

CASE FOR DISCUSSION (See case book for additional cases.)

Where Does He Fit?
Allan Zook

I did not realize they were shopping for the ideal class for their son when Allan's parents came to observe my classroom. Just before their observation, Allan had qualified for special education services as a student with multiple disabilities. But neither the school system nor the parents could decide where he could best be served. A week after their visit, my supervisor brought me Allan's folder and directed me to meet with the parents that week and develop an individualized education program for him. "You win!" she said as she patted my shoulder. My question was, "Why?"

My "prize" was seven years old. He had received speech and language services since he was two, took massive doses of anticonvulsant medication, and thought compliance with adults' requests or commands was disabling. He also had a repertoire of behaviors guaranteed to distress his teachers and peers. For example, he liked to pick his nose and wipe the results on teachers or students. He routinely exposed himself during the time he spent in mainstream classes. He was big for his age, aggressive, and had justifiably earned the description of "bully." I was not surprised to observe that he played by himself and did not approach other students. They did not approach him either.

Testing Allan was, according to the school psychologists who had tried, an extraordinary challenge. The full-scale IQ of 73 was to be taken with a grain of salt, because his responses were "unusual." Allan's academic skills were as delayed as his social skills. Most of the normative and curriculum-based measurement data placed him two to three years behind his agemates in reading and math. His fine motor skills were almost nonexistent, and any required handwriting, cutting, or painting was for him a fate worse than death. "It's too hard," he always whined before he threw a tantrum.

Individual and small-group instruction was almost impossible for Allan. Even when he tried to pay attention (which wasn't very often), he was distracted by anything and everything—people walking by the room, other students shifting in their seats, a newly decorated bulletin board, someone's clothing, or a strange noise.

Some days he came to school late because he had experienced a seizure earlier in the day. On those days, he was subdued and not so eager to misbehave, but neither did he remember many of the skills he had mastered before the seizure. If he had a seizure in school, which happened occasionally, the rest of the day was a waste as far as academic work was concerned.

"So, why me, Lord?" I asked myself repeatedly. Allan's parents and the special education administrators had considered classes designed for kids with learning disabilities, physical disabilities, and emotional disturbance, but they decided my class of kids with mild intellectual disabilities was the best place for him. They liked my highly structured, directive program. They liked the fact that my kids were happy and learning lots of social and academic skills. They believed he'd fit in better in my class than in any of the others. Besides, I had room to take another student in my class without asking for a state waiver. So I won the lottery.

Questions About the Case

1. Does Allan fit the definition of "emotional disturbance" in IDEA? Does he fit the definition of "emotional or behavioral disorder" of the National Mental Health and Special Education Coalition?

2. How would you determine which of Allan's disabilities was foremost for purposes of education?

3. Was Allan's placement in this class appropriate? Was it legal under IDEA? (You may want to revisit this question after you have read more chapters.)

4. How do you think considerations of prevalence and incidence might have played a part in thinking about the most appropriate category and program for Allan?

3 WHERE WE STARTED AND WHERE WE'RE GOING: PAST, PRESENT, FUTURE

DEVELOPMENT OF THE FIELD AND CURRENT ISSUES

Universal History Archive/UIG/Getty Images

After reading this chapter, you should be able to:

3.1 Describe key periods in the historical evolution of treatment for children and youth with EBD, from the 1800s to the present.

3.2 Describe major issues facing the field of education for students with EBD in the early part of the twenty-first century, and the connection of these issues to historical events and trends.

3.3 Describe the importance and impact of key legal developments and issues in special

education beginning with P.L. 94–142, known as IDEA in its most recent reauthorization.

3.4 Discuss the relative successes and unresolved challenges that have characterized the historical development of education and treatment for children and youth with ED.

3.5 State reasons for optimism or hope that the education and treatment of children and youth with EBD can improve in the future.

We're tempted to believe life was simpler long ago and the issues involving EBD were less difficult. Perhaps life was simpler long ago, but much of the historical literature suggests that identifying social deviance and responding to it have always been perplexing and that current ideas have long historical roots (see Kauffman & Landrum, 2006; Rodriguez, Montesinos, & Preciado, 2005).

Current issues have to be seen in the light of problems that seem to be perpetual (see Bateman, Lloyd, & Tankersley, 2015; Kauffman, 2014b; Kauffman, Nelson et al., 2017; Lloyd, Tankersley, & Bateman, 2015). We can't understand today's difficulties very well if we assume that they have no history, that they're new issues that have just popped up. Knowledge of history won't necessarily keep us from making mistakes again, but ignorance of history virtually ensures that we'll make similar mistakes over and over (Kauffman, 2014b; Kauffman & Landrum, 2006; Kauffman & Smucker, 1995).

A history of special education has to include events in other fields, particularly psychology and psychiatry (Lewis, 1974). Throughout history, some youngsters' behavior has angered and disappointed their parents or other adults and violated established codes of conduct. Teachers have *always* been challenged by the problem of disorderly and disturbing student behavior. However, special education for this population is a relatively recent phenomenon. Now it has become a field facing many difficult issues and having an uncertain future, in part because it is an inextricable part of the broader field of special education (Kauffman, 2014b, 2016; Kauffman, Anastasiou, & Maag, 2016; Kauffman & Badar, in press; Reed, Gable, & Yanek, 2014).

A BRIEF HISTORY OF THE FIELD

The Nineteenth Century

Following the American and French revolutions in the closing years of the eighteenth century, kind and effective treatment of the "insane" and "idiots" (terms then used to designate people with mental illness and intellectual disability) appeared. In that era of political and social revolution, near the beginning of the nineteenth century, emphasis on individual freedom, human dignity, philanthropy, and public education set the stage for humane treatment and education of people with disabilities.

The literature of the nineteenth century is meager compared to the literature today. However, most histories of childhood EBD consistently contain inaccuracies and distortions that underestimate the value of the nineteenth-century literature for addressing present-day problems (Kauffman, 1976).

Some psychiatrists of the early nineteenth century identified causal factors in youngsters' EBD that are taken seriously today, such as the interaction of temperament and child rearing, overprotection, overindulgence, and inconsistent discipline. Although some of the biological causes of EBD were recognized during the first half of the nineteenth century, the emphasis was on environmental factors, especially early discipline and training. It's therefore understandable that interventions in that period concentrated on providing the proper sensory stimulation, discipline, and instruction.

Many children and youth, including those with EBD, were neglected and abused in the nineteenth century. Their mistreatment included cruel discipline, forced labor, and other inhumanities suffered by many children and youth in the 1800s. Although many nineteenth-century treatments seem primitive today, some youngsters with EBD actually received better care than many such children receive today. However, when we read about the neglect and abuse of children today in institutions, schools, detention centers, communities, and homes, we might conclude that the plight of children and youth hasn't improved much since the nineteenth century.

The nineteenth century, like all centuries, was a period of changes. Important changes in attitudes toward severe and profound emotional and intellectual disabilities occurred between 1850 and 1900. Optimism, pragmatism, inventiveness, and humane care, associated with the best programs in the first half of the nineteenth century, gave way to pessimism, theorizing, rigidity, and dehumanizing institutionalization after the Civil War. The failure of private philanthropy and government programs to solve the problems of "idiocy," "insanity," and delinquency quickly, and to rectify immediately the situations of the poor, led to cynicism and disillusionment. Larger asylums and houses of refuge were cheaper per person than smaller ones, but they were not better. Things don't always get better for a society's poor and sick citizens when government or private firms change a policy; sometimes they get worse. The many complex reasons for the regression in social policy in the last part of the nineteenth century included economic, political, social, and professional factors. The same factors operate today (see Gerber, 2017; Kauffman, 2009, 2011, 2014b; Kauffman & Landrum, 2006).

By the end of the nineteenth century, several textbooks had been published about the psychiatric disorders of children and youth. These books dealt primarily with etiology and classification and tended toward fatalism—the idea that there isn't much we can do to help (see Kanner, 1960). Psychiatric disorders were assumed to be the irreversible results of widely varied causes such as masturbation, overwork, studying too hard, preoccupation with a particular topic or problem, heredity, degeneracy, or disease. The problems of obstreperous children and juvenile delinquents hadn't been solved, but people were complaining about them, searching for answers, and proposing solutions.

Early Twentieth Century: The Establishment of Intervention Programs

Concern for the mental and physical health of children expanded greatly in the early twentieth century. The first teacher training program in special education began in Michigan in 1914. By 1918, all states had compulsory education laws, and in 1919, Ohio passed a law for statewide care of children with disabilities (for many years referred to as handicapped children). By 1930, sixteen states had enacted laws allowing local school districts to recover the excess costs of educating exceptional children and youth. Educational and psychological testing was becoming widely used, and school psychology, guidance, and counseling were emerging. Mental hygiene and child guidance clinics became relatively common by 1930, and child psychiatry became a new discipline. Two professional organizations particularly important to the education of children with EBD were founded in the 1920s: the Council for Exceptional Children and the American Orthopsychiatric Association.

The Great Depression of the 1930s and the Second World War of the 1940s necessarily diverted attention and funds from the education of students with disabilities. Nevertheless, more students with disabilities were receiving special education in 1940 than in 1930, and by 1948, forty-one (of the then forty-eight) states had enacted laws authorizing or requiring local school districts to make special educational provisions for at least one category of exceptional children. The vast majority of special classes were for children with mild intellectual disabilities (then called either *mental deficiency* or *mental retardation*). Programs for students with EBD were rare, usually found only in large cities, and designed primarily for acting-out and delinquent children and youth.

The 1930s saw other developments important for educating children with EBD. The first psychiatric hospital for children in the United States, the Bradley Home (now the Emma Pendleton Bradley Hospital), was established in Rhode Island in 1931. In the 1940s, Leo Kanner of Johns Hopkins University Medical School identified the syndrome now known as autism, or *autism spectrum disorder* (he originally called it *early infantile autism*). In New York City, Lauretta Bender pioneered the education of children with schizophrenia.

By the end of the 1930s, the literature on children's emotional or behavioral disorders had grown to sizable proportions. Furthermore, various plans of special education, such as special classrooms, separate schools, and consultation with teachers, had been tried.

Mid- to Late-Twentieth Century: Elaboration of Education Programs

A wave of interest in educating children with EBD arose in the middle of the twentieth century. Education of students with EBD became a field of specialization in its own right. Before the end of the 1950s, the first book describing classroom teaching of children with EBD was published, and researchers recognized that systematic procedures were needed to identify students with EBD in the public schools. Professionals banded together in 1964 to form a new division of the Council for Exceptional Children: the Council for Children with Behavioral Disorders. Preparation of personnel to work with children with emotional or behavioral disorders received federal support in 1963. The Autism Society of America (initially called the National Society for Autistic Children) was founded in 1965.

In the last half of the twentieth century, various conceptual models were developed. Landmark books described the various conceptual approaches to working with youngsters who have EBD. These models varied in the extent to which they recommended that special educators address the supposed underlying psychological disturbances or unconscious motivations of behavior and the extent to which they considered behavior itself to be the problem.

During the 1960s and 1970s, there was a dramatic increase in interest and effort to educate children and youth with severe disabilities, including those with severe EBD. Among the models most widely adopted for children and youth with EBD was the Re-Education program, also known as Project Re-ED (see Cantrell & Cantrell, 2007). Perhaps the intervention that gained widest acceptance in this era and proved to be most effective with students having severe disabilities was behavior modification, now better known as applied behavior analysis or ABA.

During the late 1980s, calls were made for greater integration of special and regular education for all students with disabilities. In fact, some proposed a merger of regular and special education or called for the abandonment of pullout programs in which students are taught in any setting other than the regular class. These ideas grew into the full inclusion movement in the 1990s. Although inclusion in general education is desirable in many cases, the full inclusion movement also generated criticism for its lack of consideration of individual needs and the interventions feasible only in other environments (see Anastasiou & Kauffman, 2011; Kauffman, Bantz, & McCullough, 2002; Kauffman, Ward, & Badar, 2016; Mock & Kauffman,

2002; Zigmond, 2015). The issue of special education's service to very young children with EBD also emerged in the 1980s. In 1986, Congress passed P.L. 99–457, which includes incentives for states to develop early intervention programs for infants with disabilities and infants at risk, from birth to age thirty-six months (see Conroy, 2017, and chapters in her section, XII, of the *Handbook of Special Education*).

In the 1990s, the federal government attempted to establish a national agenda for the education of children with EBD (the terminology at the time was *serious emotional disturbance* or *SED*). Such students typically have low grades and other indications of unsatisfactory academic outcomes, have higher dropout and lower graduation rates than other student groups, are often placed in separate settings, are disproportionately from poor and minority families, and frequently encounter the juvenile justice system. Sufficient resources were never allocated to achieve the goals of the agenda. Whether the agenda was sufficiently specific to guide needed changes was seen by some as highly questionable (Kauffman, 1997; Kauffman & Landrum, 2006).

ISSUES OF THE TWENTY-FIRST CENTURY

Issues and trends in the field in the early twenty-first century seem to suggest a heightened level of attention to the empirical and conceptual foundations for special education. Given this circumstance, it's tempting to believe that we're finally emerging into an era of enlightenment in which progress will be coherent, dramatic, and sustained. Perhaps we are entering such an era, but careful analyses of current trends and issues in the light of history will remind us that today's issues are not new, nor are current suggestions for addressing them likely to be completely successful (Bateman et al., 2015; Kauffman, 2014b; Reed et al., 2014).

Special education has perpetual issues, including who should be served and how and where they should be served (Bateman, 1994; Bateman et al., 2015; Kauffman, 2014b; Kauffman & Landrum, 2006; Kauffman, Nelson et al., 2017). Many or most of the issues of today have been issues for nearly a century, as reflected in the following: early identification (e.g., Brown, 1943), placement options (e.g., Berry, 1936; Postel, 1937), similarities between general and special education (e.g., Baker, 1934), early identification and prevention (Martens & Russ, 1932), and training in social skills (e.g., Farson, 1940).

Our approaches to these issues may be somewhat more sophisticated today than they were many decades ago, but we clearly don't have the wisdom or the technical knowledge to put these problems entirely behind us. Although the issues and trends we review here may be prominent in the early twenty-first century, they all have historical roots many decades deep and will likely remain vexing problems for many decades to come. These issues and trends aren't entirely separate and distinct. Inevitably, we find that addressing one demands that we consider others simultaneously.

Early Identification and Prevention

A persistent and self-defeating response of educators and parents to the first signs of maladaptive behavior is to take a wait-and-see approach, which too often means letting emotional or behavioral problems fester until they become serious, if not dangerous (Kauffman, 2010c,

2014a; Kauffman & Brigham, 2009). The problems inherent in early identification and prevention have been well understood for more than fifty years (Bower, 1960), yet few measures to address the problems have been taken. We know that the early signs of EBD can be detected through careful observation or use of reliable screening instruments and that definition and identification need improvement (see Lane, Kalberg, & Menzies, 2009; Land Menzies, Oakes, & Kalberg, 2012; Walker, Yell, & Murray, 2014). We also know that many or most problems later called EBD begin in childhood or early adolescence and that most individuals with these disorders get treatment only after years of delay, if ever.

We know quite a bit about the risk factors that increase the probability of negative, destructive long-term outcomes, and we discuss these in detail in later chapters—things like poverty, abuse and neglect, harsh and inconsistent discipline, and a variety of factors related to family, neighborhood, school, and societal conditions. However, the fact that we know the path to long-term negative outcomes doesn't mean that we'll intervene early to change the child's course. For a variety of reasons, actual prevention is a hard sell, something said to be desirable but seldom done in practice (see Kauffman, 1999c, 2005, 2014a; Kauffman & Brigham, 2009).

There is now, as there has been for decades, recognition that we need early intervention in two ways:

1. Catch problems when the child is young.
2. Catch the early stages of misbehavior regardless of the person's age.

Early intervention of both types is the essence of prevention, yet early identification, intervention, and prevention remain unresolved problems.

Warning signs are often ignored, and minor deviance is allowed to escalate to hurtful, if not lethal, levels (Dunlap et al., 2006; Evans, Rybak, Strickland, & Owens, 2014; Hendershott, 2002; Kauffman, 2014a; Kauffman & Brigham, 2009; Walker et al., 2014). "Better safe than sorry" is a bromide seldom applied to the questionable behavior of children and youth. Fear of false identification encourages people to let things go. The consequences are often tragic.

Early identification and prevention are compelling ideas embraced by many special educators and psychologists (see Briggs-Gowan et al., 2006; Dunlap et al., 2006; Dunlap & Fox, 2014; Feil et al., 2014; Walker & Sprague, 2007; Walker et al., 2014). Turning these ideas into coherent, consistent, and sustained action will require scientific and political finesse that previous generations couldn't muster. Children are likely to be identified for special services only after their problems have existed for years and become severe. This is the opposite of prevention, but it remains the norm. Moreover, negative attitudes toward special education contribute to failure to identify and assist children. Appropriate special education can, however, put children on the pathway to success at school (see Strain & Timm, 2001; Walker et al., 2014).

Will schools use the knowledge and tools we have to identify students early, before problems become very serious? Having identified the students, will schools take preventative action? These are the same questions raised by Bower in 1960 and by many others in the intervening decades. The answers are in doubt for reasons that are both readily apparent and exasperating (Forness et al., 2012; Kauffman, 1999c, 2003a, 2003b, 2004, 2010a, 2010b, 2010c, 2014a). Figure 3.1 shows how the balance is tipped against early identification and prevention. Figure 3.1 doesn't show all the arguments that can be mounted on either side, but people more readily invoke and believe the arguments *against* early identification and prevention.

Figure 3.1   The Balance of Arguments Against Early Identification and Prevention

Arguments for Early Identification and Prevention	Arguments Against Early Identification and Prevention
EBD is underidentified	Too many students are already identified as EBD
	We don't want to label the student
False negatives are worse than false positives	We'd rather risk a false negative than a false positive
Special education helps students with EBD	Special education is ineffective
Earlier identification is more effective than later identification	We want to keep the child in the LRE (interpreted as regular classroom)
	We might misidentify a student because of racial or ethnic or gender bias
	Identification is based on a medical model

Education of Antisocial and Violent Students

Antisocial, delinquent, and violent behavior in schools and communities has been a perplexing issue for a very long time. In late-twentieth-century American culture, youth violence became a major problem demanding intervention on multiple fronts. In fact, the education of antisocial and violent students became a central issue in both general and special education in the 1990s (O'Mahony, 2014; Walker, Forness et al., 1998; Walker et al., 2014).

Youth violence remains a great concern, although violent crime was on a downward trajectory in the early twenty-first century (Furlong, Morrison, & Jimerson, 2004; Mayer & Leone, 2007). Youth seldom engage in violent behavior without warning signs, so research and recommendations sometimes focus on the *precursors* of violent acts. Precursors are usually defined to include such things as aggressive talk, talk of aggression, threats, intimidation, and various forms of bullying. Research suggests that students with EBD more often threaten violence than do nonidentified students in general education (Kaplan & Cornell, 2005). Best practices suggest that we should intervene to stop such precursors of more serious problems (e.g., Kauffman, 2015b; Kauffman & Brigham, 2009; Lerman & Vorndran, 2002; Sheras, 2002; Smith & Churchill, 2002). Violent behavior and its precursors are complex and demand that we struggle with difficult questions, including the following:

- When is antisocial, violent behavior legitimately declared a disability, and when should it be considered criminal or delinquent behavior for which special education is inappropriate? There is great controversy about the kind of behavior that demonstrates a disability and that which merely demonstrates delinquency, criminality, or moral failure.
- What level of antisocial and violent behavior can be tolerated in a general education classroom? No doubt behavior that is tolerated in many classrooms today wouldn't have been

in decades past. Moreover, conduct varies widely from school to school and from class to class. There is much disagreement about the kind of behavior that should be tolerated or accommodated in general education classrooms. Because behavior can't be separated from the student who exhibits it, there is much controversy about which students, if any, should be removed from general education classrooms.

- If students cross the line of what's tolerable in a classroom or school, then where and how should their education be continued? Alternative schools, special classes, homebound instruction—these placement options and the kinds of instruction offered in them are matters of much conflict.

- What are legitimate means of controlling antisocial and violent behavior? Punishment of various types and its legitimate uses provide the basis for heated arguments about the treatment of children and youth.

- How can schools best function as a part of a larger community effort to lessen antisocial and violent behavior? Most people today seem to recognize that the problem of antisocial and violent behavior isn't one the schools can handle alone. However, there is much disagreement about just what schools can and should do and how they can best work with other social agencies to address the problem.

Decades of research suggest how some of these issues might be addressed and how they might be prevented (Kazdin, 2008; Strain & Timm, 2001; Walker et al., 2004, 2014). However, the educational treatment of students who bring weapons to school, threaten and intimidate their peers or teachers, disrupt the education of their classmates, or are incarcerated will likely be controversial for decades to come. Discipline of students with disabilities, especially those with learning disabilities or EBD, is a controversial and critical issue involving the Individuals with Disabilities Education Act (IDEA) and other education laws (see Bateman, 2017; Bateman & Linden, 2012; Huefner, 2006, 2015; Yell, 2012; Yell, Crockett et al., 2017; Yell, Katsiyannis, et al., 2017).

Comprehensive, Collaborative, Community-Based Services

A strong trend of the early twenty-first century is the integration of a variety of services for children and families, "wrapping services around" children in their homes and communities rather than sending them to a succession of intervention programs in other environments (Eber, Malloy, Rose, & Flamini, 2014). These attempts to coordinate and improve the effectiveness of multiple social service programs, such as special education, child protective services, child welfare, foster care, and so on, are built on the observation that individual programs are seldom sufficient to meet children's needs and that a closer working relationship of all service providers is required.

The idea of comprehensive, coordinated social services, including general and special education, delivered through the neighborhood school is compelling. It is particularly appealing in the case of children whose lives are in great disarray, as are the lives of many children who have EBD and are also in foster care. However, implementing the ideas and demonstrating that the service delivery system is effective are far from simple. At this point, we understand relatively little about how to design and evaluate research on such complex service delivery systems. The issue is likely to be kept alive for decades because the questions listed in Table 3.1 have no ready answers.

Table 3.1   Questions About Comprehensive, Collaborative, Community-Based Services

1. If individual agencies have too few resources, then won't the combined or integrated service delivery system still leave many children ill served?
2. If wraparound services are going to be found adequate in the long run, won't specially trained and expensive personnel be required to coordinate a sufficient number of adequately trained direct-service personnel?
3. What are schools really for—that is, what is the scope of their mission, and what should be paid for out of their budgets?

The ideal of comprehensive, collaborative, community-based services is highly appealing but not new (Kauffman, 2010a; Kauffman & Landrum, 2006). Whether such services become a reality in many American communities will depend on how Americans come to view their schools and value their children. Barring a dramatic change in the political will of the nation, the promise of the ideal will remain unfulfilled for a very long time. In the early twenty-first century, deinstitutionalization appears to have failed, and quite miserably. Streets and jails have become the default placements for people with serious mental illness, at least for older adolescents and adults (Earley, 2006; Goin, 2007; Warner, 2010). This represents a return to conditions of the nineteenth century.

Focus on Academic and Social Skills

Effective instruction is at the heart of both effective special education and behavior management (e.g., Hirsch, Lloyd, & Kennedy, 2014; Kauffman, 2015a; Kauffman & Badar, 2014b; Kauffman & Hallahan, 2005b; Kauffman, Pullen et al., 2011; Lane & Menzies, 2010; Nelson, Benner, & Bohaty, 2014; Pullen & Hallahan, 2015). In fact, researchers long ago devised procedures in which teachers approached predictable misbehavior as an instructional problem and devised teaching procedures for desirable behavior similar to those used for academic instruction. Emphasis on teaching will likely continue as a trend in special education programs for at least two reasons:

1. Good instruction is now known by researchers to be the first line of defense in behavior management. That is, a good instructional program prevents many (but not all) behavior problems from arising, and an emphasis on instruction is compatible with the clearest mission of public schools. For many decades, beginning in the early 1960s, special educators working from a behavioral model emphasized the use of consequences to alter problem behavior. More recently, it has become apparent that the antecedents of behavior—the events preceding an act and the context or setting in which it occurs—are powerful teaching tools that have been neglected in working with students with problem behavior. Scholars are helping teachers understand how the classroom conditions they create and the instructional procedures they use may contribute to behavioral problems and their resolution (e.g., Alberto & Troutman, 2012; Kauffman, 2010a; Kauffman, Pullen et al., 2011; Kerr & Nelson, 2010; Lingo, Slaton, & Jolivette, 2006; Scott & Shearer-Lingo, 2002).

2. Empirical evidence to support an instructional approach to behavioral problems is accumulating, and a clear consensus may be reached that teaching appropriate behavior explicitly is a central mission of special education programs (Kauffman, 2014b; Kauffman, Pullen et al., 2011; Landrum & Kauffman, 2006; Lane & Menzies, 2010). Given that teaching both academics and appropriate social behavior are the central role of schools, there may be less tolerance for programs in which the objectives are merely behavioral containment. This trend in special education may be one of the most promising, but it's also controversial and dangerous. If students who are antisocial, disruptive, and violent are disqualified for special education and seen as simply "bad," then they may be expelled or placed in alternative programs designed to be more punitive than instructive. The controversy is whether such students should be considered to need special education; the danger is that they'll be found to deserve only exclusion from general education and that their school experience, if they continue to have one, won't emphasize instruction in academic and social skills.

Still, academic instruction is too often neglected as a research topic (Kauffman, 2015a; Mooney, Epstein, Reid, & Nelson, 2003). We hope that the future will see more attention to academic learning in programs for students with EBD.

Functional Behavioral Assessment

In a **functional behavioral assessment** (FBA), the teacher or researcher determines what specific purposes or goals the student's behavior may have. The objective then becomes teaching the student to achieve essentially the same goal but with different and more acceptable behavior (Alberto & Troutman, 2012; Cullinan, 2002; Kerr & Nelson, 2010; Martens & Lambert, 2014).

An emphasis on FBA is completely consistent with increased attention to academic and social skills curricula. It is also a more explicit and narrow focus on the environmental events that trigger undesirable social behavior and what the student obtains as a consequence of behaving in a given way. Functional assessment may reveal, for example, that a student misbehaves out of frustration, boredom, or overstimulation. It may uncover the fact that misbehavior is maintained because of the attention it garners or because it allows the student to avoid difficult tasks or unpleasant demands. Although it is a highly useful tool in teaching, conducting an FBA and basing teaching procedure on it requires careful training, especially in the case of students whose behavioral problems are severe or long-standing (see Alberto & Troutman, 2012; Cullinan, 2002; Fox & Gable, 2004; Kerr & Nelson, 2010; Walker et al., 2004). Consider these potential limitations:

- FBA is often quite complicated. Identifying the function of the behavior—what it "says" or the role it plays in the student's life—may require extensive assessment by trained observers. Without support staff trained in functional analysis, teachers may be unable to carry out the required observations and other evaluation procedures.
- Intervention procedures suggested by an FBA are sometimes difficult for classroom teachers to carry out without extra help.

- Functional assessment and functional analysis procedures were developed primarily in nonschool settings using very frequent observations of behaviors that occurred often. These procedures may not generalize to the school problems of many students with emotional or behavioral disorders, which include many serious behaviors that occur only infrequently.

Nevertheless, research on FBA will likely provide increasingly effective teaching procedures and become an important part of special education teachers' repertoire. It will be up to special educators to figure out just what the term *functional behavioral assessment* means and how to implement it in school settings in which students exhibit problem behavior of all types (see Bateman, 2017; Sasso, Conroy, Stichter, & Fox, 2001; Yell, Katsiyannis et al., 2017). It will no doubt also continue to be a controversial topic for many years.

Continuum of Alternative Placements

The inclusion of students with disabilities in general education classrooms has been perhaps one of the most controversial and divisive issues in education since the 1990s (Crockett & Kauffman, 1999; Hallahan et al., 2015; Huefner, 2015; Kauffman, Ward, & Badar, 2016; Wiley, 2015; Zigmond, 2015). Placement of students with EBD has been particularly controversial (Kauffman & Lloyd, 1995; Kauffman, Lloyd, Baker, & Riedel, 1995; Kauffman, Lloyd, Hallahan, & Astuto, 1995b). The controversy is not generated by suggestions that *some* students with EBD should be included in regular classes, but by the suggestion that *all* students should be accommodated in general education.

Many different definitions of **inclusion** have been offered, and much confusion about the term and its meaning persists. Virtually no one opposes the partial or total inclusion of most students with disabilities in as normal an educational experience as possible. In fact, placement in the least restrictive environment (LRE) has been a basic concept in special education for at least several decades. What has become a central issue of the twenty-first century is whether, as some reformers propose, the regular classroom should be considered the LRE for literally all students (cf. Huefner, 2015; Kauffman & Badar, 2016; Zigmond, 2015). As it stands in 2017, federal special education law (i.e., the Individuals with Disabilities Education Act) still requires a full continuum of placement options, as shown in Table 3.2.

Proponents of full inclusion often discuss special education with little or no reference to the different types and levels of disabilities represented and assume that no students will fail to benefit from placement in a regular classroom. This is highly objectionable to some on logical and moral grounds (e.g., Anastasiou & Kauffman, 2011; Wiley, 2015).

Reformers' suggestion that this continuum be abandoned in favor of just one (regular classroom in the neighborhood school) or very few placement options is seen by many special educators as ill advised, unworkable, and detrimental to many students with disabilities, especially to many with EBD (e.g., Anastasiou & Kauffman, 2011; Morse, 1994). In addition, under IDEA, it is illegal *not* to maintain the continuum of alternative placements and to make placement decisions on the basis of each individual student's needs (Bateman, 2017; Bateman & Chard, 1995; Bateman & Linden, 2012; Crockett & Kauffman, 1999; Huefner, 2006; Huefner, 2015; Kauffman & Hallahan, 2005a; Yell, 2012; Zigmond, 2003, 2015; Zigmond & Kloo, 2017). Nevertheless, as ideological and political pressures for full inclusion build, maintenance of placement options becomes a serious concern.

Table 3.2　Placement Options for Students with EBD

- *Regular classroom* with supports, such as aides or assistants, counseling, or psychological or psychiatric treatment
- *Crisis or resource teachers in regular schools*, including consultation and collaboration with regular classroom teachers and students
- *Self-contained special classes* in regular schools, sometimes including part-time attendance in regular classes
- *Special day schools*, sometimes serving several school districts or a region
- *Day treatment or partial hospitalization* programs that are a part of hospitals or residential centers, sometimes including placement in regular classrooms in the community
- *Residential treatment centers* and inpatient hospitals, which may send some students home on weekends and to regular classrooms in the center's community
- *Homebound instruction*, in which teachers instruct students in their homes
- *Schools in juvenile detention centers and prisons*

　　Throughout history, the purposes of placement have been to create and control social ecologies that are conducive to appropriate behavior and mental health, both of the children and their families. Table 3.3 shows some of the considerations involved in placement. It seems extremely unlikely that these purposes can be achieved without a continuum of alternative placements. Furthermore, meta-analyses (i.e., systematic statistical summaries integrating evidence from many studies) indicate that students placed in self-contained classrooms have been more likely than those placed in general education to show improved achievement and decreases in disruptive behavior (e.g., Carlberg & Kavale, 1980; Stage & Quiroz, 1997). However, advocates for

Table 3.3　Purposes of Placement

- *Education of children* in academics and other life skills and appropriate emotional responses, attitudes, and conduct
- *Education of children's families or teachers and peers* in order to provide a more supportive environment
- *Maintenance of children in a setting in which they are available for therapies*—psychotherapy, pharmacotherapy, or behavioral therapy
- *Maintenance of opportunity for observation and assessment* of children's behavior and its contexts
- *Protection of children and youth with EBD* from themselves or others
- *Protection of others* (family, community, schoolmates) from children's uncontrolled or intolerable behavior

students with EBD will undoubtedly fight a continuing battle to maintain placement options in the face of reform proposals that would eliminate or severely limit them.

Transition to Work or Further Education

Since 1990, IDEA has required that individual plans be written for the transition of older students with disabilities from high school to higher education or work (see Hallahan et al., 2015; Rojewski & Gregg, 2017; Unruh & Murray, 2014). IDEA, in combination with societal concern for education of the workforce and efforts to reform public schooling, has thus made transition an issue sure to continue.

The primary controversial issues in transition have to do with the curricular and placement options that should be available to students with disabilities at the secondary level (Bullis & Cheney, 1999; Cheney & Bullis, 2004; Edgar & Siegel, 1995). Plans for the transition of students with EBD, as well as other disabilities, may founder because of the dilemma depicted in Figure 3.2, as Edgar (1987) noted.

Different education is always controversial. If all students are not treated equally, then we assume that some are treated unfairly. We have great difficulty reconciling difference and equality despite our commitment to individualization. The dilemmas inherent in helping secondary students plan for life after school aren't easily resolved; perhaps they're unresolvable. They're likely to be issues with which every generation will continue to struggle throughout their professional lives.

Multicultural Special Education

The rapidly changing age, social class, and ethnic demographics of the United States brought multicultural concerns to the forefront of educators' thinking in the 1990s. Teaching students with any type of exceptionality demands understanding of multicultural issues (Anastasiou et al., 2016; Hallahan et al., 2015; Klingner et al., 2015). Teaching students with EBD requires particularly keen attention to the distinctive cultural aspects of behavior and behavioral change, as well as to the principles that are common to all cultures (Kauffman & Anastasiou, in press; Kauffman, Conroy et al., 2008; Osher et al., 2004).

It is difficult to know exactly how to define culture for purposes of multicultural education (see Patterson & Fosse, 2015). Cultures may differ in a variety of ways relevant to special

Figure 3.2   The Dilemma of Vocational Education for Students Who Are Not College-Bound: Which Negative Outcomes Are Worse? (What Tips the Balance?)

No Vocational Education	Vocational Education
Inappropriate (for the student) College-Bound Curriculum	Stigma of a Different Curriculum
Unprepared for Vocation	Charges of Tracking and Discrimination
Failure and Dropping Out	Second-Class Social Status

education, including the discipline procedures they recommend, condone, or reject and the experiences of their members. Moreover, a basic concept of multiculturalism is that there is enormous individual variation among the members of any culture. Although a culture, however defined, may have identifiable group characteristics, any individual member may or may not share those characteristics.

Regardless of the culture under consideration, the multicultural aspects of special education for students with EBD raise difficult questions that point to continuing controversies:

- How can behavior be assessed without cultural bias? Behavior cannot be assessed without a cultural perspective, so it's critically important to understand one's own cultural frame of reference and how it might affect perceptions and judgments.
- Why should disproportionality in identification for special education be a concern when underservice is a major problem?
- What behavior is normative and what behavior is deviant in the student's culture? Clearly, cultures differ in their standards and expectations for the behavior of children and youth, what they consider acceptable, and what they consider inappropriate or intolerable. It's essential to understand the cultural demands of the child's family and community.
- What interventions are acceptable in the culture of the student? Cultures vary considerably in what's considered appropriate behavior of adults toward children. Educators must understand how proposed interventions will be viewed by students' parents and communities.
- How might racism, sexism, and other forms of discrimination have contributed to and how might they still contribute to the creation, labeling, and inappropriate treatment of "deviance"?
- Whose culture should be the standard for making judgments about behavior and interventions? Is there any culture with only desirable or positive features? Who should decide, and how, that a cultural feature is desirable or undesirable?

The challenge of multicultural education isn't new. Americans have always faced the daunting task of dealing with cultural diversity (Hallahan et al., 2015; Kauffman & Landrum, 2006; National Research Council, 2002; Patterson & Fosse, 2015). Historically, we Americans have failed, as have most if not all other nations of the world, to provide a general culture that's inviting and supportive of all of our desirable subcultures. The next few decades may determine whether a humane, democratic American culture exists and can be sustained. If a culture welcoming of differences is to thrive, it must focus on the common humanity of all people regardless of their cultural differences (see Anastasiou, 2017; Anastasiou & Kauffman 2012; Anastasiou et al., 2016, 2017; Kauffman & Anastasiou, in press; Kauffman & Badar, in press; Kauffman, Conroy et al., 2008).

Response to Intervention

One idea put forward as "new" in the early twenty-first century is the assertion that students should not be identified for special education until they have failed to respond to good intervention (instruction and behavior management) in general education. Some have observed that this is not a new idea and that the components of what has been labeled RTI or RtI (**response to intervention**) are all strategies that are well known (Kauffman, Bruce, & Lloyd, 2012).

In fact, one of the great ironies of RtI is that it calls for evidence-based instruction, but RtI itself is supported by extremely little evidence—at least in the case of EBD (Kauffman et al., 2012). In no way does RtI address the statistical issues involved in identifying students for special education (Kauffman & Lloyd, 2017), and the claim that it will prevent failures and address the problem of disproportional representation in special education appears to be based on hope or speculation alone (Kauffman et al., 2012).

Yes, it is a good idea to address problems early, to provide effective instruction and positive behavioral support before students are referred for evaluation for special education, not to confuse cultural difference for EBD, and otherwise to provide the kind of good general education that RtI supports, and RtI can be helpful in identifying students who need special education (see Lembke, 2015). No, RtI is not at this time itself an evidence-based practice, although some of its apparent components (e.g., curriculum-based measurement, positive behavioral interventions) do have considerable support in research evidence. A major danger of RtI is that it can be used as a delay tactic for providing needed special education (see Huefner, 2015; Johns, Kauffman, & Martin, 2016). After all, students identified for special education have already failed in general education, and for some students failure to be able to do what their age peers can do is utterly predictable regardless of the quality of general education instruction. Moreover, maintenance of treatment integrity (i.e., the faithfulness with which procedures are used) in a tiered system of education is a major challenge (Gresham, 2014).

One more thing about RtI: it should be seen in the context of criticism of special education more generally. Special education has been criticized because it requires sorting children based on their abilities to do certain things, it requires labels to talk about the specific needs of students, it typically requires a different or additional curriculum, and it requires making arbitrary decisions about whether a child has or has not met a qualifying standard of performance. Adding more tiers to the two-tiered general/special education distinction requires more of nearly all the things for which special education has been criticized (Kauffman, 2016; Kauffman, Badar, & Wiley, in press).

LEGAL DEVELOPMENTS AND ISSUES

Therapeutic services of one kind or another have been provided to many individuals with emotional, behavioral, or intellectual disorders by teachers, physicians, psychologists, and psychiatrists for centuries (Kauffman & Landrum, 2006). But even with compulsory education laws in place in the United States as early as the late nineteenth century, children with disabilities, and especially those we would identify today as having EBD, didn't routinely attend public schools. Some received education in reform schools, in hospitals, or in asylums. Most were simply jailed or put out of schools and lived at home or on the streets, and thus received no formal education.

Until 1975, the education of such children depended on a patchwork of state laws, not federal law. An important marker for the development of special education as we know it today was the passage of the Education for All Handicapped Children Act of 1975, also known as Public Law 94–142 (or P.L. 94–142). The 1975 law required that all students with disabilities receive a free and appropriate public education. This included children with EBD (emotional disturbance in the language of the law).

The importance of this landmark legislation for students with disabilities and their families can be underestimated or seriously misunderstood (see Gallagher, 2007; Martin, 2013; Yell, Katsiyannis, et al., 2017). We consider the influences of the original legislation and the subsequent amendments and modifications that have occurred since its original enactment in 1975.

P.L. 94–142: Education for All Handicapped Children Act

The immediate impact of P.L. 94–142 was twofold (Yell, Katsiyannis, et al., 2017). First, it affected the estimated 1.75 million children who had been excluded entirely from public education on the basis of their disabilities prior to 1975. Moreover, it also applied to the estimated 3 million children with disabilities who had been receiving a public education but for whom educational services weren't appropriate to their needs.

The hallmark components of P.L. 94–142 have remained essentially intact, even as the law has been amended and updated since 1975. These hallmark components are shown in Table 3.4.

For students with EBD, P.L. 94–142 was important for several reasons. First, it provided the federal definition of EBD (recall that the term *serious emotional disturbance* was used in P.L. 94–142; in the IDEA amendments of 1997, the term was shortened to *emotional disturbance*). The 1975 federal definition of what we call EBD remains unchanged today, despite the controversies surrounding it, as we discussed in Chapter 2.

Second, the law offered an estimate that 2 percent of the school-aged population probably required services for EBD. This estimate was important mostly in that it contradicted professional estimates, which are much

Video Example

from

YouTube

▶

ENHANCEDetext

Video Connections 3.1

Watch this video for a simple overview of the core principles of IDEA. (https://www.youtube.com/watch?v=P--IJkVYItQ)

Table 3.4 Key Components of P.L. 94–142 and Its Revisions (IDEA, IDEIA)

Identification (Child Find)	States must make efforts to screen for and identify children and youth with disabilities.
Free Appropriate Public Education (FAPE)	All students with disabilities receive an appropriate public education at no cost to parents or guardians.
Least Restrictive Environment (LRE)	Students with disabilities are to be served in the least restrictive (most normal) environment that is appropriate to their needs.
Individualized Education Program (IEP)	A written, individualized education program (IEP) is to be developed for each student identified as having a disability.
Nondiscriminatory Evaluation	Students are to be evaluated in all areas of suspected disability in a way that is as free of bias as possible in terms of differences associated with language, culture, and disability.

higher. Soon after P.L. 94–142 was enacted, identification rates increased substantially, from about 0.4 percent to closer to 1 percent. However, the actual rate of identification in the United States has remained below 1 percent for many years. Although P.L. 94–142 had many benefits, as have subsequent revisions of the law, no federal law has resolved the problem of definition or brought the rate of identification in line with data on prevalence. In fact, federal data on actual service have never come anywhere close to even the extraordinarily low estimate of 2 percent.

Individuals with Disabilities Education Act of 1990 (P.L. 101–476)

A substantial revision of P.L. 94–142 occurred in 1990 with the passage of P.L. 101–476, which renamed the act to reflect current thinking about more appropriate, person-first terminology (i.e., use of "individuals with disabilities" rather than "handicapped children"). The Individuals with Disabilities Education Act included several important changes, including an increased focus on **transition**, or the movement of students from school to post-school settings. This new emphasis was based on mounting evidence about the dismal post-school outcomes of many students with disabilities (see Bradley, Doolittle, & Bartolotta, 2007). For students with EBD, transition has been a particular problem. Students with EBD experience problems with a host of later life adjustment issues, ranging from social difficulties, involvement with the juvenile and adult justice systems, and the need for further employment training to assistance in finding and maintaining independent housing. An additional obstacle to appropriate transition for students with such disorders into post-school life has been the extraordinary rates at which they drop out before school completion.

In part to address these concerns, the 1990 version of IDEA required a statement of needed transition services in any individual education program (IEP) for a student with a disability who is sixteen or older. Transition services were defined as:

> … a coordinated set of activities, designed within an outcome-oriented process, which promotes movement from school to post-school activities, including post-secondary education, vocational training, integrated employment (including supported employment), continuing and adult education, adult services, independent living, or community participation (20 U.S.C. S 1401[a][19]).

Individuals with Disabilities Education Act Amendments of 1997 (P.L. 105–17)

The IDEA amendments of 1997 brought about significant changes to the act that directly affected education for students with EBD. Most notable were changes that had to do with discipline. It had become problematic for many school administrators to discipline students with disabilities who violated school rules. Punishments that might be used with students without any disability—in- or out-of-school suspension, for example—came under increased scrutiny. Some educators argued that such removal from school, even if temporary, might violate a student's right to a free and appropriate public education (FAPE). School administrators, on the other hand, were increasingly concerned about keeping schools safe and orderly. The IDEA amendments of 1997 addressed these concerns in two ways.

ENHANCEDetext
Video Connections 3.2
Dr. Mark Durand provides a brief overview and example of the concept of functional behavior assessment in this video. (https://www.youtube.com/watch?v=2v1GJflTmrM)

Video Example from YouTube

ENHANCEDetext
Video Connections 3.3
In "IEPs: The BIP Isn't Working," Dr. Jonathan Tarbox addresses a parent's concern that a Behavior Intervention Plan (BIP) is not working. Though the example concerns a student with autism, attend to the description of the relationship between the FBA and BIP, as well as what parents should expect from teachers. (https://www.youtube.com/watch?v=SuC_cRR1Ezl)

First, the 1997 amendments charged school districts with proactively developing a **behavior intervention plan** (BIP) for any student with a disability who has a behavior problem. Obviously, this would apply to most or all students identified with EBD, but it would also apply to students identified with other disabilities. For example, it would not be unusual for a student with intellectual disability or a learning disability to require a BIP. Behavior intervention plans were to include positive behavior change strategies and appropriate supports. Moreover, this behavior plan was to be based on a *functional behavioral assessment* (FBA), a systematic analysis of the conditions that seem to prompt or maintain the problem behavior(s) in question. Although school districts were to act proactively in developing a BIP for any student needing one, the amendments also required that such plans be developed and implemented within ten school days of any change in placement that resulted from a behavior incident (Yell, 2012).

Although the amendments of 1997 refer to FBA by name, neither the amendments nor the subsequent regulations offered by the U.S. Department of Education specified what an FBA must entail. Presumably, educators are to rely on the professional literature on the topic to guide practice. Briefly, the professional literature suggests that an FBA requires a team of teachers first to define in concrete terms the behaviors that are of concern for a particular student. For example, "being disruptive" is not a well-defined behavior; "shouting profanities when corrected" is much more concrete. Systematic data collection involving direct observation of the student in multiple contexts then allows educators to formulate hypotheses about what causes or maintains a behavior—or what *function* it serves. Teams analyze *environmental variables* (e.g., classroom arrangement, peers), *antecedent events* that precede the problem behavior (e.g., the teacher instructs students to take out their math books), and *consequences* that follow the behavior (e.g., peers laugh; the student is sent to the office). When patterns of behavior suggest a specific hypothesis (e.g., the student seems to become disruptive mostly during math, and the result is typically that he leaves the room), the team has a working hypothesis from which to develop a BIP based on the FBA. Behavior intervention plans typically involve actions such as altering the antecedents or consequences that might be associated with a problem behavior, teaching replacement behaviors that serve the same function as the problem behavior in a more appropriate way (e.g., teaching a student to raise his hand and wait quietly for help when an assignment frustrates him), or altering environmental variables such as seating arrangements.

Related to the need for behavior intervention plans was language in the 1997 amendments about when school officials could discipline students with disabilities in the same ways they discipline students without disabilities. Central to this argument was the concept of **manifestation determination** (MD), which is a process that seeks to determine whether a student's misbehavior is a direct result of his or her disability. According to the language of the amendments of 1997, if school officials wish to change a student's placement for a period in excess of ten school days due to some behavioral incident, school officials must conduct a MD to determine whether the behavior in question is "caused by or had a direct and substantial relationship to" a child's disability (Yell, 2012, p. 347). The MD hearing is also intended to include a review of the student's IEP to determine whether it was appropriate and had been implemented. The result of the MD hearing dictates how discipline may be handled; if the misbehavior is determined to be unrelated to the student's disability, then the school may discipline him or her following the same procedures used for students without disabilities. Of course, if such discipline involves removal from school or placement in any other setting, then schools must still provide educational services delineated in the student's IEP, consistent with the fundamental requirement of FAPE in IDEA.

Manifestation determination requirements apply to any student with a disability of any type whose behavior violates school rules. In fact, courts have held that such determinations must be independent of a student's specific disability (e.g., the case of *S-1 v. Turlington*, 1981); that is, schools must not assume that the label *emotionally disturbed* implies that any behavioral infraction is related to the child's disability, just as a different categorical label (e.g., *learning disability*) shouldn't imply that behavior problems aren't related to the student's disability.

Nonetheless, these procedures are of particular concern to educators working with students with EBD, as these are students who by definition may be likely to engage in the types of behavioral transgressions that prompt discussion of suspension or expulsion. In fact, one might be justified in concluding that a student's problematic behavior itself is a disability. If behavior itself is a disability, then it's difficult to see how misbehavior could be construed as not a manifestation of disability. In those cases in which a manifestation determination is conducted for a student with EBD, the issue is likely to be whether a *new* (not previously observed) behavior is part of the student's disability.

Individuals with Disabilities Education Improvement Act of 2004 (IDEA 2004)

The federal law applying to disabilities was revised again in 2004 as the Individuals with Disabilities Education Improvement Act of 2004 (or IDEA 2004, as it is usually called). This revision of the law carried numerous changes, including the process of writing an **Individualized Education Program** or IEP, which was modified so that programmatic changes could be made with written approval of the IEP team and parents but without reconvening an IEP team meeting. Furthermore, requirements for the IEP document itself were modified so that the IEP no longer had to include benchmarks or short-term objectives (see Bateman, 2017). However, the most important changes relative to students with EBD again had to do with discipline.

The manifestation determination provision included in IDEA 2004, according to Yell (2012, p. 109), "simplifies and strengthens" the standard for determining that a behavior is directly related to a student's disability. A result of this change may be that school teams will have greater leeway to determine that behavior isn't due to disability, and thus to discipline students with a disability in the same ways that students without disabilities are disciplined.

IDEA 2004 also enhanced schools' ability to use an **interim alternative educational setting** (IAES) for disciplinary reasons. An IAES might be a separate special school serving students with behavior problems; or a separate arrangement within the public school similar to in-school suspension; or in rare cases, it might consist of providing homebound instruction, although this latter arrangement has been called into question for its inability to meet the requirements of IDEA 2004. Indeed, the law doesn't define what IAESs must be, only what they must provide. In short, the IAES must provide students with the services and modifications spelled out in their IEPs to allow them to continue to progress in the general curriculum. The IAES must also include specific programming to address and prevent the recurrence of the behavior that prompted the placement in the first place. Such settings might be used for students with serious behavior problems as a way of preserving order and manageability of the typical classroom and school.

Obviously, order and safety can be increased at least temporarily by removing the most disruptive students from schools. However, special educators and other advocates for students with EBD are also concerned about the effects such placements have on the students so removed from general education settings. In addition to drugs and weapons offenses, IDEA 2004 included *serious bodily injury to another person* among offenses that would justify a move to such an alternative placement. The new regulations also changed the length of time such a placement may be used from forty-five calendar days to forty-five school days.

Such changes in the law governing special education seem to reflect a growing movement to provide schools with greater authority to discipline students, including removing them from schools, regardless of whether they have disabilities and even in cases where misbehavior is determined to be related to a student's disability. It should be reiterated that in cases of school removal or changes in placement, protections are in place that require school districts to continue providing educational services, and this extends even to students when they are incarcerated, as long as they were identified with a disability prior to their incarceration. Many educators are concerned, however, about the nature, quality, and appropriateness of educational services that students with EBD receive in the most restrictive settings in which they ultimately may be placed.

In addition to the changes that have occurred in special education legislation over time, broader education legislation has the potential to affect the education of students with EBD in substantial ways. The most substantial of these is the No Child Left Behind Act of 2001.

No Child Left Behind Act of 2001 and Subsequent Standards-Based Policies

President George W. Bush's signature education law, known in the early years of the twenty-first century as NCLB (P.L. 107–110, a version of the Elementary and Secondary Education Act), was aimed primarily at changing general education. However, it also had very significant implications for special education. The emphasis of the law was that schools must be held accountable for the educational performance of *all* students. All identifiable groups of students (based on ethnicity, poverty, language, and disability) were to be held to the same standards of performance, and any gaps between groups in performance were to be closed.

Unfortunately, many education laws give little attention to how special education would be affected by their provisions (Gallagher, 2007). Furthermore, many laws seem to ignore the essential nature of disabilities, statistical distributions, and other realities (Kauffman, 2005, 2010c; Kauffman & Konold, 2007; Kauffman & Lloyd, 2017). Quite predictably, many students with disabilities have extraordinary difficulty meeting the standards established for the general population. Thus, the performance of students with disabilities under federal and state laws is a continuing issue.

Besides student performance, some laws have established the expectation that all teachers will be highly qualified, an assumption that is open to question. *Highly qualified* is difficult to define, and it presents particularly difficult questions for the training and licensure of special education teachers (Rock & Billingsley, 2015).

Trends in Legislation and Litigation

Many of the trends toward accountability and narrowing the differences between special and general education begun under the George W. Bush administration in the first years of the twenty-first century have continued. We may be able to note trends in legislation over past decades, but it is much more difficult to predict what will happen in future years. If there is one reliable statement we can make about legislation and litigation, it is that things will change. Just how they will change, though, isn't something that can be predicted with much accuracy (see Gallagher, 2007; Kauffman, 2014b, 2015a; Kauffman & Landrum, 2006).

Since its inception in 1975, federal law governing special education seems to us to be on an increasingly laissez-faire trajectory. That is, recent trends in laws seem to be muting the differences between special and general education and to be giving more latitude to states in interpretation. At least to some extent, this is a result of trying to "align" special and general education. Education laws appear to be an effort to make special and general education as much alike as possible, in part by holding most students with disabilities to the same academic standards as students without disabilities. Behavioral standards and expectations also appear to be increasingly the same for all students.

Whether aligning academic and behavioral standards of students with and without disabilities is advantageous for those with EBD is open to debate. Furthermore, what direction legislation and litigation will take is open to speculation. One possibility is that the distinctions between special and general education will become increasingly blurred. An alternative possibility is that the distinctions will be maintained at or near present levels. Another possibility is that the distinctions will become virtually invisible at the federal level, perhaps giving rise in future decades to recognition of the problems that prompted the first federal mandatory legislation in 1975 and sharpening the distinctions once again (Kauffman, 1999c, 2008a, 2008b, 2014b).

Implications of Legislation and Litigation

Keeping up with all the changes in laws and court judgments is difficult for anyone, practitioners in particular. In fact, teachers rely on lawyers, scholars, and administrators to interpret the law and court decisions and outline local practices that conform to legal requirements. To a large extent, teachers must rely on school and district policies regarding IEPs, discipline, and all other matters regulated by law.

One common misconception is that the law provides the best guide to ethical behavior. However, something legal can be unwise or even unethical. Whether it involves identification, programming, curriculum, placement, discipline, or any other aspect of working with students who have EBD,

---

Video Example from YouTube

▶

ENHANCEDetext
Video Connections 3.4
This video ("Discipline") provides a succinct overview by one school district of the issues around discipline for students with disabilities, including a discussion of the IEP and BIP, manifestation determination, and possible placement in an Interim Alternative Educational Setting (IAES). (https://www.youtube.com/watch?v=4N4oP2P013U)

difficult ethical issues often arise regarding what is best for the student. The law—at least the law as interpreted by some administrators or authorities—may or may not serve the best interests of the student involved. Sometimes practitioners have to weigh what is best for one person against what is best for another.

Another common misconception is that the law is based on the best evidence we have. Research does not reliably inform practice. Neither does evidence or logic necessarily underlie the law. This may well add to the dilemmas of practitioners, especially when the law assumes or demands that we ignore what we know or people reject scientific evidence (see Kauffman, 2011, 2014c; Kauffman & Konold, 2007; Kauffman, Mock, Tankersley, & Landrum, 2008; Landrum, 1997, 2015; Landrum & Tankersley, 2004; Tankersley, Landrum, & Cook, 2004).

PAST

The history of the treatment of children and youth with EBD can be discouraging. Not a single critical issue in the field seems to have been truly resolved, and current issues and trends seem only to be a recycling of those that have been with us for well over a century (cf. Bateman et al., 2015; Kauffman, Nelson et al., 2017; Reed et al., 2014; Whelan, 1999). In spite of the best intentions of those who have struggled with the problems of educating students with EBD, the most promising innovations nearly always seem to have gone awry, to have produced results that are disappointing to many people, or to have been abandoned at least temporarily in the face of evidence supporting them. Our disappointment may be partly a result of unrealistic expectations and partly a result of our failure to see that good intentions are not enough to ensure success.

Success in teaching students with EBD is especially hard to define. If special education really works, then what would we expect the outcomes of it to be? For many or most students who have severe disorders of conduct, it's unrealistic to expect a complete cure, especially if intervention isn't begun early (Kauffman & Brigham, 2009). How much improvement under what conditions would we define as success? These are important questions that are seldom directly, explicitly addressed among special educators. Too often, perhaps, our expectations simply aren't reasonable, and we define ourselves or our programs as failures by criteria that are quixotic—extravagantly, unreasonably idealistic.

Many of the efforts special educators have made have been at least moderately successful by a reasonable standard (Walker, 2003), but few have been *spectacularly* successful, and none has been *totally* successful in every case. Charges of failure and calls for radical reform have been based in some cases on distorted perceptions of the effects special education might be expected to produce, given the resources allocated to the effort. We must constantly strive to balance the recognition that special education needs improvement and should produce better outcomes than it does for children with the acknowledgment that special education has a history of improving the lives of many students. In a sense, our situation is like that of the students with whom we work: We need to recognize our failures, limitations, and need for improvement without becoming unrealistic in our expectations for change, success, or perfection.

The road special education has traveled in the past century from eugenics to euphemisms has been paved with good intentions. The people who, in retrospect, we may see as monsters who set out to stigmatize, dehumanize, and disenfranchise children and youth with disabilities are *bogeymen*, not the real people who chose labels, built institutions, established special classes, emptied institutions, tinkered with new labels, mainstreamed students and called for full inclusion, or wrote the laws and regulations we see as cumbersome, inadequate, or counterproductive. Their intentions were good, but good intentions aren't and never have been enough to make all our hopes realities.

If it had succeeded as planned, special education's history would be a tale of success—of caring and cures, fully realized potential, freedom from stigma and discrimination, efficient management, and social harmony. Well-laid, best-intentioned plans can miss their mark for many reasons, including the failure of planners to see their designs in a social-historical context and to adhere strictly to what's actually known at the time about intervention in human behavior. Our failure to see how our own designs are enmeshed in the context of current sociopolitical trends and our false claims of knowledge about our interventions could make us the bugbears of future generations. If we're going to avoid many mistakes of the past, then we need to proceed with greater awareness of our history, more caution in assuming that any change will bring real progress, and heightened attention to staying within the scientific foundations of our work (see Bateman et al., 2015; Crockett, 2001; Kauffman, 2010c, 2011; Kauffman, Anastasiou, & Maag, 2016; Lloyd & Hallahan, 2007; Reed et al., 2014; Sasso, 2007; Walker, Forness et al., 1998).

PRESENT AND FUTURE

Textbooks often end with speculation about the future. We have chosen instead to comment on the past here in the first section of this book because we believe the best prediction of future developments is based on past events (see Kauffman, 2014b; Kauffman & Landrum, 2006; Nelson & Kauffman, 2009). In the past, we've seen an ebb and flow of concern for the plight of students with EBD and periods of progress and regression in effective intervention. Professionals have expressed enthusiasm for new methods and disillusionment when the solution turns out to be less than final. A solely legal-bureaucratic approach to fulfilling society's obligation to students with disabilities has failed in the past and shows no particular promise for the future. Laws like the Individuals with Disabilities Education Act, the No Child Left Behind Act, and subsequent legislation may set forth legal standards and promises, and these may be extremely important, but they can be circumvented or changed; there seem always to be "loopholes" or ways around the law. But effective and humane education of students with disabilities has always depended on the individual actions of competent, caring teachers and other individuals, as will be the case in the future, regardless of legal mandates or prohibitions.

What *has* happened is always a harbinger of what *will* happen, and it's wise to know how today's problems are related to the past (see Gerber, 2017; Lloyd et al., 2015). We're living today with the backdraft of pressures for reductions in human services and supports for those in need—reductions defended with rhetoric intended to cover the painful consequences for children and their families. Children and youth at risk don't benefit from the sloganeering, denial, self-contradiction, posturing, and irrational, antiscientific, or unintelligible statements that have become popular in talk and writing about reforming education (Kauffman, 2010c, 2011, 2014b; Kauffman, Anastasiou, & Maag, 2016).

Today, denigrating special education has become popular. True, special education is less than perfect and does need improvement, so that it becomes far more reliably what it can and should be. However, it's neither the horror nor the self-serving institution that is described by some, nor would the changes suggested by some critics be likely to improve it significantly

(Kauffman, 2009, 2014b). It's wise to remember that special education and related disciplines solve more problems than they create, are greater sources of hope than of despair, and stand more for healing wounds than for making them (Kauffman & Hallahan, 2005b; Walker, 2003; Walker, Forness et al., 1998).

We live in what Zigmond, Kloo, and Volonino (2009) have called "the climate of full inclusion," in which the emphasis is on placement of students with disabilities in general education. A part of this climate is the notion that general and special education really aren't very different and shouldn't be very different—that the solution for students with disabilities is making general education better so that it serves *all* children well. Special education has been described as disgraceful, but as Zigmond and Kloo (2017) have observed, if there is disgrace it is that many people believe that special education is *not* special and that a general education teacher can teach students with disabilities well while teaching the rest of the class (see also Zigmond, 2015).

The issues today parallel those of the last century, although the potential for helping students with EBD is greater today than it was then because of our broader base of scientific knowledge and experience. We have reason, then, for guarded optimism. Quick and easy cures aren't possible for most problems. People must care, but their caring has to include searching diligently for reliable answers to the questions of how youngsters come to have EBD. Even more important is finding out how to help children and youth learn appropriate behavior when they have these disorders. To the extent that people dedicate themselves to finding such answers and putting those answers to work in practice, we can have confidence that progress will ultimately outweigh regression.

SUMMARY

Children and youth with EBD have been recognized throughout history. Efforts to educate these students began in the nineteenth century. The second half of the twentieth century was a period of rapid growth in educational interventions. Diverse theories and divergent educational practices were proposed. Many current issues are a recycling of

concerns that have never been and may never be completely resolved.

The history of the field cannot be captured merely by reviewing a chronology of events, but a chronology can help one grasp the development of ideas and trends. Some of the important events in the history of the field are listed in Table 3.5.

Table 3.5   Chronology of Important Events Relating to Students with EBD, 1799–2004

Year	Event
1799	Itard publishes his report of the wild boy of Aveyron
1825	House of Refuge, first institution for juvenile delinquents in the United States, founded in New York; similar institutions founded in Boston (1826) and Philadelphia (1828)
1841	Dorothea Dix begins crusade for better care of the insane

(continued on next page)

Table 3.5   *(continued)*

Year	Event
1847	State Reform School for Boys, the first state institution for juvenile delinquents, established in Westborough, Massachusetts
1850	Massachusetts incorporates school for idiotic and feebleminded youth at urging of Samuel Gridley Howe; Edward Seguin moves to the United States
1866	Edward Seguin publishes *Idiocy and Its Treatment by the Physiological Method*
1871	Ungraded class for truant, disobedient, and insubordinate children opens in New Haven, Connecticut
1898	New York City Board of Education assumes responsibility for two schools for truant children
1899	First U.S. juvenile court established in Chicago
1908	Clifford Beers publishes *A Mind That Found Itself*
1909	National Committee for Mental Hygiene founded; Ellen Key publishes *The Century of the Child*; William Healy founds the Juvenile Psychopathic Institute in Chicago
1911	Arnold Gesell founds the Clinic for Child Development at Yale University
1912	Congress creates the U.S. Children's Bureau
1919	Ohio passes law for statewide education of the handicapped
1922	Council for Exceptional Children founded
1924	American Orthopsychiatric Association founded
1931	First psychiatric hospital for children in the United States founded in Rhode Island
1935	Leo Kanner publishes *Child Psychiatry*; Lauretta Bender and others begin school for psychotic children at Bellevue Psychiatric Hospital in New York City
1943	Leo Kanner describes early infantile autism
1944	Bruno Bettelheim opens the Orthogenic School at the University of Chicago
1946	New York City Board of Education designates 600 schools for disturbed and maladjusted pupils; Fritz Redl and David Wineman open Pioneer House in Detroit
1947	Alfred Strauss and Laura Lehtinen publish *Psychopathology and Education of the Brain-Injured Child,* based on work at Wayne County Training School in Northville, Michigan
1950	Bruno Bettelheim publishes *Love Is Not Enough*
1953	Carl Fenichel founds the League School, first private day school for severely emotionally disturbed children, in Brooklyn
1955	Leonard Kornberg publishes *A Class for Disturbed Children*, first book describing classroom teaching of disturbed children
1960	Pearl Berkowitz and Esther Rothman publish *The Disturbed Child*, describing permissive, psychoanalytic educational approach
1961	William Cruickshank et al. publish *A Teaching Method for Brain-Injured and Hyperactive Children*, reporting results of a structured educational program in Montgomery County, Maryland; Nicholas Hobbs and associates begin Project Re-ED in Tennessee and North Carolina

(continued on next page)

Table 3.5   *(continued)*

Year	Event
1962	Norris Haring and Lakin Phillips publish *Educating Emotionally Disturbed Children*, reporting results of a structured program in Arlington, Virginia; Eli Bower and Nadine Lambert publish *An In-School Process for Screening Emotionally Handicapped Children* based on research in California
1963	P.L. 88–164 provides federal money for support of personnel preparation in the area of the emotionally disturbed
1964	William Morse, Richard Cutler, and Albert Fink publish *Public School Classes for the Emotionally Handicapped: A Research Analysis*; Council for Children with Behavioral Disorders established as a division of the Council for Exceptional Children
1965	Nicholas Long, William Morse, and Ruth Newman publish *Conflict in the Classroom*; Autism Society of America founded; first annual Conference on the Education of Emotionally Disturbed Children held at Syracuse University
1968	Frank Hewett publishes *The Emotionally Disturbed Child in the Classroom*, reporting use of an engineered classroom in Santa Monica, California
1970	William Rhodes begins Conceptual Project in Emotional Disturbance, summarizing theory, research, and intervention
1974	Association for Persons with Severe Handicaps founded
1975	Nicholas Hobbs publishes *Issues in the Classification of Children and the Futures of Children*, reporting the work of the Project on the Classification of Exceptional Children
1978	P.L. 94–142 (enacted in 1975) requires free, appropriate education for all handicapped children, including the seriously emotionally disturbed; federal funding for National Needs Analysis studies at University of Missouri
1986	P.L. 99–457 enacted, extending provisions of P.L. 94–142 to all handicapped children three to five years of age by school year 1990–1991; statistics show that about 1 percent of students enrolled in public schools are receiving special education services as seriously emotionally disturbed, only about one half of a conservative estimate of prevalence
1987	National Mental Health and Special Education Coalition formed; C. Michael Nelson, Robert B. Rutherford, and Bruce I. Wolford publish *Special Education in the Criminal Justice System*
1989	Federation of Families for Children's Mental Health founded; National Juvenile Justice Coalition formed
1990	Individuals with Disabilities Education Act (IDEA) amends P.L. 94–142; National Mental Health and Special Education Coalition proposes new definition and terminology
1997	National Agenda for Students with Serious Emotional Disturbance proposed; IDEA amended; *seriously* dropped from the designation of *emotionally disturbed* in federal language
2004	IDEA reauthorized as the Individuals with Disabilities Education Improvement Act

Definition, prevalence, and terminology remain current issues of great importance to special educators. Issues of increasing importance revolve around the settings in which students with EBD should be taught. Proposals to merge or radically integrate regular and special education have, however, met with considerable skepticism, particularly as such integration might be applied at the secondary level. Extension of special education to incarcerated youth and provision of special services to very young children with EBD are emerging trends. Conceptual models are evolving into more sophisticated and integrated approaches that address students' behavior and cognitions in social systems. New coalitions of parents, professionals, and advocates and a new organization for parents and families have brought renewed hope to the field.

In the early twenty-first century, issues and trends include early identification and prevention; education of antisocial and violent students; comprehensive, collaborative, community-based services; a focus on instruction in academic and social skills; functional assessment of behavior; maintaining a continuum of alternative placements; transition of students to work or further education; multicultural education; response to intervention; and a variety of legal issues, including amendments of federal special and general education laws.

✔ ENHANCEDetext **END-OF-CHAPTER 3 QUIZ**

Click on the checkmark icon to access an end-of-chapter quiz. Answer the questions to gauge your understanding of chapter concepts and better prepare you for case discussions.

CASE FOR DISCUSSION (See case book for additional cases.)

She's All Yours.

Cindy Lou

I began my teaching career in a special self-contained class in a small town in the South. I wasn't certified to teach, but the school district was desperate for someone to take positions in special education. Two days before my first students arrived, the principal handed me a cumulative folder and said, "Mrs. Jones and I have decided that this young man would do better in your room." He offered no verbal or written explanation about why the young man in question would do better in a class for students with mild mental retardation (intellectual disabilities). As the year progressed, I began to understand how students qualified for my class. If the principal and the regular classroom teacher agreed, they pulled that child's folder from behind the regular classroom teacher's name in the file drawer and placed the folder behind my name. He or she was then "retarded." It was that simple—a process uncluttered by procedures the teacher and principal deemed unnecessary.

The most interesting student in my class that year was Cindy Lou, one of the few who had actually had a score on an IQ test. Her full-scale score, obtained four years before she came to my class, was 92.

Cindy Lou always sat in the back of the room in spite of my best efforts to place her anywhere else. I soon learned to appreciate her self-imposed exile. Whenever she completed seat work, she talked and muttered to herself constantly. Sometimes she supplemented this soliloquy with yells and threats directed at anyone unfortunate enough to catch her eye. Early on, some of my other students laughed at her or teased her about talking and muttering to herself. But they soon learned to keep a healthy distance from Cindy Lou. She was a big girl and not above punching someone who offended her. And it soon became apparent that she didn't require an excuse to knock someone into the middle of next week. Any insult, real or imagined, would suffice.

In spite of Cindy Lou's angry outbursts, she was the best student in my room—when she was there. She was always first to grasp a concept, complete her work, and answer oral and written questions correctly. But even with my efforts combined with those of her mother, the principal, and the school social worker, Cindy Lou was absent at least one day each week.

Cindy Lou was a seventh grader who had been retained twice. She was large, full-bosomed, and sexually active. It wasn't long before the town madam called me to say, "Listen here, you restrain that Cindy Lou!" According to her, Cindy Lou waited outside her establishment, offering herself for less money than the whores inside. "She's undercutting my girls. And furthermore, I'll have you know I run a clean establishment. None of my girls is underage!" she bellowed.

Just before Christmas, Cindy Lou brought me a pretty glass candle holder shaped like a star. Since we spent part of every day in angry confrontation with each other, I was touched that she would give me a present. An hour later, the principal asked me to come to his office. The manager of a store was there. He had seen Cindy Lou take the candleholder. When he confronted her, she had become violent, and he had retreated. There were other witnesses, and he intended to press charges unless someone paid for the candleholder. I was new, unskilled, and a bit stupid. I paid for the candleholder.

Questions About the Case

1. In what historical period do you think this case could have taken place? Why?

2. In what historical period do you think this case did take place? What developments in the field lead you to this conclusion?

3. Historically, what attempts have been made to guard against misidentification and misplacement of students with special needs? Can you propose better safeguards than have been devised so far?

PART 2 Possible Causes

INTRODUCTION

Disturbing behavior is a puzzle. When we see it, we wonder why people act the way they do. "Why, why, *why?*" we ask.

Our typical response is to search for a conceptual model that'll help us understand what's gone wrong. Maybe one reason is that we want to know what or whom to blame. We think we'll know how to correct the problem and perhaps prevent future occurrences if we can just figure out *why*. The chapters in this section discuss the four most frequent answers to the "why" question about EBD: biology, culture, family, and school. As you read these chapters, keep the following questions in mind:

- How are causal factors interrelated?
- How is knowledge of cause related to intervention?
- What are the implications of the way we assess blame?

The fact that we discuss biological, cultural, family, and school causal factors in separate chapters doesn't mean that they're entirely separate issues. In fact, biological, cultural, family, and school factors are all interrelated. Seldom, if ever, does one factor alone cause EBD (see Cook & Ruhaak, 2014). Seldom can we answer the "why" question about EBD with much confidence. Only rarely can we pinpoint a single cause. In most cases, we should think about how causal factors work together—what each factor contributes to the individual's risk or vulnerability and what might contribute to their resilience (see Gerber, 2014; Hayden & Mash, 2014). As we consider the factors that heighten an individual's risk for EBD, we should also be thinking about those factors that offset risk—the conditions that build up a person's resilience and help prevent disorders. We need to ask not only what supporting role these factors play in creating conditions under which EBD is likely to develop but also what events and conditions help counteract risk factors.

Often we assume that knowing the cause of troublesome behavior will help us find a better way to deal with it. If we believe an individual's behavior is a sign of "illness" or "disorder," then we may hope that finding the cause will lead to a cure. But finding a contributing cause doesn't always lead us directly to an intervention because we may have no feasible way of changing the causal condition. For example, we might know that watching many television programs is associated with increases in the aggressive behavior of already hyper-aggressive children, but we may not have any effective means of controlling a child's television watching. Furthermore, finding an effective cure or intervention doesn't necessarily imply that we know the cause. We might find that medication reduces a child's hyperactivity, but we can't conclude from that finding that the child's hyperactivity has a biochemical cause. Some medications work, even though physicians don't understand how they're related to the cause of the illness. Reasoning backward from effective treatment to a cause is a common error of logic: post hoc, ergo propter hoc (after the fact, therefore because of it). To take an example from medicine, the observation that penicillin cures strep throat doesn't lead logically to the conclusion that a lack of penicillin causes strep throat. Similarly, in classroom practice, the observation that praise for a student's on-task behavior increases attention to the task doesn't necessarily support the conclusion that lack of reinforcement for on-task behavior caused this student's inattention. In considering what we know about causal factors, you might ask yourself these questions:

- What does knowing or suspecting this cause suggest I should do?
- Are there effective ways of dealing with this problem, even if we don't know the cause?

These are important questions for teachers, and at the end of each chapter in this section we summarize the implications for educators of what we know about causal factors. How we think about blame or responsibility for behavior is crucial in determining the interventions we choose for children and youth who are troubling to us.

The relationship between presumed cause and blame has important implications not only for our choice of intervention but also for the survival of a humane society. An enduring moral precept of our society is that we don't hold people responsible for misfortunes that are beyond their control. Sick people aren't usually blamed for their illnesses. To the extent that we assume children or youth are suffering from mental illness or social circumstances beyond their control, we don't blame them for their misconduct. In the present-day United States and in most Western cultures, we seldom blame children or youth for serious misconduct. In most cases, we shift blame to something other than the individual—to a biological disorder, parental mismanagement or abuse, dissolution of the family, peer pressure, teachers' incompetence, bad school organization, or social decadence.

To what extent should we depersonalize blame and attribute misbehavior to external factors? Under what conditions should we view young people who exhibit unacceptable behavior as victims of their environments or biology rather than as responsible persons who should be held accountable for their choices? The depersonalization of blame may carry substantially different implications depending on the nature, seriousness, and severity of social deviance and the age of the person who exhibits it. Blaming children and youth with schizophrenia— assuming that they choose to behave the way they do and holding them morally responsible for their deviant behavior—hardly seems justifiable on any grounds, partly because evidence so clearly connects schizophrenia with biological processes. Nevertheless, children and youth who exhibit disorders in which biological factors are less obvious and personal volition is more clearly involved—conduct disorders and juvenile delinquency, for example—might be expected to share some measure of moral responsibility for their behavior. Perhaps a teenage sniper or a youth who shoots up a school can't be held blameless. But what of a youth who has schizophrenia and, as part of his determination to get money for a surgical procedure that he only *imagines* he needs, robs a bank?

Questions about the attribution of cause and personal responsibility are pervasive and critical issues in the field of EBD. They're at the heart of the controversy regarding whether students with conduct disorders or "social maladjustment" should be considered to have a disability or to behave in ways that merit prosecution and punishment. They're at the center of the idea of "manifestation determination," the requirement that school authorities determine whether a student's misbehavior is or is not a manifestation of a disability. In common parlance, school authorities are to determine whether to conclude "that's the disability talking" when a student misbehaves or, alternatively, to conclude that the student could have chosen to behave differently and that the disability is "no excuse."

The personalization of blame almost certainly accounts for the punitive approaches to dealing with most students who misbehave in school and the under identification of students who have EBD. Yet the depersonalization of blame may also have undesirable outcomes, including disproportionate increases in social attention and benefits to youngsters who misbehave and a depreciation of individual integrity. In an era of concern for individual responsibility and self-actualization, special educators must weigh carefully the evidence that individual students are able to exercise self-control, as well as the evidence that they are victims of circumstances and have little or no personal, moral responsibility for their behavior. Perhaps blame can be assessed, but if so, it must be done with careful judgment.

4 BIOLOGY

After reading this chapter, you should be able to:

4.1 Explain why biological factors have such great appeal as explanations for deviant behavior.

4.2 Describe the contributions of genetic factors to risk for developing EBD and the factors that make the odds of developing a disorder better or worse.

4.3 Explain the relationship between brain damage or dysfunction and EBD.

4.4 Describe the relationship between diet or nutrition and children's emotional and behavioral development.

4.5 Define temperament and describe how it might affect pupil–teacher interactions.

4.6 Discuss the appropriate role of educators in interventions for EBD that may involve medications prescribed by physicians or psychiatrists.

THE APPEAL OF BIOLOGICAL FACTORS AS CAUSAL EXPLANATIONS

A biological view of EBD has particular appeal because, on the one hand, psychological models of behavior can't account for all behavioral variations in children (Cook & Ruhaak, 2014; Pinker, 2002). On the other hand, advances in genetics, physiology, and medical technologies such as imaging and medications make the suggestion of a biological basis for all EBD seem plausible. Moreover, research suggests that a high percentage of students with severe EBD have neuropsychological problems (Cooper, 2014; Kuniyoshi & McClellan, 2014; Mattison, Hooper, & Carlson, 2006).

Completion of the Human Genome Project was announced in April 2003 (Collins, 2003; Collins, Green, Guttmacher, & Guyer, 2003). That is, the "mapping" of all the genes in human DNA was completed. This accomplishment may well allow preventive medicine to make great progress and even have benefits for the prediction and early treatment of certain mental disorders. It was said by its director to have enormous potential to revolutionize medicine (Collins, 2003). However, enthusiasm for advances in understanding genetic codes has to be tempered with the understanding that genes *alone* don't determine the way people behave (Scull, 2015). Still, this understanding that genes alone don't determine behavior should not obscure the fact that advances in gene editing and gene manipulation pose serious questions of medical ethics (Achenbach, 2015; Kauffman & Hallahan, 2009).

For many decades, we have understood that the central nervous system is involved in all behavior, and all behavior involves neurochemical activity. Furthermore, scientists long ago established that genetic factors alone are *potentially* sufficient to explain all variation in human behavior (Eiduson, Eiduson, & Geller, 1962; Weiner, 1999). It may seem reasonable to believe, therefore, that disordered emotion or behavior always implies a genetic accident, bacterial or viral disease, brain injury, brain dysfunction, allergy, or some other biochemical imbalance (Linnoila, 1997). And we can find cases in which serious antisocial behavior is attributable to such neurological problems as brain tumors (e.g., Burns & Swerdlow, 2003) or biological factors provide a predisposition to develop antisocial behavior (e.g., Dodge & Pettit, 2003; see also Earley, 2006; Sedgwick, 2007).

As attractive as biological explanations may appear on the surface, however, the assumption that disorders are simply a result of biological misfortune is misleading, as is the suggestion that disorders are simply a result of social or cultural conditioning. Although biological processes have a pervasive influence on behavior, they affect behavior only in interaction with environmental factors (see Jensen et al., 2001; Pinker, 2002; Plomin, 1995; Rutter, 1995; Scull, 2015).

Knowing that a disorder has a biological cause doesn't always lead to a prescription for treatment. This doesn't mean that biologically-based disorders are untreatable; it means that scientists may not be able to devise a biological treatment designed to reverse the cause but may only be able to treat its effects, the symptoms of the biological process. Furthermore, because biological and environmental processes are interactive, sometimes the best treatment for a biological disorder is an alteration of the environment—arrangement of the social environment to ameliorate the effects of the biologically-based disorder. For example, Tourette's disorder, a neurological disorder with symptoms including tics and often accompanied by obsessions, compulsions, hyperactivity, distractibility, and impulsivity, may be treated with a combination of medication and cognitive-behavioral approaches involving changes in the social environment. The social environment may have significant effects on the symptoms of Tourette's disorder, although the basic cause of the disorder is neurological. Medication may be the single most effective treatment alternative for most children with attention deficit–hyperactivity disorder (ADHD) and related learning disabilities, but for many, especially those showing defiant and disruptive behavior in addition to ADHD, the combination of medication and psychosocial intervention (behavior therapy) works better (see Hallahan, Kauffman, & Pullen, 2015; Hallahan, Lloyd, Kauffman, Weiss, & Martinez, 2005; Jensen et al., 2001; Pullen, Lane, Ashworth, & Lovelace, 2017; Rooney, 2017).

The biological processes involved in behavioral deviance are extremely complex, and new discoveries are being made rapidly. Moreover, nearly every type of biological factor has been suggested as a possible cause of nearly every type of psychopathology. We may conclude that the effects of biological factors on behavioral development are considerable but frequently neither demonstrable nor simple. And although biological factors influence behavior, environmental conditions modify biological processes. Knowledge of biological causes may carry significant implications for prevention or medical treatment, but such knowledge usually has few direct implications for the work of educators. Educators work almost exclusively with environmental influences, relying on biological scientists and medical personnel to diagnose and treat the physiological aspects of EBD. Thus, educators should have basic information about biological factors but focus primarily on how the environmental conditions they may be able to control might affect students' behavior.

With these points in mind, we discuss several biological factors that may contribute to the development of disordered emotions or behavior: genetics, brain injury or dysfunction, nutrition and allergies, and temperament. We can't discuss the role of every possible biological factor in every type of disorder. Clearly, such things as the mother's substance abuse during pregnancy *can* contribute to emotional or behavioral problems in children. However, our discussion is brief and focused on representative examples of known or presumed biological causes and disorders in which such factors may play a role.

GENETICS

Children inherit more than physical characteristics from their parents; they also inherit predispositions to certain behavioral characteristics. Not surprisingly, genes have been suggested as causal factors in every kind of emotional or behavioral difficulty, including criminality, attention deficits, hyperactivity, schizophrenia, depression, Tourette's disorder, autism, and anxiety (see Asarnow & Asarnow, 2003; Kuniyoshi & McClellan, 2014; Levy & Hay, 2001). Research indicates that, indeed, genes have a strong influence on the development of all types of behavior, both desirable and undesirable. In fact, the evidence that there are significant genetic influences on behavior had become so overwhelming even before the twenty-first century that the question was not whether but *how* genes affect behavior (Grigorenko, 2014).

Genes linked to some specific diseases or vulnerabilities have been identified, but gene therapy, in which genes are manipulated, has been oversold by some scientists and the news media. However, genetically determined differences in children's behavior are observed by scientists not only in their research but also in their everyday lives.

In the early twenty-first century, we are learning that cloned animals (and, by extension, humans) do not necessarily have the same behaviors as their genetic matches. The same is true for identical twins (naturally occurring clones). Scientists have very good reason to conclude that behavioral characteristics are not determined solely by genes. Environmental factors, particularly social learning, play an important role in modifying inherited emotional or behavioral predispositions.

Furthermore, at the level of specific behaviors, social learning is nearly always far more important than genetics. Little or no evidence supports the suggestion that specific behaviors are genetically transmitted; however, some type of genetic influence obviously contributes to the major psychiatric disorders of children and adolescents and to many other disorders as well. What is inherited is a predisposition to behave in certain ways, a tendency toward certain types of behavior that may be made stronger or weaker by environmental conditions. The predisposition is created by a very complex process involving multiple genes. Seldom does EBD involve a single gene or an identifiable chromosomal anomaly. Moreover, **comorbidity**—multiple disorders involving complex gene interactions—is common (Grigorenko, 2014; Hay & Levy, 2001; Kuniyoshi & McClellan, 2014).

Genetic factors are suspected in a wide variety of disorders. However, a disorder in which genetic transmission is particularly well recognized is schizophrenia. The onset of schizophrenia occurs only rarely in young children, but onset in middle and late adolescence is relatively common (Asarnow & Asarnow, 2003; Kuniyoshi & McClellan, 2014). In most cases, the first symptoms of schizophrenia are observed in people ranging from fifteen to forty-five years of age. The features of schizophrenia are similar in children and adults, although onset in childhood may be associated with a severe form of the disorder. The major characteristics are delusions, hallucinations, disorganized speech, and thought disorders.

The exact genetic mechanisms responsible for a predisposition to schizophrenia and other disorders such as depression and bipolar disorder (formerly called manic depression) are still unknown, but research decades old clearly shows an increase in risk for schizophrenia and schizophrenic-like behavior (often called *schizoid or schizophrenic spectrum behavior*) in the relatives of schizophrenics. More recent research has not overturned the basic findings of a genetic link (see Youngstrom & Algorta, 2014). The closer the genetic relationship between the child and a schizophrenic relative, the higher the risk that the child will develop the condition. Heightened risk can't be attributed to the social environment or interpersonal factors alone. A higher level of risk goes with increasingly close genetic relatedness to a person who has schizophrenia. For example, having a sibling with schizophrenia increases a person's risk, but having an identical twin with schizophrenia increases an individual's risk a lot more.

Many people misunderstand the implications of increased risk for schizophrenia or other disorders. Does a heightened genetic risk for schizophrenia mean a person will necessarily develop the disorder? No. Do the genetic factors in schizophrenia mean that prevention is impossible? No. Some people with a genetic predisposition to become schizophrenic won't have the disorder. Although having blood relatives who have schizophrenia may increase someone's risk for it significantly, the chance that someone will develop schizophrenia is less than 50 percent, even for those at highest genetic risk—those having an identical twin or both parents with

Video Example from YouTube

ENHANCEDetext
Video Connections 4.1
In this video a physician talks about the familial risk of schizophrenia and some environmental factors that might serve as triggers for the development of schizophrenia. (https://www.youtube.com/watch?v=iuquAP3R-lk)

schizophrenia (see Sedgwick, 2007, for a family tree that highlights the notion of genetic risk, and includes a description of personal history involving depression). Furthermore, risk factors can be lowered by altering the social environment and avoiding circumstances that might trigger the disorder (see Gerber, 2014).

The causes of schizophrenia are likely multiple and complex, with genetic factors being only one predisposing factor (see Mukherjee, 2016). However, schizoid behavior or full-blown schizophrenia can apparently be triggered by a bad drug trip as well as environmental stressors. Those at highest risk for schizophrenia (i.e., those with close blood relatives with the disorder) would be well advised to avoid experimenting with drugs (Gottesman, 1987, 1991).

Implications of Genetic Factors

A common misperception is that disorders arising from genetic accidents are not treatable—that once the genetic code is set, the related deviant behavior is immutable. But this isn't necessarily so. As with schizophrenia, environmental as well as biological factors are involved in causing deviant behavior. When the biochemical mechanisms underlying genetic transmission are discovered, there's hope that effective interventions will be found to prevent or alter the course of behavioral development. Nevertheless, the effects of prevention are invisible. That is, no one sees what is prevented (Kauffman, 1999c; Specter, 2009).

Genetic factors are known to contribute to a variety of behavioral and physiological problems, perhaps even to most. In some severe disorders, such as schizophrenia, the level of the genetic contribution is clear, but how the gene system works isn't clear. For most types of EBD, the genetic contributions remain unclear, and environmental factors appear to be far more important for educators (see Grigorenko, 2014; Pinker, 2002; Specter, 2009).

As Kazdin (2008) pointed out, parents and teachers often jump too quickly to a conclusion that a program involving changes in what they do in response to behavior won't work. True, there are cases in which environmental changes aren't effective. In an extreme example, Kazdin notes, children might have uncontrollable tantrums that the usual techniques of behavior management just won't change, no matter what is tried. But in the vast majority of cases, even in those in which there is a genetic contribution to the misbehavior, the skillful use of environmental consequences—altering the antecedents and consequences of behavior—is effective (see Foxx, 2016b; Walker & Gresham, 2014).

Evolutionary biology strongly suggests that many behaviors are influenced by genetic makeup and the mixing of genes from unrelated individuals. Genetic mixing ordinarily helps species perpetuate their kind. However, genetic mutations—random changes or errors in genes—also occur (Batshaw, 2002b; Grigorenko, 2014; Judson, 2002). Sometimes these are destructive and don't help a species survive. We don't really know how to determine whether EBD is a mutation and whether it helps perpetuate *Homo sapiens* in any way.

BRAIN DAMAGE OR DYSFUNCTION

The brain can be traumatized in several different ways before, during, or after birth, and such damage may contribute substantially to antisocial behavior (Batshaw, 2002a; Hallahan et al., 2015; Lajiness-O'Neill, Erdodi, & Lichtenstein, 2017). Physical insult during an accident or during the birth process may destroy brain tissue. Prolonged high fever, infectious disease, and toxic chemicals (such as drugs or poisons taken by the child or by a woman during pregnancy) may also damage the brain. A frequently suspected or known cause of brain damage in children, however, is **hypoxia** (also known as **anoxia**), a seriously reduced supply of oxygen. *Hypoxia* often occurs during birth but can also occur during accidents or as a result of disease or respiratory disorders later in life.

The brain may function improperly for a variety of reasons. Tissue damage from traumatic injury may cause dysfunction. In the case of **traumatic brain injury**, we know that the brain's function has been impaired by documented damage at a specific location or locations. However, the brain may not function properly because of structural anomalies (i.e., malformation of certain parts of the brain) that are present at birth or are part of a disease process or because of a neurochemical imbalance resulting from a disease or drugs. In some cases, scientists don't know exactly why the brain isn't working as it should, although it obviously isn't. For example, schizophrenia has been clearly established as a brain disorder, but we don't yet know exactly what's wrong with the brain of a person who has schizophrenia. Researchers are also working to find the brain mechanisms underlying **obsessive-compulsive disorder** (OCD) (see Nutt, 2016).

A very wide range of EBD has been attributed to known or suspected brain damage or dysfunction. Learning disabilities and the related problems of hyperactivity, impulsivity, and inattention historically have been assumed to be caused by brain injury or dysfunction, although the exact nature of the injury or dysfunction has not been demonstrated (Hallahan et al., 2005, 2015). Subtle brain injury before, during, or shortly after birth is an important contributing cause of serious juvenile delinquency and adult criminality, according to some researchers. Other researchers have found neuropsychological problems involving language and attention in a high percentage of students with severe EBD (Mattison et al., 2006).

Nearly every sort of serious emotional or behavioral problem could be hypothesized to be, at some level, a matter of structural or chemical problems of the brain. For purposes of illustration, consider a category of acquired disability that was made a separate special education category under federal law in 1990: *traumatic brain injury*, often known as TBI.

The effects of TBI may be misattributed to other causes if the brain injury isn't diagnosed and understood. In many cases, violence and other disturbing behavior can't be connected to brain damage, and it's important not to attribute such behavior to brain damage in the absence of medical evidence of damage. However, we also know that TBI can cause violent aggression, hyperactivity, impulsivity, inattention, and a wide range of other emotional or behavioral problems, depending on just what parts of the brain are damaged. The possible effects of TBI include a long list of other psychosocial problems, some of which we list here:

- Inappropriate manners or mannerisms
- Failure to understand humor or read social situations
- Becoming easily tired, frustrated, or angered
- Unreasonable fear or anxiety
- Irritability
- Sudden, exaggerated mood swings
- Depression
- Perseveration (getting stuck on one thought or behavior)

The emotional and behavioral effects of TBI are determined by more than the physical damage to the brain. These effects also depend on the student's age at the time of injury and the social environment before and after the injury occurs. Home, community, or school environments that foster misbehavior of any child or youth—disorganization, lack of adult supervision, dangerous circumstances, or lack of safety precautions, for example—are known to be associated with higher risk for acquiring TBI. Such environments also are extremely likely to make any emotional or behavioral problem resulting from TBI worse.

Creating an environment that's conducive to and supportive of appropriate behavior is one of the great challenges of dealing effectively with the **sequelae** (aftereffects, or consequences) of brain injury (Best, Heller, & Bigge, 2010). Medical treatment usually can't undo the effects of TBI. Emotional or behavioral problems may be known to have resulted from brain injury, but these problems must be addressed primarily through environmental modifications—changing other people's demands, expectations, and responses to behavior.

TBI often shatters an individual's sense of self. Recovering one's identity may require a long period of rehabilitation and may be a painstaking process requiring multidisciplinary efforts (see Lajiness-O'Neill et al., 2017). Effective education and treatment often require not only classroom behavior management but also family therapy, medication, cognitive training, and communication training.

Brain damage or dysfunction can produce a wide variety of emotional and behavioral disorders. Brain damage or dysfunction isn't the only cause of such disorders, however, and it's important to remember that environmental factors can make a significant difference in the effects of brain injury on behavior.

NUTRITION, ALLERGIES, AND OTHER HEALTH ISSUES

We've known for decades that severe malnutrition can have catastrophic effects on children's cognitive and physical development. Malnutrition is especially devastating to the development of very young children. It reduces the child's responsiveness to stimulation and produces apathy. The eventual result of serious malnutrition (especially severe protein deficiency) is retardation in brain growth, irreversible brain damage, diminished intellectual ability, or some combination of these effects. Apathy, social withdrawal, and school failure are expected long-term outcomes if children are severely malnourished. Furthermore, it's well recognized that hunger and inadequate nutrition interfere with the ability to concentrate on academic and social learning. Thus, the concern for children's adequate nutrition in poor families is well justified (Tanner & Finn-Stevenson, 2002).

The belief that less-severe nutritional inadequacies (such as not enough vitamins or minerals) or excesses (such as too much sugar or caffeine) cause children to misbehave has been popular for many years. Disorders ranging from hyperactivity to depression to autism to delinquency have been attributed by some to what youngsters eat or don't eat. True, hypoglycemia (low blood sugar), vitamin or mineral deficiencies, and allergies can influence behavior, and teachers should be aware of these potential problems. However, the role of specific foods and allergies in causing cognitive, emotional, or behavioral problems has often been exaggerated.

Although we know that some children are allergic to certain foods and a variety of other substances (e.g., medications, pollens, dust, insect stings), there is little evidence that these allergies are often causes of emotional or behavioral problems. However, teachers, like parents, may prefer the belief that diet is a major factor in causing misbehavior (Williams & Foxx, 2016). Biases and expectations appear to maintain the superstition that foods and allergies often cause behavioral or emotional problems. Adequate nutrition is crucial; excluding or severely restricting certain food substances seldom is.

A wide variety of other health-related disorders are found in the child population, including obesity, sleep disorders, injuries, and diseases (Peterson, Reach, & Grabe, 2003). Many health issues are associated with poverty (Pascoe et al., 2016). In some cases, these involve problems of mental health as well as physical health. However, it's important not to assume that *all* health-related problems are created by either poverty or EBD.

TEMPERAMENT

Beginning in the 1960s, researchers began to explore the centuries-old notion of **temperament**. The definition and measurement of temperament and the stability or continuity of temperament across time are still matters of considerable controversy (see Keogh, 2003; Rimm-Kaufman & Kagan, 2005). Temperament has been variously defined as "behavioral style," or the "how" rather than the "what" and "how well" of behavior; as the "active and reactive qualities" of infant behavior; and as "measurable behavior" during infancy. It has been measured by questionnaires given to parents or teachers and by direct observation of children's behavior. Despite differences in the ways in which researchers define and measure it, we can describe the concept of temperament in general terms: Individuals tend to have consistent, predictable reactions to certain types of circumstances or events, and their typical way of responding—their temperament—is partly determined by basic biological processes as well as environmental factors.

The point is that infants begin life with an inborn tendency to behave in certain ways. The newborn has a behavioral style that's determined predominantly by biological factors, and how a baby behaves at birth and in the first weeks and months thereafter will influence how others respond. But temperament can be changed by the environment in which the child develops; what the child experiences and how the child is managed may change temperament for better or worse (Chess & Thomas, 2003; Keogh, 2003; Nelson, Stage, Duppong-Hurley, Synhorst, & Epstein, 2007). A difficult temperament may increase the child's risk for emotional or behavioral disorders. However, temperament is an initial behavioral style that may change in interaction with environmental influences. Based on their now classic longitudinal study, Thomas, Chess, and Birch (1968) described nine categories of temperamental characteristics:

1. *Activity level:* how much the child moves about during activities such as feeding, bathing, sleeping, and playing
2. *Rhythmicity:* the regularity or predictability with which the child eats, sleeps, eliminates, and so on
3. *Approach or withdrawal:* how the child responds initially to new events such as people, places, toys, and foods
4. *Adaptability:* how quickly the child becomes accustomed to or modifies an initial reaction to new situations or stimuli

5. *Intensity of reaction:* the amount of energy expended in reacting (positively or negatively) to situations or stimuli

6. *Threshold of responsiveness:* the amount or intensity of stimulation required to elicit a response from the child

7. *Quality of mood:* the amount of pleasant, joyful, and friendly behavior compared with unpleasant, crying, and unfriendly behavior exhibited by the child

8. *Distractibility:* the frequency with which extraneous or irrelevant stimuli interfere with the ongoing behavior of the child in a given situation

9. *Attention span and persistence:* the length of time a child will spend on a given activity and the tendency to maintain an activity in the face of obstacles to performance.

Thomas and colleagues (1968) found that children with any kind of temperament might develop EBD, depending on the child-rearing practices of their parents and other adults. Besides the characteristics listed, other more inclusive or general temperaments have been described. As Keogh (2003) pointed out, some children may be described as "easy." An easy temperament is characterized by regularity, adaptability, and positive response to new stimuli, mild or moderate intensity of response, and positive mood. Children with "difficult" temperaments are more likely to develop troublesome behavior. A difficult temperament is characterized by irregularity in biological functioning, mostly negative (withdrawing) responses to new stimuli, slow adaptation to changes in the environment, frequent displays of negative mood, and mostly intense reactions. Some children can be described as "slow-to-warm-up" in temperament. Other temperament types include "undercontrolled," "inhibited," "confident," "sluggish," and "well adjusted."

Keogh (2003) pointed out that the "difficulty" of a child depends on the social context in which the child is behaving—the particular situation or circumstances and the cultural expectations. The key point is that what is perceived as a "difficult" temperament may elicit negative responses from a child's caretakers; a baby with a difficult temperament isn't easy to care for and may increase parents' irritability, negative mood, and tendency to ignore or punish the child. If infant and parents adopt a pattern of mutual irritation, their negative interactions may increase the probability that the youngster will exhibit inappropriate or undesirable behavior in future years. Longitudinal research by other investigators also points to the potential for temperament to partially explain or predict later behavior. For example, inhibited and uninhibited temperaments in infancy have been shown to be associated with differences in observed kindergarten behavior (Rimm-Kaufman & Kagan, 2005); difficult temperament at an early age has been shown to be predictive of behavioral problems in adolescence (Caspi, Henry, McGee, Moffitt, & Silva, 1995); an easy or positive temperament has been found to be associated with children's resilience in responding to stress (Keogh, 2003); and temperament interacts with parenting behavior to place children at risk or make them resilient (Nelson et al., 2007; Ungar, 2011).

The concept of difficult temperament has its critics. Some suggest that what researchers believe are inborn biological characteristics of infants are merely the subjective interpretations of mothers' reports. That is, "difficult temperament" reflects social perceptions of an infant's behavior and may not be within-the-individual characteristics. A baby is said to have a difficult temperament on the basis of the mother's report rather than more objective evaluations;

therefore, the mother's perceptions (and the researcher's) are being assessed rather than a biological characteristic of the baby. Keogh (2003) and others, however, interpret their research as confirming the reality of inborn behavioral characteristics or temperaments that are altered by environmental conditions. There appears to be a consensus regarding the interaction of environmental and inborn factors in shaping children's behavior:

1. Environmental effects such as family dysfunction, neighborhood violence, poor schools, and other unfortunate conditions are responsible for a substantial proportion of children's behavioral disorders.

2. Intrinsic factors explain some disorders formerly thought to be caused by the social environment. We now understand, for example, that autism and learning disabilities and perhaps other problems such as obesity are caused primarily by biological processes. These disorders are likely to exist under a wide range of environmental conditions.

3. A poor fit between a child's normal temperament and the values and expectations of the child's caregivers can cause stress, leading to EBD.

Both environmental and intrinsic, biological factors contribute to EBD. Environmental and intrinsic factors combine to shape temperament. Moreover, a mismatch of social environment and the child's typical behavior can exacerbate a difficult temperament. A difficult temperament may increase a child's risk of EBD, but the risk may be either heightened further or lowered by the way in which parents and teachers manage the child's behavior (Keogh, 2003; Nelson et al., 2007).

A few researchers have investigated teachers' ratings of children's temperaments in the classroom (see Keogh, 2003, for a review). Their general findings are that children do exhibit a consistent behavioral style or temperament in the classroom and that teachers tend to take children's temperaments into account in planning, instruction, and management. Moreover, teachers have a temperament, which may be a good or bad fit with the child's temperament.

Temperament may play a significant role in the development of EBD, but it does so only in interaction with environmental conditions. A consistent behavioral disposition or temperament such as irritability or impulsivity may heighten the risk for EBD. Research doesn't indicate that temperament is the direct or exclusive result of biological factors, but it does suggest that students exhibit a consistent behavioral style that teachers recognize and should consider in instruction and accommodation of behavioral diversity among students.

IMPLICATIONS FOR EDUCATORS

The biological factors that may have a significant negative effect on behavior are many and complex. It's important for educators to understand how genetics, parental neglect or abuse, malnutrition, and neurological damage may be linked to school failure and impulsive or antisocial behavior. Biological and social risk factors together offer the best explanations of the causes of antisocial behavior, and the same applies to other forms of EBD. Genetic predisposition, neglect, abuse, malnutrition, and brain injury all are more likely to be significant contributors to maladaptive behavior when they are accompanied by inconsistent or ill-suited behavior management at home and school.

However, it's wrong to assume that EBD always has a biological origin and that there-fore all such disorders are best handled by medical intervention. Not only is the tie between many of these disorders and specific biological causative factors tenuous, but also a biologi-cal cause may have no direct implications for change in educational methodology. Educators should work with other professionals to obtain the best possible medical care, nutrition, and physical environment for their students. However, educators cannot provide medical intervention and they have only very limited influence over their students' physical health. Although teachers should be aware of possible biological factors and refer students for evalu-ation by other professionals when appropriate, they must not allow speculation regarding biological etiologies to excuse them from teaching appropriate behavior when they can—the academic and social skills that will enable students to be happy and successful in everyday environments.

Pharmacological (drug) treatment of EBD is becoming more common, systematic, and effective (see Konopasek & Forness, 2014; Mattison, 2014; Nutt, 2016). Medications can sometimes be extremely helpful in controlling EBD (see Earley, 2006, for a description of its importance in managing schizophrenia and other serious mental disorders). Unfortunately, there appears to be a strong anti-medication bias among many educators. Part of this bias may be because of teachers' lack of awareness of the purposes and possible benefits of medications and to their failure to understand that careful monitoring of classroom behavior is necessary to determine whether the drug is working, should be discontinued, or needs a dosage adjustment to obtain maximum benefits with minimum side effects.

Although a teacher is not able to prescribe medications or adjust dosages, the teacher's observations provide critical information for the physician (Mattison, 2014). Teachers should be aware of the major types of drugs that may be prescribed for their students and the possible effects and side effects those drugs may have on classroom behavior and performance.

We suggest that teachers should first clarify the medications and dosages prescribed for their students with families or directly with prescribing physicians when appropriate (e.g., when the family or physician has initiated contact with the teacher to seek input on the effects or side effects of medication that might be observed in the school setting). Teachers should also consult with a school nurse on specific concerns about a particular medication and its potential effects. The internet—used carefully—can be a good source of information about drugs used in treatment (i.e., therapeutic drugs, which may be abused or used for illicit pur-poses) and illicit drugs, which are never prescribed but may nonetheless be used and abused by some students with EBD.

Teachers should certainly seek additional facts relevant to particular cases. There are many categories and subcategories of psychotropic drugs, such as antidepressants, stimulants, antipsychotics, and mood stabilizers. New drugs are constantly being introduced, and the effects and side effects of a given drug may vary greatly depending on the dosage level and the individual. The teacher should consult a nurse, physician, or professional publications for more detailed information about drug categories as well as specific therapeutic drugs and dosages. A student's parents or physician should inform the teacher that the student is taking a particular medication and ask the teacher to monitor its effects on the student's classroom behavior and academic performance. If the teacher isn't so informed and isn't asked to participate in evalu-ating the drug's classroom effects but becomes aware that the student is taking a psychotropic medication, he or she should approach the parents or the school nurse about monitoring the way in which the student is using and responding to the drug.

SUMMARY

Biological factors have special appeal because all behavior involves biochemical, neurological activity. Among the many biological factors that may contribute to the origins of EBD are genetics, brain damage or dysfunction, nutrition or allergies, and temperament.

Genetic factors have been suggested as the causes of nearly every type of disorder. Genetics are known to be involved in causing schizophrenia, but little is known about how the gene system that causes the disorder works. Environmental factors appear to trigger schizophrenia in individuals who are genetically vulnerable. The fact that a disorder has a genetic cause doesn't mean that the disorder is untreatable.

Brain damage or dysfunction has been suggested as a cause of nearly every type of EBD. Traumatic brain injury involves known damage to the brain and may cause a wide variety of emotional and behavioral problems. Schizophrenia is now recognized as a biological disorder, although neither the exact nature nor the reasons for the brain dysfunction are known. In both TBI and schizophrenia, environmental conditions can be significant in managing the disorder.

Severe malnutrition has devastating effects on young children's development. However, the popular notion that EBD is often caused by diet or allergies hasn't been supported by a consistent body of research. Teachers should be aware of possible dietary problems and allergies of students, but concern for these possible causes shouldn't distract attention from instructional procedures.

Temperament is a consistent behavioral style or predisposition to respond in certain ways to one's environment. Although temperament may have a biological basis, it's also shaped by environmental factors. Skillful management by parents and teachers can lower the risk of EBD associated with difficult temperament.

When biological factors contribute to EBD, they don't operate in isolation from or independently of environmental (psychological) forces. The most tenable view at this time is that biological and environmental factors interact with one another to cause disorders. It seems reasonable to propose a continuum of biological causes ranging from minor, undetectable, organic faults to profound accidents of nature and a related continuum of EBD, ranging from mild to profound, to which these biological accidents contribute. Implications of biological factors for the day-to-day work of teachers may in some cases be nil, but teachers should be aware of possible biological causes and refer students to other professionals when appropriate. Teachers should be aware of the possible effects and side effects of psychotropic medications and be involved in monitoring drug effects.

✔ ENHANCEDetext END-OF-CHAPTER 4 QUIZ

Click on the checkmark icon to access an end-of-chapter quiz. Answer the questions to gauge your understanding of chapter concepts and better prepare you for case discussions.

CASE FOR DISCUSSION (See case book for additional cases.)

She Goes On and On.

Lorna

Fifteen-year-old Lorna sometimes talks on and on, even though what she's saying is confusing to others. Members of her family sometimes try to clue her in by saying to her, "Lorna, you're going on and on." Her younger brother sometimes tells her that nobody wants to hear everything she's saying. But Lorna just chalks it up to the way brothers talk to their sisters. Lorna's mother once said that a listener has to share an experience with Lorna to be able to understand what she is talking about. Even then, the mother admits, understanding Lorna is difficult for anyone.

Excessive talking is sometimes called *verborrhea* or *logorrhea*—an excessive use of words. Regardless of the technical or psychiatric term, going on and on or talking too much can be a sign of serious emotional or behavioral problems.

Lorna's tendency to talk on and on was one of the first things a psychiatrist noticed in forming his opinion that something was seriously wrong with her. He suggested further evaluation, which revealed another problem. Lorna tended to talk on and on, but she tended to go on and on in writing, too, often not making sense because she left out words or didn't finish writing words. Her sentences tended to get really long, and she typically became very confused about a topic and was

not be able to write more than a paragraph or two on any topic.

Source: Based on Anonymous (1994)

Questions About the Case

1. Imagine that Lorna is in your 10th-grade class. Would knowing that she has schizophrenia and is taking medication for it make a difference in how you respond to her going on and on? If not, why not? If so, how?

2. As her teacher, what strategies might you try to help Lorna learn to converse more normally (i.e., not to go on and on)?

3. If Lorna were a student in a regular 10th-grade class, how would you help her classmates respond kindly and helpfully to her when she goes on and on?

5 CULTURE

After reading this chapter, you should be able to:

5.1 Describe the conflicts between cultures and how they create stress for children and youth.

5.2 Be able to describe the steps educators can take to avoid the problems of bias and discrimination against students whose cultures differ from their own.

5.3 Explain how cultural factors might contribute to behavioral deviance.

5.4 Describe how TV viewing might influence children's antisocial and prosocial behavior.

5.5 Characterize a neighborhood that supports the development of children's appropriate social behavior.

APPEAL OF CULTURAL FACTORS AS CAUSAL EXPLANATIONS

A variety of social influences help determine, in part, how youngsters behave. We discuss in the next two chapters the influence of families (Chapter 6) and schools (Chapter 7) on children's behavior, but even these do not include all the social influences that impact children and youth. Children, families, and teachers are part of a larger culture that molds their behavior. Parents and teachers tend to hold values and set behavioral standards and expectations that are consistent with those of the cultures in which they live and work. Children's attitudes and behavior gravitate toward the cultural norms of their families, peers, and communities. We must therefore evaluate behavior in the context of cultural differences and changes. Family relationships change across time and are different in different cultures. Although we may find certain patterns or characteristics of successful child rearing that are the same across time and in all cultures, it's also clear that the same specific behaviors that are adaptive in one circumstance may not be in another (e.g., inner city versus affluent suburb; time of peace versus time of war; economic stability and growth versus economic depression; rearing by parents versus rearing by grandparents; one-parent versus two-parent families). Therefore, the findings of studies conducted in 2015 or 2020 or 2025 may tell us less than we might imagine about American families in 2030 or later because of changing conditions and demographics (see Hayden & Mash, 2014; Patterson & Fosse, 2015; also www.virginia.edu/marriageproject/).

Culture involves behavioral expectations, but it is more than that (Anastasiou & Kauffman, 2011; Anastasiou, Kauffman, & Michail, 2016; DeLuca, Clampet-Lundquist, & Edin, 2016). Culture may include values, typical or acceptable behavior, languages and dialects, patterns of nonverbal communication, awareness of cultural identity, and worldviews or general perspectives. Nations and other large social entities have a shared culture or national culture. Within the larger society are many smaller groups with differing values, styles, languages, dialects, ways of communicating nonverbally, awareness, frames of reference, and identification (often called subcultures, not because they are dominated or of lesser importance but because they are only a part of the whole). How do we maintain American culture and at the same time respect the subcultures that form it? The answer is neither obvious nor easy (see Anastasiou et al., 2016; Hallahan et al., 2015; Kauffman & Anastasiou, in press; Learoyd-Smith & Daniels, 2014; and Skiba, Middelberg, & McClain, 2014 for further discussion of multiculturalism and education, including special education for children and youth with EBD).

The United States has often been called a cultural melting pot—an amalgam of various nationalities and cultures. We have come to believe that its diversity of citizens makes the United States strong and good. But we realize that if we don't make a true alloy of the diverse ingredients of our culture—if we don't amalgamate our diverse elements into a single, uniquely American identity—we can be neither strong nor good as a society. *E pluribus unum* (out of many, one), a slogan stamped on our coins, seems to present an increasing paradox. We value cultural diversity, but common cultural values hold our society together. The tension between our separateness and our togetherness—our distinctiveness and our oneness—obviously can set the stage for disordered emotions and behavior, as well as conflicts among groups on nearly every issue. But it is togetherness, oneness, unity, and commonality that provide the glue holding any society together. An emphasis on differences to the exclusion of seeing the common sets the stage for cultural conflicts, racism, hatred, and war. Moreover, the same fundamental principles of behavior and instruction seem to apply to all cultures (Kauffman, Conroy et al., 2008).

When the child's, family's, school's, or teacher's values or expectations conflict with other cultural norms, emotional or behavioral development may be adversely affected or school behavior may become a difficult issue. To the extent that different cultural forces tug a youngster's behavior in different directions, they create conflicting expectations and increase the probability that he or she will violate cultural norms and be labeled deviant. A lot of attention has been given in the literature to "race," which is not a scientifically defensible biological fact even though many people believe it is. This is not to say that the cultural construct of race is unimportant, only that it has no basis in biology (Anastasiou & Kauffman, 2012). Neither is this to say that a student's ethnic identity and community is unimportant (Fosse, 2015; Patterson, 2015a, 2015b).

CONFLICTING CULTURAL VALUES AND STANDARDS

It's easy to find examples of conflicting cultural values and standards and the stress they create for children and youth. Television shows, movies, and magazines glamorize the behavior and values of high-status models that are incompatible with the standards of many children's families; youngsters' imitation of these models results in disapproval from parents. Religious groups may forbid certain behaviors that are normative in the larger community (such as dancing, attending movies, dating, or masturbating). Youngsters who conform to these religious teachings may be rejected by peers, stigmatized, or socially isolated, whereas those who violate these prohibitions may feel extreme guilt. The values children attach to certain possessions or behavior because they are highly regarded by their peers or teachers (such as wearing particular items of clothing or achieving or not achieving at school) may be incomprehensible to their parents. Differences between parents' and children's values may become the focus of parental nattering.

Hitting and aggression are generally considered unacceptable in our society (see Kimonis, Frick & McMahon, 2014). However, physical (corporal) punishment has been an integral part of how parents discipline their children throughout history, and data suggest that as many as 95 percent of American parents spank their young children (Gershoff, 2002; Taylor, Manganello, Lee, & Rice, 2010). Although some nations of the world have outlawed the corporal punishment of children, the United States has not. Attitudes among various cultural groups toward corporal punishment and knowledge of the effects of spanking remain matters of considerable controversy.

Children of mixed ethnicity—of so-called "interracial" marriages—may have difficulty developing a sense of identity, particularly during adolescence. They may have major problems reconciling their dual identifications into a single, personal identity that affirms the positive aspects of each heritage and acknowledges society's ambivalence toward biracial persons. At the same time, the demographic trends in America are toward a mixing of national, ethnic, and racial categories, and just how or when someone takes on a particular cultural identity is not known (see Kauffman, Conroy et al., 2008). Moreover, it is clear to those who embrace a scientific view of the world that sometimes a long-held or traditional cultural belief must yield to one better grounded in empirical evidence, or what some call a Western view of reality, if children are to be treated humanely.

Conflicting cultural influences on behavior are sometimes perverse; the culture provides both inducements for a given type of behavior and severe penalties for engaging in it.

This kind of temptation or pressure with one hand and punishment with the other is especially evident in the areas of violent behavior and sexuality. Our society fosters violence through its glorification of high-status, violent models in the mass media, yet it seeks severe punishment for youngsters' imitative social aggression. Consider teenage pregnancy—the cultural forces that foster it and society's responses to it. During the past several decades, sexual mores have changed so that adolescents now have much greater freedom and added responsibilities for preventing pregnancy. Our society tempts adolescents, offering them freedoms and responsibilities they aren't equipped to handle, yet it does nothing to help them deal with these freedoms and responsibilities and in fact punishes them for abusing freedom and behaving irresponsibly. Movies, the internet, social media, and commercials highlight sex appeal and sexual encounters, providing models of behavior that are incompatible with efforts to encourage sexual abstinence or avoid pregnancy. Teenagers often pressure their peers to become sexually active; at the same time, conservative politicians have attempted to restrict sex education and make contraceptives less available to teens. Education for family life and child rearing is often inadequate.

MULTICULTURAL PERSPECTIVE

Besides the conflicts that differing cultural standards create, children's and adults' own cultural values may bias their perceptions of others. A full discussion of cultural bias in education is far beyond the scope of this chapter, but it's important to note that problems of bias and discrimination carry serious implications for evaluating youngsters' behavior (see Patterson & Fosse, 2015).

Ultimately, nearly all behavioral standards and expectations—and therefore nearly all judgments regarding behavioral deviance—are culture-bound. That is to say, value judgments can't be entirely culture-free. In our pluralistic society, which values multicultural differences, the central question for educators is whether they have made sufficient allowance in their judgments for behavior that's a function of a child's particular cultural heritage (see Cartledge, Kea, & Ida, 2000; Osher et al., 2004; Patterson, 2015a; Skiba et al., 2014). Cultural differences that don't put the youngster at risk in the larger society should be accepted; only values and behaviors that are incompatible with achieving the larger goals of education (self-actualization, independence, and responsibility) should be modified.

Who determines the larger goals of society? We all tend to view our own cultural orientation as the standard against which others should be judged. Because the United States has been dominated by European subcultures, the focus of multicultural concerns has been on non-European minority cultures.

It isn't easy to establish rules for applying a multicultural perspective. Teachers and school administrators must make daily decisions about which standards of conduct represent their personal value systems and which represent justifiable demands for adaptation to the larger society. For example, is it really necessary for students to remove their hats in the classroom? What is "polite" English, and is it necessary that students use it to address adults in school? What values and behaviors are inconsistent with a youngster's success and happiness in society at large? When do the values of a particular culture place a student at risk for school failure? Under what conditions is risk of school failure a fault of the school itself—how it's organized and the demands it makes of students?

These and similar questions have no ready answers. They'll continue to be part of our struggle for fairness and justice in a multicultural society. At the same time, we note that the greatest fairness to students is achieved by offering them instruction that is evidence-based (Kauffman, Mock, Tankeresley, & Landrum, 2008; Walker & Gresham, 2014).

PROBLEMS IN EVALUATING CULTURAL FACTORS

Besides the family and the school, which are topics of separate chapters, the most frequently researched cultural factors include the mass media, peer group, neighborhood, ethnic origin, social class, religious institutions, urbanization, and health and welfare services. Evaluating the role of these factors in EBD is extremely difficult, primarily for three reasons.

First, the interrelationships among the many cultural influences are so strong that untangling the effects of most of the individual factors is impossible. Hodgkinson (1995) observed long ago that concern with racial and ethnic differences has diverted our attention from the more pervasive effects of poverty (see Pascoe et al., 2016). Although poverty may be correlated with racial or ethnic identities, the best strategy for improving the lives of children who are members of racial or ethnic minorities and those with disabilities may be to focus on poverty itself.

Second, research related to several of the factors is limited or nearly nonexistent. Religious beliefs and institutions, for example, probably have a strong influence on family life and child behavior, yet there is little research on the effects of religion on child behavior and family life.

Third, culture and temperament are interrelated in ways that make identification of problem behavior difficult. Is the problem in the child's behavior, the teacher's expectations, or the lack of fit between the two (Keogh, 2003)?

Despite these difficulties in understanding cultural factors, available research does suggest relationships between certain cultural characteristics and the development of behavioral deviance. For example, violence in the media and the ready availability of guns, two prominent features of contemporary American culture, are consistently linked to aggressive conduct of children and youth (Huesmann, MoiseTitus, Podolski, & Eron, 2003; Walker et al., 2004). Understanding and sustaining cultural diversity that enhances the human condition while modifying cultural patterns of behavior that destroy the human spirit is a tremendous challenge.

Mass Media

Mass media include printed materials, radio, television, motion pictures, music, and electronic information available on the internet. Societal concern for the effects of mass media on the behavior of children and youth began when books and magazines became widely available. A few generations ago, concerns about the effects of radio programs and comic books were frequently expressed. Jazz was once thought to be a corrupting influence. Present controversies rage over the effects of textbooks, pornographic magazines, novels, motion pictures, electronic games, hip-hop, and information and pornography available on the internet on the thinking and behavior of the young.

That what people read, see, and hear influences their behavior is hardly questionable, yet relatively little sound research is available to explain how—with the exception of advertising material. Publishers and broadcasters do market research to show the effectiveness of sponsors' ads; they know a lot about what sells and what influences the buying habits of specific segments of their audiences, including children and adolescents. Nevertheless, the influence of the media on youngsters' social behavior is often dubious or hotly disputed. Ironically, the same individuals (television network executives) who express confidence in the behavioral effects of television commercials argue that the effects of television violence on children's social behavior are negligible.

Today, the effects of television on behavioral development are by far the most serious media issue. Watching lots of television appears to have adverse effects on the cognitive abilities of young children (Zimmerman & Chistakis, 2005) and to be associated in adolescence with risk for development of problems in attention, learning, and schooling (Johnson, Cohen, Kasen, & Brook, 2007). Moreover, researchers and policy makers are interested in how watching television may increase children's aggression and their prosocial behavior (for example, helping, sharing, and cooperation). Research clearly links watching television to increases in aggression, but the link is a statistical probability, not a one-to-one correspondence. Some highly aggressive children do not watch much television, and some children who watch television almost incessantly aren't aggressive. Yet television viewing is clearly a contributing factor to some children's antisocial conduct, and it's important to understand how television viewing can be involved in causation. One obvious way in which television violence can facilitate aggressive conduct is through observational learning; youngsters imitate what they see. This explanation is probably a gross oversimplification, however; research now suggests that much more complicated processes are involved.

The most likely explanation of the effects of television viewing fits a social cognitive model described long ago (Bandura, 1986). That is, the effects involve reciprocal influence among three components: person variables (thoughts and feelings), the social environment, and behavior. In the case of television violence and aggression, Bandura's triadic reciprocation involves the child's thoughts and feelings about aggression and the television characters who model it, the child's environment (including school, home, and community), and the child's selection of violent television programs and aggressive responses to problem situations. But general social circumstance—the social ecology in which aggression is exhibited, including friendship patterns and school performance—must also be considered.

Watching a lot of TV violence apparently dramatically increases the risk that a child will grow up to exhibit violent interpersonal behavior in adulthood (Huesmann, Moise-Titus, Podolski, & Eron, 2003). Violent media action appears to instigate antisocial acts in some cases, to desensitize children to acts of aggression (i.e., to make them more apathetic to displays of aggression and less likely to help others), and to perceive their environment as a more aggressive and dangerous place. Some violent video games appear to provide effective training in violent acts through emotional preparation and behavioral rehearsal. Although research may not indicate clearly that watching television violence consistently causes children (including those with EBD) to be violent, there are good reasons to limit children's television viewing and direct their attention toward more constructive activities. Decreasing the violence depicted on television and in movies may well help to lower the level of violent behavior among children and youth.

The role of the mass media (not just television but all print, film, music, video, and broadcast media) in the development of EBD is a concern

Video Example from YouTube

▶

ENHANCEDetext
Video Connections 5.1

In this video, a researcher describes his study of the effects of television watching on young children's behavior. He discusses both potentially positive impacts of watching positive television shows, as well as the potentially negative effects of viewing violence, even in young children's programming like cartoons. (https://www.youtube.com/watch?v=ox8vlSRI1IM)

to those who wish to construct a more prosocial and humane society. For example, teenage suicidal behavior appears to increase following media coverage of teen suicides. Motion pictures that glorify violent solutions to problems may add to the effects of television violence. It is difficult to conclude that print or electronic materials featuring violence and pornography play any *positive* role in behavioral development or conduct.

A concern of some is the influence of hip-hop (rap) lyrics. Although some rap lyrics use words or phrases that some people find offensive, this is not true of all rap. Furthermore, the same could be said of nearly all—if not literally all—vocal music genres. Probably, disapproval of hip-hop per se is incompatible with understanding the youth of any culture today (Marshall, 2015).

Perhaps decreasing the portrayal of undesirable behavior and increasing prosocial programming and reporting of prosocial acts would make our culture less self-destructive and more humane. Yet the solution to the media problem isn't apparent; censorship isn't compatible with the principles of a free society. Personal choice and responsibility in patronage may be the only acceptable way to approach the problem. How to increase responsible personal choice in media production, viewing, and listening remains unknown.

Finally, we note that if high-profile, powerful individuals in a society use language that is aggressive, threatening, degrading, demeaning or belittling of others, or mocks others, lies and denies realities—and especially if other powerful, high-profile individuals do not clearly condemn, reject, or punish such conduct—the positive perception of such characteristics is likely to increase. Models of antisocial behavior and attention to and reward of such models play a significant role in what we call **conduct disorders** (discussed in Chapter 9). Combined with romantic portrayal of disabilities and denial that antisocial conduct is a form of disability, media (especially television) may contribute to the ready acceptance of some forms of EBD and admiration of those who display behaviors characteristic of EBD (Kauffman & Badar, in press).

Peer Group

The peer group is a possible contributing factor to EBD in two ways. First, the establishment of positive, reciprocal peer relationships is critical for normal social development. Children who are unable to establish positive relationships with classmates are at high risk because the peer group is an important link to social learning (LeBlanc, Sautter, & Dore, 2006). Second, some children and youth are socially skilled and have high social status but are enmeshed in a peer group that exerts pressure toward maladaptive patterns of behavior (Farmer, 2000; Walker et al., 2004).

Absence of Positive Peer Relationships

Peer relationships are extremely important for behavioral development, especially during middle childhood and early adolescence. We can now identify problematic relations with peers in children as young as five years of age, and these problems tend to persist over time (Walker et al., 2004). Behavioral characteristics associated with emergence and maintenance of social status in the peer group and relationships between peer status and later behavioral problems are becoming clearer.

In general, high status or social acceptance is associated with helpfulness, friendliness, and conformity to rules—to prosocial interaction with peers and positive attitudes toward others. Low status or social rejection is associated with hostility, disruptiveness, and aggression in the peer group. To complicate matters, aggressive youngsters, compared to nonaggressive youngsters, seem more likely to attribute hostile intentions to their peers' behavior, and they are more likely to respond aggressively even when they interpret their peers' intentions as nonhostile. Low social status among peers is also associated with academic failure and a variety of problems in later life, including suicide and delinquency. In fact, poor peer relations, academic incompetence, and low self-esteem are among the primary factors in an empirically derived model of the development of antisocial behavior.

The evidence that antisocial children and youth are typically in conflict with their peers as well as with adult authorities is overwhelming, as is the evidence that antisocial youngsters tend to gravitate toward deviant peers. Youngsters who don't learn about cooperation, empathy, and social reciprocity from their peers are at risk for inadequate relationships later in life. They're likely to have problems developing the intimate, enduring friendships necessary for adequate adjustment throughout life. Thus, the peer group is a critical factor in creating social deviance.

These generalizations don't do justice to the complexity of the research on relationships between social status among peers and children's behavioral characteristics. Social status can be measured using peer nominations, teacher ratings, or direct behavioral observations. Depending on the source of data, different pictures of social acceptance or rejection emerge. Normal or expected behavior in the peer group differs with age and sex, so the same type of behavior can have different implications for peer relations depending on age and sex. The social processes that lead to social rejection may be quite different from those that lead to social isolation or neglect. The same classroom conditions can produce different effects on social status and friendship patterns for students of different races, and bias in peers' social perceptions can produce different outcomes in terms of social acceptability for two individuals who exhibit similar behavior.

All sources of information regarding children's social acceptance indicate that better-liked youngsters are those who are considerate, helpful, and able to appeal to group norms or rules without alienating their peers. Social rejection is related to opposite characteristics—violating rules, hyperactivity, disruption, and aggression—although the antisocial behavior that characterizes rejected youngsters changes with age. As children grow older, they tend to exhibit less overt physical aggression. The ways in which they irritate others, and so become rejected, become more complex, subtle, and verbal. Physical aggression is more often a factor leading to rejection in boys' groups than in girls'.

Social withdrawal is often associated with peer rejection, but the causal relationship isn't always clear. Apparently, social withdrawal isn't as prominent as aggression in young children's thinking about relations with their peers. As children grow older, however, withdrawal correlates more closely with rejection, perhaps because rejected children are acquiring a history of unsuccessful attempts to join social groups. This correlation suggests that withdrawal is the result of rejection, a way of dealing with repeated social rebuffs. Youngsters who withdraw following repeated rejection may become the targets of taunts and abuse, perpetuating a cycle of further withdrawal and further rejection.

We know less about the behavior of socially neglected children than about those who are actively rejected, partly because it's difficult to study the characteristics of children who are all but invisible to their peers. Nevertheless, it appears that their peers see them as shy and withdrawn, that they engage in solitary play more frequently than most children, and that they are less aggressive and higher achieving than even popular youngsters. Neglected children sometimes appear to exhibit relatively high levels of prosocial behavior and conformity to teacher expectations, but their general lack of assertiveness may result in their peers not perceiving them as socially competent.

Given that we have identified social skills in which rejected, withdrawn, and neglected youngsters are deficient, establishing programs to teach those skills is a logical intervention. Social skills training programs are now readily available (Gresham & Elliott, 2014; McGrath, 2014). Nevertheless, social skills training often yields equivocal results, perhaps in part because training programs are typically implemented poorly or inconsistently.

Moreover, we often don't know exactly what skills need to be taught. The notion that we can easily identify critical social skill deficits without careful assessment is a deceptive oversimplification (Gresham & Elliott, 2014). Social competence is much more complex than previously thought. Social competence may relate to the ability to display specific skills in specific situations, but precise identification of skills and exact specifications of performance in given situations are extremely difficult to determine. Moreover, identifying social skill deficits that cause youngsters to have problems with their peers isn't always possible. The causes of peer rejection or neglect are typically multiple and complex.

An important aspect of the analysis of peer relations and social skills training, and one that hasn't always been considered in research, is the development of expectations that bias youngsters' perceptions of their peers' behavior. If, for example, a youngster acquires a reputation among his or her peers for aggression or for popularity, others respond to this reputation. They expect behavior that is consistent with their attributions of the motives of an individual whose reputation they accept as valid, and they interpret behavioral incidents accordingly. If one child throws a ball that hits another child on the head, peers are likely to interpret the incident in terms of their beliefs about the motives of the child who threw the ball. If the child is popular and doesn't have a reputation for aggression, they're likely to interpret the incident as an accident; if the child has a reputation for aggression, they're likely to interpret it as aggressive. The reciprocal interaction of biased perceptions and actual behavior must be taken into account in trying to understand why some youngsters are rejected, whereas others who behave similarly aren't.

Effective social skills interventions must, therefore, include provisions for dealing with peer-group response to the youngster with EBD as well as teaching skills that enhance social acceptance. Only when the social ecology of the peer group can be altered to support appropriate behavioral change are social skills likely to result in improved status of the target child. Knowing that a youngster lacks specific social skills necessary for social acceptance and being able to teach those skills isn't enough; one must also change the youngster's reputation—the perceptions and attributions of peers.

Undesirable Peer Socialization

An important causal factor in some EBD, especially antisocial behavior and delinquency, is peer pressure and socialization to deviant peer groups. The assumption that students who exhibit antisocial tendencies will observe and imitate the desirable behavior of their regular classroom peers appears to be based on myth rather than facts about observational learning. Antisocial students often reject prosocial models and gravitate toward a deviant peer group.

Peer pressure toward rejection of academic tasks, as well as toward antisocial behavior, appears to be a serious problem in many communities. Pressure of the peers of some students toward academic failure and classroom disruption may involve not wanting to act or being accused of acting in ways that are seen as undesirable. Such pressure is not exclusive to any ethnic group. In any ethnic or racial group and in any social stratum, we may find groups of peers who express disdain for those who are studious, high achieving, and tractable. Furthermore, sometimes a student is seen as popular among peers even though he or she exhibits behavior that is highly problematic, such as bullying (Leff, Waanders, Waasdorp, & Paskewich, 2014; Thunfors & Cornell, 2008). And in some schools, a high proportion of students exhibit behavior that is seriously, persistently maladaptive and incompatible with learning. The stressors or risk factors that students in these schools experience can in combination create a school culture in which noncompliance is typical and peer reinforcement leads students to expect and accept disruptive behavior of other students (Warren et al., 2003).

Teachers must thus be aware of how their efforts to induce and maintain appropriate behavior in their students can be undermined by negative peer pressure. They must also understand both the "pull" of the street and the ways in which some students resist being pulled into a deviant subculture (Rosenblatt, Edin, & Zhu, 2015). More important, teachers need to find ways, perhaps through peer tutoring or other means, to build a peer culture that supports kindness and achievement. This may be accomplished for most students when they are given regular opportunities to learn, with proper training and supervision, to nurture and teach younger children. Moreover, special classroom settings may be required for the most effective instruction in desirable social behavior for youngsters with EBD (Kauffman, Anastasiou, Badar, Travers, & Wiley, 2017; Kauffman, Bantz, & McCullough, 2002; Kauffman, Ward, & Badar, 2016).

Neighborhood and Urbanization

Neighborhood refers not only to residents' social class and the quality of physical surroundings but also to the available psychological support systems. Separating the neighborhood from other causal factors in social deviance, particularly social class, has proved difficult, if not impossible. The neighborhood and community may play important roles in the prevention of certain types of highly visible behavioral deviance, such as conduct disorder and juvenile crime. For example, a community sense of moral order, social control, safety, and solidarity may be extremely difficult to achieve in a neighborhood in which crime rates are high. Interventions aimed at individuals will probably not succeed because of the lack of neighborhood monitoring and mutual support. Students who carry weapons to school have been found to perceive less social support from parents, teachers, classmates, and friends (Malecki & Demaray, 2003). Group-oriented community interventions that promote a shared sense of being able to cope with deviance may be more likely to help prevent juvenile delinquency and crime in high-crime neighborhoods. An emphasis on community cohesion may also play a part in reducing certain psychiatric disorders (Grapen et al., 2011). A neighborhood in which violence is "normative" may actually foster the use of violence among children and youth (see Ng-Mak, Salzinger, Feldman, & Stueve, 2002). Some people express enthusiasm for the virtues and healing powers of rural retreats and agrarian cultures, but there is not much evidence that they are superior to urban environments in producing mentally healthy and high-achieving children. The overriding factors associated with deviance appear to be low socioeconomic status and the breakdown of family and community ties. Recent reports of economic and social conditions in rural America leave no doubt that inner cities are not our only disaster areas for families and children. If rural ever meant "safe," "healthful," or "educationally superior" for children, it is clear that it does not necessarily mean those things in the present era.

Ethnicity

Ethnicity has been the focus of much contemporary concern for understanding cultural diversity and forging multicultural education. Nevertheless, ethnic identity is increasingly difficult for many Americans to define, and we must be careful to separate ethnic influences on behavior from those of other factors such as economic deprivation, social class, the peer group, and so on (see Anastasiou & Kauffman, 2011; Anastasiou et al., 2016; Anastasiou, Morgan et al., 2017; Kauffman & Anastasiou, in press; Morgan, Farkas, Cook et al., 2016).

In one of the largest and most carefully controlled studies of prevalence of behavioral problems in children and adolescents, which has become a classic, Achenbach and Edelbrock (1981) found very few racial differences. They did, however, find substantial differences in behavioral ratings from different social classes, with children of lower class exhibiting higher problem scores and lower social competence scores than did those from higher class. Cullinan and Kauffman (2005) didn't find that teacher judgment of emotional or behavioral problems was biased by ethnicity of students or that bias in referral explained the disproportional representation of African American students in special education for students with EBD. Roberts, Roberts, and Xing (2006) didn't find differences among psychiatric disorders among African, European, and Mexican American adolescents. Neighbors and colleagues (2007) did find that African Americans tend to underuse mental health services.

When the effects of social class and academic achievement are controlled, ethnicity apparently has little or no relationship to EBD. The risk factors that may appear to accompany ethnicity are probably a function of the poverty of many ethnic minority families and low academic achievement (see Anastasiou, Morgan et al., 2017; Noble et al., 2015).

Ethnicity is often suggested as a factor in juvenile delinquency because studies show higher delinquency rates among Black than among White youngsters, but we must question the meaning of differences in rate for at least two reasons. First, discrimination in processing may account for higher official delinquency rates among African American youth. Second, ethnic origin is difficult or impossible to separate from other causal factors, including family, neighborhood, and social class. Thus, it is not clear that ethnicity is related to delinquency independent of other factors.

Our tendency has been to make sweeping judgments regarding ethnic groups without taking individual backgrounds and experiences into account. This leads to stereotypes based on ethnic identity alone. Ethnic identity plays a part in how youngsters, particularly adolescents, are treated in our society, and much of what appears to be attributable to ethnicity is more likely a result of other factors (see Anastasiou, Morgan et al., 2017; Kauffman & Anastasiou, in press; National Research Council, 2002; Sampson, 2015).

The issues surrounding ethnicity are complex because the values, standards, and expectations of ethnic groups are shaped not only internally by members of these groups but also by external pressures from the larger culture of which they are a part. Thus, we must be careful in analyses of the effects of ethnicity to separate the influences of ethnic background from the effects of the dominant cultural groups' treatment of other ethnic groups.

Given the long history of maltreatment of ethnic groups with relatively little power by the dominant American ethnic groups, we should not be surprised to find that membership in an ethnic minority that has comparatively little political or social power presents barriers to the achievement of academic competence, economic security, and mental health. Moreover, it is important to recognize that most ethnic minority youngsters do not succumb to the risk factors they experience (see Patterson & Fosse, 2015).

An important point is that the disproportionality of ethnic groups in special education or juvenile justice doesn't mean that a very high percentage of youngsters from an ethnic group are in special education or juvenile justice. For example, it is an egregious error to conclude that half of all African American students are emotionally disturbed if half of the students in special education with emotional disturbance are African Americans. This is the kind of logical and mathematical error that fosters stereotypes (see Kauffman, Nelson et al., 2017).

Social Class and Poverty

One ordinarily measures children's social class in terms of parental occupation, with children of laborers and domestic workers representing one of the lower classes and children of professional or managerial workers representing one of the higher classes. Although lower social class is often associated with psychopathology, the meaning of this finding is controversial.

The relationship between social class and specific types of disordered behavior doesn't hold up as well as the relationship to EBD in general. Furthermore, family discord and disintegration, low parental intelligence, parental criminality, and deteriorated living conditions seem to be much more influential than parents' occupational prestige in accounting for children's behavior. Although it's true that many parents in low-prestige occupations may be described by the characteristics just cited, it isn't clear that low social class in itself is a contributing factor in children's social deviance; social class may be a factor only in the context of these other parental and family characteristics (see Roberts et al., 2006).

Economic disadvantage—poverty, with all its deprivations and stress—is apparently a factor in the development of disordered behavior, but social class, at least as measured by occupational prestige of parents, probably isn't (cf. DeLuca et al., 2016; Park, Turnbull, & Turnbull, 2002; Pascoe et al., 2016; Qi & Kasiser, 2003; Roberts et al., 2006). Merely being poor doesn't make people inadequate or destroy families or account for children's school failure or EBD. However, we do know that many of the conditions that often are part of poverty, especially in its extreme, are strong negative influences on children's neurological development associated with school learning (Noble et al., 2015) and cognitive and social development as well. Poverty is associated with inadequate shelter, food, and clothing; exposure to chaotic living conditions and violence; and lack of opportunities to learn from nurturing, attentive adults (see Pascoe et al., 2016; Vance, 2016). Occasionally, poverty is glorified, or at least its ravages are denied and the right to be poor is defended, usually by those who haven't experienced poverty themselves or haven't seen it up close.

Gender

The role of females in many cultures has been subservience to males. In fact, most of the cultures making up the larger American culture have been sternly patriarchal. Women are often treated unfairly, and male domination of females has often been a test of masculinity. Poverty and inequalities contribute to violence against women. Gender equity is important in all cultures, and in addressing the problem of gender inequity it is important to include both males and females (Miller, 2015). Schools should make certain that gender inequality in educational opportunities does not contribute to problematic behavior.

IMPLICATIONS FOR EDUCATORS

Educators should be aware of how cultural factors may be contributing to their students' EBD and of the possibility of cultural bias in evaluating behavioral problems. We can seldom untangle the effects of isolated factors from the mix of circumstances and conditions associated with disordered behavior. Parental attitudes toward behavior and its correction can't be understood without reference to cultural and community norms, especially for such controversial issues as corporal punishment and touching students.

Sometimes the difference between teacher and students in culture or ethnicity is jarring, and teachers are caught completely by surprise. For example, Nakamura (2003) described his surprise at the contempt students showed for him in a Japanese high school, where he found that, as in America, a large number of students were being treated poorly.

Specific factors that might lead to disorders have important implications for prevention, especially if intervention can be aimed at improving children's individual circumstances. For example, reducing television violence and providing more prosocial television programming, for example, would probably help reduce the level of aggression in our society, as would simply reducing the amount of time many children spend watching television.

Much could be done to address the needs of children reared under adverse conditions in which their health and safety, not to mention intellectual stimulation and emotional development, are at stake. But social changes demand large-scale efforts that educators can't achieve alone. More Americans need to speak out about the physical and mental health risks of children. Programs to serve children and youth living in poverty will have enormous consequences for the nation's future. An open question is the extent to which local, state, and national governments will ask taxpayers to fund programs for poor and disadvantaged children and youth.

Of the causal factors discussed in this chapter, the peer relations of rejected and neglected students are perhaps the most important consideration for the daily work of teachers. We now recognize the great significance of students' poor peer relations and association with deviant peers. However, we know relatively little about the most effective means of intervening to improve their status or change their social affiliations once patterns of maladaptive behavior have become well established. Developing school-based, early interventions for target children and their peers should be a priority for researchers and teachers. These interventions may play an important role in the prevention of social adjustment problems (see Evertson & Weinstein, 2006; Ispa-Landa, 2015; Martella, Nelson, Marchand-Martella, & O'Reilly, 2012).

SUMMARY

Children, families, and teachers are influenced by the standards and values of the larger cultures in which they live and work. Conflicts among cultures can contribute to youngsters' stress and to their problem behavior. Not only conflicts among different cultures, but mixed messages from the same culture can be a negative influence on behavior. Cultures sometimes both encourage and punish certain types of behavior; for example, youngsters may be tempted or encouraged by the media to engage in sexual behavior, yet our society creates penalties for teenage pregnancy.

We must guard against bias and discrimination in our pluralistic, multicultural society. Cultural differences in behavior that don't put the child or youth at risk in the larger society must be accepted. Educators should seek to change only behavior that's incompatible with achievement of the larger goals of education. However, clear rules for applying a multicultural perspective haven't been established. Teachers and school administrators must continue to struggle with decisions about what behavior puts a child at risk in society at large.

Besides family and school, cultural factors that influence behavior include mass media, peer group, neighborhood, urbanization, ethnicity, and social class. A major difficulty in assessing most of these and other cultural factors is that they're so intimately intertwined. It's difficult, for example, to untangle

the factors of social class, ethnicity, neighborhood, urbanization, gender inequality, and peer groups. Social class, ethnicity, the neighborhood, and urbanization haven't been shown to be, *in themselves*, significant causal factors in emotional and behavioral disorders. They're apparently significant only in the context of economic deprivation and family conflict.

Other cultural factors are more clearly involved in causing disordered behavior. Watching television causes rising levels of aggression among children who are already aggressive. Rejection by peers also increases the upward spiral of aggression among youngsters who are uncooperative, unhelpful, disruptive, and aggressive. Socialization to deviant peers also may be a significant factor in antisocial behavior. In both cases—television violence and peer rejection or social gravitation to bad companions—youngsters' behavior, their environments (including others' reactions to their behavior), and their perceptions are factors in the development of increasing social deviance.

The literature on peer relations and social skills training has the clearest and most direct implications for educators. Teachers must be concerned about teaching the social skills deviant students need, but they must also be concerned with the responses and perceptions of the peer group and the deviant social networks that students with behavioral disorders may establish.

✓ ENHANCEDetext END-OF-CHAPTER 5 QUIZ

Click on the checkmark icon to access an end-of-chapter quiz. Answer the questions to gauge your understanding of chapter concepts and better prepare you for case discussions.

CASE FOR DISCUSSION (See case book for additional cases.)

How Can You Win Them Over?
James Winters

James grew up in a middle-class—and all white—neighborhood, and throughout his childhood spent many afternoons playing football or baseball with

his friends in the park at the end of his street. He walked two blocks to the elementary school he attended for six years and did well enough in his large suburban high school to be accepted into the four-year state university about two hours south, where at least twenty of his classmates also went to school. He chose special education early on as a major and found that the teacher preparation program was mostly fun and interesting. James was a bit apprehensive upon graduation, as were most of his classmates, but he told himself he was smart, had done well in school, and was well prepared to be a special education teacher.

His optimism led to his decision to accept what he thought, and even hoped, would be a challenging position in a middle school in a medium-sized city only about fifty miles from where he grew up and went to school. He looked forward to the challenge of working with kids who really needed help the most, and he knew that the school would have a high percentage of kids from more impoverished backgrounds than he had experienced. He did know, for example, that all of the students in his self-contained class for students with EBD would be receiving free lunch. He had not given much thought, however, to the fact that more than half of the students in his new school were black, including *every* student in his class. As his students walked in that first day, he greeted them at the door in a wrinkled oxford shirt and tie, saying with a boyish grin, "Hey, fellas, come on in. You can sit anywhere you like." He was proud of this latter comment, as he had cleverly arranged the seats into a pattern that had all students facing the center of the room, but with ample space between each desk so students would be less inclined to chat and disrupt each other. With this pre-planning, he thought, assigned seats would not even be necessary, and he might even win over a few kids with this "pick your own seat" gimmick.

His optimism about his new job began to fade as each student entered the classroom, walking right past him without words. None—*none*—so much as made eye contact with him. He did notice more than one eye-roll and head-shake as a student strolled right past him and his greeting. His seating arrangement also took a blow. After the first student took a seat, the next student literally took a seat, sliding it halfway across the room and plopping down next to his friend. Before long nearly all the seats had been moved, and a group of about

seven students were near the back corner, some in desks, some sitting atop desks facing their friends or out the window, all talking and all completely ignoring their new teacher. James's stress about his decision to accept this job was rising rapidly. He glanced nervously at the stack of worksheets arranged neatly on his desk. There was a word-find, a vocabulary crossword puzzle, and a graphic organizer labeled "Hypothesize!" all xeroxed early that morning in preparation for his very first lesson: a review of the scientific method. The bell for the start of first period rang, but the students seemed not to notice at all, and they continued their rather loud conversations. He couldn't make out much of what the students were saying, though their frequent use of profanity was obvious. He did catch a few phrases, most memorably a barely audible comment about "... some white boy coming in here thinking he's some kind of teacher ..."

Questions About the Case

1. James became less optimistic, and even nervous, as he met his students on his first day of school. What caused this? What perceptions might he have had that didn't match the reality of his new position?

2. James seems to sense that his plan for instruction might not be very successful. Does he need to change his approach or adjust his instruction? How so? Why?

3. What could James have done differently to prepare for his first day of school? What, if anything, should he have done differently that very first day as he met his students for the first time?

4. In what ways does this case illustrate preconceptions, stereotypes, cultural misunderstanding or mismatch, or other issues of culture discussed in this chapter?

5. Consider the above case now with James, the teacher, as an African American male, and the students as all Caucasian. Would your reactions be any different to the case, or to the preceding questions?

6 FAMILY

Scott Cunningham/Pearson Education, Inc.

After reading this chapter, you should be able to:

6.1 Discuss the interplay between family structure and family interactions and their contributions to children's social and emotional development.

6.2 Describe reasons children living in single-parent homes or in substitute care are not inherently at greater risk for EBD, and discuss factors associated with those living arrangements that can heighten risk.

6.3 Name several features of parental child management, and describe the styles of parenting that seem to be associated with the best and worst effects of children's behavioral development.

6.4 Explain how coercive family interactions are related to the development of antisocial behavior.

6.5 Define and give an example of a negative reinforcement trap.

6.6 Describe the interactional–transactional model of family influence for families with abused children.

6.7 Explain how parents might be able to contribute to a child's success or failure in school.

APPEAL OF FAMILY FACTORS AS CAUSAL EXPLANATIONS

When youngsters misbehave, our natural tendency may be to blame parents for mismanaging their child or blame the disintegration of the family. Given the importance of family relationships in children's social development, it's understandable that we look for the origins of EBD in the structure, composition, and interactions of family units. However, family relationships alone don't provide a straightforward prediction of EBD. Like other causal factors, those related to the family are complex and influenced by genetic factors as well as a wide variety of environmental events and conditions. We have to be on our guard against adopting simple explanations of EBD and rely instead on researchers' more complex and reliable predictors of child psychopathology (see Brigham, Bakken, & Rotatori, 2012; Scull, 2015).

Family characteristics appear to predict emotional and behavioral development only in complex interactions with other factors, such as socioeconomic status; support from somebody outside the family; and the child's age, sex, or temperament. The concept of *risk* is important here: The idea is that we're dealing with *probabilities* and that particular events or conditions may increase or decrease the chance that we'll see a particular outcome, such as an EBD. When risk factors occur together—for example, a parent's antisocial behavior, community violence, *and* difficult temperament—they might have the effect of increasing the chance of EBD more than when there's only one. Combined risk factors might more than double the chance that a child will develop a disorder. So, for example, if a second risk factor is added, the risk of EBD might go up by more than a factor of two, and if a third factor is added, the chance of EBD might be several times higher yet (see Mash & Barkley, 2014; Pascoe et al., 2016; Seeley, Rohde, Lewinsohn, & Clarke, 2002).

However, risk also has to be weighed in the light of other factors that can protect a youngster or provide resilience. So, sometimes things may not be as bad as they would seem to be based on a risk factor because there are other helpful factors in the mix.

Let's take an example. Generally speaking, a family breakup puts a child at risk. However, it's not *always* true that separation of the child from one or both parents impairs a child's psychological and behavioral development. In a family that stays together, parental discord might do more damage to the child than parental separation. A good relationship with one parent can sustain a child, even in the face of parental discord or separation. The interaction of the child's constitutional or temperamental characteristics with parental behavior may be more important than parental separation or disharmony. In addition, factors outside the home (school, for instance) may lessen or heighten the negative influence of family factors.

For some reason, some children don't succumb to extreme disruption or disintegration of their families. We don't know precisely why some children are vulnerable and others invulnerable to negative family influences. A positive, or easy, child temperament (recall our discussion of temperament in Chapter 4) and maternal warmth appear to be factors that may heighten resilience, but these factors may be insufficient to buffer children against psychopathology in violent families. Research also suggests that high cognitive skills, curiosity, enthusiasm, ability to set goals for oneself, and high self-esteem are associated with resilience. Many intervention programs now focus on reducing risk factors and fostering resilient behaviors in at-risk children (Beardslee, Versage, Van de Velde, Swatling, & Hoke, 2002; Gerber, 2014; Hayden & Mash, 2014; Olsson, Bond, Burns, Vella-Brodrick, & Sawyer, 2003; Place, Reynolds, Cousins, & O'Neill, 2002; Singer, Maul, Wang, & Ethridge, 2017).

Conversely, we know that certain features of family relationships, especially parental deviance and discord, harsh and unpredictable parental discipline, and lack of emotional support, increase children's risk for developing EBD. Yet a family environment that creates high risk does not necessarily cause a child to have a disorder. Causation is more complex than that.

The concept of *heightened risk*, as opposed to a simple cause–effect relationship, is important in disordered behavior. What happens in families in which risk of EBD is high? We can answer this question in general terms, but we can't make confident predictions of outcomes for individual children for two reasons. First, each child is affected individually by the family environment. A younger, more compliant child may experience her family quite differently than her older, more disobedient brother. Second, whether life circumstances or environmental conditions are positive or negative for a child, and whether they heighten or reduce the child's risk of EBD, depends on the processes involved. Processes or mechanisms—not merely the presence of risk variables but how children cope with degrees and patterns of exposure to those variables—determine how vulnerable or resilient a child will be. The shared family context simply does not offer uniform experiences to all children in the family (Jenkins, Rasbash, & O'Connor, 2003; Pinker, 2002).

We understand little about the processes involved in producing vulnerability and resilience, but a key ingredient for each individual appears to be the pattern, sequence, and intensity of exposure to stressful circumstances. We do know that the accumulation of stressful life events is an important factor in determining how a child will be able to cope. Stressful life events may occur within the family, but they're related to the larger social environment in which the family itself functions. Therefore, it's important to consider both the interpersonal transactions that occur between the child and other family members and the external pressures on the family that may affect those interactions.

Whereas the research of thirty years ago tended to focus on the general processes thought to be the basis for the development of child psychopathology, more recent research has examined specific, focused interactions that may contribute to causing or exacerbating EBD. The empirical evidence increasingly points to **social learning** as the basis for a lot of EBD; research suggests that parental **modeling, reinforcement,** and **punishment** of specific types of behavior hold the keys to how families influence children's behavioral development. For example, researchers have documented that children who demonstrate high levels of anxiety often have families in which caution and avoidance are modeled and reinforced. In such instances, parents may reward avoidance of risk and social disengagement and thereby foster the development and expression of fear and anxiety (Dadds, 2002; Heubeck & Lauth, 2014; Singer et al., 2017).

Evidence from longitudinal studies increasingly points to families as critical factors, but not the only factors, in the development of antisocial and delinquent behavior. In a sample of approximately 1,500 boys, Loeber, Farrington, Stouthamer-Loeber, and Van Kammen (1998a) found a correlation between early onset of behavioral problems and deviant parental behavior. However, these authors also argued that such findings demonstrated a clear need for interventions aimed at introducing protective factors in the lives of these at-risk youth. Thus, familial factors may be critical, but they aren't powerful enough alone to determine a child's fate (see Reinke, Frey, Herman, & Thompson, 2014).

The structure and interaction patterns in families clearly influence children's success or failure at school and, ultimately, in life. In turn, family interactions may be shaped by external influences; we consider in particular the potentially powerful influences of factors such as poverty and parental employment. We also discuss the implications for educators of what we know about families, especially families of children with EBD. The scope and complexity of family-related research are enormous, however, and we reiterate that this overview highlights only a few dimensions of this complex topic and only scratches the surface of this vast literature.

FAMILY DEFINITION AND STRUCTURE

Although the intact mother–father–children concept of family remains the ideal for many in mainstream American culture, a variety of diverse family forms fit the realities of contemporary life. The essential functions of families are to:

- Provide care and protect children.
- Regulate and control children's behavior.
- Convey knowledge and skills important for understanding and coping with the physical and social worlds.
- Give affective meaning to interactions and relationships.
- Facilitate children's self-understanding.

Regardless of how families define themselves, the key is that the individuals involved see each other as family and agree to protect and care for one another. They are a group of people affiliating with each other regardless of their blood relationships. Given these considerations, it may be important to examine whether or to what extent family structure affects children's behavior.

The effects of family size and birth order on behavioral development have been studied extensively, but such elements of family configuration are far outweighed by factors related to divorce and other circumstances resulting in single-parent homes or other nontraditional family structures. Family composition or configuration may have an effect on children's behavior, but other factors involving *interactions* among family members and the social contexts in which they live appear to be far more important contributors to behavior problems than family structure alone.

Research clearly suggests that family form by itself has relatively little effect on children's emotional and behavioral development. Although children reared in single-parent families may be at heightened risk, the risk factors appear to be conditions associated with a single-parent family structure (e.g., economic distress), not single parenting itself. Being reared by substitutes for one's biological parents may be associated with heightened risk but only insofar as abuse, neglect, or other traumatic circumstances affect children before they are removed from their biological parents or after they enter foster care. In short, family structure is far less important than what happens in the family—the interactions among family members—regardless of how the family is constituted. Nevertheless, we briefly examine the effects of single-parent families and substitute care (e.g., foster care, adoption, care by relatives other than parents) on children's behavior.

Marriage and family continue to go through changes in our society (Wilcox, 2010; see also www.virginia.edu/marriageproject/). Attitudes toward traditional marriage, same-sex marriage, and single-parent families are changing, particularly among different demographic groups, with those having less education and fewer economic resources making the most dramatic changes—specifically, declining faith in traditional marriage.

Single-Parent Families

A substantial proportion of children are now reared in single-parent families, usually because of divorce but also often because of out-of-wedlock births or military assignment. According to the Pew Research Center (www.pewresearch.org), more than one-third (34 percent) of children lived in single-parent homes in 2013, and this represents an increasing trend in the U.S.; in 1960 only 9 percent of children lived in single parent homes, and in 1980 this had grown to 19 percent. It's understandable that, given the high percentage of American children being reared by a single parent, people ask whether the presence of only one parent in a family puts children at risk for EBD. We begin by considering the effects of divorce on children's behavior.

Divorce is traumatic, not only for parents and children but also for extended family and friends. The lasting psychological pain and fear felt by many children with parents who have divorced have been well known for a long time. Yet overwhelming evidence shows that most children adjust to divorce and go on with their lives without developing chronic emotional or behavioral problems.

How children adjust to divorce depends on factors beyond family dissolution. These factors are numerous and include concerns such as the child's age when the divorce occurs, characteristics of the custodial parent, and the child's cognitive and affective characteristics related to coping with stress. There isn't a general formula for predicting child psychopathology following divorce.

The absence of fathers in homes and families is a common feature of contemporary life. What effect father or mother absence has on a child depends a great deal on the child's relationship with the custodial parent, as we discuss in the section on family interaction.

Substitute Care

Children in foster care and those living with relatives who are not their parents appear to be at high risk for EBD and school-related problems. Researchers have only begun to examine the specific nature of stress and strain on nonparental caregivers of students with EBD (e.g., Taylor-Richardson, Heflinger, & Brown, 2006).

Some children are placed in substitute care because of the death or incapacitation of their parents, but the great majority—and an increasing percentage—are placed under the care of the child protection system because of their parents' neglect and abuse. During 2013, for example, the U.S. Department of Health and Human Services (2015) reported that 679,000 children were victims of neglect or abuse—this translates into a rate of 9.1 out of every 1,000 children in the U.S. (0.91 percent, or 1 out of every 110 children). We note that these numbers are based on *reported* cases of neglect or abuse. Children are virtually never placed in any form of substitute care unless they have suffered trauma that is highly likely to result in at least short-term emotional or behavioral problems (except in the case of adopted infants). Abused children are known to have more behavioral problems than those who are not maltreated. Yet much remains unknown about why and how children are placed in protective care.

A major problem in providing substitute care is finding or training caregivers who are highly motivated and skilled in child rearing. Many foster parents have little or no training for the task, and few are well trained in dealing with difficult children. Although long-term foster care has demonstrated positive outcomes, many foster children are placed for short periods in many different foster homes, and the risk for negative behavioral and emotional outcomes appears to increase with the number of different placements. The lack of stability, continuity, attachment, and nurturing that goes with numerous foster placements and unskilled foster parents is likely to promote EBD.

Adoptive families, like biological families, have a variety of structures. The influence of adoptive families on children's emotional and behavioral development can be predicted to parallel the influence of biological families. Controversy sometimes arises regarding the adequacy of adoption by single parents or adoptive families that involve differences in sexual orientation (e.g., gay fathers or lesbian mothers) or differences in the color or ethnicity of children and parents (e.g., Caucasian parents adopting children of color). Here, too, we might expect familial determinants to function as they do in any other family structure. In short, the color, ethnicity, sex, and sexual orientation of the parent or parents are not the determining factors in children's EBD.

FAMILY INTERACTION

When we think of family factors, our tendency is to ask, "What kinds of families produce children with EBD?" However, it's also reasonable to ask, "What kinds of families do children with EBD produce—what effects do youngsters with EBD have on their families?"

Those who study child development now realize that children's influence on their parents' behavior is significant in determining family interactions. A child from a broken family may well exhibit behavioral characteristics that would break nearly any family (see Pinker, 2002; Scull, 2015). The idea that parents influence their children a lot but children don't have much influence on their parents is very outdated. Researchers found decades ago that undesirable parenting behavior and negative family interactions are in part a reaction of family members to a deviant youngster. Reciprocity of influence can be observed from the earliest parent–child interactions, strengthening and manifesting in all subsequent interactions. This dynamic is especially evident in child management and child abuse.

Child Management

Parental management or discipline comes up as a topic in almost every discussion of children's EBD. We shall return to family interactions as potential causal factors in each of the chapters in Part 3. Here, we review general findings on parental management of children but focus on the role of family interactions in causing the disorder people usually consider first in discussions of family factors: the impulsive, aggressive, acting-out behavior generally known as **conduct disorder**. In fact, we know more about the effects of parental discipline on disruptive, oppositional, aggressive behavior than we do about the effects of parental behavior on children's anxiety, fear, and depression (Ehrensaft et al., 2003; Kazdin, 2008).

The effects of discipline techniques are complex and not highly predictable without considering both the parents' and the child's general behavioral characteristics and ongoing stress in the family. Nevertheless, we can suggest some general guidelines for discipline that can help parents avoid the types of interactions that research strongly suggests are mistakes, and these principles may hold across all cultural groups (see Kazdin, 2008). Consider some now classic studies.

Many years ago O'Leary (1995) identified three types of mistakes typically made by mothers of two- to four-year-old children that still apply: laxness, over-reactivity, and verbosity. Laxness refers to giving in, failure to enforce rules, and giving positive reinforcement like attention for misbehavior. Over-reactivity refers to anger, meanness, and irritability. Verbosity refers to the tendency to engage in lengthy discussion of misbehavior even when talking to the child about it is ineffective. Parents can be very "nice" to their children but ineffective in discipline because they're unable or unwilling to set consistent, firm, unambiguous limits. These parents may use long, delayed, and gentle (but imprudent) reprimands that actually make the child's behavior worse. Others may make the mistake of using harsh reprimands for misbehavior but paying little attention to the child when he or she is behaving well.

Researchers describe two primary dimensions of discipline: *responsiveness* (which involves warmth, reciprocity, and attachment) and *demandingness* (involving monitoring, firm control, and positive and negative consequences for behavior). Parents who provide the best management of their children are both highly responsive and highly demanding. That is, they are highly committed to their children. More specifically, parents who discipline most effectively are sensitive to their children's needs, empathic, and attentive. They establish a pattern of mutually positive, reciprocal interactions with their children, and their warmth and reciprocity form the basis for emotional attachment or adult–child bonding. These parents are also demanding of their children. They monitor their children's behavior, providing appropriately close supervision for the child's age. They confront their children's misbehavior directly and firmly rather than attempting to manipulate or coerce their children. They provide unambiguous instructions and demands in a firm but non-hostile manner and consistently follow through with negative but non-abusive consequences for misbehavior. They provide positive reinforcement in the forms of praise, approval, encouragement, and other rewards for their children's desirable behavior.

Parental discipline that is both demanding and responsive is sometimes referred to as **authoritative** (as opposed to *authoritarian* discipline, which is demandingness without responsiveness) and is typically found to have the best effects on children's behavioral development. Researchers have even found a relationship between authoritative parenting and decreased tobacco and alcohol usage among children and youth, decreased violence among adolescents, and decreased levels of anger and alienation among middle-school students (Adamczyk-Robinette, Fletcher, & Wright, 2002). Authoritative discipline balances what is asked of the child with what is offered to the child, and this balance may be the key characteristic of effective parental discipline in various cultures. It may be, in fact, the key to effective discipline by all caretakers of children, but it is not the pattern of interaction typically found in families of children who exhibit antisocial behavior.

The work of the late Gerald Patterson and his colleagues at the University of Oregon over a period of decades has given us insight into the characteristics of interactions in the families of antisocial youngsters. His research group's methods involve direct observation of parents' and children's behavior in the home, revealing an identifiable family pattern. They show that interaction in families with aggressive children is characterized by exchange of negative, hostile behaviors, whereas the interaction in families with nonaggressive children tends to be mutually positive and gratifying for parents and children. In families with aggressive children, not only do the children behave in ways that are highly irritating and aversive to their parents but the parents also rely primarily on aversive methods (hitting, shouting, threatening, and so forth) to control their children. Thus, children's aggression in the family seems both to produce counter-aggression and to be produced by punitive parenting techniques (see especially Patterson, Reid, Jones, & Conger, 1975; Patterson, Reid, & Dishion, 1992; Reid & Eddy, 1997).

Decades ago, Patterson (1980) studied mutually aversive interactions between mothers and children, and his findings have not been overturned by new data (go to www.oslc.org to see many research citations and reports of research at the Oregon Social Learning Center, some of the research very recent and some going back for forty years or more). Patterson's research group focused on families of aggressive children and found that many of the undesirable behaviors are maintained by negative reinforcement. **Negative reinforcement** involves escape from or avoidance of an unpleasant condition, which is rewarding (negatively reinforcing) because it brings relief from psychological or physical pain or anxiety.

Patterson calls such interactions **negative reinforcement traps** because they set the stage for greater conflict and coercion; each person in the trap tends to reciprocate the other's aversive behavior and to escalate attempts to use *coercion*—controlling someone by negative reinforcement. In the long run, the parent falls into the trap of being coerced into giving up. Patterson and his colleagues have found that, unlike normal children, children with conduct problems tend to increase their disruptive or irritating behavior in response to parental requests or punishment. Predictably, therefore, the families of aggressive children seem to foster undesirable child behavior, to encourage and even teach the very behavior they find problematic.

Here's an example of how we suggest it might work involving a school issue, as shown in Table 6.1 and as explained as a process by Patterson (1980). Let's suppose the child hasn't

Table 6.1 How a School-Related Negative Reinforcement Trap Might Work in a Family

NEGATIVE REINFORCEMENT TRAP AT HOME INVOLVING HOMEWORK		
First →	Second →	Third
Mother notices child's homework isn't done and says, "Do your homework now!"	Child complains	Mother gives up and stops asking child to complete homework
	Immediately	**Long-Term (the Trap)**
What the Mother Gets	Relief from irritation when the child stops complaining	If mother asks and child complains, mother is more likely to give up or not ask
What the Child Gets	Relief from irritation when the mother stops demanding	When the child's homework isn't done, mother is less likely to ask child to complete it
Result	The homework wasn't completed	Child is more likely to use complaining to get mother to stop asking that homework be completed

completed homework, which is an aversive condition for the mother. First, the mother asks the child to complete the homework, whereupon the child complains, perhaps saying that it's too difficult or too much to do, perhaps whining and crying, too (also aversive for the mother). The child's complaints are so aversive to the mother that after a while she stops asking the child to do the homework or, as the child sees it, demanding or nagging. The mother's asking (or demand) is painfully aversive to the child, who finds that his or her complaints will stop the mother's demands or nagging. In other words, the child learns, "If I just keep up my complaints about my homework, my mother stops reminding me to do it." In the short run, both mother and child escape from their irritation or pain—the child stops complaining and the mother stops demanding. However, the child's homework isn't getting done. In the long run, the mother avoids asking the child to do the homework, and the child learns to use complaining to stop the mother's demands. Both mother and child are negatively reinforced by the avoidance of or escape from aversive consequences. However, the problem condition (the uncompleted homework) still exists as a potential source of future negative interactions. And it's highly likely that this scenario will be repeated because, eventually, the mother can't stand it that the child isn't doing the homework and is likely to fail at school, drawing her even more deeply into the issue.

Although Table 6.1 illustrates how a negative reinforcement trap might involve a child's mother, we caution that the same kind of negative reinforcement trap could involve a child's teacher. In Chapter 7, we discuss negative reinforcement in schools and suggest that such negative reinforcement traps can occur in classrooms and involve teachers, not only parents.

In effect, the members of families with aggressive children "train" each other to be aggressive and to use negative reinforcement. Although the major training occurs in transactions between an aggressive child and parent(s), it spills over to include siblings. Patterson (1986b) reported that siblings of an aggressive child are no more aggressive toward their parents than are children in families without an aggressive child. Interactions between siblings in families of antisocial youngsters, however, are more aggressive than those in families without an aggressive child. Coercive exchanges between aggressive children and their parents appear to teach siblings to be coercive with each other. Not surprisingly, these children then tend to be more aggressive in other social contexts, such as school. In fact, school conflict and school failure are frequently associated with antisocial behavior at home (cf. Kazdin, 2008; Kerr & Nelson, 2010; Walker, Ramsey, & Gresham, 2004).

It's difficult to delineate the development of overt behavioral disorders; however, the model emerging from Patterson's research group suggests that they arise from parents' failure to punish effectively the most common, seemingly innocuous coercive behaviors of their children. The child begins winning battles with the parents, and parents become increasingly punitive but ineffective in responding to coercion. Coercive exchanges escalate in number and intensity, increasing sometimes to hundreds per day and progressing from whining, yelling, and temper tantrums to hitting and other forms of physical assault. The child continues to win a high percentage of the battles with parents; parents continue to use ineffective punishment, setting the stage for another round of conflict. This coercive family process may occur in concert with other conditions associated with high risk for psychopathology: social and economic disadvantage, substance abuse, and a variety of other stressors such as parental discord and separation or divorce. During the process, the child receives little or no parental warmth and is often rejected by peers. School failure is another typical concomitant of the process. Understandably, the child usually develops a poor self-image (see Kazdin, 2008; Kerr & Nelson, 2010).

Patterson's suggestion that parents of aggressive children do not punish their children effectively doesn't mean he believes punishment should be the focus of parental discipline. Instead, his work suggests that parents need to set clear limits for children's behavior, provide a warm and loving home environment, provide positive attention and approval for appropriate behavior, and follow through with non-hostile, nonphysical punishment for coercive conduct.

Patterson and other researchers have shown that the pattern of coercive exchanges characterizing families of antisocial children can be identified early (e.g., Walker et al., 2004). In addition, these and other findings suggest that children with conduct disorders are at risk from an early age, partly because they are infants with difficult temperaments and have parents who may lack coping skills (cf. Nelson, Stage, Duppong-Hurley, Synhorst, & Epstein, 2007). For children demonstrating disordered behaviors, inconsistent discipline and family conflict often become the norm. Although data don't uniformly support the conclusion that punitive parents *cause* their children to become aggressive—the relationship does not appear that direct—researchers have observed that parent education can, in some circumstances, modify children's aggression (Kazdin, 2008; Serbin et al., 2002). However, spanking and other forms of corporal punishment may increase the risk of the child's aggression (Taylor, Manganello, Lee, & Rice, 2010).

Child Abuse

We may now know something about how coercive interactions begin and are sustained in families of aggressive children and how parents sometimes provide ineffective or counterproductive discipline. However, we must not forget the old and repeatedly confirmed wisdom that most likely there are many ways to be a good parent, and these will vary with the personal characteristics of both parents and children and with influences of the environment (Becker, 1964).

When is ineffective child management abusive or neglectful? This question is not easily answered. Much depends on the developmental level of the child, specific circumstances, professional and legal judgments, and cultural norms. If there is a consensus about how to define *child abuse*, it likely is centered on parental behavior that seriously endangers or delays the normal development of the child.

Given the difficulty in defining *abuse*, it isn't surprising that reliable estimates of child abuse and family violence are difficult to find. Nevertheless, without belaboring the issue, we may conclude that family violence and child abuse—physical, psychological, and sexual—are problems of great magnitude; abuse very likely involves more than a million children per year in the United States. Although abuse of all types is serious and has important consequences, we focus our discussion here on physical abuse.

Most people give little thought to children's and parents' interactive effects on each other in cases of abuse. Child abuse is often seen as a problem of parental behavior alone, and intervention has often been directed only at changing parents' responses to their children. The **interactional–transactional model** considers abused children's influence on their parents and suggests that intervention deal directly with the abused child's undesirable behavior as well as with the parents' abusive responses. This perspective is valuable even when the child's challenging behavior is not what initially provoked abuse on the part of a caregiver, but the child has been drawn into an abusive relationship and is now exhibiting inappropriate behavior in response. Intervention typically needs to be directed toward the entire family and its social context.

One hypothesis about parent–child interaction in child abuse is that their children's responses to punishment inadvertently "teach" parents to become increasingly punitive (recall our prior discussion of how family members may train each other to be coercive). For example, if the child exhibits behavior that is aversive to the parent (perhaps whining), the parent may punish the child (perhaps by slapping). If the punishment is successful and the child stops the aversive behavior, then the parent is negatively reinforced by the consequence; the parent is, in effect, rewarded for slapping by the child's stopping the aversive behavior. The next time the child whines, the parent is more likely to try slapping to get relief from the whining. If at first the child doesn't stop whining, the parent may slap harder or more often to try to make the child be quiet. Thus, the parent's punishment becomes increasingly harsh as a means of dealing with the child's increasingly aversive behavior. Although abusive parents aren't usually successful in punishing their child, they continue to escalate punishment. They seem not to understand or not be able to use a more positive or less harsh alternative means of control. Although abused children suffer in the bargain, they often hold their own in the battle with their parents; they may stubbornly refuse to knuckle under to parental pressure. Parent and child may become trapped in a mutually destructive, coercive cycle in which they cause and are caused physical or psychological pain (recall Table 6.1 and the accompanying discussion).

The negative reinforcement trap can escalate behavior to the level of abuse. Such a coercive struggle is characteristic of conduct disorder, and the developmental consequences for children are severe (see Kazdin, 2008; Walker et al., 2004). Moreover, abuse is likely to be transmitted across generations through such processes because children with conduct disorder are likely to become parents with antisocial behavior and poor child management skills. For example, Serbin and colleagues (2002) conducted a longitudinal study spanning approximately twenty-five years and documented that the more aggressive mothers were as children, the more aggressive their children are likely to be. Of course, such observations could also confirm genetic tendencies (see Pinker, 2002).

The conclusion that the child's behavior is *always* a reciprocal causal factor in an abusive relationship with a parent is not warranted, however. Abusive relationships are extremely varied, both in abusive behaviors and in abused–abuser relations. Sexual abuse in families, for example, takes many forms and may involve incestuous relationships between siblings, parent and child, or other family members (for example, uncle or aunt, stepparent or grandparent) and child. Because it is a social problem surrounded by many taboos, sexual abuse is a difficult, yet not impossible, topic to research. Existing research studies have failed to demonstrate that children contribute to their own sexual victimization, particularly when the abused child is very young. A history of sexual abuse or observation of overt sexual behavior may cause some children to be sexually provocative, which may contribute to, but not cause, their further abuse.

Much has been written about the characteristics of abusive parents, and stereotypes abound. One stereotype is that they are socially isolated; another is that they themselves were abused as children; still another is that they are mentally ill. Although all three impressions hold for some cases, none is supported by research as an abusive parent prototype. Nevertheless, we can point to several psychological characteristics that frequently accompany abusive parenting. For example, abusive parents tend to exhibit deficits in empathy, role taking, impulse control, and self-esteem, and an external locus of control.

Children who are abused by their parents have been shown by research to be at risk for the full range of emotional and behavioral disorders, including both internalizing problems such as depression and externalizing problems such as conduct disorder. Teachers, parents, and peers are all likely to see higher levels of behavioral problems in physically abused children than in children who are not maltreated.

In devising intervention programs for abused children and youth, it's important to recognize that their behavior may be directly related to family violence and that attempting merely to modify their behavior in school may be insufficient. Teachers, as well as others with responsibility for children's welfare, must report suspected abuse and work toward comprehensive services that meet all the student's needs. These individuals can play pivotal roles in cultivating the resilience of children suffering from abuse (Doyle, 2003).

FAMILY INFLUENCES ON SCHOOL SUCCESS AND FAILURE

Because the responsibility for children's learning is regularly delegated to schools, the family's contribution to school performance often plays a secondary role. Parents nevertheless contribute to or detract from their child's success at school in several ways: their expressed attitudes toward education, their own school experience, and their attitudes toward appropriate school-related behaviors, such as attending regularly, completing homework, reading, and studying. When an educational orientation is missing at home or the home environment is one in which education isn't important, the children in that home are particularly likely to have learning or behavior problems at school. The social training children receive at home may be an important factor in determining school success. Furthermore, poor peer relations in school, especially rejection by peers, is highly predictive of academic problems (Walker et al., 2004).

Parental discipline, parent–school relations, and parent–child relationships play important roles in school success and school failure. We have known for a long time that the authoritative parental discipline described previously (both responsive and demanding) is likely to support students' achievement (cf. Rutter, 1995). Parents who are positively involved with their child's education tend to have youngsters who perform at a higher academic level. Conversely, families in which a coercive process is at work are likely to send students to school unprepared to comply with teachers' instructions, to complete homework assignments, or to relate well to their peers. Unprepared for the demands of school, these students are virtually certain to fail to meet reasonable expectations for academic performance and social interaction (Reinke et al., 2014; Walker et al., 2004).

EXTERNAL PRESSURES AFFECTING FAMILIES

Family interactions are influenced by external conditions that put stress on parents and children. Poverty, unemployment, underemployment, homelessness, community violence—it is not surprising that these conditions influence the ability of families to cope from day to day, of parents to nurture children, and of children to behave well at home and perform well in school (Walker et al., 2004). Homelessness affects not only entire families but, in some cases, adolescents alienated from their families, sometimes because of external influences that destroyed parent–child bonds.

Poverty is perhaps the most critical problem undermining families (see Fujiura & Yamaki, 2000; Pascoe et al., 2016). Severe economic hardship is known to be associated with abusive or neglectful parental behavior and children's maladaptive behavior. Poverty often means that families live in inadequate or dangerous housing (if they are not homeless) in neighborhoods rife with substance abuse and violence. These neighborhood conditions often contribute to parents and children being victimized and to their feelings of inadequacy, depression, and hopelessness.

Predictably, there is a substantial link between poverty and risk of disability and school difficulty (Berliner, 2010; Fujiura & Yamaki, 2000; Pascoe et al., 2016). Neighborhoods characterized by low family income, high unemployment, transient populations, high concentrations of children living in single-parent families, and high rates of violence and substance abuse are places in which families are at heightened risk of dysfunction and disintegration, and children are at heightened risk for psychopathology and school failure (Fitzgerald, Davies, & Zucker, 2002). Violent victimization, whether by family members or others, puts children and youth at risk for EBD and school problems of a wide variety. Furthermore, in communities characterized by danger of victimization, restrictive parenting may be adaptive.

A common misperception of poor families is that the parents typically are unemployed or uninterested in work. Although unemployment and lack of work skills are problems of a substantial percentage of poor parents, the majority of poor parents are workers. Parental unemployment is a stressor of enormous proportions, but parental employment that does not pay a decent wage is not far behind in its effects. Employment of both parents places stress on middle-class families and requires extraordinary parental efforts to provide adequate monitoring and nurturing for children, but when such employment does not allow the family to escape poverty, the stress is multiplied. Poverty and the social and personal problems stemming from it are issues our society must address more effectively if we wish to reduce family stress and child psychopathology. As poverty and income disparities increase (see Norton & Ariely, 2011; Saez, 2010), such problems become more prevalent.

IMPLICATIONS FOR EDUCATORS

We must begin with a strong cautionary note. Findings that higher ratings on behavioral problem scales for children living in homes in which a family member is receiving mental health services should not be interpreted to mean that all children with behavioral problems have parents with mental illness, nor should such findings be interpreted to mean that all parents with mental illness have children with behavioral problems. Familial factors in behavioral problems are multiple, complex, and interactive—they are seldom direct and straightforward (see chapters in Pascoe et al., 2016; Patterson & Fossee, 2015; Pinker, 2002; Scull, 2015).

Given what we know about the family's role in children's EBD, educators would be foolish to ignore the influence of home conditions on school performance and conduct. Still, blaming parents of troubled students is unjustified. Very good parents can have children with very serious EBD. The teacher must realize that the parents of a youngster with EBD have undergone a great deal of disappointment and frustration and that they, too, would like to see the child's behavior improve, both at home and at school. We find the strongest indicators for family causal contributions to antisocial behavior. However, even for conduct disorder and delinquency, we shouldn't assume that parents are usually the primary cause.

ENHANCEDdetext
Video Connections 6.3

In this video, we see an example of how one school implemented several strategies to involve parents in their children's education in positive ways.

Educators must be careful not to become entangled in the same coercive process that may characterize the antisocial student's family life. Harsh, hostile, verbal, or physical punishment at school is likely to function as a new challenge for antisocial students who may have been trained, albeit inadvertently, by their parents to step up their own aversive behavior in response to punishment. To win the battle with such students, school personnel must employ the same strategies that are recommended for parents: clearly state expectations for behavior, emphasize positive attention for appropriate conduct, and punish misbehavior in a calm, firm, nonhostile, and reasoned manner (Kauffman & Brigham, 2009; Kauffman, Pullen et al., 2011; Kazdin, 2008; Pullen, 2004; Walker et al., 2004). Teachers need to be both responsive and demanding. They must not allow their students' disadvantaged home lives to become an excuse for poor teaching.

For far too long, educators, and many others in our society as well, have not only blamed parents for students' EBD but have viewed parents as likely adversaries rather than potential sources of support for their troubled children. More positive views of parents and their role in helping their children is in large measure a result of effective parent advocacy. The organization of the Federation of Families for Children's Mental Health in 1989 brought parents together to advocate more effectively for mental health and special education programs for their children. Parent groups in many states have established resource centers that provide information and guidance for parents who want to become more actively involved in seeing that their children get appropriate education and mental health services. Hanson and Carta (1996) suggested that teachers enlist the help and support of other professionals to do the following:

- Provide critical positive interactions with students and demonstrate these for parents.
- Find and support the strengths of individual families.
- Help families find and use informal sources of support from friends, neighbors, coworkers, or others in the community.
- Become competent in understanding and valuing cultural differences in families.
- Provide a broad spectrum of coordinated services so that families receive comprehensive, flexible, and usable services that address their needs.

SUMMARY

Although many look to the family as a likely source of deviant behavior, the factors that account for children's disordered behavior are multiple and complex. Some family factors, notably conflict and coercion, are known to increase a youngster's risk for developing EBD. We don't fully understand why some children are more vulnerable to risk factors than others and some are more resilient than others.

Families are best defined by their functions. They provide protection, regulation, knowledge, affect, and self-understanding to children. Family structure, by itself, appears to have negligible effects. Divorce doesn't usually produce chronic disorders in children, although we can expect temporary negative effects. Children living in single-parent families may be at risk for behavioral problems, but we don't know precisely why. When children are cared for by substitutes for their biological parents, any negative effects stem primarily from traumas experienced before their separation or from a continuation of dysfunctional parenting.

An interactional–transactional model of family influence suggests that children and parents exert reciprocal effects; children affect their parents' behavior as surely as parents affect their children's. Parental discipline is a significant factor in behavioral development. Discipline that is authoritative—characterized by high levels of responsiveness and demandingness—usually produces the best outcomes. Ineffective discipline often involves lax supervision, harshness, and inconsistency.

We can view both conduct disorder and child abuse in terms of the interactions and transactions of parents and their children. In both cases, parent and child become involved in an aversive cycle of negative reinforcement, escalating aversive behavior and obtaining reinforcement through coercion. A child's difficult temperament and a parent's lack of coping skills may contribute to the initial difficulty; the coercive process then grows from nagging, whining, and yelling to more serious and assaultive behavior such as hitting.

Parental behaviors affect children's school performance and conduct. External factors such as poverty and employment may have substantial effects on family functioning. Many children grow up in poverty, even if their parents work, and their living conditions put them at risk for EBD.

Educators should be concerned about the family's influence on children's conduct at school, but they must not blame parents for children's misbehavior. School personnel must avoid becoming enmeshed in the same coercive process that antisocial students are probably experiencing at home and should use the same intervention strategies that are recommended for parents. Educators must work with other professionals to obtain comprehensive services for families.

✔ ENHANCEDetext END-OF-CHAPTER 6 QUIZ

Click on the checkmark icon to access an end-of-chapter quiz. Answer the questions to gauge your understanding of chapter concepts and better prepare you for case discussions.

CASE FOR DISCUSSION (See case book for additional cases.)

He's Our Son, You Know.
Weird Nick

Earlier in the day I had taken Nick to the principal's office because he had refused to restore the classroom computer password. He was a genius at computers, and it had taken no time at all for him to discover the school password and replace it with one only he knew. He liked the power this action had given him, knowing it had infuriated me. He loved it when people took his bait, as I had, whether it was in the form of a bomb threat, a detailed drawing of a stabbing, or his consistent proclamation that "Satan rules!"

Nick had sat quietly in the principal's office. He looked the part of a satanic cultist in his black jeans, black shirt, and black shoes. His black hair hung in stringy curls over his pale face. His fingers were busily drawing a pentagram. Was this just the image building of a middle school student plagued by self-doubt, or was it really an expression of belief in the occult?

I remembered how Nick seemed to get a special kick out of leaving the school building, forcing support staff to track him visually, walkie-talkies in hand. He knew that leaving the school grounds would necessitate our calling the police, so he would walk the perimeter of the property, running ahead if an adult came too close. All the other kids were afraid of "Weird Nick," as they called him. They kept their distance from this tall, powerful loner. And he distanced himself from his family, his classmates, and his teachers, unable to connect with anyone. All of us on the staff shared the concern that someday we would be hearing about Nick on the evening news.

Now his mother sat with me and the principal in my classroom after school, nervously twisting her gloves as if wringing out a rag, staring out the window at the freezing rain and growing darkness. "I just don't know what to do with him. I take him to church with me every chance I get. You know I go to church every day. Why is he doing this to me? He knows that his fascination with Satanism hurts us deeply. Is he going to hurt us? He's our son, you know. What are we supposed to do?"

Questions About the Case

1. If you were Nick's teacher, how would you respond to his mother's obvious distress?

2. Given Nick's pattern of behavior, what focus would you suggest for his school program? That is, what would be your primary concerns and teaching or management strategies?

3. Would you advise Nick's teacher and principal to make special efforts to work with Nick's parents? Why, or why not? If so, how?

7 SCHOOL

Monkey Business Images/Shutterstock

After reading this chapter, you should be able to:

7.1 Explain why educators, especially teachers, must consider how the school might contribute to students' disordered behavior.

7.2 Describe the levels of intelligence, academic achievement, and social skills typical of students with EBD.

7.3 Describe the relationship between intelligence, achievement, and antisocial behavior and school success and failure.

7.4 List and describe several ways that schools might inadvertently contribute to the development of EBD.

7.5 Explain the role of teachers in meeting the complex demands students with EBD present in school and how teachers can help students develop self-control.

THE APPEAL OF SCHOOL FACTORS AS CAUSAL EXPLANATIONS

Besides the family, the school is probably the most important socializing influence on children and youth. In our culture, success or failure in school is tantamount to success or failure as a person. This is because school is the occupation of all children and youth in our society—and for some it becomes a preoccupation. As high-stakes testing and universal standards are increasingly mandated by federal and state laws, school performance becomes even more a matter of concern. Little wonder that school should make some students extremely anxious.

Academic success is fundamentally important for social development and opportunities outside school. As nearly any student, teacher, or parent can tell you, certain types of behavior are unacceptable in school. Yet many people, including many educators, seem to be unaware of how the school environment can inadvertently contribute to the very behavior that teachers, parents, and students find objectionable!

The school environment is the only causal factor over which teachers and principals have direct control. It's true that some youngsters develop behavior problems before they begin school, and some develop problems because of events outside of school. Even so, educators should consider how the school itself might make the problem either better or worse. And because many youngsters don't exhibit EBD until after they start school, educators must recognize the possibility that the school experience could be a significant causal factor or play an important role in prevention (see Cannon, Gregory, & Waterstone 2013; Conduct Problems Prevention Research Group, 2011).

An ecological approach to understanding behavior includes the assumption that all aspects of a youngster's environment are interconnected; changes in one element of the ecology have implications for the other elements. Yes, what happens *outside* of school may affect what the student does *in* school, but what the student experiences *in* school also affects what happens *outside* of school. In short, success or failure at school affects behavior at home and in the community; effects of school performance ripple outward. Consequently, success at school assumes even greater importance if a youngster's home and community environments are disastrous. Furthermore, anything required before a student is evaluated for special education implies that the current classroom environment might be involved in making the problem better or worse. Most special educators recognize the importance of eliminating possible school contributions to misconduct before saying that a student has a disability.

Before discussing social–interpersonal behavior and its school and classroom contexts, we must consider the characteristics of students with EBD that are relevant to a central mission of the school: academic learning (see Kauffman, 2010a, 2015a; Kauffman, Nelson et al., 2017). Intelligence and academic achievement are the two characteristics most closely linked to the way in which students respond to the expectations and demands of the school.

INTELLIGENCE

Intelligence tests are most reasonably viewed as tests of general learning in areas that are important to academic success. IQ refers only to performance on an intelligence test. IQs are moderately good predictors of how students will perform academically and how they will adapt to the demands of everyday life. Standardized tests are the best single means we have to measure general intelligence, even though performance on a test is not the only indicator of intelligence and may not tap abilities in specific areas that are important in everyday life (see Hallahan et al., 2015).

The definition and measurement of *intelligence* are controversial issues, with implications for the definition of *giftedness*, *intellectual disability*, and other exceptionalities for which special education may be needed (see Hallahan et al., 2015; Kauffman, 2010c, 2011, 2015d). Psychologists agree that intelligence comprises a variety of abilities, both verbal and nonverbal. The ability to direct and sustain attention, process information, think logically, perceive social circumstances accurately, and understand abstractions, for example, are distinguishable parts of what makes a person "smart." But scholars continue to debate the merits of the concept of *general intelligence* versus the idea of *multiple intelligences* (e.g., Chan, 2006). Some have called the theory of multiple intelligences "scientifically untenable" and question practices based on it, but debating these issues is beyond the scope of this book (see Lloyd & Hallahan, 2007; Willingham, 2009). Although the theory of multiple intelligences is widely held to be legitimate, there are no (or very few) proven applications of it to teaching. We do not intend to imply that intelligence can be reduced to a single score or performance, but we do suggest that the idea of many intelligences remains unproven.

Intelligence of Students with Emotional or Behavioral Disorders

Authorities on EBD have traditionally assumed that students with such disorders fall within the normal range of intelligence—that is, within a couple of standard deviations above or below the average on intelligence tests. If the IQ falls below 70, the student may have an intellectual disability, even when behavioral problems are a major concern. Occasionally, however, students with IQs in the disability range are said to have EBD or learning disabilities rather than intellectual disability as their *primary* disability, on the presumption that emotional or perceptual disorders prevent them from performing to their true capacity on intelligence tests (cf. Hallahan et al., 2005, 2015).

The average IQ for most students with EBD is in the low normal range, with a dispersion of scores from the severe intellectual disability range to the highly gifted level. Over many decades, numerous studies have yielded the same general finding: Average tested IQ for these students is in the low 90s. We have accumulated enough research on these students' intelligence to draw this conclusion: Although the majority fall only slightly below average in IQ, a disproportionate number, compared to the normal distribution, score in the lower end of the normal range and the range generally associated with mild intellectual disability, and relatively few fall in the upper ranges. Research findings suggest a distribution like that in Figure 7.1. The hypothetical curve for most students with EBD shows a mean of about 90 to 95 IQ, with more students falling at the lower IQ levels and fewer at the higher levels than in the normal distribution. If this hypothetical distribution of intelligence is correct, then we can expect a greater than normal frequency of academic failure and socialization difficulties for these students.

Implications of Low IQ

Research clearly suggests that students with EBD tend to be lower than average in IQ and that the most severely disabled students also tend to be (but, of course, are not always) those with the lowest IQs. The correlation between intelligence and level of disorder, however, doesn't

Figure 7.1   Hypothetical Frequency Distributions of IQ for Students with Emotional or Behavioral Disorders as Compared to a Normal Frequency Distribution

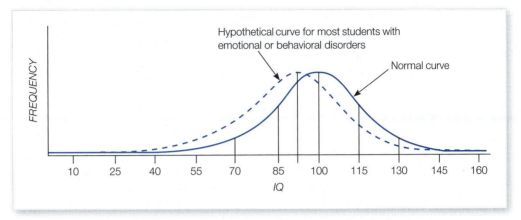

imply a causal relationship. The predictive power of IQ for achievement and future social adjustment of students with EBD probably approximates the predictive power of IQ for students in the normal distribution: significant but far from perfect.

ACADEMIC ACHIEVEMENT

Although academic achievement is usually assessed by standardized achievement tests, it's dangerous to place too much confidence in them because they aren't highly accurate measures of academic aptitude nor highly precise measures of the academic attainment of the individual student. Scores on achievement tests do, however, allow comparisons between the performances of normative and nonnormative groups, which are valuable in assessing and predicting students' school success.

Achievement of Students with Emotional or Behavioral Disorders

The academic achievement of students with EBD and juvenile delinquents has been studied for many years. Collectively, research leads to the conclusion that most such students are academically deficient, even taking into account their mental ages, which are typically slightly below those of their chronological age-mates. Although some students with EBD work at grade level and a very few are academically advanced, most function a year or more below grade level in most academic areas.

Implications of Academic Underachievement

Low achievement and behavior problems go hand in hand; they are highly related risk factors (Lane, 2004; Lane & Menzies, 2010). In most cases, it isn't clear whether disordered behavior causes underachievement or vice versa. Sometimes the weight of evidence may be more on one side of the issue than the other, but in the majority of instances the precise nature of the relationship is elusive. As we'll see, there's reason to believe that underachievement and disordered behavior affect each other reciprocally. Disordered behavior apparently makes academic achievement less likely, and underachievement produces social consequences that are likely to foster inappropriate behavior. In any case, we've known for a long time that the effects of educational failure on future opportunity should cause alarm for the plight of students with EBD (Kauffman, 2010a; Kauffman & Brigham, 2009; Lane, 2004; Nelson et al., 2014; Walker et al., 2004).

SOCIAL SKILLS

Interest in the social skills that make people attractive to others and enable them to cope effectively with difficult interpersonal circumstances is many decades, if not centuries, old. Obviously, people who are considered to have EBD lack certain critical social skills. However, it's often not so obvious just what those skills are, and how to teach people the skills they lack is even less apparent (see Gresham & Elliott, 2014; McGrath, 2014).

Social skills related to schooling may be those that allow a student to establish and maintain positive interpersonal relationships, be accepted by peers, and get along well in the larger social environment. Students with EBD often don't know how to make and keep friends, especially friends whose behavior is not problematic. They frequently behave in ways that anger and disappoint their teachers and classmates. They find it difficult or impossible to adjust to changing expectations when they move from one social environment to another.

A list of the most important social skills encompasses many that are necessary for academic and social success in school. They include listening to others, taking turns in conversations, greeting others, joining in ongoing activities, giving compliments, expressing anger in socially acceptable ways, offering help to others, following rules, being adequately organized and focused, and doing high-quality work. Knowing what these skills are is important; assessing the extent to which individual students have mastered them is critical in dealing effectively with antisocial behavior.

At the heart of social skills is the ability to communicate verbally and nonverbally—to use language competently. In fact, lots of students with EBD have language disorders (Rogers-Adkinson, 1999, 2003). Although these students may have problems in any area of language competence (e.g., they may have difficulty with word sounds, word forms, grammar, and so on), they tend to be particularly deficient in **pragmatics**—the practical, social uses of language. Acting out youngsters may know how to use language very effectively to irritate, intimidate, and coerce others, but they do not have skills in using language effectively for positive, constructive social purposes. A functional analysis of their language skills is likely to indicate that they need to learn to use language to obtain desired consequences in socially acceptable ways. Withdrawn students lack the sophisticated language repertoires their normal peers have for engaging others in discourse. We may conclude that a lack of social skills, especially pragmatic language skills, may underlie many of the behavior problems that are predictive of school failure. Students with EBD may need instruction in specific language-based social skills such as these:

- Identifying, labeling, and expressing needs, wants, and feelings
- Describing and interpreting emotions of oneself and others
- Recognizing incipient emotions, providing control over them, and integrating them into appropriate social behavior.

Instruction in the pragmatics of language can improve the language skills of students with EBD (Hyter, Rogers-Adkinson, Self, & Jantz, 2002).

Behavior Predictive of School Success and Failure

Educational researchers are interested in identifying the classroom behavior associated with academic accomplishment in the hope that teachers can teach those behaviors. For instance, if attentiveness is positively correlated with achievement, then teaching students to pay better attention might improve academic performance. Similarly, if achievement correlates negatively with certain dependence behaviors, then reducing dependency behaviors might be successful. The implicit assumption is that the identified behavioral characteristics will have more than a correlational relationship to achievement; there will be a causal link between certain overt behaviors and achievement.

The causal relationship between classroom behavior and academic success or failure isn't entirely clear. Although a frequent strategy of teachers and educational researchers has been to modify behavior (such as task attention) in the hope of improving performance on academic tasks, direct modification of academic skills has proved most effective in preventing failure or remediating deficits. For decades, we've known that in some cases direct reinforcement of academic performance eliminates classroom behavior problems (Kauffman, Pullen et al., 2011). Increasing a student's correct academic responses is often effective in reducing classroom behavior problems (Lane & Menzies, 2010). Nevertheless, classroom success or failure is determined by more than academic competence; doing the academic work is critical, but it is not the whole story.

Success and failure in school correlate with a variety of academic and social characteristics. Students who are low achieving and socially unsuccessful tend to exhibit:

- Behavior requiring teacher intervention or control, such as teasing, annoying, or interfering with others
- Dependence on the teacher for direction
- Difficulty paying attention and concentrating
- Becoming upset under pressure
- Sloppy, impulsive work
- Low self-confidence

High-achieving and popular students, on the other hand, tend to exhibit:

- Rapport with the teacher, including friendly conversation before and after class and responsiveness in class
- Appropriate verbal interaction, asking relevant questions, volunteering, and participating in class discussions
- Doing more than the minimum work required, taking care to understand directions and to master all details
- Originality and reasoning ability, quickness to grasp new concepts and apply them
- Sensitivity to the feelings of others

However, we must also consider the teacher's expectations and responses to students' behavior. Sometimes, as we shall discuss further, the mismatch between a student's and teacher's temperaments seems to be the primary reason for academic failure (Keogh, 2003).

School Failure and Later Adjustment

Low IQ and academic failure often foretell difficulty for students. A higher proportion of those with low IQ and achievement than of students with high IQ and achievement will experience adjustment difficulties as adults; those with low IQ are disproportionately represented among people who commit criminal acts. A high proportion of schizophrenic and antisocial adults are known to have exhibited low academic achievement as children.

However, low IQ and achievement alone don't *necessarily* mean that the individual is going to have terrible behavior problems. Most youngsters with mild intellectual disabilities, whose achievement may lag behind even their mental ages, don't turn into social misfits, criminals, or institutional residents in adult life; they're considered to have significant problems only during their school years. The same can be said of most youngsters with learning disabilities, whose academic delays usually mark them as school failures. Even among children and youth with EBD, the prognosis is not *necessarily* poor just because the student has a low IQ or fails academically.

However, when school failure is accompanied by serious and persistent antisocial behavior—conduct disorder—the risk for mental health problems in adulthood is most grave (Walker et al., 2004). The earlier the onset and the greater the number of antisocial behaviors, the greater the risk. Even when conduct disorder is accompanied by low intelligence and low achievement, we must be careful in drawing causal inferences; if a causal connection does exist between achievement and antisocial behavior, however, then it has implications for education.

To reiterate, low IQ and school failure alone aren't as highly predictive of adult psychopathology as when they're combined with conduct disorder. The outlook for a youngster is particularly grim when he or she is at once relatively unintelligent, underachieving, and highly aggressive or extremely withdrawn. If conduct disorder is fostered by school failure, then programs to prevent school failure may also contribute to prevention of antisocial behavior (see Lane, Kalberg, & Menzies, 2009; Lane, Menzies, Oakes, & Kalberg, 2012; Sutherland & Conroy, 2010).

INTELLIGENCE, ACHIEVEMENT, AND ANTISOCIAL BEHAVIOR

Given that antisocial behavior (for example, hostile aggression, theft, incorrigibility, running away from home, truancy, vandalism, sexual misconduct), low intelligence, and low achievement are interrelated in a complex way, it may be important to clarify their apparent interrelationship. Figure 7.2 shows a hypothetical relationship among the three characteristics. The various shaded areas in the diagram represent the approximate (hypothesized) proportions in which various combinations of the three characteristics occur. The diagram illustrates the hypothesis that relatively few youngsters who exhibit antisocial behavior are above average in IQ and achievement (area A), most are below average in IQ and achievement (area D), and a few are below average in only IQ (area B) or only achievement (area C). Whereas the majority of underachieving youngsters are low in IQ (areas D and G), they are usually not antisocial (area G is much larger than area D). Some youngsters are low in IQ but not achievement (areas B and E) or vice versa (areas C and F), but relatively few of these youngsters are antisocial (area E is much larger than area B, and area F is much larger than area C).

Keep in mind that additional factors enter the picture to determine the adult outcome for children and youth with a given combination of characteristics. The severity of the antisocial behavior, the parents' behavioral characteristics, and perhaps parental socioeconomic

Figure 7.2 Hypothetical Relationships Among Below-Average IQ, Below-Average Achievement, and Antisocial Behavior

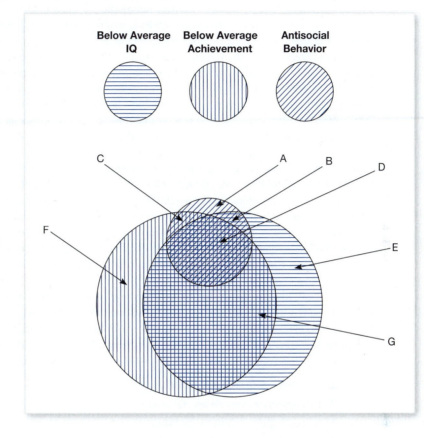

circumstances influence the probability that behavioral difficulties will persist into adulthood. To the extent that youngsters exhibit many antisocial behaviors in a variety of settings and at high frequency, have parents who are themselves antisocial or abusive, and come from a lower social class, they have a greater chance of being hospitalized as mentally ill or incarcerated as a criminal when they become adults. Also, remember that many children and youth who are low in intelligence, low in achievement, high in antisocial behavior, or some combination of these don't exhibit serious behavioral disorders as adults. Any prediction of adult behavior based on childhood behavioral characteristics is subject to substantial error in prediction for the individual case.

SCHOOLS' CONTRIBUTION TO EMOTIONAL AND BEHAVIORAL DISORDERS

The demands of school and the student's social and academic repertoire probably affect each other reciprocally. For decades, we have known that a circular reaction occurs between the student and the social context of the classroom. Students who are healthy, intelligent, upper-middle class, high achieving, high in self-esteem, and adroit in interpersonal skills (likely to be perceived as "easy" and "teachable" by a teacher) enter the classroom at a distinct advantage. They're likely to make positive approaches to others, who in turn are likely to respond positively, and these advantaged students will be sensitive to others' responses toward them and be able to use their intelligence to further enhance their personal power and social status. Intelligence and achievement beget social acceptability, self-esteem, accurate social perception, and status, all of which in turn induce positive social responses from others and facilitate achievement. This perspective on the student's reciprocal interaction with the social ecology of the classroom is entirely consistent with research (Keogh, 2003; Wong & Donahue, 2002). Moreover, the same coercive process found in families of antisocial boys can too often be found in schools. Educators (like parents) and classroom peers (like siblings) can become entangled in escalating contests of aversiveness, in which the individual who causes greater pain is the winner, obtaining negative reinforcement and digging in for the next round of conflict (see Kauffman & Brigham, 2009; Kazdin, 2008; Walker et al., 2004).

The same type of interaction between the student's temperament and the parents' child-rearing techniques appears to occur between the student's temperament and the school's social and academic demands. The student who is slow to approach others, has irregular work habits, is slow to adapt to new situations, and is predominantly negative in mood is most likely to have difficulty in school, although any temperamental characteristic is susceptible to modification with proper handling (Keogh, 2003).

The school, like the family and biological factors, doesn't operate in isolation from other factors. However, we can identify classroom conditions and teacher reactions to pupil behavior that make behavioral difficulties more likely or could be changed to reduce the likelihood of acting out and other emotional or behavioral problems. The school might contribute to disordered behavior and academic failure in one or more of the following ways:

1. Insensitivity to students' individuality

2. Inappropriate expectations for students

3. Inconsistent management of behavior

4. Instruction in nonfunctional and irrelevant skills

5. Ineffective instruction in critical skills

6. Destructive contingencies of reinforcement

7. Undesirable models of school conduct

Besides these factors, others such as crowded and deteriorated schools and classrooms are associated with aggression and other problems. The physical conditions under which students are taught will surely affect their behavior for better or worse.

Insensitivity to Students' Individuality

Special educators of all persuasions recognize the necessity of meeting pupils' individual needs. Some speculate, in fact, that a large proportion of the schoolchildren identified as having learning and behavioral disorders reflect the failure of the education system to accommodate individual differences. Although not making reasonable accommodations to individual needs undoubtedly contributes to some students' failures or maladjustment, reasonable requirements for conformity to rules and standards clearly don't account for the failure or deviance of many others. In fact, just the opposite may be the case for some students; they may fail and behave antisocially because reasonable rules and expectations for conformity to standards of achievement and civility aren't made clear enough (cf. Kauffman & Brigham, 2009; Kauffman, Pullen et al., 2011; Landrum & Kauffman, 2006).

However, rigidity and failure to tolerate differences do demand scrutiny. By making the same academic and behavioral requirements of each student, schools can force many students who are only slightly different from most into roles of academic failures or social deviants. Through inflexibility and stultifying insistence on sameness, schools can create conditions that inhibit or punish healthy expression of individuality. In an atmosphere of regimentation and repression, many students will respond with resentment, hostility, vandalism, or passive resistance to the "system."

For students unfortunate enough to differ more than slightly from the norm in learning or behavior, the message in some classrooms is clear: To be yourself is to be bad, inadequate, or unacceptable. This might increase as standards of learning become more universal or expectations for performance become more the same for *all* students. These students' self-perceptions are likely to become negative, their perceptions of social situations distorted, and their intellectual efficiency and motivation weakened. They can become caught in a self-perpetuating cycle of conflict and negative influence.

Insensitivity to individuals doesn't, of course, emanate from the school as an abstraction. Policy makers, administrators, teachers, and other pupils are the people who are sensitive or insensitive to expressions of individuality. School administrators can create a reasonably tolerant or a repressive mood in the way they deal with students and adults. Teachers are primarily responsible for the classroom emotional climate and for how restrictive or permissive, individualized or regimented the student's school day will be. Peers may demand strict conformity regarding dress, speech, or deportment for social acceptance, especially in the higher grades. On the other hand, peers may be an easygoing, open group in which a fellow student can find acceptance even though he or she is quite different from the group.

Teachers and administrators who are sensitive to students but have clear and positive expectations for academic performance seem to foster appropriate behavior. We shouldn't assume, though, that a positive and productive school climate is fostered merely by an emphasis on talking to students about their family and emotional problems or a policy of all-inclusiveness. Teachers must not abandon their role as adult authority figures in attempts to develop better relationships with their students. A critical key to generally improved student behavior is a clear, consistent plan for behavior management in the classroom and for school-wide discipline (Kauffman, Pullen et al., 2011; Lewis et al., 2014; Martella et al., 2012).

In classic developmental studies, Thomas and Chess (1984) and Thomas and colleagues (1968) showed that EBD is accelerated by adults' failure to treat youngsters in accordance with their temperamental individuality (see Keogh, 2003). Little experimental evidence suggests that EBD is caused by insensitivity alone. However, we can readily find anecdotal evidence that insensitivity may be a feature of many students' school experience. Unfortunately, insensitivity and rigidity in school environments are not relics of the past. They have always been problematic, and they remain a bane of education. Such environments appear to be a breeding ground for antisocial behavior.

The foregoing discussion is decidedly not intended as an indictment of all rules, regulations, or demands for conformity in the classroom or school. Certainly, reasonable rules must be maintained for the safety and well-being of all. No social institution can exist without some requirements of conformity, and we can't interpret an appeal for tolerance of individual expression to mean that *everything and anything* should be accepted. Nevertheless, insensitivity to students as individuals and needless repression of their uniqueness can contribute to behavior problems in the classroom. Students like to have a piece of the action, and allowing them to participate in self-determination of their classroom lives often results in improved behavior and academic performance.

Inappropriate Expectations for Students

The expectations teachers *do* hold for their students, and the expectations they *should* hold, are continuing sources of controversy in American education. Two facets of the problem of expectations are the effects of what teachers are led to believe about their students (especially the possible biasing effects of diagnostic or administrative labels) and teachers' classroom standards of behavior and academic performance.

Effects of Labels

Concern about labeling is decades old, and probably older than special education itself. Some claim that many of the problems of exceptional children originate with and are perpetuated by the labels we use to designate them, as discussed by Kauffman and others (e.g., Kauffman, 2003a, 2005, 2011, 2012a, 2015c; Kauffman & Badar, 2013, 2014a). Some have assumed that a label such as *emotionally disturbed* carries with it an expectation of misbehavior and lower academic performance. The teacher's lower expectation for students labeled *exceptional* will be communicated in subtle ways to the students, and they will indeed fulfill this expectation. Moreover, there is concern about the stigma that goes with receiving a label denoting exceptionality, especially disability. Students' own expectations may also influence their performance.

Ultimately, we must face the fact that labels of some type are necessary for communication (Kauffman, 2012a; Kauffman & Konold, 2007; Kauffman, Mock, Tankersley, & Landrum, 2008). They simply cannot be avoided unless we refuse to discuss students' problems. The issues, then, should be how we understand and use labels and how we work with the larger problem—our perceptions of the people whose characteristics we refer to when we use labels (Kauffman, 2011, 2012a).

A popular assumption is that receiving special education services destroys students' self-esteem and social status, regardless of the particular label under which they are served. Research suggests that this assumption may be unfounded for children with learning disabilities and EBD. Studies indicate that students receiving special education for learning or behavioral disorders—students receiving these labels—may have lower self-concepts or social status than do students without learning or behavioral problems. They have not, however, been found to have lower self-perceptions and status than do nonlabeled students who have academic or behavioral problems. Students appear to suffer damage to self-esteem and social status as a consequence of learning and behavior problems, not as a result of being labeled; the label follows the problem, not vice versa. In fact, a label for their difficulties appears to give many people with disabilities a sense of relief and to provide others with an understandable reason for differences that, unlabeled, result in social rejection. Besides, high self-esteem has not been shown to cause better academic performance, interpersonal success, or happiness.

Effects of Classroom Standards

The early twenty-first century is marked by an emphasis on higher academic and social standards in American public schools. For students with disabilities and serious academic or social problems, these increased expectations, if interpreted as universal standards demanded of all students, create the certainty of failure without extraordinary supports and a high probability of failure even with the most effective interventions known (Hallahan et al., 2015; Kauffman, 2010c, 2011). Especially for students with EBD, alternative placements in which the expectations are adjusted to fit the students' prior learning and abilities are essential if their education is to be appropriate.

The research and speculation on effects of teacher bias don't lead logically to the conclusion that simply expecting normal behavior will help students with EBD improve. After all, it's quite clear that most such students are lower in tested intelligence, academic achievement, and social adjustment than are average students. Many are far below their age-mates in numerous areas of development, and expecting normal performance from them is unrealistic.

For many years, we've had good reason to suspect that a discrepancy between the child's ability and adults' expectations for performance contributes directly to the development of disordered behavior. If the expectations are too high or too low, the student may become disinterested, dispirited, and disruptive. We do know that students with EBD often are motivated by **negative reinforcement**—by behaving in ways that allow them to escape or avoid demands or expectations for performance.

If expectations that are too low become self-fulfilling prophecies, and if expectations that are too high are frustrating and depressing and prompt attempts to avoid them, then what level of expectation will avoid the risk of contributing to development of disordered behavior? Expectations of improvement are always in order—assuming, of course, that the teacher knows the student's current level of academic performance or adequate social behavior and can specify a reasonable level of improvement along a measurable dimension. If pupil and teacher define *reasonable* together, then the expectations should be neither too low nor too high.

Research doesn't suggest that teachers' expectations and demands are typically well attuned to students' abilities and characteristics. Teachers' expectations can be a significant problem for students with EBD, regardless of whether they're in a special or general education class and regardless of whether they're elementary or secondary students.

What do teachers expect or demand of their students? Most teachers have *dos* and *don'ts*, which are generally things like these:

1. Follow the classroom rules.

2. Listen to my instructions and do what I say.

3. Do assignments and do them well.

4. Don't steal or engage in inappropriate or suggestive behavior.

5. Don't react negatively when you're corrected.

6. Don't damage things.

Given teachers' standards and expectations, it shouldn't be surprising that students with EBD and their teachers frequently disappoint each other, which sets the stage for conflict and coercion. We shouldn't inappropriately generalize to *all* teachers or assume that high standards and low tolerance for misbehavior are undesirable. Some teachers apparently make few demands and have great tolerance for deviance, and others are just the opposite. Compared

Video Example from YouTube

ENHANCEDetext
Video Connections 7.1
This video shows a classroom scene in which the teacher is not proactive in establishing expectations or standards nor responding to misbehavior. Notice how the students respond. (https://www.youtube.com/watch?v=XMhIUo2a1iE)

to regular classroom teachers, special education teachers may be somewhat more tolerant of misbehavior and judge students' behavior as less deviant. Teachers' expressed tolerance for troublesome behavior may be affected by several factors, including their self-perceived competence, the availability and quality of technical assistance, and the difficulty of the particular group of students they're teaching. Teachers who have higher standards and lower tolerance for disorderly behavior may also provide more effective instruction. Also, the teacher's temperament in interaction with the child's seems to be a critical factor in many school problems.

Inconsistent Management of Behavior

A major hypothesis underlying a structured approach to educating students with EBD is that a lack of structure or order in their daily lives contributes to their difficulties. When youngsters can't predict adults' responses to their behavior, they become anxious, confused, and unable to choose appropriate behavioral alternatives. If at one time they're allowed to engage in a certain misbehavior without penalty and at another time they're punished for the same misconduct, the unpredictability of the consequences of their behavior encourages them to act inappropriately. If they can't depend on favorable consequences following good behavior, they have little incentive to perform well.

We find strong support in the child development literature for the contention that inconsistent behavior management fosters disordered behavior. If one can extrapolate from the findings that inconsistent parental discipline adversely affects children's behavioral development, then it seems highly likely that inconsistent behavior-management techniques in the school will also have negative effects. Capricious, inconsistent discipline in the classroom will contribute nothing toward helping students learn appropriate conduct. School-based studies of antisocial behavior such as vandalism also indicate a connection between punitive, inconsistent discipline and problem behavior. Even though inconsistent management may not be the root of all EBD, it obviously contributes to the perpetuation of behavioral difficulties (Kauffman & Brigham, 2009; Kauffman, Pullen et al., 2011; Kerr & Nelson, 2010; Landrum & Kauffman, 2006; Walker et al., 2004; see also chapters in Walker & Gresham, 2014).

Instruction in Nonfunctional and Irrelevant Skills

One way in which a school increases the probability that students will misbehave or be truant is in offering instruction for which pupils have no real or imagined use. Not only does this kind of education fail to engage pupils, but it also hinders their social adaptation by wasting their time and substituting trivial information for knowledge that would allow them to pursue rewarding activities, thus increasing the likelihood that they will drop out of school (Garner, 2014; Hirsch et al., 2014; Nicholson, 2014; Witt, VanDerHayden, & Gilbertson, 2004).

The problem of making education relevant to students' lives has plagued teachers for a long time. The question we need to ask is more than whether the teacher or other adults know that instruction is important for the student's future. To resolve the question, the youngster must be convinced that the learning he or she is asked to do is or will be important. The teacher must convince the student that the instruction is in some ways worthwhile; otherwise, the classroom will be merely a place for the pupil to avoid or to disrupt. For some students with a history of school problems, convincing them will require provision of artificial reasons to learn, such as extrinsic rewards for behavior and performance.

Ineffective Instruction in Critical Skills

Social acceptance and positive self-perceptions are greatly enhanced by academic competence and skills in interacting with one's peers and authority figures. Thus, the classroom must be a place in which all class members learn critical academic skills and the social skills critical for success in general education. Ineffective instruction in either area—academic or social learning—dooms many students to academic or social failure or both. Nevertheless, many classrooms are not places where students are taught effectively but places where they are left to fend for themselves instructionally, to pick up whatever skills they might acquire through incidental learning or self-discovery (Hirsch et al., 2014; Kauffman, 2010a, 2010c, 2011; Kauffman, Conroy et al., 2008).

We cannot overemphasize the importance of academic learning to emotional well-being and behavioral development. For all students, being able to meet everyday expectations is critical to mental health. Faced with constant failure and unfavorable comparisons to peers, nearly anyone will succumb to feelings of frustration, worthlessness, irritability, and rage (see Willingham, 2009). Competence on the job is an elixir; incompetence compared to one's peers is an emotional and behavioral poison. The job of students is academic learning, and teachers who are not as effective as they could be in helping students achieve academic competence are contributing to students' emotional and behavioral problems.

Unfortunately, most of general public education has adopted instructional practices that are not effective, especially for students who come to school without the skills that most economically privileged students acquire outside school (Heward, 2003; Silvestri & Heward, 2016; Kauffman, 2010c, 2011). Child-directed, "holistic," "discovery learning" approaches and heterogeneous grouping, for example, are instructional practices virtually certain to fail with students at risk of failure. Special education classes are also too often places in which effective academic instruction is not provided. Direct instruction is effective in helping students with disabilities acquire academic skills, and using such instruction could improve the learning of students in both general and special education (Engelmann & Carnine, 2011; Hirsch et al., 2014; Kauffman, 2010b, 2010c).

Also unfortunate is the fact that most of general public education often has failed to adopt explicit programs for teaching social skills and rewarding desirable behavior. Specific social skills need to be assessed and taught explicitly and systematically to many individuals and groups if they are to learn the basic skills needed for positive interaction with others (Kavale, Mathur, & Mostert, 2004; Walker et al., 2004). Yet few schools provide such assessment or instruction. Moreover, classrooms need to be places where desirable conduct is explicitly, frequently, and effectively rewarded. Yet most classrooms are characterized by very low rates of positive consequences for appropriate behavior. Popularization of the notion that rewards undermine intrinsic motivation and that positive reinforcement amounts to bribes (e.g., Kohn, 1993) has further impeded the adoption of positive behavioral strategies for managing classroom behavior (Kauffman, 2010c, 2011; Maag, 2001). However, overwhelming empirical evidence indicates that rewards appropriately used don't undermine intrinsic motivation and that rewards are essential for effective, positive classroom management, especially of difficult students (see Alberto & Troutman, 2012; Frey, Lingo, & Nelson, 2008; Kauffman, Pullen et al., 2011; Kazdin, 2008; Kerr & Nelson, 2010; Lewis, Lewis-Palmer, Stichter, & Newcomer, 2004; Walker et al., 2004).

Destructive Contingencies of Reinforcement

From the viewpoint of behavioral psychology, the school can contribute to the development of emotional or behavioral disorders in several obvious ways:

- Providing positive reinforcement for inappropriate behavior
- Failing to provide positive reinforcement for desirable behavior
- Providing negative reinforcement for behavior that allows students to avoid their work.

The following section defines what we call positive and negative reinforcement and gives examples of how each may work in a classroom environment. We recognize that in the behavior analysis research community, the distinction between positive and negative reinforcement is a matter of debate, but in our opinion the distinction is helpful in thinking about what happens in teaching–learning interactions in classrooms.

Positive and Negative Reinforcement: A Dynamic Duo

Reinforcement—especially negative reinforcement—is often misunderstood. Many teachers don't understand how positive and negative reinforcement typically work together and how both may be involved in maintaining either desirable or troublesome classroom behavior. In many interactions, students with emotional or behavioral disorders get a double dose of reinforcement, one positive and one negative, and often for the wrong behavior.

Reinforcement, whether positive or negative, is a reward or consequence that makes the behavior it follows more likely to recur. The "reward" may be something one gets (i.e., a positive reinforcer) or something one gets rid of or avoids (i.e., a negative reinforcer). It may be helpful to think of people looking for work and having signs stating what they want. Some signs might say, "Will work FOR _____." Other signs might say, "Will work TO GET OUT OF _____." Still others might say, "Will work FOR _____ AND TO AVOID _____." What someone will work *for* provides **positive reinforcement**; what someone will work *to get out of or avoid* provides **negative reinforcement**. Most of us will work for money, and most of us will work to get out of debt or to avoid losing our job. Most of us will work for course credit and, at the same time, work to avoid embarrassment or a bad grade. In fact, in most cases our behavior is motivated by two consequences at once: 1) something we *get* and 2) something we *avoid* (or at least escape temporarily). We work for money and also to get out of work (the negative reinforcement—escape from work that we call vacations).

We all experience both positive and negative reinforcement in everyday life, and both types of reinforcement play important roles in motivating our adaptive behavior. However, positive and negative reinforcement become problematic rather than helpful in the classroom or any other environment when they are misused or poorly arranged. Misuse or poor application may be the result of either of two major mistakes:

- *Misidentification.* A teacher may believe that criticisms or reprimands are negative reinforcers that a student will work to avoid, when they are actually positive reinforcers. Being reprimanded is something the student will work to get because of the attention it brings from the teacher and classroom peers (for many of us, attention is something we crave, whether it is criticism or praise; being ignored is what we will work hardest to avoid). A teacher may also fail to see that academic assignments are negative reinforcers for a student who exhibits disruptive classroom behavior; academic work may be something the student will misbehave to get out of. Whatever behavior allows this student to escape from the work (or postpone it) will be reinforced; the student will misbehave so that he or she does not have to do the work.

- *Malcontingency.* The contingencies in a classroom are destructive if they result in either positive reinforcement or negative reinforcement for undesirable behavior. Students may learn this: I get lots of attention when I misbehave (positive reinforcement, even if the attention is in the form of intended punishment such as scolding); in addition, I get out of my academic work (negative reinforcement).

The dynamic duo of positive and negative reinforcement can be harnessed to give desirable behavior a double boost. Students get a double good deal when the classroom contingencies involving both positive and negative reinforcement are constructive: attention for desirable behavior (positive reinforcement) and little vacations from work (negative reinforcement) as a reward for work done promptly and well.

How Things Often Go Wrong

Destructive rather than constructive contingencies of reinforcement are in place in many classrooms, both in general education and in special education. Appropriate conduct typically goes unrewarded, whereas both positive and negative reinforcement for misconduct are frequent. A great deal of evidence suggests that constructive reinforcement contingencies can be arranged to teach appropriate behavior even to students whose behavior is seriously disordered. In study after study over the past several decades, experimental research has shown that providing teacher attention during appropriate behavior but withholding it during undesirable behavior results in improvement (Alberto & Troutman, 2012; Kauffman, Pullen et al., 2011; Kerr & Nelson, 2010; see chapters in Walker & Gresham, 2014).

In many classrooms, the contingencies of reinforcement are inadvertently arranged to promote the very behavior the teacher deems undesirable. The use of constructive consequences for adaptive behavior is consistent with a conceptual model that assumes interactive effects of students' and teachers' responses. An interactional or transactional model suggests that youngsters and adults exert reciprocal influence on each other. It's reasonable to believe that teachers' and problem students' mutual praise and criticism become important factors in the maintenance of behavior and that mutual hostility could be defused beginning with either teacher or pupil. Thus, in some cases, children with developmental disabilities and problem behavior have been taught to help their teachers provide positive reinforcement for their desirable behavior. Too often, classroom peers are allowed to provide additional reinforcement for misconduct.

Peer tutoring is another strategy designed to provide more positive reinforcement for desired behavior in the typical classroom (Tournaki & Criscitiello, 2003). Whether involving only specific pairs of students (one of whom tutors the other) or class-wide peer tutoring (in which all members of the class are engaged in tutoring one another), the strategy has been shown to benefit many students whose behavior is problematic by increasing their engagement in academics and the positive interactions they have with their peers. Moreover, a skillfully implemented program of peer tutoring could be a key strategy in teaching social skills to all students and teaching students nurturing responses to others, which would help make

Video Example

from

YouTube

▶

ENHANCEDetext
Video Connections 7.2
This animated clip provides an excellent overview of the basic concepts and procedures involved in implementing class-wide peer tutoring. (https://www.youtube .com/watch?v=V9i5yWzz79s) ·

schools and the larger society kinder and gentler places in which to live. In too many cases, students are abusive of each other and their teacher, instead of helpful or nurturing.

Abundant empirical evidence shows that students' classroom behavior can be altered by manipulating the contingencies of reinforcement, even when the reinforcement is as natural a part of the classroom as teacher and peer attention (see Alberto & Troutman, 2012; Kauffman, Pullen et al., 2011; Kerr & Nelson, 2010). It's easy to see the potential implications of this evidence in the school's contributions to the development of EBD. Students whose behavior is a problem often receive abundant attention for misbehavior but little or no attention for appropriate conduct. Even though the attention they receive for misbehavior is often in the form of criticism or punishment, it's still attention and is likely to reinforce whatever they are doing at the time it's dispensed. The effect of attention for misbehavior and non-attention for good deportment is likely to be perpetuation of the miscreant's deeds, regardless of the intentions of the teacher or another adult.

Undesirable Models of School Conduct

Children and youth are great imitators. Much of their learning is the result of watching others and mimicking their behavior. Youngsters are particularly likely to imitate the behavior modeled by people who are socially or physically powerful, attractive, and in command of important reinforcers. Unless the modeling process is carefully controlled, students who act out and disrupt the classroom are likely to gravitate toward other peers who are disruptive. Teachers must find ways to call attention to and reward the appropriate behavior of high-status peers.

Exemplary behavior on the part of the teacher encourages like conduct in pupils. Maltreatment by the teacher of any student in the class is very likely to encourage students to treat each other with hostility or disrespect. Teachers whose attitude toward their work is cavalier or who are disorganized may foster similar carelessness and disorganization in their students. Corporal punishment—still used in some schools and classrooms—is a horrid example of aggressive misconduct by adults that may be mimicked by students in their relationships with others. A teacher's lack of self-awareness is likely to encourage a lack of self-awareness on the part of pupils (Richardson & Shupe, 2003).

Peers exert considerable social pressure on students' behavior in school, particularly at the high school level. Schools in which high-status students either refuse to perform academic tasks or exhibit serious misbehavior with impunity are likely to see the spread of academic failure and social misconduct.

IMPLICATIONS FOR EDUCATORS

The teacher of students with EBD must be prepared to work with pupils who are below average intellectually and academically as well as deviant in their social behavior. Some of these students are superior intellectually and academically, but most aren't. Teaching these students demands not only the ability to instruct pupils across an extremely wide range of intellectual and academic levels but also the ability to teach social and other nonacademic

Table 7.1 How Teachers Can Help Students Learn Self-Control

√ Provide a model of self-control.

√ Demonstrate knowledge of the student's family, pets, and preferences.

√ Make the classroom pleasant and friendly, yet orderly, predictable, and a nice place to work.

√ Insist that classroom peers be treated respectfully and encourage peer friendships.

√ Emphasize reward for approved behavior and minimize use of punishment.

√ Avoid shaming and harsh punishment.

√ Keep classroom rules simple and reward students who comply with them.

behaviors that make scholastic success possible, such as good work habits, attention strategies, and independence. The most crucial tasks of the teacher as a preventive agent are to foster academic success and to lessen the student's antisocial conduct. Academic failure and antisocial behavior limit future opportunities and make future maladjustment likely.

The teacher's primary task is to modulate the school environment in ways that will contribute to adaptive, prosocial behavior and academic growth. The first requirement of appropriate education for students with EBD is that they be provided with effective instruction in academic skills (Hirsch et al., 2014). In addition, every special education classroom should be characterized by the strategies of teachers who are also effective in preventing discipline problems and promoting self-control. Such characteristics are listed in Table 7.1.

Regrettably, many teachers of students with EBD are poorly prepared for the task. Moreover, the effectiveness of many special education programs is undercut by lack of support from administrators and parents. The challenge we face is not just preparing more and better teachers but also providing the supports that will facilitate their success and keep the best in the field longer.

BIOLOGY, CULTURE, FAMILY, AND SCHOOL: A TANGLED WEB

Genes and environments have considerable influence on behavior and the creation of culture. Thus, cultures, including families, schools, and other features of societies, are partly a result of social learning and partly a result of biological fates.

When we think of cultural factors, we think of social institutions—nations, ethnic groups, religions, schools, and families. These and other social institutions are interconnected in ways that defy simple explanations of causal influences on children's behavior. For each possible combination of social institutions, we must ask how one affects the other. To what extent does the nation make its schools, and to what extent do its schools make that nation? To what degree can schools succeed without the support of families, and to what degree can families be successful without schools that teach what their children need to learn? What are the cultural factors, other than families and schools, that shape children's behavior, and how do families and schools create, enhance, or counteract these other influences? The answers to these questions are neither simple nor obvious, but they are critical to our understanding of the roles of schools and teachers in our society.

The role of schools in American culture—the extent to which schools merely reflect our national character and the extent to which they are responsible for creating it—is frequently a matter for discussion. Perhaps the increasing use of guns in the United States is peculiarly American. If it is a part of American culture, then it is no wonder it has invaded our schools.

We cannot, however, ignore the fact that schools and teachers have a special responsibility to influence the families and communities for whom they exist—the other parts of our culture that they also reflect. True, parents must be involved with and support the work of teachers if the schools are to succeed. And meaningful engagement can occur only if schools offer instruction that addresses the concerns of families and communities. Many poor minority children have been shortchanged by an exclusive focus on "progressive" methods of instruction that cater to the learning of middle-class White students. Yet the affection of the public and educators for "progressive" methods seems to other writers to continue to stymie the progress of many students, especially ethnic minorities and children with disabilities or other disadvantages (see Heward, 2003; Kauffman, 2010c; Silvestri & Heward, 2016; Snider, 2006). There is great irony in the fact that many advocates of so-called culturally sensitive instruction embrace constructivist ideas that are inimical to the success of students whose cultures and languages are different from those of the larger society.

Many see the role of schools in American culture changing in large measure because of the increasingly troublesome behavior, attitudes, and social needs of students. American culture itself is shaped in significant ways by the distribution of wealth among its citizens, and increasing economic disparities are a troublesome part of American culture. Poverty is a part of American culture that we obviously have not addressed effectively (see Pascoe et al., 2016). The cultural context of American public schools in the twenty-first century includes extraordinary disparities of wealth, widespread poverty among children, and the deterioration of families and other social institutions that previously offered more support for schools. The role of special education for children and youth with EBD in this context will likely be a matter for increasingly hot debate because it is clear that special education has not adequately addressed the problems our society wants to see solved.

When we think about the causes of EBD, oversimplifications and overgeneralizations are great temptations. We're inclined to assume that highly inappropriate behavior is simply a result of inadequate parenting or teaching, physiological problems, or cultural influences. We're too often tempted to believe that [whatever] is destiny, whether the [whatever] stands for biology, culture, or anything else. Keogh (2003) noted how biological factors don't always have the negative consequences for human relationships that we might expect. She described watching preschoolers' social interactions with peers and teachers: Her message isn't that temperament is destiny. It simply must be considered for the complex role it plays in children's development—and not just the temperament of the child, but the temperament of parents and teachers as well.

As we hope you understand from reading the four chapters in Part 2, physiology, culture, parenting, and teaching can be significant causal factors, but we must be extremely cautious in drawing conclusions about the individual case. Before concluding that a student's undesirable classroom behavior is a result of the teacher's ineptitude or that the child's disorder is caused by poor parenting, for example, we must examine carefully what transpires in the interactions between student and teacher or child and parent. However, even if we observe these interactions and find that the adult clearly is behaving toward the child in a less-than-admirable manner, we also must be careful not to jump to the conclusion that we've found the root of the problem. A child with serious EBD may be extremely difficult for anyone to live with; he or she may be highly effective in frustrating and bringing out the worst in just about anyone.

Recognizing that causal effects aren't so simple or unidirectional as they first appear should help us maintain a reasonable level of humility in evaluating our own work with children and youth and give us caution in placing blame on the other adults who work with them as well.

We know more today about some of the origins of EBD than we knew twenty-five or even ten years ago, but researchers now realize that causal mechanisms are far more complex than we thought. At the same time that research is showing us the incredible complexity and interconnectedness of causal factors, it's opening up new possibilities for intervention. Old ideas that the course of psychopathology is set by early life experiences or biology and effective intervention is impossible have given way to more hopeful attitudes for most disorders. At the same time, newer ideas about the positive influences of therapeutic environments are being tempered by the realization that many patterns of behavior reflect genetics and other biophysical processes and that teachers and parents shouldn't be blamed for them or held responsible for correcting these problems solely through interpersonal interventions.

Skepticism is important in trying to find out why people behave as they do. The scientific frame of mind is critically important (Kauffman, 2011, 2014c). Thinking or believing something does not make it true (Polsgrove, 2003). Remember the message of the bumper sticker that reads, "Don't believe everything you think."

SUMMARY

The role of the school in causing EBD is a particularly important consideration for educators. In our society, school failure is tantamount to personal failure. The school environment is not only critically important for social development but is also the factor over which educators have direct control.

As a group, students with EBD score below average on intelligence tests and are academic underachievers. Many of them lack specific social skills. The behavior they exhibit is not associated with school success. Disordered behavior and underachievement appear to influence each other reciprocally; in an individual case, which causes the other is not as important as recognizing that they are interrelated. Academic failure and low intelligence, when combined with antisocial behavior or conduct disorder, increase the likelihood of social adjustment problems in adulthood. The school may contribute to the development of EBD in several ways:

- School administrators, teachers, and other pupils may be insensitive to the student's individuality.
- Teachers may hold inappropriate expectations of students.
- Teachers may be inconsistent in managing students' behavior.
- Instruction may be offered in nonfunctional (that is, seemingly irrelevant) skills.
- Ineffective instruction may be offered in skills that are critical for school success.
- School personnel may arrange destructive contingencies of reinforcement.
- Peers and teachers may provide models of undesirable conduct.

Teachers of students with EBD must be prepared to teach youngsters who are underachieving and difficult to instruct, and instruction must be provided in both academic and social skills.

✔ ENHANCEDetext END-OF-CHAPTER 7 QUIZ

Click on the checkmark icon to access an end-of-chapter quiz. Answer the questions to gauge your understanding of chapter concepts and better prepare you for case discussions.

CASE FOR DISCUSSION (See case book for additional cases.)

You Had Better Get on Them.

Bob Winters

Bob Winters had been prepared to teach preschoolers with disabilities, but he accepted a job teaching a special class of students with mild mental disabilities in a middle school. When he was hired, the principal, Mr. Dudley, had told him, "You're the expert. We'll give you a lot of leeway for making decisions about these students because you're the one who's trained to work with difficult students. Mr. Arter, the teacher last year, had lots of trouble with these kids. You'll have to come down on them hard."

Bob struggled to develop appropriate instructional programs for his students. Other teachers were coming to him for advice, but he had little or nothing to offer. He ended up assigning lots of worksheets emphasizing basic skills. He tried to keep the kids busy, but as the days and weeks rolled by, his class became more and more rowdy, and he felt his classroom control slipping away. The students raced through their assignments and then wandered around the room laughing and joking in small groups and verbally abusing each other. Poor grades did not bother them. In fact, they bragged about getting bad grades and were particularly glad to show off a paper that had the lowest score in the class.

Bob's class became so unruly and noisy that Mr. Dudley occasionally came down the hall to open the classroom door and glare or shout at Bob's students. The students laughed and joked about Mr. Dudley after he left. "He thinks he's bad," one would say, and the others would nod their heads in agreement. Bob was determined to get tougher. He simply had to get control over this class. He began trying Mr. Dudley's shouted directions. As punishment, he began requiring students to copy pages out of the dictionary, something they seemed to dread. But one Thursday he invoked this punishment when

Ronnie disrupted the class as he returned from the restroom. Ronnie grinned impishly and declared, "Okay, I *love* copying the dictionary." He copied more pages than Bob had assigned. But the next day Ronnie flatly refused to copy any pages at all, and Bob eventually ordered him to the office.

Eventually, Bob decided to arrange the students' desks facing the classroom walls. Maybe this way they wouldn't distract each other so much and would get more work done, he reasoned. But then they began moving their desks together without permission. They met his reprimands with saucy comments such as "Oh, big man!" and "Yeah, he thinks he's going to do something!" When Gerald jumped out of his seat and ran over to whack Mike playfully on the back of the head, Bob lashed out. "Get your ass in the chair!" he bellowed. Gerald froze. The others stared silently at Bob as he went on, "I don't give a damn what you all want to do. You're going to do as I say." Cathy nudged Ronnie, who sat beside her, and they began to giggle. Bob descended on Cathy immediately, shouting, "Go to the office!" With flashing, angry eyes, Cathy stalked out and slammed the door. Her classmates shook their heads and exchanged scowls.

Ten minutes later, Mr. Dudley was at Bob's door. "Mr. Winters, may I see you outside?" As he walked to the door, Bob heard Amber say, "He's going to be in trouble." Bob guessed she was right.

Questions About the Case

1. How do Bob's teaching and management strategies illustrate the concepts presented in this chapter? What was Mr. Dudley's role in contributing to the problems with this class?

2. If you were Bob's friend and colleague, what advice would you give him about improving his teaching performance?

3. Where does the responsibility lie for preventing situations like the one depicted here?

PART 3 Types of Disordered Behavior

INTRODUCTION

In the preceding chapters, we discussed EBD primarily in the general case, with only occasional and brief attention to specific types or categories of disorders. In Part 3, we revisit earlier questions with which we dealt mostly in the general case, this time giving closer scrutiny to specific types of disorders. For each major type of disorder, we attempt to provide succinct answers to as many of the following questions as possible:

- How is this disorder defined? What is its prevalence?
- What do we know about its causes and its possible prevention?
- What are the primary approaches to intervention and education?

Although we are able to provide at least tentative, brief answers to these questions for most of the major disorders, we are not able to answer all the questions for all the disorders or their subtypes.

We call Part 3 "Types of Disordered Behavior" to indicate that the types of problems we discuss are merely different aspects of what we call EBD. The classification of the disorders known as EBD is complex and inevitably produces ambiguous categories. Disorders of all types seem to be interconnected, so in discussing one type, we necessarily consider several others as well. For example, hyperactivity, conduct disorder, and delinquency are interrelated problems. True, one might find a youngster who is hyperactive yet is not considered to have a conduct disorder and has not been designated **delinquent**. We occasionally may find a seemingly "pure" case of any given type of disorder, one in which the youngster's problem is apparently neatly limited in character. Nevertheless, these "pure" cases are not typical. In most instances, we find multiple problems, clusters of disorders, behavior that is characteristic of several different facets of what we call EBD.

How, then, shall we decide what constitutes a distinctive *type* or *facet* of disordered behavior? Clearly, anyone's answer to this question will be arbitrary in some ways. We have chosen to divide this part of the book into six chapters, partly on the basis of empirical evidence of the way in which behavioral problems are clustered or factored statistically and partly according to what we believe will facilitate the clearest discussion. We begin with the disorders that are among the most prevalent: disorders of attention and activity, often referred to as attention deficit–hyperactivity disorder (ADHD), and conduct disorders (overt aggression and covert antisocial behavior). In the subsequent chapter, we discuss anxiety and a variety of related disorders that do not fit neatly under any other category (fears and phobias; obsessions and compulsions; and disorders involving speaking, eating, eliminating, moving, and sexual behavior). Depression and suicide, which we examine next, are increasingly recognized as serious problems among children and adolescents. Next, we address the disorders known variously as psychoses, or pervasive developmental disorders, which are among the least prevalent.

Finally, we turn to some of the special problems of adolescents, including juvenile delinquency and substance abuse, early sexual experience, and other problems closely related to conduct disorders and attention problems.

We hope the chapters in Part 3 bring you a better understanding of the specific ways in which children and youth can exhibit EBD. As you read these chapters, you should ask yourself how specific disorders are interrelated and how they are distinctive. Here is a sample of the kinds of questions you might ask:

- What distinguishes conduct disorder from depression?
- When we see a youngster who has a conduct disorder, for example, might we also be seeing one who is depressed (that is, might conduct disorder and depression be comorbid conditions)? Could the same set of circumstances give rise to both conduct disorder and depression?
- To what extent are interventions that are effective for conduct disorder also appropriate or inappropriate for a student who is depressed?
- What do we know about the comorbidity of depression and excessive fears?
- Under what circumstances are we likely to see a pervasive developmental disorder and hyperactivity or attention deficits in the same person? When we do, what are the implications for teaching?
- How are teenage sexual activity and teenage parenthood linked to delinquency, substance abuse, and other disorders?

Questions such as these are not easily answered, and our brief discussions of specific disorders cannot do justice to the complexity of these problems and their interconnections.

The serious study of EBD calls to mind the old idea that a little bit of inaccuracy saves a lot of explanation. Although we strive to be as accurate as we can be, we recognize the fact that eliminating every inaccuracy and overgeneralization is impossible. However, we hope reading the next six chapters will leave you with a new appreciation of the complexity of EBD.

8 ATTENTION AND ACTIVITY DISORDERS

Anthony Magnacca/Pearson Education, Inc.

After reading this chapter, you should be able to:

8.1 Give a more complex definition of *hyperactivity* than simply being overly active.

8.2 List the kinds of behavior that are most closely associated with attention deficit–hyperactivity disorder (ADHD).

8.3 Explain why students with attention and activity disorders are typically unpopular with their peers.

8.4 Describe the behavioral interventions that are frequently used to manage hyperactivity and related problems.

8.5 Summarize general conclusions about using self-monitoring to manage off-task behavior and improve academic performance.

DEFINITION AND PREVALENCE

We said in the introduction to Part 1 and in Chapter 2 that youngsters with EBD often induce negative feelings and behavior in others. Among the many characteristics that are bothersome or irritating to others and make others respond negatively are disorders of attention and activity. During the past several decades, individuals with these disorders have been described by a variety of terms, including *hyperactive* and *hyperkinetic*. Severe and chronic problems in regulating attention and activity are now commonly known as **attention deficit–hyperactivity disorder** (ADHD). The inability to control one's attention has replaced hyperactivity as the core problem of concern. The prevailing opinion is that hyperactivity usually, but not always, accompanies attention deficits. ADHD is a term about which there is still much uncertainty and controversy (see Hallahan et al., 2015; Hallahan, Lloyd, Kauffman, Weiss, & Martinez, 2005; Nigg & Barkley, 2014; Rooney, 2017).

In this chapter, we use the term *ADHD* because we are concerned primarily with children and youth who have attention *and* activity disorders, and who have problems that are more severe than most. These youngsters with extreme attention and activity problems may also be categorized as having EBD or learning disabilities (LD). Youngsters whose attention deficits are accompanied by hyperactivity and *impulsivity* are more likely to have conduct disorders than are those who show attention deficits and disorganization without hyperactivity. Our concern here is with youngsters who have serious social or emotional problems and whether they are related to hyperactivity or other manifestations of attention deficits in addition to problems attending to their schoolwork. We have known for a long time that children with disorders of attention and activity have lots of social problems (e.g., Nigg & Barkley, 2014; Whalen & Henker, 1991).

ADHD is among the most controversial disorders, even though it is not new. Like LD, ADHD is still seen by some people as a real and serious disability and by others as an attempt to legitimize teachers' or parents' inadequacies, or as a ruse or excuse for getting undeserved, special attention. Good teaching and good discipline at home and school would, according to some skeptics, resolve the problem of ADHD in all but a very small percentage of cases. Others see ADHD as a true developmental disability for which there is no cure. Professional disagreement and public confusion have been found at almost every point of research and practice.

We believe that ADHD does exist and that a consensus among professionals regarding its nature and treatment is gradually emerging. Contrary to much popular opinion, the emerging consensus, based on decades of research, is that ADHD is neither a minor problem nor a temporary characteristic of childhood that kids typically outgrow. It is a distinctive set of problems and a real disability (Barkley, 2003; Hallahan et al., 2005; Hallahan et al., 2015; Nigg & Barkley, 2014; Rooney, 2017). Most definitions of ADHD suggest that it is a developmental disorder of attention and activity, is evident relatively early in life (before the age of seven or eight), persists throughout the life span, involves both academic and social skills, and is frequently accompanied by other disorders.

The difficulties in focusing and sustaining attention, controlling impulsive action, and showing appropriate motivation that characterize

---

Video Example

from

YouTube

▶

ENHANCEDetext
Video Connections 8.1
Dr. Thomas Brown from
Yale University describes
the basic characteristics of
ADHD in this short video clip.
(https://www.youtube.com/
watch?v=vVZ2qbMgMPs)

ADHD can make a person with the disorder—regardless of his or her age—a trial for parents, siblings, teachers, classroom peers, or coworkers. Hyperactive, distractible, impulsive young-sters upset their parents and siblings because they are difficult to live with at home; at school, they often drive their teachers to discomposure. They are often unpopular with their peers, and they do not typically make charming playmates or helpful workmates. Incessant move-ment, impulsiveness, noisiness, irritability, destructiveness, unpredictability, flightiness, and other similar characteristics of students with ADHD are not endearing to anyone—parents, siblings, teachers, and schoolmates included. Whalen (1983) provided a classic description of how unpleasant a child with ADHD might be. For example, a boy with ADHD might place his dirty hands on a wall his mother has just cleaned, insist on changing the rules while play-ing a game with his siblings or neighbors, ask his teacher to give directions after the directions were given to the class, make unusual noises that disturb and irritate everyone who can hear him, recklessly destroy what his classmates have painstakingly created, carelessly spill his juice or food, trip over things that are not problems for others walking in the same area, or acci-dentally disconnect or turn off the TV in the middle of a program others are watching with great interest. And such a child often seems not to understand how and why he makes himself unpopular or makes other people frustrated and angry. He or she is not really malicious, just socially inept and unaware.

Teachers need to be aware of the developmental aspects of attention and understand what distinguishes the student with ADHD from one who exhibits normal levels of inattention and impulsivity. We frequently see a high level of seemingly undirected activity, short attention span, and impulsive behavior in normally developing young children. As children grow older, however, they gradually become better able to direct their activity into socially constructive channels, to pay attention for longer periods and more efficiently, and to consider alternatives before responding. Thus, only when attention skills, impulse control, and motoric activity level are markedly discrepant from those expected at a particular age is the child's behavior considered to require intervention. Children with ADHD stand out from their age peers, often from an early age. Moreover, the characteristics of ADHD usually aren't subtle; they tend to be "in your face" behaviors that make most of the child's peers and most adults want to exclude the child from their environment or resort to "in your face" reprisals. In fact, it is becoming more and more apparent that ADHD is frequently a component of other disorders (see Nigg & Barkley, 2014).

Relationship to Other Disorders

Disorders of attention and activity are very frequently seen in children and youth with a wide variety of other disorders. Nearly all teachers, parents, and clinicians agree that many youngsters with other types of EBD—conduct disorders, autism, depression, or anxiety, for example—have difficulty controlling their attention to academic and social tasks and are disruptive.

Figure 8.1 shows the central role that not paying attention and disruptive behavior play in a variety of EBD, not just ADHD. When we observe the core symptoms of inattention and disruptive behavior, therefore, we need to look further to know whether these behaviors are part of ADHD. Very similar behaviors often characterize conduct disorder (overt or covert antisocial behavior), affective disorders such as depression and irritability, anxiety disorders

Figure 8.1 Hypothetical Overlap Among Different Types of EBD and ADHD

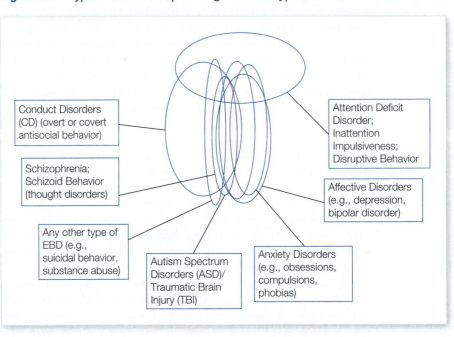

(e.g., obsessions and compulsions), schizophrenia or other thought disorders, and autism spectrum disorders or brain injury.

Not paying attention and being disruptive are key components in lots of diagnostic categories. To complicate the picture further, a given child may have multiple disorders. Inattention may thus be part of the complex, multiple problems of an individual child. Thus, as illustrated in Figure 8.1, many specific types of EBD may be overlapping, and problems of attention and controlling impulsive, disruptive behavior may be a part of nearly any or all of them. That is, virtually any disorder can occur along with virtually any other disorder or a variety of other disorders, and ADHD is a component of most disorders. Figure 8.1 also illustrates the messiness of diagnosis and labeling, the difficulty of disentangling the many types of EBD that an individual may have, and the relationships among these disorders, in addition to their common relationship to attention problems.

In combination with other developmental problems such as conduct disorders or juvenile delinquency, ADHD greatly increases the risk of school failure and severity of symptoms, especially in boys (see Hallahan et al., 2015; Nigg & Barkley, 2014; Rooney, 2017). In fact, hyperactivity, inattention, and impulsiveness appear to play a key role in the development of antisocial behavior, at least for boys.

Nearly all researchers who recognize that disorders of attention and activity exist conclude that although ADHD is a separate, distinctive disorder in its own right, there is great overlap between ADHD and other diagnostic categories (Barkley, 2003; Gershon, 2002; Nigg & Barkley, 2014; Rooney, 2017; Satterfield et al., 2007). Whether ADHD should become a separate category under federal laws and regulations has been a matter for hot debate.

Whether there are unique features of ADHD and, if so, where the boundaries between ADHD and other disorders should be drawn are points of considerable controversy. Most experts believe that a significant percentage (perhaps about 30 percent) of the children with ADHD have not been served under any category of special education and that a high percentage (perhaps 50 percent to 70 percent) of those with LD or EBD also have ADHD. The confusion about the nature of ADHD and its relationship to other disorders is heightened by the fact that the children referred for mental health services often are those with extreme attention problems, with or without hyperactivity. Children and youth with EBD typically have difficulty relating to their peers, often being actively rejected by peers because of their inappropriate social behavior. Although many children with attention deficits do not have problems with peers, some are rejected. If they have extreme attention deficits, their peer problems may be understandable; people (both children and adults) do not usually prefer as companions those who are extremely "flighty." We may conclude the following:

- Many children and youth with ADHD will not be found to have EBD.
- A sizable percentage of those with extreme ADHD will be identified as having EBD.
- Many of those receiving special education because of other types of EBD will have ADHD.
- LD may accompany any combination of disabilities.

We might speculate that the relationships among the populations of individuals having ADHD, EBD, and LD are approximately those shown in Figure 8.2. EBD and LD may occur alone or in combination with each other and with ADHD.

Prevalence

Controversy regarding definition makes the prevalence of a disorder extremely hard to estimate, as we noted in Chapter 2. Most authorities estimate the prevalence of ADHD at 3 percent to 5 percent of the school-age population, making it one of the most common disorders of children and youth and putting it among the most common reasons for referral (Hallahan et al., 2015). Moreover, ADHD is not merely an American phenomenon and is being studied in many nations. Among those referred for ADHD and related disorders, boys far outnumber girls. Gender bias may be a partial explanation for the predominance of boys, but the size of

Figure 8.2 Hypothetical Relationships Among ADHD, EBD, and LD

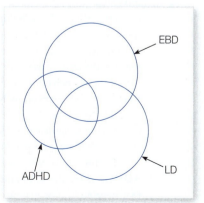

the disparity suggests that there may also be biological gender differences that contribute to the disorder (see Nigg & Barkley, 2014; Gershon, 2002).

CAUSAL FACTORS AND PREVENTION

Historically, brain dysfunction has been the presumed cause of what is now known as ADHD (Hallahan et al., 2015; Rooney, 2017). Today, researchers are investigating biological causes through more sophisticated anatomical and physiological tests involving blood flow to the brain, neurotransmitters, and so on (e.g., electrical potentials in brain tissue, magnetic resonance imaging). As yet, no reliable evidence shows precisely what neurological problem is the basis of ADHD, although many researchers suspect an underlying biological cause for most cases (Nigg & Barkley, 2014).

Various food substances (e.g., dyes, sugars, preservatives), environmental toxins (e.g., lead), and allergens have been suggested as causes of hyperactivity and related disorders. None of these has been demonstrated to be a cause of many or most cases of ADHD, although evidence does suggest that such factors may be a cause in a small number of cases. Claims that foods, toxins, or allergies are *frequent* causes are not substantiated by credible research.

Genetic factors appear to increase risk for ADHD, although the genetics of the disorder are very poorly understood. We do know that ADHD is more common among the biological relatives of children who have the disorder than in the general population, suggesting that ADHD is genetically organized in some way. It is plausible that genetic factors may give some individuals a predisposition toward attention problems and impulse control and that it leads to ADHD in combination with other biological or psychological factors (see Rooney, 2017).

A difficult temperament—an inborn behavioral style characterized by irritability, high activity level, short attention span, distractibility, and so on—has been suggested as a possible starting point for ADHD. Children with ADHD are often identifiable as toddlers or preschoolers (Barkley, 2003). Temperamentally, they fit the description of the "difficult child." They are children who in preschool and early elementary grades show a variety of problems with attention, impulse control, noncompliance, and aggression. Yet temperament alone does not explain all the problems of these youngsters. In short, evidence does not clearly and consistently link any particular biological factor to ADHD. It is plausible, however, that biological factors are involved in most cases, but precisely what they are and how they operate remain unknown.

Hypothesized psychological causes of ADHD range from psychoanalytic explanations to those involving social learning theory. For instance, numerous studies of modeling and imitation illustrate how children could acquire deviant behavior patterns through observation of frenetically active parents or siblings. The literature is replete with examples of how children's inappropriate behavior can be manipulated by social attention, suggesting that parents and teachers could inadvertently teach youngsters to behave in the manner that characterizes ADHD. Nevertheless, research has not demonstrated that ADHD is primarily a matter of undesirable social learning, and therefore it is inappropriate for us to lay responsibility for the creation of ADHD on parents or teachers.

To summarize what we know about causes, we do not know exactly why children have ADHD. There doesn't appear to be a single cause. In the vast majority of cases, we suspect that neurological or genetic factors launch the child toward ADHD and that these factors, in combination with other influences in the child's physical and social environment, produce the inattentive or hyperactive behavior (Nigg & Barkley, 2014).

We know more about how to control the problems related to this disorder once it has appeared than we know about its origins, so prevention is largely a matter of intervening early in the families and classrooms of youngsters who are difficult to manage. Effective primary prevention—keeping ADHD from emerging during the child's development—would require knowledge of neurology and genetics that we don't have now, in addition to training in child care and management that would eliminate possible environmental causes. Secondary prevention—reduction and management of problems that have emerged—is the most feasible approach.

Much of the responsibility for secondary prevention falls on educators, who must manage the child's behavior in school and provide instructional programs that will foster academic success and social adjustment. ADHD appears to be a persistent set of problems that follows children into adolescence and adulthood. It interferes with academic achievement and peer relations. Lack of achievement, feelings of failure, social isolation or rejection, and low motivation make for high rates of socially inappropriate behavior. The student with ADHD becomes trapped in a self-perpetuating pattern of negative self-perceptions, inappropriate behavior, and negative interactions with others. Prevention of later and more serious difficulties depends on breaking this cycle.

ASSESSMENT

Assessment of ADHD usually involves a medical examination, a clinical interview by a psychologist or psychiatrist, and parent and teacher ratings of behavior (Nigg & Barkley, 2014; Rooney, 2017). The clinical assessment of ADHD by a psychologist or psychiatrist and the educational assessment of ADHD by teachers or other school personnel may differ considerably. Clinicians will likely be interested primarily in determining whether the child meets certain diagnostic criteria; teachers will be more interested in devising a plan for management of classroom behavior and instruction. Parents will want to know why their child behaves as he or she does and how they should respond.

Although the characteristics of ADHD may be noticed by parents or others before the child enters school, it is often not until the child is confronted by the demands of the classroom that someone—usually a teacher—becomes aware of the seriousness of the child's problems. In the context of school, ADHD often becomes intolerable, and the child's behavior is perceived as provoking a crisis. Children with ADHD often exhibit social behavior about which teachers are understandably upset. Teachers' concerns about their students' academic performance apparently most often lead them to refer students for special education. However, many pupils with ADHD present both behavioral and academic concerns.

The primary means of assessment of ADHD useful in school settings are teacher and peer rating scales, direct observation, and interviews. A wide variety of rating scales have been used; some are specific to ADHD, whereas others are the broader, more inclusive scales. The value of any of these rating scales is that they allow someone to organize and quantify teachers' and peers' perceptions of the student's academic and social behavior. These perceptions are important, but they may not correspond well to direct observation of the student's behavior. One of the problems in assessing ADHD is determining whether the youngster shows problems related to attention deficits, aggression, or both. ADHD may be distinguished by disrupting the classroom, exhibiting problems in daily academic performance, being unprepared for class, not having required materials, and so on. These problems may or may not be accompanied by aggressive behavior or other indications of EBD. The distinction may be important in judging the seriousness of the student's problems and designing an intervention plan.

Direct observation of the youngster's behavior in various school settings—classroom, playground, lunchroom, hallways—and careful daily records (as opposed to teacher ratings) of academic performance are critical aspects of assessment. These can pinpoint the behavioral aspects of the problem of ADHD and serve as an objective measure of the effectiveness of interventions. Both objective records of behavior and performance and subjective judgments regarding the nature and acceptability of the student's behavior and performance are important in managing ADHD.

INTERVENTION AND EDUCATION

In most cases, ADHD involves a cluster of related behavioral characteristics, including problems in regulating attention, motivation, hyperactivity, and socially inappropriate responses. Consequently, many different intervention techniques have been tried in both home and classroom settings. The two most common and successful approaches have been medication and training parents and teachers how to manage the student's behavior (psychosocial interventions). The vast majority of cases require multiple interventions involving both parents and teachers (Barkley, 2003,; Hallahan et al., 2015; Kazdin, 2008; Rooney, 2017).

Medication

No method of dealing with ADHD has been so controversial as medication (Hallahan et al., 2015; Rooney 2017). The medications usually given are psychostimulants, such as Ritalin, Dexedrine, Cylert, or Adderall, or a nonstimulant drug called Strattera. Opponents of medication have described the drugs' possible negative side effects, unknown long-term effects on growth and health, possible negative effects on perceptions of personal responsibility and self-control, and possibility of encouraging drug abuse. The statements of some of the opponents of medication have been unfounded and hysterical; others have been thoughtful and cautious, based on reliable evidence that stimulant drugs are not a panacea and do, like all medications, carry risks as well as benefits. You might consider the cases of John (for Chapter 1) and Danny (for Chapter 8) in the accompanying case book and the thoughts of their mothers about the management of ADHD.

Research clearly indicates that the right dosage of the right drug results in remarkable improvement in behavior and facilitates learning (makes the student more teachable) in about 90 percent of youngsters with ADHD (Hallahan et al., 2015; Rooney, 2017). It is important to recognize that a higher-than-optimal dosage may impair learning rather than facilitate it, that a medication may not have effects on all the youngster's problem behaviors (e.g., it may improve hyperactivity but have little or no effect on aggression), and that the effects of medication may be different in different settings (e.g., more improvement in school than at home). Children with other disorders in addition to ADHD, such as anxiety or depression, may not respond well to stimulant drugs.

Research clearly points to medication as the single most effective treatment of ADHD (see Forness, Freeman, & Papparella, 2006). However, there is absolutely no reason to choose between medication and other interventions. As is the case with virtually all EBD, both medication and other treatments together can be used to best advantage. A combination of medication and behavior management provides even better outcomes for children with ADHD than medication alone (Gully et al., 2003). In fact, stimulant drugs may improve the effects of good behavior management strategies, and good behavior management may improve the effects of medication.

When reasonable precautions are taken in their use and the dosage and effects are carefully monitored, stimulant drugs are a safe and sane way of augmenting parents' and teachers' other strategies for managing ADHD (Hallahan et al., 2015), but good psychopharmacology demands careful monitoring of the effects of medication. Teachers should offer parents and physicians their observations about the effects (or noneffects) and side effects of medications on the behavior and learning of a medicated student who is in their class (Mattison, 2014).

Psychosocial Training Involving Parents and Teachers

Medication alone is not the most effective means of bringing the behavior of children with ADHD under control. Parents typically have serious difficulty managing these children at home, and teachers often have difficulty managing these children in school. Consequently, systematic training of parents and teachers in behavior management skills is an approach frequently used by psychologists who serve children with ADHD and their families (Alberto & Troutman, 2012; Barkley, 2003; Kazdin, 2008). The objective of this training is not to cure or eliminate ADHD but to help parents and teachers learn how to manage children's behavior more effectively. The training is organized around principles of behavioral psychology and involves teaching parents and teachers to interact more positively with their children during ordinary activities, avoiding the coercive interactions that are hallmarks of families with aggressive and hyperactive children and adolescents. The procedures parents and teachers are taught to use may include a token reinforcement system for encouraging appropriate behavior and response cost (withdrawing some part of an earned reward) or time-out (brief social isolation or temporary suspension of the opportunity to earn reinforcers) for misbehavior.

Ultimately, parents may be taught techniques for managing behavior in public places and generalizing the training to new problems and settings. This type of training is not possible with all parents, nor is it always successful when parents are receptive to it. However, it has been used successfully with many parents. The psychologist working with parents will typically involve teachers as well in a behavior management plan because little change is likely in school unless similar behavior management procedures are used in the classroom. Parents may also need suggestions for how to manage everyday events for families, such as an adolescent learning to drive.

The problems of students with ADHD are usually most evident in the classroom, where compliance and focused attention to task are essential for success. Teachers should be helped to understand the likely functions of

Video Example from YouTube

ENHANCEDetext
Video Connections 8.2
Although this recent news story erroneously refers to well-established behavioral procedures like praise as a "new" approach, it provides an excellent example of the benefits of combining medical and behavioral interventions for ADHD. (https://www.youtube.com/watch?v=02b_ftlesoA)

ADHD and related behavioral problems in the classroom, which they may discover through careful behavioral assessment.

Response to Intervention and Tiered Education

Response to intervention (RTI or RtI) and other education involving tiers (sometimes called MTSS for multi-tiered system of supports) are most often mentioned with reference to LD. Similarly, a framework of tiers is called positive behavior interventions and support (PBIS). However, these approaches are an issue with all types of troubling behavior (Kauffman & Brigham, 2009; Kauffman et al., 2012). Certainly, RtI, MTSS, and PBIS or other tiered frameworks are good ideas in many ways, but their success with students having ADHD or any type of EBD depends on the skill with which their components are implemented. The components of RtI and other tiered education are well known, but they often have been implemented poorly, if at all, when schools say they are using them (Johns et al., 2016).

Behavioral interventions and cognitive strategy training are the two most widely recommended approaches to managing the problems of ADHD, and both are often components of tiered education. Teachers must be trained in how to use these approaches if they are to have a reasonable chance of success; they are not intuitive methods or ones that every teacher learns.

Behavioral Intervention

A basic behavioral principle is that behavior is affected by its antecedents and consequences (see Alberto & Troutman, 2012; Kauffman, Pullen et al., 2011; Landrum, 2017; Landrum & Kauffman, 2006). Behavioral intervention is not likely to be successful unless the person who is trying to use it both understands the principles that make it work and is attuned to the student's individual characteristics and preferences. It is a powerful tool—but a good one only in the hands of a perceptive and sensitive teacher. Adept use of behavioral interventions results in warm, caring relationships between students and teachers (Kauffman, Pullen et al., 2011; Kerr & Nelson, 2010; Landrum, 2017; Walker, Ramsey, & Gresham, 2004).

Behavioral intervention means making certain that rewarding consequences follow desirable behavior and that either no consequences or punishing consequences follow undesirable behavior. As is true with parents, rearranging consequences to support desirable behavior and not support undesirable behavior may be as simple as shifting attention from inappropriate to appropriate behavior. More powerful consequences such as *token reinforcement, response cost*, and *time-out* may be needed as well.

In many cases, it is helpful to make the contingencies of reinforcement and punishment more explicit by writing a *contingency contract*. In addition to the procedures used in the classroom, the parents may be involved in a home–school behavior modification program in which behavior at school earns the pupil rewards provided by the parents at home (see Hallahan et al., 2005). The emphasis must be on positive consequences for appropriate behavior, but prudent negative consequences for misbehavior may be necessary.

Other behavioral intervention procedures involve altering classroom conditions or instruction to make them more attractive to students. These procedures do not in any way make consequences unimportant. They are simply an additional means of putting behavior principles to work in helping students with ADHD behave more appropriately and learn more.

Figure 8.3   Graph Showing a Functional Relationship Between Behavior and Intervention

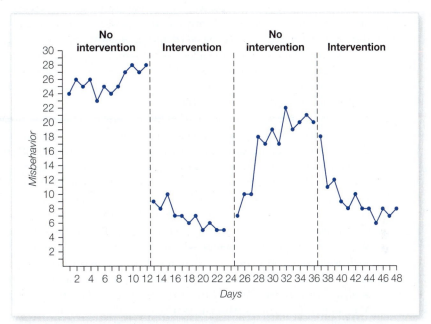

It is important to understand what maintains undesirable behavior—attention from others versus escape from effortful tasks, for example. If undesirable behavior is maintained by escape from effortful tasks, then giving a student a choice of assignments may be helpful. However, if the undesirable behavior is maintained by attention from others, then giving the student choices may have no effect at all (see Kauffman, Pullen et al., 2011).

Behavioral interventions are not foolproof for controlling problems of ADHD or any other EBD, but research has demonstrated that noisy, destructive, disruptive, and inattentive behavior can usually be changed for the better by controlling the contingencies of reinforcement. Like medication or any other intervention, behavioral interventions can be abused and misused. Even when used skillfully, they can have unanticipated or undesirable outcomes, and they will not necessarily make a student with ADHD appear normal. Nonetheless, behavioral interventions may be the best tool available to teachers and parents. Figure 8.3 shows the kind of change in undesirable behavior that has been demonstrated in many studies—that is, a functional relationship between an intervention and behavior. The intervention might be giving a student a choice of what to do, or it might be teacher attention to desirable rather than undesirable behavior. The point is that many studies of behavioral intervention have demonstrated that behavior can often be improved substantially by making the consequence of desired behavior more positive.

Cognitive Strategy Training

The interventions falling under the general rubric of cognitive training or cognitive strategy training include self-instruction, self-monitoring, self-reinforcement, and cognitive–interpersonal problem solving (see Reid, Trout, & Schartz, 2005). All have the goal of helping individuals become more aware of their responses to academic tasks and social problems and actively engage in the control of their own responses. We are aware that cognitive strategy training in some academic areas, such as mathematics, may not be supported by the empirical evidence. Nevertheless, there is strong evidence supporting other types of cognitive strategy training.

We describe just three strategies—**mnemonics**, self-instruction, and self-monitoring—because they are the most widely used in classroom settings. However, other strategies that involve students cognitively and actively in their self-management, such as goal setting, are also valuable in working with ADHD.

Mnemonic strategies are ways of helping students remember things. These methods include teaching students with memory problems to use first-letter strategies, key words, and peg words. For example, a teacher might use the acronym HOMES to help a student remember the names of the five Great Lakes of North America by associating the acronym with the first letters of the lakes: Huron, Ontario, Michigan, Erie, and Superior. Using key words involves choosing a picture and a phonetically similar word to retrieve a definition. For example, a teacher might help a student picture a bear acting as a lawyer to remember the meaning of the word barrister. Peg words use rhyming. For example, Washington might be remembered by thinking of (or picturing) a gun being washed, with wash and gun being the rhyming elements used to remember the first president of the United States. Mnemonic strategies have been found to be effective in helping students with many types of disability remember important information (see Scruggs, Mastropieri, Brigham, & Milman, 2017).

Self-instruction involves teaching students to talk to themselves about what they are doing and what they should do. Teaching students to label stimuli and to rehearse the instructions or tasks they have been given appears to have merit as an instructional strategy in many cases. For example, a student may be told to verbalize each arithmetic problem or its operation sign while working a problem, to say each letter of a word aloud while writing it, or to rehearse a reading passage before reading it aloud to the teacher.

Typically, self-instruction training requires a series of steps in which verbal control of behavior is first modeled by an adult, then imitated by the student, and finally used independently by the student. On a given task or in a given social situation, the adult first performs the task or response while verbalizing thoughts about the task requirements or social circumstance. The adult may talk about relevant stimuli or cues, planning a response, performing as expected, coping with feelings, and evaluating performance. Then the adult and student might run through the task or response to the social situation together, with the student shadowing the adult's verbal and nonverbal behavior. Eventually, the student tries it alone while verbalizing aloud and finally with subvocal self-instruction. Teaching students to use their own language to regulate behavior has been a successful approach with some impulsive children and youth in academic or social situations. Telling impulsive students to slow down and be careful before responding may not work, yet if these same students can be taught to tell themselves in some way to stop and think before they respond, they might improve their behavior considerably.

Self-monitoring has been widely used for helping students who have difficulty staying on task in the classroom, particularly during independent seat-work time. A tape recorder, phone, or other electronic device is used to produce tones (prerecorded to sound at random intervals ranging from ten to ninety seconds, with an average interval of about forty-five seconds) that

Figure 8.4   Example of a Self-Monitoring Form

Was I Paying Attention?					
	Yes	No		Yes	No
1			11		
2			12		
3			13		
4			14		
5			15		
6			16		
7			17		
8			18		
9			19		
10			20		

cue the student to ask, "Was I … [usually paying attention]?" and self-record the response on a form. This simple procedure has been found effective in increasing the on-task behavior of many students, ranging from children as young as five years to adolescents who have ADHD and a variety of other disorders. Variations on the procedure have been used to improve academic productivity, accuracy of work, and social behavior.

Figure 8.4 shows an example of a simple recording sheet that might be used with a student who is self-monitoring his or her attention to a task (or to the teacher) during a lesson. Figure 8.5 shows examples of broader self-monitoring activities that might be used to help students remember various academic-related skills that are necessary if they are to be successful in typical classroom instruction. Self-monitoring can be adapted to a variety of circumstances and types of behavior. For example, researchers have used a combination of token reinforcement, explicit feedback to students about rule following, matching self-evaluation with teacher evaluation of behavior, and self-evaluation alone to lower the disruptive behavior of several students with ADHD and related problems. The students can be gradually moved from more extrinsic, teacher-determined rewards to self-management. Research on self-monitoring has led to the following general conclusions:

1. Self-monitoring procedures are simple and straightforward, but they cannot be implemented without preparing the students. Brief training is necessary, in which the teacher talks with the student about the nature of off-task and appropriate behavior, explains the procedure, role-plays the procedure, and has the student practice.

2. Self-monitoring of on-task behavior increases time on task in most cases.

Figure 8.5   Example of a Recording Sheet for Broader Self-Monitoring Activities

Daily Assignment Recording Sheet			
Name:	**Class:**	**Date:**	
Did I remember to:		yes	no
1. Bring all materials to class (notebook, textbook, pen or pencil)			
2. Complete my homework and place it in the homework folder			
3. Copy down today's homework assignment in my planner			
4. Raise my hand before asking a question or giving an answer			
5. Listen quietly while others were speaking			

3. Self-monitoring of on-task behavior also typically increases academic productivity.

4. Improvement in on-task behavior and performance usually lasts for several months after the procedure is discontinued.

5. The beneficial effects of self-monitoring are usually achieved without the use of backup reinforcers; extrinsic rewards, such as tokens or treats for improved behavior, are seldom necessary.

6. The recorded tones (cues) prompting self-monitoring are a necessary part of the initial training procedure and implementation, although they can usually be discontinued after a period of successful self-monitoring.

7. Students' self-recording—marking answers to their self-questioning—is a necessary element of initial training and implementation but can be discontinued after a period of successful self-monitoring.

8. Accuracy in self-monitoring is not critically important; some students will be in close agreement with the teacher's assessment of their on-task behavior, but others will not be.

9. The cueing tones and other aspects of the procedure are usually minimally disruptive to other students in the class.

Notwithstanding enthusiasm for cognitive strategies and the many reports of their success in dealing with a wide variety of problems, they have not produced the generalized changes in behavior and cognition in ADHD that researchers and others had hoped for. Cognitive training in all its various forms clearly is not a panacea for the problems presented by disorders of attention and activity. Moreover, cognitive training is not as simple as it might first appear. The teacher who wishes to use any of the techniques effectively must understand their theoretical basis and carefully construct procedures to fit the individual case (Hallahan et al., 2005).

A PERSPECTIVE ON INTERVENTION

Nearly every type of intervention that has been used with any kind of troublesome behavior has been tried with ADHD. Perhaps that in itself is a commentary on the seriousness with which adults approach the problem. Psychotherapy, providing an optimal level of sensory stimulation, biofeedback, relaxation training, dietary control—you name it, and it has probably been experimented with or even touted as a breakthrough, a revolutionary treatment, or an outright cure.

The lure of the idea that we should be able to find a way to "fix" this common and perplexing malady of children and youth is strong, perhaps irresistible. Over the past several decades, various intervention strategies have been devised by leading scholars and researchers, investigated with initial excitement, adopted widely, and endorsed enthusiastically by many as a solution, if not the cure, for the problems we now call ADHD. Each strategy eventually has been found not to be the fix. This initial overenthusiasm for an intervention—one said to be so powerful that the developmental disorder disappears—and the eventual disappointment it leads to has been the history of our approach to every developmental disability, including intellectual disability, autism, cerebral palsy, and other developmental disorders. Leading researchers now suggest that ADHD is, indeed, a developmental disability for which we have no cure, and we are not likely to find one soon (Hallahan et al., 2005).

Recognition of the fact that we have no cure for ADHD should not deter us from seeking and implementing the most effective interventions possible. We do have interventions and approaches to education that will help us reach important goals. We know that medication can be extremely helpful, especially in combination with psychological interventions. Medication can make students more teachable, but alone—without good behavior management—it is certainly not going to have maximum effect. For teachers, the most important tools, whether the child is taking medication or not, are 1) *a highly structured classroom* in which the student's attention is clearly and consistently focused, 2) *behavioral interventions* that are consistently and explicitly implemented, and 3) *self-management* that is taught systematically. See Box 8.1 for an example of a simple, structured intervention that can help focus students' attention and improve their learning.

Given our present level of understanding, we should not have the unrealistic expectation that we can eliminate the disability known as ADHD, but our goal should be managing it as effectively as possible while recognizing that it is a chronic, disabling condition.

Box 8.1

Teaching Social Skills to Students with ADHD

What social skill problems in students with ADHD will be most important to address?

We've described in detail that the child with ADHD will be a tremendous challenge to teachers in any classroom. These students are described as busy-bodies, always in motion, or simply having a "high motor." This is often coupled with distractibility, impulsivity, and inattention, and thus students with ADHD, particularly those with more severe forms, will

(continued)

Box 8.1   *(continued)*

bring few academic and social survival skills to the classroom (e.g., sitting still or staying in their place, raising hand before being called on, taking turns in either academic or social contexts, listening to or focusing on the teacher or other speaker when required to do so). Conversely, they will often bring many of the social behaviors that teachers and peers find undesirable or intolerable (constant talking or interruption, frequently being out of place, or "poking their noses in other people's business").

What are appropriate targets for intervention?

Any of the behaviors listed above could be targets for individually designed interventions. But we often think of these types of behaviors as falling under the larger umbrella of "self-control." Given the nature of these behaviors, it's quite understandable that *self-control* is the term teachers often use to describe the most important or desirable characteristic they say students need in order to succeed in their classroom. Moreover, any of these behaviors, many of which occur in combination, will almost certainly have a negative—sometimes devastating—impact on students' academic performance. Thus, when we think of interventions, it may be important to think broadly about arrangements that will limit students' displays of these distractible, off-task behaviors, and get them more engaged in appropriate academic work.

What types of intervention show promise?

We've already mentioned a number of behavioral, cognitive-behavioral, or psychosocial intervention approaches, including reinforcement, response cost, and self-management systems. But a promising approach that has combined elements of structure, routine, consistency, frequent positive consequences, and corrective feedback, all with an academic focus, is classwide peer tutoring.

An example—classwide peer tutoring

Classwide peer tutoring (CWPT) is a simple intervention that has shown promise in improving the behavior and academic performances of students with ADHD (and students with other disabilities, as well as students without disabilities). Briefly, teachers establish tutoring pairs, and each pair is assigned to one of two teams that are competing for a group reward. The teacher provides students with explicit training up front on how to tutor. CWPT generally involves the tutor asking the tutee a question (typically to spell a spelling word or define or identify a vocabulary word's meaning); providing praise for each correct response or immediate corrective feedback for each incorrect response (providing the correct answer and having the student repeat or practice the correct response); and recording points. The pair earns two points for each initial answer that is correct, and one point for each correction successfully completed following an error. Points are publicly posted, and the winning team each week (teams are reformed each week) receives a social reward. Peer tutoring is typically implemented four days a week (with one day a week reserved for pre- and/or post-testing what has been or will be learned), and follows a very structured schedule. The teacher sets a timer for each part of the tutoring session, with a signal after ten minutes for the tutoring pair to switch roles. Numerous studies of CWPT have demonstrated good effects on students' academic performances, as well as their task-related social behavior. The structure, routine, academic engagement focus, and positive consequences associated with CWPT all fit well with the learning and behavioral characteristics of students with ADHD.

Where to find more information about classwide peer tutoring:

Bowman-Perrott, L. (2009). Classwide peer tutoring: An effective strategy for students with emotional and behavioral disorders. *Intervention in School and Clinic, 44*(5), 259–267.

Maheady, L., & Gard, J. (2010). Classwide peer tutoring: Practice, theory, research, and personal narrative. *Intervention in School and Clinic, 46*(2), 71–78.

Maheady, L., Harper, G., & Mallette, B. (2003). Class-wide peer tutoring. *Current Practice Alerts, 8*, 1–4. Retrieved from http://TeachingLD.org/alerts

SUMMARY

Attention deficit–hyperactivity disorder is now the most widely-used term for disorders of attention and activity. There is still considerable controversy and confusion regarding terminology and definition. However, most definitions suggest that ADHD is a developmental disorder of attention and activity level that is evident before the age of seven or eight, persists throughout the life span, involves both academic and social problems, and is frequently accompanied by or symptomatic of other disorders. The core problems of concern are regulation of attention, cognition, motivation, and social behavior. ADHD, LD, and EBD are overlapping, interrelated categories. About 3 percent to 5 percent of the school-aged population is diagnosed with ADHD, with boys greatly outnumbering girls.

Brain injury or dysfunction has long been suspected as a cause of ADHD. Many other biological causes, including food substances, environmental toxins, genetic factors, and temperament, have been researched. Various psychological causes have also been suggested, but as yet research does not clearly and reliably point to any specific biological or environmental cause. Leading researchers suggest that poorly understood neurological factors instigate the problem, which is then exacerbated by a variety of factors in the physical and social environment. Prevention of ADHD and related disorders consists primarily of managing problems once they are evident.

Assessment for teaching and assessment for clinical treatment may differ considerably. School personnel and parents are interested primarily in assessment that helps them design an intervention program. Teacher and peer rating scales and direct observation of troublesome behavior in various school settings are most useful to educators.

The most widely-used and successful approaches to intervention and education with ADHD and related disorders are medication, parent training, and teacher training. Medication is very controversial, but research clearly indicates its value when it is properly managed, and alternative approaches have not been as successful as medication or medication in combination with behavioral interventions. Medication cannot teach skills or resolve all problems, but it can make the youngster more teachable. Parent or teacher training typically involves instruction in behavior management skills. Teacher training usually involves implementing behavioral interventions (e.g., token reinforcement, response cost, contingency contracts) or cognitive training strategies (e.g., self-instruction or self-monitoring). It may be important to articulate classroom behavior modification with a home-school program involving contingencies managed by parents.

Nearly every known type of intervention has been suggested and attempted with ADHD and related disorders. None has provided a cure. The goal of intervention should be to manage the youngster's problems as successfully as possible, realizing that a cure is not available and that coping strategies for parents and teachers are important for dealing with this chronic, disabling condition.

✔ ENHANCEDetext **END-OF-CHAPTER 8 QUIZ**

Click on the checkmark icon to access an end-of-chapter quiz. Answer the questions to gauge your understanding of chapter concepts and better prepare you for case discussions.

PERSONAL REFLECTIONS

Attention and Activity Disorders

Tina Radford, M.A.T., is currently Team Leader of the Exceptional Child Education Department at Fern Creek Elementary School in Louisville, KY, where she teaches students with Emotional and Behavior Disabilities (EBD). She has taught students with a range of emotional, behavioral, autism spectrum, and mild mental disabilities, including students with EBD, for sixteen years at the elementary (K–5) level.

Think of a student you have worked with who exhibited an attention or activity disorder (i.e., ADHD). How did these concerns come to your attention (what did the student's behavior and academic performance look like)?

Cal is currently a senior in high school, but he first came to my attention as a kindergarten student who was in a regular education classroom for about sixteen to eighteen weeks before being placed in my self-contained EBD classroom. Cal struggled with attending to tasks, sitting still, focusing, listening, completing assignments, remaining in his assigned area, transitioning, and following directions. Cal had poor peer relationships and difficulty making friends. His behavior was deemed out-of-control, obstinate, oppositional, defiant, and stubborn. He would hit, spit, throw objects, and use profanity to gain control of a situation. His teacher at the time was at her wits end and couldn't get anything out of him. Cal would refuse to do anything for her. She just couldn't motivate Cal to work or get a handle on his misbehavior. He liked to be in control and had a hard time with limits. After several interventions had been tried, unsuccessfully, a meeting was held and it was decided that Cal should be placed in my self-contained classroom. I saw this move as a challenge that I welcomed. Cal was young, and at this age I believed he could be taught replacement behaviors for some of the more challenging behaviors he used to control situations, as well as techniques he could use to calm himself. He needed positive ways to vent and ways to make friends.

Cal was extremely smart for a five-year-old. He knew all 220 Dolch sight words, and was reading on a third-grade level. In fact, Cal would sometimes shut down over his work because he felt it was too easy. This lack of compliance seriously impacted his daily performance and grades; although he was above average in all academic areas, he was not passing because of his inability to complete tasks/assignments. After reviewing all the data we had on Cal, assessing him myself, conferencing with his dad, and making necessary accommodations and modifications to his behavior plan, one conclusion for me was that Cal needed to be challenged. I also allowed him movement breaks and offered him various choices in his work. At first, Cal was reluctant, but he soon learned that I wanted nothing more for him but success, and that I was willing to make modifications necessary for him to be successful. He was offered choices on assignments. I completed a survey with him on things he liked to do and things that interested him (e.g., coloring sheets, toys, snacks, treats). Cal was given advanced warnings about changes to routine or schedule. He was given clearly stated consequences, rewards, and incentives for the various behavioral choices he might make. I made Cal a leader within the classroom, allowing him to tutor, pass out papers, and even to read to the class.

How did this student's attentional and behavioral concerns impact his or her educational progress and overall school success?

Cal's attentional and behavioral concerns could have seriously impacted his educational progress and school success if necessary adjustments weren't made. In fact, Cal's kindergarten year was somewhat unsuccessful. His noncompliant and defiant behavior made him one of our most challenging students to teach. He would frequently interrupt instruction, he did poorly academically, and he showed little interest or motivation to learn. It wasn't until his first grade year that a difference could be seen academically and behaviorally. While there were no magical strategies or cures for his misbehavior, I achieved the best outcome by remaining calm, following through consistently with intervention strategies, and not arguing or engaging in power struggles. Also, I knew I must form a positive relationship with him, one built on mutual trust and respect. I embraced and fostered high expectations and belief in him. Cal knew I believed in him and wanted nothing but the best in him all the time. It was also important to engage Cal in high interest activities. This helped keep Cal on task and interested in what he was learning. I also made lessons more appealing and more real world to allow him to see the importance of what was being taught. Cal was able to adjust to these expectations and routines with our support, and he was included in regular education settings for half the day beginning in fourth grade. His progress continued, and when Cal entered middle school, he was totally exited from special education services for EBD.

What did you or other teachers or staff find most successful in working with this student?

Working with Cal was highly rewarding. He grew each year I had him in class, and in fact flourished over time. Not only did Cal learn from me, but I learned from him as well. Cal loved learning and was very artistic. Every day was a learning adventure. He needed and wanted someone to care about him. He needed behavioral supports and strategies to assist him with his inability to attend to task but also needed some freedom to move around the classroom. He also needed to learn to express himself properly. Over time, he learned all these things and more. Cal was capable of performing all academic assignments at very high levels. He was working well above grade level in every subject. As Cal acquired more skills and behavioral self-control, he became even more motivated to succeed, and by the time he reached high school, he clearly desired to show everyone just how much he had grown and that he was a success.

In your opinion, what is the long-term prognosis for this student? What will be the greatest concerns for this student in the future?

Although ADHD is generally a life-long disability, most individuals become better equipped to deal with it as they get older, and this was clearly the case with Cal. The strategies we taught him and the social skills lessons we delivered certainly helped him along this pathway. In my opinion, Cal has a bright future! Currently, he is a senior and ready to graduate with honors. He is working two jobs and often performs with a youth performing arts group playing his violin. I have kept in touch with Cal and continue to offer any support he may need or just a listening ear or pat on the back. He continues to flourish. Cal has developed many tools and knows what he needs to do to be successful in terms of his ADHD and issues with impulse control. My only concern for him is outside influences from peers. Peer pressure is very difficult for all students, but it is especially difficult for students with disabilities like ADHD. However, given that Cal has always been headstrong, I believe he will only do what he chooses to do, and more often than not will continue to make good choices.

Questions for Further Reflection

1. How would you explain to parents the difference between a child being very active or inattentive, and a child having ADHD?

2. At what point should a child who displays inattention, impulsivity, or a high level of activity be referred to evaluation for possible EBD?

3. What evidence would you need before arguing with a school psychologist or other school personnel or parents that a particular student's ADHD (already identified as such) was not merely ADHD but an indication of other problems or disorders as well?

9 CONDUCT DISORDER

OVERT AGGRESSION AND COVERT ANTISOCIAL BEHAVIOR

Mandy Godhehear/123RF

After reading this chapter, you should be able to:

9.1 Identify what distinguishes aggressive anti-social behavior from the behavior problems associated with typical development.

9.2 Describe the types of behavior that apply to both overt and covert antisocial conduct, and what is different between the two.

9.3 Explain why social factors must be taken into account when defining and dealing with aggression.

9.4 Define the environmental conditions most closely associated with a high risk for conduct disorder.

9.5 Discuss strategies for assessing antisocial behavior, including the particular difficulties in assessing covert antisocial behavior.

9.6 Describe the types of prevention programs that are particularly relevant for children with covert antisocial behavior.

9.7 List and describe the phases of the acting out behavior cycle, and where in the cycle interventions are most effectively used.

DEFINITION, PREVALENCE, AND CLASSIFICATION

Definition

All normally developing children and adolescents exhibit some form of antisocial behavior at some point. It is just a part of growing up. They might throw a temper tantrum, get in a fight with siblings or peers, cheat, lie, be physically cruel to animals or other people, refuse to obey their parents, or destroy their own or others' possessions. Normally, as they grow up, children learn through socialization by their parents and other adults and children that such behavior is not acceptable. Some children learn very quickly and may do these things only once or twice. Normally developing youngsters don't perform antisocial acts in *most* social contexts, nor do they do so with such persistence and frequency in any context that they become social outcasts among their peers or excessively problematic to their parents and teachers.

The children we're talking about in this chapter engage in these antisocial behaviors repeatedly, after the age at which most children conform to social norms, and usually in multiple contexts (home, school, community). A child or youth who is diagnosed with **conduct disorder** (CD) exhibits a persistent pattern of antisocial behavior that significantly impairs everyday functioning at home or school or leads others to conclude that the youngster is unmanageable. Many of these children become bullies. Their antisocial behavior may include such things as theft, vandalism, fire setting, lying, truancy, and running away from home. The common element in all behavior of this type is that the child violates major social norms. Conduct disorder means a pattern of antisocial behavior that impairs everyday functioning at home or school and leads many people to see the child or adolescent as unmanageable.

Two broad forms of conduct disorder are often distinguished, one we see and one we typically don't. The form we see is referred to as *overt aggression*, typically characterized by acting out toward others verbally or physically. Parents, teachers, and peers not only see these behaviors but are often the targets. The form that isn't often seen (though its effects are seen after the fact) is referred to as *covert antisocial behavior*, which is characterized by more secretive antisocial acts such as vandalism or fire setting. As we discuss later, if there are witnesses to covert antisocial behavior, these are likely to be equally deviant peers engaged in the same behaviors, out of sight of parents, teachers, and authority figures. In fact, another set of terms used to distinguish these two types is *undersocialized conduct disorder* (for overt aggression) and *socialized conduct disorder* (for the covert form). We have been aware of different forms of conduct disorder for many decades, but reliable empirical evidence of the different forms emerged primarily from large-scale studies in the 1980s. These studies were based on statistical probabilities. The probabilities also indicated that some children are "versatile," showing both overt and covert forms. CD is also closely related to **oppositional-defiant disorder** (ODD)—very negative, hostile, defiant behavior that persists beyond the developmental age at which most children stop acting that way. Some CD begins in childhood, and some begins in adolescence (see Kimonis, Frick, & McMahon, 2014).

Youngsters who are versatile generally have more severe problems, and their prognosis is usually worse than for those who engage in only one type of antisocial behavior. Even versatility itself is a matter of degree, however; some youngsters are especially versatile, others more specific in their antisocial conduct.

Video Example from YouTube

ENHANCEDetext
Video Connections 9.1
The speaker in this brief video provides a quick overview of signs of conduct disorder. (https://www.youtube.com/watch?v=g58qUHEq6fU)

Conduct disorder of both types is often difficult to distinguish from other disorders, especially juvenile delinquency. In fact, the socialized (covert) form typically involves delinquent activities, often with bad companions or gangs and often involving alcohol or other drug use. *Delinquency* is a legal term, however, and connotes behavior that is the topic of Chapter 13.

As should be obvious, assessment and management of overt and covert forms of antisocial behavior present different challenges to educators. Whereas overt antisocial behavior is easy to see—in fact, it's hard to miss—covert antisocial behavior is by definition difficult to observe and assess. Children and youth with covert antisocial behavior aren't trustworthy; they're good at manipulating others (including both peers and adults) and at hiding their behavior from authority figures. In fact, overt and covert antisocial behavior may represent different ends of a single behavioral dimension, with *noncompliance*—sassy, negative, persistent disobedience—as the most common or keystone characteristic of both extremes (see the case of George in the accompanying case book).

Again, the children we're talking about here—particularly those displaying overt antisocial behavior—engage in serious problem behaviors at a much higher rate and at a much later age than do normally developing children. A youngster with aggressive conduct disorder may match the problem behaviors of the normally developing child by a ratio of 2 to 1 or more.

In a now classic study, Patterson and his colleagues spent many hours observing in the homes of both normally developing children and aggressive children (Patterson et al., 1975). They identified noxious behaviors, measuring the rates at which they were performed by normally developing children and contrasting them to the rates at which they were performed by aggressive children whose behavior might fit the definition of CD. They found, for example, that an aggressive child can be expected to be noncompliant about every ten minutes, as well as to hit and to tease about once every half hour. In contrast, a nonaggressive child might be expected to be noncompliant once in twenty minutes, to tease once in about fifty minutes, and to hit once in a couple of hours. Patterson's description of Don (see the accompanying case book) illustrates the types of behaviors that extremely socially aggressive young children exhibit at home and school. Don's interactions with his family are characterized by coercive exchanges. Without effective intervention to break the coercive cycle at home and school, Don seems virtually certain to experience a high rate of failure in school and continuing conflict in the community.

As we've mentioned, CD must be judged with reference to chronological age. Ordinarily, children tend to exhibit less overt aggression as they grow older. Compared to nonaggressive youngsters, children and youth with CD typically show age-inappropriate aggression from an earlier age, develop a larger repertoire of aggressive acts, show aggression across a wider range of social situations, and persist in aggressive behavior for a longer time (Patterson et al., 1992; Walker et al., 2004). For example, a temper tantrum in a three-year-old (while no fun for a parent) is decidedly easier to accept and deal with than the temper tantrum of a twelve-year-old. Similarly, the infant who pushes a caregiver's hand away at feeding time or pushes an entire plate of food off a high chair tray and onto the floor is probably signaling frustration, tiredness, or maybe that he or she just doesn't want any more food. In contrast, should an eight- or nine-year-old push away a caregiver or throw food on the floor, parents probably should be concerned, and even more so if this happens repeatedly. A significant percentage of children and adolescents with CD show the characteristics of oppositional defiant disorder (ODD) at an earlier age. That is, they show a pattern of negativistic, hostile, and defiant behavior that is quite different from normally developing children of the same age.

Characteristics include having frequent temper tantrums and often arguing with adults, refusing to obey adults, deliberately annoying other people, and acting angry and resentful (Eddy, Reid, & Curry, 2002; Hinshaw & Lee, 2003; Kazdin, 2008; Kimonis et al., 2014).

CD is often comorbid with (occurs at the same time as) other disorders, such as **attention deficit–hyperactivity disorder** (ADHD). We know that ODD, ADHD, and CD are closely linked, although having one of these disorders doesn't necessarily mean that a youngster will have one or both of the others. In fact, several subtypes of CD are now well established, and all types of CD may be comorbid with ADHD, depression, anxiety, delinquency, substance abuse, and sexual acting out (see Kessler, Berglund, Demler, Jin, & Walters, 2005; Kessler, Chiu, Demler, & Walters, 2005; Kimonis et al., 2014).

Prevalence

Estimates of the prevalence of CD range from 6 percent to 16 percent of boys and 2 percent to 9 percent of girls under age eighteen. In one nationally representative sample, Nock, Kazdin, Hiripi, and Kessler (2006) found the overall prevalence of CD to be 9.5 percent, with rates of 12.0 percent among boys and 7.1 percent among girls. (Recall our comments in Chapter 2 on identification rates for EBD in schools, which persistently hover just below 1 percent, remembering that CD is a psychiatric diagnosis and not a school-based decision that a student needs special education; we discuss psychiatric classification further in Chapter 15.) The preponderance of boys with CD may reflect a combination of biological susceptibilities and socialization processes involving social roles, models, expectations, and reinforcement (see Costello et al., 2005, 2006). This gender split has been supported in school-based screenings for EBD as well; in a three-year study of more than 15,000 students in grades six through nine, boys outnumbered girls among those identified as at risk for EBD at a rate of 3:1. Moreover, the ratios of males to females were 5:1 for risk of externalizing disorders and 2:1 for risk of internalizing disorders (Young, Sabbah, Young, Reiser, & Richardson, 2010).

The prevalence of each subtype of conduct disorder hasn't been estimated precisely, but some generalities are evident; these include evidence of gender differences (Talbott, Celinska, Simpson, & Coe, 2002). For example, boys with CD tend to exhibit fighting, stealing, vandalism, and other overtly aggressive, disruptive behavior; girls are more likely to exhibit lying, truancy, running away, substance abuse, prostitution, and other less overtly aggressive behavior.

Measurement, prediction, and comorbidity are critical issues in studying the antisocial behavior of girls. Comorbidity may be a unique aspect of gender difference. Although boys generally tend to display higher rates of antisocial behavior than girls, there is a "gender paradox" in that girls may be at risk for greater comorbid symptoms—that is, they may be at increased risk for related problems (e.g., drug abuse, mental health problems) when they do display conduct disorder (see Kimonis et al., 2014; Kroneman, Loeber, Hipwell, & Koot, 2009; Zahn-Waxler, Shirtcliff, & Marceau, 2008). Moreover, the aggressive and disruptive behavior of girls is both similar to and different from that of boys, depending on the developmental stage at which it is measured. Much remains to be learned about gender differences in antisocial conduct, particularly the way in which biological and social factors influence the developmental course of antisocial behavioral patterns of boys and girls.

In summary, the consensus among researchers is that the problems associated with conduct disorder affect at least the officially estimated percentage of children and youth who may have CD and that the prevalence is probably increasing. Moreover, the severity of the disorder is perceived as increasing, and a delay of years in treatment after the onset of the disorder is common (see Hinshaw & Lee, 2003; Kimonis et al., 2014; Wang et al., 2005).

Classification

One way of classifying CD is by age of onset. Researchers have consistently found that children with early onset of CD and delinquency (before age ten or twelve) typically show more severe impairment and have a poorer prognosis than those with later onset. CD may be classified as mild (resulting in only minor harm to others), moderate, or severe (causing considerable harm to others).

Undersocialized conduct disorder includes characteristics such as hyperactivity, impulsiveness, irritability, stubbornness, demandingness, arguing, teasing, poor peer relations, loudness, threatening and attacking others, cruelty, fighting, showing off, bragging, swearing, blaming others, sassiness, and disobedience. Note that any of these would make the child stand out to teachers, parents, and peers. Undersocialized conduct disorder is also closely associated with violent behavior—a widespread and long-standing concern, especially to educators and others concerned with children's development. *Socialized conduct disorder* is characterized by more covert antisocial acts such as negativism, lying, destructiveness, stealing, setting fires, associating with bad companions, belonging to a gang, running away, truancy, and abuse of alcohol or other drugs. Note here that many of these specific behaviors would escape the notice, at least temporarily, of teachers or parents. However, antisocial behavior of all types is closely linked to delinquency and substance abuse.

AGGRESSION AND VIOLENCE IN SOCIAL CONTEXT

Aggression has been a common feature of American life for a long time (Goldstein, Carr, Davidson, & Wehr, 1981). In fact, this now old reference seems all the more apropos in the early decades of the twenty-first century. Aggression is not new to American children, their homes and families, or their schools. Even a cursory examination of *Children and Youth in America* (Bremner, 1970, 1971) and other histories (e.g., Scull, 2015) quickly reveals that coercion, violence, and brutality have always been practiced by and toward children and youth.

Recognizing the historical presence of violence does not in any way, however, reduce the unacceptable level of aggression in the present-day lives of American children. Through the media, children are exposed to brutal acts of aggression at a rate that may be unprecedented in the history of civilization (Huesmann, Moise-Titus, Podolski, & Eron, 2003). Although this concern was once limited to movies, and then television, it has grown in the early part of the twenty-first century to encompass all manner of media that might convey messages or images of violence, including music, video games, and of course vast and essentially unregulated internet content (e.g., Ybarra, Diener-West, Markow, Leaf, Hamburger, & Boxer, 2008). Moreover, most of these violent portrayals are readily available to children and youth, many on portable, handheld devices like smartphones. Technology carries additional unfortunate side effects, of course, and students in school are also known to record fights or other misdeeds to share through social media or other internet outlets. Indeed, cyberbullying has evolved in the first part of the twenty-first century and is reported to have effects equal to or worse than

Video Example

from

YouTube

▶

ENHANCEDetext
Video Connections 9.2
This video is geared directly at
parents, but note the overview
provided regarding the sources and
amounts of media violence children
are exposed to and the potential
effects of this media violence.
(https://www.youtube.com/
watch?v=7CXqZWW9yRQ)

"traditional" bullying (e.g., Smith, Mahdavi, Carvalho, Fisher, Russell, & Tippett, 2008). Cyberbullying can include sending text or voice messages, pictures, or videos directly to victims, or simply posting such material on publically available outlets.

Assaultive behavior, disruptiveness, and property destruction in schools have grown commonplace. Violence and weapons in schools are problems now apparent in small towns as well as big cities, in small schools as well as big ones, and in affluent as well as poor schools. We do not mean to misrepresent school violence generally with these figures on the rates of CD among children and youth. Media portrayals of extreme forms of school violence, such as school shootings, sexual assault, and bullying, may lead to the erroneous conclusion that schools are extremely dangerous places. However, data suggest that extreme school violence was on a steady decline in the first decade of the twenty-first century (Mayer & Furlong, 2010). What concerns us more are chronic instances of incivility, disruption, and both overt and covert antisocial behavior directed toward others and toward property. We know of no evidence to contradict the conclusion that such behaviors remain common in schools.

Aggression as a Multicultural Issue

Aggression and violence are multicultural issues in that all subcultural groups in the United States are affected, and stereotypes regarding various cultural groups are common. African American and Latino cultures are frequently miscast as tolerant of violence and aggression, and violence among Native American and Asian-Pacific island American youth is poorly understood. Particularly vulnerable populations are often overlooked in discussions of violence, including children with disabilities and other marginalized groups (see Kimonis et al., 2014; chapters in Patterson & Fosse, 2015).

We don't suggest overlooking the fact that some groups do have special vulnerabilities and needs, but we think it's important to recognize the commonalities of sociocultural conditions and needs for nurturing among all children and youth, regardless of color or ethnic background. The same risk factors for socialization are probably at work among youths from all ethnic groups.

Intervention programs designed for particular groups of aggressive students, such as African American males or Latino students, have been suggested by some (see Patterson & Fosse, 2015). Cultural sensitivity and multicultural competence are important, but they are no substitute for effective interventions that transcend ethnic and gender identity (Kauffman, Conroy, Gardner, & Oswald, 2008; Kimonis et al., 2014; National Research Council, 2002).

Regardless of color, ethnicity, gender, and other personal characteristics, children and youth are placed at risk by common factors such as poverty, family disruption, abuse, neglect, racism, poor schools, lack of employment opportunities, and other social problems that create stress in people's lives. Likewise, the most effective remedies for these risk factors and the protective factors that increase children's resilience are essentially the same across all cultural groups (see Kimonis et al., 2014 for a summary of risk and protective factors).

Still, the definitions of psychopathologies are grounded in cultures. Moreover, it is important to recognize the special considerations that must be made in assessing and treating psychopathology. Cultural factors are not simply a matter of racial identity, ethnic identity, or social class but a combination of these factors (see Anastasiou, Kauffman, & Michail, 2016).

Knowing the difference between pathological behavior and behavior that is simply an expression of cultural heritage is no easy matter. We note that millions of voters elected President Donald Trump, a Caucasian whose xenophobia, love of aggression, and CD have been on full display. More research is needed to help us make definitive statements about the differences between behavior that is merely cultural and behavior that represents pathological aggression.

Aggression in the Context of School

General education teachers must be prepared to deal with aggression because it's likely that at least one of their students will be highly disruptive, destructive, or assaultive toward other students or the teacher. Teachers of students with EBD must be ready to handle an especially large dose of aggression, because conduct disorder is one of the most common, exasperating, challenging indicators of EBD that ultimately brings students into special education.

The future special education teacher who expects most students to be withdrawn, or who believes that students with CD will quickly learn to respond kindly and appropriately to their peers' and teachers' attempts at interaction, will be shocked. Without effective means for controlling aggression, the teacher of students with EBD must develop a superhuman tolerance for interpersonal nastiness.

Observations in schools and studies of school records suggest that we can expect highly problematic, disruptive classroom behaviors from aggressive youngsters in most classrooms. This is not to say that we accept these behaviors; we suggest only that teachers in these roles should be aware of what they're getting into and come equipped not only with the right mind-set and realistic expectations but also an array of strategies for dealing with a variety of unpleasant, aggressive behaviors. These behaviors are frequently accompanied by academic failure. Not surprisingly, students who exhibit aggressive conduct disorder are often rejected by their peers and perceive their peers as hostile toward them. When children exhibit aggressive antisocial behavior and academic failure beginning in the early grades, the prognosis is particularly grim, unless effective early intervention is provided (see Garner, Kauffman, & Elliott, 2014; Lane et al., 2012; Walker & Gresham, 2014).

The high rates of antisocial behavior and the significant impairment of everyday functioning of youngsters with undersocialized aggressive conduct disorder do not bode well for their futures. Such youngsters tend to exhibit a relatively stable pattern of aggressive behavior over time, and the evidence is overwhelming that their problems don't tend to dissipate but continue into adulthood, especially when the onset is early and the child displays multiple and complex problems. Because aggressive antisocial behavior tends to keep people in contact with mental health and criminal justice systems, and because the behavior inflicts considerable suffering on victims of physical assault and property loss, the cost to society is enormous.

Boys with a history of serious antisocial conduct before age fifteen have higher chances in adulthood of externalizing psychopathology (aggression, criminal behavior, alcohol and drug abuse). Girls with such history have a higher probability as adults of both externalizing disorders and internalizing disorders (e.g., depression, phobias). We have known for many years that CD gives a child a particularly high risk of adult dysfunction. Thus, finding effective interventions for conduct disorder is a priority among social scientists and educators.

CAUSAL FACTORS

Though we have discussed key differences between overt and covert forms of antisocial behavior, the causal factors that seem to underlie them appear to be the same, and further seem to influence both boys and girls in very similar ways (see Eddy et al., 2002). Gerald Patterson and his colleagues have been instrumental in describing a model that seems to explain the development of much antisocial behavior. The basic ideas underlying their "coercive" model are listed in Table 9.1. In their model, a number of environmental factors in a child's life provide the context for their development and adjustment (e.g., family socioeconomic status [SES], infant temperament, other stressors impacting the family). These personal, family, and social contexts provide the background for the more direct influences on children's development, namely parents' or caregivers' monitoring of the child, managing behavior, and providing positive interactions. It is predictable that a host of negative contextual factors (e.g., low SES, difficult infant temperament, divorced or otherwise stressed parents or caregivers) can contribute to poor behavior management on the part of parents, who may be unskilled in monitoring and disciplining their children and fail to use positive reinforcement and problem solving in family interactions. The outcome is heightened risk of social incompetence and antisocial behavior of the child. We think it's important to note that we can't simply say that poor parenting *causes* antisocial behavior. Rather, research suggests that poor parenting is one characteristic among many that seem to occur in the environments of the great majority of children and youth who exhibit antisocial behavior.

Table 9.1   How Context Influences Children's Adjustment

Potential Environmental or Contextual Influences

1. Socioeconomic status of the family
2. Infant temperament
3. Parents' behavioral characteristics
4. Marital status of parents
5. Characteristics of neighborhood
6. Stressors impacting family
7. Capacity of extended family

Direct Influences on Child's Adjustment

1. Parents' or family's capacity to monitor the child
2. Parents' skills in managing behavior
3. Frequency of positive reinforcement received by child
4. Ability of family to solve problems constructively

Potential Outcomes when Difficult Environmental Conditions Intersect with Poor Parental or Family Influences

1. Child with antisocial behavior
2. Socially incompetent child

In some studies comparing overt to covert antisocial children, families of those who exhibited covert antisocial behavior are characterized by lower rates of aversive, coercive behavior on the part of parents and children and less supervision or monitoring on the part of parents. Other studies, however, have found no differences between overtly and covertly antisocial youngsters on family process variables such as parental rejection. A fairly consistent finding is that youngsters with versatile antisocial behavior come from the most disturbed families in which child-rearing practices are the most inadequate.

As perhaps the most common defining characteristic of overt antisocial behavior, aggression has historically been an object of study for scientists in many disciplines, and many alternative explanations have been offered for it. Psychoanalytic theories, drive theories, and simple conditioning theories have not led to effective intervention strategies, and they've been largely discounted by alternative explanations based on scientific research. Biological and social learning theories are supported by more reliable evidence (Dodge & Pettit, 2003; Grigorenko, 2014; Kimonis et al., 2014). In some cases, medication for aggressive behavior may be helpful, particularly when aggression is related to ADHD (see Konopasek & Forness, 2014).

Although genetic and other biological factors apparently contribute to the most severe cases of conduct disorder, their role in milder cases of aggression isn't clear; in both severe and mild forms of conduct disorder the social environment obviously contributes to the problem. Furthermore, it is now apparent that there is not a single cause of conduct disorder and related problems.

Sociobiology is an intriguing and controversial topic (Pinker, 2002), but it has little to offer developmental psychologists who are seeking more immediate causes of aggression. In fact, decades of research by numerous scientists strongly suggest that an individual's social environment is a powerful regulator of neurobiological processes and behavior; social learning may be the most important determinant of aggression and prosocial behavior (Eddy et al., 2002; Walker et al., 2004). The many factors that place children and youth at risk for development of a conduct disorder include a) child factors, b) parent or family factors, and c) school-related actors. Child factors associated with risk for conduct disorder include difficult temperament in infancy; deficits in the neuropsychological functions related to the use of language; early signs of difficult behavior, particularly if these are evident in multiple forms and in multiple situations (home, school, community); and academic deficits or lower IQ. Parent and family factors associated with risk for CD include complications during or after pregnancy, including low birth weight or prematurity; a history of antisocial or criminal behavior in either parents or siblings; lax supervision of children; harsh and inconsistent punishment; family and marital discord or difficulties; large family size; and poverty and its associated challenges. Finally, school-related factors that may contribute to CD include a low emphasis on academic success, lowered expectations, and little reward or acknowledgment for schoolwork. Examining this list of factors, it should not be hard to see why a child experiencing even a few of these factors is at heightened risk for CD, and that generally speaking, the more factors a child is exposed to, the greater the risk.

Among the several psychological explanations of aggression, one that stands out as most clearly supported by careful, systematic, scientific research is the *social learning theory*. We focus on these social learning explanations for aggression and its prevention. We first summarize the general findings of social learning research and then highlight personal, family, school, peer group, and other cultural factors and review Patterson's model of the coercive process that produces and sustains aggression.

General Conclusions from Social Learning Research

A social learning (or social cognitive) analysis of aggression includes three major controlling influences: 1) the environmental conditions that set the occasion for behavior or that reinforce or punish it, 2) the behavior itself, and 3) cognitive-affective (person) variables (Bandura, 1986; Bandura & Locke, 2003). Whether a person exhibits aggressive behavior depends on the reciprocal effects of these three factors and the individual's social history. Social learning theory suggests that aggression is learned through the direct consequences of aggressive and non-aggressive acts and through observation of aggression and its consequences. Research in social learning supports several generalizations about how aggression is learned and maintained:

- Children learn many aggressive responses by observing models or examples. The models may be family members, members of the child's subculture (friends, acquaintances, peers, and adults in the community), or individuals portrayed in the mass media (including real and fictional, human and nonhuman).
- Children are more likely to imitate aggressive models when the models are of high social status and when they see that the models receive reinforcement (positive consequences or rewards) or do not receive punishment for their aggression.
- Children learn aggressive behavior when, given opportunities to practice aggressive responses, they either experience no aversive consequences or succeed in obtaining the rewards they're after by harming or overcoming their victims.
- Aggression is more likely to occur when children experience aversive conditions (perhaps physical assault, verbal threats, taunts, or insults) or decreases in or termination of positive reinforcement. Children may learn through observation or practice that they can obtain rewarding consequences by engaging in aggressive behavior. The probability of aggression under such circumstances is especially high when alternative (appropriate) means of obtaining reinforcement are not readily available or have not been learned and when aggression is sanctioned by social authorities.
- Factors that maintain aggression include three types of reinforcement: *external reinforcement* (tangible rewards, social status rewards, removal of aversive conditions, expressions of injury or suffering by the victim), *vicarious reinforcement* (gratification obtained by observing others gain rewards through aggression), and *self-reinforcement* (self-congratulation or increased self-esteem following successful aggression).
- Aggression may be perpetuated by cognitive processes that justify hostile action: comparing one's deeds advantageously to more horrific deeds of others, appealing to higher principles (such as protection of self or others), placing responsibility on others (the familiar "I didn't start it" and "He made me do it" ploys), and dehumanizing the victims (perhaps with demeaning labels such as *nerd, dweeb, trash, pig, drooler, wimp, mental*).
- Punishment may also serve to heighten or maintain aggression when it causes pain, when there are no positive alternatives to the punished response, when punishment is delayed or inconsistent, or when punishment provides a model of aggressive behavior. When counterattack against the punisher seems likely to succeed, punishment maintains aggression. The adult who punishes a child by striking out not only causes pain, which increases the probability of aggression, but provides a model of aggression as well.

Video Example from YouTube

ENHANCEDetext
Video Connections 9.3
This video describes one of Dr. Albert Bandura's best-known studies about the effects of modeled aggression on children's behavior, and highlights the importance of social learning theory to children's behavioral development. (https://www.youtube.com/watch?v=zerCK0lRjp8)

A social learning analysis of aggression generates testable predictions about environmental conditions that foster aggressive behavior. Research over several decades has led to the following empirically confirmed predictions about the genesis of aggression:

- Viewing televised aggression may increase aggressive behavior, especially in males and in children who have a history of aggressiveness; similar findings are beginning to emerge on the effects of playing or viewing violent video games.
- Delinquent subcultures, such as deviant peer groups or street gangs, will maintain aggressive behavior in their members by modeling and reinforcing aggression.
- Families of aggressive children are characterized by high rates of aggression on the part of all members, by coercive exchanges between the aggressive child and other family members, and by parents' inconsistent, punitive control techniques and lack of supervision.
- Aggression begets aggression. When one person presents an aversive condition for another (hitting, yelling, whining), the affronted individual is likely to reply by presenting a negative condition of his or her own, resulting in a coercive process. The coercive interaction will continue until one individual withdraws his or her aversive condition, providing negative reinforcement (escape from aversive stimulation) for the victor.

Family, school, and cultural factors involving social learning were discussed in previous chapters. These factors undoubtedly play a major role in the development of aggressive conduct disorders. By providing models of aggression and supplying reinforcement for aggressive behavior, families, schools, and the larger society teach youngsters (albeit inadvertently) to behave aggressively. This insidious teaching process is most effective for youngsters who are already predisposed to aggressive behavior because of biological (i.e., genetic) factors or their previous social learning. And the process is maintained by reciprocity of effects among the behavior, the social environment, and the child's cognitive and affective characteristics. The teaching–learning process involved in aggression includes reciprocal effects such as these:

- The social environment provides aversive conditions (noxious stimuli), including social disadvantage, academic failure, peer rejection, and rejection by parents and other adults.
- The youngster perceives the social environment as both threatening and likely to reward aggression.
- The youngster's behavior is noxious to others, who attempt to control it by threats and punitive responses.
- The youngster develops low self-concept and identifies himself or herself in primarily negative terms.
- In coercive bouts, the youngster is frequently successful in overcoming others by being more aversive or persistent, thereby obtaining reinforcement for aggression and confirming his or her perceptions of the social environment as threatening and controlled by aggressive behavior.

All of these factors contribute to the development of antisocial behavior and, over time, cement it into a pattern very resistant to change. The major causal factors described by Patterson and colleagues (1992) as contributing to antisocial behavior are listed in Table 9.2. We next examine major contributing factors and how they are interrelated in a coercive process.

Associating with deviant peers
Problems with self-esteem
Problems with socialization
Being rejected by peer group
Failure of parents to manage routine behavior problems
Failure of parents to adequately supervise
Parents resorting to physical punishment
Rejection by parents
Failure in school

Table 9.2   Factors Associated with the Development of Delinquency and Antisocial Behavior

Personal Factors

As we discussed in Chapter 4, children are born with dispositions or temperaments that, although modifiable, tend to be fairly consistent over a period of years. Many children with difficult, irritable temperaments are at risk for developing antisocial behavior (Center & Kemp, 2003). Their difficult temperaments as infants may evolve through social interaction with their caretakers into high rates of noncompliance and oppositional behavior in the early childhood years. These children are likely to develop low self-esteem and depressed affect as well as to have major problems in peer relations and academic achievement. In short, they may begin life with personal attributes that make social rejection likely, and these characteristics may be exacerbated by cycles of negative interaction with caretakers, peers, and teachers. Although demographic factors such as low socioeconomic status and family factors such as parental substance abuse are important, the personal characteristics of attention problems and especially fighting are predictive of the early onset of conduct disorder in boys.

Peer Group Factors

From an early age, normally-developing children tend to reject their peers who are highly aggressive and disruptive in play and school activities. Antisocial students may achieve high status among a subgroup of peers, but they are likely to be rejected by most of their nonantisocial peers. Further, peer rejection in childhood may also be related to the persistence of aggressive behavior into adulthood (Rabiner, Coie, Miller-Johnson, Boykin, & Lochman, 2005). To achieve some sense of competence and belonging, antisocial children and youth often gravitate toward a deviant peer group (Gest, Farmer, Cairns, & Xie, 2003; Parker, Rubin, Erath, Wojslawowicz, & Buskirk, 2006; Rubin, Coplan, & Bowker, 2009). If poor parental monitoring and other family risk factors are present, along with academic failure, it is easy to see how adolescents would be likely to identify with deviant peers and be drawn into delinquency, substance abuse, and antisocial behavior that only create additional barriers to their opportunities for further education, employment, and development of positive and stable social relationships.

Family Factors

The families of antisocial children tend to be characterized by antisocial or criminal behavior of parents and siblings. Often homes and family relationships are chaotic and unsupportive of normal social development or are characterized by physical or sexual abuse. There are often many children in the family. The families are often broken by divorce or abandonment and characterized by high levels of interpersonal conflict. Parental monitoring of children's behavior tends to be lax or almost nonexistent, and discipline tends to be unpredictable but harsh—precisely the opposite of that suggested by those well versed in the topic of rearing well-socialized children (Kazdin, 2008). Often many generations live together, and grandparents or other relatives living in the home also typically lack child-rearing skills. As discussed in Chapter 5, the children and parents often become enmeshed in a coercive cycle of interaction in which parent and child increase the pain they cause the other until one party "wins." Despite growing evidence of these family patterns, we should be careful not to assume that all families of antisocial children can be characterized this way. However, these are the typical family characteristics of children who are antisocial. Domestic violence, poverty, poor parental education, family members' criminality, and other adverse conditions increase the risk (i.e., chances) that a child will be aggressive or exhibit other emotional or behavioral disorders, such as depression.

The stages in the growth, development, and perpetuation of antisocial behavior are listed in Table 9.3. Patterson and others (1992) compared this stage model of the growth of antisocial behavior to the growth of a "vile weed." Their coercive model begins with background factors (e.g., antisocial or substance-abusing parents, stressful life circumstances, difficult temperaments), where the social and family context can lay the groundwork for later problems. These contextual factors increase the odds of producing an antisocial child with low self-esteem (the first stage). In the second stage of their model, school failure, rejection by parents and peers, and depression all contribute to one another and further strengthen the child's antisocial tendencies. In the third stage, the youngster associates with antisocial peers and engages in delinquent acts and substance abuse. Now the youth has become enmeshed in social relationships and behavioral patterns that often lead to the fourth stage, in which the antisocial youth becomes an antisocial adult who is unable to hold a job and is at high risk

Table 9.3   How Conduct Disorder Grows from Background Factors to Adulthood

Background Factors: Parents who are antisocial or substance abusers, unskilled or deviant grandparents or other caretakers, stressful circumstances, difficult temperament
First Stage (Early Childhood): Poor discipline and monitoring by caretakers, associated with antisocial child behavior and low self-esteem
Second Stage (Middle Childhood): Poor school achievement, rejection by parents and peers, depression
Third Stage (Adolescent): Substance abuse, gravitation toward deviant peers, delinquency
Fourth Stage (Adult): Disappointing employment or career, marital failure, institutionalization

for incarceration or other institutionalization and a disrupted marriage. Clearly, any offspring of an adult in the fourth stage of this model is likely to have the same background factors in place, and is thus at high risk for perpetuating the cycle by passing through the same stages. So antisocial behavior can be passed from one generation to the next, perhaps in part through genetics but also through the conditions of the home and community. Eddy and colleagues (2002) depicted similar coercive interactions and conditions as causes of antisocial behavior.

School Factors

Most antisocial students will find little success in school; they experience academic failure and are rejected by both peers and adults. In many cases, the schools they attend are deteriorated or crowded buildings. The discipline they experience in school is often little better than the parental discipline they experience at home: highly punitive, erratic, escalating, and with little or no attention to their nonaggressive, positive behaviors or their efforts to achieve. The academic work they are given is often not consistent with their achievement level or relevant to their eventual employment, forcing them to face either failure or boredom most every day they attend school. As with family factors, though, we need to be careful not to accuse *all* teachers and school administrators of failing to teach and manage difficult students well. However, the typical school experience of antisocial students is highly negative, contributing to further maladjustment, as discussed in Chapter 7.

ASSESSMENT

The antisocial behavior characterizing conduct disorder is included on nearly all behavior problem checklists and behavior rating scales. Moreover, a variety of instruments have been designed specifically to measure the antisocial behavior of children and adolescents through self-reports or ratings of parents, teachers, or peers. These measures of antisocial behavior are often helpful, but they must always be supplemented by direct observation of the children or youth in several different settings to obtain more precise information about the problem (Freeman & Hogansen, 2006).

We cover assessment instruments and practices appropriate for students with EBD more extensively in Chapter 15, and guidelines presented there certainly apply to the assessment of CD. The following additional suggestions for assessing CD should also be taken into account (see Kazdin, 2008):

1. Use rating scales that have multiple dimensions because children with CD are likely to have other problems as well.

2. Make sure to assess prosocial skills (behavioral strengths or appropriate behavior) as well as CD.

3. Compare the child to norms for others of the same age and gender.

4. Assess the social contexts, including family, community, and school.

5. Make provisions for periodic reassessment to measure progress or the impact of intervention.

It is important to know what social skills a student has and what his or her standing is in peer groups. Another aspect of assessment is functional behavioral assessment or functional analysis, the goal of which is to find out what purpose the student's behavior serves (i.e., what consequences, gains, or benefits it provides; see Lane, Menzies, Bruhn, & Crnobori, 2011). A functional analysis can provide guidance for making alterations in the environment (e.g., tasks, commands, reinforcement) that will prevent or ameliorate problems. Unfortunately, the behavior of many disruptive students is motivated in large measure by negative reinforcement—escape from academic demands (see Kauffman, Pullen et al., 2011; Kerr & Nelson, 2010).

It is common for students with EBD, including those with conduct disorder and especially those with ADHD, to try to avoid tasks that require much effort. Neutral and negative teacher commands dominate the typical classrooms of students with behavioral problems. Teachers too seldom give students with EBD work at which they can succeed and too seldom provide immediate and frequent positive reinforcement for behaving as expected. Helping teachers change this pattern is not easy. However, teachers must begin by asking questions related to their instruction and how their students are responding to it as well as their own (teachers') responses to students (see Kauffman, Pullen et al., 2011).

As mentioned in our discussion of prevention, precorrection strategies are based on the premise that assessment of the context in which antisocial behavior is likely to occur will help teachers find ways of short-circuiting misbehavior and coercive struggles. Ultimately, assessment is of little value unless it suggests the variables that could be changed to alter antisocial behavior (Kauffman, Pullen et al., 2011; Walker et al., 2004).

INTERVENTION AND EDUCATION

Prevention

Prediction and social control of violent behavior are among the most controversial and critical issues involving American youth. Prediction—*anticipation*—of antisocial behavior is essential to prevention, simply because no one can prevent what he or she does not anticipate (Kauffman, 2010c, 2012a, 2014a; Landrum, Scott, & Lingo, 2011). Research during the past two decades has yielded a wealth of evidence about community, family, school, peer, and personal characteristics that place children and youth at high risk of adopting antisocial behavior patterns. Nevertheless, most individuals in our society are hesitant to intervene early to prevent later problems (Kauffman, 1999c, 2003a, 2004, 2005, 2010c, 2012a, 2012b, 2014a). This is an unproductive if not maddening denial of realities that many have observed.

We can now make more recommendations regarding the prevention of aggressive behavior with considerable confidence. Clearly, we need to address antisocial behavior at all levels of prevention: *primary* (to prevent serious antisocial behavior from emerging), *secondary* (to remediate or ameliorate antisocial behavior once it is established), and *tertiary* (to accommodate or attenuate the negative effects of antisocial behavior that is unlikely to be changed).

Many members of our society, including professional practitioners in education and related disciplines as well as politicians and policy makers, have been reluctant to take the steps that we have good reason to believe would prevent or lessen antisocial behavior. Although all may agree that the level of antisocial behavior and violence in our society is unacceptable, many are opposed to the coherent, sustained, and costly programs of government at all levels that are necessary to address the problem effectively.

The steps research suggests we should take might be summarized as follows:

1. *Provide effective consequences to deter aggression.* Antisocial behavior is less likely to recur if it is followed by consequences that are nonviolent but immediate, certain, and proportional to the seriousness of the offense. Violence as a means of controlling aggression frequently results in counteraggression, setting the stage for further coercion. Aggression is reduced in the long term if the consequences are swift, assured, and restrictive of personal preferences (e.g., temporary loss of certain privileges) rather than harsh or physically painful. Antisocial children and youth are typically punished capriciously and severely; the consequences of their behavior are often random, harsh, and unfair, cementing the pattern of counteraggression. The belief that harsher punishment is more effective is a deeply ingrained superstition. If teachers, parents, and others dealing with antisocial behavior learn to use effective nonviolent consequences, then the level of violence in our society will decline.

2. *Teach nonaggressive responses to problems.* Aggressive behavior is, to a significant degree, learned. So is nonaggressive behavior. Teaching youngsters how to solve personal conflicts and other problems nonaggressively isn't easy, nor will teaching nonaggression help them solve all problems. A school curriculum including nonaggressive conflict resolution and problem solving could lower the level of violence, but that effect would be multiplied many times were the media, community leaders, and high-profile role models to join forces with educators in teaching that nonviolence is a better way.

3. *Stop aggression early before it takes root.* Aggression begets aggression, particularly when it's successful in obtaining desired ends and when it has become well practiced. Aggression often escalates from relatively minor noncompliance and belligerence to appalling acts of violence. Nonviolent consequences are more effective when applied early in the sequence. We need intervention that is early in two ways: first, early in that we intervene with young children; second, early in that we intervene from first instances of antisocial behavior, the earliest behaviors in a chain of aggressive interactions.

4. *Restrict access to the instruments of aggression.* Aggressors use the most efficient tools available to damage their targets. True, some will show aggression with whatever tools are available. The more important truth is that having more efficient weapons (e.g., guns rather than knives) enables aggressors to accomplish violent ends with less immediate risk to themselves and to escalate the level of violence easily. More effective restriction of access to the most efficient tools of aggression would help to check the rise in violence: Restrictions on the manufacture, distribution, and possession of both the tools themselves and of the parts that make the most efficient weapons of violence operable.

5. *Restrain and reform public displays of aggression.* We've learned that the behavior children and adolescents observe affects their own thinking and overt behavior. Much of the fare marketed by the entertainment industry is saturated with aggressive acts, desensitizes observers to aggression and its consequences, and disinhibits expressions of aggression. Broadcasts of admired athletes and other public figures often depict them bragging, intimidating their opponents,

bullying, or fighting. They are often portrayed as swaggering winners or sore losers, in either case as very bad role models. Reducing the amount and type of antisocial behavior purveyed to the public as entertainment and requiring that the realistic consequences of aggression be depicted would contribute to the goal of a less-violent society. Athletes, politicians, musicians, and others who eschew both violence and braggadocio could add immeasurably to this effect.

6. *Correct the conditions of everyday life that foster aggression.* People tend to be more aggressive when they are deprived of basic necessities, experience aversive conditions, or perceive that there is no path to their legitimate goals other than aggression. Poverty and the deprivations and aversive conditions that come with it affect an enormous proportion of American children and youth, and these conditions of everyday life provide fertile ground for aggressive conduct. Social programs that successfully address poverty, unemployment, and related social inequities would help to remove the conditions that breed aggression. Opportunities for supervised recreation or other productive activity during nonschool hours can provide alternatives to antisocial behavior. A reasonably supportive society cannot abolish poverty or remove all of life's dangers, but it can keep many children from living in abject fear, misery, and hopelessness. We must have more effective social programs involving government, the private sector, local communities, religious groups, families, and individuals.

7. *Offer more effective instruction and more attractive educational options in public schools.* Achieving academic success and engaging in study that they see as interesting and useful in their lives reduces the likelihood that youngsters will behave aggressively. By adopting instructional methods known to produce superior results—putting instruction on a solid scientific footing—schools could ensure that more students achieve success in the basic skills needed to pursue any educational option. We think that a specific, relentless emphasis on basic reading and math skills in the earliest grades is absolutely critical to later school success, and even staying in school. Moreover, by offering highly differentiated curricula, especially in the later grades, school systems could help more students find options that interest them and prepare them for life after high school.

Prevention of covert antisocial behavior in many ways parallels prevention of overt aggression. Character training or moral education seems to the casual observer particularly relevant to the prevention of stealing, lying, vandalism, and so on. The effects of typical moral and character education, however, haven't shown great promise. Moral behavior often doesn't match moral judgment. Children and youth, as well as adults, often do wrong even though they know what's right. Moral behavior tends to be controlled at least as much by situational factors as by moral or character traits; youngsters are honest or altruistic at some times and in some situations but not in others. Teachers' talk about classroom conventions, procedures, and moral issues has little effect on children's reasoning about morals. For schools to have much influence in teaching prosocial values, they must develop coherent and pervasive programs of character education that include discussion, role-playing, and social-skills training to help students recognize moral dilemmas, adopt moral values, and select moral behavioral alternatives.

Although preventive efforts may have some effect if implemented in any single social context (e.g., school or family), they will have maximum effect only if implemented as a coherent package of interventions involving multiple facets of the problem (see Conduct Problems Prevention Research Group, 1999, 2011; Strain & Timm, 2001). This knowledge should not deter educators or any other professionals from implementing preventive practices immediately, regardless of what happens in spheres outside their immediate responsibility or direct influence.

Most important for educators is understanding how instruction is a key tool for prevention. Being confronted daily, if not hourly, by academic and social tasks at which they are failures is known to contribute directly to students' tendency to exhibit antisocial behavior. Many antisocial students don't know how to do the academic tasks and don't have the social coping skills to be successful in the typical classroom, and each failure increases the probability of future antisocial responses to problems.

The most effective approaches to school-based prevention of antisocial behavior are *proactive* and *instructive*: planning ways to avoid failure and coercive struggles regarding both academic and social behavior and actively teaching students more adaptive, competent ways of behaving. Antisocial behavior should prompt teachers to ask what prosocial skills the student needs to learn as a replacement for aggression and to devise an explicit instructional strategy for teaching those skills.

Major Features of Social Learning Interventions

Many conceptual approaches to intervention for CD once it has emerged have been suggested. These have included psychodynamic therapies, biological treatments, and behavioral interventions. Parent management training, problem-solving training, family therapy based on systems theory and behaviorism, and treatments addressing multiple social systems (family, school, community) as well as the individual are among the most promising approaches. Interventions based on social learning principles have generally been more successful than have those based on other conceptual models (e.g., Dean, Duke, George, & Scott, 2007; Kauffman, Pullen et al., 2011; Kazdin, 2008; Walker & Sprague, 2007; Walker et al., 2004). A social learning approach offers the most direct, practical, and reliable implications for the work of teachers, so we confine discussion here to interventions based on social learning concepts.

A *social learning approach* to the control of aggression includes three primary components: specific behavioral objectives, strategies for changing behavior by altering the social environment, and precise measurement of behavioral change. These components allow us to judge the outcome of an intervention qualitatively as well as quantitatively against an objective goal.

Social learning interventions sometimes appear quite simple, but the apparent simplicity is deceptive because it is often necessary to make subtle adjustments in technique to make them work. Tremendous sensitivity to the variations in human communication is necessary to become proficient in the humane and effective application of behavioral principles. The range of possible techniques for an individual case is extensive, calling for a high degree of creativity to formulate an effective and ethical plan of action.

School-based social learning interventions designed to reduce aggression may include a wide variety of strategies or procedures (Kauffman, Pullen et al., 2011; Landrum & Kauffman, 2006). In a classic book, Walker (1995) discussed twelve intervention techniques for managing the acting-out student, providing guidelines for correct application, special issues, and advantages and disadvantages of each. His treatment remains one the clearest summaries of decades of research on management techniques, and research continues to support these basic premises of effective intervention (see Lane et al., 2011 and chapters in Walker & Gresham, 2014). The twelve techniques (and others) may be used individually or in combination. The following thumbnail sketches of the twelve techniques provide a beginning point for understanding how effective interventions for conduct disorder may be constructed:

1. *Rules*—clear, explicit statements defining the teacher's expectations for classroom conduct. Clarity of expectations is a hallmark of corrective or therapeutic environments for students with conduct disorder. A few clear rules let students know how they should behave and what is prohibited; they are important guidelines for classroom conduct and teacher behavior as well. Positively stated rules, which should predominate, guide the teacher's praise, approval, and other forms of positive reinforcement. Negatively stated rules, which should be kept to a minimum, guide the teacher's use of punishment.

2. *Teacher praise*—positive verbal, gestural, or other affective indications of approval (kind words, smiles, gestures). Teacher praise for desirable, nonaggressive student conduct is one of the key ingredients in successful behavioral management. Despite claims to the contrary in the popular press, research consistently demonstrates that praise is an effective tool for encouraging positive behavior and that it is grossly underused by teachers, especially toward students who probably need it most (e.g., see Bayat, 2011). Used skillfully, teacher praise is perhaps the most important element in a program of positive reinforcement. Moreover, rules alone are much less effective than are rules combined with frequent, skillful teacher praise for following them.

3. *Positive reinforcement*—presentation of a rewarding consequence that increases the future probability or strength of the behavior it follows. Such consequences can be extremely varied in form. Rhode, Jenson, and Reavis (2010) suggested that to be most effective, praise and other forms of positive reinforcement should be given a) immediately after appropriate behavior, b) frequently, c) with enthusiasm, d) with eye contact from the teacher, e) after or with description of the behavior that earned the reward, f) in ways that build excitement and anticipation for obtaining them, and g) in great variety. Sometimes, token reinforcers are given that can be exchanged later for desired objects or privileges (much like any other economic exchange or monetary system). The effective use of positive reinforcement requires differential responding to the student's behavior (called *differential reinforcement*). That is, the desired behavior is to be reinforced; undesirable behavior is to be ignored (not reinforced). The basic idea of positive reinforcement is very simple; its skillful implementation is not, especially with difficult antisocial students (see Kauffman, Pullen et al., 2011).

4. *Verbal feedback*—information about the appropriateness or inappropriateness of academic or social behavior. Teachers' responses to students' academic performance and conduct (the content, emotional tone, and timing of what they say and do in reaction to students' behavior) are crucial factors in how students learn to behave. Giving clear feedback, keeping it primarily positive, steering

clear of arguments, and finding the most effective pace and timing are critical issues. Using verbal feedback effectively requires much experience, training, and reflection.

5. *Stimulus change*—alteration of antecedent events or conditions that set the stage for behavior. Sometimes antecedents can be changed easily, resulting in a marked decrease in problem behavior. For example, making instructions or assignments shorter and clearer may result in greatly improved levels of compliance. Presenting tasks or commands in a different way may also defuse resistance to them. Increasing attention is being given to the effects of the context in which aggression occurs, and modification of the context is often found to be both feasible and effective in reducing aggression.

6. *Contingency contract*—a written performance agreement between a student and teacher (or parents, or both teacher and parents), specifying roles, expectations, and consequences. Simply put, a behavioral contract spells out what the student will do (academic and behavioral expectations), and what consequences he'll receive (both for meeting, and for not meeting, expectations). Contracts must be written with the student's age and intelligence in mind. They should be simple, straightforward statements. Successful contracts are clearly written, emphasize the positive consequences for appropriate conduct, specify fair consequences to which all parties agree, and are strictly adhered to by the adults who sign the document. Contracts are not generally successful if they are used as the only or primary intervention strategy. They are useful primarily for individuals for whom specific problem behaviors can be clearly delimited.

7. *Modeling plus reinforcing imitation*—showing or demonstrating the desired behavior and providing positive reinforcement for matching responses. Learning through watching models and imitating them—*observational learning*—is a basic social learning process. The models may be adults or peers, but it is critical that the student who is to learn more appropriate behavior be taught whom to watch, what to look for, and what to match; models without explicit instruction are not typically effective in remediating academic or social problems (see Kauffman, Pullen et al., 2011). Effective modeling and reinforcement often must be done in private one-on-one sessions with the teacher, and procedures must be used to help students exhibit in everyday circumstances the improved behavior they learn through observational learning.

8. *Shaping*—a process of building new responses by beginning with behavior the student already can perform at some level and reinforcing successive approximations of the desired behavior. The key factor in shaping is identifying and reinforcing small increments of improvement; the teacher reinforces the student when his behavior gets just a little better each time. This typically requires careful attention to the student's current behavior in relation to a behavioral goal. It also requires ignoring behavior that doesn't represent progress toward the goal. As is true of positive reinforcement, the basic idea is simple, but the skillful implementation is not.

9. *Systematic social skills training*—a curriculum in which the skills taught are those that help students a) initiate and maintain positive social interactions,

b) develop friendships and social support networks, and c) cope effectively with the social environment. Social skills involve getting along with authority figures such as teachers and parents, relating to peers in a variety of activities, and solving social problems in constructive, nonaggressive ways. Problems with social skills involve both skill deficits (the student does not have the skill) and performance deficits (the student has but does not use the skill). A useful social skills training program must not only be intensive and systematic but also aimed at demonstration and practice of the skills in natural or every-day environments in which they are needed to avoid coercive struggles and aggressive behavior.

10. *Self-monitoring and self-control training*—consistent tracking, recording, and evaluating of one's own specific behaviors with the intention of changing those behaviors. These procedures may involve not only keeping track of one's own behavior but also prompting oneself or applying consequences to oneself. These procedures require explicit training and rehearsal, as well as the motivation to use them. As discussed in Chapter 8, self-monitoring is a strategy frequently used with students who have ADHD. Self-monitoring may be an inappropriate strategy for serious aggressive behavior and for students who don't have the cognitive awareness or social maturity to carry out the procedures.

11. *Time-out* (formally known as *time-out from positive reinforcement*)—the temporary removal or suspension of a student's opportunity to obtain positive reinforcement based on his or her display of a specific misbehavior. Time-out may involve removing a student from the group or classroom, although that isn't always necessary (e.g., it can simply involve the teacher's turning away and refusing to respond or a time during which the student cannot earn points or other rewards). Time-out is generally reserved for serious behavioral problems. Like any punishment procedure, it's easily misunderstood, misused, and abused (especially the form of time-out known as *seclusionary time-out*). Used knowledgeably and skillfully and in combination with other positive procedures, however, time-out is an important nonviolent tool for reducing aggressive behavior, and teachers of students with EBD would be wise to become knowledgeable about the benefits of time-out, especially of nonexclusionary time-out, as well as the potential dangers of seclusionary time-out (see Ryan, Sanders, Katsiyannis, & Yell, 2007).

12. *Response cost*—the removal of a previously earned reward or reinforcer (or a portion thereof) contingent on a specific misbehavior. Response cost is a fine or penalty incurred for each instance of an inappropriate behavior. Minutes of recess, free time, or access to another preferred activity or points toward earning a reinforcing item or activity may be lost for each misbehavior. Like any other punishment procedure, response cost is subject to misunderstanding and misuse. Moreover, it's ineffective without a strong program of positive reinforcement; that is, students must have ample opportunities to earn reinforcement so that small portions of it can be removed. However, of all types of punishment procedures, it's probably the least likely to engender strong emotional side effects and resistance.

The Uses and Misuses of Punishment

Many people in the United States appear to embrace corporal punishment and other highly punitive approaches to child discipline (e.g., Gershoff, 2002). Indeed, numerous studies have confirmed the low rates of positive reinforcement for appropriate behavior and high rates of aversive conditions for students in typical U.S. classrooms, as discussed in Chapter 7. In reaction to excessive and ineffective punishment, some have advocated a ban on most or all forms of punishment, arguing that positive measures alone are sufficient and punishment in any form is unethical. Research does not support a complete abandonment of punishment as a means of child management, but it does suggest great care in the use of punishment procedures (see Arnold-Saritepe, Mudford, & Cullen, 2016; Foxx, 2016a; Kauffman, Pullen et al., 2011; Mulick & Butter, 2016; Newsom & Kroeger, 2016).

Although teaching appropriate behavior is important in social learning interventions, some behaviors may require punishment because they are intolerable or dangerous, or have not been responsive to alternative positive interventions. It may be difficult or impossible to establish adequate classroom control, particularly with students who have learning and behavioral problems, without using negative consequences for misbehavior in addition to positive reinforcement of appropriate conduct. Judicious use of negative consequences for misconduct can even enhance the effectiveness of positive consequences (Lerman & Vorndran, 2002).

We have to be extremely careful in the use of punishment, however, because ill-timed, vengeful, and capricious punishment, especially in the absence of incentives for appropriate behavior, provides a vicious example for youngsters and encourages their further misbehavior. Harsh punishment provokes counteraggression and coercion. Punishment is a seductive, easily abused approach to controlling behavior. Harsh punishment typically has an immediate effect; because it frequently results in immediate cessation of the individual's irritating or inappropriate behavior, it also provides powerful negative reinforcement for the punisher (e.g., a teacher is negatively reinforced when yelling or scolding gets an obnoxious student to stop, even temporarily, his or her disruptive behavior). Thus, it is often the beginning point of a coercive style of interaction in which the punished and the punisher vie for the dubious honor of winning an aversive contest. And because people mistakenly believe that punishment makes the individual suffer, physical punishment is frequently thought to be more effective than milder forms. These dangers, misconceptions, and abuses of punishment appear to underlie the coercive relationships that characterize families of aggressive antisocial children (cf. Patterson et al., 1992). Consequently, it is crucial to carefully consider punishment in educational settings to avoid having the school become another battleground for aversive control.

A pervasive misconception about punishment is that it requires inflicting physical pain, psychological trauma, or social embarrassment. None of these is required; punishment can be defined as any consequence that results in a decline in the rate or strength of the punished behavior. Thus, a mild, quiet reprimand, temporary withdrawal of attention, or loss of a small privilege can be effective punishers in many instances. For persistent and serious misbehavior, stronger punishment may be necessary, but mild forms of social punishment such as restrictions or loss of rewards are most effective if the youngster's environment also provides many opportunities for positive reinforcement of appropriate behavior.

The social learning literature clearly supports the assertion that punishment, if carefully and appropriately administered, is a humane and effective tool for controlling serious misbehavior (Kauffman, Pullen et al., 2011; Lerman & Vorndran, 2002; Newsom & Kroeger, 2016;

Walker et al., 2004). Effective punishment may actually be necessary to rear a nonaggressive, socialized child. However, clumsy, vindictive, or malicious punishment is the teacher's or parent's downfall. And it is a mistake not to offer positive reinforcement for desired alternative behavior at the same time punishment is employed (Kazdin, 2008; Maag, 2001; Newsom & Kroeger, 2016). Punishment that is out of proportion to the seriousness of the offense has no place in humane treatment. Before using punishment procedures, educators must be sure that a strong program of teaching and positive consequences for appropriate behavior is in place, and they must carefully consider the types of behavior that are priorities for punishment. Teachers should study the use of punishment procedures in depth before implementing them in the classroom. Following are general guidelines for humane and effective punishment:

- Punishment should be reserved for serious misbehavior that is associated with significant impairment of the youngster's social relationships and behaviors that positive strategies alone have failed to control.
- Punishment should be instituted only in the context of ongoing behavioral management and instructional programs that emphasize positive consequences for appropriate conduct and achievement; punishment should involve response cost (loss of privileges or rewards or withdrawal of attention) rather than aversives.
- Whenever possible, punishment should be related to the misbehavior, enabling the youngster to make restitution or practice a more adaptive alternate behavior.
- Punishment should be discontinued if it is not quickly apparent that it is effective. Unlike positive reinforcement, which may not have an immediate effect on behavior, effective punishment usually results in an almost immediate decline in misbehavior. It is better not to punish than to punish ineffectively, because ineffective punishment may merely increase the individual's tolerance for aversive consequences. Punishment will not necessarily be more effective if it becomes harsher or more intense; using a different type of punishment, making the punishment more immediate, or making the punishment more consistent may make it more effective.
- There should be written guidelines for using specific punishment procedures. All concerned parties—students, parents, teachers, and school administrators—should know what punishment procedures will be used. Before implementing specific punishment procedures, especially those involving time-out or other aversive consequences, they should be approved by school authorities.

As we have discussed, children and youth with CD have typically experienced lax monitoring and inconsistent, harsh punishment with little positive reinforcement for appropriate behavior. Their discipline has typically contributed to their CD, not because it has included punishment per se but because it has included too little positive reinforcement for the right kind of behavior and punishment that isn't appropriate. Effective intervention in CDs may often require punishment, but of a different kind.

THE ACTING-OUT BEHAVIOR CYCLE AND PRECORRECTION

Social learning interventions focus on stepping in early to prevent the escalation of aggression and the blowups in which it often terminates. Based on the work and writing of Colvin and his associates (e.g., Colvin, 1992), Kauffman, Pullen, and colleagues (2011) described a conceptual framework that teachers might use to think about intervention. They describe the phases children and youth typically go through in a cycle of acting-out behavior.

A highly significant feature of this acting-out cycle is that it begins with a *calm* phase in which the student is behaving in ways that are expected and appropriate. The student is cooperative, compliant, and task oriented. Most students with CD exhibit appropriate behavior at least some of the time, but teachers typically ignore this behavior. We note that many teachers of students with EBD will say their students are *never* calm, but for even the most disruptive, aggressive students, we find that there are at least brief moments during the school day when the student is at least compliant, observant, or not disruptive. Major emphasis should be placed on recognizing and showing approval of students in the calm phase; the obvious goal is for teachers to help students remain in the calm phase for a longer period of time.

An unresolved problem in or outside of school—being teased, for example—may be a trigger for a student. The *trigger* is often the first thing that sets off a student headed for a major blowup. At this point, a teacher may stop further escalation if they recognize the triggering events or conditions and move quickly to help the student resolve the problem.

If triggering problems are not resolved, the student may move into a state of *agitation*, in which overall behavior is unfocused and off task. If the teacher recognizes indications of agitation, further escalation of aggressive behavior may be prevented by the teacher's getting closer to or further away from the student, engaging the student in alternative activities, involving the student in a plan of self-management, or using other strategies designed to help the student avoid a blowup.

Agitation, if responded to inappropriately, can lead to a stage of the cycle called *acceleration*. In this phase, the student engages the teacher in a coercive struggle. Acceleration is characterized by attempts to draw the teacher into arguments or demand teacher attention through noncompliant, highly disruptive, abusive, or destructive behavior. At this point, it is extremely important for the teacher to avoid getting drawn in, to use crisis-prevention strategies to extricate himself or herself from the struggle. By the time the student gets to this point, it is very difficult to de-escalate the behavior; this phase is sometimes thought of as a time when teachers realize things are getting out of hand but also realize that there's little they can do to *stop* the misbehavior. Instead, the goal becomes one of minimizing further damage (literally and figuratively), and getting the student through the crisis with as little further escalation as possible. Clear consequences for such behavior need to be established and communicated to the student beforehand, so that at this point the teacher can deliver the needed information to the student matter-of-factly and allow him or her a few seconds to make a decision (e.g., "Roger, you must stop throwing stuff around now, or I will call the principal. Take a couple of seconds to decide"). Prompt and unequivocal follow-through in applying the consequence is extremely important.

In the *peak* phase of the cycle, the student's behavior is out of control, and the safety of all concerned becomes the paramount concern. It may be necessary to call the police or the student's parents or remove the student from the classroom or school. Preparation at a schoolwide level for such out-of-control behavior is essential so that the involved adults are as calm, systematic, and effective as possible in preventing injury or damage so that the de-escalation phase can be entered as quickly as possible. Frequent out-of-control behavior should be a signal to educators to examine the environment and schoolwork for conditions that need to be changed.

During *de-escalation* following a peak phase, the student typically is beginning to disengage from the struggle and is in a confused state. Behavior may range from withdrawal, to denial and blaming others for what happened, to wanting to make up, to responsiveness to directions and willingness to engage in simple tasks. It is important to take measures to help the student cool down, restore the environment as much as possible (e.g., pick up books and chairs, clean up a mess), and get back to routine activities. This is not yet the time to talk to the student about his or her behavior. Debriefing at this point in the cycle is likely to be counterproductive; the student is likely to be reluctant to talk at all or may not be able to think clearly about the incident, what led to it, and how similar problems might be avoided.

Finally, the student enters a *recovery* phase in which he or she is eager for busywork and a semblance of ordinary classwork but still reluctant to discuss what happened. It is important to provide strong reinforcement for normal routines and to avoid negotiations about the negative consequences that may have been applied to the serious misbehavior. However, it is very important at this point to *debrief* the student, to review what led up to the problem and what alternative behaviors the student might have chosen. Any effort of the student to problem-solve should be acknowledged, and the student should be helped to devise a step-by-step plan for avoiding repetitions of the blowup. The student needs reassurance that he or she can succeed and avoid such out-of-control incidents with help.

Educators often place a great deal of emphasis on Phases 4 and 5 of the acting-out behavior cycle, where most of the drama occurs, but they virtually ignore the first three phases, particularly Phase 1 (calm). This is counterproductive. The opposite emphasis is recommended by decades of research: Focus attention on the earlier phases of the cycle, on attention to and reinforcement of calm behavior, removing or ameliorating triggers, and intervening early and nonthreateningly when students begin showing signs of agitation. Strong reinforcement for appropriate behavior is important, but an intervention called *precorrection* by Colvin, Sugai, and Patching (1993) begins with examination of the context in which misbehavior is likely and how conditions might be altered and instructional (as opposed to correctional) procedures used to prevent the misbehavior from occurring—how triggers and agitation can be avoided. Figure 9.1 shows an example of a precorrection checklist and plan devised by a sixth-grade teacher for Timmy, a student in her class.

Most of the problems involving episodes of aggression start with something that doesn't at first seem significant at all. Astute teachers perceive the potential for triggers and agitation and move quickly and positively to help students learn to avoid them, not just to deal appropriately with the early stages of acting out. Many of the most effective interventions involve expert management of seemingly ordinary events.

School Violence and Schoolwide Discipline

There is strong consensus among those who study schools and behavioral deviance that the problems of student misconduct have increased enormously in seriousness and pervasiveness during the past two decades. Such episodes will not be managed well or lessened without a coherent schoolwide plan of behavior management in addition to strategies designed for individuals and classroom groups (Algozzine & Algozzine, 2014; Lewis, Mitchell, Johnson, & Richter, 2014).

In many schools today, especially middle schools, students are concerned about the violent behavior of their peers. Teaching peace and conflict-resolution skills has been suggested as an effective strategy for reducing violence, and perhaps such instruction can contribute to safer, less-violent schools. However, it is possible that the most effective approach to school

Figure 9.1 Precorrection Plan for Timmy

A Sample Precorrection Plan

Teacher: <u>Lydia Hassey</u>   Student: <u>Timmy Lindle (6th grade)</u>   Date: <u>Oct. 11, 2016</u>

1. Context [where and when; situation, circumstances, or conditions in which predictable behavior occurs]

   During science or social studies classes, especially when group work is required

   Predictable Behavior [the error or misbehavior that you can anticipate in the context]

   Timmy complains loudly about the assignment ("Why do we have to do this crap!") or about his peers, calling them names ("stupid," "retard"); he is especially cruel when other students respond to a teacher question, making fun of or mimicking them.

2. Expected Behavior [what you want the student to do instead of the predictable behavior]

   Timmy will work cooperatively in a group, talking only about the assignment or work-related topics, and speaking to or about his peers only in positive terms.

3. Context Modification [how you can change the situation, circumstances, or conditions to make the predictable behavior less likely and the expected behavior more likely to occur]

   When groups are formed for a class activity, ask Timmy what role he'd like to take (e.g., recorder, materials manager, researcher). Question him as group begins work on what his role is, what that means, and what he'll accomplish during this class period.

4. Behavior Rehearsal [practice; dry run; try out; drill]

   Review group members' roles with Timmy in private in the morning on the day that an afternoon group activity is planned; ask him to name and describe the roles of each group member. Role-play a brief group activity with Timmy, asking him task-related questions and requiring him to talk about the assignment.

5. Strong Reinforcement [special reward for doing the expected behavior]

   Acknowledge and praise Timmy for appropriate talk during group work on at least three occasions per day. Allow Timmy ten minutes on computer each day he completes a group activity with zero instances of teasing, name-calling, or inappropriate talk.

6. Prompts [gestures or other signals indicating "remember; do it now"]

   Use hand signal to remind Timmy that he is expected to work cooperatively and talk appropriately during group work (and thumbs up when he is working and talking appropriately).

7. Monitoring Plan [record of performance; indicator of success that you can show someone]

   Timmy and I will record whether his group work and talk were appropriate—only at the end of each group activity.

violence is focused primarily on the more ordinary, routine interactions that characterize class-rooms and other school environments and that are natural extensions or refinements of basic educational practices rather than special curricula. In fact, schoolwide discipline plans may be thought of as universal interventions that help to prevent more severe disorders from ever developing.

An important concept in the prevention of violence is that violent acts, like the more mundane acts of aggression that characterize CD, typically follow a pattern of escalating conflict. The most effective strategies for controlling school violence, therefore, are those that modify the conditions under which lower levels of aggressive acts are most likely to occur, deal quickly and nonviolently with the earliest indications that aggressive behavior is on an escalating path, and organize the school staff to support consistent, schoolwide implementa-tion of discipline procedures. With a good schoolwide plan, the entire school staff functions as a team to set clear behavioral expectations, establish a positive school climate in which desirable behavior is frequently recognized and reinforced, monitor student behavior continu-ously, apply consistent and planned consequences for unacceptable behavior, provide collegial support, and maintain clear communication about both behavioral expectations and problem incidents (see Lane et al., 2009; Lewis et al., 2014).

Much of the problem of antisocial behavior in schools is in the form of bullying—coercion, intimidation, and threats that often start as mean-spirited teasing and progress to extortion and physical attack. Bullying is now recognized as a serious problem in the schools of many nations throughout the world. It is a serious problem that is often a pre-cursor to school violence. Antisocial students are typically the bullies, not the victims, although they sometimes suffer the same fate as those they bully. Any student who is particularly passive, submissive, or provocative is a potential victim of bullies. Effective intervention in bullying typically requires a schoolwide, if not communitywide, effort, as well as individual intervention, because much of the bullying occurs outside the presence of any one adult. The general features of effective antibullying interventions include the following (see Gregory, Cornell, Fan, Sheras, Shih, & Huang, 2010; Walker et al., 2004 for further discussion):

- A school climate characterized by a warm, positive, supportive school atmosphere in which adults set clear and firm limits on unacceptable behavior
- Nonhostile, nonphysical sanctions applied immediately and consistently to violations of behavioral expectations
- Continuous monitoring and surveillance of student activities in and around the school
- Adult mediation of student interactions and assumption of authority to stop bullying when it is observed
- Discussion of the issue of bullying with bullies, victims, parents, and neutral students (non-participants) to clarify school values, expectations, procedures, and consequences

We would like to think that all schools are responsible for all children and that no child should be excluded from a school because of his or her disability. However, some students with severe conduct disorder are disabled in ways that make their inclusion in regular classrooms and neighborhood schools inadvisable on ethical grounds, if not a mockery of social justice (Kauffman, Anastasiou, Badar, Travers, & Wiley, 2017; Kauffman, Ward, & Badar, 2016). Violent behavior cannot and must not be tolerated in schools if nonviolent students and their teachers are to maintain a viable social and instructional environment.

Interventions Specific to Covert Antisocial Behavior

Because of similarities in the nature and causes of the problems, intervention and education in overt and covert forms of conduct disorder share many features, but they also have important differences (cf. Eddy et al., 2002; Walker et al., 2004). Consequently, the particular problems, as well as the approaches to intervention, may differ somewhat for specific types of covert anti-social acts. For example, families of children who steal more often than families of aggressive children who do not steal are extremely difficult treatment targets. Sometimes family therapy or parent discipline training is simply unfeasible or ineffective. Vandalism is often a particular problem in schools, and some intervention programs may therefore be primarily school based. Fire setting may be only tangentially related to school programs, but schools may be targets of arson by students with academic difficulties. Truancy is by definition an educational problem, although it is associated with delinquency, and programs to encourage school attendance may involve both the school and other community agencies.

Stealing

A common behavior problem that parents of young children report is that they don't recog-nize and respect the property rights of others. Many young children simply take what they want when they see it, without regard for ownership; in short, they steal. If this behavior persists beyond the age of five or six, the child may become known as a stealer and get into trouble with peers and adults. The most useful analyses of the origins and management of stealing come from a behavioral or social learning perspective (Eddy et al., 2002).

Some scholars have systematically researched the characteristics of aggressive children who steal (see Eddy et al., 2002). These generalizations have emerged:

- Stealers exhibit lower rates of observable out-of-control (negative–coercive and antisocial) behavior than do aggressive children who don't steal.
- Families of stealers demonstrate lower rates of both positive–friendly and negative–coercive behaviors than do families of aggressive children who don't steal.
- The differences in positive–friendly and negative–coercive behavior rates are almost com-pletely because of the mothers' behavior.

Many stealers appear to exhibit high rates of antisocial behavior only away from home or at home when no observers are present. Many stealers are likely to confine their antisocial behavior to settings outside the home, disturbing the community rather than their parents by their theft and leaving their parents with little motivation to work on the problem. Parents of stealers tend to blame the stealing on someone else, thus refusing to recognize the problem and failing to follow through on intervention plans.

Families of stealers appear to be loosely structured and characterized by lack of parental supervision or emotional attachment to the children. The stealer may, therefore, learn that tak-ing others' possessions is acceptable behavior, that no one will care what he or she takes, and that no adverse consequences will follow theft. The child who learns to steal may be motivated to seek stimulation and reinforcement outside the family.

The difficulty in treating theft isn't surprising. Theft generally occurs out of sight of any authority figure, so it's highly unlikely that any swift consequence or correction can be delivered. As important, if one takes a behavioral view, it's easy to see how theft itself is immediately reinforced—by the object stolen. Overcoming such contingencies is indeed a tall order. Despite these difficulties, and the destructive family interaction patterns of stealers, relatively successful behavioral interventions have been devised. An effective anti-stealing program has several essential components. Before implementing such a program, a fundamental problem must be resolved: parental definition of stealing. Parents of stealers are usually hesitant to accuse the child of theft and may be unlikely to take disciplinary action. Because they seldom, if ever, actually observe the child in the act of taking something, parents may accept their child's explanation for how something came into his or her possession. Many parents blindly accept the child's claims of finding, borrowing, trading, winning, or receiving as payment whatever item was stolen. When their child is accused by teachers, peers, or police, parents of stealers frequently argue that the child is being unjustly attacked. By blaming others—making it somebody else's problem—the parents avoid having to deal with the problem themselves. Even when the behavior occurs at home, parents often do not adequately define *stealing*. Some parents consider it theft to take food from the refrigerator without specific permission, whereas others view all family possessions as common property. The value of an item is also an issue because many parents of stealers cannot bring themselves to apply consequences for stealing something they consider to be worth very little.

The first step in dealing with theft is to recognize that the child is in difficulty because he or she steals more than other children of the same age do, may steal valuable objects, and has been labeled by others as a thief. The antitheft strategy must include steps to help the child stop being accused of theft and being viewed with suspicion. The child will not lose the stigma associated with the label until he or she learns to avoid even the appearance of wrong-doing. Following is the recommended strategy for parents:

1. Agree to define *stealing* as the child's possession of anything that doesn't belong to him or her or taking anything he or she doesn't own.

2. Only the parents decide whether a theft has occurred. They may base their judgment on either their own observation or on the report of a reliable informant.

3. When it's determined that the child has stolen, the parents state that according to their rules, the child has stolen and a consequence will be applied. The parents must not shame or counsel the child at the time they discover the theft and apply the consequences, but they are encouraged to discuss the theft with him or her at another time.

4. Every instance of stealing must receive consequences.

5. Parents are advised to keep their eyes open and ask about "new" property rather than use detective tactics such as searching the child's room or clothing.

6. Consequences for stealing are either a specified interval of useful work or a period of grounding or restriction. Stealing more expensive items receives more severe consequences. Harsh consequences, such as humiliation or beating, are prohibited.

7. No positive reinforcement is given for periods of nonstealing because it's impossible to know that successful covert stealing has not occurred.

8. The program should stay in effect for at least six months following the last episode of stealing.

If the child steals both at home and at school, parents and teachers must implement consistent antitheft programs in both environments (Williams, 1985). Effective and early management of stealing is particularly important; the younger the age at which children begin stealing and the longer they persist, the more likely they are to become chronic stealers and adjudicated delinquents. In general, the more severe the conduct disorder, the less likely it is that intervention will be successful. Management of stealing at school, particularly with older students, becomes particularly complex, and legal issues arise, including the need for schools to attend carefully to local policies and laws regarding matters like searches and seizures.

Lying

Parents and teachers consistently rate lying as a serious problem behavior of childhood, yet there has been little research on the subject (see Mash & Barkley, 2003; Shinn, Walker, & Stoner, 2002). Research continues to explore the nature and development of lying in children (e.g., Ahern, Lyon, & Quas, 2011). However, validated interventions for dealing with lying aren't available. Like stealing, lying presents a particular challenge for intervention in that in many cases, the lie isn't known to be a lie at the moment it happens; parents or teachers often only learn well after the fact that a child was intentionally deceitful. Thus, any correction, consequence, or punishment cannot happen swiftly.

Developmental changes clearly occur in the understanding of lies and liars, but the relationship of these changes to the development of pathological lying isn't understood. Apparently, children often lie in attempts to escape punishment. Adults consider lying a serious problem not only because it is an attempt at concealment but also because it is associated with other antisocial behaviors such as stealing and truancy. In the classroom, lying and cheating are functionally similar behaviors.

As one might expect, lying is related to the same sort of family process variables, especially lack of parental monitoring or supervision, that characterize stealing. Although lying is a serious problem and may be a stepping-stone to the development of other conduct problems, only a small body of research is available to guide intervention. In addition to careful monitoring, providing reinforcement for honest behavior and punishment of lying and cheating is necessary. It's important to determine whether the student can discriminate truth from nontruth, to find the probable reason for the student's telling untruths (e.g., to avoid consequences or work), and to avoid getting caught up in arguments about the veracity of what the student has said.

Fire Setting

The fires that children set frequently cause injury, loss of life, and property damage. In fact, youthful arsonists account for more than half of all set fires. The lifetime prevalence of fire setting has been estimated at 1.0 percent in the general population, though evidence suggests strong associations between fire setting and a host of other risk factors, including antisocial behavior in the child, a family history of antisocial behavior, drug and alcohol use, and other psychiatric disorders (e.g., obsessive-compulsive disorder) (Vaughn et al., 2010). Although fire setting has been a behavior of scientific interest for more than 150 years, we still don't understand very well the causes and management of this behavior in children (Kolko, 2002). Fanciful psychodynamic explanations that connect fire setting to sexual excitement have only recently begun to give way to conceptualizations grounded in reliable empirical evidence. However, social learning may account for risk factors, which seem to include playing with fire. Children learn attitudes and behaviors from early experiences, such as watching parents or older siblings working or playing with fire. Children of fire fighters, furnace stokers, smokers, and adults who otherwise model behavior dealing with fire may be more likely to set fires.

We see interest in fire and playing with fire in a high percentage of young children. The ready availability of incendiary materials to children (see Henderson & Mackay, 2010) who are interested in fire and observe models who set or manage fires may set the stage for fire setting. Another major factor, however, is the personal repertoires that may heighten the risk of fire setting. Children may be more likely to set fires if any of the following are true:

- They don't understand the danger of fire or the importance of fire safety.
- They don't have the necessary social skills to obtain gratification in appropriate ways.
- They engage in other antisocial behaviors.
- They're motivated by anger and revenge.

Finally, stressful life events; parental psychopathology; and lack of parental supervision, monitoring, and involvement can increase the chances that a child will set fires (see Kolko, 2002). Although research doesn't clearly distinguish different types of fire setters, all fires obviously aren't set under the same conditions or for the same reasons. Some fires are set accidentally by children playing with matches or lighters, some by angry children who are seeking revenge but don't understand the awful consequences, others by delinquents who know full well the consequences of arson and are seeking to conceal another crime they have committed, some in response to deviant peer pressure, some in attempts to injure the fire setters themselves, and still others by youngsters whose behavior is related to anxiety and obsessions or compulsions.

Most school-aged youngsters who set fires have a history of school failure and multiple behavioral problems. Schools are sometimes their targets, so educators are among those who have an interest in identifying and treating fire setters. Fire safety education and cognitive-behavioral treatment are among the more frequent interventions used with fire setters and their families, but research on the outcomes of these approaches is scant (Kolko, Herschell, & Scharf, 2006). Thus, at this point, we can make few research-based recommendations for intervention or prevention. Both intervention and prevention will probably require efforts similar to those suggested for managing other covert antisocial behaviors such as stealing, vandalism, and truancy. However, educators may have a unique role to play in finding out about the motivations and behavior of fire setters and finding interventions that work (Pinsonneault, Richardson, & Pinsonneault, 2002).

Vandalism

Deliberate destruction of school property costs hundreds of millions of dollars each year, and vandalism in other community settings results in much higher costs. Destructiveness and violence against people are often linked, and both are on the increase (Mayer & Sulzer-Azaroff, 2002; Walker et al., 2004). It appears to increase dramatically in antisocial boys after age seven and to peak in the middle school years; in one study, vandalism peaked at about age fourteen and was closely linked to physical aggression and alcohol and drug use (van Lier,

Vitaro, Barker, Koot, & Tremblay, 2009). The typical response of school administrators and justice officials to violence and vandalism is to tighten security measures and provide harsher punishment. Unfortunately, punitive measures may only aggravate the problems.

Vandalism in schools appears to be, at least in part, a response to aversive environments. More specifically, students tend to be disruptive and destructive when school rules are vague, discipline is punitive, punishment is rigidly applied regardless of students' individual differences, relationships between students and school personnel are impersonal, the school curriculum is mismatched with students' interests and abilities, and students receive little recognition for appropriate conduct or achievement. Decreasing the aversiveness of the school environment by adjusting school rules, teachers' expectations, and consequences for desirable and undesirable behavior might be more effective in preventing vandalism than increasing security and making punishment more severe (see Mayer & Sulzer-Azaroff, 2002; Walker et al., 2004).

Truancy

Truancy has been a problem for schools since the beginning of compulsory education in the United States more than a century ago (e.g., Leyba & Massat, 2009), and it remains a major factor in school failure and delinquency. Attendance at school certainly doesn't guarantee academic success, but chronic unexcused absence virtually ensures failure. Frequent truancy is serious not only because of probable school failure but because chronic truants are at risk for later unemployment or employment failure, criminal convictions, substance abuse, and a variety of other difficulties. Dissatisfaction with school programs and failure to attend school regularly are important signals that the student may drop out (Walker et al., 2004).

The problem of truancy isn't new, and neither are the most effective approaches to reducing it. Interventions based on social learning principles continue to produce better results than do other approaches (see Kerr & Nelson, 2010; Walker et al., 2004). These interventions are intended to make school more attractive by recognizing and praising attendance, setting up systems in which attendance earns special rewards or privileges, giving the student work that is more interesting to him or her and at which he or she can be successful, connecting school with work or later education that is important to the student, stopping harassment by peers or other social punishment in school, and, if possible, decreasing the satisfaction or fun the student has outside school during school hours. It's often necessary to have the cooperation of the student's parents to make school more attractive and alternatives less attractive. A review of truancy intervention research by Sutphen, Ford, and Flaherty (2010) supported these general guidelines. Interventions that had shown promise were grouped into four categories: student- and family-based interventions (including primarily reward or punishment-based interventions); school-based interventions (including school reorganization efforts designed to provide more appealing and appropriate career tracks, focused instructional support for struggling students, and afterschool programs); and community-based interventions (which included primarily punitive measures, such as schools notifying parents, or referring children and families to social services or mental health agencies, or ultimately to law enforcement).

Youngsters with CD of any kind will tax any teacher's skill. In Box 9.1, we summarize the social skills these students need most and suggest a technique a teacher might try.

Box 9.1

Teaching Students with Conduct Disorder the Social Skills They Need Most

What learning or social skills present the greatest challenges for teachers?

Students with conduct disorder will be difficult to manage, displaying frequent disruptive behavior and aggression toward peers, adults, or their environment (e.g., destroying materials). They are likely to be noncompliant, frequently failing to follow teacher directions, and may leave their designated place without regard for classroom or school rules (ranging from simply being "out-of-seat" to leaving the classroom or even school grounds without permission). Though their intelligence and potential academic achievement may be in the normal range, they will undoubtedly experience academic difficulties and deficits. It's unclear which came first—the academic failure or the problem behavior—but it's generally accepted that each is made worse by the other. Probably the social skill they need most is following directions—compliance with reasonable instructions and requests.

What are appropriate targets for intervention?

There will be no shortage of problem behaviors from which teachers might choose when deciding what new skills such students need, or what negative behaviors they'd like to see less of. Reducing the number and severity of disruptions or acts of aggression toward others would be logical priorities if students are to participate meaningfully and positively in classroom activities. Staying in seat (or appropriate location), completing assignments, and positive social skills involved in interacting with others in a variety of contexts (peers in the classroom, lunchroom, or on the playground; teachers in instructional settings) will undoubtedly be behaviors teachers would like to increase. Because being "difficult to manage" often describes students with conduct disorder, we think a logical approach to intervention might be simply to increase "compliance." Compliance includes following teachers' routine directions (e.g., "take out your math book," "please line up for lunch") as well as more pointed requests or directions based on potential misbehavior (e.g., "you need to return to your seat," "please put your cell phone in your backpack"). By definition, compliance subsumes many of the behavioral excesses and deficits a student with conduct disorder might display, and increasing compliance would certainly be a welcome change for any teacher.

What types of interventions show promise?

As we have discussed, interventions based on a behavioral view, or more specifically, based on the principles of applied behavior analysis, probably provide teachers with the best and most effective tools suitable for classroom use. Strategies that show promise include simple positive reinforcement, which might be delivered in the forms of specific teacher praise or more systematically and overtly through the use of a token economy or point system. More specific procedures such as precision requests and behavioral momentum might be particularly useful.

(continued)

Box 9.1   *(continued)*

An example—behavioral momentum

Behavioral momentum refers to exactly what the name implies; teachers can create momentum toward compliance by giving students a series of easy requests before giving them a difficult request. Research has shown that the odds of compliance with a difficult task (referred to as a low-probability request) increase when students successfully complete a series of easy tasks (referred to as high-probability requests) before being asked to comply with the more challenging request. To implement behavioral momentum, teachers must analyze a particular student's pattern of compliance to determine those tasks or requests that typically cause trouble for the student, and those tasks or requests with which a student is likely to comply. Momentum is built when the student complies with the easy requests, which notably gives the teacher the opportunity to reinforce the student for compliance (something a student with conduct disorder probably experiences too infrequently). Consider the following example involving Cedric, a fifth grader in Ms. Jones' general education classroom. Though he is not identified as having any disability, Ms. Jones knows from his parents that Cedric has been diagnosed with conduct disorder. In her classroom, Cedric is frequently noncompliant and his failure to follow directions often results in escalating, highly disruptive battles between student and teacher. Ms. Jones decides to use behavioral momentum to increase the likelihood that Cedric will comply. Note that behavioral momentum does not guarantee that a student will comply with a difficult request (joining a group and opening a book in the example below), but research does suggest that the *odds* of compliance increase when the difficult request is preceded by several high-probability requests.

Ms. Jones: "Cedric, will you pass out these papers for me?"

Cedric complies.

Ms. Jones: "Thank you, Cedric; you passed those out quickly and quietly. Now, will you get the markers from the shelves and give one box to each group?"

Cedric complies.

Ms. Jones: "Thank you again, Cedric. I really appreciate your help. Now, please join your group and open your book to page 147."

Where to find more information on behavioral momentum:

Belfiore, P. J., Lee, D. L., Scheeler, C., & Klein, D. (2002). Implications of behavioral momentum and the academic achievement for students with behavior disorders: Theory, application, and practice. *Psychology in the Schools, 39,* 171–179.

Landrum, T. J., & Sweigart, C. A. (2015). Simple, evidence-based interventions for classic problems of emotional and behavioral disorders. *Beyond Behavior, 23*(3), 3–9.

Lee, D. L., Belfiore, P. J., & Budin, S. G. (2008). Riding the wave: Creating a momentum of school success. *Teaching Exceptional Children, 40*(3), 65–70.

Also see: http://www.interventioncentral.org/student_motivation_high_probability_requests

SUMMARY

Conduct disorder is characterized by persistent antisocial behavior that violates the rights of others as well as age-appropriate social norms. It includes aggression toward people and animals, destruction of property, deceitfulness and theft, and serious violation of rules. We distinguish youngsters with conduct disorder from those who are developing normally by their higher rates of noxious behaviors and by the persistence of such conduct beyond the age at which most children have adopted less aggressive behavior. CD is often comorbid with other disorders. It's one of the most prevalent psychopathological disorders of childhood and youth, estimated to affect 6 percent to 16 percent of males and 2 percent to 9 percent of females under the age of eighteen. CD may be classified by age of onset, and those with early onset typically show more serious impairment and have a worse prognosis. Other subtypes include overt aggressive (undersocialized); covert antisocial (socialized), such as theft, lying, and arson; and versatile (both socialized and undersocialized).

Aggressive behavior has long been a common phenomenon in American culture, but aggression, violence, and incivility have become a much greater concern in schools during the past two decades. Aggression and violence are multicultural issues, although most contributing factors and interventions appear to apply equally across all subgroups. Both general and special education teachers must be prepared to deal with the aggressive behavior of students.

Many contributing causes of aggression have been identified, but social learning theory provides the best-supported and most useful conceptualizations for educators. We know that aggression may be learned through processes of modeling, reinforcement of aggression, and ineffective punishment. The risk of aggressive behavior is increased by a wide variety of personal, family, school, peer, and other cultural factors. These factors are often combined in a coercive process leading to aggressive behavior that is passed from one generation to the next.

Steps likely to be effective in preventing CD include consequences that deter aggression, instruction in nonaggressive responses to problems, early intervention, restriction of the tools of aggression, restraint of public displays of aggression, correction of everyday living conditions, and more effective and attractive school options. A proactive, instructional approach to prevention is of greatest value to educators.

A variety of rating scales are useful in assessing CD, but direct observation of behavior in various settings must supplement the ratings. Assessment requires evaluation of a variety of domains, including both academic and social problems and behavior at home and school. Assessment must include prosocial skills as well as social deficits. Ongoing assessment to monitor progress is essential. Social skills must be assessed to guide instruction. Functional assessment of behavior to determine what consequences, gains, or benefits it provides the student will help guide intervention.

Interventions based on social learning are the most reliable and useful for teachers. These may include strategies such as rules, teacher praise, positive reinforcement, verbal feedback, stimulus change, contingency contracts, modeling and reinforcement of imitation, shaping, systematic social skills instruction, self-monitoring and self-control training, time-out, and response cost. Particular care must be taken in the use of punishment because it is seductive and easily misused. The focus must be on positive strategies. The concepts of the acting-out behavior cycle and precorrection help keep the focus of intervention on positive strategies applied early in the sequence. The acting-out cycle includes the phases *calm, trigger, agitation, acceleration, peak, de-escalation,* and *recovery*. Greatest emphasis should be placed on intervention in the first three phases of the cycle. Precorrection plans help to keep the focus on earlier phases in the cycle. Schoolwide discipline plans may help decrease the level of violence in schools by focusing efforts on positive attention to appropriate behavior, clear expectations and monitoring of student behavior, staff communication and support, and consistent consequences for unacceptable behavior.

Covert antisocial behavior consists of acts such as stealing, lying, fire setting, vandalism, and truancy. These also are best addressed by application of social learning principles to problem reduction or resolution.

✔ ENHANCEDetext END-OF-CHAPTER 9 QUIZ

Click on the checkmark icon to access an end-of-chapter quiz. Answer the questions to gauge your understanding of chapter concepts and better prepare you for case discussions.

PERSONAL REFLECTIONS

Aggressive Conduct Disorder

Lisa Funk Njoroge is originally from Ohio and completed her undergraduate degree at Cleveland State University in Ohio and her master's of science in special education at the California State University of Long Beach. She has spent the past fourteen years educating middle school and high school students with emotional and behavioral disorders in various settings. She wrote this reflection about Marko, a student she last worked with when he was an eighteen-year-old high school student.

Think of a particular student who exhibits a conduct disorder. How does this student manifest the disorder?

Marko is an eighteen-year-old Hispanic male who receives his education in a non–public school setting, which is the most restrictive environment next to home schooling and hospitalization available in California. Beginning in the fourth grade, Marko began arguing with peers, which quickly escalated to routine violence toward peers. Marko usually shows his conduct disorder through violent behavior and fighting, but his conduct disorder isn't limited to that kind of behavior.

His conduct disorder also comes out in his relationship with his mother, his attitude toward au-

thority, and his response to the law. He has been arrested several times in the past two years for fighting with his mother. Consequently, their relationship has become so strained that she currently questions whether she can continue to live with him and support him. He's also been hospitalized following a fight involving several known gang members. Marko suffered extensive injuries, requiring stitches in his mouth, eye, and cheek, and staples in his scalp. This hospitalization did nothing to lessen his propensity toward fighting, and immediately after his discharge from the hospital, Marko went looking for the people involved. Finally, Marko routinely breaks the law by driving without a license, among other things. Most of his behavior in the classroom that's associated with his diagnosis relates to his difficulty with being told "no."

What procedures have you found most useful in working with this student?

One of the most effective tools I used while working with Marko for two years was one-on-one emotional processing. This means that when he entered the classroom visibly upset, I made it a point to pull him aside and directly address the difference in his demeanor. I would later follow up when time permitted to give him an opportunity to let me know what was going on. This was not possible in the beginning of his time in my classroom, as it takes months (or more) to build the necessary trust to implement such an intervention. Knowing this, in the beginning I had him keep a journal about his thoughts/emotions and turn it in at the end of the day.

Another method that worked well with Marko was giving him constant praise. Although this may seem obvious to some, it isn't always regularly implemented. Students who regularly receive attention for negative reasons need exponentially more praise for improved behavior due to this fact. He would always respond with a warm "thank you" when acknowledged for progress in his impulse control and decision-making. Although it was difficult, it was imperative that I build a relationship with his mother as well. We even attempted a home-school contract which rewarded Marko for following his mother's directions at home and treating her respectfully with privileges in the classroom that were important to him. This contract helped to improve the communication between the home and school, which helped to stabilize Marko's behavior. Another method that proved effective with Marko was to have him evaluate his own behavior after each academic period and at the end of each day. This tool helped Marko to begin looking at his behavior honestly and forced him both to take credit for his positive behavior and responsibility for his negative behavior throughout the day.

What do you see as the biggest long-term problems this student will face?

Marko has received his high school diploma. He plans to attend vocational school or a community college to enhance his skills in the area of musical engineering and production. I believe that if he finds early success in his classes or has professors who take an interest in guiding him, he will complete his goal of augmenting his talents with education. I do believe that although he has the potential to succeed, many factors could potentially prevent his success. Some of my fears for him include his mother deciding that she has had enough and withdrawing financial and housing support. I also fear his getting into trouble for a serious offense leading to jail. In addition to the difficulty he may have finishing school without a mentor or guiding adult, he will need this, too, in terms of making decisions in relationships and in working. One of Marko's greatest strengths has been his ability to listen to adults whom he trusts and heed their advice to the best of his ability. If he continues in therapy or is taken under the wing of a stable adult figure, I have no doubt that he can accomplish what he sets out to do in this world that is positive. (See the accompanying case book for Ms. Njoroge's interview of Marko.)

Questions for Further Reflection

1. How would you argue with someone who insisted that overt conduct disorder is not an emotional disturbance but an indication of social maladjustment that should not be included in special education?

2. What level of aggression or violence, if any, would you argue justifies removal of a student from a regular classroom or from a typical neighborhood school?

3. What are the things you can do as a teacher to keep acting-out, aggressive behavior in your classroom to a minimum, and how are these related to cultural diversity?

10 ANXIETY AND RELATED DISORDERS

Gem Photo/Shutterstock

After reading this chapter, you should be able to:

10.1 Explain how anxiety is related to a variety of EBDs.

10.2 Specify the conditions under which manifestations of anxiety should prompt concern and possible intervention by educators and others.

10.3 Describe the most effective intervention strategies for anxiety disorders.

10.4 Identify the major defining characteristics of eating and elimination disorders, and discuss educators' roles in dealing with these.

10.5 Describe the role the peer group may play in effective intervention in social isolation.

Chapters 8 and 9 dealt mostly with problems that fall under the general dimension of *externalizing disorders*. This chapter turns to problems designated generally as *internalizing*. We point out that the classification of internalizing (versus externalizing) disorders, referred to as *broadband* classification, is well established by research. In contrast, most of the specific categories and disorders that fall under it are not. In short, there is more confusion and controversy over terminology and classification for internalizing problems than for externalizing problems, which makes discussion of internalizing disorders difficult.

Regardless of how we group internalizing problems for discussion, it's important to note that they may occur along with other internalizing disorders, and even with externalizing problems. When internalizing and externalizing disorders do occur together, the child is at particularly high risk. Anxiety, social withdrawal, and other internalizing behavior problems often occur together and sometimes are comorbid—coexisting—with externalizing behavioral problems (Albano, Chorpita, & Barlow, 2003; Gresham & Kern, 2004; Higa-McMillan, Francis, & Chorpita, 2014; Kazdin, 2001), although this is not always the case (Bagwell, Molina, Kashdan, Pelham, & Hoza, 2006; Higa-McMillan et al., 2014). Eating disorders and reluctant speech may both involve specific fears or anxieties, stereotyped movement disorders may involve obsessions or compulsions or both, and so on. Anxiety is a frequent component of other disorders, and anxiety disorders of all types may be comorbid with a variety of other disorders. Comorbidity is the rule, not the exception, among students with EBD.

The relationships among the various problems involving anxiety and other internalizing problems are complex and confusing. We won't attempt to summarize definition, prevalence, causal factors, prevention, assessment, intervention, or education for the general case or for all specific disorders because these disorders are so varied and loosely related. The problems we discuss are representative of those most frequently described in the literature. We begin with anxiety disorders because they're the broadest category; anxiety appears to be a significant component of all the others.

ANXIETY DISORDERS

Anxiety is a normal reaction to stress. The distress, tension, or uneasiness that goes with fears and worries is also a part of the normal development of young children (Albano et al., 2003; Dadds, 2002; Hintze, 2002; Woodruff-Borden & Leyfer, 2006). At birth, for example, infants have a fear of falling and of loud noise; fear of other stimuli (strange persons, objects, situations) ordinarily develops during the first few months of life. These fears probably have survival value, and they're considered normal and adaptive, not deviant. As children grow into the middle childhood years they develop additional fears, especially about imaginary creatures or events (e.g., Beesdo, Knappe, & Pine, 2009). But it's only when fears become excessive or debilitating that we consider anxiety a disorder; if anxiety is so severe that it prevents the child from engaging in normal social interaction, sleep, school attendance, or exploring the environment, then anxiety is a problem, rather than a normal, protective human trait. Indeed, children who have no fears at all are not only highly unusual but also likely to endanger themselves because of inappropriate brashness and risk-taking.

Children's anxieties or fears may be mild and short-lived enough that they don't seriously interfere with social growth. In fact, the study of the prevalence of anxiety in childhood has been concentrated on school phobia or resistance and fears that aren't considered pathological.

Reviews of research suggest that 5 percent to 8 percent of children and youth may have persistent anxiety at a given time (Curry, Marsh, & Hervey, 2004) and that 15 percent to 20 percent of children or adolescents may experience some form of anxiety disorder at some time (Beesdo et al., 2009). Not all of these anxieties require intervention (Woodruff-Borden & Leyfer, 2006). Again, some anxiety and even fear of rightfully fearful situations is quite normal and even useful. When fear unnecessarily restricts the child's activity, however, intervention is called for. A child or youth may be in a chronic state of anxiety about a broad range of things, in which case he or she may be described as having a generalized anxiety disorder. However, a youngster may also have a more specific anxiety. An extreme, irrational fear that is out of proportion to reality and leads to automatic avoidance of the feared situation is called a **phobia** (see Higa-McMillan et al., 2014). In the past, the child who showed extreme anxiety and social withdrawal had been assumed to be more disturbed and to have a worse prognosis for adult adjustment than the hostile, acting-out child with an externalizing disorder. Research doesn't support this assumption.

Characteristics associated with anxiety and withdrawal are usually more transitory and responsive to treatment than are those associated with conduct disorder, and anxiety doesn't typically put a child at risk for later development of schizophrenia or other major psychiatric disorders in adulthood. Compared to their awareness of peers' aggressive and disruptive behavior, children's awareness of their peers' anxiety and withdrawal isn't as keen or as early to develop. At least among typical children, those with high levels of anxiety appear to see themselves in more negative terms than do their peers whose anxiety is lower. There is growing evidence, however, that severe anxiety disorders may be a precursor to later problems with substance abuse (Beesdo et al., 2009; see also Higa-McMillan et al., 2014).

Anxiety-withdrawal in its typical form is not the greatest concern to knowledgeable professionals who work with children and youth who have EBD. Perhaps because professionals are more wary of children who are violent or act out, those who are withdrawn may be overlooked or simply perceived as well-behaved, compliant students. Nevertheless, in their extreme forms, anxiety and related disorders *do* result in serious impairment of functioning. Extreme social isolation, extreme and persistent anxiety, and persistent extreme fears, for example, can seriously endanger social and personal development and demand effective intervention. Some children and adolescents experience severe panic attacks, generally defined as intense periods of discomfort and stress, often lasting no more than ten minutes, associated with an irrational fear and accompanied by observable physical symptoms. The physical symptoms may include rapid heart rate, sweating, trembling, difficulty breathing, nausea, dizziness, and numbness. The individual having the panic attack may fear he or she is losing control, "going crazy," or even dying. True panic attacks are quite rare, though the individual who has them repeatedly will undoubtedly suffer tremendous social consequences. Those who have occasional panic attacks may become even more socially isolated, fearing that going out or putting themselves in certain situations will trigger such an attack.

Problems with anxiety disorders are complicated by their frequent comorbidity with depression, conduct disorder, learning disabilities, and other disorders. The prevalence of anxious-withdrawn behavior appears to be approximately the same as that of conduct disorder, placing it among the most common categories of childhood EBD (Higa-McMillan et al., 2014; Woodruff-Borden & Leyfer, 2006). And in marked contrast to externalizing disorders, females outnumber males in diagnosed anxiety disorders. This gender difference first appears early in childhood, but it reaches a factor of 2:1 or 3:1 by adolescence (Beesdo et al., 2009).

The causes of anxiety aren't entirely clear, though a combination of learning and biological factors almost certainly plays a role. Humans learn fears in a variety of ways. Infants and young children undoubtedly learn certain fears through classical or respondent conditioning. If a naturally fright-producing stimulus is paired with another object or event, the child may come to fear that object or event. Comments, corrections, and other verbal communications of parents (especially the mother) and other adults about objects, activities, places, persons, or situations induce fearfulness in children who have acquired language skills (see Turner, Beidel, Roberson-Nay, & Tervo, 2003). Adults' and other children's nonverbal behavior can also have a powerful influence on a child's learning fear. That is, a child may learn fear vicariously. For example, a child who is overly fearful of dogs may have acquired the fear in one or a combination of ways. A dog may have frightened the child by barking or growling, jumping, knocking the child down, biting, and so on. The parents or someone else may have warned the child in an emotional way about the dangers of dogs, or the child may have heard people talk about a dog's meanness and dangerousness. Or the child may have seen a parent, sibling, or other child (or someone in a movie or on television) attacked or frightened by dogs.

In addition to social learning, anxiety appears in some cases to be affected by physiological factors. Anxiety disorders of various types tend to run in families, and it's suspected that genetic or other physiological factors may be involved in the origins of these disorders as well as social learning principles. Other risk factors like those that increase risk for other kinds of EBD also play a role. Anxiety disorders tend to be more prevalent among families that are economically stressed, among individuals with lower educational achievement, among children who are abused, and among females. Temperament also is suspected of playing a role, but teasing out the effects of any one variable or risk factor remains difficult. Suffice it to say that a female born with an anxious temperament into a family living in poverty, with a parent or sibling who has an anxiety disorder, whose parents are overprotective, or who is abused is surely at heightened risk for anxiety disorder herself (Beesdo et al., 2009; Rapee, Schniering, & Hudson, 2009).

Some children develop fears or phobias about separation, and leaving home or their parents—even for a short time—may be extremely traumatic. Some are extremely anxious about going to school. School phobia may more appropriately be called social phobia in some cases because it's a fear of the social interactions that are an expected part of school attendance (Beidel & Turner, 1998; Higa-McMillan et al., 2014). Of course, a student may have extreme anxiety about both separation from home or parents and social interaction in school.

Social learning principles can help resolve both children's and adults' excessive or irrational anxieties and fears. Rapee et al. (2009) describe approaches to treatment as falling under two categories: skills-based or cognitive-behavioral treatment (CBT). The point of most interventions is to help children identify and understand their anxiety and what triggers it, and to teach them skills that allow them to face, rather than avoid, fear-producing events or situations. Three approaches, which can be used in combination, have been particularly successful: modeling, desensitization, and self-control training. With these techniques, clinicians have helped children and youth overcome a wide array of fears and phobias (see Dadds, 2002; King, Heyne, & Ollendick, 2005). Teachers may be asked to assist in implementing these procedures in school settings. Medications to reduce anxiety may also be helpful (Garland, 2002; Konopasek & Forness, 2014).

Having fearful children watch movies in which other youngsters are having fun (at a party or playing games) while approaching the feared object without hesitation (for example,

Video Example

from

YouTube

ENHANCEDetext
Video Connections 10.1
This video briefly discusses the general approaches to treating childhood anxiety, including medication therapy and cognitive/behavioral interventions. (https://www.youtube.com/watch?v=ayTUqqkM708)

the youngsters in the movie may be handling dogs or snakes while playing) may reduce fear in the observers and make them more willing to approach the thing they fear. Having individuals with phobias watch several different peer models unanxiously approach several different feared objects and showing films that display the actual feared object (rather than a replica) have increased the effectiveness of this method of fear reduction. Positive reinforcement of the fearful person's approach to the feared object adds to the fear-reducing effects of watching models. Filmed modeling procedures have also been effective in preventing children from acquiring maladaptive fears of medical and dental procedures, as well as in dealing with children who have already become fearful.

Procedures variously referred to as systematic desensitization, reciprocal inhibition, and counterconditioning have also been effective in lowering fears of children and adults. The central feature of these procedures involves the individual's gradual and repeated exposure to the fear-provoking stimuli (either in real life or in purposeful fantasy of them), while the person remains unanxious and perhaps engaged in an activity that is incompatible with or inhibits anxiety (such as eating a favorite treat or relaxing comfortably in a chair). Gradual approach to a feared object, repeated exposure to it, and maintenance of an unanxious state during exposure are thought to weaken the conditioned or learned association between the object and the fear response it elicits.

In self-control training, fearful individuals learn to talk through a variety of techniques for managing anxiety. They may learn relaxation, self-reinforcement, self-punishment, self-instruction, visual imagery, or problem-solving strategies. The trainer might help the individual develop images that represent calm or pleasant feelings that are incompatible with anxiety and that the subject can recall when he or she encounters anxiety-provoking circumstances.

Interventions based on behavioral principles have been quite successful in remediating the problem of school phobia and other social fears. Specific techniques vary from case to case, but general procedures include one or more of the following:

- Desensitization of the child's fear through role-playing or in vivo (real-life) approximations of attending school for an entire day
- Reinforcement for attending school even for a brief period, gradually lengthening the time the child is required to stay in school
- Matter-of-fact parental statements that the child will go back to school, avoiding lengthy or emotional discussion
- Removal of reinforcers for staying home (such as being allowed to watch television, play a favorite game, stay close to their mother, or engage in other pleasurable activities)

Many maladaptive fears of school are preventable (see Albano et al., 2003; Kearney & Albano, 2007). Prevention involves desensitizing young children to school by introducing future teachers, school routines, play activities, and so on. Transitions to middle school and senior high school similarly can be made less anxiety provoking by preparing students for their new environments and new expectations. Although many schools attempt to provide orientation experiences, they are often not carefully planned.

Individual students may need to learn coping skills to deal with irrational thoughts and to learn adaptive behavior (such as asking a teacher or a peer for assistance) through modeling, rehearsal, feedback, and reinforcement. Increasingly, it is clear that the causes, prevalence, and responsiveness to particular treatments are extremely complex for all manner of anxiety disorders (Higa-McMillan et al., 2014).

Obsessive-Compulsive Disorders

Obsessions are repetitive, persistent, intrusive impulses, images, or thoughts about something, not worries about real-life problems. **Compulsions** are repetitive, stereotyped acts the individual feels he or she must perform to ward off a dreaded event, although these acts aren't really able to prevent it (e.g., turning a light switch off and on three times). Sometimes the obsessions or compulsions are seen as bizarre, as when a young person is obsessed with the idea that he or she might turn into someone or something else (e.g., become a "transformer") or take on some undesired characteristic (Piacentini, Chang, Snorrason, & Woods, 2014; Volz & Heyman, 2007).

Both obsessions and compulsions may be part of ritualistic behavior an individual uses in an attempt to reduce anxiety. Such disorders occur along a continuum or spectrum (Piacentini et al., 2014). When such behavior causes marked distress, is inordinately time-consuming, or interferes with a person's routine functioning in home, school, or job, it's considered an obsessive-compulsive disorder (OCD). Children with OCD often don't understand that their behavior is excessive and unreasonable, although adults with OCD typically do.

OCD affects perhaps as many as 1 in 200 children and adolescents, making it a relatively rare disorder (see Albano et al., 2003). It may involve many types of ritualistic thoughts or behaviors, such as:

- Washing, checking, or other repetitive motor behavior
- Cognitive compulsions consisting of words, phrases, prayers, sequences of numbers, or other forms of counting
- Obsessional slowness, taking excessive time to complete simple everyday tasks
- Doubts and questions that elevate anxiety

<table>
<tr><td>

Video Example

from

YouTube

▶

ENHANCEDetext
Video Connections 10.2
This video provides an excellent overview of OCD in children and makes the point that OCD becomes a disorder when it gets in the way of normal activity. (https://www.youtube.com/watch?v=oO5Agg3zAbc)

</td><td>

Many children and adolescents with this disorder aren't diagnosed, in part because they are often secretive about their obsessional thoughts or rituals or because the rituals don't interfere with or disrupt most daily activities. However, in its extreme form, OCD can result in significant impairment in social and academic impairment.

If a student's problems with OCD are severe, then a first course of treatment may be medication prescribed and monitored by a physician or psychiatrist. But the most effective interventions for OCD that teachers will encounter are based on social learning principles, particularly strategies employed for reduction of anxiety. Medications to reduce anxiety may also be helpful, and in many cases the combination of medication and behavioral or cognitive-behavioral interventions produces the best outcomes (Beer, Karitani, Leonard, March, & Sweda, 2002; Garland, 2002). Teachers may play an important role in detecting OCD, especially when the student is secretive about thoughts or rituals, and careful observation and questioning are necessary to discover why the student is having socialization or academic difficulties. Special educators may be expected to assist in intervention by implementing features of anxiety-reduction procedures in the classroom,

</td></tr>
</table>

and may be called upon to provide data (behavioral checklists or rating scales) to help physicians monitor the effects of medication therapy.

Posttraumatic Stress Disorder

Posttraumatic stress disorder (PTSD) refers to prolonged, recurrent emotional and behavioral reactions following exposure to an extremely traumatic event (or multiple events) that could have resulted in death or serious injury to oneself or others. The person's response at the time of experiencing the event(s) must include intense fear, helplessness, or horror (children may show disorganized or agitated behavior). Although many, if not most, children will experience at least one traumatic event before the age of twenty, most of them don't develop PTSD (Copeland, Keeler, Angold, & Costello, 2007). Because children with PTSD are often at risk for other disorders, often related to anxiety or depression, it's difficult to estimate precisely how many children have PTSD. Some have estimated that rates of PTSD are between 1 percent and 10 percent among children and youth, with slightly higher rates for girls than for boys (see Hawkins & Radcliffe, 2006). PTSD is also presumed to be related directly to the number and intensity of traumatic events to which a child is exposed. The events giving rise to PTSD may occur in early childhood or later in life (see Lyons-Ruth, Zeanah, Benoit, Madigan, & Mills-Koonce, 2014; Nader & Fletcher, 2014).

PTSD is characterized by persistent cognitive, perceptual, emotional, or behavioral problems related to the event. For example, people with PTSD may reexperience the traumatic event in a variety of ways, such as through recurrent and intrusive thoughts, images, or dreams. They may avoid stimuli associated with the event or experience a general emotional numbing or unresponsiveness. Their symptoms may also include increased arousal (e.g., difficulty sleeping or concentrating; see Fletcher, 2003; Mindell & Owens, 2003).

Video Example from YouTube

ENHANCEDetext
Video Connections 10.3
In this video, a professor of pediatrics talks about the potential for post-traumatic stress disorder (PTSD) in children who have witnessed or been exposed to violence. (https://www.youtube.com/watch?v=J3cbyoXgobl)

Until relatively recently, children's delayed emotional and behavioral reactions to extreme stress were largely ignored. PTSD was seldom studied unless the traumatic stress occurred in adulthood. Since the mid-1980s, however, mental health workers have recognized that extremely traumatic experiences can cause delayed EBD in children as well as adults (Copeland et al., 2007; Fletcher, 2003; Nader & Fletcher, 2014). By the mid-1990s, it was well recognized that extreme stress or life-threatening experiences not only can produce depression, anxiety, fears, and other reactions in children but also can result in PTSD. Some common characteristics acquired through extreme childhood trauma include:

- Visualized or otherwise repeatedly perceived memories of the trauma
- Repetitive behaviors that may be similar to obsessions or compulsions
- Fears linked specifically to the traumatic event
- Altered attitudes toward people, life, or the future, reflecting feelings of vulnerability

Individuals respond to traumatic events in tremendously different ways. However, researchers are finding that accidents, wars, terrorism, natural disasters such as earthquakes or hurricanes, and domestic or community violence may produce PTSD in children and adolescents.

Treatment of these disorders may involve a variety of approaches, such as group discussion and support activities, crisis counseling, and individual treatment to reduce anxiety and improve coping strategies. Prevention involves not only efforts to reduce accidents and violence but also planning for the traumas that are likely if not inevitable.

Events producing PTSD may occur in school or the community. Sexual and physical abuse or school shootings, for example, may give rise to PTSD. As more immigrant children from war-torn countries enter our schools, we will no doubt see an increase in the number of children showing posttraumatic stress. Meese (2005) reported that more than 80 percent of foreign-born children adopted by U.S. citizens in the decade prior to 2002 had lived for one or more years in institutions. Although the nature and quality of care in foreign orphanages varies tremendously, Meese suggested that a number of factors, including the reasons that children were placed in orphanages in the first place, put them at heightened risk for PTSD in addition to cognitive delays and behavioral difficulties. Regardless of the location at which the traumatic event occurs, the student with PTSD is likely to have serious problems in school. Anxiety and related responses to the trauma may make it very difficult for the student to concentrate on academic work or engage in typical social activities. Consequently, it is important that teachers be aware of the indicators of possible PTSD, refer students for evaluation, and participate in efforts to reduce anxiety to manageable levels.

Historically, recognition and treatment of disabilities in civilians has followed the return of injured soldiers. Because PTSD is one of the major problems of soldiers returning from foreign wars, perhaps the public will become more aware of and demand better treatment of youngsters with PTSD.

Stereotyped Movement Disorders

Stereotyped movements are involuntary, repetitious, persistent, and nonfunctional acts over which the individual can exert at least some voluntary control under some circumstances but not total control in all circumstances. Stereotyped movements include self-stimulation and self-injury. However, they may also include repetitive movements related to anxiety (Albano et al., 2003; Piacentini et al., 2014; Himle, Flessner, Bonow, & Woods, 2006).

Most stereotyped movements that aren't labeled self-stimulation or self-injury are referred to as **tics**. Tics that involve only the facial muscles and last only a short time are common; nearly one-fourth of all children will at some time during their development display these tics, and they are best ignored. Tics involving the entire head, neck, and shoulders, however, typically require intervention. Tics may be vocal as well as motor; the individual may make a variety of noises or repeat words or word sounds, with or without accompanying motor tics.

Chronic motor tics that last more than a year and involve at least three muscle groups simultaneously are more serious than those involving fewer muscles or lasting a shorter time. There are a variety of tic disorders, but the most severe variety and the one on which most research has been done is Tourette's disorder or **Tourette's syndrome** (TS). TS is typically called a disorder if it begins before age eighteen and the person has both multiple motor and one or more verbal tics occurring many times a day (usually in clusters) nearly every day or intermittently for more than one year. The prevalence of Tourette's syndrome has been estimated as high as 1 percent (Kurlan, 2010). It occurs across diverse racial and ethnic groups, and more often in males than in females. The tics associated with TS generally resolve on their own in about one-third of cases, and are substantially reduced in another third of cases, by age thirteen. For the remaining cases, the tics can be a lifelong condition, with little reduction in symptoms.

In the 1990s, TS became a focus for much research on obsessive-compulsive and anxiety disorders. Because it has been so misunderstood until recently, TS has carried extraordinary social stigma. The symptoms of TS may be very mild and not readily apparent to the casual observer. However, a person with severe symptoms may find that others respond with fear, ridicule, or hostility to their bizarre behavior (e.g., twitching, grunting, shouting obscenities or words inappropriate to the circumstances). The diagnosis of TS in high-profile athletes (e.g., baseball player Jim Eisenreich, former NBA star Mahmoud Abdul-Rauf [formerly Chris Jackson], long-time U.S. Soccer goalkeeper Tim Howard), the brilliant writing of the late neurologist Oliver Sacks (see "A Surgeon's Life" in Sacks, 1995, the story of a surgeon and pilot with TS), and the work of the Tourette Syndrome Association have done much to dispel ignorance, discrimination, and cruelty shown toward children and adults with TS.

We now know that TS is a neurological disorder, although the cause and precisely what is wrong neurologically aren't known. TS is a multifaceted problem with social and emotional as well as neurological features. It may have a genetic component. It can vary greatly in severity and nature of symptoms, and it's often a comorbid condition with a variety of other disorders, especially attention deficit–hyperactivity disorder (ADHD) and OCD. In fact, some researchers suggest that TS is a specific form of attention disorder or obsessive-compulsive disorder and that OCD in children with TS may become more severe with age (Bloch et al., 2006, Kurlan, 2010). Some symptoms of TS may involve tic-like ritualistic behavior (e.g., stereotyped touching or arrangement of objects, repetition of words or phrases). In some cases, the person with TS has difficulty inhibiting aggression, and TS can be mistaken for or comorbid with conduct disorder. Although the symptoms of TS may become more severe under specific conditions, especially with the experience of anxiety, trauma, or social stress, this is not always predictable, and the fact that symptoms seem to come and go or lessen and worsen at seemingly unpredictable times makes treatment and acceptance of TS even more difficult for teachers and peers (see Kurlan, 2010; Piacentini et al, 2014).

TS is becoming better understood as diagnosis becomes more accurate and research reveals more about its nature and treatment. The most effective treatments are cognitive-behavioral therapies and medications or a combination of the two (Piacentini et al., 2014; Walkup, 2002). Many individuals with TS do not like the side effects of neuroleptics and other medications that may be prescribed to attenuate their symptoms. Management of tics by other means, including allowing them to occur under many circumstances and educating others to understand and accept them, are often the preferred strategies (see the report of Kane in the accompanying case book).

Special educators are likely to encounter students with TS because it's often comorbid with other disorders and because misunderstanding of TS often leads to stigma and social rejection or isolation. Effective intervention often requires involvement of the family and school as well as the student with TS (see Albano et al., 2003). A major aspect of the educator's role is understanding and communicating to others the nature of TS, ignoring the tics that can't be controlled, and focusing on the student's capabilities.

Selective Mutism

Children who demonstrate the capacity for normal or nearly normal speech in some situations but who don't speak in situations in which speaking is socially expected (e.g., school)

Video Example from YouTube

ENHANCEDetext
Video Connections 10.4
Notice how the speaker in this video distinguishes between selective mutism that is associated with broader anxiety and social withdrawal, and selective mutism in which the child may interact with others but simply not speak. (https://www.youtube.com/watch?v=J3cbyoXgobI)

are said to have **selective mutism** (SM). A common example is a child who doesn't speak to teachers or peers at school, but will converse with parents or siblings at home. Other terms used to describe their problems include *elective mutism, speech inhibition, speech avoidance, speech phobia,* and *functional mutism.* SM is a rare disorder, estimated to occur in well under 1 percent of children. Because typically developing children vary tremendously in their sociability and use of language, SM is difficult to diagnose. Clinicians understand that it's unwise to diagnose SM during the first weeks of school, for example, when anxiety, shyness, and withdrawal wouldn't be unusual; the diagnosis of SM also generally requires that the child experience social and academic impairment due to his or her lack of speech. These children present a puzzling behavior problem to teachers (Brigham & Cole, 1999; O'Connell, 2015). Brigham and Cole (1999) noted that most children with SM are first identified by educators when they enter school, but most teachers have not been confronted by this rare disorder and feel defeated by it.

Selective mutism appears to be a result of social anxiety in most cases, a specific fear of talking to certain individuals or groups of people (Bergman, Piacentini, & McCracken, 2002). But the causes of selective mutism are apparently diverse, including both genetic and environmental factors (Viana, Beidel, & Rabian, 2009; Higa-McMillan et al., 2014). Families of children with SM, for example, typically display some form of anxiety or social phobia themselves, and often are either overprotective or otherwise conflicted in their parenting style.

Because the selectively mute youngster doesn't need to acquire normal speech but merely to learn to use speech under ordinary circumstances, remediation is often believed to be easier than for a child who lacks speech (i.e., is mute) or has some other speech or language disorder (e.g., echolalia). But the research literature on effective interventions for SM remains limited. Behavioral or cognitive-behavioral interventions, either alone or combined with pharmacological interventions, have shown the most promise. As with other fears, social learning principles have been the basis for the most successful approaches to treating selective mutism. Strategies involve alteration of the demands or conditions under which the child is expected to speak, desensitization to the fear of speaking, and reinforcement for gradual approximations of speaking freely to the person(s) in whose presence the child has been mute (Cohan, Chavira, & Stein, 2006).

Selective mutism is poorly understood (even mysterious) and an extremely rare condition, but it can be an extraordinarily challenging problem for teachers. In some cases, the child simply starts talking more normally without treatment. Therefore, the first decision of concerned adults must be whether to implement intervention—whether the child's behavior is such a serious problem that intervention should be attempted. Usually, it's better to intervene than to wait for spontaneous resolution (Bergman et al., 2002; Higa-McMillan et al., 2014; Pionek, Stone, Kratochwill, Sladezcek, & Serlin, 2002). If intervention is initiated, then it's important for the teacher to work with other professionals, especially speech-language pathologists and those involved with the student's family. It's also important to implement a nonpunitive, behavioral approach to encouraging speech in the classroom and to realize that in many cases, successful intervention requires long-term treatment.

EATING DISORDERS

Eating disorders receive much attention in the press because the nation's affluence makes it acceptable to waste food and because of the near obsession many people—particularly those of high social status—have with slenderness. Among eating disorders, anorexia nervosa (or simply **anorexia**), bulimia nervosa (or simply **bulimia**), binge eating, and obesity garner the most attention (Macera & Mizes, 2006; Von Ranson & Wallace, 2014; Wilson, Becker, & Heffernan, 2003). Anorexia and bulimia are primarily, but not exclusively, problems of females, especially adolescent girls, and they appear to be more prevalent among White than among Black women (Robb & Dadson, 2002; Striegel-Moore et al., 2003). Medication is one possible treatment of such disorders.

Anorexia is an obsession with low body weight and fear of gaining weight. Individuals with anorexia are obsessively concerned with losing weight and extremely anxious about getting fat. They starve themselves down to an abnormally low weight, often exercising compulsively as well as severely restricting caloric intake. They endanger their health, sometimes dying of self-starvation. Anorexia is more prevalent in females than males by a factor of 3:1, but this ratio is much lower than the historical belief that anorexia was almost exclusively a female disorder (Treasure, Claudino, & Zucker, 2010). Anorexia occurs most frequently in adolescents and young adults.

Bulimia involves binge eating followed by behavior designed to offset the food intake, such as self-induced vomiting, using laxatives or enemas, or extra exercise. People with bulimia often try to keep their eating binges and related behavior a secret. They often feel depressed and unable to control their eating habits.

Despite public fascination with anorexia and bulimia and the assumption that they are epidemic among high school and college females in the U.S., we have relatively little understanding of the nature, prevalence, causes, or effective treatments of eating disorders, especially when the onset of these disorders is in childhood. One problem is that eating disorders are often well hidden by those who have them, or at least go unreported to treatment providers. In 2007, Hudson, Hiripi, Pope, and Kessler reported the following estimates of diagnosed eating disorders in the U.S.:

- Anorexia: 0.9 percent of females; 0.3 percent of males
- Bulimia: 1.5 percent of females; 0.5 percent of males
- Binge eating disorder: 3.5 percent of females; 2.0 percent of males

Researchers now recognize that the problems associated with eating disorders are multidimensional and require multimodal treatment approaches. The cultural ideal of thinness may be a factor in precipitating some cases of eating disorders. Family conflicts about eating and difficulty in communicating with other family members are known to be associated with adolescents' maladaptive attitudes toward food and eating. However, genetic predisposition to eating problems is increasingly recognized by researchers (Von Ranson & Wallace, 2014; Wilson et al., 2003), and comorbidity with other psychiatric disorders (including autism spectrum disorders, ADHD, OCD, and anxiety disorders) is common (Treasure et al., 2010). Behavioral analyses of causes and behavioral or cognitive-behavioral interventions have been encouraging in the short run, but long-term follow-up evaluations indicate the need for more comprehensive assessment and treatment approaches. Effective intervention requires consideration of the eating behaviors themselves and the thoughts and feelings associated with anorexia and bulimia, plus the social environment in which the patterns have developed and are maintained.

Other eating disorders, typically associated with more severe disorders, include **pica** (eating inedible substances such as paint, hair, cloth, or dirt), **rumination** (self-induced vomiting, which usually begins in infancy), highly exclusive food preferences, binge eating, and obesity (Von Ranson & Wallace, 2014). These problems severely limit a child's social acceptability and endanger health.

Childhood and adolescent *obesity* is a growing problem in most Western cultures, particularly the USA, and carries significant health risks, usually results in a poor self-image, contributes to poor social relations and may be exacerbated by social relationships, and tends to persist into adulthood (Christakis & Fowler, 2007; Peterson, Reach, & Grabe, 2003; Wilson et al., 2003). Obese children often experience social rejection or neglect. Although causes of obesity include genetic, physiological, and environmental factors, the basic problem is that the individual eats more calories than he or she expends in activity. Successful management of obesity therefore requires not only changing eating habits but also increasing physical activity. Obesity has often been thought to be a result of the individual's learning undesirable eating patterns and poor nutritional habits, but socialization to accept obesity undoubtedly plays a critical role (Christakis & Fowler, 2007). It's important to remember that avoidance of obesity requires a combination of proper diet and exercise—a regimen harder for some than for others but possible for nearly everyone.

Special educators will often deal with students who have eating disorders. These disorders shouldn't be addressed by special educators alone, and teachers shouldn't independently assume responsibility for eating problems. Students with eating disorders may display high levels of anxious or obsessive-compulsive behavior in the classroom. The role of special education in such disorders is to provide instruction and support for proper nutrition and exercise as needed and to work with other disciplines in managing students' food intake.

ELIMINATION DISORDERS

Attitudes toward toileting vary widely among cultures and within social groups. In Western culture, toilet training is considered very important and is generally begun at a young age. Although the extreme practice of beginning toilet training in the first few weeks of life is ill advised, behavioral research shows that most children can be taught by sixteen or eighteen months. In the U.S., school attendance (including preschool) is often predicated on the assumption that children can toilet with little or no assistance. When children continue to wet or soil themselves after the age of five or six, they are considered to have a problem that demands intervention. **Enuresis** may be either diurnal (wetting during waking hours) or nocturnal (bed-wetting). About twice as many boys as girls are enuretic, and 2 percent or 3 percent of children are enuretic at age fourteen. At the time they begin first grade, approximately 13 percent to 20 percent of children are enuretic. **Encopresis**, or soiling, usually occurs during the day and is not as common as enuresis.

Toilet training is usually a gradual process, and stress and illness have an effect on bowel and bladder control. Thus, the younger the child and the more stressful the circumstances, the more one can expect accidents to occur. Enuresis and encopresis are not matters of infrequent accidents; the child has a chronic problem, after the age at which children are expected to be continent of urine and feces; that is, in retaining urine or feces and releasing it only in the toilet (Peterson et al., 2003).

Psychodynamic ideas attribute enuresis and encopresis to underlying emotional conflicts, usually conflicts involving the family. Although these psychodynamic ideas aren't supported by reliable evidence, family factors obviously play an important role if the family is inconsistent or unreasonable in toilet training. At the least, wetting and soiling can sour parent–child relationships regardless of the cause of the problem. Not many parents can face these problems with complete equanimity, and rare is the child who is completely unaffected by adults' reactions to misplaced excrement. Thus, one must recognize that negative feelings about the problem often run high in families of children with elimination disorders. Treatment must be planned to avoid further parental anger and abuse of the child.

Enuresis is seldom the child's only problem; the child with enuresis often has other difficulties—perhaps stealing, overeating, underachievement, or other behavior problems (Ramakrishnan, 2008). This is especially true of children who have what is referred to as *secondary enuresis*—they established and demonstrated bladder control for a period of at least six months, but have "relapsed" into bedwetting or daytime enuresis. It's important to note that after the age of ten, children whose problem is primary nocturnal enuresis (bedwetting) don't typically have comorbid behavioral problems (Ramakrishnan, 2008). Nearly all children with encopresis have multiple problems, often of a severe nature. Diurnal enuresis and encopresis at school are intolerable problems for teachers and result in peer rejection. Understandably, most youngsters with elimination disorders have low self-esteem.

In a few cases, elimination disorders have physiological causes that can be corrected by surgery or medication, but the vast majority of cases have no known anatomical defect, and medication isn't particularly helpful. These disorders are in the vast majority of cases a matter of failure to learn how to control the bladder or bowels, and the effective methods of treating them involve habit training or practice. Intervention may thus involve training the child in urine retention, rapid awakening, and practice in toileting as well as reward for appropriate toileting or mild punishment for wetting. For many children, a urine alarm system in the bed or pants has successfully eliminated enuresis.

Although many approaches to enuresis have been tried and many behavioral techniques have been highly successful, no single approach has been successful for every child, and combinations of techniques are often used. Encopresis is sometimes treated by training children in biofeedback so that they learn to control their sphincters more deliberately. Those who soil themselves may be required to clean themselves rather than receive solicitous attention and cleaning from an adult. Selecting a successful technique for enuresis or encopresis depends on careful assessment of the individual case.

Special educators who work with students having more severe disorders are particularly likely to encounter those who have elimination disorders. These disorders can be extremely troublesome in school, making students unwelcome to adults and peers alike and becoming the central issue in behavior management. Special educators need to work with professionals from other disciplines, particularly psychology and social work, to address the problems created by elimination disorders in the classroom.

SEXUAL PROBLEMS

Promiscuous sexual conduct is often thought to connote moral misjudgment, and promiscuity is often involved in delinquency. Early sexual intercourse and teenage pregnancy are serious problems for teenagers and their children, as discussed in Chapter 13. Dating and related sexual relationships are of great concern to teens and their adult caretakers. Sexual relationships and sexual behavior can be sources of enormous anxiety and obsessive-compulsive behavior for children and teens. Scarcely anyone condones exhibitionism, sadomasochism, incest, prostitution, fetishism, and sexual relations involving children (pedophilia), and these behaviors usually carry serious social penalties. American social mores don't condone all sex practices—some sexual behavior is clearly taboo, and incest is taboo in nearly every society. However, most people now recognize the wide variety of normal sexual expression that is a matter of preference or biological determination.

Autoerotic behavior (masturbation) is not inherently maladaptive, although it is viewed as undesirable or prohibited by some religious groups. When carried to excess or done publicly, sexual self-stimulation is considered disordered behavior by nearly everyone. Although many or most teachers have observed children masturbating publicly, little research has been done on the problem of children's public masturbation, perhaps because masturbation has for so long been looked upon as evil (Hare, 1962; Stribling, 1842) and is still condemned by some religions, as is homosexuality.

Classifying gender-related behavior of any kind as a disorder raises serious questions of cultural bias and discrimination. The consensus is that some forms of sexual expression are deviant and should be prevented—incest, sexual sadism or masochism, pedophilia, and public masturbation, for example. Today, however, many people feel there is nothing deviant about other sex-related behaviors, such as preference for clothing styles, stereotypical masculine or feminine mannerisms, and homosexuality. Clothing styles and accepted sex roles have changed dramatically since about 1970. *Androgyny* (having the characteristics of both sexes) is apparent in many fashions and in role models. Problems related to sexual preference may be seen as primarily a matter of cultural or personal intolerance (often justified by religious beliefs or political inclination), so we must be sensitive to the possibility of cultural and personal bias in judging sex-related behavior, just as we must be aware of personal biases toward racial and ethnic identity. Individuals who view themselves as a different gender than their assigned (biological) gender are at risk of developing **gender dysphoria**; note that this term replaced the previously used term *gender identity disorder* in the latest revision of the DSM. This revision reflects growing recognition and acceptance of gender nonconformity, and the diagnostic criteria make clear that gender nonconformity itself is not a mental disorder. Rather, it is only when the stressors that may accompany the condition result in impairment in social or other functioning that a disorder might be diagnosed. In children, gender nonconformity may be seen in an insistent desire to be the opposite sex, strong preference for or insistence on dressing like the other sex or adopting the opposite sex role, strong preference for playmates of the other sex, and persistent wishes to have the physical features of the opposite sex. Again, as with the behaviors associated with many other disorders we have discussed, only when such characteristics cause significant distress or impairment of social functioning are they considered a disorder. LGBT (lesbian, gay, bisexual, or transgender) persons are no longer considered to have a disorder because of their sexual orientation, although persons of any sexual orientation may have EBD. Discrimination against LGBT persons, regardless of whether motivated by religious conviction or political motivation or both, may indeed be a primary source of stress in the lives of individuals of any sexual orientation, but particularly those who are not "straight." Attitudes toward homosexuality vary with culture (see Goldstein, 2014; Sacks, 2015; Scull, 2015).

Sexual behavior that involves intimidation, harassment, and other forms of aggression are, as noted in prior chapters, more accurately associated with conduct disorder and delinquency. However, many individuals who exhibit sexual aggression may experience high levels of anxiety as a comorbid condition.

Special educators, especially those who deal with adolescents, are certain to be confronted by students' sexual behavior and knowledge (or lack of it), which are of great concern. Maintaining an open mind about sexual preferences and alternative modes of sexual expression is important; so is an understanding of pathological behavior and the necessity of addressing it. Teachers must be ready to work with psychologists, psychiatrists, social workers, and other professionals in identifying and managing deviant sexual behavior.

SOCIAL ISOLATION AND INEPTITUDE

Many of the behaviors we've discussed in this and previous chapters may isolate a child with EBD from his or her peers socially. The student with EBD may withdraw intentionally, may simply lack the skills needed to interact appropriately with peers, or may inadvertently drive them away with bizarre or troubling behavior (see Farmer, 2000; McClelland & Scalzo, 2006; Rubin, Burgess, Kennedy, & Stewart, 2003). Sometimes, the inept or bizarre behavior that results in social difficulty signifies autism spectrum disorder (ASD), but often it does not. Some socially isolated youngsters lack basic social approach skills, such as looking at, initiating conversation with, asking to play with, and appropriately touching their peers or adults. Usually, they also lack responsiveness to others' initiations of social contact. Others may be neglected by their peers for reasons that aren't well understood. What is known is that rejected, socially isolated children don't engage in the *social reciprocity* (exchange of mutual and equitable reinforcement between pairs of individuals) that is characteristic of normal social development.

Social isolation is not an all-or-nothing problem. All children and youth sometimes exhibit withdrawn behavior and are socially inept, and this varies across contexts; many typical children, and adults for that matter, are socially inept in a new or unfamiliar setting. This behavior may occur with any degree of severity as well, ranging along a continuum from a normal social reticence in new situations to the profound isolation of psychosis. In nearly any classroom, from preschool through adulthood, however, some individuals are distinguished by their lack of social interaction. Their social isolation can often be accompanied by immature or inadequate behavior that makes them targets of ridicule or taunts. This is often true of children and youth with ASD. They can become friendless loners who are apparently unable to avail themselves of the joy and satisfaction of social reciprocity. Unless their behavior and that of their peers can be changed, they are likely to remain isolated from close and frequent human contact and the attendant developmental advantages afforded by social interaction. Their prognosis, then, isn't good without intensive intervention.

Causal Factors and Prevention

Social learning theory predicts that some children, particularly those who have not been taught appropriate social interaction skills early in life, and those who have been punished for attempts at social interaction, will be withdrawn. A mildly or moderately withdrawn youngster is likely to be anxious and have a low self-concept, but the conclusion that anxiety and low self-concept *cause* withdrawal and social isolation is not justifiable. It's more plausible that anxiety and low self-concept result from the child's lack of social competence. Indeed, a cycle can develop in which withdrawal and isolation limit opportunities to develop skills and friendships, which leads to further isolation, and so on.

There is no doubt that biological factors also contribute to some individuals' social isolation. Genetic factors almost certainly play a role. Particularly in cases in which children are diagnosed with some form of autistic spectrum disorder, the social difficulties are determined at least in part by brain dysfunction.

Parental overrestrictiveness or social incompetence, lack of opportunity for social learning, and early rebuffs in social interaction with peers may contribute to a child's learning to play in isolation from others and to avoid social contact. Parents who are socially obtuse are likely to have children whose social skills aren't well developed, probably because socially awkward parents provide models of undesirable behavior and are unable to teach their children the skills that will help them become socially attractive (Dadds, 2002; Higa-McMillan et al., 2014). Aversive social experiences, including abuse by parents or siblings, may indeed produce anxious children who have little self-confidence and evaluate themselves negatively. Anxiety and self-derogation may then contribute to reticence in social situations and help to perpetuate social incompetence. Nevertheless, the child's temperamental characteristics, in combination with early socialization experiences and the nature of the current social environment, probably account for the development of social isolation (Keogh, 2003). The social learning view of isolate behavior, which focuses on the factors of reinforcement, punishment, and imitation, carries direct implications for intervention and suggests ways we might remediate isolation by actively teaching social skills. Effective prevention of social isolation, however, involves more than teaching youngsters how to approach and respond to others; it requires arranging a social environment that is conducive to positive interactions.

Assessment

The definition of *social isolation* includes active rejection by peers or neglect of peers. Measurement of rejection and acceptance frequently includes use of a questionnaire or sociometric assessment tool that asks youngsters to choose or nominate classmates for various roles. Students may be asked to indicate which of their peers they would most like to play, sit, or work with, or invite to a party, and with whom they would least like to interact. The results of this procedure are then analyzed to see which individuals have high social status in the group (to whom many peers are attracted), those who are isolates (not chosen as playmates or workmates by anyone), and those who are rejected (with whom peers want to avoid social contact). Farmer (2000) pointed out the importance of a key distinction that emerges from sociometric research with regard to the children we're concerned with in this chapter—those who aren't popular among, nor even connected in a positive way, to their peers. He noted that rejected status is very distinct from neglected status, even though both can be seen as isolated. Children typically have no trouble in naming others they find obnoxious, aggressive, cruel, or disturbing; it's easy for them to indicate that they'd rather not work with or sit next to such students. But students who are found to be neglected on the basis of sociometric research have simply escaped the notice of their peers. They aren't judged harshly, but neither are they perceived in a positive light. The student who receives neither positive nominations nor any negative nominations from their peers may be at risk for further and potentially worsening social isolation. In addition to sociometrics, teachers may obtain more precise measurement of social interaction of individual children by direct daily observation and recording of behavior. We can thus define *social isolates* as children who have a markedly lower number of social interactions than do their peers.

Sociometric status and direct measurement of social interactions, although both are valuable in assessment, don't necessarily reveal what causes a youngster to experience social isolation. A student could, for example, have a relatively high rate of positive social interaction and still be a relative social isolate; his or her interactions might involve relatively few peers and be characterized by a superficial or artificial quality (Walker et al., 2004). Consequently, assessment should also include teacher ratings and self-reports. Adequate measurement of social skills or social isolation requires attention to the rate of interactive behaviors, qualitative aspects of social interactions, and children's perceptions of social status.

As social skills research becomes more sophisticated, the nuances of appropriate social interaction become more difficult to capture. Much of our knowledge about the nature of children's social skills is superficial. Children's social intentions (*why* as well as *what* they do) may be an important area to research; we may need to assess their pragmatic reasons for interacting with peers in specified ways to fully understand social isolation and social acceptance.

Intervention and Education

One approach to the problem of withdrawal is to try to improve the youngster's self-concept, on the assumption that this will result in a tendency to engage more often in social interactions. We can encourage children to express their feelings about their behavior and social relationships in play therapy or in therapeutic conversations with a warm, accepting adult. As they come to feel accepted and able to express their feelings openly, their self-concepts will presumably become more positive. The incidence of positive social interactions should then increase as well. Unfortunately, data don't support targeting self-concept itself for intervention.

Attempts to remediate social isolation without teaching specific social skills or manipulating the social environment are usually ineffectual. Few data show that self-concept can be improved without first improving behavior. If youngsters' appraisals of their own behavior are unrealistic, then bringing self-perceptions into line with reality is, to be sure, a worthy goal. If youngsters are indeed socially isolated, then attempting to convince them of their social adequacy without first helping them learn the skills for social reciprocity may be misleading. After their behavior has been improved, however, there is a foundation for improving self-image.

Arranging appropriate environmental conditions helps teach socially isolated youngsters to reciprocate positive behavior with their peers (Swan, Cummings, Caporino, & Kendall, 2014). Situations that are conducive to social interaction contain toys or equipment that promote social play and bring the isolated youngster into proximity with others who have social interaction skills or who require social interaction from the target child. Specific intervention strategies based on social learning principles include these:

- Reinforcing social interaction (perhaps with praise, points, or tokens)
- Providing peer models of social interaction
- Providing training (models, instruction, rehearsal, and feedback) in specific social skills
- Enlisting peer confederates to initiate social interactions and reinforce appropriate social responses

Of course, all four strategies may be used together, and experimental research shows the effectiveness of these procedures in modifying certain behaviors. Social learning strategies for defining, measuring, and changing youngsters' deficient social behavior show great promise. Nevertheless, current social skills training methods don't adequately address the problems of producing behavioral changes that actually make children and youth more socially acceptable, that generalize across a variety of social situations, and that are maintained after intervention is terminated. As Strain, Odom, and McConnell (1984) noted decades ago, social skills involve *reciprocity*—an exchange of behavior between two people. Interventions that focus exclusively on changing the isolated individual's behavior miss that vital aspect of social adaptation: social interaction. The goal of intervention must be to help the socially isolated individual become enmeshed or entrapped in positive, reciprocal, self-perpetuating social exchanges, which can be done only by carefully choosing the target skills. One must select target skills with these questions in mind:

- Are the particular social behaviors likely to be maintained after intervention is terminated?
- Are the skills likely to generalize across different settings (as in different areas of the school and during different types of activities)?
- Do the target skills relate to peers' social behavior so that peer behavior prompts and reinforces performance of the skill (that is, are the skills part of naturally occurring, positive social interactions)?

To the extent that we can answer these questions with "yes," the effects of social skills training are more likely to last.

Some children and youth aren't social isolates but still don't fit in well with their peers and are hampered by inadequate social sensitivity or ineptness in delicate social situations. Children whose previous social experience is at odds with the majority of their peers, adolescents making their first approaches to members of the opposite sex, and adolescents interviewing for their first jobs are often quite tactless or unskilled in the social graces demanded for acceptance. Some individuals have irritating personal habits that detract from social adequacy. The results of social ineptitude may be negative self-image, anxiety, and withdrawal.

One can often eliminate or avoid bungling social behaviors by teaching important social cues and appropriate responses. Offering group and individual counseling, showing the youngster recorded replays of his or her own behavior, modeling appropriate behavior, and providing guided practice (or some combination of these strategies) have been used to teach social skills (Wheeler & Mayton, 2014). A social learning view of the origin and remediation of interpersonal ineptness is clearly a functional view for the special educator, for it implies that direct instruction is most effective.

The design of intervention strategies depends partly on the age of the student and the nature of the student's relationship to peers. Older students with a long history of socialization difficulties and victimization by peers may need a safe haven, such as a special school or class, in which to learn new skills (as illustrated by the case of Pauline in the accompanying case book). While some may assume that the student who is anxious or withdrawn is somehow easier to deal with than a student with acting out, disruptive behavior disorders, both can be challenging for a teacher, and intervention is no less important for the long-term success of the student. An example related to teaching social skills to students who lack them is provided in Box 10.1.

Box 10.1

Teaching Social Skills to Students Who Are Anxious or Withdrawn

What social skills, or lack thereof, will be of greatest concern for teachers?

As we have discussed, students with anxiety or related disorders will sometimes escape the notice of teachers because their behavior is not of the externalizing variety. Anxious students may withdraw and choose not to—or be unable to—interact with either peers or teachers. They are often simply quiet; they can be shy, withdrawn students who seldom, if ever, volunteer in class or initiate conversation with peers, even in social environments like the playground or lunchroom. As we also discussed, some children with anxiety will engage in odd, even bizarre behavior, such as repetitive movements or tics or other obsessive-compulsive behaviors. In either case, their lack of positive social skills required to engage with peers, and the potential for bizarre behaviors that will be off-putting at best among peers, put them at increasing risk for further social isolation.

What are appropriate targets for intervention?

The student who is isolated from or rejected by peers is at great risk for worsening of social ineptitude, and potentially for the development of other disorders. As such, interventions designed to encourage positive peer interaction are critical. Specific targets are generally simple behaviors, and can be thought of as the "survival" skills any child would need to navigate peer groups in school or social situations. Examples include initiating social conversations and greetings, responding appropriately to the initiations of others, gaining entree into a game or activity (e.g., "May I play?"), and engaging in sharing in either a work, play, or social context (e.g., "May I use those crayons?," "Do you want to borrow my markers?"). More sophisticated social skills will be needed as well to build upon these initiations and interactions; this is especially true of older children. These skills will include such things as reducing or eliminating bizarre or negative behaviors as well as developing higher level conversational skills (e.g., understanding and using humor, sarcasm, double meanings, etc.).

What types of interventions show promise?

Social skills have long been recognized as a problem for students with EBD and other mild disabilities, and there is no shortage of social skills curricula, materials, and intervention packages to choose from. But in the 1990s several reviews of social skills interventions led to a perhaps oversimplified conclusion: social skills training doesn't work. Two observations led to this conclusion. First, it was indeed true that many packaged social skills curricula showed little promise of improving the social skills of children. Second, even when intervention did promote change in social behavior, the changes typically didn't last—that is, transfer to other settings, times, and places. Scholars have generally decided that it was premature to conclude simply that "social skills intervention doesn't work." What can be said is that early packaged social skills curricula, some of which simply focused on one skill a week, should not have been expected to change the behavior of individual students who undoubtedly have very unusual strengths and needs. Indeed, we know that social skills intervention must be based on careful, individual analysis of problem situations that tells the teacher what contexts cause social problems for a given child; what behaviors the student displays, or fails to display, that contribute to this problem; and what skills the student needs to be successful. Moreover, we know that for behavior change to last, plans for maintenance and generalization to other contexts must be built into our interventions (e.g., what steps can we take to increase the odds that Johnny will display this positive social skill on the playground next week?).

An example—a social skills lesson

Mr. Lankton decides that Rusty, an eighth grader identified with EBD, is a social isolate due to a lack of social skills. That is, Rusty doesn't display aggression or any bizarre behavior to drive peers away, but merely lacks the social skills needed to engage in conversations or join in games with peers. Mr. Lankton decides to teach Rusty an initiation skill for joining a game of basketball on the playground. He uses several teaching strategies. First, he uses direct instruction to teach Rusty the skill in a model-guided practice—that is, an independent practice format. That is, Mr. Lankton first demonstrates the skill for Rusty (i.e., "watch me"). After Mr. Lankton has demonstrated the skill once, he asks Rusty to show how he would ask to join a game of basketball, but walks through the skill with him (i.e., guided practice; "let's do it together"). Once he feels Rusty is comfortable he asks him to repeat the skill by himself (i.e., independent practice; "Show me how you would ask to join the game"). Now that he believes Rusty understands the skill involved, Mr. Lankton arranges for Rusty to practice the skill in a role-play setting in the classroom with a couple of his peers. Finally, after several days of role-playing practice, Mr. Lankton speaks to other teachers to find out when they will be on the playground in the coming week so he can set up a real-life scenario for Rusty to go out and practice his newly learned skill. Note that throughout his training, Mr. Lankton has offered Rusty plenty of praise and positive feedback as he acquired the new skill (and could have offered tangible reinforcers, points, etc., as well, if needed). Once they move to the natural context of the basketball game on the playground, the reinforcer

(continued)

Box 10.1   *(continued)*

Rusty may earn will be a natural one—if he displays the new social skill properly, he will be reinforced by getting to join the basketball game.

Where to find more information about social skills instruction:

Bremer, C. D., & Smith, J. (2004). *Teaching social skills.* Information Brief, National Center on Secondary Education and Transition. Minneapolis, MN: University of Minnesota. Available at http://www.ncset.org/publications/info/NCSETInfoBrief_3.5.pdf

Gresham, F. M., Van, M. B., & Cook, C. R. (2006). Social skills training for teaching replacement behaviors: Remediating acquisition deficits in at-risk students. *Behavioral Disorders, 31,* 363–377.

McIntosh, K., & McKay, L. D. (2008). Enhancing generalization of social skills: Making social skills curricula effective after the lesson. *Beyond Behavior, 18,* 18–25.

Wheeler, J. J., & Mayton, M. R. (2014). The integrity of interventions in social emotional skill development for students with emotional and behavioral disorders. In P. Garner, J. M. Kauffman, & J. G. Elliott (Eds.), *The Sage handbook of emotional and behavioral difficulties* (2nd ed.) (pp. 385–398). London, U.K.: Sage.

SUMMARY

Grouping anxiety and related disorders for discussion is problematic because the disorders are loosely interrelated. Subcategories of anxiety disorders aren't well defined, and anxiety disorders are frequently comorbid with a variety of other disorders.

Anxiety—uneasiness, fears, and worries—is part of normal development. However, extreme anxiety and fears (phobias) can be seriously debilitating. Anxiety disorders are generally more transient and are associated with lower risk for adulthood psychiatric disorder than are behaviors related to externalizing disorders. As many as 15 percent to 20 percent of children and adolescents experience some form of anxiety disorder at one time or another. Anxiety may be at least part of the problems in 20 percent to 30 percent of youngsters referred to clinics for behavior problems. Girls are affected by anxiety disorders slightly more frequently than boys during childhood, and this difference increases with age such that adolescent females with anxiety disorders outnumber males by two or three to one. Anxiety disorders appear to have both social and biological causes and

to be most amenable to social learning approaches to intervention, sometimes combined with medication.

Anxiety appears to play a significant role in a variety of related disorders. Obsessive-compulsive disorder involves ritualistic thinking or behavior intended to ward off feared events. It may take many forms and is potentially a serious detriment to school attendance and performance. Posttraumatic stress disorder (PTSD) is now recognized as a disorder of children and adolescents as well as adults. The anxiety and other problems associated with PTSD can seriously impede students' progress in school. Stereotyped movement disorders include Tourette's syndrome, a disorder involving multiple motor and vocal tics and now recognized as a neurological problem. TS is often comorbid with other disorders and appears to be particularly closely associated with anxiety, attention disorders, and obsessive-compulsive disorders. *Selective mutism* is extreme, persistent anxiety about speaking in the presence of certain individuals or in certain contexts. Intervention is typically designed to reduce anxiety in situations demanding speech.

Eating disorders include anorexia, bulimia, and binge eating, which often involve anxiety about food, eating, and body weight, as well as obesity. Elimination disorders include enuresis and encopresis. These disorders are extremely problematic in school settings and must be resolved if children are to develop normal peer relations. Sexual problems are difficult to define because of societal attitudes toward sexual behavior. However, some types of sexual behavior, such as public masturbation, incest, and masochism, are clearly taboo.

Socially isolated children and youth don't have the social approach and response skills necessary to develop reciprocally reinforcing relationships. They may lack these skills because of inappropriate models of social behavior at home, inadequate instruction or opportunity to practice social skills, or other circumstances that inhibit social development. Intervention and prevention call for teaching social skills that are assumed important for social development, but there is a great deal of controversy concerning which are the most appropriate skills and the most effective instructional methods. In general, effective social skills training involves modeling, rehearsal, guided practice, and feedback, either for individual students or for groups. Peer-mediated interventions that alter both the socially isolated youngster's behaviors and those of peers in naturally occurring interactions may be the most effective strategies.

✅ ENHANCEDetext **END-OF-CHAPTER 10 QUIZ**

Click on the checkmark icon to access an end-of-chapter quiz. Answer the questions to gauge your understanding of chapter concepts and better prepare you for case discussions.

PERSONAL REFLECTIONS

Anxiety and Related Disorders

Chris Sweigart is a regional special education and behavior consultant in Kentucky, and he formerly taught middle school students with emotional and behavioral disorders. He completed his Master of Arts in Teaching and Ph.D. in Curriculum and Instruction at the University of Louisville, where he developed a passion not just for teaching students with EBD but also for supporting and training those who work with them. He wrote this reflection about Kendrick, a student he last worked with when Kendrick was a 13-year-old middle school student.

Think of a student you worked with who displayed a severe anxiety disorder. In what ways did this student's behavior demonstrate that he/she experienced anxiety?

A seventh grade student I taught my very first year of teaching students with EBD in a middle school comes to mind when I think about severe issues with anxiety. Kendrick was a charming kid with a big smile who could easily make you laugh—even in the midst of some pretty challenging situations. He had experienced significant upheaval, transitions, and difficulties in his childhood—things that would be pretty challenging for an adult to manage, let alone a child. Due to frequent moves, he had changed schools often, including switching to my school partway through his seventh grade year.

Kendrick's anxiety was quickly apparent. He was constantly worried about and asking about his mom and almost always desperate to talk to her, to see her, to get her to bring him home with her. This manifested at times as minor behavior problems, such as asking to call home dozens of times a day or sneaking to the office to have his temperature taken in hopes of a spontaneous fever so he could be sent home. In fact, I once discovered he was stopping by the bathroom sink to run hot water in his mouth to spike the temperature reading on the thermometer.

All too often, his anxiety manifested as more extreme and concerning behaviors. For example, when he wasn't allowed to call or go home on one occasion, he sat in his math class and slowly, methodically—bracket by bracket—ripped out his own braces from his mouth. He had completely removed the top set and was struggling with the bottom wire, which he pulled out partially and twisted upward into a smile around his lips to draw the attention of his teacher. This was quite effective at getting him access to his mom! On another more humorous—yet still dangerous—occasion, he tried to sneak out of the school by climbing through the ceiling tiles in the bathroom to try to access a vent to escape as if he were in a movie; this was less effective. When we developed a more comprehensive and individualized behavior intervention plan for Kendrick to help him be successful in school, which included limiting calls home and keeping him at school, he ramped up the intensity of some of his behavior, which included destroying some of my classroom and emailing my administrators detailed descriptions of how he was going to kill me. I never once actually felt threatened by him, and his behaviors—including the threats—pretty clearly were intended to serve the functions of access to his mom and escape from school. On many past occasions, if Kendrick managed to talk to his mom, she would come pick him up from school; further, school administrators had suspended him fairly often for the more severe problem behaviors.

What strategies did you find most successful or useful in helping Kendrick deal with his anxiety?

We worked with a team of people to develop an individualized behavior intervention and support plan. The team included myself, my paras, administrators, the guidance counselor, a student assistance counselor, a social worker, Kendrick, his mom, and his grandparents. Everyone had roles in the development and implementation of supports for the student. We wanted to develop a positive and supportive plan that would help Kendrick to be more successful in school.

We had determined that Kendrick had severe anxiety and that the primary functions of his problem behavior were to access his mom and escape school. For the school side of things, we used these functions to guide the development of an intervention plan. For example, we came to an agreement with Kendrick's mom that we would generally no longer call home (with Kendrick) unless he had a fever or there was a legitimate emergency. We also agreed that his mom would generally never pick him up early nor would the school send him home early or suspend him, as these merely reinforced problem behavior. Further, we developed a reinforcement component for Kendrick displaying appropriate behavior: He could earn a call home to mom close to the end of the school day. We also built in a 10-minute break timer that Kendrick could use to allocate himself breaks throughout each school period as a way to get more appropriate escape from school activities. Finally, we also built in some adjustable behavior contracts where Kendrick could earn other reinforcers of his choice.

We also developed a plan to teach Kendrick appropriate replacement behaviors, such as expressing his anxiety more appropriately or requesting to use the break timer. In addition to this school-based plan, the social worker began to work with both Kendrick and his mom outside of school to provide wraparound supports. She got Kendrick into a program that allowed a mental health worker to visit him at school and home to provide therapy and to teach him (and my team) tools for managing his anxiety. We incorporated the therapist's suggestions throughout the school year. For example, we provided a quiet space for him to take requested breaks, a journal, and a box of comfort items he could access during the breaks. We were also available to talk to him if he wanted during these break times.

When we first implemented this plan, there was a burst in the intensity of Kendrick's problem behavior, which I referred to above. He destroyed parts of my room and made threats to kill me. I had to persuade my administrators at this time that I did not feel threatened and that it was critical that we keep Kendrick in school that day and not call his mom as we agreed upon in the plan to prevent his problem behavior from serving the previous functions. They agreed and over time we were able to see some significant (yet not perfect, of course) improvements in Kendrick's behavior and success in school. He still clearly had significant anxiety but it manifested less frequently as extreme problem behavior, and he was more likely to use the other appropriate supports we offered.

What are/were your biggest concerns about Kendrick's future?

Kendrick's anxiety could be crippling, and the problem behavior he engaged in could be quite severe. He's now an adult and the consequences of such behaviors for an adult can be extreme. Kids with EBD have some of the poorest long-term outcomes—lack of employment and post secondary education or training, lack of housing, involvement with the justice system, etc. I worry for Kendrick that he might face such poor outcomes and have a hard life; I especially worry that if he continues to

engage in some of the more extreme behaviors in his repertoire, he has a high probability of negative encounters with law enforcement and perhaps imprisonment as well. Despite the challenges, he really was a fantastic and charismatic young man with gifts to offer the world. I hope that he has continued to develop his skills for managing his own anxiety and behavior, so that he can be successful in life.

Questions for Further Reflection

1. What indications would lead you to believe that a student of yours is anxious to the point of having EBD?

2. Given your information to this point, what possible changes in behavior might you anticipate if a student who is taking medication for an anxiety-related disorder discontinues taking it?

3. If a student of yours were socially inept, how would you approach this student (what would you try to accomplish, and what would you say to him or her)?

11 DEPRESSION AND SUICIDAL BEHAVIOR

Anne Vega/Pearson Education, Inc.

After you read this chapter, you should be able to:

11.1 Tell someone how the federal definition of *emotionally disturbed* includes internalizing disorders and depression.

11.2 Explain how comorbidity and the episodic nature of mood disorders complicate the assessment of depression.

11.3 Discuss the relationship between age, gender, ethnicity, and suicide rates.

11.4 Describe how teachers can help reduce suicide risk and how they should treat students following a suicide threat or attempt.

One of the five distinguishing characteristics of children defined in federal regulations as having emotional disturbance is "a general, pervasive mood of unhappiness or depression." Just whom federal officials meant to identify by this characteristic is not entirely clear. A general, pervasive mood of unhappiness or depression is more narrow and restrictive than the broadband behavioral dimension of *internalizing* disorder, yet it doesn't correspond exactly with narrower dimensions, such as anxiety or social withdrawal. But the term *unhappiness* also doesn't seem consistent with the clinical criteria for a major depressive episode. Rather, it may approximate a less-severe condition that might be called *dysthymia* by clinicians. Still, depressed mood might be considered the prototypical internalizing disorder (Reynolds, 2006). A reasonable conclusion is that the federal definition of *emotionally disturbed* should probably be interpreted to include a wide range of internalizing disorders such as anxiety-withdrawal and clinical depression.

Depression has been relatively neglected in special education research, even though it's clear that depression is closely related to a variety of other disorders, as well as to academic and social difficulties. It's recognized as an important disorder of childhood and adolescence that increases in prevalence with age, often coexists with other disorders, and is associated with long-term risks of mental illness and suicide (Geller & DelBello, 2003; Hammen, Rudolph, & Abaied, 2014). The relationship between depression and suicidal behavior concerns all educators, especially those who work with students identified as having EBD.

DEPRESSION

Definition and Prevalence

Childhood depression has been a controversial topic for decades. Traditional psychoanalytic theory suggests that depression cannot occur in childhood because psychological self-representation isn't sufficiently developed. For example, it's been argued that young children can't conceive of concepts such as hopelessness, at least not in the same way that

adults do. Some scholars suggest that children's depression is masked by other symptoms—expressed indirectly through symptoms such as enuresis, temper tantrums, hyperactivity, learning disabilities, truancy, and so on. However, most researchers long have agreed that depression in childhood parallels adult depression in many ways, though the specific types of behavior the depressed person exhibits will be developmentally age appropriate. Both children and adults can thus be characterized by depressed mood and loss of interest in productive activity, but adults may develop problems around work and marriage, whereas children may have academic problems and exhibit a variety of inappropriate conduct such as aggression, stealing, social withdrawal, and so forth.

Depression isn't among the disorders that are usually first diagnosed in infancy, childhood, or adolescence. Nevertheless, child psychiatrists do recognize that depression is something found among youngsters with EBD (Mattison, 2014). A major depressive episode may be signaled by significant weight loss when not dieting or weight gain. In children, this signal of depression might be failure to make expected weight gain for their age or

Video Example

from

YouTube

ENHANCEDetext
Video Connections 11.1
This video provides an excellent, thorough overview of the signs and symptoms of childhood depression. (https://www.youtube.com/watch?v=BVpsXJD_iSY)

being overweight. To some extent, however, the assumption that depression is the same phenomenon in children and adults may be misleading. We must remember that children aren't merely scaled-down versions of adults, that childhood depression may be accompanied by other disorders or difficulties (e.g., attention deficit–hyperactivity disorder, conduct disorder, anxiety disorders, learning disabilities, and school failure), and that children's limited experience and cognitive capacity may give them feelings or experiences of depression that are different from those of most depressed adults.

Childhood depression was at one time thought to be just a normal part of human development, an idea we now realize is erroneous. After the abnormality of childhood depression had been recognized, some saw it as the underlying problem behind all other childhood disorders, another view that clearly isn't accurate. If aggression, hyperactivity, noncompliance, learning disabilities, school failure, and other problems of nearly any sort are all attributed to underlying depression in the absence of core features of depressed behavior (depressed mood, loss of interest in most or all normal activities), then depression becomes meaningless as a concept and diagnostic category. A more defensible perspective is that childhood depression is a serious disorder in its own right that may or may not be accompanied by other maladaptive behavior or be comorbid with other disorders (Hammen et al., 2014; Mattison, 2014; Seeley, Rohde, Lewinsohn, & Clarke, 2002; Seeley, Severson, & Fixsen, 2014; Waslick, Kandel, & Kakouros, 2002).

Depression is part of a larger category of **mood disorder**. One's mood may be elevated or depressed, and mood disorders may involve different levels of severity of symptoms in both directions (or toward both poles, as in **bipolar disorder**). Depressed mood is characterized by **dysphoria**, feelings of unhappiness or unwellness not consistent with one's circumstances. In children and adolescents, dysphoria may be shown as irritability as well as by unhappiness. Elevated mood is characterized by the opposite—**euphoria**, a feeling of extraordinary and often unrealistic happiness or wellness. Dysphoric mood or irritability that lasts for a protracted period of time (a year or more for children and adolescents) but doesn't reach an intense level is called *dysthymia*. Euphoria and frenetic activity are known as *mania*.

Some mood disorders are *unipolar*, such as depressive disorder in which mood varies between normal and extreme dysphoria (depression) or normal and extreme euphoria (mania). Others are *bipolar*, in which mood swings from one extreme to the other. *Bipolar* has largely replaced the earlier terminology *manic-depressive*. Whether children with bipolar disorder are typically appropriately diagnosed has been controversial, but it is increasingly recognized as existing in children's experience (Groopman, 2007; Youngstrom & Algorta, 2014).

Although we might provide detailed diagnostic criteria for the clinical diagnosis of various mood disorders in adults and make notes regarding diagnosis in children and adolescents, considerable uncertainty remains about just how these criteria should apply to children and adolescents. The same general characteristics apply to adults and children, but the exact characterization of these disorders in children awaits much more research. Generally speaking, the symptoms one looks for in depression and related mood disorders in children and adolescents include the following:

- Dramatically diminished interest or pleasure in all or almost all activities
- Depressed mood or general irritability
- Disturbance of appetite and significant weight gain or loss
- Disturbance of sleep (insomnia or hypersomnia)
- Psychomotor agitation or retardation

- Loss of energy, feelings of fatigue
- Feelings of worthlessness, self-reproach, excessive or inappropriate guilt, or hopelessness
- Diminished ability to think or concentrate; indecisiveness
- Ideas of suicide, suicide threats or attempts, recurrent thoughts of death

These symptoms indicate depression only if several are exhibited over a protracted period of time and if they aren't temporary, reasonable responses to life circumstances (e.g., a romantic breakup, a death in the family, or even of a pet; we would expect several symptoms associated with depression during a period of grieving; see the case of Buddy in the accompanying case book for an example of childhood depression).

Depression and other mood disorders tend to be episodic and of long duration. That is, people are said to have "bouts" of depression, and those who have repeated bouts, or a major episode in terms of intensity or duration, are at high risk for more. Children and adolescents with long-standing depression (two years or longer) have been found to have more significant impairments, greater anxiety, and lower self-esteem, and to show more acting-out behavior. Depressive behavior may result in peer rejection, particularly if it's exhibited under conditions of low stress and there is no apparent reason for depressive behavior, which is often the case.

Depression affects a substantial percentage of children and adolescents, and many young people who are depressed remain untreated for the disorder (Seeley, Rohde, Lewinsohn, & Clarke, 2002; Hammen et al., 2014). At any given time, it's estimated that as many as 15 percent of children and adolescents display some symptoms of depression, but the true prevalence of major depression in children and adolescents is probably in the range of 3 percent to 5 percent. Rates of depression increase significantly after puberty, at which time females begin to outnumber males in likelihood of diagnosis; by age fourteen, approximately twice as many females as males are diagnosed with depression; this ratio also persists for the next thirty-five to forty years (Bhatia & Bhatia, 2007; Hammen et al., 2014; Seeley, et al., 2002). Adolescents who are diagnosed with depression are subsequently two to four times more likely to be diagnosed with depression as adults. Although there is still considerable uncertainty about the definition and diagnosis of many mood disorders, bipolar disorder is increasingly diagnosed in adolescents with major mental health problems and recognized as a topic needing research. Also, the comorbidity of depressive disorders with other disorders, particularly conduct disorder and attention deficit–hyperactivity disorder, is increasingly recognized (Papolos, 2003; Seeley et al., 2002; Seeley, Severson, & Fixsen, 2014). Depression has also been found to affect some children diagnosed with pervasive developmental disorders (see DeJong & Frazier, 2003; Hammen et al., 2014), though clearly more research is needed on these findings.

Assessment

The formal diagnosis of depression and other mood disorders in children and adolescents is left to psychologists or psychiatrists, though educators can play a key role in aiding the assessment of these disorders (Mattison, 2014). Competent assessment requires a multimodal approach in which several sources of information are tapped: self-reports, parental reports, peer nominations, observation, and clinical interviews. A substantial number of tools are available for assessing depression, including rating scales and structured interviews (Reynolds, 2006). However, the most important contribution of teachers to assessment may be careful observation of students' behavior that may reflect depression.

The types of behavior indicating possible depression include four categories of problems: affective, cognitive, motivational, and physiological. We can expect the depressed student to show depressed affect—to act unusually sad, lonely, and apathetic. Cognitive characteristics may include negative comments about oneself that indicate low self-esteem, excessive guilt, and pessimism. Depressed students often avoid demanding tasks and social experiences, show little interest in normal activities, and seem not to be motivated by ordinary or even special consequences. Finally, depressed students often have physical complaints of fatigue or illness or problems with sleeping or eating. If a student exhibits such characteristics frequently for a period of weeks, the teacher should consider the possibility that the student is suffering from a mood disorder and refer him or her for evaluation. However, it's important not to overlook the possibility that other behaviors, such as general irritability or acting out, are also sometimes signs of depression, especially in children and adolescents. Difficulty in expressing anger appropriately is one characteristic associated with depression, so a student's behavior might be mistakenly thought to reflect an externalizing disorder. Adolescents who are depressed may also become involved in substance abuse, as a means of self-medicating their depression (Bhatia & Bhatia, 2007).

Comorbidity of depression with other disorders makes assessment particularly difficult, as does the episodic nature of mood disorders and the fact that an individual can have more than one mood disorder. If the student exhibits conduct disorder or attention deficit–hyperactivity disorder, for example, it may be easy to overlook indications of depression. When an individual is recovering a more normal mood after a depressive episode, it's easy to assume that the depression wasn't serious or that the risk of another episode is low. If the student has a dysthymic disorder but is going through a major depressive episode, the low-grade depression may be misinterpreted as normal.

Causal Factors, Relationship to Other Disorders, and Prevention

As with most disorders, in most cases we don't know exactly what causes depression. Instead, we can identify risk factors that may contribute to the development of depression. Some cases are evidently *endogenous* (a response to unknown genetic, biochemical, or other biological factors); other cases are apparently *reactive* (a response to environmental events, such as death of a loved one or academic failure). Predictably, child abuse, parental psychopathology (especially a history of depression), and family conflict and disorganization are frequently linked to children's depression (see Hammen et al., 2014 for a discussion of risk factors).

An area where clearer evidence is accumulating involves the significant correlation between parents' (especially mothers') depression and a variety of problems in their children, including depression (see Beardslee, Versage, Van de Velde, Swatling, & Hoke, 2002; Ohannessian et al., 2005; Seeley et al., 2002, 2014). Despite this evidence, it would be erroneous to conclude that all children of depressed mothers develop serious psychopathology. In a study of the psychosocial outcomes for children of mothers with depression or bipolar disorder, although there was a general trend for the parents' grown children to have received a psychiatric diagnosis and to have accessed mental health services, significant variability was observed in the adult outcomes these children experienced (Mowbray & Mowbray, 2006). This relationship undoubtedly reflects some genetic influence on behavior, but it is extraordinarily difficult to separate biological or genetic influences from family or behavioral influences. Depressed parents may provide models of depressed behavior (which their children imitate), reinforce depressive behaviors in their children, or create a home environment that is conducive to depression (by setting unreasonable expectations, providing few rewards for achievement or initiative, emphasizing punishment, or providing noncontingent rewards and punishments). Depressed mothers are known to lack parenting skills, which could account for at least some of their children's behavioral and affective problems. In short, the child born to and raised by a parent with depression is at heightened risk for depression on both biological and environmental grounds.

Educators are in a particularly good position to identify depression and should give special attention to the ways in which a student's depression may affect and be affected by school performance (Seeley et al., 2002, 2014). Young children who are depressed engage in less play and exhibit more undirected activity than do typical children (Lous, de Wit, De Bruyn, & Riksen-Walraven, 2002). Depression appears to be associated with lowered performance on some cognitive tasks, lowered self-esteem, lowered social competence, deficits in self-control, and a depressive attributional style in which children tend to believe that bad outcomes are a result of their own unmodifiable and global inadequacies. This includes a poor academic self-image (Hammen et al., 2014; Masi et al., 2000). There is an inverse relationship between depressive symptoms and problem-solving abilities; better problem solvers tend to show fewer depressive symptoms.

These findings suggest that school failure and depression may be reciprocal causal factors: depression makes the student less competent and less confident, both academically and socially; failing academically and socially makes the student feel and act more depressed and reinforces the attribution of failure to unalterable personal characteristics. Depression and failure may thus become a vicious cycle that is hard to break. This cycle may often be a part of conduct disorder and, to a lesser extent, learning disabilities. Yet teachers and other school personnel have been slow to recognize the signs of depression and even slower to provide intervention.

Preventing depression is important because childhood depression, at least in its severe and chronic form, is linked to adult maladjustment and sometimes to suicidal behavior. However, research provides little guidance for preventive efforts. We might guess that an accumulation of major stressful life events is an important factor in some youngsters' depression and suicide. However, more typical daily hassles can also put adolescents at risk for depression, particularly in the late childhood and early adolescent years. Primary prevention may therefore involve efforts to reduce all manner of stressful life events for all children, but such broad-based, unfocused efforts are unlikely to receive much political or fiscal support. There is a better chance for support and success if efforts focus on relieving stress for abused and neglected youngsters and others whose lives are obviously extremely stressful. Another approach to primary prevention, somewhat more focused and feasible, is parent training for depressed parents (Beardslee et al., 2002; Swan et al., 2014). Secondary and tertiary-level prevention are still more focused and feasible, giving depressed youngsters behavioral or cognitive-behavioral training in overcoming their specific difficulties. This training is preventive in that it keeps the child's current situation from worsening and may forestall the development of long-term negative outcomes and recurrent episodes of depression.

Intervention and Education

Treatment for childhood depression generally involves cognitive-behavioral therapy or counseling, either alone or in combination with antidepressant medications (Bhatia & Bhatia, 2007; Swan et al., 2014). Following initial concerns about using medication to treat depression in children before it had been adequately studied in this population, research has continued to accrue on pharmacological treatment of childhood depression. Concerns have now shifted to the effectiveness of medication with children, as well as concerns about the side effects of such medications (Hammen et al., 2014; Konopasek & Forness, 2014; Kusumakar, Lazier, MacMaster, & Santor, 2002; Ryan, 2002; Warner, 2010). A particularly critical concern has been raised with the suggestion that one potential side effect of certain antidepressants in adolescents is increased suicidal behavior. This concern only heightens the need for adolescents with depression to be treated only by physicians or psychiatrists who specialize in childhood depression, and for any use of medication for depression to be closely monitored. A number of studies have compared behavioral to psychopharmacologic treatments for depression, and early evidence suggests that a combined approach—one using both behavioral interventions and medication—may be most efficacious (Forness, Freeman, & Paparella, 2006). When medications are prescribed, teachers need to carefully monitor the effects on behavior and learning. As is the case in nearly every type of disorder, successful intervention requires collaborative, multimodal treatment involving a variety of professionals.

A very controversial treatment for depression in adults is electroconvulsive treatment (ECT, sometimes called electroconvulsive or electroshock treatment) (Wang, 2007). At one time, ECT was frequently used for depression, but it is now rarely used because of its history of abuse. It is now used only in cases in which depression is severe and not responsive to drug therapies, and it's extremely unlikely to be used with adolescents.

Teachers are most likely to be directly involved in interventions that are behavioral or cognitive-behavioral. These interventions are based on theories of depression that highlight the roles of social skills, productive and pleasurable activity, causal attributions, cognitive assertions, and self-control (see Maag & Swearer, 2005; Seeley et al., 2002; Swan et al., 2014).

The common signs of depression that might point to interventions to which teachers might contribute directly include those first identified by Kaslow, Morris, and Rehm (1998) two decades ago:

1. Low activity level
2. Social skills deficits
3. Self-control deficits
4. Depressive attributional style
5. Low self-esteem and feelings of hopelessness
6. Limited self-awareness and interpersonal awareness

Teachers can be extremely helpful, if not the key players, in implementing strategies to overcome depression.

SUICIDAL BEHAVIOR

Definition and Prevalence

The definition of *completed suicide* is straightforward and without controversy: successfully killing oneself intentionally. However, determining that a given death was a suicide is often difficult because the circumstances, particularly the intentions of the deceased, are often in question. Suicide is socially stigmatizing, so the label *suicide* is likely to be avoided if death can be reasonably attributed to accident. Accidents are the leading cause of death among adolescents aged fifteen to twenty-four, and many researchers suspect that in this age group, many deaths attributed to accident are disguised or misreported suicides.

The term *parasuicide* sometimes refers to unsuccessful or uncompleted suicidal behavior. *Attempted suicide* is difficult to define because studies often differ in distinctions between suicidal gestures (suicidal behavior that is interpreted as not serious in intent), thoughts of suicide or self-injury, threats of suicide, and self-inflicted injury requiring medical treatment (see Cha & Nock, 2014; Spirito & Overholser, 2003).

Regardless of how we define them, suicide, suicide attempts, and self-injury of adolescents (and, to a lesser extent, younger children) remain a major mental health concern in the U.S.; only accidents and homicides are more often the cause of death among youth between the ages of fifteen and twenty-four (Cha & Nock, 2014). Rates of suicide have trended differently over the past forty years, and age, gender, and ethnicity breakdowns create an even more complicated picture. According to the Centers for Disease Control and Prevention (search the Internet for the center or go to https://www.cdc.gov), the rates of suicide among males aged ten to twenty-four years decreased gradually from 1991 to 2006, but this trend generally reversed in about 2006, and rates of suicide for all age groups, and for both males and females, was higher in 2014 than it was in 1999. The CDC's figures highlight quite obviously the preponderance of adolescent males who commit suicide. Not only do adolescent males have a higher suicide rate than do females, this sex difference becomes more marked with age; overall, approximately four times as many males as females die from suicide in the U.S. each year. Among older adolescents and young adults, parasuicides (attempted suicides), however, are more common for females than for males. Among children, the gender difference is reversed, with suicide attempts more common for boys than for girls.

In the United States, Native American youth continue to have the highest rates of suicide, with both males and females committing suicide at a rate more than double that of their counterparts of any other ethnicity. While Black males had traditionally been thought to have lower rates of suicide than White males, there is evidence that this difference has decreased over time, and it may no longer be possible to say that the risk is any different for White versus Black males. Finally, the trend suggests that Hispanic females are at increasing risk for suicide. The complexity of reasons underlying these changing trends are far from known, and while research continues to examine factors that contribute to risk, and of course what can be done to lessen risk, it isn't possible to predict whether or how rates of suicide and parasuicide for different racial, ethnic, age, or gender subgroups will trend in the future.

Although suicide is rarely reported in children under ten years old and is relatively infrequent even in prepubertal children, we do occasionally encounter reports of suicide attempts and successful suicides of very young children. Regardless, rising suicidal behavior among young people and the high rate at which children and youth kill or attempt to kill themselves are alarming. Greater understanding of the causes and more effective prevention programs must be priorities. We also need better means of dealing with suicidal individuals after an attempted suicide, and with survivors after a completed suicide.

Causal Factors and Prevention

Most authorities agree that biological and nonbiological factors interact in complex ways in the causation of suicide and depression. There appear to be genetic and other physiological contributions to depressive behavior, as we have already noted, and these factors may increase risk for suicidal behavior and nonsuicidal self-injury (NSSI) as well (see Cha & Nock, 2014). However, educators focus primarily on the environmental factors involved. The many complex factors that contribute to children's and adolescents' suicidal behavior include major psychiatric problems, feelings of hopelessness, impulsivity, naive concepts of death, substance abuse, social isolation, abuse and neglect by parents, family conflict and disorganization, a family history of suicide, parasuicide, or NSSI and cultural factors, including stress caused by the educational system and attention to suicide in the mass media. Youth with EBD, especially those who use alcohol or illicit drugs, are at particularly high risk of suicidal behavior (Carr, 2002; Cha & Nock, 2014; Spirito & Overholser, 2003).

The common thread among all causal factors is that suicidal individuals believe they have little impact on the world around them. They often don't know that help is available for dealing with their problems, believing that no one cares and that they must deal with their problems alone. Culp, Clyman, and Culp (1995) studied 220 students in grades six through twelve. Nearly half of those who reported feelings of depression didn't ask for help, most often because they didn't know about services available to them in the school or, if they did, believed they had to take care of their problems by themselves. Feelings of loneliness and especially hopelessness appear to be among the best predictors of suicidal thoughts and intentions (Spirito & Overholser, 2003).

Hopelessness has long been recognized as a characteristic of the thinking of those prone to suicide (Cha & Nock, 2014; Esposito, Johnson, Wolfsdorf, & Spirito, 2003). Hopelessness and intent to commit suicide correlate more highly than do depression and suicide intent. Apparently, all individuals who feel hopeless are depressed, but not all who are depressed feel hopeless. Those who feel hopeless are convinced that things won't get better, can't get better, so they might as well give up hope. Hopelessness may represent the final stage of depression that tends to precede suicidal intent, the stage at which an individual concludes that suicide is justified.

Many children and adolescents who commit suicide or parasuicide have a history of EBD and school failure. In fact, school performance of adolescents who show suicidal behavior is almost uniformly poor, and most teenagers' suicides and parasuicides occur in the spring months, when school problems (grades, graduation, college admission) are highlighted.

Other factors increase the likelihood of suicide attempts, besides mood disorders, which are common to most suicide attempts. West, Swahn, and McCarty (2010), for example, found that sadness (perhaps part of a mood disorder), substance use, and violent victimization were related to suicide attempt in both male and female high school students. Hills, Afifi, Cox, Bienvenu, and Sareen (2009) found the presence of externalizing disorders (in addition to internalizing disorders) to be predictive of suicide attempts; they speculated that impulsivity in particular was the key factor in the individual acting upon a suicidal thought. Of all risk factors, it continues to be the case that the best single predictor of suicide attempt is a previous suicide attempt.

Some have suspected that social stress related to homosexuality or other sexual differences or sexual abuse are risk factors in suicide, but research continues to be mixed on whether this is the case (see Cha & Nock, 2014). In an extensive summary of research, Haas and colleagues (2010) found no reliable connection between sexual orientation and suicide, though the few studies on the topic have been criticized for methodological problems. In their review, Haas and others did note a dramatically elevated risk for suicide *attempt*—two to seven times greater risk—for adolescents who identified themselves as lesbian, gay, or bisexual (LGB) compared to students who were heterosexual. The precise nature of risk in this population is difficult to determine, however, as rates of other disorders are also elevated in the LGB population, including major depression, anxiety disorder, conduct disorder, and substance abuse problems. Still, Haas and colleagues concluded that these related disorders don't account for all of the increased risk for suicide attempt in LGB youth, and that stigma, prejudice, and discrimination, and the obvious stress they bring, most likely contribute to an increased risk of suicide attempt.

It isn't surprising from a social learning perspective that suicidal behavior appears to be learned, at least in part, through observation of the behavior of others in family and social contexts. Outbreaks of suicide attempts are particularly likely to occur in institutional settings and psychiatric hospitals, or even in high schools or communities (e.g., Cha & Nock, 2014; Insel & Gould, 2008), probably partly as a result of imitation or competitive bids for attention and status.

Primary suicide prevention presents enormous problems of identifying individuals who are at risk because, in any attempt to make predictions, the number of false positives is extremely high and the consequences of false negatives are extremely severe. Because only a relatively small percentage of the population commits or attempts suicide, and because suicidal and nonsuicidal individuals have many common characteristics, any general screening procedure turns up many false positives—individuals who aren't actually at high risk. But the consequences of identifying as "not at risk" those who are in fact likely to attempt or commit suicide (the false negatives) are obviously grim. Consequently, most primary prevention programs are aimed at entire school populations.

Assessment

Suicidal behavior isn't always preceded by recognizable signals, although some characteristics and circumstances are danger signals for which educators and other adults should be on the lookout. Adults' and peers' awareness of indications that a child or youth might be at risk for suicidal behavior is an important aspect of assessing the general school population (Carr, 2002; Cha & Nock, 2014; Spirito & Overholser, 2003). These are some indications of risk in the general school population:

- Sudden changes in usual behavior or affect
- Serious academic, social, or disciplinary problems at school
- Family or home problems, including parental separation or divorce, child abuse, or running away from home
- Disturbed or disrupted peer relations, including peer rejection and breakup of romantic relationships or social isolation
- Health problems, such as insomnia, loss of appetite, sudden weight change, and so on
- Substance abuse
- Giving away possessions or talk of not being present in the future
- Talk of suicide or presence of a suicide plan
- Situational crisis such as death of a family member or close friend, pregnancy or abortion, legal arrest, loss of employment of self or family member

Part of any assessment of risk involves systematic evaluation of the characteristics of individuals who are thought to be at higher than usual risk. A personal characteristic associated with most suicides, parasuicides, and thoughts of suicide is depression, so it's important to assess depression. However, depression may be accompanied by aggressive behavior, conduct disorder, or a variety of other problems (Mattison, 2014).

Intervention and Education

Adults should do the following:

- Take all suicide threats and attempts seriously.
- Seek to reestablish communication.
- Provide emotional support or sustenance that relieves alienation.

Although dealing adequately with the problem of suicidal behavior requires a complex, multifaceted effort, the general notion is that the suicidal individual must be helped to establish and maintain as many points of contact as possible with significant others, including adults and peers. The child or adolescent must be shown ways that are not self-destructive to solve problems and get attention from others. Teachers can aid in suicide prevention by realizing that they can identify students who are at risk; school systems can play a part in prevention by providing curricula that acquaint students with others' experience of normal physical and social development.

The educator's role in intervention is primarily to provide information about suicide and refer students who appear at risk to other professionals. A comprehensive program of suicide awareness and prevention has several parts: administrative guidelines specifying school policy, faculty in-service to obtain support of teachers and provide them with basic information and skills in dealing with students, and curricular programs for students. In addition, hotlines, peer counseling, and programs designed to reduce and manage stress may be implemented.

Managing children and adolescents after their suicide attempts or threats is the joint responsibility of counselors or other mental health personnel and teachers. Although teachers should not attempt to offer counseling or therapy themselves, they can provide critical support by encouraging students and families to obtain help from qualified counselors or therapists. Teachers can also help by reducing unnecessary stress on students and being willing and empathic listeners. An example of how a teacher might work with a student who shows signs of depression is presented in Box 11.1.

Video Example
from
YouTube

ENHANCEDetext
Video Connections 11.2
This very dramatic video from the Mayo Clinic is aimed at parents, and it provides an excellent description of signs that an adolescent might be considering suicide, as well as suggestions for parents in how to talk to teens. (https://www.youtube.com/watch?v=3BByqa7bhto)

Box 11.1

Teaching Social Skills to Students with Depression

What social skill problems will be most important to address in the context of dealing with depression?

It's not surprising that students who are depressed will think and talk about themselves in negative ways, sometimes referred to as a negative, or depressed, attributional style. They'll often make statements about how "dumb" they are, how they are failures at everything they try, or how they have no friends. Signs of hopelessness creep into their assessment of any task or activity they are faced with (e.g., "Why even try? I know I can't do it"). Such consistently negative statements can frustrate any teacher, but even more maddening are the extreme negative assessments students sometimes make that are wildly inconsistent with reality. Students' negative attributions can be remarkably consistent in that they assume the worst about themselves—if they fail at a task, it is because they are stupid, incompetent, or unathletic, etc. And on the chance that they succeed or do well at something, they likewise fail to take credit (e.g., "You made the test too easy on purpose!"). The skills teachers would like to see more of are positive self-statements, or at minimum accurate self-assessments. And of course at the same time teachers would like to see fewer harsh, often extreme, negative self-assessments.

What are appropriate targets for intervention?

As we have said, the goal is often simply to increase the student's self-awareness in ways that lead to accurate assessments and interpretations of the events around them. Beck (1976) has been credited with describing an important framework for understanding the way individuals with depression view their world: a) they interpret most experiences negatively, b) they consistently view themselves in a negative way, and c) they perceive that the future will hold only negative outcomes. Accordingly, interventions must target some or all of these erroneous perceptions. We want students to replace negative perceptions of events with accurate assessments—to view themselves accurately, including having the self-awareness to make realistic appraisals of both strengths and weaknesses. We want them to understand that future outcomes are in their control, at least to some extent, and that positive outcomes are certainly possible.

What types of intervention show promise?

Cognitive-behavioral interventions are a common treatment approach for depression, though we note that even in school settings, these are often implemented by school or clinical psychologists. As we also noted earlier, these are often supplemented by medication for severe depression, but of course medication is prescribed and should be monitored closely by a physician or psychiatrist. The role of teachers in these cases is to support intervention by providing opportunities for students to practice the skills they are working on, and of course reinforcing students when they display positive behaviors (e.g., positive self-statements).

An example—cognitive restructuring

Cognitive-behavioral intervention will often include a component or process known as *cognitive restructuring*. In cognitive restructuring, the therapist attempts to help the student think through and reframe a negative thought. Often, any number of negative thoughts are part of a student's negative attributional style, and these become so ingrained in their thinking that they become automatic statements that students repeat in multiple contexts, without really thinking about them (upon starting a difficult task, taking a spelling test, or being assigned a complicated lab with a new partner, they assume failure is imminent, because "I'm stupid"). But in cognitive restructuring, the therapist helps the student analyze particular situations that tend to prompt an automatic, negative statement

(continued)

Box 9.1   *(continued)*

and help the student reframe the event. Suppose a student in fact gets a bad grade on a spelling test, and says, "See, I told you I was stupid." A therapist might examine this scenario with the student, asking whether and how the student prepared for the test, whether they know what words will be on the next test, and how they plan to prepare next time. The immediate goal is for students to come to the conclusion that they didn't do well because they didn't prepare. An obvious long-term goal—one for which the teacher must assume primary responsibility—is helping students prepare better for a challenging assignment, and hopefully obtain a better grade. Note that the need for cognitive restructuring may kick in again if the student in fact earns a better grade, as the student is sure to respond to success with yet another negative attribution (e.g., "That's just because you helped me," or "You made this one easy"). In this case, the therapist obviously helps students think through the idea that maybe they did better this time because they studied. Such a simple intervention helps students see not only that their negative self-assessment was inaccurate (they are not stupid), but also that they do in fact have some degree of control over future events. As with most any interventions, the key to success will be consistency, repeated practice, and reinforcement of successes along the way.

Where to find more information about cognitive-behavioral interventions:

Cha, C. B., & Nock, M. K. (2014). Suicidal and nonsuicidal self-injurious thoughts and behaviors. In E. J. Mash & R. A. Barkley (Eds.), *Child psychopathology* (2nd ed., pp. 317–342). New York, NY: Guilford.

Maag, J. W., & Swearer, S. M. (2005). Cognitive-behavioral interventions for depression: Review and implications for school personnel. *Behavioral Disorders, 30*, 250–276.

Shirk, S. R., Kaplinski, H., & Gudmundsen, G. (2009). School-based cognitive-behavioral therapy for adolescent depression. *Journal of Emotional and Behavioral Disorders, 17*, 106–117.

SUMMARY

The federal definition of *emotionally disturbed* suggests that youngsters with internalizing problems, including depression, should be eligible for special education, although the definition describes depression and related disorders ambiguously. Childhood depression has only recently become a topic of serious research. Consensus is emerging that depression is a major disorder of childhood that parallels adult depression in many respects, but particular behaviors exhibited in response to depressed affect will be developmentally age appropriate. Both adults and children who are depressed experience depressed moods and lose interest in productive activity. Depressed children may exhibit a variety of inappropriate behavior, and depression is often comorbid with other conditions.

Depression is part of the larger category of mood disorders, which includes unipolar and bipolar disorders involving elevated or depressed mood. Indications of depression include the inability to experience pleasure in most activities, depressed mood or irritability, disturbances of sleep or appetite, psychomotor agitation or retardation, loss of energy or fatigue, feelings of self-derogation or hopelessness, difficulty thinking or concentrating, and suicidal ideation or attempts. Several of these symptoms are exhibited for a protracted period and are not a reasonable response to life events. Prevalence of depression is higher among older adolescents than young children, and girls are more affected at older ages. Depression is estimated to occur in 3 percent to 5 percent of the child and adolescent population, but researchers suspect that many cases aren't identified.

Assessment of depression must be multifaceted and should include self-reports, parental reports, peer nominations, observations, and clinical interviews. The judgments of teachers shouldn't be overlooked. Teachers should be on the lookout for four categories of problems: affective, cognitive, motivational, and physiological.

Some cases of depression clearly result from unknown biological factors, but the causal factors in most cases are indeterminable. In some cases, depression represents a reaction to stressful or traumatic environmental events. We find significant correlations between parents' depression and problems of their children, including depression. Educators should give special attention to how depression and school failure can be reciprocal causal factors. Prevention of depression is important because severe chronic depression is associated with adult maladjustment and suicidal behavior. Prevention may involve reducing stress, training in parenting, or teaching specific cognitive or behavioral skills.

Antidepressant drugs may be useful in some cases of depression, but their effects and side effects should be monitored carefully by physicians or psychiatrists who specialize in treating childhood depression. Behavioral or cognitive-behavioral interventions are based on theories that attribute depression to inadequate social skills, maladaptive thought patterns, and lack of self-control. Selecting intervention strategies depends on analyzing the depressed individual's specific cognitive and social characteristics. Teachers can play a major role in teaching social skills and engaging students in higher levels of productive activities as well as assisting in other approaches.

Suicide and suicidal behavior (parasuicide) of children and youth are a major public heath concern in the U.S. Factors increasing the risk of suicidal behavior include both biological and environmental factors, especially a history of difficulty or failure in school, stress related to family dysfunction or abuse, substance abuse, family members or acquaintances who have completed suicide, depression and feelings of hopelessness, and aggressive behavior.

Prevention of suicide is extremely difficult because of the problems associated with false positives and false negatives. Prevention programs are typically aimed at entire school populations and consist of guidelines for teaching, in-service training for teachers, and instructional programs for students and parents. Assessment of suicide risk involves recognizing danger signals and evaluating the individual's sense of hopelessness. Evaluation of statistically based risk factors and the student's ability to perform specific coping tasks is required to determine whether a suicide attempt is imminent.

Teachers and other adults should take all suicide threats and attempts seriously, seek to reestablish communication with students who feel alienated and help them establish as many points of contact as possible with significant others, and provide emotional sustenance and support. Schools should have a plan for follow-up intervention when a suicide occurs.

✔ ENHANCEDetext END-OF-CHAPTER 11 QUIZ

Click on the checkmark icon to access an end-of-chapter quiz. Answer the questions to gauge your understanding of chapter concepts and better prepare you for case discussions.

PERSONAL REFLECTIONS

Depression and Suicidal Behavior

Adam Brown, M.S. Ed., is a principal for the Re-Education Program (Re-ED) and Tidewater Regional Alternative Educational Program (TRAEP) for the Southeastern Cooperative Educational Programs (SECEP) in Virginia Beach, Virginia. These programs serve students with a range of emotional and behavioral disabilities in grades kindergarten through twelve. Before his current role as an administrator, Adam was a teacher in the Re-ED program for four years.

Describe the school in which you currently work and your professional role in that school.

In my current role, I oversee two separate school buildings. A majority of the students served in these buildings are placed in the Re-ED program. The Re-ED program is based on the Twelve Principles of Re-Education developed by the psychologist Nicholas Hobbs. This philosophy is based on the premise that all students can be provided a safe learning environment in which they can be taught to manage their behaviors in a way that can be generalized outside of the classroom while receiving quality instruction from qualified teachers.

In a typical Re-ED classroom, there are two teachers for an average of eight to twelve students. The two teachers—a special education teacher and a general education teacher—provide instruction in the core academic areas as well as provide instruction in social-skills and behavior regulation. Our emphasis on the emotional well-being of students, while also implementing strong instructional practices, requires a special educator who is able to implement a variety of interventions targeting multiple skills on a daily basis.

The TRAEP program serves students in both general and special education who have not been able to demonstrate academic success in a more traditional classroom. Classrooms average ten to fifteen students in this program. The TRAEP program serves students at the secondary grade levels and individualizes programming so that students receive additional credit hours, work towards obtaining their GED, and demonstrate behaviors that can allow them to return to a more comprehensive setting. Like the Re-ED program, TRAEP focuses on social-skills training and instruction on behavior management. A strong emphasis on the emotional well-being of the student is enforced throughout the program.

As a principal for these programs, I serve as the instructional leader. I ensure that IEPs, instructional content, and programming meet the needs for all students in an effort to provide them with successful outcomes. This requires the facilitation of a wide range of professional development opportunities that provide our teachers with the skills necessary to establish a welcoming environment for our stakeholders.

It is also my role to ensure that staff and students maintain a safe environment that provides the opportunity for students to generalize the skills they have learned to other settings. These opportunities include a variety of field trips including overnight camping trips, conducting a plant sale with plants grown by students participating in our career and technical education class, and trips to local job fairs for students who are close to graduating or who have demonstrated workplace readiness skills.

Think of a student you have worked with who exhibited depression or suicidal thoughts or behavior. How did these concerns come to your attention (what did you observe)?

Working with this student population, I have seen a wide range of behaviors whose functions can be attributed to each student's unique past experiences and desires. These include physical aggression (hitting, kicking, and biting), verbal aggression (cursing, specific threats, and inappropriate comments), elopement, and self-injurious actions. While these behaviors are highly observable, students who exhibit signs of depression or suicidal ideations often exhibit a more withdrawn and internalized affect. As such, they are often overlooked, as aggressive actions tend to gain quicker staff response to maintain safety.

I am reminded of a student named Johnnie. Johnnie did display some of the behaviors listed in the previous paragraph, but they were infrequent and would often result from an antecedent event that was easily identifiable. For example, he became upset over an assignment that he could not complete which resulted in him flipping a desk and attempting to run out of the classroom. Johnnie was an introverted student and had difficulty maintaining peer and staff relationships. He rarely engaged in conversations and it appeared that only a few staff members felt that they had established a strong connection with Johnnie.

His infrequent acting out behaviors and quiet demeanor led to teachers assuming that his needs were being met through the normal structure and routine that was being provided on a daily basis. However, it became apparent that Johnnie's introvert behavior masked inner turmoil that was occurring. As the school year progressed, Johnnie began to display behaviors with no obvious antecedents or triggers. These included spontaneous fits of crying that would last for over twenty minutes, acts of physical aggression towards random individuals, and overt displays of self-injurious behavior, which included frequent attempts to wrap shoe strings and belts around his neck. This required intensive safety plans to be implemented to ensure Johnnie's safety. The support system (parent, teachers, psychologist, and mentor) for Johnnie continued to seek out various ways to validate to him that he had individuals who cared for him, but it appeared that his internal struggle was an extremely difficult barrier to break through.

What was the impact of this student's behavioral and emotional concerns on his or her educational progress and overall school success?

Due to Johnnie's long history of behaviors, he spent a large amount of time outside of the classroom before coming to SECEP. In a more comprehensive setting, Johnnie spent a lot of time in administrator and counselor offices, and resource rooms, and received in-school and out-of-school suspensions. This resulted in lost instructional time and severe academic deficiencies before he entered a more restrictive environment. He exhibited deficiencies in literacy and numeracy, which impacted his performance in all academic subjects. These deficiencies led to frequent frustration that resulted in behaviors that provided Johnnie with a way to escape task demands. This is a common trait for a majority of this student population.

In addition to these behaviors, Johnnie's depression was another element that he struggled with during the academic day. Due to his deficiencies, he would often receive remedial instruction along with the grade-level curriculum in an effort to help improve his academic performance. Johnnie was self-conscious about how his peers perceived him and would exhibit problem behaviors if he felt that peers saw that his work was easier than their work. Additional elements that impeded his progress were the supports needed to accommodate Johnnie's bouts with depression. At times, Johnnie needed to take time outside of the classroom when he had difficulty maintaining his emotions. These breaks were often spent in another classroom or taking walks. Johnnie would often not talk at all to the staff member supervising him and would only talk to indicate to staff that he was ready to return. It became a common practice for staff to let Johnnie deal with his emotions on his own terms, which they felt was necessary to maintain a safe learning environment. Regardless, these additional supports delayed his academic progress.

What did you or other teachers or staff find most successful in working with this student?

Johnnie was able to form a strong relationship with a staff member who had worked with him for several years. He would engage in some conversation and showed an interest in participating in activities with this staff member. Through frequent communication with the parent, teachers, and psychologist, it was determined that this relationship could serve as a pathway towards increased confidence and an ability to interact with more staff and students in the building. Johnnie was able to start earning various rewards and participate in activities that involved other students. Johnnie enjoyed playing basketball and started being able to select peers to play with when he met certain criteria that were agreed upon between the staff member and himself.

It is often stressed with this student population that you must meet them where they currently are performing academically in order to help them progress to grade-level performance. What is often missed is that students with emotional disabilities have to be met where they are currently functioning on an emotional level as well. The day must be individualized and adaptable in order to provide the necessary supports to meet the emotional needs of each student. Depression serves as an additional barrier towards being able to understand what supports are needed. For a student with depression, it is vital to find the teacher or other adult who can best form a strong relationship with that student and start building from there.

In your opinion, what is the long-term prognosis for this student? What will be the greatest concerns for this student in the future?

As Johnnie begins to enter his teenage years, he has made some gains in regard to his behavior management and relationship building. However, there is still a lot of room to grow. He continues to struggle academically and with his depression. He is entering a time where he will begin to pursue his high school diploma and look at his future. My greatest concern for this student is that he will not be able to find effective measures to handle his depression independently. I fear that with his disability and bout with depression, he will seek out negative avenues to find the supports he requires. This could come in the form of gang activity, substance abuse, or violence in the community.

As educators, it is our responsibility to provide the programming necessary to provide Johnnie with a pathway towards a positive outcome. Through the supports provided in our program, we must continuously seek out various ways to promote his emotional well-being. I hope to see Johnnie as a successful member of our community when he completes his education, but it is imperative that the community provide him with supports necessary to achieve this.

Questions for Further Reflection

1. How would you tell the difference between depression and other problems that one of your students is experiencing?

2. In your opinion, what are the kinds of events that would cause your students to legitimately experience a depressed mood?

3. What are the most helpful things you could do as a teacher to prevent depression and suicide attempts among your students?

12 DISORDERS OF THINKING, COMMUNICATING, AND STEREOTYPICAL BEHAVIOR

Photographee.eu/Shutterstock

After reading this chapter, you should be able to:

12.1 Define the term *psychotic* and discuss how schizophrenia fits, or does not fit, the definition.

12.2 Describe the specific signs or symptoms associated with schizophrenia and how they might be mistaken for other disorders in children.

12.3 Describe the nature of communication disorders and the features of intervention that are associated with the best outcomes.

12.4 Discuss the primary causes of and interventions for unacceptable stereotyped behavior.

In this chapter we briefly summarize information regarding the nature and causes of **schizophrenia** and other severe disorders—problems involving thinking and communicating. We also discuss unacceptable stereotyped behavior—stereotypical behavior, sometimes called **stereotopy** (abnormal repetitive behavior). Keep in mind that schizophrenia is now included explicitly in the federal definition of *emotionally disturbed*. Also, remember that severe disorders of thinking, communicating, and stereotypical behavior often occur along with other disabilities besides EBD. Some texts on severe disabilities don't include discussion of schizophrenia and related disorders. However, researchers and clinicians increasingly recognize that psychopathology, including schizophrenia and related disorders, occurs across the full spectrum of intellectual ability and co-occurs with intellectual disabilities (formerly referred to as mental retardation).

Schizophrenia is typically referred to as a psychotic disorder, and many pervasive developmental disabilities (PDD) have often been called psychoses as well. However, the term **psychotic** has had many definitions, none of which is universally accepted. Broadly, the term *psychosis* refers to a break with reality. Accordingly, psychotic disorder most often will include delusions (ideas that are not consistent with reality) and/or hallucinations (imaginary sensory experiences, such as hearing voices or noises that don't exist or seeing imaginary objects or events).

Schizophrenia is usually diagnosed by a psychiatrist (see Kuniyoshi & McClellan, 2014; Mattison, 2014). Several subtypes of schizophrenia may be named, including paranoid type, disorganized type, catatonic type, and so on. Sometimes a particular form of schizophrenia is diagnosed, such as schizophreniform disorder (like schizophrenia, but shorter in duration, usually just one to six months in duration; a relatively short episode of schizophrenia) or schizoaffective disorder (schizophrenia that includes an affective or mood disorder, such as bipolar disorder or depression, as well).

A variety of disorders other than schizophrenia may fall under the general heading of *psychotic*. These might include such diagnoses as delusional disorder, substance-induced psychotic disorder, and so on. The major feature of these psychotic disorders in all cases is an inability to distinguish reality from unreality.

Pervasive developmental disorders (PDD) affect multiple aspects of a child's development. Some behaviors that are severely problematic and may be considered to indicate EBD in their own right (e.g., persistent and pervasive mutism, extreme self-stimulation, or self-injury) are sometimes seen in children with PDD. An important point about the emotional and behavioral problems associated with schizophrenia and related disabilities is that they're now recognized as having their origins primarily in biological factors, as noted in Chapter 4. Although researchers are increasingly finding a biological basis for many types of EBD, the scientific evidence of biological factors is stronger for more severe disorders.

We first discuss schizophrenia. Then we turn our attention to behavior often seen in youngsters with severe disabilities, regardless of their diagnostic labels: socialization problems, communication disorders, and stereotypy, especially self-stimulation and self-injury. As you can imagine, behaviors like these are severely debilitating and often present persistent and significant challenges to teachers and others who work with children and youth who have schizophrenia or other severe disorders.

Video Example from YouTube

▶

ENHANCEDetext
Video Connections 12.1

This video shows several examples of children with different types of psychoses, including childhood schizophrenia. Note that the psychiatrist in the video points out that disorders this severe are rare. (https://www.youtube.com/watch?v=PVHNGZ0Omx0)

SCHIZOPHRENIA

Definition, Prevalence, and Characteristics

Schizophrenia is a disorder in which people usually have two or more of the following symptoms:

- Delusions
- Hallucinations
- Disorganized speech (e.g., they may frequently get derailed or be incoherent)
- Grossly disorganized or catatonic behavior
- Negative symptoms such as lack of affect, inability to think logically, or inability to make decisions (Asarnow & Asarnow, 2003; also, see Kuniyoshi & McClellan, 2014)

The definition of schizophrenia is not simple. It is a complex, multifaceted disorder (or group of disorders) that has defied precise definition for more than a century (Cepeda, 2007). Defining schizophrenia in children is even more problematic than defining it in adults (the usual age of onset is between ages eighteen and forty years) because children usually have more difficulty explaining themselves. Nevertheless, no one any longer questions the fact that schizophrenia occurs in children and has manifestations similar to schizophrenia in adults. Moreover, children can have schizophrenia and another disability, including intellectual disability (Kuniyoshi & McClellan, 2014; Matson & Laud, 2007).

Schizophrenia affects about 1 in 100 adults, but it's rarely seen in children and youth under the age of eighteen; as we noted, it's typically first diagnosed in individuals between the ages of eighteen and forty. Delusional thinking is uncommon in children, but sometimes young children are easily convinced that their fantasies are real, or even that the delusions of other people might be real. Normal children, particularly typical young children, often engage in fantasies during play. Fantasies are considered normal in some contexts, but not in others. When fantasies persist beyond the bounds of acceptable "pretend play," especially in older children, or the child has difficulty distinguishing reality from fantasy, the child's socialization or academic learning may suffer. The cases of Wanda and Carmen in the accompanying case book illustrate the extent to which children can become caught up in their fantasies.

Table 12.1 shows examples of the types of psychotic symptoms that are most often seen in schizophrenia: hallucinations and delusions. Hallucinations and delusions take a wide variety of forms. In addition to these examples, the delusions of children and adolescents frequently have sexual or religious content. Children having delusions and hallucinations are not always diagnosed as having schizophrenia (Polanczyk et al., 2010). They may be diagnosed as having bipolar disorder, or they may have comorbid disorders, such as schizophrenia along with conduct disorder, attention deficit–hyperactivity disorder (ADHD), depression or bipolar disorder, or another diagnosable psychiatric disorder (Asarnow & Asarnow, 2003; Kuniyoshi & McClellan, 2014).

In many cases, the diagnosis of schizophrenia in children is difficult because the onset is hard to detect, perhaps beginning with conduct problems, anxiety disorders, or ADHD. Symptom patterns may go unrecognized if they are mild, or may be confused with other disorders. Sometimes, children who show violent aggression and have serious school problems are later found to have schizophrenia.

Table 12.1 Examples of Psychotic Symptoms

Hallucinations—experiencing something through one of the five senses that does not exist, or that others cannot perceive:

1. *Visual*—seeing things that aren't there
2. *Auditory*—hearing things (voices, most commonly) that aren't real
3. *Tactile*—feeling something (e.g., something touching your skin) that isn't there
4. *Olfactory*—smelling things that others can't smell (or not smelling things that others do)
5. *Gustatory*—sensing a taste when no food is present

Delusions—holding a strong belief about oneself, with no evidence that it is true, and even in the face of clear contradictory evidence:

1. *Paranoid delusions or delusions of persecution*—most commonly, believing that others are "out to get you"; believing that bad things are happening to you (whether or not they are) AND attributing that to malicious intent of real or imagined foes
2. *Delusions of reference*—believing that there is some link between you and things in the environment when there isn't, or, in some cases, which can't possibly be true (e.g., falsely believing that a television news reporter is talking about you; believing that aliens are listening to your telephone conversations)
3. *Somatic delusions*—false beliefs about your body (e.g., you have some terrible illness; there are foreign objects in your body)
4. *Delusions of grandeur*—believing that you have special powers or abilities (e.g., you're a movie star, famous athlete, or celebrity)

Some children who are diagnosed with some sort of PDD are later diagnosed as having schizophrenia, but that is not typical. Most children with schizophrenia never lose their symptoms completely, although some do (Asarnow & Asarnow, 2003; Kuniyoshi & McClellan, 2014).

Causes and Prevention

As discussed in Chapter 4, the causes of schizophrenia are known to be in large measure biological, but the exact biological mechanisms responsible for the illness aren't known. Genetic factors are known to play a critical role, but which genes are involved and how they work we don't know yet. It's quite likely that schizophrenia isn't a single disease entity but a cluster of highly similar disorders in the same way that cancer isn't a single disease.

The same causal factors seem to operate whether schizophrenia is first diagnosed in childhood or adulthood. However, onset of schizophrenia in childhood or adolescence seems to carry a worse prognosis than adult-onset schizophrenia, particularly when the symptoms are severe (Eggers, Bunk, & Drause, 2000; Kuniyoshi & McClellan, 2014; Lay, Blanz, Hartmann, & Schmidt, 2000).

We know that in the vast majority of cases, if not all, biological and environmental factors work together to cause schizophrenia. Families in which the parents exhibit deviant behavior may contribute to the development of schizophrenia. Primary prevention consists of assessing genetic risks and avoiding behavior that may trigger schizophrenia in vulnerable persons, especially substance abuse and extreme stress. Secondary prevention consists mainly of psychopharmacological treatment and structured environments in which symptoms can be managed most effectively (Konopasek & Forness, 2014; Mattison, 2014).

Education and Related Interventions

It's not possible to describe a specific educational intervention, or even a set of interventions, for children and youth with schizophrenia because the symptoms and educational needs of these students vary tremendously. Moreover, it's safe to say that education will be only one of several interventions used because pharmacological treatment is almost always called for, as are therapeutic family-based interventions (Konopasek & Forness, 2014). When special education is necessary, it appears that a highly structured, individualized program that provides a feeling of safety and routine may help the student keep symptoms in check as much as possible.

Schizophrenia is nearly always treated with antipsychotic drugs (known as neuroleptics), which don't cure schizophrenia but are designed to reduce its symptoms. In brief, neuroleptics are prescribed to reduce intrusive thoughts, hallucinations, and delusions. Many drugs don't work well for all children and youth (or adults for that matter), and they may have serious side effects. Research is ongoing into the effects and side effects of adult medications, and the development of new medications to treat schizophrenia specifically in children, but the consensus remains that pharmacological intervention is probably a necessary component of the effective treatment of both children and adults.

The outcomes for children and youth with schizophrenia are extremely variable. As we've noted, the prognosis for children diagnosed with schizophrenia is generally not as good as the prognosis for those first diagnosed with schizophrenia as adults. A substantial proportion of these students don't make good overall adjustment as they progress into adulthood. Some cases, however, turn out quite well (as illustrated by the case of Bill in the accompanying case book).

In summary, schizophrenia is a rare and disabling disorder of childhood. The onset is often insidious and confused with other disorders. Intervention nearly always involves psychopharmacology, along with social and educational interventions. A structured, individualized educational program is often necessary. With appropriate intervention, some children and youth with schizophrenia lose many or most of their symptoms.

SOCIALIZATION PROBLEMS

As we've noted, socialization depends in large part on competent communication. Unfortunately, language and communication deficits are classic symptoms of childhood schizophrenia. In addition to language, broader social skill problems are also typically evident. The odd, unresponsive, and rejecting patterns of behavior shown by such children may severely limit their learning to play with, befriend, and be befriended by others. Teaching self-control, social skills, and appropriate alternative behavior to youngsters with any type of EBD is difficult. Teaching these to students with intellectual disabilities (which are evident in a large number of children and youth with schizophrenia) is even more complicated.

Most children with any type of PDD have extreme problems with social skills of nearly every type. Many critical social skills can't be taught one-on-one by an adult teacher or with a group of other equally unskilled children, so it isn't surprising that most intervention requires interaction with normally developing peers. Peers may be trained to serve as models, to initiate interactions, and to respond appropriately to the student with severe disorders in home, classroom, or community settings.

Students with schizophrenia and other PDD exhibit a wide range of emotional and behavioral problems and often have comorbid disorders. Consequently, the full range of interventions used with disorders discussed in other chapters, including attention deficit–hyperactivity disorder, conduct disorder, depression, and so on, may be needed.

COMMUNICATION DISORDERS

Teaching children with any type of pervasive developmental disorder to use communication effectively is one of the greatest challenges their teachers face. Educational programs for children who do not speak have been based on applying behavior principles to teaching language. The child's attempts to follow commands or approximate vocalizations are rewarded, typically with praise, hugs, and food given by the teacher immediately following the child's approximation of what the teacher expects. For example, at the earliest step in the sequence, a child might be reinforced for merely establishing eye contact with the teacher. The next step might be making any vocalization while looking at the teacher, next making a vocalization approximating a sound made by the teacher, then imitating words spoken by the teacher, and finally replying to the teacher's questions. Of course, this description is a great oversimplification, but through such methods nonverbal children are often taught basic oral language skills.

A disappointing outcome of early research on language training was that few of the children acquired truly useful or functional language, even after intensive and prolonged training. Their speech tended to have a mechanical quality, and they often didn't learn to use their language for many social purposes. A current trend in language intervention is emphasis on pragmatics (making language more functional in social interaction) and motivating children to communicate. Instead of training children to imitate words in isolation or to use syntactically and grammatically correct forms, we might train them to use language to obtain a desired result. For example, the child might be taught to say, "I want juice" (or a simplified form: "juice" or "want juice") to get a drink of juice. Increasingly, language intervention for children with limited communication skills involves structuring opportunities to use language in natural settings. For example, the teacher may set up opportunities for children to make requests by using a missing item strategy (e.g., give the child a coloring book but not crayons, prompting a request for the crayons), interrupting a chain of behavior (e.g., stopping the child on her way out to play, prompting a request to go out), or delaying assistance with tasks (e.g., waiting to help a child put on his coat until he asks for assistance).

Progress in teaching functional communication skills comes slowly through careful, programmatic intervention and ongoing research. Claims of breakthrough interventions are almost always misleading and disappointing. The language training procedures based on

Table 12.2   Recommendations for Teaching Communication Skills

1. Early intervention is important, so teaching should begin as soon as it is evident that communication skills are lacking.
2. The program should involve parents and other family members and provide instruction in as normal or natural an environment as possible.
3. Teachers should make the most important information in communication as obvious as possible by using highlighting.
4. Teachers should be highly organized and use a lot of repetition; better to repeat too much than not enough.

operant conditioning applied to natural language contexts have not led to dramatic break-throughs or a cure. However, research over a period of decades now supports the use of these procedures in most cases. Table 12.2 summarizes recommendations on teaching students with communication difficulties, regardless of the nature of a child's specific disability or disorder (see Gerenser & Forman, 2007). Thorough evaluation of speech and language skills is necessary before these teaching practices are used (see Conroy, Stichter, & Gage, 2017; Gerenser & Forman, 2007; Justice, 2006; Lonke, 2017). A broader discussion of teaching the social skills associated with communication to children and youth with schizophrenia is presented in Box 12.1 at the end of this chapter.

STEREOTYPY (ABNORMAL REPETITIVE MOVEMENT)

Children and adults with severe emotional, behavioral, or cognitive disabilities may engage in persistent, repetitive, seemingly meaningless behavior. Their stereotypical patterns of behavior, or **stereotypy**, may or may not result in serious self-injury. Stereotypy is an umbrella term and refers to a broad class of behaviors that involve repetition, rigidity, invariance, inappropriateness, and lack of adaptability or acceptability. Such repetitive movements may have been caused by biological or environmental factors, or both.

Often, repetitive movement seems to serve the primary or sole purpose of providing sensory feedback and thus is referred to as self-stimulation. In its most severe and troubling form, these repetitive behaviors result in an individual's physical injury. We briefly discuss both noninjurious self-stimulation and self-injury.

Video Example from YouTube

ENHANCEDetext
Video Connections 12.2
This very short video is intended for clinicians, but note the examples of stereotypy in children and description of the basics of intervention. (https://www.youtube.com/watch?v=__3_FAt8WpA)

Self-Stimulation

Self-stimulation can take an almost infinite variety of forms, such as repeatedly staring blankly into space, body rocking, hand flapping, eye rubbing, lip licking, or repeating the same vocalization over and over. Depending on the *topography* (particular movements) of self-stimulation and the rate or intensity, it can result in physical injury—for example, eye rubbing at a high rate and pressure might impair vision.

Self-stimulation is apparently a way to obtain self-reinforcing or self-perpetuating sensory feedback. It's not likely to stop for long unless demands for other incompatible responses are made or it is actively suppressed. This appears to be true of some self-stimulatory behavior, such as nail biting, of typically developing children and youth (and adults). We could probably find some form of self-stimulation in nearly everyone's behavior, varying only in subtlety, social appropriateness, and rate. It's a pervasive characteristic of normally developing infants, for example, and nearly everyone engages in higher rates of some type of self-stimulatory behavior when bored or tired (e.g., bouncing or tapping feet, hair twirling). Thus, like most behaviors, self-stimulation is considered abnormal or pathological only when it occurs in certain social contexts or at a high intensity or rate.

High rates of self-stimulation sometimes require highly intrusive, directive intervention procedures because students are unlikely to learn academic or social tasks when engaged in such behavior. Many procedures have been researched, among them using self-stimulation or alternative sensory stimulation as reinforcement for appropriate behavior, medications, and changing the environmental conditions in which self-stimulation tends to occur (see Bodfish, 2007). As we learn more about the nature of self-stimulation and related behavior, we are coming to understand that the context in which it occurs (e.g., highly structured tasks or relatively unstructured recreation) has a lot to do with the success of the procedures used to control it.

There is no one best method of controlling self-stimulation. Effective intervention varies according to the individual. In fact, intervention is not always justified. For some, reducing self-stimulation may serve no therapeutic purpose. When self-stimulation doesn't a) result in physical injury or deformity, b) interfere significantly with learning, or c) prevent participation in normal activities, then intervention may not be justified. Again, whether to intervene depends on the topography, rate, duration, and typical social consequences of the behavior. Intervention should attempt to find the function that the repetitive behavior serves (i.e., the reason or reasons the person does it) and provide positive support for appropriate behavior.

Self-Injury

Like self-stimulation, some types of self-injury may occur in people whose behavior is considered normal (see Cha & Nock, 2014). For example, body piercing and tattooing, although typically performed by others at the request of an individual, may be considered deliberate self-injury. Only the social context and rate or level of most behaviors distinguish what is acceptable from what is unacceptable. Nearly any behavior is maladaptive and considered socially inappropriate when it is engaged in at a very high level, but normal and acceptable at a lower level or under certain conditions. Consider the difference between a small tattoo, discretely placed on an arm or shoulder, versus tattoos covering the face. Or, one might consider relatively modest piercing with more extreme forms of piercing.

Some youngsters injure themselves repeatedly and deliberately in the most brutal and socially unacceptable fashion. We find this kind of *self-injurious behavior* (SIB) in some individuals with severe intellectual disability, but it is a characteristic often associated with multiple disabilities—for example, intellectual disability and schizophrenia. Most people with SIB don't have well-developed oral language. They are often either mute or have very limited language.

In fact, one frequent approach to SIB is to try to figure out what function such behavior has, what it communicates, and what noninjurious consequences it produces (e.g., attention or escape from adults' demands, sensory stimulation; see Bodfish, 2007; Cha & Nock, 2014).

A more recent concern is children and youth with normal intelligence and language skills who deliberately injure themselves, without the intent of killing themselves. The prevalence of such behavior, sometimes referred to as **nonsuicidal self-injury** (NSSI), appears to have risen dramatically since the 1990s. Some estimates suggest that 6 percent to 7 percent of adolescents may injure themselves in this way in a given year, with anywhere from 12 percent to 37 percent engaging in NSSI at some time in their lives (Cha & Nock, 2014; Whitlock, 2010). Distinct from the more culturally accepted tattooing or piercing, behaviors included under the category of NSSI once included primarily "cutting," but now also include burning; scratching; self-hitting; carving on one's body; and biting, tearing, or ripping the skin. NSSI appears to occur in nearly as many adolescents without any comorbid disorders as it does in those with other diagnosed disorders. Injuries to the face, eyes, neck, breasts, or genitals may be indicative of greater pathology than injuries inflicted elsewhere on the body. It has been presumed that NSSI is closely associated with depression or thoughts of suicide, but some researchers have now suggested that NSSI may in fact be a way that adolescents relieve stress and, in essence, avoid suicide. But because the practice of NSSI is a relatively new phenomenon among U.S. teens, and research on this topic is only beginning, little is known about the nature, causes, and treatment of NSSI or its long-term outcomes.

Whatever their causes or functions, the atavistic (primitive) behaviors known as SIBs take a variety of forms, and if left unchecked, they share the consequence of bodily injury. Without physical restraint, protective gear, or effective intervention, there is risk that the youngster will permanently disfigure, incapacitate, or kill himself or herself.

The deviant aspects of SIB are its rate, intensity, and persistence. Perhaps 10 percent of young, nondisabled children under the age of five occasionally engage in some form of self-injurious behavior. It is considered normal, for example, for very young children in the midst of temper tantrums to bang their heads or hit themselves. Deviant self-injury, however, occurs so frequently and is of such intensity and duration that the youngster cannot develop normal social relationships or learn self-care skills and is in danger of becoming even more severely disabled.

Evidence indicates that SIBs could in some cases be a result of deficiencies in biochemicals required for normal brain functioning, inadequate development of the central nervous system, early experiences of pain and isolation, sensory problems, insensitivity to pain, or the body's ability to produce opiate-like substances in response to pain or injury. But no single biological explanation is now supported by research (Bodfish, 2007; Cha & Nock, 2014). However, biological factors need not, and probably usually don't, operate independently of social factors in causing SIB. Perhaps, in many cases, biological factors cause initial self-injury, but social learning factors exacerbate and maintain the problem. Self-injury, like other types of behavior, may be reinforced by social attention. This notion has important implications for intervention because it suggests ways of teaching alternatives to self-injury.

Some children appear to use SIBs as a means of getting adults to withdraw demands for performance, which the children experience as aversive. When presented with a task that demands their attention and performance, these children begin to injure themselves; the demands are then withdrawn. The social interaction and attention involved in teaching and learning is reinforcing for some children, and withdrawal of attention contingent upon SIB is, for some, an effective extinction or punishment procedure. The same type of interaction and attention is apparently aversive for other children, and withdrawal of attention contingent on SIB is negatively reinforcing for them; it makes the problem worse instead of better.

The assessment of self-injury is at once straightforward and complex. It is straightforward in that assessment involves direct observation and measurement; self-injurious behaviors should be defined, observed, and recorded daily in the different environments in which they occur. It's complex in that the causes aren't well understood, and care must be taken to assess possible biological and subtle environmental causes (see Bodfish, 2007; Cha & Nock, 2014). Possible biological causes include genetic anomalies and factors such as ear infections and sensory deficits. SIB may occur more often in some environments than in others, and a change in environmental conditions (such as demands for performance) may dramatically alter the problem. So it's important to assess the quality of the youngster's surroundings and social environment as well as the behavior itself, and it's particularly important to assess the social consequences of SIB.

Many different approaches to reducing SIB have been tried. No approach has been entirely successful, although some show much better results than others. Among the least successful have been various forms of psychotherapy, "sensory-integration therapy," and "gentle teaching," approaches that are nonaversive (i.e., don't involve punishment) but are supported by very little scientific evidence that they reduce SIB (see Foxx & Mulick, 2016). The most effective nonaversive strategies yet devised involve functional analysis (to find the purpose the behavior serves) and arranging an environment in which alternative behaviors are taught or SIB is less likely to occur (see Bodfish, 2007; Foxx & Mulick, 2016). The emphases of research and practice in the early twenty-first century are on functional analysis, nonaversive procedures, and pharmacological treatments.

Box 12.1

Teaching Social Skills to Students with Schizophrenia or Severe Disorders

What social skill problems in students with schizophrenia or severe disorders will be most important to address?

Unlike the other disorders associated with EBD we've discussed in previous chapters, schizophrenia and other severe disorders bring a host of such severe social skill problems that it is difficult to know where to begin. In fact, it is a fundamental, defining characteristic of schizophrenia that extreme socialization problems are sure to be present (except, perhaps, in a small percentage of the mildest of cases). These social skill problems can range from almost complete lack of connection to or interaction with the environment or others in it—in essence, a complete lack of social skills—to an array of such bizarre, inappropriate, unpredictable behaviors that virtually no one, peer or adult, finds it easy to be around the child (see the case of Carmen in the accompanying case book and think about what social skills problems she might have in a regular classroom or with a teacher who was not keenly sensitive to her differences). As we discussed in this chapter, the lack of positive social skills, the array of bizarre behavior, and lack of connectedness to others might be summarized as a problem of *communication*. That is, the student lacks skills needed to communicate or interact with others or has so many odd behaviors that communication efforts and attempts to interact positively are routinely thwarted.

What are appropriate targets for intervention?

It's often possible to analyze some of the problem behaviors of children with schizophrenia from the perspective of simply attempting to figure out a child's communicative attempt, and then teaching the child a more appropriate means of making his or her wishes known. More broadly construed, communication can take many forms, and the social skills that make up communication, or that lay the foundation for effective communication, are many. Targets for intervention for children and youth with schizophrenia might include things like a) social perceptions (reading the emotions of others); b) responding or sending skills (using verbal or nonverbal communication to effectively send intended messages); c) interactional skills (initiating, maintaining, or ending a conversation); and d) affiliative skills (expressing affection to family or friends in contextually appropriate ways). Keep in mind, too, that working with a child with schizophrenia requires extremely good social skills on the part of the teacher.

What types of intervention show promise?

As we've suggested, there are no treatments that are universally effective, and a continuing problem is generalization. That is, even when a structured instructional approach results in some learned skills in a classroom or clinical setting, it remains very difficult to get children and adolescents to put those social skills to use outside of training settings, in the natural contexts in which the skills are needed the most. Despite these concerns, it seems that several components are probably necessary to increase the odds of effectively enhancing the social and communication skills of children and youth with schizophrenia or other severe disorders: a) comprehensive assessment of a students' present skills in socialization and communication (strengths and needs); b) direct instruction in the specific communication or social skills targeted for change (i.e., modeling, guided practice, independent practice); c) extensive practice, repetition, and reinforcement of the skills targeted for a given individual; and d) training in a variety of natural contexts (various locations throughout the school, community, and home), and involving a variety of individuals (e.g., other teachers or adults in school, including staff; peers on the playground or in the cafeteria; friends or family members in home and community settings). Finally, if skills are targeted and prioritized well, the notion of naturally maintaining contingencies (which we mentioned in Chapter 10) should be taken advantage of whenever possible. For example, the child who learns to communicate effectively with staff in the cafeteria will be able to successfully purchase the ice cream he wants, and the student who learns to communicate in a normal tone about appropriate topics may be welcomed more readily to join a group of peers involved in an academic task or even a game.

An example—social skills training for adolescents with schizophrenia

Children and adolescents with schizophrenia will be a particular challenge in terms of social skills instruction for two key reasons. First, the early onset of childhood schizophrenia

(continued)

Box 12.1   *(continued)*

means that many basic social interaction skills that typically developing children acquire easily and naturally during childhood often have been missed. Thus, such basic things as eye contact may be a brand new skill for that student. Second, we know that cognitive function is often impaired in children and adolescents with schizophrenia, so our attempts at instruction are even more challenging. For these reasons, researchers recommend the following:

1. Begin with simple, basic skills (e.g., eye contact, smiling, appropriate speech volume).
2. Break down skills into their component parts (i.e., use task analysis).
3. Model the behavior you want to see (use either therapist or peer models).
4. Use role-play extensively.
5. Provide immediate, frequent, positive feedback (including corrective feedback as needed); for more sophisticated older children, social skills may be taught in groups, and peers can be taught to provide positive feedback.
6. Assign social skill homework (or practice in naturalistic settings).

Where to find more information about social skills training for schizophrenia:

Bellack, A. S., Mueser, K. T., Gingerich, S., & Agresta, J. (2004). *Social skills training for schizophrenia: A step-by-step guide.* New York, NY: Guilford.

Kopelowicz, A., Liberman, R. P., & Zarate, R. (2006) Recent advances in social skills training for schizophrenia. *Schizophrenia Bulletin, 32* (suppl 1), S12–S23.

Mattai, A. K., Hill, J. L., & Lenroot, R. K. (2010). Treatment of early onset schizophrenia. *Current Opinion in Psychiatry, 23,* 304–310.

SUMMARY

In the federal category "emotional disturbance," schizophrenia is explicitly included. Schizophrenia and pervasive developmental disorders are rare, severe disorders of children and youth in which emotional and behavioral disorders are manifested.

Schizophrenia is a major psychiatric disorder falling under the general category of "psychotic disorders." Symptoms include hallucinations, delusions, and grossly aberrant behavior or thinking. Schizophrenia is unusual in individuals under eighteen years of age, especially in preteens. The onset is often insidious and may be confused with other disorders. However, schizophrenia seems to be essentially the same disorder in children and adults. The causes appear to be primarily biological, although they aren't well understood. Effective education is usually highly structured and individualized. Psychopharmacological treatment is essential. Some children with schizophrenia recover, although many make little improvement and continue to have major symptoms in adulthood.

The socialization problems of children and youth with schizophrenia and pervasive developmental disorders are extremely varied. Schizophrenia may be comorbid with a wide variety of other disorders, such as conduct disorder, ADHD, depression, or intellectual disability.

A full range of intervention strategies is needed to address the socialization problems of these children and youth. Communication disorders are a central feature of many severe disorders. Language interventions now focus on naturalistic applications of operant conditioning principles in communication training.

Stereotypy consists of repetitive, stereotyped acts that seem to provide reinforcing sensory feedback.

Stereotypies may be merely self-stimulatory or self-injurious. Self-stimulation may interfere with learning. The best method of control depends on its topography and function. Self-injurious behavior appears to have multiple causes, both biological and social. It may serve the function of getting attention from others or allowing the individual to escape from demands. Current trends in research and intervention emphasize functional analysis, nonaversive procedures, and psychopharmacological treatment.

✔ ENHANCEDetext END-OF-CHAPTER 12 QUIZ

Click on the checkmark icon to access an end-of-chapter quiz. Answer the questions to gauge your understanding of chapter concepts and better prepare you for case discussions.

PERSONAL REFLECTIONS

Disorders of Thinking, Communicating, and Stereotypical Behavior

Jeanmarie Badar completed her master's degree in special education at Kent State University and her Ph.D. in special education at the University of Virginia. She taught special education for elementary-age children with emotional and behavioral disorders and a variety of other disabilities for twenty-five years and is now a personal trainer. She taught in Ohio, Virginia, and Singapore.

Describe your experience teaching or working with students with pervasive developmental disorders.

As an elementary special education teacher for many years, I frequently encountered students diagnosed as having a pervasive developmental disability (PDD). In my experience, I seldom or never saw a young child who had only one type of problem,

such as the bizarre thinking that we associate with schizophrenia.

Most of the children who have severe or pervasive developmental disabilities have multiple problems that include deficits in thinking and communicating plus a variety of extremely problematic, stereotypical behavior, such as screaming, rocking, throwing things, or aggressive or self-injurious behavior. For most of my years of teaching, my classroom was a relatively separate, self-contained setting within a regular public school, and I found that a student with PDD was likely to have an IEP that designated placement in such an environment. Placing such students in regular, general education classrooms seems to me very unlikely to help anyone for obvious reasons.

Think of a particular student who had a serious disorder. What were the unique or most challenging aspects of this student's disorder?

One student, in particular, stands out in my memory as presenting very complex challenges and whose needs I found extremely difficult to meet on a day-to-day basis. "Jesse" was a seven-year-old first grader when I began working with him. I was new to this particular position and school, but I had been teaching in similar settings for over twenty years at the time. Jesse had a full-time aide assigned only to him, and his IEP stated that he would receive all of his academic instruction in my self-contained classroom, but he would participate with general education classes for "specials" (Music, Art, P.E.), lunch, recess, and field trips. He was described as completely non-verbal with cognitive skills significantly below average. Some of Jesse's problem behaviors included screaming and yelling, hitting, biting, throwing things, and refusing to complete tasks. Also noted was the fact that Jesse was not toilet-trained and, therefore, wore diapers. In addition, he needed assistance with all self-care tasks such as eating, dressing, and personal hygiene. Physically, Jesse was described as "frail," and he had a history of being underweight and undernourished, very pale, frequently ill, lacking muscle tone, and wearing braces on his legs.

As is often the case, the IEP I received was not particularly helpful in preparing me to work with Jesse, especially given the fact that I had nine other students in grades K–2 who would also be in my classroom for all or most of their academic instruction. I would have one classroom aide who, like Jesse's aide, was not paid to attend any of the preparatory "work days" before the start of school or required to be at work during any time when students were not also present (i.e., before or after school). Both aides were entitled to a thirty-minute lunch break and two fifteen-minute breaks during the school day.

The academic goals on Jesse's IEP struck me as extremely sparse: five goals altogether. In a nutshell, Jesse was to learn to count and identify numbers to five; recognize five basic colors and four basic shapes, and sort objects accordingly; recognize, spell, and write his first name; match upper- and lower-case letters of the alphabet; and recognize ten basic sight words. The behavioral goals were even less helpful: "Jesse will reduce incidents of _____ to one or fewer per day." Fill in the blanks with each of his problem behaviors (e.g., screaming, hitting, biting, throwing things). No instructional or behavioral

strategies were suggested, nor were his current academic levels or behavior frequencies provided. Almost as an afterthought, a statement on the IEP indicated that Jesse had begun using a picture schedule throughout the school day toward the end of his kindergarten year.

Before the school year began, I tried to be as prepared as possible for Jesse. I designed a series of "work-jobs" for Jesse that aimed to assess his current levels and begin to teach the "readiness" skills listed on his IEP. I used sturdy cafeteria trays; a variety of plastic and wooden blocks, letters, numbers, etc.; and LOTS of Velcro to create what I hoped would be relatively indestructible manipulative instructional materials. I designated a roomy corner of the room as "Jesse's Work Station" and an adjacent area as "Jesse's Play Area." I created what seemed like a reasonable picture schedule, which incorporated the "Premack Principle" to allow for frequent play breaks and pleasurable activities following successful completion of work-jobs. I met briefly with the woman who would be Jesse's aide. She had not met Jesse yet either and had no experience or training in working with students with Jesse's characteristics. Jesse's mother did not have a home telephone and did not show up for "Back-to-School Night" the week before school started. She also did not respond to the postcard I had sent offering to visit her at home or meet somewhere nearby (it was a sprawling rural school division, and many families lived quite a distance from school).

I need to add here that the nine other students assigned to me appeared to have very, very different needs from Jesse's. They ranged in ages from six to eight and had significantly below-average academic skills, but all were verbal and quite capable of dressing, eating, and toileting on their own. Many had problem behaviors like inattention, noncompliance, poor peer relations, and even frequent temper tantrums, but all appeared on-track to become readers and writers and master basic math skills.

My intuition was correct. As I got to know all my students and began to design academic instruction and behavioral programming that was appropriate for them, Jesse was clearly an outlier who needed something quite different and, frankly, much more intensive intervention than I was able to provide. He showed no interest in the work-jobs I had created for him, other than to put each and every piece in his mouth and/or throw it to the floor. His screaming was so intense and so constant that I found myself taking the rest of the students to another room whenever possible in order to have some quiet time for instruction. I spent countless hours reading, planning, consulting with others, inviting observers to the classroom, conferring with Jesse's mom, and attending workshops to learn more about working with students like Jesse. In the end, I did find a few interventions that were somewhat successful, at least in the short term.

First, I learned more about picture schedules and realized that developmentally, Jesse was probably not ready to understand the relationship between the pictures and what they represented. We experimented with an "object schedule," for which a series of objects directly related to scheduled activities were lined up on the shelf. For example, a clean diaper represented a bathroom break; the small pillow we used on Jesse's chair represented a desk activity or work-job; his "sippy cup" represented snack time. Over time, we were able to help Jesse understand that snack time was coming soon, but he needed to finish his desk job first.

Secondly, I had to rethink the design of Jesse's work-jobs. I made the activities drastically shorter—two or three discreet trials as opposed to ten or twelve. I used much larger objects in order to stop Jesse from putting everything in his mouth. His work-jobs were now stored in laundry baskets instead of on desktop trays.

Third, I worked with Jesse's aide to try to reduce his screaming behavior, which was the most disruptive, if not the most serious, of his behavioral issues. We actually scheduled "Quiet Training" into Jesse's day, and these five-minute sessions were focused on teaching, modeling, and rewarding quiet behavior, beginning with ten-second intervals of no screaming, after which Jesse received a food reward. We sliced Skittles into tiny, tiny pieces because this was the only food we could find

that motivated Jesse to comply. Of course, we also spent a great deal of time brushing Jesse's teeth several times throughout the day!

These are just a few examples of interventions and techniques that we tried over the course of the year. Some worked; many more failed. Jesse's aide requested a transfer halfway through the school year, and despite my frustration at having to train a whole new person for this difficult job, the new aide had better teaching and behavioral instincts, in my opinion, AND was willing to put in extra (unpaid) hours to consult and problem-solve with me.

In the end (two years later), Jesse was re-evaluated and found to have multiple disabilities. His placement was changed to a separate school setting where everyone was highly trained in ABA techniques, and the staff-to-student ratio was much greater. However, all of these changes came about only after numerous requests by me (and other staff) for a re-assessment of the appropriateness of Jesse's IEP. Jesse's mother always blocked any attempt to explore more appropriate services for her son because she wanted him to attend the same elementary school she had attended as a child. Finally, when some parents of other students in the class started to complain that their children's education was being negatively affected by one individual, administrators began to put pressure on Jesse's mom to reconsider. Admittedly, I often think about how much time was lost in the lives of these other students—as well as for Jesse—because of our inability to provide FAPE for this student whose disabilities were so complex and difficult to manage.

Questions for Further Reflection

1. How would you respond to someone who believes that students like Jesse should be included in general education?

2. What do you think are reasonable long-term goals for students like Jesse?

3. What advantages and disadvantages do you see in Jesse's placement in a separate school rather than a special class in a regular public school?

13 SPECIAL PROBLEMS OF ADOLESCENTS

DELINQUENCY, SUBSTANCE ABUSE, AND EARLY SEXUAL ACTIVITY

George Dodson/Pearson Education, Inc.

After reading this chapter, you should be able to:

13.1 Explain the similarities in and differences between conduct disorder and delinquency.

13.2 Give arguments for the view that most or all incarcerated youngsters have disabilities and need special education.

13.3 List the primary causes and prevention strategies related to substance abuse.

13.4 Name the substances that children and youth most commonly abuse and state why they are not the focus of most concern about drugs.

13.5 Explain the primary reasons for concern about early sexual activity.

In this chapter, we focus on delinquency, substance abuse, and early sexual activity because these particular problem behaviors often have been found to occur together (see Siegel & Welsh, 2011), and the personality disorders of adolescents typically involve multiple, complex problems (Shiner & Tackett, 2014). Bear in mind that even the concept of adolescence continues to evolve, as do the definitions of problem behaviors associated with being an adolescent.

PROBLEM BEHAVIORS IN ADOLESCENCE AND EARLY ADULTHOOD

Juvenile delinquents rarely display only one isolated problem behavior. More often, they engage in a constellation of a number of interrelated problem behaviors, including delinquency, sexual activity at an early age, and substance abuse (Jessor, 1998; Jessor, Van Den Bos, Vanderryn, Costa, & Turbin, 1995; Siegel & Welsh, 2011). As we will discuss, these behaviors often go hand in hand, with each potentially contributing to the others, and frequently developing in the context of certain risk factors. Further, youngsters who are delinquent, abuse substances, and engage in early sexual behavior often participate in other antisocial activities as well (Ensminger & Juon, 1998).

Most adolescents engage in some risky behaviors, but most stop short of serious involvement and either reduce the intensity of risky behavior or stop such behavior altogether by the time they are adults (Donovan & Jessor, 1985; Siegel & Welsh, 2011). For example, many, if not most, adolescents will experiment with drugs, but relatively few become regular users or addicted to drugs. Attention deficit–hyperactivity disorder (ADHD), lack of guilt, poor communication with parents, low achievement, and anxiety are all characteristics of adolescents who exhibit escalating levels of problem behavior that are likely to continue into adulthood (Chang, Chen, & Brownson, 2003; Chassin, Ritter, Trim, & King, 2003; Siegel & Welsh, 2011; Silbereisen, 1998). Adolescents with those characteristics are predicted to have the highest levels of problem behaviors, and the presence of problem behaviors in adolescence is the strongest predictor of problem behaviors in adulthood (Brigham, Weiss, & Jones, 1998; see also Jolivette & Nelson, 2010a; Shiner & Tackett, 2014).

Loeber, Farrington, Stouthamer–Loeber, and Van Kammen (1998a, 1998b) found that measures of eight forms of problem behaviors were all highly related to each other: delinquency, substance abuse, ADHD, conduct problems, physical aggression, covert behavior such as lying and manipulation, depressed mood, and shyness or being withdrawn. That is, high scores in one of these areas of problem behavior were often accompanied by high scores in the other seven areas. Externalizing behaviors were more interrelated to each other than they were to internalizing behaviors so that physical aggression was strongly related to substance abuse, but shyness and being withdrawn were not. Boys with high levels of problem behaviors were also characterized by high levels of delinquency, sexual precocity, and substance abuse. Such behaviors are often a symptom of more complex psychiatric disorders and societal dysfunction that require complex services (see Gagnon, 2010; Nelson, Jolivette, Leone, & Mathur, 2010; Shiner & Tackett, 2014). Although many of these disorders are detected after a series of punitive interventions aimed at the most superficial aspects of the problem, researchers have been able to identify groups of variables that reliably predict the development of these complex disorders (Jolivette & Nelson, 2010b; Nelson et al., 2010; Leech, Day, Richardson, & Goldschmidt, 2003).

Research supports the importance and plausibility of early identification. Although the remainder of this chapter is organized around different categories of problem behaviors, remember that it's highly unlikely that any individual will display one and only one element of problem behavior. Problem behavior theory (Jessor & Jessor, 1977; Shiner & Tackett, 2014; Siegel & Welsh, 2011) and observations of comorbidity of problem behaviors with complex psychiatric disorders suggest that addressing only one or a few aspects of the problem behaviors described in this chapter will be of limited use. Rather, these problems are likely to respond only to more complex interventions that combine educational, mental health, family, and psychopharmocologic interventions (Forness et al., 1999; Garfinkel, 2010; Nelson et al., 2010).

JUVENILE DELINQUENCY

Definition

When someone who is not legally an adult (i.e., a juvenile) commits an act that could result in apprehension by police, he or she is said to have committed a **delinquent** act. Because many delinquent acts don't result in arrests, the true extent of **juvenile delinquency** is difficult to determine. Some laws are vague or loosely worded so that delinquency isn't clearly defined (e.g., it's not clear when a particular act would result in apprehension by police). Some acts are illegal if committed by a juvenile but not if they are committed by an adult (such as buying or drinking alcoholic beverages). Other delinquent acts are clearly criminal; they're considered morally wrong and punishable by law regardless of the age of the person who commits them (such as assault or murder; see cases in the accompanying case book). Many aggressive children's behavior just skirts legal delinquency. Much of their behavior is irritating, threatening, or disruptive, but not delinquent in a legal sense. Truly delinquent behavior is that which brings a juvenile into contact with law enforcement.

It's important that we distinguish between delinquent behavior and official delinquency. Any act that has legal constraints on its occurrence may be considered delinquent behavior. Juveniles may commit *index crimes*—crimes that are illegal regardless of a person's age and that include the full range of criminal offenses, from misdemeanors to first-degree murder. Common index crimes committed by juveniles are vandalism, shoplifting, and various other forms of theft such as auto theft, armed robbery, and assault. Acts that are illegal only when committed by a minor are called *status offenses*. Status offenses include truancy, running away from home, buying or possessing alcoholic beverages, and sexual promiscuity. They also include a variety of ill-defined behaviors described by labels such as *incorrigible, unmanageable*, or *beyond parental control*. Status offenses are a grab-bag category that can be abused in determining whether a child is a juvenile delinquent; it is a category that encompasses serious misdeeds but that adult authorities can expand to include mere suspicion or the appearance of misconduct (Blackburn, 1993; see also Sims & Preston, 2006; Jolivette & Nelson, 2010b).

The differences between official delinquency and delinquent behavior are significant. Surveys in which children and adolescents report whether they engage in specific delinquent acts indicate that the vast majority (80 percent to 90 percent) have done so. Self-reports appear to be by far the best way to estimate the true extent of delinquent behavior (Siegel & Welsh, 2011, 2012). Research studies have provided data indicating that self-reported delinquent behavior correlates positively with depressed mood (Beyers & Loeber, 2003) and negatively with parental awareness of a child's delinquent behavior (Laird, Pettit, Bates, & Dodge, 2003). Only about 20 percent of all minors are at some time officially delinquent; in a given year, approximately 2 million youths are arrested (Siegel & Welsh, 2011). Official delinquents are found disproportionately among lower socioeconomic classes and ethnic minorities (Laub & Lauritsen, 1998; Loeber, Farrington, Stouthamer-Loeber, & Van Kammen, 1998a; Penn, Greene, & Gabbidon, 2006; Siegel & Welsh, 2011).

Delinquent behavior, conduct disorder, and official delinquency are overlapping phenomena. Although data support a positive correlation between conduct disorder and delinquent behaviors (Vermeiren, Schwab-Stone, Ruchkin, De Clippele, & Deboutte, 2002), not all youngsters with conduct disorder of either the overt or covert variety will engage in delinquent behavior or become an official delinquent.

Few delinquents begin their criminal behavior with extreme behaviors such as violent crime. Rather, they ease into their delinquency through a series of minor offenses. The earlier the series of behaviors begins, the more likely it is that the individual will eventually show more serious examples of problem behavior and violence. Therefore, educators must not be lulled into a sense of false security that a young misbehaving youngster will outgrow his or her behavior patterns. Quite the opposite is implied by research. Children who exhibit problem behaviors at an early age very often grow into more serious problem behaviors.

Types of Delinquents

Researchers have attempted to delineate homogeneous groups of delinquents based on behavioral characteristics, types of offenses, and membership in subcultural groups (e.g., Achenbach, 1982; Quay, 1986a; see also Siegel & Welsh, 2011; Sims & Preston, 2006). However, it may be more helpful to distinguish between those who commit only one or a few delinquent acts and those who are serious repeat offenders, especially those who commit violent crimes against persons. Some have argued that because a majority of adolescents commit delinquent acts, the differences between those who are convicted and those who are not are largely a reflection of police or court biases, but this argument has not been supported by data. It can be argued that the correspondence between official arrest records and self-reports of delinquent and criminal acts, plus the ability of self-reports to predict future convictions, indicates that both self-reports and convictions are valid measures that distinguish the worst offenders. This view is supported by the finding that a prior arrest for a violent crime and a history of family violence and criminality are the best predictors (e.g., better than prior gang involvement or heavy alcohol and drug use) of a youth's likelihood of committing a violent crime (see Farrington, 2007; Lattimore, Visher, & Linster, 1995; see also Siegel & Welsh, 2011).

Another useful way of thinking about different types of delinquents is the age at which they commit their first offense. Prior research has indicated that the prognosis for those who begin a delinquent pattern of behavior before the age of twelve is much worse than it is for those who are late starters (Dinitz, Scarpitti, & Reckless, 1962; see also Sayre-McCord, 2007; Shiner & Tackett, 2014), though there is evidence that poorer prognosis for early starters is more typical of boys than of girls (see Bryant et al., 1995; Kratzer & Hodgins, 1999). The data appear to be consistent with the observation that more serious delinquent behavior is associated with a coercive family process that trains children in antisocial behavior from an early age (Patterson, Reid, & Dishion, 1992). In addition, research seems to indicate a correlation between parental dysfunction and child delinquency that is not explained by observational learning (Tapscott, Frick, Wootton, & Kruh, 1996).

Prevalence

We've pointed out that most children and youth commit at least one delinquent act. But because authorities don't detect most illegal acts, hidden delinquency remains a major problem. There are estimates that 3 percent to 4 percent of youth are adjudicated delinquent each year in the U.S., but remembering that most delinquent acts go unreported, there's no doubt that the rate at which youth engage in delinquent behavior is much higher. About half of the juveniles who become official delinquents are adjudicated for only one offense before they become adults. But it's juveniles who commit repeated offenses (**recidivists**) who account for the majority of official delinquency. Recidivists commit more serious offenses, begin performing delinquent acts at an earlier age (usually before they are twelve years old), and tend to continue their antisocial behavior as adults (Tolan, 1987; Tolan & Thomas, 1995).

Males continue to commit most juvenile offenses, particularly serious crimes against people and property, though females are increasingly involved in all types of offenses (Schaffner, 2006; Siegel & Welsh, 2011, 2012). Females comprised 19 percent of all cases of delinquency in 1985, but by 2007, this had risen to 27 percent of all cases (Knoll & Sickmund, 2010). Race, drug use, poor school performance, truancy, risk-seeking, and conflicts with parents, in addition to gender, are all factors associated with delinquency recidivism (Chang, Chen, & Brownson,, 2003). Official delinquency rates rise and fall. For example, the total number of cases of delinquency rose steadily from 1985 to its peak in 1997, increasing by 62 percent during that time to a high of more than 1.7 million cases. Rates then fell steadily from 1997 through 2013, decreasing by 44 percent. For the year 2013, the U.S. Department of Justice estimated that 1.1 million cases were handled by juvenile courts, which represents 9 percent fewer cases than in 1985. For the most current data on juvenile delinquency, visit the website of the Office of Juvenile Justice and Delinquency Prevention: ojjdp.gov/.

The peak ages for juvenile delinquency are ages fifteen to seventeen, after which delinquency rates decline. Orientation to drugs and delinquency related to drugs, especially alcohol abuse, are pervasive concerns of parents, educators, and other adults for this age group.

Causal Factors and Prevention

Delinquency isn't just law-violating behavior but also involves the responses of adult authority to it (Farrington, 2007). Incarceration and other forms of punishment have failed to control delinquency. Many social-cultural factors, including our society's failure to control access to firearms, contribute to delinquency. The problem is not merely young people's criminal behavior but adult responses that tend to exacerbate rather than reduce delinquency (Nelson et al., 2010; St. George, 2011). The scope of the problem is great, and the issues in delinquency have complex legal, moral, psychological, and sociological implications. Criminologists have suspected social–environmental, biological, familial, and personal causal factors (see Siegel & Welsh, 2011, 2012). We focus here on explanations of the origins of delinquency that have the greatest implications for educators.

Longitudinal research in England and New Zealand, as well as the United States, has led to remarkably consistent findings and hypotheses about the risk factors for delinquency and suggestions for prevention. Research consistently reveals that the following characteristics put preadolescents at high risk for later delinquency:

- History of child abuse
- Hyperactivity, impulsivity, and problems in paying attention
- Low intelligence and low academic achievement, as well as a general pattern of disengagement from school
- Lax parental supervision and harsh authoritarian discipline
- A family history of criminality and family conflict, including aggression between siblings
- Poverty, large family size, densely populated neighborhood, poor housing
- Antisocial behavior or conduct disorder, including especially aggressive behavior and stealing

Researchers have formed hypotheses about how these and related factors work in leading to delinquency. Three general models of influence appear in the delinquency literature: a) delinquent behavior is the result of stable antisocial personality traits located within the delinquent individual, b) delinquent behavior is mostly the product of external environmental factors and circumstances, and c) delinquent behavior is primarily the result of interactions between the personal characteristics of the individual (e.g., hyperactivity, ability) and the environment. Most researchers endorse the third option and suggest that no single factor can account for delinquent behavior (Siegel & Welsh, 2011).

Youngsters who are at risk for delinquent behavior are often disengaged from school and work, and school disengagement may precede engagement in other problem behaviors (see Fosse, 2015; Patterson & Rivers, 2015). Engagement in school may be more important as a protective factor than disengagement is as a risk factor. Students who are engaged in school have more to lose (e.g., positive peer group, good education, entrance into college, a good job) if they become involved in deviant behavior. So, school engagement may be important for delinquency prevention. Educators, especially special educators, should focus on reengaging delinquents in school (Nelson et al., 2010).

The parents of youngsters with conduct disorder typically don't monitor their children's behavior well. Fridrich and Flannery (1995) found that parental monitoring and susceptibility to antisocial peer influence characterized early adolescent delinquents regardless of their ethnicity. Long ago, Patterson and colleagues (1992) described a concatenation or linking of actions and reactions leading to delinquency—a series of interconnected, interdependent events and conditions leading through several stages in a wave-like pattern toward a criminal career. Patterson and authors describe five stages that reflect a back-and-forth, reciprocal cycle between the child and others in his or her life. For example, Stage 1 involves the initial symptoms of antisocial behavior (e.g., noncompliance, coercion; the child's reactions), which result in reactions from others at Stage 2 (e.g., peer rejection, parental rejection), which in turn result in additional reaction from the child (e.g., depression, gravitating toward a deviant peer group). You may recall that this "my turn, your turn" sequence is part and parcel of the acting-out cycle that we see in school. Patterson and colleagues (1992) see it as the essence of the coercive process leading to antisocial behavior and, left unchecked, eventually to a criminal career. It is important to note that this model does not suggest that delinquent behaviors are learned solely through parental modeling. Blaming parents holds intuitive appeal, but data do not necessarily support this conclusion (see Frick & Loney, 2002).

Delinquency, Disabling Conditions, and the Need for Special Education

Educating juvenile delinquents presents difficult problems for public schools and correctional institutions because of unclear definitions of disabling conditions (see Nelson et al., 2010; Nelson, Leone, & Rutherford, 2004). Are juvenile delinquents disabled and therefore included under the Individuals with Disabilities Education Act (IDEA)? We think it would be easy to argue that most or all incarcerated delinquents logically fall into the IDEA category of "emotionally disturbed." Unfortunately, the decision isn't that clear-cut. The current federal definition specifically excludes youngsters who are "socially maladjusted but not emotionally disturbed." Thus, when delinquent behaviors are attributed to social maladjustment rather than emotional disturbance, students are denied the protections and services mandated by IDEA—unless they have intellectual disabilities, learning disabilities, physical or sensory impairments, or some other disabling condition (see Leone, Rutherford, & Nelson, 1991; Nelson et al., 2004).

Researchers have consistently found that disabilities are in fact common in delinquents, with learning disability the most prevalent disabling condition (Gagnon, 2010; Nelson et al., 2004; Preston, 2006; Siegel & Welsh, 2012). Nevertheless, the ambiguous wording of current law precludes using adjudication or assignment to a correctional facility as the basis for identifying an emotional or behavioral disability. It requires curious turns of logic, however, to conclude that many incarcerated youths don't have emotional or behavioral disorders and are not entitled to special education under the law. If behavioral disorders include both overt and covert antisocial behavior, then finding incarcerated youth who don't have behavioral disorders is a logical impossibility (except, of course, children or youth who are held unjustly).

We know that mentally ill youngsters are often incarcerated and that a diagnosis of conduct disorder is often used as a rationale for incarcerating rather than providing mental health services to children and youth (see Jolivette & Nelson, 2010b; Preston, 2006). We also know that conduct disorder is frequently accompanied by other types of EBD. If higher levels of delinquent conduct indicate higher levels of psychopathology, and if youth who commit more frequent and more serious delinquent acts are more likely to be incarcerated, then the argument that all or nearly all incarcerated youth are disabled is supported. Finally, if behavioral disorders are not defined as disabling conditions under the law, then logically indefensible distinctions are drawn between emotional disturbance and social maladjustment.

Assessment of Delinquents' Educational Needs

Delinquents' disruptive behavior, bravado, and lack of cooperation often make them inaccessible, and they may be very good at covering up their academic deficits. However, the assessment of their educational needs doesn't differ in any essential way from the assessment of other students' needs; evaluation should focus directly on the skills in which instruction is to be offered (see Nelson et al., 2010; Overton, 2009). Because many delinquents have cognitive and academic deficits in addition to social and vocational skills deficits, their assessment must often be multifaceted. Disabilities make their assessment, treatment, and transition back to the community after incarceration all the more difficult (Clark & Unruh, 2010; Sprague, Jolivette, & Nelson, 2014; Unruh & Bullis, 2005). Assessment must often be done hurriedly and without relevant background information because delinquents are often in detention centers or special facilities where student populations are transient, educational records unavailable, and communication with other agencies difficult. Finally, because there is little agreement about the most important skills for delinquents—social, academic, or vocational—the focus of assessment is often questionable.

Intervention in Juvenile Delinquency

There are no easy or surefire solutions for any facet of the problem of delinquency, and the issues in treating violent juvenile delinquents are particularly complex (Jolivette & Nelson, 2010a, 2010b; Nelson et al., 2010; Sims & Preston, 2006; Sprague et al., 2014). The cyclic history of interventions and the failures of our legal system to deal with the problems of crime and violence, including delinquency of minors, seems characterized by a recurrent pattern of enthusiasm for proposed solutions having a scant research base followed by failure to win support sufficient for success. It isn't surprising that some people would abandon the very notion of juvenile justice (see Caeti & Fritsch, 2006).

We seem to be in an era of pessimism regarding government social programs and enthusiasm for harsher punishment. Although an exclusive reliance on harsher punishment is clearly inadvisable on scientific grounds (Alberto & Troutman, 2012; Jolivette & Nelson, 2010b; Kern, 2017), some have argued that we need to lower our typical expectations when working with persistent antisocial behavior.

Effective intervention, like prevention, must include the astute, persistent, multifaceted efforts of a variety of individuals and agencies, focusing not only on risk factors but also on those factors that have demonstrated protective effects (Arthur, Hawkins, Pollard, Catalano, & Baglioni, 2002; Gavazzi, Wasserman, Partridge, & Sheridan, 2000; Nelson et al., 2010). That is, our efforts are more likely to produce benefit when we work toward enhancing protective factors, as well as reducing children's exposure to risk factors.

Families

Make no mistake: parents who are loving, nurturing, and skilled in child rearing *can* have delinquent children. Still, neglectful parents with poor discipline skills are far more likely to have delinquent children. In fact, parent–child relationships have been linked to the quality of children's social interaction into adulthood, and parents need to be involved in treatment programs (Eber et al., 2014; Ford, 2006; Garfinkel, 2010; Sayre-McCord, 2007; Shiner & Tackett, 2014).

The typical parents of chronic delinquents don't monitor and nurture their children closely. They punish aggressive, delinquent behavior unpredictably, harshly, and ineffectively. They often show little concern when their children offend the community by stealing or fighting outside the home. As long as they don't have to deal with the misbehavior, they choose not to see their children as a serious problem. Within the home, they show little motivation to change their own behavior to decrease the coercion and violence that characterize their interactions with their children. Other parents may not believe that they have the ability to make a difference in the lives of their children.

Intervention in the families of chronic offenders is extremely difficult. Changing long-standing patterns of coercion may be impossible in families in which parents are unmotivated and have limited cognitive and social skills themselves. Patterson and his colleagues (Patterson et al., 1992) reported success in significantly reducing aggressive behavior and stealing in many families of aggressive children, but the long-term outcome for stealers and chronically delinquent adolescents is guarded at best. There appears to be no effective substitute for a family social system that has failed—at least when the criterion for effectiveness is "cure," or permanent behavioral change that requires no further treatment. Researchers have suggested that serious antisocial behavior and delinquency should be considered a social disability requiring long-term treatment involving multiple agencies (Eber et al., 2014; Garfinkel, 2010; Shiner & Tackett, 2014; Walker, Ramsey, & Gresham, 2004).

Juvenile Courts and Corrections

Juvenile courts were instituted in the United States in about 1900 to offer more humane treatment of juvenile offenders than the nineteenth-century reform schools had provided. Judges were empowered to use their discretion in determining the consequences of a child's misconduct. Although the intent was good, the institution has become mired in an overload of cases, and the rights of children—if children are considered to have constitutional rights equal to those of all other citizens—have been blatantly abridged. Consequently, the juvenile court system and the question of children's rights have come under close scrutiny (see Siegel & Welsh, 2011, 2012; Sims & Preston, 2006; Sprague et al., 2014; St. George, 2011).

Although we frequently hear proposals for drastic reform, the juvenile court system is likely to remain as it is for a considerable time. A sizable proportion of children and youth will make appearances before a juvenile court during their school years, and teachers could profit from familiarity with the court's workings. Whatever the failures in the social systems of families and schools, one can find equal disasters in the procedures and institutions devised by lawyers and judges.

Under the juvenile justice system, juvenile court judges have wide discretion in handling cases. They may release juveniles to the custody of their parents, refer youngsters to social service agencies, or assign them to a variety of correctional programs ranging from probation to restitution to community attention homes to state detention centers or even to private, less-monitored wilderness-challenge experiences or boot camps. The effectiveness of the various juvenile justice and corrections options is widely and hotly debated (see Caeti & Fritsch, 2006; Siegel & Welsh, 2012), and abuses seem frequent. Most researchers conclude that harsher punishment is counterproductive in the vast majority of cases, contrary to the opinions of many holding political office.

The *restorative justice model* is a response to crime and delinquency that focuses on accountability for illegal behavior and the development of competencies that prevent reoffending (see Umbreit, Greenwood, & Coates, 2000; White, 2006). In this way, offenses are responded to on individual bases, focusing on compensation for the victim(s), not on punishment.

Schooling

A substantial proportion of all juvenile crime occurs in school buildings or on school grounds. Each month during the academic year, thousands of teachers and millions of children in U.S. schools are assaulted or otherwise victimized. Theft, assault, drug and alcohol abuse, extortion, sexual promiscuity, and vandalism occur all too frequently, not just in deteriorated inner-city schools but in affluent suburban and rural communities as well.

Punishment and increased focus on security are schools' usual responses to delinquent behavior. The typical punishment (detention) or exclusion (office referral, suspension, disciplinary transfer, or expulsion) is usually ineffective in reducing the problem behavior and improving the student's academic progress. In short, the typical school's response to disruptive behavior is woefully inadequate and does little more than maintain a semblance of order and prevent total abandonment of its traditional programs (Jolivette & Nelson, 2010b; Sprague et al., 2014; Walker et al., 2004).

We discussed earlier schoolwide discipline and positive, nonpunitive procedures designed to reduce antisocial behavior in school. Furthermore, such positive behavior management procedures, as well as effective instruction, literacy development, and transition programming, are as important for youngsters in juvenile corrections facilities as they are for those in regular public schools (see Clark & Mathur, 2010; Clark & Unruh, 2010; Houchins, Shippen, & Lambert, 2010; Mathur & Schoenfeld, 2010; Sprague et al., 2014). Box 13.1 at the end of this chapter provides a discussion of promising school-based interventions for the social skill problems associated with delinquency.

Education of children and youth with disabilities in detention is governed by the same federal laws and regulations as is education of youngsters in public schools (Nelson et al., 2004; Sprague et al., 2014). Those in detention facilities are guaranteed all the procedural protections and requirements for nonbiased individualized assessment, individual education programs (IEPs), and so on afforded under IDEA and related laws and regulations. Ideally, therefore, assessment of students in detention is functionally related to an appropriate curriculum, and the instruction of students is data-based and prepares them with critical life skills. Nevertheless, incarcerated children and youth often don't receive assessment and education. Given the following difficulties, it isn't surprising that many delinquent youngsters' needs aren't met:

- Criminal justice officials and the public often take the attitude that delinquent and criminal young people are *not* entitled to the same educational opportunities as are law-abiding citizens.
- Some psychologists, psychiatrists, and educators take the position that many incarcerated youths are *not* disabled.
- There is a shortage of qualified personnel to staff good special education programs in correction facilities.
- Some of the provisions of IDEA, such as regulations requiring education in the least-restrictive environment and parental involvement in educational planning, are particularly difficult to implement in correctional facilities.
- The student population of correctional facilities is transient, making educational assessment and planning especially difficult.
- Interagency cooperation and understanding are often limited, which hampers obtaining student records, designating responsibility for specific services, and working out transition from detention to community.
- Administrators of correction facilities often consider security and institutional rules more important than education.
- Funds for educational programs in correction facilities are limited.

Street Gangs

An increasing problem related to delinquency is gang activity. Gangs have proliferated across the world, and now most cities and towns, even small towns and relatively rural areas, have problems of some type with gangs and gang violence. Gang activity is also prevalent in many schools. And gang activity includes so-called "preppie gangs" of preteens and teens who live in rich, gated communities or have upper-middle-class backgrounds (see Crews, Purvis, & Hjelm, 2006; Logan, 2009).

Misconceptions about gangs and gang activities abound; misunderstandings are often created or perpetuated by distorted media coverage, misinformed professionals, or both, and research on gangs is difficult (Klein, 1995, 2006; Sims & Preston, 2006). Among the most egregious misimpressions is that most youth street gangs are organized to distribute drugs. Drug involvement by street gangs has increased, and it is true that some gangs have drug trade as their primary activity, but this isn't true of most street gangs. Researchers draw a distinction between gangs that operate primarily around drugs, and thus have a business or entrepreneurial focus, and those that are built around a common cultural group focus (see Capuzzi & Gross, 2014). There is certainly concern about gangs that are organized around serious crime, including drug trafficking, both within and outside of the U.S., but these gangs are different from the more loosely affiliated "street gangs" or "youth gangs" that are more prevalent. The misperception that one who joins a gang is in the gang for life, for example, may apply to the more structured, sophisticated gangs that operate multimillion-dollar crime organizations, but in fact most youth who affiliate with a street gang do so between the ages of thirteen and fifteen, for a relatively brief period of time, averaging less than one year (Maxson, 2011). The street gang is probably the greater concern for teachers.

Gangs have been studied for several decades, and here we summarize only a small part of the extensive and complex literature on gangs that is most relevant to educators. The definition of *gang* is difficult and controversial. Although there are many different kinds of gangs organized for different purposes, we are concerned here primarily with what are known as *street gangs,* which Klein (1995) defined as aggregations of youth who recognize themselves as a group and are oriented toward delinquent acts. It's important to recognize that some gang members aren't delinquents and that many delinquents aren't gang members.

Gang membership is a means of obtaining affiliation, protection, excitement, and money, objects, or substances that members desire. The two characteristics that most clearly set an aggregation of youth apart as a gang are a) commitment to a criminal orientation and b) self-recognition as a gang, as signified by special vocabulary, clothing, signs, colors, and graffiti-marked territory. Gang members are overwhelmingly male, mostly adolescent, and predominantly homogeneous groups of ethnic minorities. Minority groups differ in the nature or focus of their gang activities (Logan, 2009; Rosenblatt et al., 2015). However, increases in younger and older members, female members, and White supremacist gangs were seen in the 1990s (see Delaney, 2006; Short & Hughes, 2006a, 2006b). Early research in this area indicated that members of gangs tend to come from families that place less importance on intrafamial socialization, youth supervision, and outward expressions of affection. The typical gang member is thought to exhibit one or more of the following characteristics:

- A notable set of personal deficiencies—perhaps difficulty in school, low self-esteem, lower impulse control, inadequate social skills, a deficit in useful adult contacts

- A notable tendency toward defiance, aggressiveness, fighting, and pride in physical prowess
- A greater-than-normal desire for status, identity, and companionship that can be at least partly satisfied by joining a special group like a gang
- A boring, uninvolved lifestyle, in which the occasional excitement of gang exploits or rumored exploits provides a welcome respite. (Klein, 1995, p. 76)

Street gangs spend most of their time just hanging out together. Contrary to popular perception, researchers who have spent decades studying street gangs portray them as inactive most of the time. Both gang-related and non-gang-related homicides are highly concentrated in disadvantaged, racially isolated neighborhoods. Such disadvantages may be more powerful predictors of violence than gang affiliation alone. Though precise data are difficult to obtain, gang homicides are much more likely to be a problem in large cities with well-entrenched, long-standing gangs than in smaller communities.

The onset of gang organizations may be fostered by poor social and economic conditions, but they aren't necessary for the organization of gangs (Crews et al., 2006; (Short & Hughes, 2006b). Gang behavior may exacerbate crime, minority segregation, and other negative community conditions, but gangs are maintained by things that threaten members, legitimize the need for the gang, and increase the cohesiveness of the group. These maintaining factors include institutions that oppose the gangs (e.g., police); gang rivalries that threaten personal safety, possessions, or status; perceived barriers to alternatives to gang membership and activities; and gang intervention programs that inadvertently strengthen the gang's cohesion— for example, attempts to use the gang structure to redirect members toward noncriminal activities.

Interventions designed to reduce gang membership and gang-related delinquent behaviors are matters of considerable controversy (Nelson et al., 2004; Short & Hughes, 2006b). Success has historically been quite limited, though promising approaches are beginning to emerge. To be effective in reducing gang activity, communities must include elements of prevention, intervention, and suppression in their efforts (e.g., Spergel, Wa, & Sosa, 2006). Prevention involves working with at-risk youth before they become gang-involved, with the target of preventing them from joining in the first place. Intervention refers to efforts to work with the youngest gang-involved youth to encourage their separation from gangs. Finally, suppression refers to the efforts of law enforcement to deal with well-established gang members to stop or reduce criminal activity. The difficulty, of course, is that gang members have extensive contact with like-minded individuals with similar behavioral, educational, and socioeconomic backgrounds (see Hagedorn, 2007). This pattern of association exacerbates the problems associated with gang memberships (e.g., exposure to violence) and insulates many gang members from interventions designed to assist them in creating more favorable life circumstances. Intervention programs typically have lacked intensity and comprehensiveness or have relied primarily on punitive measures (e.g., a crackdown by law enforcement) or other approaches that exacerbate the problem. Truly effective programs to stem the tide of gangs and gang violence would require an unlikely scenario given the current political climate. Such programs would need to include massive and sustained efforts that accomplish the following: a) reduce poverty, b) provide job

Video Example

from

YouTube

▶

ENHANCEDetext
Video Connections 13.1
Gang prevention efforts involving after-school and recreational sports programs are highlighted in this brief video. (https://www.youtube.com/watch?v=1WjnHlhJvlQ)

training and well-paid jobs for youth, c) provide decent housing in inner cities, d) rebuild and reform deteriorated schools and their instructional programs, and e) reduce racism and other social blights.

The Problems of Overreaction and Punitive Responses

Public misconceptions about delinquency, violence, and gangs have led to major problems, especially overreaction and punitive responses. Many schools are running scared, approaching problems primarily through scare tactics, tightened security, and punitive measures, often with the help of law enforcement (Jolivette & Nelson, 2010b; Sprague et al., 2014; St. George, 2011). Overreaction of the public, under the misimpression that there is a juvenile crime wave or that juveniles are becoming extremely violent, is a major problem, and harsh punishment makes the problem worse.

Although school safety is an important and legitimate concern, schools should put their primary efforts into positive schoolwide discipline plans and restructured programs designed to meet more of the social and educational needs of students (Kauffman, Nelson et al., 2017; Liaupsin, Jolivette, & Scott, 2004; Martella et al., 2012; Nelson et al., 2010; Sprague et al., 2014). In their obsession with college-bound youth, schools fail to provide the work-oriented high school programs that keep youth in school and help them find employment (Clark & Unruh, 2010; Spergel, 2007). Schools could play a major role in the reduction of delinquency and gang membership if they focused on positive discipline, effective instruction and remediation, a differentiated curriculum with courses leading directly to work for those who are not headed for college, coordination of efforts with other community agencies, and an array of extracurricular activities designed to attract all students into meaningful alternatives.

SUBSTANCE ABUSE

We use the term *substance abuse* rather than *drug abuse* because not all abused chemicals are drugs. Abused substances other than drugs include gasoline, cleaning fluids, glue, and other chemicals that can cause psychological effects. The substances under discussion here are those deliberately used to induce physiological or psychological effects (or both) for other than therapeutic purposes. *Abuse* usually is defined as use that contributes to health risks, disruption of psychological functioning, adverse social consequences, or some combination of these.

Substance abuse disorders cannot exist without the availability of the substance and a willing user. Many substances are readily available, and many people are willing or anxious to use or abuse them. These facts imbue much of the discussion of substance abuse with a moralistic tone (the notion that substance abusers are simply evil or weak willed) and encourage the assumption that interdiction of supply will be effective in reducing use and abuse.

Definition and Prevalence

Although the illicit use of alcohol and drugs may have declined in recent years, the prevalence remains relatively high (Donohue, Karmely, & Strada, 2006; also, search the Internet for

National Institute on Drug Abuse or go to https://www.drugabuse.gov). Prevalence studies suggest that the use of psychoactive substances is more likely to be experimental or episodic for most adolescents. Most teenagers will drink alcohol and experiment with drugs at least once. But what is the difference between experimentation and abuse? Does a single episode of use by a child or adolescent constitute abuse? At what level of use should an adolescent be considered to have a substance abuse disorder? It is clear that most adolescents take or use substances but that only a minority of them (perhaps 6 percent to 10 percent of users) become chronic abusers.

Adolescent substance abuse is in many ways similar to substance abuse in adulthood, but there are key differences. Many adolescents who use or abuse substances don't become adults with substance abuse disorders. The definition of *substance abuse* is clouded by controversy regarding specific criteria, changing social attitudes, and political use of the issue (Donohue et al., 2006).

The topic of drug use is especially prone to distortion of fact and hysterical rhetoric because the definition of *adolescent substance abuse* is anchored in cultural tradition, social fad, and political positioning as well as scientific evidence. Moreover, controversy regarding definition makes many prevalence figures suspect. Nevertheless, nearly all authorities on the topic agree that substance use and abuse are alarmingly high among American children and youth and that effective measures to reduce both use and abuse of substances are needed.

A common misperception is that substance abuse has to do primarily with illegal drugs such as cocaine, marijuana, and heroin or with illicit use of prescription medications such as barbiturates. However, alcohol and tobacco are and have always been the largest problems for children and youth because they are readily available to adults, they are advertised for sale, most people view their use by adults as permissible, and children usually receive their first exposure to and first experiment with these substances in the home. The earlier the child's first experience with alcohol and tobacco, the more likely he or she will become a regular user. Early use of alcohol and tobacco, as well as other substances, correlates with family problems, low socioeconomic status, school failure, and psychiatric disorders, especially conduct disorder (Upadhyaya, Brady, Wharton, & Liao, 2003).

Because the negative health consequences of alcohol and tobacco are staggering, preventing children and adolescents from beginning to smoke and drink seems wise. Indeed, according to the U.S Department of Health and Human Services, the most common cause of death among teenagers in the United States is unintentional accidents, with auto accidents being the major contributor to this (Heron, 2016). In adults, tobacco-related mortality (including cancers and heart disease) accounts for more deaths than any other preventable cause (search the Internet for Centers for Disease Control and Prevention, or go to https://www.cdc.gov; see also Roll, 2005). Thus, any "war on drugs" has not been focused on what likely should be its primary targets.

Another common misperception is that substance abuse is disproportionately a problem of ethnic minorities. Contrary to many racial stereotypes, some drugs have higher abuse rates among white adolescents (Yacoubian, 2003). Despite racial targeting, researchers have found that among individuals arrested for drug offenses, White arrestees were found more than twenty times as likely to be guilty of certain drug offences (e.g., possession of the drug ecstasy) than non-White arrestees (Urbach, Reynolds, & Yacoubian, 2002).

Some youngsters, primarily adolescents age fifteen or older, do abuse substances other than alcohol and tobacco. Following is a list of several major types of drugs of abuse, along with a few examples of each. Some of these drugs are prescribed for therapeutic purposes, so they have legitimate purposes as well as potential for abuse. We also list some of the most typical effects or symptoms of serious intoxication with the drug and of drug withdrawal:

- Depressants: Alcohol, Phenobarbital, Valium, Quaalude
  Signs of intoxication: Drowsiness, irritability, disinhibition, extreme relaxation or sedation
  Signs of withdrawal: Tremors, fever, anxiety, hallucinations
- Stimulants: Nicotine, caffeine, cocaine, amphetamines, and methamphetamines
  Signs of intoxication: Dilated pupils, restlessness, loss of appetite, paranoia, hallucinations
  Signs of withdrawal: Fatigue, mental and physical slowness or depression
- Stimulant hallucinogens: Phencyclidine (PCP), MDMA (ecstasy), ketamine
  Signs of intoxication: Agitation, irritability, grandiosity, dilated pupils, fine tremors, sweating, rapid speech and movement, hallucinations, dry mouth and throat, uncontrolled jaw movements, repetitive movements
  Signs of withdrawal: Anxiety, agitation, depression, fatigue, sleeplessness, panic attacks, increased appetite, psychosis, suicidal thoughts
- Narcotics: Morphine, methadone, codeine, Darvon
  Signs of intoxication: Drowsiness, slurred speech, constricted pupils, poor physical coordination, analgesia (insensitivity to pain)
  Signs of withdrawal: Vomiting, cramps, fever, chills, "goose flesh"
- Inhalants: Glues, aerosols, paint thinners, cleaning fluids, fuels
  Signs of intoxication: Confusion, hallucinations, exhilaration or depression, poor balance
  Signs of withdrawal: Inconsistent
- Marijuana: cigarettes or forms taken by mouth
  Signs of intoxication: Sleepiness, poor concentration, confusion, anxiety, paranoia, distorted perceptions
  Signs of withdrawal: Psychological distress
- Hallucinogens: Mescaline, psilocybin, lysergic acid diethylamide (LSD)
  Signs of intoxication: Dilated pupils, hallucinations, altered perceptions of body or time, problems focusing attention, emotional lability
  Signs of withdrawal: Not well established.

As we mentioned earlier, the substances that become popular or receive intensive media attention in any given period of time are highly variable and affected by fads and other social phenomena. For example, in the mid-1990s, Ritalin became a popular drug of abuse, and national media attention heightened concern about its prescription and control. In the late 1990s, media attention shifted to ecstasy abuse, especially among adolescents and young adults attending raves. Much of what we know about the effects of this drug is based on anecdotal evidence; clinical research has been plagued with problems including an unethical risk of neural brain injury to participants in such studies (Ricaurte, Yuan, Hatzidimitriou, Cord, & McCann, 2003). Despite varying trends in media attention, marijuana is the most widely used illegal drug in Western societies, including among adolescents. In 2013, for example, 8.8 percent of adolescents aged twelve to seventeen in the U.S. were estimated to be current users of illicit drugs, and about 80 percent of this group (7.1 percent of all adolescents) used marijuana (search the Internet for SAMHSA [Substance Abuse and Mental Health Services Administration], or go to https://findtreatment.samhsa.gov). We note that while illicit drug use overall declined slightly from 2002 to 2013 (from 11.6 percent of youth aged twelve to seventeen to 8.8 percent), marijuana use specifically remained essentially flat during those years, ranging from 6.7 percent to 8.2 percent of youth aged twelve to seventeen. A major societal shift began in the second decade of the twenty-first century, as several states legalized the sale of marijuana (to adults) for recreational use; four states voted to legalize recreational marijuana use in 2016, bringing the total number of states where such use is legal to eight, plus the District of Columbia (even though federal law still prohibits marijuana use) (e.g., Lindsay, 2016). Whether the increasing legal availability of marijuana to adults has any impact on illicit use of marijuana by children and youth is not known. In the SAMSHA survey, the next most frequently abused substances were prescription drugs, which were estimated to be used by 2.2 percent of adolescents in 2013 (a significant decline from 2002). In addition to those we have listed, people may abuse many other preparations, including *designer drugs*—new concoctions made up in illegal laboratories and represented as well-known drugs or touted to produce euphoria. The street names of various drugs are numerous, and new names are constantly being invented.

Two consistent patterns of substance abuse persist over time. First, experimentation with alcohol and other substances begins in adolescence and declines significantly for most individuals with transition to young adulthood. Prosocial processes associated with marriage and employment are consistently associated with declines in substance use across the early adult years. However, the second pattern suggests that there are risks for adult adjustment based on adolescent behavior. The adolescent substance abuser who becomes a substance-abusing adult typically abuses multiple substances. In addition, adolescent problem behavior and patterns of nonconformity predict adult substance abuse better than level of substance use does.

The emotional and behavioral problems associated with substance abuse include both the effects produced by using the substance and the effects of abstinence after a period of use (i.e., withdrawal). Terms commonly used in discussion of substance use include the following:

- *Intoxication* indicates symptoms of a toxic amount of substance in the bloodstream (enough to have physiological or psychological effects).
- *Tolerance* refers to physiological adaptation to a substance so that an increasing amount is required to produce the same effects; tolerance typically increases with repeated use and decreases after a period of abstinence.
- *Addiction* indicates compulsive use of a substance and that obtaining and using the substance has become a central concern and pattern of behavior.
- *Dependence* refers to the need to continue using a substance to avoid physical or emotional discomfort or both.
- *Withdrawal* designates physical or emotional discomfort associated with a period of abstinence.

An important feature of advanced substance abuse is its insidious onset, progressing through various stages. A substance abuser rarely becomes a habitual user immediately; rather, experimentation, perhaps under peer pressure, is followed by occasional social or recreational use, then use in certain circumstances or situations (perhaps to relax after a stressful event, to stay awake to perform a demanding task, or to sleep). Situational use may intensify and become part of daily routine; eventually, the substance can become the individual's central focus. Clearly, substance use and abuse do not always progress to the obsessive-dependent addiction stage. However, teachers and other adults should be aware of the danger signals of the transitions from experimentation to social–recreational and to situational–circumstantial use. Teachers may first observe changes in social behavior and academic performance at the point of transition to situational use (Severson & James, 2002).

An additional concern regarding substance abuse since the 1980s is contracting the human immunodeficiency virus (HIV) through unprotected sex or the use of contaminated needles for intravenous injection of drugs. The probability of sexual activity, including sexual intercourse without a condom, is greatly increased by the use of alcohol and other substances that alter mood and cognitive control. Adolescents who are runaways, homeless, or substance abusers are a particularly high-risk group for sexual promiscuity and for contracting HIV or any number of sexually transmitted infections (STIs).

It's difficult to estimate the extent of substance abuse among children and adolescents. We do know that students with EBD are at higher risk than is the general population of students. The level of use and abuse of specific substances by adolescents reflects adult patterns and is affected by fads, social attitudes, and prohibitions. Use of hallucinogenic drugs was lower in the 1980s than in the previous two decades, but in the 1980s cocaine became a major concern, and marijuana use, which in previous decades caused much alarm and sometimes resulted in legal penalties of absurd proportions, was considered comparatively safe. Beginning in the mid-1980s, there was a steady decrease in the use of most illicit drugs, followed by an increasing trend starting in about 1992 (Johnston, O'Malley, Bachman, & Schulenberg, 2009). From 2002 through 2011, the rates of substance abuse among adolescents remained fairly stable, at around 10 percent, but rates then dropped to their lowest point in eleven years by 2013 (to 8.8 percent; see SAMHSA, https://findtreatment.samhsa.gov). While a number of scholars have speculated on the causes of these trends, no explanation seems to capture a single reason or even set of factors that undoubtedly contribute to the complex issues surrounding adolescent substance abuse. Trends in the coming years in rates of drug use, or fads in terms of what substances adolescents are likely to abuse, are impossible to predict.

Causal Factors and Prevention

A variety of theories have been offered to explain adolescent substance abuse, including models that view it as a disease (metabolic or genetic abnormality), a moral issue (lack of willpower), a spiritual problem (needing the help of a higher power), or a psychological disorder (learned maladaptive behavior or intrapsychic conflicts). Most researchers have concluded that no single cause has been or is likely to be found and that substance abuse has multiple causes. The focus is on assessing factors that heighten risk or tend to protect against risk (Severson & James, 2002).

Family factors known to increase risk are poor and inconsistent parental discipline, family conflict, and lack of emotional bonding of family members. Family members may provide models of substance abuse and introduce children to the use of substances. Undoubtedly, genetic factors contribute risk, perhaps by making some individuals more susceptible to the physiological and psychological effects of drugs. Socialization with a deviant peer group may play a major role in substance abuse, as may media exposure to substance use and abuse. All aspects of the culture in which the youngster is embedded may have a substantial influence on initiation to substance use (see Shiner & Tackett, 2014).

Community conditions of joblessness and deteriorated living conditions are also risk factors. Certainly, substance abuse is no stranger to middle-class and upscale communities. Still, the lack of socioeconomic opportunity, hopelessness, crowding, and violence that characterize many poor urban communities are very significant risk factors.

Age of onset of substance use is a known risk factor. The earlier the age at which a youngster has his or her first experience with substance use, the greater the risk of later abuse. Risk of **polydrug** use, use of more than one substance within a four-week period, seems to increase with age during adolescence (Smit, Monshouwer, & Verdurmen, 2002).

Substance abuse disorders often occur with a variety of other disorders or psychiatric illnesses. Externalizing behavior problems (aggression and other characteristics of conduct disorder) are especially likely to increase risk. The polysubstance abuser typically has multiple disorders, all of which are intertwined and need to be addressed. It's important to note the reciprocal influences of substance use and other disorders. Some disorders, such as schizophrenia, depression, and personality disorders, may be precipitated or exacerbated (started or made worse) by substance use. A variety of disorders may both contribute to substance abuse and be exacerbated by it (Severson & James, 2002).

Different factors may be associated with drinking level compared with drinking problems. Across a number of studies, the results suggest that drinking level is more closely tied to peer groups, whereas drinking problems are associated with familial and psychological problems. People who are problem drinkers experience difficulties compared to nonproblem drinkers, even at the same level of consumption.

Protective factors include not only the opposite of family characteristics associated with high risk but personality characteristics, perhaps extending from early temperament, such as low anger and aggression, school achievement, compliance, and responsibility (Shiner & Tackett, 2014). Researchers have also found that factors associated with resilience and safe sex attitudes, such as HIV/AIDS knowledge, self-esteem, and hopefulness, were in fact negatively related to drug and alcohol use among adolescents (Chang, Bendel, Koopman, McGarvey, & Canterbury, 2003). Thus, the very same strengths that may work to prevent incarceration and HIV/AIDS infection may also serve to prevent substance abuse.

Social and cultural influences such as peer support and societal disapproval can help influence children and youth to avoid substance use during adolescence or at least delay the age at which they have their first experience with substance use. Communities in which there are jobs and alternative activities to substance abuse are also protective.

A variety of targets for prevention have been suggested, including prevention of use or abuse (especially early onset of use), consequences of use, and the risk factors associated with use and abuse. Prevention can also be aimed at increasing the protective factors that lower risk. The most effective prevention efforts we can devise will address all of these concerns. Moreover, prevention strategies should encompass and be matched with all risk factors, including peer-related factors, individual factors (e.g., poor academic and social skills, conduct disorder), family factors (e.g., parental discipline), biological factors (e.g., use of medications), and community factors (e.g., socioeconomic conditions). Interventions can be classified according to whether they target individuals or the larger environment. Simplistic prevention programs such as teaching children to "just say no" are doomed because alcohol and drug experimentation has become a largely normative behavior in adolescent development. Adolescents who break the "just say no" taboo and find no immediate negative consequences may disregard all subsequent substance abuse warnings. Clearly, a more intensive and reasoned approach to prevention is called for. General recommendations for prevention strategies are that they should be developmentally appropriate, focused on high-risk populations, comprehensive (address multiple risk factors), coordinated with changes in social policies in the community, and long term.

Most relevant for discussion here are the skills-based interventions that form educational efforts to prevent adolescent substance abuse—interventions aimed at helping students understand the effects and consequences of substance use and abuse. Curricula designed to help students learn a variety of skills and allow them to do the following things may be helpful (see Rosenblatt et al., 2015):

- Resist peer pressure
- Change attitudes, values, and behavioral norms related to substance use
- Recognize and resist adult influences toward substance use
- Use problem-solving strategies such as self-control, stress management, and appropriate assertiveness
- Set goals and improve self-esteem
- Communicate more effectively

Prevention is preferable to intervention after substance abuse has become a reality. But, if it is to be effective, it must be intensive, comprehensive, and sustained, focusing on high-risk youth in high-risk neighborhoods, especially on improving the social and economic conditions in the communities of youth at highest risk. Unfortunately, public sentiment and social policy in the United States indicate less willingness to support effective prevention programs.

Intervention and Education

Substance abuse prevention programs are highly desirable, but they do little to help those who are already using drugs. A wide range of intervention approaches and combinations of treatments are employed in treating adolescent substance abuse, including medication (see Mirza, 2002) and behavioral approaches (see Roll, 2005; Martella et al., 2012). Traditional methods include twelve-step programs such as those suggested by Alcoholics Anonymous and Narcotics Anonymous. Group therapy, family therapy (either single families or groups of families), cognitive-behavior modification, and psychopharmacological treatment are alternatives frequently employed. Family involvement and programs that are consistent with cultural traditions are critical features of prevention and intervention efforts (see Eber et al., 2014; Severson & James, 2002). Though research remains limited, increasing evidence suggests that family therapy and cognitive behavioral therapies may offer promise in the treatment of adolescents who are drug dependent (Liddle, Dakof, Turner, Henderson, & Greenbaum, 2008). Some programs provide a comprehensive approach to prevention and intervention involving the entire spectrum of intervention agents: schools, peer groups, families, the media, communities, law enforcement, and the business sector (see Eber et al., 2014). It is important that treatment be designed for the individual case and that careful consideration be given to inpatient versus outpatient treatment.

Our primary concern here is educational intervention. One important feature of successful substance abuse education programs is getting accurate and useful information into the hands of teachers, parents, and students in an accessible, abbreviated form. Tables 13.1 and 13.2 are examples of the type and amount of information that can be made available. Drug abuse prevention has expanded from efforts focused on keeping children and youth from abusing illegal substances to the concern about the abuse of prescription drugs, as indicated in Table 13.2.

Table 13.1   Commonly Abused Drugs

Substance Category and Name	Examples of *Commercial* or Street Names	Acute Effects	Health Risks
Cannabinoids			
Marijuana	Dope, grass, herb, joints, pot, reefer, green	Euphoria; relaxation; slowed reaction time; distorted sensory perception; impaired balance and coordination; increased heart rate and appetite; impaired learning, memory; anxiety; panic attacks; psychosis	Cough, frequent respiratory infections; possible mental health decline; addiction
Hashish	Boom, hash, hash oil, hemp		
Opioids			
Heroin	*Diacetylmorphine:* smack, horse, brown sugar, dope, H, junk, skag, skunk, white horse, China white; cheese (with OTC cold medicine and antihistamine)	Euphoria; drowsiness; impaired coordination; dizziness; confusion; nausea; sedation; feeling of heaviness in the body; slowed or arrested breathing	Constipation; endocarditis; hepatitis; HIV; addiction; fatal overdose
Opium	*Laudanum, paregoric:* big O, black stuff, block, gum, hop		
Stimulants			
Cocaine	*Cocaine hydrochloride* blow, bump, C, candy, Charlie, coke, crack, flake, rock, snow, toot	Increased heart rate, blood pressure, body temperature, metabolism; feelings of exhilaration; increased energy, mental alertness; tremors; reduced appetite; irritability; anxiety; panic; paranoia; violent behavior; psychosis	Weight loss, insomnia; cardiac or cardiovascular complications; stroke; seizures; addiction **Also, for cocaine**—nasal damage from snorting

(continued)

Table 13.1   *(continued)*

Substance Category and Name	Examples of *Commercial* or Street Names	Acute Effects	Health Risks
Amphetamine	*Biphetamine, Dexedrine*: bennies, black beauties, crosses, hearts, LA turnaround, speed, truck drivers, uppers		Also, for methamphetamine—severe dental problems
Methamphetamine	*Desoxyn*: meth, ice, crank, chalk, crystal, fire, glass, go fast, speed		
Club Drugs			
MDMA (methylenedioxy-methamphetamine)	Ecstasy, Adam, clarity, Eve, lover's speed, peace, uppers	Mild hallucinogenic effects; increased tactile sensitivity; empathic feelings; lowered inhibition; anxiety; chills; sweating; teeth clenching; muscle cramping	Sleep disturbances; depression; impaired memory; hyperthermia; addiction
Flunitrazepam (associated with sexual assaults)	*Rohypnol*: forgetme pill, Mexican Valium, R2, roach, Roche, roofies, roofinol, rope	Sedation; muscle relaxation; confusion; memory loss; dizziness; impaired coordination	Addiction
GHB (associated with sexual assaults)	*Gamma-hydroxybutyrate*: G, Georgia home boy, grievous bodily harm, liquid ecstasy, soap, goop, scoop, liquid X	Drowsiness; nausea; headache; disorientation; loss of coordination; memory loss	Unconsciousness; seizures; coma

Substance Category and Name	Examples of *Commercial* or Street Names	Acute Effects	Health Risks
Dissociative Drugs			
Ketamine	*Ketalar SV:* cat Valium, K, Special K, vitamin K	*For all dissociative drugs*— Feelings of being separate from one's body and environment; impaired motor function	Anxiety; tremors; numbness; memory loss; nausea
PCP and analogs	Phencyclidine: angel dust, boat, hog, love boat, peace pill	**Also, for ketamine**— analgesia; impaired memory; delirium; respiratory depression and arrest; death	
Salvia divinorum	Salvia, Shepherdess's Herb, Maria Pastora, magic mint, Sally-D	**Also, for PCP and analogs**— analgesia; psychosis; aggression; violence; slurred speech; loss of coordination; hallucinations	
Dextromethorphan (DXM)	Found in some cough and cold medications: Robotripping, Robo, Triple C	**Also, for DXM**—euphoria; slurred speech; confusion; dizziness; distorted visual perceptions	
Hallucinogens			
LSD	*Lysergic acid diethylamide:* acid, blotter, cubes, microdot, yellow sunshine, blue heaven	*For all hallucinogens*— altered states of perception and feeling; hallucinations; nausea **Also, for LSD and mescaline**— increased body temperature, heart rate, blood pressure; loss of appetite; sweating; sleeplessness; numbness, dizziness, weakness, tremors; impulsive behavior; rapid shifts in emotion	*For LSD*—Flashbacks, Hallucinogen Persisting Perception Disorder
Mescaline	Buttons, cactus, mesc, peyote		
Psilocybin	Magic mushrooms, purple passion, shrooms, little smoke	**Also, for psilocybin**— nervousness; paranoia; panic	

(continued)

Table 13.1   *(continued)*

Substance Category and Name	Examples of *Commercial* or Street Names	Acute Effects	Health Risks
Other Compounds			
Anabolic steroids	*Anadrol, Oxandrin, Durabolin, Depo-Testosterone, Equipoise*; roids, juice, gym candy, pumpers	No intoxication effects	Hypertension; blood clotting and cholesterol changes; liver cysts; hostility and aggression; acne; in adolescents—premature stoppage of growth; in males—prostate cancer, reduced sperm production, shrunken testicles, breast enlargement; in females—menstrual irregularities, development of beard and other masculine characteristics
Inhalants	Solvents (paint thinners, gasoline, glues), gases (butane, propane, aerosol propellants, nitrous oxide), nitrites (isoamyl, isobutyl, cyclohexyl): laughing gas, poppers, snappers, whippets	(varies by chemical) Stimulation, loss of inhibition; headache; nausea or vomiting; slurred speech; loss of motor coordination; wheezing	Cramps; weight loss; muscle weakness; depression; memory impairment; damage to cardiovascular and nervous systems; unconsciousness; sudden death

Information is critical, but there is no reason to believe that merely providing information on illegal and prescription drugs will necessarily change behavior; more specific, targeted action is needed. Such actions in schools might include: a) clear, well-defined policies for teachers and students spelling out how drug use or possession will be handled; b) basic, simple drug education at all grade levels; c) increased teacher awareness about local drug problems and community service agencies; d) group discussions about topics such as adolescent

Table 13.2 Prescriptions Drugs That Are Abused

Substance Category and Name	Examples of *Commercial* or Street Names	Intoxication Effects	Potential Health Consequences
Depressants			
Barbiturates	*Amytal, Nembutal, Seconal, Phenobarbital*; barbs, reds, red birds, phennies, tooies, yellows, yellow jackets	Reduced pain and anxiety; feeling of well-being; lowered inhibitions; slowed pulse and breathing; lowered blood pressure; poor concentration; sedation; drowsiness	Confusion, fatigue; impaired coordination, memory, judgment; respiratory depression and arrest; addiction; dizziness **Also for barbiturates**—depression; unusual excitement; fever; irritability; poor judgment; slurred speech
Benzodiazepines (other than flunitrazepam)	*Ativan, Halcion, Librium, Valium, Xanax*; candy, downers, sleeping pills, tranks		
Opioids and Morphine Derivatives			
Codeine	*Empirin with Codeine, Fiorinal with Codeine, Robitussin A-C, Tylenol with Codeine*; Captain Cody, Cody, schoolboy; (with glutethimide) doors & fours, loads, pancakes and syrup	Pain relief, euphoria, drowsiness	Respiratory depression and arrest; nausea; confusion; constipation; sedation; unconsciousness; coma; tolerance; addiction **Also, for codeine**—less analgesia, sedation, and respiratory depression than morphine
Fentanyl	*Actiq, Duragesic, Sublimaze*; Apache, China girl, China white, dance fever, friend, goodfella, jackpot, murder 8, TNT, Tango and Cash		

(continued)

Table 13.2   *(continued)*

Substance Category and Name	Examples of *Commercial* or Street Names	Intoxication Effects	Potential Health Consequences
Morphine	*Roxanol, Duramorph*; M, Miss Emma, monkey, white stuff		
Other opioid pain relievers (oxycodone, meperidine, hydromorphone, hydrocodone, propoxyphene)	*Tylox, OxyContin, Percodan, Percocet*; oxy 80s, oxycotton, oxycet, hillbilly heroin, percs *Demerol, meperidine hydrochloride*; demmies, pain killer *Dilaudid*; juice, dillies *Vicodin, Lortab, Lorcet*; *Darvon, Darvocet*		
Stimulants			
Methylphenidate	*Ritalin*; JIF, MPH, R-ball, Skippy, the smart drug, vitamin R	Increased heart rate, blood pressure, metabolism; feelings of exhilaration, energy, increased mental alertness; possible increase or decrease in blood pressure; psychotic episodes	Rapid or irregular heartbeat; reduced appetite, weight loss, heart failure; digestive problems

See: National Institute on Drug Abuse, https://www.drugabuse.gov/drugs-abuse/commonly-abused-drugs-charts, retrieved February 16, 2016.

development and drug use; e) one-to-one and group counseling using community resources such as community counseling centers and drop-in centers within the school; and f) peer-group approaches with positive role models for group or individual support.

Many students with substance abuse problems have belief systems that lead to either increased risk of substance abuse or decreased ability to respond to intervention efforts. Individuals who are at the greatest risk for initial substance abuse problems are more likely to report beliefs that they are unable to avoid using substances or to resist peer pressure. After becoming involved with drug use, problem substance users more often report beliefs that they are unable to control their drug use or minimize the harmful effects of drug use. For such individuals, treatment must involve more than information and admonitions to abstain from drug use. Supportive environments that help individuals reinterpret environmental cues and develop more positive belief systems over time, although difficult to realize, are clearly necessary. Without such supports, individuals with maladaptive efficacy beliefs who are learning to manage their substance abuse are likely to interpret minor setbacks and difficulties as additional evidence of their inability to effect change in their own lives. Consequently, they may abandon their efforts to limit their substance use and its damaging effects. Treatments affecting efficacy beliefs are, for the most part, rare in schools and other public institutions. However, the high rates of relapse associated with substance abuse interventions suggest that this element is a promising addition to existing interventions.

Teachers need to know how to manage suspected substance abuse episodes and suspected intoxication or withdrawal crises in school. Their role is to manage and refer students appropriately, not to become investigators or counselors. Although educators must be aware of indications of substance abuse, they should not automatically assume that certain physical or psychological symptoms are the result of intoxication or withdrawal. Referral to counselors or medical personnel is appropriate to determine the cause. A clear school policy regarding detection and management helps teachers and administrators respond correctly to suspected abuse and crisis situations. In the event of an emotional–behavioral crisis, the teacher should remain calm and nonconfrontational. We have known for a long time that safety is more important than demonstrating disciplinary control.

EARLY SEXUAL ACTIVITY AND TEEN PARENTHOOD

Delinquency, substance abuse, and sexual activity are often linked. Sexual activity itself may be defined as a juvenile status offense, but some juveniles commit index sex crimes such as rape or molestation (see Dwyer & Laufersweiler-Dwyer, 2006). However, most early sexual intercourse is a concern because it is associated with a high risk of teenage pregnancy and premature parental responsibility, contracting STIs, and a wide variety of psychological and health risks (Kotchick, Shaffer, Miller, & Forehand, 2001; Schofield, Bierman, Heinrichs, Nix, & Conduct Problems Prevention Research Group, 2008). In earlier times, sexuality was less often discussed and assumed to be a feature of adult life. However, sexuality is not only a problem of adults but is clearly part of adolescent behavior. Sexual intercourse itself is of much less concern when it is engaged in by an eighteen-year-old than by a thirteen-year-old. That is, the level of concern is inversely proportional to the age of the child or youth.

Adolescents with psychological problems are at particularly high risk for contracting HIV and other STIs through casual sexual encounters, which are often linked with substance abuse. Sexual activity of young teenagers is also associated with social and emotional maladjustment and inadequate child-care skills. Many adolescents have distorted perceptions of their own high-risk behavior; they see having sex as relatively low in risk and high in benefit for them. Students with EBD tend to have distorted ideas about sexual behavior that put them at high risk of contracting HIV. Teenage pregnancy and parenthood present enormous problems for young people, and these problems are only exacerbated when other risk factors are present, including poverty, antisocial behavior, and substance abuse. It would be easy to understand how pregnancy and parenthood could overwhelm an already at-risk teen.

The sexual behavior of teens may be motivated by a variety of factors other than physiological urges. The social and psychological conditions that encourage early sexual activity are many and complex; they include the family and cultural factors we discussed previously. Sexual abuse by older individuals may initiate the sexual activity of some teenagers, and they may suffer long-term psychological stress or dysfunction as a result. Many sexually active teenagers appear to be seeking a sense of belonging, emotional closeness, or importance that they are unable to achieve in other ways. They may romanticize parenthood, believing that their child will give them the love they have not found from others. Some appear to be addicted to sex and love. In a study of approximately 200 adolescents aged twelve to nineteen years of age, Donenberg, Bryant, Emerson, Wilson, and Pasch (2003) found that three variables enabled the researchers to predict which girls initiated sexual activity at or before fourteen years of age: hostile parental control, peer influence, and externalizing psychopathology. The psychological and physical risks are grave for these young teenagers. The realities and personal costs of teenage parenthood—to the teenagers and to their children—are staggering.

There are also differences in the reasons that adolescents engage in sexual intercourse that are related to the sex of the individual as well as the culture in which he or she lives. Eyre and Millstein (1999) asked eighty-three adolescents between the ages of sixteen and twenty to list the qualities they preferred in a sexual partner as well as the reasons to have or abstain from having sexual intercourse. A core of beliefs related to reasons to have sex emerged across all of the groups included in the study. They included familiarity with the partner and the partner's sexual history, the partner's overall level of intelligence, and ease of communication as positive factors. The absence of these factors was associated with reasons not to have sex with a person. This study also found variations in attitudes and sexual behavior between males and females, as well as between African American and White adolescents. Males of both races described sexual arousal as a reason for engaging in intercourse, whereas females more often described concerns regarding personal respect and the individual's prospects for the future as reasons to have sex. African American adolescents who were sexually active more often reported association of such activity with love, marriage, and parenthood, whereas White adolescents (particularly males) more often reported sexual activity in relation to drinking.

The facts of teenage sexual activity and parenthood are often assumed to imply a need for education about sexuality, family life, and parenting. In the U. S., however, this topic is often debated from political, moral, or religious viewpoints, rather than on the basis of reliable evidence. Indeed, perhaps because of these debates, trustworthy data are difficult to find. It is perhaps ironic that the U.S. has higher rates of STIs and teen pregnancy than most other industrialized nations. One argument that has been central to this debate in the twenty-first century concerns the content of sex education classes in school, and indeed whether sex ed should be taught at all. Many religious groups promote an abstinence-only approach (teaching students that they simply should not engage in sexual activity before or outside of marriage), while others argue that adolescents need information about all aspects of sexuality, including contraception and the notion of "safe sex." Those promoting an abstinence-only approach sometimes argue further

Video Example from YouTube

▶

ENHANCEDetext
Video Connections 13.2
This video, produced by the Centers for Disease Control, is targeted at health care providers but provides an overview of several key facts regarding teen sexual activity and pregnancy prevention. (https://www.youtube.com/watch?v=Vjdd41VbNvk)

that providing education about and access to contraception will only encourage earlier sexual activity. Though more research is needed, evidence has emerged to suggest that comprehensive sex ed programs result in clearly better outcomes than no sex ed at all, result in lowered teen pregnancy rates than abstinence only programs, and do not result in any increase in teen sexual activity or rates of STIs (e.g., Kohler, Manhart, & Lafferty, 2008; Lindberg & Maddow-Zimet, 2012). Similarly, in an evaluation of abstinence-only programs, Trenholm and colleagues (2007) found no differences between abstinence-only and control groups at forty-two and seventy-eight months after beginning the program in abstaining from sex, age of first sexual activity, number of partners, and condom use. It remains to be seen how educators will approach the issue of sex education, but the fact remains that the impact of early and unprotected sexual activity is devastating to teens, and undoubtedly more so for those impacted by the constellation of risk factors that typically accompany EBD.

Box 13.1

Teaching Social Skills to Students Who Are Juvenile Delinquents

What social skill problems of juvenile delinquents present the greatest challenges for teachers?

It is unfortunate but true that students who are juvenile delinquents may be most known to teachers for their absence from or avoidance of school altogether, particularly in late adolescence. In early adolescence (when they are more likely to still be in regular schools and classrooms), the characteristics of juvenile delinquents, or those at risk for delinquency, will be among the most challenging that teachers will encounter. Such students may be hostile, belligerent, and disruptive; they may well be seen as bullies. At minimum, they are likely to be distractible, inattentive, and difficult to engage in learning activities. In short, they are likely to be very similar to students with conduct disorder, and in fact, many will have been diagnosed as such. Indeed, conduct disorder is a precursor to juvenile delinquency in most cases.

What are appropriate targets for intervention?

Like students with conduct disorder, there will be no shortage of problem behaviors from which teachers might choose when deciding how to intervene. But an additional defining characteristic of delinquency in the majority of cases is a marked disconnect, or disengagement, from school. (Disengagement from family, as well as community, is also characteristic of many juvenile delinquents, but we focus here on school-based concerns.) Delinquent students will struggle academically, in part because of their problems with distractibility and impulsivity. Thus the obvious concern for educators is how to engage students who have little interest in being in school and, further, probably lack many of the basic skills needed to succeed in school.

(continued)

Box 13.1   *(continued)*

What types of interventions show promise?

Researchers who have studied the development of delinquency have consistently noted that students with fully developed repertoires of delinquent and antisocial behavior (especially those considered "versatile," exhibiting both overt and covert antisocial behavior) have much poorer prognoses, and effective treatment remains elusive. As such, researchers also consistently call for efforts to be focused more on the prevention side, working with younger children who show signs of risk so that delinquency never fully develops. Loeber, Farrington, and Petechuk (2003) suggested that promising interventions designed primarily for preventing delinquency before it occurs might fall in the following categories:

- Classroom and behavior management programs
- Multicomponent classroom-based programs
- Social competence promotion curriculums
- Conflict resolution and violence prevention curriculums
- Bullying prevention
- Afterschool recreation programs
- Mentoring programs
- School organization programs
- Comprehensive community interventions

Note that the last four areas listed involve providing programs that enhance students' *engagement*. To this list we would add the notion that one reason students disengage early is academic failure; thus a prevention program should also include some element of ensuring that students receive the best possible instruction in basic academic skills (reading, writing, math) beginning in their earliest school years.

An example—a multicomponent aggression-prevention intervention

The Metropolitan Area Child Study Research Group (2002) assessed the effects of a multicomponent aggression-prevention intervention with high-risk elementary aged students to determine whether increasing levels or layers of intervention would enhance academic achievement and reduce aggression. The intervention consisted of three components, and different groups receive one, two, or all three components. The first level of intervention was termed "classroom general enhancement only," and consisted of biweekly seminars for two years focused on classroom management, cultural diversity, encouraging prosocial behavior, and managing conflict. In addition, trained teacher collaborators supported each teacher, and all teachers were trained in the Yes I Can curriculum; participating teachers focused specifically on teaching students to understand their own and others' feelings, to develop solutions and action plans for problems, and to reduce their display or acceptance of aggression. The second level of intervention added small group sessions, held weekly, focused on changing students' beliefs about aggression, and established a prosocial "norm" within the group. Topics covered in these sessions included initiating social interactions, maintaining social interaction, solving interpersonal conflicts, understanding ambiguity, dealing with victimization, and developing friendships. Finally, a third layer of intervention included family involvement. This component targeted the improvement of families' communication and parenting skills, as well as networking with other families. Large group meetings with multiple families, individual family meetings, weekly telephone calls with families, and homework assignments for families were all used to teach and reinforce the skills covered.

The results of this comprehensive intervention were generally positive in both preventing aggression and increasing academic achievement in young elementary school students, with a couple of interesting caveats. First, the intervention seemed to work best when delivered a) earlier, rather than later, in the elementary years and b) in communities that had adequate resources (as compared to distressed, inner-city communities). The authors conclude that their results lend yet more support to the notion that "earlier is better," but also that interventions for older children with high risk for delinquency, especially in schools or communites that are already distressed, remains a significant challenge.

Where to find more information on working with delinquents:

Burns, B. J., Howell, J. C., Wiig, J. K., Augimeri, L. K., Welsh, B. C., Loeber, R., & Petechuk, D. (2003). *Treatment, services, and intervention programs for child delinquents.* Bulletin. Washington, D.C.: U.S. Department of Justice, Office of Justice Programs, Office of Juvenile Justice and Delinquency Prevention.

Henggeler, S. W., & Schoenwald, S. K. (2011). Evidence-based interventions for juvenile offenders and juvenile justice policies that support them. Social Policy Report, Volume 25, Number 1. *Society for Research in Child Development.*

Loeber, R., Farrington, D. P., & Petechuk, D. (2003). *Child delinquency: Early intervention and prevention.* Bulletin. Washington, D.C.: U.S. Department of Justice, Office of Justice Programs, Office of Juvenile Justice and Delinquency Prevention.

Tolan, P., Henry, D., Schoeny, M., Bass, A., Lovegrove, P., & Nichols, E. (2013). Mentoring interventions to affect juvenile delinquency and associated problems: A systematic review. *Campbell Systematic Reviews, 9*(10).

SUMMARY

Children and adolescents with EBD often engage in delinquency, substance abuse, and precocious sexual behavior. These behaviors rarely occur in isolation from each other. Rather, troubled adolescents more often display a constellation of interrelated behavioral difficulties. The behaviors discussed in this chapter are related to the persistence and aggravation of such problems in adult life.

Juvenile delinquency is a legal term indicating violation of the law by an individual who is not yet an adult. Acts that are illegal only if committed by a minor are *status offenses*; *index crimes* are illegal regardless of the individual's age. The vast majority of youngsters commit delinquent acts; a small percentage are apprehended. Delinquent children and youth often have other emotional or behavioral disorders, especially conduct disorder. However, not all delinquents are identified as having conduct disorder, and not all youngsters with conduct disorder are delinquents. The most important distinctions are probably between those who commit few delinquent acts and those who are chronic offenders, especially those who repeat violent offenses against persons.

About 20 percent of all children and youth are at some time officially delinquent, and about 3 percent are adjudicated each year. About half of all official delinquents commit only one offense before reaching adulthood. Recidivists account for the majority of official delinquency. Peak ages for juvenile delinquency are ages fifteen to seventeen. Most adjudicated delinquents are male.

Causal factors in delinquency are numerous and include antisocial behavior, hyperactivity and impulsivity, low intelligence and school achievement, family conflict and criminality, poverty, and poor parental discipline. Delinquency appears to grow from environmental disadvantages, weakened social bonds (to family, school, and work), and disrupted social relationships between youths and social institutions in the community. Effective prevention would have to address all the conditions that increase risk of delinquency.

We might logically take the position that nearly all incarcerated delinquents have EBD requiring special education. Assessment of delinquents' educational needs is extremely difficult because of the behavioral characteristics of delinquents and the social agencies that serve them.

Intervention in delinquency, if it is to be successful, must involve families, juvenile justice, schools, and communities. Parents need training to monitor and discipline their children more effectively. Juvenile justice may involve a variety of strategies, ranging from diversion to incarceration. The recommendations of researchers are typically for interventions that keep all but violent offenders in the community. Schools typically respond to disruptive and delinquent behavior with heightened punishment and a focus on security, but schoolwide discipline and emphasis on attention to appropriate behavior are more successful. Education in the corrections system should include functional assessment of students' needs, a curriculum that teaches important life skills, vocational training, supportive transition back to the community, and a full range of educational and related services from collaborating agencies.

Street gangs are an increasing problem in many cities, but misperceptions of these gangs are common. Street gangs are aggregations of youth who define themselves as a group and are committed to a criminal orientation. Most do not have drug distribution as a primary focus, and most of gang members' time is spent doing noncriminal and nonviolent acts. Gang members typically have notable personal deficiencies, are antisocial, desire status and companionship, and lead mostly boring lives. The causes and approaches to prevention of gangs are similar to those for delinquency, and many of the same intervention strategies apply, especially addressing problems of poverty and joblessness. However, gangs are maintained by perceived external threats and interventions that strengthen their cohesiveness. Many schools are running scared and approach gangs in ways that are counterproductive. A particular educational need is a differentiated curriculum that includes programs for non-college-bound youth.

Substance abuse is not easy to define. However, a substance may be considered abused when it is deliberately used to induce physiological or psychological effects (or both) for other than therapeutic purposes and when its use contributes to health risks, impaired psychological functioning, adverse social consequences, or some combination of these. The most pervasive substance abuse problems involve alcohol and tobacco. Substance abuse typically progresses through several stages: from experimentation to social–recreational use to circumstantial–situational use, which may become intensified and lead to obsessional dependency. Teachers are most likely to observe the first indications of substance use during the transition from experimentation to social–recreational or to circumstantial–situational use. The causes of substance abuse are varied and include family, peer, community, and biological factors. Substance abuse is often accompanied by other disorders. Effective prevention programs are expensive, multifaceted, and controversial. Intervention in substance abuse must be designed for the individual case. School-based interventions require clear school policies regarding drugs, systematic efforts to provide information, referral to other agencies, and involvement of families and peers. In addition, interventions related to substance abuse may need to target the individual's beliefs that he or she actually can effect change in his or her patterns of substance use.

Early sexual activity is of concern primarily because of the risk of pregnancy, sexually transmitted diseases, and psychological and health problems. The sexual activity of juveniles may be motivated by a variety of factors, but the risk of negative consequences is always high. Teachers may be involved in educational programs, but current school-based intervention programs may be ineffective.

✔ ENHANCEDetext **END-OF-CHAPTER 13 QUIZ**

Click on the checkmark icon to access an end-of-chapter quiz. Answer the questions to gauge your understanding of chapter concepts and better prepare you for case discussions.

PERSONAL REFLECTIONS

Problem Behaviors of Adolescence

Michele M. Brigham, M.Ed., has been teaching for over thirty years. She has been a high school special education resource teacher and music teacher and works with general education teachers. She has also been the choral director for her school and has directed its musicals. She has been an adjunct faculty member for the University of Virginia, teaching special education courses in Falls Church, Virginia.

How would you describe the academic needs of most of the high school students you teach?

Most of them face three sources of tension in dealing with their academic needs. First, they have severe deficits in basic skills. Schools are reluctant to provide direct remediation of basic skills because that would mean setting up specialized treatments, removing them from some inclusive environments and some parts of the standards-based curriculum. Second, they're not passing their classes, so instead of remediation they get tutoring. Even with tutoring, many students still have trouble passing their classes and the proficiency examinations. Consequently, many of them won't earn a standard diploma. Third,

one result of standards-based curriculum reform is a drastic reduction in vocational education. So, besides not getting a standard diploma, they're unlikely to leave school ready for skilled or semiskilled labor.

They're far behind their peers in reading and writing skills. Lots of the seniors in my practical English classes read at the third- to eighth-grade level. They lack the decoding skills needed for fluent reading, and so they have poor comprehension, too. Their reading skills are so deficient that they don't consider reading a pleasure or a reasonable way of getting information. They resist reading aloud, which is the best way to gain accuracy. Long before they get to high school, teachers have given up getting them to read aloud. So, they've been unable to make much progress in fluency and comprehension, so they don't really have access to the general curriculum either.

Predictably, my students are also deficient in writing. They have difficulty with grammar, syntax, and pragmatic language. Their problems in writing include basic mechanics—things like spelling and punctuation. They need to be taught to write complete sentences and organize ideas into complex sentences and paragraphs. Their compositions lack elaboration and provide only sketchy information. Writing is slow and laborious for them, and they often have poor handwriting and keyboarding skills. Therefore, it's easy to see that skills that are automatic for most students at this level are distractions from the cognitive skills required to craft both expository and narrative prose.

There's a complex interaction between these skill deficits and general verbal abilities. My students lack confidence in their ability to understand others and express themselves. Consequently, they often mask their confusion with apparent belligerence or nonchalance. Although some of them are disruptive, many of them are using these behaviors to mask their insecurity or their inability to compete with their peers. The skills they need are rarely taught explicitly at this level in general education. Consequently, students who fail to acquire them before they reach high school are unlikely to profit substantially from exposure to the general curriculum.

The interaction of these skill deficits leads to an even larger problem for my students, which is a deficient store of background knowledge. Their background knowledge deficits make it difficult for them to participate meaningfully in many aspects of general education classes. Put simply, they just don't understand what their teachers and peers are talking about. Consequently, many of my students dismiss the general education curriculum as "stupid" or irrelevant.

Most of my teaching is in language arts, but I've observed similar deficits in my students' ability to keep up with their peers in mathematics, science, and social studies. It's easy to see how their skill deficits in reading and writing cause similar problems in these areas.

To what extent do these youngsters need social skills training?

Most of them have serious social problems. However, the extent to which they would profit from direct social skills training is somewhat questionable. To many educators, social skills training means instruction in specific interactional skills such as making eye contact, shaking hands, and polite conversation. At the high school level, social skills intervention with those who don't have intellectual disabilities probably should be more about their belief that

appropriate behavior is worth the effort. There's a difference between knowing the skills and using them. Most of my students know and have the social skills they need, but they use maladaptive behavior because they've found it more effective and efficient in attaining their immediate goals. Their previous interactions have led them to believe they'll never achieve competence in the prized academic skills, so they focus on escape and avoidance.

Many psychologists and guidance officials make anger management plans for my students that allow them to leave the instructional environment when they become upset. These plans don't teach students how to cope with difficult demands. I'm not convinced that this is always the best way to support my students in reaching their long-term goals because it a) deprives them of the academic instruction they need and b) keeps them from learning the coping skills they need for independence and employment.

Here's an example: One of my students supported by such a misguided anger management plan was unsuccessful in work-study during his senior year and couldn't hold a job after he graduated. Whenever he got negative feedback from a supervisor, he used the same strategy he was taught in school—he walked off his job. This inability to meet the demands of the working world leads me to doubt his ability to successfully meet the commitment of marriage, parenting, and other social relationships that enhance quality of life.

What advice would you offer to teachers of typical high school students?

Interestingly enough, many teachers already know the techniques that would be most successful with my students. These include maximizing engaged time on task, with students actively participating in instructional activities and making sure the content is covered with appropriate pacing, well-defined and prioritized objectives, and structured delivery of information that includes a statement of the objectives, review and repetition of the important points, ample opportunities for practice, and frequent and explicit feedback using techniques such as curriculum-based measurement. Teachers need to use good teaching techniques that have been identified through empirical research. It's important for students like mine to have much more frequent feedback so they can see for themselves that they're making progress. Structure and consistency are important for my students so they feel secure enough to try to learn material that's difficult for them.

What are the most important things a teacher can do to help students who have begun to abuse substances?

Dealing with substance abuse is a bigger problem than most teachers should handle by themselves because our training prepares us for instructional–behavioral issues in school. We should respect the limits of our training.

The first step should always be to refer the student to appropriate professionals. In my school, our guidance professionals, school nurse, and school psychologist are the front line for working with students with substance abuse problems. However, in thinking about things that can be done in the classroom, it's hard to imagine that the kinds of good teaching methods that help students with disabilities would be completely ineffective with students who have begun to abuse substances. Clear and explicit feedback, focus on accomplishments, frequent reinforcement for accomplishment, and helping students understand the relationship between effort and outcome are tools teachers can use effectively with students engaging in substance abuse.

What are the most common behavioral problems that you must deal with?

The major problems are refusal to participate, truancy, and tardiness. Refusal to participate takes many forms, including gestures and language that some see as requiring punishment instead of attempts to escape work. I believe that whatever form the refusal to participate takes, the real problem that we should deal with is the attempt to withdraw from the instruction. I see my students in two very controlled settings outside of the core content classes—a resource–tutorial setting and a dedicated practical English class. Although many

people prefer the word *segregated*, that implies involuntary separation. Most of my students are terrified that they will be forced to return to general education, where they are well aware that their skill level will keep them from success and they will experience personal humiliation. Even within these homogeneous settings, I experience high levels of resistance to instruction from many students. Task avoidance behaviors such as refusal to participate in instruction, refusal to attempt to do assignments or otherwise participate in classroom activities, tardiness, and truancy have been inadvertently rewarded in both regular and special education.

When students present general education teachers with the choice of ignoring disengagement or dealing with disruption, the teachers are overwhelmed by the size of their classes and the amount of material to be covered. These teachers can ill afford to devote substantial amounts of instructional time to a few students at the expense of the rest of the class. Support staff, parents, and IEP teams too often excuse students from instructional demands rather than provide them with the requisite skills to benefit from instruction. By the time they get to high school, many of these students are so overwhelmed by their cycle of failure they are no longer willing to take the risks or make the effort required for success in learning.

What are the kids you teach actually like? Give us a thumbnail sketch of several.

Carrie is a sophomore, but still considered a freshman because she hasn't passed enough classes or state competency exams. She's living with her grandmother. She's had a lot of difficulty in her classes and has lost a job she really liked because of her inability to control her temper, work with people she doesn't like, and tell the truth. She has an emotional or behavioral disorder and a behavior plan, and she's being considered for placement in a special school but hasn't been placed yet because of inadequate documentation of her problems.

Kate is a junior with a learning disability and has become quite successful in her practical level classes. She takes classes half the school day and has been placed for work-study in a job she really enjoys. Though she's very proud of her job, it's currently in jeopardy because she's been unable to pass her driver's test.

Larry is also a junior and probably the most successful of the three in understanding and working with his disability. He will take standard-level classes during his senior year. He's involved with his community and is active in a theater company. He's a very talented artist as well. Though he describes himself as a former "hoodlum," Larry has mastered the social skills he needs to be successful in school.

Questions for Further Reflection

1. What are the things you can do as a teacher to help steer students away from the most serious problems of adolescence?

2. What should you do, and how should you do it, if you become aware that one of your students (of any age) is abusing substances?

3. As a teacher, how would you talk to a student who comes to you with accounts of early sexual experience? What would you ask? What would you say, and how would you say it?

PART 4   Assessment

INTRODUCTION

As you read the next two chapters, we hope your self-questioning will turn to important practical matters having to do with intervention. If we're going to do something about EBD, we first have to determine who has a disorder. We also have to decide what kind of information we're going to rely on in screening, classifying, and teaching the students we believe have EBD. The major problems we address in Part 4 might be expressed as two questions:

- How do we turn a definition into practical procedures for identifying students who have disorders and classifying their disorders in a useful way?
- How do we obtain and use information about students that will help us teach them most effectively?

We begin Chapter 14 with a brief overview of reliability and validity of assessment procedures. These are foundational concepts by which all assessment procedures must be evaluated.

We don't go into the details of calculation of reliability and validity. Our presentation is designed only to give readers a basic understanding of these concepts and to provide suggestions for how to interpret test results or other assessment data with these criteria in mind. We try to address these questions: Why do people do assessments? How would we know a good assessment from one that isn't good?

We then turn to issues of screening. At first blush, screening seems an easy problem to tackle. After all, children and youth with severe EBD are usually easy for anyone to identify. They typically stand out immediately and clearly as different—obviously peculiar or deeply troubled in the eyes of most observers. Rational people don't usually have much difficulty reaching a consensus that certain ways of behaving are deviant, and most people will admit that clearly deviant behavior requires some sort of intervention. If we were interested only in children and youth with the most severe disorders, screening would be a snap. But EBD isn't *always* severe or isn't *always* obvious in *all* settings. So, some youngsters with EBD aren't as readily identified. Still, the *severity* of a disorder may be more important to know than the psychiatric classification or label. The majority of the students that schools identify as having EBD have *severe* disorders (Forness et al., 2012; Mattison, 2014). EBD shouldn't be considered a mild disability given what we know about the special education category "emotionally disturbed."

In fact, most emotional or behavioral disorders aren't so severe that they're immediately obvious to the casual observer. They're serious enough that at least one adult is upset or concerned. But they're either mild enough or infrequent enough that someone might argue that most of the youngster's behavior is within the normal range and that the problem will work itself out with little or no help. Indeed, mild disorders fade into normal behavior in a haze of conjecture about where to draw the line or what to make of a particular behavior. As Kauffman, Bruce, and Lloyd (2012) point out, EBD is often characterized by long periods of normal behavior punctuated by infrequent instances of very serious misconduct, so someone who doesn't see one of those infrequent "earthquakes" might mistakenly assume that there's no problem. Differences of opinion about whether an individual should be identified as having EBD are common, even among experts. Consequently, it's often helpful to use screening procedures to help focus attention on the marginal cases. Screening procedures are designed to answer questions like these:

- Which students should we be most concerned about?
- How should we select those we're going to study more carefully by collecting more in-depth assessment data?
- How do we decide that one student has problems but doesn't need special education, but that another student with problems does need special education?

The variety of youngsters' perplexing behavior is dazzling, even to people who have had many years of experience working with those who have EBD. Saying that a student has EBD and needs special education is thus not very informative. "What kind of disorder does this student have?" is a reasonable question to ask, and the answer must be a category or classification. The classifications we use should tell us more about what kind of behavior the student exhibits—the problems we might expect.

Children and youth are certainly individuals, but we can't treat every individual in *every* respect as a unique case. We have to identify the similar or critical features of cases so that we have some basis for communicating about types of problems and deciding what interventions to try. Classification isn't just basic to all science; it's essential for effective communication and intervention. The issue, then, is this: What is the most helpful way to categorize or classify the types of problems we encounter? Important questions about assessment include how the information is related to what we do in the classroom:

- What kinds of information are most helpful in planning an educational program?
- How should I use the information I have about a student in writing an educational plan, choosing a curriculum, and evaluating progress?

Significant changes in the assessment of exceptional children and youth have occurred in recent years. One change is a shift in terminology. Psychologists and educators still occasionally use the term *diagnosis*, and psychiatrists typically use that term with reference to EBD. However, *diagnosis* has largely been replaced in the language of educators by *evaluation* or *assessment*, because *diagnosis* connotes the classification of disease. In the vast majority of cases, there is no evidence that disordered emotion or behavior is a disease in any physiological sense, even with recent advances in brain imaging and genetics. *Evaluation* and *assessment* are more appropriate for educational purposes because they connote measurement of nonphysiological and nonmedical factors that are related to social learning and adaptation.

The availability of assessment devices and technical information about the assessment process have increased dramatically in recent years. If you're preparing to teach students with EBD, you'll need to study assessment procedures in greater detail.

Besides the increase in available instruments and technical information, legal issues have recently taken a prominent place in assessment. A student who's referred for special education must be evaluated to determine whether he or she is eligible for services under the Individuals with Disabilities Education Act (IDEA) and related state legislation. Federal regulations require that this assessment be completed by an interdisciplinary team of qualified specialists because the results will be useful not only for determining eligibility for special education but also for planning instruction, regardless of the student's placement in special or general education classes. If the student receives special education, then the evaluation data must be used in writing an individual education program (IEP). The law now also requires a *functional behavioral assessment* (FBA), meaning that special educators must try to figure out why the student is behaving inappropriately and devise a positive, proactive behavior intervention plan to address the student's needs as part of the IEP.

The assessment of a student's abilities and problems is no easy task. It can easily be botched in either of two ways. On one hand, it's easy to be too imprecise—so subjective and so reliant on general impressions that we miss important details or end up with a decision that simply doesn't fit the objective facts of the case. On the other hand, it's easy to get so absorbed in precise measurement and quantitative details that we miss the big picture or ignore the affective, human aspects of the case. Perhaps assessment is the task that presents the greatest challenge to maintaining a balance between objective data and subjective interpretation. We think the challenge of becoming skilled at assessment is much like the challenge of becoming a sensitive scientist, and we hope you will complete your reading of the last chapter with an appreciation of the difficulty of giving balanced attention to what can be recorded objectively and what can only be sensed.

14 MEASUREMENT ISSUES, SCREENING, AND IDENTIFICATION

After reading this chapter, you should be able to:

14.1 Describe the essential requirements and protections included in IDEA regarding special education evaluation.

14.2 Define and discuss the importance of reliability and validity, in particular as they relate to assessment of EBD.

14.3 Define screening and its purpose, as well as some ways that screening for EBD can be conducted in schools.

14.4 Describe what must happen by law, as well as what constitutes good practice, in prereferral intervention for students suspected of having EBD.

14.5 Describe the process of evaluation for eligibility for special education services.

Although we have outlined and will discuss four purposes of assessment (screening, eligibility, evaluation for instruction, and classification), we can think of two of these processes as central to the day-to-day work of educators and other professionals working directly with students with EBD. In general, students suspected of having disabilities or students who have been identified as having disabilities are assessed by those who work with them for one of two broad purposes. The first is to determine whether a student is eligible for special education. The second is to plan the student's educational program. Although these are compatible goals, the instruments and procedures used for each purpose are sometimes different. Typically, assessment directly linked to intervention is the most useful for teachers who must plan and implement instruction (Bateman & Linden, 2012; Lane & Walker, 2015; Shapiro, 2011). However, the legal mandates of identifying a specific group of children who are to receive special treatment appear to be most efficiently conducted through norm-referenced assessments (Landrum, 2000). There has been considerable movement away from exclusive reliance on norm-referenced instruments and toward somewhat more informal but more instructionally useful procedures (e.g., curriculum-based assessments or other instruments useful for academic or behavioral progress-monitoring; see Caldarella, Larsen, Williams, Wehby, Wills, & Kamps, 2016). However, we can learn much about a student from norm-referenced instruments despite the criticisms leveled at them (e.g., Sacks, 1999). Eliminating them from the repertoire of educational and psychological evaluators would be premature (Kauffman, 2010c, 2011; Kauffman & Konold, 2007).

In this chapter, we consider the procedures typically used to assess students with or suspected of having EBD. Note that we focus on different purposes of assessment, and while we approach topics in sequence, these don't necessarily proceed in a lock-step fashion in real world practice. It's also important to note that the purpose of assessment should drive decisions about specific procedures and instruments to use. For example, a screening tool provides valuable information if the question asked is: How many students in our school show early signs of problem behavior that might require more in-depth assessment to determine the nature and extent of a problem, if one even exists? But the information gained from such screening would likely be of little use to a classroom teacher working with an individual child with EBD. Moreover, certain assessment purposes are more suited to norm-referenced assessment procedures (e.g., assessment for eligibility), while other purposes of assessment are more suited to more informal procedures (evaluation for planning instruction or progress monitoring). The major topics we cover in this chapter are a) screening, b) evaluation for eligibility for special education services, c) evaluation for instruction, and d) classification. Before we discuss each of these in greater depth, we begin with an overview of some legal and policy foundations of assessment for students with disabilities, and a brief introduction to some of the major concepts underlying sound assessment (e.g., reliability and validity).

The procedures for assessment, identification, and classification of students with disabilities are very important. In fact, according to Bateman and Linden (2012) and Huefner (2006), it's difficult to overstate the importance of a full assessment prior to the development of the individualized education program (IEP). Bateman and Linden's and Huefner's emphasis on the importance of good assessment is based on the understanding that an accurate evaluation of the child's strengths, weaknesses, and current levels of performance is the basis for all that will follow. Assessment involves procedures to identify the distinguishing features of an individual case. Whether we are classifying disorders, determining eligibility for special education, or planning and monitoring the effects of instruction, assessment of children and youth with EBD must be based on the most sound procedures we have at our disposal.

GENERAL RULES FOR EVALUATION FOR SPECIAL EDUCATION

The following general rules governing evaluation for special education are laid down by federal law in the Individuals with Disabilities Education Act (IDEA) and its accompanying code of regulations. State rules may be no less strict than the federal rules; however, state rules may mandate requirements that are more stringent than the federal rules (see Bateman & Linden, 2012; Huefner, 2006; Yell, 2016).

Parents Must Participate

Parents must be members of the teams making decisions about eligibility for special education, writing individualized education programs, and determining appropriate placements. Further, schools must include parents in the initial assessment process, in large part because parents can provide valuable input into many aspects of the process. Parents, for example, can help identify areas of particular concern or strength, as well as settings or events that are either problematic for the student, or conversely, are associated with the student exhibiting acceptable behavior. Parents may also participate in reevaluations of the student. Some parents may decline to participate in the assessment-evaluation process, but by law they must be invited to do so. If assessment proceeds without parental involvement, the school must carefully document its good-faith efforts to include the parents.

Multiple Disciplines Must Be Involved

An evaluation entails individualized assessment of the student's educational needs. It typically includes four components: medical, psychological, social, and educational. All evaluation procedures must be completed before the student's eligibility for special education can be determined. The assessment must be completed by a group of professionals qualified to evaluate the student's problems, at least one of whom must be a teacher or specialist qualified to teach students with disabilities like the one the child is suspected of having.

All Known or Suspected Disabilities Must Be Assessed Accurately and Fairly

The student must be assessed in each area of known or suspected disability. Evaluation must be carried out using methods or tests that are not racially or culturally discriminatory, and assessments must be administered in the student's native language or usual mode of communication. The tests must have evidence of reliability and validity for the purposes for which they are used. Furthermore, *no single test or method of evaluation can be used as the sole criterion for determining the student's eligibility for special education*. After parental permission for evaluation is obtained, the school must complete all components and determine eligibility within sixty days (Yell, 2016). (Note: Sixty days is a federal requirement; some state laws may set a limit of less than sixty days.)

Assessment Results Must Be Confidential

All test results and other records about the student being evaluated for eligibility must be kept confidential. No one except teachers and other professionals who work with the student is allowed to review the records without parental permission. It's unprofessional and illegal to share information from the evaluation with anyone—including other professionals—who are not directly involved with the student's education. Parents, of course, must by law be informed of the results of the evaluation in language they can understand, and the school must allow parents to see their child's records if they so request. In addition, regulations of the IDEA provide that each regular and special education teacher and service provider responsible for implementing a child's IEP must a) have access to the child's IEP and b) be informed of his or her specific responsibilities under the IEP, and of the specific accommodations, modifications, and supports that must be provided for the child in accordance with the IEP.

Parents Have a Right to Mediation or a Due Process Hearing

If parents disagree with the school's evaluation data, they have a right to have their child evaluated by someone not affiliated with the school and to present the results to the school. Then, if parents and the school can't reach an agreement about an accurate evaluation, by law either party may request a hearing. Mediation of disputes about evaluation issues is encouraged, but participation in mediation must be voluntary and can't be used to delay or avoid a due process hearing.

Periodic Reevaluation Is Required

After a student is determined to be eligible and is placed in special education, his or her progress is assessed at least annually. Usually, the teacher or the specialist providing the services to meet the relevant educational goals or objectives conducts evaluations, rather than assembling an entire team of evaluation specialists. At annual review, the questions asked include, "Is the student making adequate progress toward the annual goals spelled out in the IEP?" and "Do goals, objectives, or services provided need to be adjusted, modified, or updated?" In addition to annual review, a comprehensive reevaluation involving an interdisciplinary team must be completed at least every three years. This is called a **triennial evaluation** and should mirror the process and procedures used during the initial evaluation for special education eligibility. During triennial evaluations, assessment teams review the assessment data collected during the student's recent evaluations to determine the adequacy of the information. The team may consider the information currently available about the student, administer assessments to update previously obtained information, and obtain new data regarding a given student. At the point of triennial evaluation, the issue at hand is whether the student still needs special education services. The question the team asks at triennial evaluation should be the same that was asked at initial evaluation: "Does this student have a disability under IDEA and require special education services for that disability?"

Transition Planning Must Be Part of the IEP for Students Aged Sixteen or Older

Plans for making the transition to further education or to work must be included in the IEP for students aged sixteen or older. This requires assessment of the student's probable educational and employment futures. In addition, older students should be active participants in planning transition programs to ensure that the student's interests and preferences are included (Clark & Mathur, 2010; Wehmeyer, 2001).

Students with EBD Must Be Included in General Assessments of Educational Progress

All students with disabilities, including those with EBD, must be included, if appropriate, in any state- or district-wide standardized or general assessment of educational progress. If appropriate, the student with a disability must be included with adaptations or accommodations for his or her disability. Decisions about whether and how to participate (e.g., with accommodations) are made by the IEP team and are spelled out specifically in the student's IEP.

Positive Behavior Intervention Plans Based on a Functional Behavioral Assessment Must Be Included in IEPs

If a student's behavior is interfering with his or her learning (a given in the case of a student with an EBD), then the IEP must include a plan to use positive strategies (i.e., not merely a plan for punishment of misbehavior) to address or prevent the problem behavior. The behavior intervention plan must be based on a **functional behavioral assessment** (FBA). These legal requirements become particularly important when questions arise around disciplinary issues involving suspension, expulsion, or change of placement. However, the intent of the law clearly is to have FBAs included in IEPs before such disciplinary actions are contemplated (Yell, 2016). Furthermore, the FBAs must be meaningful. Many school districts have adopted procedures that create a document called an FBA, but too often the document is an exercise in checking boxes on preprinted forms to accomplish superficial compliance with state and federal regulations. Many times, such documents are filed without consideration of the results in terms of the child's educational program or disciplinary decisions. It's unlikely that such practices would withstand legal challenges.

Whether evaluation is for eligibility or intervention, two considerations are important: The source of referral and the initial appearance of a problem. Young children almost never refer themselves for evaluation, and even older youths seldom do. Children and youth are usually brought to the attention of mental health workers or special educators by their parents, teachers, or other adults. The evaluation is thus almost always prompted by adults' judgments of youngsters' behavior rather than by the children's opinions of themselves. Adult referral of children and youth has two immediate implications:

1. The evaluation must involve appraisal of at least one referring adult as well as the youngster. Appraisal of the adult who refers the child or youth is necessary to validate the concern about the disturbing behavior and to discover how the adult's responses to the student might be contributing to the problem.

2. Attempts must be made to determine the youngster's own view of the situation.

No humane and ethical approach to EBD can disregard or trivialize the child's opinions of his or her problems and treatment. Some youngsters' opinions are not accessible because of their lack of communication skills, and some young people's opinions must be overruled because they are clearly not in their own best interests. Nevertheless, the rights of children and youth must be protected, and their opinions, when they can be determined, should be weighed seriously in decisions about identification and treatment. Emotional or behavioral problems are not always what they seem at first. Sometimes an explanation is difficult to find, not because the disorder is buried deep in the individual's psyche but simply because some of the most relevant facts are hard to extract from the situation. Sometimes evaluation focuses too much on the student's behavior and doesn't tap some critical item of information, which is often difficult to obtain. If the student's behavior is understood in the context of the circumstances of his or her life, then decisions regarding eligibility and intervention can be made with greater confidence.

GENERAL CRITERIA FOR ACCEPTABLE ASSESSMENTS

To be of any use, assessments must meet a basic set of requirements. Among these are that a) they must assess what they say they are assessing; b) the assessment domain must reflect agreed-on definitions of the target behavior(s) or constructs; c) the assessment must be as free from error as possible; and d) the assessment should yield similar results when administered by different evaluators or when administered a second time within a reasonably close time period (see Gresham, 2015).

The forgoing list of desirable test characteristics is far from complete. The American Educational Research Association, the American Psychological Association, and the National Council for Measurement in Education jointly developed statements regarding assessment requirements and competencies for assessment professionals (see American Educational Research Association, American Psychological Association, & National Council on Measurement in Education, 2014). A complete discussion of those standards is beyond the scope of this chapter. However, professionals who are engaged in formal assessment procedures would be wise to become familiar with the principles illustrated in the professional standards of those organizations.

The psychometric characteristics of an assessment tool can be lumped roughly into two issues: **reliability** and **validity**. Issues of random measurement error and the stability of measures over time or between different evaluators are related to the reliability of the measure. The extent to which a test measures what it says it does in a manner that is consistent with agreed-on definitions of the phenomenon and without bias is related to the validity of the procedure (see Bagner, Harwood, & Eyberg, 2006; Lane et al., 2012).

Reliability and validity are interrelated, but their relationship is sometimes confusing. Reliability refers to how consistently a measure performs, while validity refers to the extent to which we are really measuring what we believe we are. Suppose a thermometer consistently and repeatedly shows a person's body temperature to be 80 degrees. Such a thermometer is highly reliable, producing the same or very similar results consistently. But it's far from valid—it's highly doubtful that it is truly measuring the person's actual body temperature. The relationship that exists between reliability and validity by definition is highlighted in this example: A measure cannot be considered valid unless it has a significant degree of reliability. But note that the converse is not true: A measure can be highly reliable with little or no evidence of validity. Consider another example; suppose a bathroom scale shows a person's weight to be 180 pounds one day, 160 the next day, and 200 the following day. Given that it would be virtually impossible for weight to fluctuate so dramatically, a logical conclusion is that the scale is not reliable—it doesn't produce consistent results. We must further conclude that the scale is also not valid—it can't be considered a valid measure of body weight if its results can't be trusted to be reasonably accurate estimates of what it is supposed to measure. Indeed, we can never be sure exactly what an unreliable instrument is measuring. It's these very concepts—reliability and validity—that educators should keep in mind when administering or interpreting the results of educational or psychological tests.

Reliability of Assessment

Reliability refers simply to how *consistently* a test measures whatever it measures. However, we know that all measurement contains error (Brigham, Tochterman, & Brigham, 2001; Kauffman & Konold, 2007; Kauffman & Lloyd, 2017); thus our goal is not to eliminate error entirely (an impossible task) but to make sure that assessments, and consequently the decisions based on them, are as free from bias and random error as possible. When assessments are characterized by lots of error or bias, they waste time and money, have the potential to harm students, and undermine the credibility of those attempting to help individuals with EBD. Random results and bias are both forms of error, but we discuss bias in the validity section because it tends to be a consistent, systematic form of error and thus is related more to validity than to reliability.

There are several different types of reliability that might be considered in regard to a given measure, and we briefly consider three that may be particularly important to the assessment of EBD: Test–retest reliability, alternate forms reliability, and inter-rater reliability.

Types of Reliability

Test–retest reliability refers to the extent to which an assessment yields similar results at different times (typically separated by not more than one or two weeks). This form of reliability speaks to the trustworthiness of test results by addressing this question: If we assessed this individual again one or two weeks later with the same instrument, would we get basically the same results? Obviously, test–retest reliability is an important consideration only for characteristics that aren't likely to change dramatically in a short period of time. Intelligence tests and measures of general functioning, for example, should have good evidence of test–retest reliability.

Some measures are available in multiple forms (e.g., Form A and Form B), which is useful when it's necessary to assess a student repeatedly (for example, to monitor progress over time). In such cases, test developers should provide evidence of *alternate forms reliability*. This is an indication of the extent to which two or more forms of the same instrument yield the same results; that is, regardless of which form we administered, we would obtain basically the same results. However, not all tests have alternate forms of the same instrument and thus must rely on a test–retest method to establish evidence of reliability.

A third form of reliability that may be particularly important to the assessment of EBD is called *inter-rater reliability*. Inter-rater reliability refers to the extent to which different individuals using a particular assessment tool to rate the same individual or event obtain the same results. Inter-rater reliability is particularly important in behavioral observation and other assessments that involve subjective appraisals (e.g., judging writing assignments).

Reliability is typically expressed as a correlation coefficient, which may range from −1.0 through zero to +1.0. A negative coefficient indicates that high scores on one measure are associated with low scores on the other measure and vice versa. A positive coefficient indicates that there is some level of systematic agreement between the measures (i.e., high scores on one measure are associated with high scores on the other measure, and low scores on one measure are associated with low scores on the other measure). Correlation coefficients at or near zero indicate that there is little or no systematic relation between the measures. Depending on the particular instruments being compared, a positive or a negative correlation can indicate high reliability. The point to remember is that a larger difference from zero indicates a stronger relationship and, thus, greater reliability.

Inter-rater reliability data are usually expressed as a percent of agreement between raters across observation or evaluation opportunities; these range from 0, which indicates no agreement, to 100 percent, which indicates perfect agreement on all opportunities. Obviously, as with test reliabilities, the rule is that higher agreement coefficients (those approaching 100 percent) are more desirable than lower coefficients.

Interpreting Reliability Data

Guidelines have been suggested for judging reliability, but note that we never say that a test "is reliable"; the best we (or those developing tests) can do is report evidence of reliability. One rule of thumb that is sometimes suggested is that reliability coefficients of at least .80 are necessary for any group administered test, and that coefficients of .90 or greater are preferred for assessment tools when they are used to make decisions about an individual student. However, there are no absolute rules for evaluating instruments' reliability, other than that stronger indications of reliability (i.e., greater difference from zero) are better (Mills & Gay, 2016). An important point to keep in mind is that reliability becomes increasingly important when data are used to make high-stakes decisions; when determining eligibility for special education services, for example, professionals should use assessment tools that have the best evidence of reliability. For our purposes, it's sufficient to state that evaluators should be aware of the reliability estimates of the instruments they use, regardless of purpose, and select the most reliable tools they can find.

Standard Error of Measure

There's another concern with regard to the reliability of assessments that influences all measures. As we mentioned earlier, *perfect* measures of human characteristics don't exist; all measurement contains error. Variations in test scores can be due to factors such as the motivation of the person being assessed, the situation in which the measure is taken, the person administering the measure, or random errors in administration and scoring, to name only a few. Theoretically, there's a "true" score that one would obtain if a perfect measure existed, but it's better to acknowledge that error exists and try to estimate that error. An estimate of the variability of obtained scores around true scores due to error in any measurement is called a *standard error of measurement* (SEM). SEM is an extraordinarily complex topic, even for psychometricians and statisticians (see Belia, Fidler, Williams, & Cumming, 2005; Kauffman & Lloyd, 2017), but we mention it here because the concept of SEM will come into play with many assessments that are used for children and youth with EBD. A SEM is usually expressed as a range of scores (plus or minus a certain number from the obtained score) within which the individual is likely to score on a readministration of the measure. Using the concept of a normal distribution around a mean, we can compute confidence intervals (CI) around an obtained score to give our estimates of error even more meaning. For example, we can predict that if we administer a measure multiple times, the scores we obtain would fall within one SEM of the original score 68 percent of the time, and within two SEMs 95 percent of the time. Thus, if a student obtained a score of 70 on a given measure that has a SEM of three, we would estimate that if we administered this assessment repeatedly, his scores would fall between 67 and 73 (70 ± 3) 68 percent of the time and between 64 and 76 (70 ± 6) 95 percent of the time.

Again, SEM is a fairly complex topic, and our discussion of it here is meant only to alert practitioners to the implications of SEM. The concept of SEM may be particularly important when considering cutoff scores; for example, in the context of assessment for eligibility. If a student's score on a particular assessment falls within one or even two SEMs of some type of cutoff score (telling us that in some percentage of repeated assessments with this instrument or test, his score would be on the other side of that cutoff), teams would be wise to examine carefully all other sources of information on that student before making any high-stakes decisions.

Unfortunately, we're unable to specify the exact actions that should be taken in the face of uncertainty; however, failure to consider the error of a given measure falls far short of standards for professional practice in educational and psychological evaluation. The concept of error in assessments is also a reason that no important educational decision (e.g., eligibility for special education services, graduation, grade retention) should ever be made on the basis of the score a student receives on a single assessment.

Validity of Assessment

The *validity* of an assessment refers to the extent to which it measures what it's intended to measure (Mills & Gay, 2016). In the context of EBD, the validity of assessments can be a particularly complex topic in that people attempting to measure some aspect of EBD must share a high level of agreement about what they're after. But as we discussed in Chapter 2, the definition of EBD itself has been criticized for its vagueness and historically hasn't been subject to widespread agreement. As an example, in the early to mid-twentieth century, some individuals were diagnosed with "hysterical paralysis." Few practitioners today believe there is such a thing. Assessments of "hysterical paralysis" would now be regarded with suspicion or disbelief by most professionals. Conversely, conditions such as depression in children, although often dismissed in the distant past, are now well supported by research. Assessments of children's depression now appear in the repertoires of many mental health workers and educators.

Another issue related to validity of an assessment is the ability to isolate particular behaviors or behavioral clusters from other characteristics of the person (e.g., socioeconomic status, ethnicity, gender, educational opportunity, and language abilities and differences). Most professionals consider measures that fail to isolate the target skill or behavior to be contaminated by other influences—error or biases. A clear example of measurement contaminated by additional factors (and thus rendered essentially invalid) is a math test requiring children to read and solve mathematical word problems. For students with adequate reading ability, the measure primarily taps their ability to conceive of the mathematical situation described and use the correct operations to reach a solution. However, the picture is much more complicated for students with limited reading ability. Failure to arrive at correct solutions under such circumstances could be related to a student's reading deficiencies, the student's mathematical ability, or an interaction of these factors. Validity requires freedom from bias, measuring the target variable(s) of concern instead of some extraneous factor, measuring variables that are sensible, and measuring with accuracy.

Types of Validity

Four types of validity are traditionally discussed: a) *construct validity* (what the test is really measuring), b) *concurrent criterion-related validity* (the degree to which scores on one test are similar to scores on some other assessment administered at the same time), c) *predictive criterion-related validity* (the extent to which a test can predict how well a person will perform on another assessment in a future situation), and d) *content validity* (the extent to which a test measures or adequately covers its intended content area). (For an overview and succinct definitions, see Lane et al., 2012.)

Different indications of validity are used for different purposes. For example, if one is attempting to identify children whose behaviors are not yet highly problematic but are likely to become so without intervention, then a high degree of predictive validity is required. If one desires a standardized measure of achievement that indicates how well the child is progressing through school learning tasks, then high content validity is essential.

Concurrent validity indicators are often used by producers of new tests attempting to demonstrate the adequacy of their assessment instruments. If a new procedure yields scores that are highly similar to another, well-accepted procedure, then the publisher is able to claim that the new test is at least as useful as the older procedure. Finally, construct validity is normally used to demonstrate the importance of the phenomenon under consideration.

Interpreting Validity Data

As with reliability calculations, hard and fast rules about validity in measurement are difficult to specify. Assessments that have good evidence of validity can be quite useful in identifying children who are in need of special education and suggesting appropriate treatments for them. Measures that lack adequate validity will be of no constructive value to educators or the students they serve. Worse, some of these measures actually can be detrimental to children by promoting misclassification, providing misleading results, or focusing attention on fruitless educational or behavioral treatments. Practitioners are advised to attend to the evidence of validity for any measure used to evaluate children and youth with EBD, and especially to consider the types of validity (construct, concurrent, predictive, and content) for which evidence is provided in relation to the purpose for which an assessment tool is used.

The Importance of Reliable and Valid Measures for Students with EBD

The technical adequacy of assessment tools is particularly important because students with disabilities are entitled to certain rights that don't apply to their peers who don't have disabilities (Bateman, 2017; Huefner, 2006; Yell, 2016; Yell & Dragow, 2000). Among these are procedural safeguards, including: a) informed parental consent for initial assessment and any reevaluations that are to be conducted; b) use of a variety of assessment tools that are validated for their purpose and administered in the child's native language or mode of communication, unless it is not feasible; c) tests administered by trained personnel in accordance with the instructions provided by the test producer; and d) assessment in all areas of suspected disability. In addition, federal law requires assessment that yields information directly relevant to the team that determines the educational needs of the student. Many of the procedures and instruments used to determine eligibility of students with EBD can provide insight into the general educational needs of a given student. There are four major purposes for which professionals might assess students with or suspected of having EBD: screening, eligibility, evaluation for instruction, and classification. We consider screening and evaluation in the remainder of this chapter, and turn to evaluation for instruction and classification in Chapter 15.

SCREENING

Ideally, the identification and evaluation procedure for students who show signs of behavioral difficulties should move from brief, general measures applied to large groups—*screening*—through a series of more elaborate and focused steps converging on a determination that a given student is eligible for special education services. In some of the most important early work on screening, Walker and colleagues (1988) called these increasingly focused steps *multiple gating procedures*. Many times, however, schools do a poor job of screening for EBD in the general population, preferring to wait until a student's behavior can no longer be ignored or tolerated to begin evaluation procedures (Dunlap et al., 2006; Kauffman, 2012a; 2014a; Lane et al., 2009, 2012). In addition, when individuals exhibit highly unusual or completely intolerable behaviors, school personnel may skip the initial screening stage. In this section, we describe the rationale for screening as well as some of the procedures for screening preschool and school-aged students.

Screening is a brief procedure that samples a few behaviors across skills or a domain (Overton, 2016), with the general purpose of identifying students whose behavior may be indicative of a serious problem and who thus should be assessed more thoroughly. In short, screening is used to determine the need for additional assessment. However, because screening samples no areas in depth, the information generated is inappropriate for anything other than selecting students for more study. By definition, screening is economical and efficient. Therefore, a large number of students can be screened with minimal expense and time, allowing schools to identify students who may be in need of assistance long before their behaviors become so intolerable that they arouse the concerns of even the most hardened observer (Kauffman, 2004, 2012a, 2014a).

Early Identification and Prevention

Screening is often justified by the argument that early identification will lead to prevention. Although this argument is both rational and supported by research, translating concern for prevention into effective screening has proven difficult. Chief among the difficulties are defining the disorders to be prevented and separating serious from trivial problems. Effective screening must eliminate concern for common problems that do not carry serious consequences or that are virtually certain to resolve themselves without intervention, and instead focus attention on precursors that are most likely to be associated with serious later consequences if no further action is taken. Efforts to prevent problems demand a developmental perspective that takes into account developmental milestones associated with chronological age, life events, different environments, and intervention strategies (Forness & Kavale, 1997).

Prevention can be thought of in several forms, including primary, secondary, and tertiary (or *universal, selective,* and *indicated*; see O'Connell, Boat, & Warner, 2009). The purpose of screening for EBD is usually *secondary prevention* as opposed to *primary prevention.* Primary prevention keeps disorders from occurring at all. It involves the universal application of safety and health maintenance interventions that reduce risk. If primary prevention is successful, then secondary prevention isn't needed. Once a disorder has emerged (is detectable), primary prevention is no longer possible for that individual. Then the issue is secondary prevention. Secondary prevention is designed to stop the disorder from getting worse and, if possible, to reverse or correct it. *Tertiary prevention* is designed for disorders that have reached advanced stages of development and seem likely to have significant side effects or complications. Tertiary prevention is intervention designed to keep the disorder from overwhelming the individual and others in his or her environment (Kauffman, 1999c, 2003b, 2005, 2010c, 2012a).

Screening for EBD among infants and preschool children is particularly problematic. Children with pervasive developmental disorders such as autism often have been perceived by their parents as "different" from birth or from a very early age. Pediatricians often identify these and other cases in which extremely troublesome behavior is part of a pervasive developmental disorder. But trying to select infants and preschoolers who need special education and related services because of relatively mild disorders is quite another matter. Several factors make selection difficult.

First, large and rapid changes occur during development from infancy to middle childhood. Infants and preschoolers have not yet acquired the language skills that are the basis for much of the older child's social interaction.

Second, a child's behavioral style or temperament in infancy interacts with parenting behavior to determine later behavior patterns. For example, "difficult" behavior x at the age of ten months isn't necessarily predictive of inappropriate behavior y at six years. The responses of others to child behavior and behavior management techniques that parents and teachers use from ten months to six years need to be taken into account.

Third, parents vary markedly in their tolerance of emotional and behavioral differences in children. Because a problem *is* a problem primarily by parental definition in the preschool years, it's difficult to decide on a standard set of behaviors that are deviant (Hayden & Mash, 2014). (Exceptions, as we have said, are obvious developmental lags.)

Finally, the school itself is a potential source of problems. Its structure, demands for performance of new skills, and emphasis on uniformity may set the stage for disorders that simply don't appear until the child enters school. Despite these concerns with identifying problems at a very early age, a growing body of evidence suggests that it's possible to identify children in the primary grades or even in preschool who are at high risk for developing antisocial behavior and other serious behavioral problems (see Briggs-Gowan et al., 2006; Dunlap et al., 2006; Nelson et al., 2007). Unfortunately, despite our increased ability to identify children at risk for EBD at earlier ages, data don't suggest that schools are actually doing so (Dunlap et al., 2006; Walker, Nishioka, Zeller, Severson, & Feil, 2000). Many scholars agree with what Walker and colleagues (2000) suggested some time ago: "the majority of behaviorally at risk students are not identified until well after the point where early intervention could have a substantive, positive impact on their problems" (p. 30) (see Briggs-Gowan et al., 2006; Dunlap et al., 2006).

Dunlap and authors (2006) provided summary statements that represent the consensus of researchers about EBD ("challenging behaviors") in young children. In our words, Dunlap and colleagues offered three consensus statements that are particularly relevant to prevention: First, if children with serious emotional and behavioral problems aren't identified quickly and provided appropriate education and treatment, then their problems tend to be long-lasting and require more intensive services later; second, if young children's inappropriate behavior isn't addressed quickly and effectively, then it's more likely that the child's progress in school will be slow, peers will reject the child, mental health services will be required in adulthood, and there will be adverse effects on the family and community; third, although systems and tools for early identification of children with EBD are available, the actual identification of these children is infrequent, and appropriate services are seldom provided. As you can see, researchers agree that screening and early identification are critically important but seldom practiced.

We noted that EBD often co-occurs with learning disabilities (LD), or at least significant academic and learning problems. We also know that professionals and parents may be reluctant to identify students—particularly very young students—with EBD, and also that LD may be perceived by many as a less stigmatizing label. Perhaps because of these reasons, there is evidence that many students who would benefit from services for EBD are identified as eligible for special education but placed in programs for students with learning disabilities (Forness & Kavale, 1997). This is a truly unfortunate situation because credible evidence suggests that early intervention can keep problems from becoming more serious (Dunlap et al., 2006; Serna, Lambros, Nielsen, & Forness, 2002; Serna, Nielsen, Lambros, & Forness, 2000).

Criteria for Selecting and Devising Screening Procedures

Some screening procedures are more effective and efficient than others. When we think of the nature and purpose of screening tools and procedures, it's clear that we must strike a balance between scientific rigor and practicality and ease of use. A number of researchers have addressed this need to balance the importance of using psychometrically sound screening tools with the need for schools to have access to relatively brief, easy-to-administer screeners that fit into the day-to-day demands on teachers in schools, particularly in the emerging context of multi-tiered systems of support (MTSS). MTSS may encompass both Response-to-Intervention (RTI) and Positive Behavior Interventions and Supports (PBIS) frameworks (e.g., Lane, Kalberg, Lambert, Crnobori, & Bruhn, 2010; Lane et al., 2009, 2012; Walker et al., 2010). Care is required to select procedures that meet both reasonable psychometric and practical criteria for use in schools. Walker and others (2004) suggested four criteria for screening and identifying antisocial behavior, and the same criteria could be applied to all types of EBD:

1. The procedure should be proactive rather than reactive. The school should take the initiative in seeking out students who are at high risk for exhibiting disorders, not simply wait for these students to demonstrate serious maladaptive behavior and then respond.

2. Whenever possible, a variety of people (e.g., teacher, parent, trained observer) should be used as sources of information, and students' behavior should be evaluated in a variety of settings (e.g., classroom, playground, lunchroom, home).

The objective should be to obtain as broad a perspective as possible on the nature and extent of any problems that are detected.

3. Screening should take place as early as possible in students' school careers, ideally at preschool and kindergarten levels. If screening is to serve its intended function well, then target students need to be identified and intervention programs begun before the child develops a long history of maladaptive behavior and school failure.

4. Teacher nominations and rankings or ratings are appropriate in the beginning of the screening process but should be supplemented, if possible, by direct observation, examination of school records, peer or parent ratings, and other sources of information that might be available. The process should be increasingly broad and thorough at successive stages to minimize the chances of misidentification.

Alternative Screening Instruments

Hundreds of behavioral rating scales are available, nearly all of which are potentially useful as screening instruments. Many other procedures, including self-reports, sociometrics, direct observation, and interviewing, can also be used to assess children's social–emotional behavior. Use and interpretation of these instruments require careful study of the test materials and manuals (see Lane et al., 2012; McLean, Wolery, & Bailey, 2004; Pierangelo & Giuliani, 2006).

One concept that is increasingly recognized is strength-based assessment (Epstein, 2004: Hurley, Lambert, Epstein, & Stevens, 2015). In the strength-based model developed by Epstein and colleagues (2004), the focus of assessment is on the social, emotional, and behavioral skills children and youth might already be able to apply positively to their schoolwork; to social relationships with both peers and adults, both in and out of school; and to the difficulties and stressors they may encounter in school and later life.

Epstein (2004) formalized strength-based assessment in an instrument known as the *Behavioral and Emotional Rating Scale* (BERS-2). The BERS-2 includes a Youth Rating Scale (a self-report form) in addition to Teacher and Parent Rating Scales. The instrument has fifty-two items organized into five separate subscales:

1. *Interpersonal strengths*, which measures the ability to control emotions or behaviors in social situations

2. *Family involvement*, which measures the individuals' participation and relations within the family

3. *Intrapersonal strength*, which assesses the individual's perception of competence and accomplishment

4. *School functioning*, which measures the individual's competence in school and classroom tasks

5. *Affective strengths*, which measures the individual's ability to accept affect from others and to express her or his own emotions

The instrument known as Systematic Screening for Behavior Disorder (SSBD), first published in 1990, deserves particular attention as a screening device (Walker & Severson, 1990;

Walker, Severson et al., 2014). It's designed for use in elementary schools based on the assumption that teacher judgment is a valid and cost-effective (though greatly underused) method of identifying students with EBD. Teachers tend to over-refer students who exhibit externalizing behavior problems—those who act out or exhibit conduct disorder. Teachers tend to under-refer students with internalizing behavior problems—those who are characterized by anxiety and social withdrawal (Gresham & Kern, 2004). To make certain that students aren't overlooked in screening and to minimize time and effort, a three-step or "multiple gating" process is used (Walker et al., 1988).

In the first step or "gate" of the SSBD, the teacher lists and rank-orders students with externalizing and internalizing problems, listing those who best fit descriptions of externalized problems and internalized problems, and ranking them from most like to least like the descriptions.

The second step requires that the teacher complete two checklists for the three highest-ranked students on each list—those who have passed through the first "gate." One checklist asks the teacher to indicate whether the pupil exhibited specific behaviors during the past month (e.g., "steals," "has tantrums," "uses obscene language or swears"). These items constitute a Critical Events Index (CEI) of behaviors that, even if they occur at a low frequency, constitute what Gresham, Macmillan and Bocian (1996) aptly called "behavioral earthquakes" that place children at very high risk of being identified as having EBD. The other checklist requires that the teacher judge how often ("never," "sometimes," "frequently") each student shows certain characteristics (e.g., "follows established classroom rules," "cooperates with peers in group activities or situations").

The third step requires observation of students whose scores on the checklists exceed established norms—those who have passed through the second "gate." Students are observed in the classroom and on the playground by a school professional other than the usual classroom teacher (a school psychologist, counselor, or resource teacher). Classroom observations indicate the extent to which the student meets academic expectations; playground observations assess the quality and nature of social behavior. These direct observations, in addition to teacher ratings, are then used to decide whether the student has problems that warrant full evaluation for special education.

The procedures that Walker and his colleagues devised are the most fully developed screening system currently available for use in school settings; indeed Lane and authors (2010) referred to the SSBD generally as the "gold standard" among systematic screeners for EBD.

The Early Screening Project (ESP) was an important extension of the SSBD (Walker, Severson et al., 2014), and this work was a catalyst for subsequent work on an important early intervention project known as First Steps to Success (see Frey, Small, Feil, Seeley, Walker, & Golly, 2013). The ESP was designed and normed specifically for children aged three to five. As noted by Feil (1999), "the beginning of antisocial behavior patterns can be identified at an early age, and these behaviors can be prevented from escalating into more serious and intractable problems" (p. 53). Preliminary studies documented positive effects of the ESP on teachers' ratings of adaptive behavior, maladaptive behavior, and aggression, as well as observation of students' academic engaged time (Walker & Sprague, 2007). Nevertheless, as we have noted, there are strong forces working against prevention, including resistance to the idea of identifying young children as exhibiting serious problem behavior (Kauffman, 2012a, 2014a).

A second instrument that has received perhaps renewed interest due to increasing demand for brief screeners that schools can use as part of their schoolwide (i.e., PBS) efforts is the

Student Risk Screening Scale (SRSS; Drummond, 1994). The SRSS is a brief, one-page screening tool that is available free of charge. Teachers complete the screener by rating each student in their classroom on seven items; total scores are used to predict externalizing behavior problems. A noted potential limitation of the SRSS is a focus on externalizing behavior problems more so than on internalizing problems. Based on a series of studies of the utility of the SRSS, Lane and colleagues suggested that the SRSS had acceptable psychometric properties (e.g., internal consistency, test–retest reliability) and was comparable to the SSBD in predicting externalizing behavior disorders, though less so for predicting internalizing behavior disorders (Lane et al., 2008; Lane et al., 2010). Lane and colleagues suggest that schools evaluate their screening needs carefully and choose from among available screeners based on their unique circumstances and needs.

The *School Archival Records Search* (SARS) is designed to code and quantify existing school records of elementary students (Walker, Block-Pedego, Todis, & Severson, 1991). It involves collecting and systematically coding certain information from a student's school records. Eleven variables are examined: demographics, attendance, achievement test information, school failure (i.e., retentions in grade), disciplinary contacts, within-school referrals, certification for special education, placement out of the regular classroom, receiving chapter 1 services, out-of-school referrals, and negative narrative comments. The SARS was originally intended as a fourth level of screening in the SSBD, but it can be used for a variety of other purposes. Because it is a systematic way of searching out important data about a student's school career, however, the SARS can be used to assist in three other decision-making tasks: identifying students who are at risk for dropping out of school, validating school assessments, and determining eligibility for special programs.

Screening as Convergence and Confirmation of Concerns

A key provision of professional practice in assessment, and indeed a requirement under IDEA with regard to eligibility decisions, is that no single procedure or data source should ever be used to make important decisions (Yell, 2016). The risk of one person reaching an unjustified conclusion about a student is too great to be ignored. It's often difficult for an individual who holds an unsupported opinion to reanalyze the evidence and alter his or her conclusion without external supports. Furthermore, as we have discussed, all tests and measures are characterized by a certain amount of error, leading to random fluctuation of scores taken at specific times or with specific instruments (Sternberg & Grigorenko, 2002). Therefore, it's never defensible for one person's opinion or a single score on a rating scale or other instrument to be considered adequate for screening.

A student should be selected for further evaluation (the purpose of screening) only when several observers share the suspicion that he or she may have a disorder and their shared suspicion is confirmed by data obtained from structured observations or ratings from multiple sources. Otherwise, the risk is too high that the student will be unnecessarily evaluated, potentially identified with a disability when none exists, and erroneously labeled and perhaps stigmatized; or that his or her privacy rights will be violated, and that resources will be wasted on fruitless evaluations.

The goal of screening should be to obtain information from a variety of sources and to use instruments that facilitate the development of hypotheses regarding the reciprocal influence of the behavior, the environments in which it occurs, and the student's personal perspectives. This goal is consistent with an ecological approach and with a social-cognitive conceptual model.

A special concern in screening and identification is the accommodation of cultural diversity and individual differences. Students who are members of ethnic or cultural minorities are at particularly high risk for identification as having disabilities requiring special education or other special services, whereas other ethnic groups are at risk of underidentification (see Forness et al., 2012; Osher et al., 2004; Oswald, Coutinho, Best, & Singh, 1999). On one hand, behavioral differences that aren't truly disorders may be misinterpreted if the person doing the assessment isn't sensitive to cultural or ethnic patterns of behavior. On the other hand, misperception or misunderstanding of cultural or ethnic patterns of behavior could lead to serious behavioral problems being overlooked or dismissed as of little consequence.

Bias about the characteristics of various cultural groups could thus result in overidentification or underidentification of students with these characteristics. Teachers often need guidance in how to evaluate the influence of culture on students' behavior. The available data suggest that African American students are overidentified in the category of EBD (Harry & Klingner, 2014). The precise reasons for this and solutions to the problem, however, remain elusive (Wiley, Brigham, Kauffman, & Bogan, 2013). Nevertheless, no ethnic group, including African American students, is served in special education programs for students with EBD at or above the level that prevalence estimates suggest is appropriate, and racial bias in identification hasn't been shown to be the primary cause of disproportionality (Cullinan & Kauffman, 2005). Underservice to all ethnic groups appears to be the larger problem (see Dunlap et al., 2006; Forness et al., 2012; Kauffman, Mock, & Simpson, 2009; Wiley et al., 2013).

Using Functional Behavioral Assessment in Screening

Functional behavioral assessment (FBA) has been suggested as a useful tool for identifying children with EBD at an early age (McLean et al., 2004; see also Landrum, 2017). FBA is a procedure required in IDEA to address challenging school behaviors that are likely to result in severe disciplinary actions or removal from the schools (Yell, 2016). However, researchers have also considered the application of FBA procedures to younger children (Alter, Conroy, Mancil, & Haydon, 2008; Conroy & Davis, 2000; Conroy, Davis, Fox, & Brown, 2002). Note that the use of FBA procedures for designing interventions has been researched extensively (e.g., Scott & Alter, 2017); here we consider the potential for FBA to serve a screening function.

FBA helps practitioners answer a basic question about a child's challenging behavior: What *function* does the behavior serve? Does the child obtain something of value (e.g., a tangible reinforcer such as food, access to an activity, or attention)? Or does the child escape or avoid something, such as a demanding task? With answers to these questions, FBA practitioners can design interventions that alter or eliminate factors supporting the undesirable behavior. At present, no single preferred FBA procedure exists, and the law doesn't spell out specific strategies for conducting FBA (Conroy et al., 2002; Pierangelo & Giuliani, 2006). However, it's possible to identify several steps shared by most FBA procedures. These are a) defining the target behavior clearly and specifically, b) determining broad environmental events and factors that may increase the occurrence of the behavior, c) identifying antecedents and consequences of the behavior, d) developing hypotheses regarding the function of the behavior, e) testing hypotheses through experimental manipulation, and f) developing and implementing behavioral interventions that address the factors that contribute to and maintain the behavior.

Conroy and her colleagues (2002) adapted the functional behavioral assessment model to create a multigating, multilevel system of assessment that can be used to identify children with EBD. Their system contains three levels. At Level 1, a broad environmental assessment is conducted, and interventions that should benefit all children in the classroom are implemented. By ensuring that elements of the environment (both the physical and the instructional environment) that support undesirable behavior are reduced and elements that support positive behavior are increased, minor problems can be eliminated, secondary problems can be prevented, and the number of false positives greatly reduced (Brigham & Kauffman, 1998; Kauffman & Brigham, 2009). Evaluations at Level 1 are conducted through interviews, checklists, and sometimes direct observation of the environment in which the problem behavior occurs across several days. Aspects of the environment that are identified as potential contributors to problem behavior are addressed, and the behavior of the target children is observed.

For many, but not all, children who exhibit undesirable behavior in school, Level 1 intervention is sufficient. Some children continue to exhibit undesirable behavior after Level 1 environmental intervention has been implemented. These students are the focus of assessment at Level 2, which focuses on high-risk behavior and intervention. To identify children who are at risk for development of EBD at this level, Conroy and others (2002) suggested using standardized screening instruments (e.g., Walker, Severson, et al., 2014) or informal techniques such as teacher nomination. At this stage, identification focuses on examination of the social and communication skills of the target children. Behavioral problems can be the result of skill deficits (Wehby, Symons, & Canale, 1998). Children who are found to have deficits can be provided with training in social and communication skills, as well as general compliance training (e.g., Bellipanni, Tingstrom, Olmi, & Roberts, 2013; Brown, Musick, Conroy, & Schaffer, 2001; Ford, Olmi, Edwards, & Tingstrom, 2001).

Children who resist interventions at Levels 1 and 2 and who continue to exhibit undesirable behaviors are candidates for further assessment and intervention at Level 3 of the Conroy and colleagues (2002) assessment model. During Level 3 screening in this model, FBA procedures are employed to target the specific antecedents and consequences of target behaviors and to develop, implement, and monitor behavioral interventions for the child in question. Assessment at this level is far more intensive, time-consuming, and individually focused than were efforts at Levels 1 and 2. Very few children are likely to need this type of attention, and it's probable that those children will fall into the group of children identified as having EBD.

EVALUATION FOR ELIGIBILITY

If students have passed through screening efforts (or "gates") and remain high on the list of concerns of school personnel, and universal interventions haven't resulted in improvements in their behavioral functioning in school, a concerted effort on the part of educators to address the problem is still necessary before making a formal referral for evaluation for potential eligibility for special education services. This step is known as prereferral intervention, and it is linked to an RTI or MTSS framework (see Kauffman, Badar, & Wiley, in press).

Prereferral Strategies and Response to Intervention

Before students are evaluated for special education services, teachers must try to accommodate their needs in regular classes. These efforts must be documented and must show that the student isn't responding well to reasonable adaptations of the curriculum and the behavior management techniques used in the regular classroom.

IDEA 2004 allows *response to intervention* (RTI), but the practice of RTI may be abused (Johns, Kauffman, & Martin, 2016). RTI is the idea that before a student is considered for referral to special education, the teacher must show that the student isn't responding to evidence-based practices (O'Connor, Sanchez, & Kim, 2017). That is, the teacher has implemented practices that scientific evidence indicates should be effective, but the student hasn't responded as expected. Although RTI has usually been considered as it applies to instruction and academic learning, the concept of response to intervention also applies to social behavior (Fairbanks, Sugai, Guardino, & Lathrop, 2007; Kauffman, Bruce, & Lloyd, 2012). Before making a referral to special education for problem behavior, a teacher must make sure that appropriate positive behavioral supports have been provided in the context of the regular classroom.

The success of prereferral intervention may depend on the support provided for such activities by the school administration (Burns & Symington, 2002; Fairbanks et al., 2007). Schools in which adequate training and support are provided often report effects of prereferral intervention that are far superior to many other schools. Furthermore, involvement of university-based consultant teams also appears to be associated with positive outcomes for prereferral interventions (Burns & Symington, 2002).

Prereferral strategies aim to reduce the number of false positives (i.e., to avoid the misidentification of those who don't actually have a disorder) and to avoid wasting effort on unnecessary formal evaluations. The functional behavioral approach to screening for EBD (Conroy et al., 2002) described earlier in this chapter contains many elements of prereferral activities as a part of the screening procedure itself.

Screening should result in prompt attempts to find solutions to the problems of selected students in general education without evaluating them for special education. Failure to find solutions within a reasonable time should result in prompt referral for evaluation; eternal hope should not spring from failure (see Kauffman, 2014b; Kauffman et al., 2012). Furthermore, specialized prereferral procedures shouldn't be conducted without parental consent, and keeping students in general education classrooms when prereferral procedures haven't been successful could be a violation of IDEA (see Katsiyannis, 1994). When has a teacher done enough to circumvent referral? The answer requires careful consideration of the individual. Suggestions are provided in Box 14.1.

Box 14.1

What Do I Do Before Making a Referral?

Before making a referral, you will be expected to document the strategies you have used in your class to meet the student's educational needs. Regardless of whether the student is later found to have a disability, your documentation will be useful in the following ways: a) You will have evidence that will be helpful to or required by the committee of professionals who will evaluate the student, b) you will be better able to help the student's parents understand that methods used for other students in the class are not adequate for their child, and c) you will have records of successful and unsuccessful methods of working with the student that will be useful to you and any other teacher who works with the student in the future.

Your documentation of what you have done may appear to require a lot of paperwork, but careful record keeping will pay off. If a student is causing you serious concern, then you will be wise to demonstrate your concern by keeping written records. Your notes should include items such as the following:

- Exactly what you are concerned about
- Why you are concerned about it
- Dates, places, and times you have observed the problem
- Precisely what you have done to try to resolve the problem
- Who, if anyone, helped you devise the plans or strategies you have used
- Evidence that the strategies have been either successful or unsuccessful

Prereferral strategies sometimes result in successful management of the student in a general education classroom without the need for special education. Early detection of problems increases the likelihood of finding effective solutions without removing the student from the problem situation. Even with the best available prereferral strategies and flawless teamwork by general and special educators, however, some students' needs will not be met in regular classes (see Bateman, 2017; Kauffman, 2010c; Kauffman et al., 2012; Kauffman, Bantz, & McCullough, 2002; Kauffman & Brigham, 2009; Mock & Kauffman, 2002).

Evaluation for Eligibility Determination

After prereferral or response-to-intervention strategies have been tried in earnest but little improvement has been noted, a formal referral for special education evaluation will follow. Federal regulations require that evaluation for eligibility involve multiple sources of data and assessment by a multidisciplinary team (MDT). One of the most important tools to guide the assessment team is the definition of EBD that they're required to use. The definition that schools must use, of course, is found in IDEA. A starting point for identifying students eligible for services under the category of EBD is the five subpoints of the EBD definition in IDEA (as we discussed in Chapter 2). Assessment procedures should generally address the extent to which the student exhibits:

1. An inability to learn that cannot be explained by intellectual, sensory, or health factors
2. An inability to build and maintain satisfactory interpersonal relationships with peers and teachers
3. Inappropriate types of behavior or feelings under normal circumstances
4. A general, pervasive mood of unhappiness or depression
5. A tendency to develop physical symptoms or fears associated with personal or school problems.

Landrum (2000, 2017) pointed out that the field of behavioral disorders has yet to adequately define the population of students with whom we are working. Consequently, the determination that a student is or isn't eligible for services under the EBD category is often controversial and difficult to make, except in the more extreme instances.

Consider each of the subpoints of the definition. Learning is clearly an important issue for schools, and one would certainly fall short of any professional standard in ascribing learning problems to emotional disturbance when they were indeed caused by another problem. Therefore, evaluation of academic performance is critical because most students suspected of or identified as having EBD have serious academic problems as well as problems of social adjustment (Lane, Carter, Pierson, & Glaeser, 2006; Nicholson, 2014). Evaluations of physical status and cognitive development are also important because problems in one of these areas can contribute substantially to EBD. Evaluations of the social environment of the home and the student's emotional responses to parents, teachers, and peers are essential for understanding the social influences that may be contributing to the problem (see Epstein & Cullinan, 1998).

We now recognize that language disorders and EBD are often closely linked (Chow & Wehby, 2016; Hollo, Wehby, & Oliver, 2014; Nelson, Benner, & Cheney, 2005; Nelson, Benner, & Rogers-Adkinson, 2003). Students with EBD often have difficulty understanding the meanings of others' language and behavior and have difficulty expressing themselves appropriately and effectively (Rogers-Adkinson & Griffith, 1999).

Ideally, the MDT carefully weighs information obtained from evaluations in all these areas before deciding the student's eligibility for special education. Unfortunately, the MDT seldom functions with ideal care and reliability. In practice, decisions are often made with information from limited sources, and the decision-making process tends to be unreliable—not predictable on the basis of objective data from tests and observations alone. One reason for the lack of predictability is the absence of guidelines specifying exactly how the MDT must function. That is, the federal guidelines speak to various safeguards and global concepts around professional and ethical approaches to assessment, but specific, step-by-step procedures for exactly what the members of the MDT do are left for states and school districts to determine. Another reason is the lack of clear criteria for defining disorders; members of the MDT may interpret parts of the definition of EBD differently. Still another reason is the tendency of some evaluation procedures to turn up irrelevant or unhelpful information; for example, some physiological or psychological tests may have little value for educational decisions. Decision-making might become more objective along some dimensions by tightening the criteria for definition and by using expert systems in which computer programs use multiple sources of data to establish complex and entirely objective criteria. Such efforts to objectify the decision-making process don't, unfortunately, take into consideration the fact that the definition of disordered behavior is necessarily subjective, as we discussed in Chapter 2. More objective and reliable instruments and computer programs may help people make better decisions, but they can't become the sole basis for decision making.

A major problem in evaluation is that the decisions of those who declare a student eligible for special education tend to be unreliable (unpredictable or inconsistent) when judged against criteria such as standardized test scores and objective behavioral observations. Different groups and different individuals may evaluate according to different criteria; they may use different criteria for students who differ in gender, race, socioeconomic status, and so forth. Inconsistency is a serious concern because it can indicate bias or inappropriate discrimination in evaluation. However, the solution is not to make the judgments conform to objective psychometric criteria alone (such as test scores or quantitative values in computer programs), nor is it to abandon the goal of more reliable, predictable, or consistent decisions. The most desirable response is to stress professional responsibility in decision making. These are key actions in discharging that responsibility:

- Obtaining inservice training in appropriate evaluation procedures
- Refusing to use evaluation procedures that you aren't qualified to use and refusing to accept evaluation data from unqualified personnel
- Functioning as a member of an MDT to ensure that a single individual doesn't make the eligibility decision
- Insisting that multiple sources of data be made available to the MDT and that the eligibility decision be made on the basis of all relevant data
- Requiring implementation of documented prereferral strategies before evaluation for eligibility
- Involving parents and, if appropriate, the student in the eligibility decision to be sure they're aware of the nature of the problem and the implications of identification
- Documenting disordered behavior, its adverse effects on the student's education, and the need for special education and related services
- Considering the interests of all parties affected by the eligibility decision: Student, peers, parents, and teachers
- Estimating the probable risks and benefits of identifying and not identifying the student for special education
- Ensuring that any special education program proposed as a result of identification is likely to confer educational benefit to the student
- Remaining sensitive to the possibility of bias in the use of procedures and interpretation of data

SUMMARY

Instruments used for any purpose of assessment—screening, determining eligibility, evaluation for instruction, and classification—must be selected carefully using criteria that apply to any measurement. *Reliability* refers to the stability of the measured characteristic across time, observers, and forms of an instrument. *Validity* refers to the extent to which an instrument measures what it supposedly measures. Understanding the concepts of reliability and validity is important for selecting the means by which individuals with or suspected of having EBD will be assessed.

Screening means narrowing the field to those students most likely to have EBD. It involves becoming a good "suspection," so that incipient cases and those that are not immediately obvious are reliably identified. Although IDEA requires the identification of all children with disabilities, few

school systems use systematic screening procedures to identify students with EBD. If schools were to use such screening procedures, they would be likely to identify more students than could be served by special education.

One rationale for screening is that early identification will result in effective early intervention. Although this rationale is supportable, translating concern into screening procedures is difficult. Screening for EBD involves, for the most part, secondary prevention: preventing complications and exacerbation of existing problems. Effective screening of infants and young children with mild disorders is particularly difficult for educators because young children's behavior is sensitive to parental management, and parents, not teachers, define preschoolers' problem behavior. Criteria for selecting screening instruments include proactive (rather than reactive) procedures, information obtained from a variety of sources, implementation in the early grades, and use of teacher identification followed by additional procedures such as direct observation and ratings by parents and peers.

Many rating scales and other instruments can be used for screening. Screening should never consist of a single individual's judgment or be based on data from a single instrument. Convergence of judgments based on confirmation from a variety of sources should be the basis for screening decisions. Accommodation of cultural diversity and individual differences is necessary to avoid bias in screening children and youth who are members of ethnic or cultural minorities.

Prereferral strategies are a necessary intermediate step between screening and referral for evaluation. Before formal evaluation for special education, school personnel must make documented efforts to resolve the student's problems and provide appropriate education in the regular classroom, including response to intervention. Functional behavioral assessment may be thought of as one type of prereferral intervention.

When prereferral strategies fail, the teacher should not delay in referring the student for evaluation. The formal evaluation to determine eligibility for special education services is conducted by a multidisciplinary team, and this work is guided by a set of procedural safeguards spelled out in IDEA.

✔ ENHANCEDetext END-OF-CHAPTER 14 QUIZ

Click on the checkmark icon to access an end-of-chapter quiz. Answer the questions to gauge your understanding of chapter concepts and better prepare you for case discussions.

15 ASSESSMENT FOR INSTRUCTION

After reading this chapter, you should be able to:

15.1 Describe the ways assessment for instruction differs from assessment conducted for other purposes.

15.2 List and briefly describe the benefits of several key assessment approaches useful in evaluating students with EBD, to include: standardized, norm-referenced tests; behavior ratings; direct observation; interviews; and curriculum-based measures.

15.3 Define the purposes and approaches used in a manifestation determination.

15.4 Define functional behavioral assessment, and state why is it an important aspect of evaluation for instruction.

15.5 Discuss the appropriate inclusion of students with EBD in general education assessments.

15.6 Describe the use of assessment data in developing appropriate and useful IEPs for students with EBD.

15.7 State why it is important to work toward a useful and coherent classification system for EBD.

ASSESSMENT FOR INSTRUCTION

Federal language included in IDEA is clear: Assessment information obtained as part of the process of determining eligibility for special education services should be used in planning the educational program for that student. In the preceding chapter, we examined assessments used primarily for screening purposes or for determining eligibility. We turn now to assessment specifically for the purpose of planning and monitoring the effects of instruction. Note that we construe the term *instruction* to mean more than academics, for we must also plan and monitor behavioral interventions as well. But make no mistake; as we argued in Chapter 1, strong academic instruction provides the first line of defense, and the foundation for all that follows, in the education and treatment of students with EBD. Assessments for screening and eligibility (and for classification, which we discuss later in this chapter) answer questions related to how behavior deviates from normative samples or the extent to which it is similar to the behavior of other individuals with EBD. Assessments for instruction are intended to answer questions about what a student has learned and needs to learn.

To be useful for classroom instruction, assessments must be sensitive to small changes in behavior so that the teacher can use them to guide decisions about instruction. Teachers of students with EBD routinely collect information on both academic and social or interpersonal behavior. In addition, they often monitor outcomes of medical interventions (e.g., medications prescribed by physicians or psychiatrists) and related services such as speech and language therapy by completing checklists or otherwise reporting on behavioral and academic performance in the classroom. Many formal, commercially produced measures are on the market; however, informal, teacher-created measures are often more effective for guiding instruction.

CURRENT TRENDS IN EDUCATIONAL ASSESSMENT FOR INSTRUCTION

Few educational issues are currently in the spotlight as much as assessment of the extent to which students are mastering various academic and social skills. It's difficult to follow a leading news source for longer than a week without seeing at least one feature on the failures of American schools and the pressures on schools and educators brought about by current standards-based reforms and accompanying accountability measures that are purportedly designed to improve schools (Lindstrom, 2017). The news is rarely flattering for educators. In fact, as Bracey (2007) has observed, the news about the failure of American public schools is dominated by fear mongers. News of the accomplishments of special educators is even less often positive than for general educators. Even some of those identified as special educators portray it as, at best, unhelpful (e.g., Brantlinger, 2006; Harry & Klingner, 2006, 2007). Probably, neither general education nor special education is the abject failure that is portrayed by some (see Hallahan, Kauffman, & Pullen, 2015; Kauffman, 2009; Kauffman & Hallahan, 2005b).

Regardless of their failures and successes, the improvement of both general and special education is of course highly desirable. Several very strong instructional technologies clearly could lead to higher student achievement and improved conduct for students with EBD (see Berkeley & Riccomini, 2017; Kauffman & Landrum, 2007; Landrum & Kauffman, 2006; Lane, 2004; Lane, Barton-Arwood, Rogers, & Robertson, 2007; Lane, Menzies, Bruhn, &

Crnobori, 2011; Morris & Mather, 2008; Walker & Sprague, 2007). Selecting the proper instructional tool for the job requires a clear determination of the instructional needs of individual students.

Most students with EBD present several instructional problems. It's sometimes easier to identify the problems facing a given student than to prioritize them to decide which will receive intervention. One reason for the difficulty in prioritizing intervention is that different teachers, schools, and communities put higher values on certain aspects of educational programming than they do on others (Zigmond, 2003, 2007).

Schools vary widely from one community to another, but they nevertheless command the endorsement of their constituents. For example, some schools stress creativity and expression, whereas others stress basic skills or demanding academic curricula. It shouldn't be surprising that test manufacturers have responded to the various niches created by these school models. Consequently, the sheer number of tests available is overwhelming. Worse, the claims regarding many of the tests on the market are, to be kind, overstated. Teachers are often told that a certain test can identify not only specific educational needs but also the precise methods by which a given student should be taught. Let us be clear: As of 2017, any credible evidence for such a claim simply doesn't exist.

Rather than looking for a test that will provide guidance about how to teach a given student, the teacher must approach instructional decision making as a scientific problem-solving task. Typically, the first step in any problem-solving task is to define the problem. Behavioral issues are usually defined as excesses or deficits in particular skills or classes of behavior. Academic achievement problems exist primarily as deficits in skills, the ability to use the skills, the individual's fund of general information, or some manifestation of one or more of these difficulties.

It's also a very good idea to consider the academic strengths of a given student. Part of the process of defining the problem is collecting evidence to validate the decisions that are being made. All of the procedures that are used to generate evidence regarding the nature and extent of the problem, finding its possible causes and exacerbating factors, designing methods for changing it, and monitoring the outcome are considered to be assessments.

Tests are one form of assessment, but assessment of individuals with EBD can include many more tools (see Berkeley & Riccomini, 2017). For example, observations of the student's behavior in different settings and contexts should be included. Often interviews of the target student, members of the student's peer group, family, and teachers lead to insights unavailable through other means (Orvaschel, 2006; Sharp, Reeves, & Gross, 2006).

Many assessment techniques are available to educators of students with EBD. To ensure that a complete picture of the student's educational needs is developed, teachers should carefully consider the evidence they require and select a variety of tools to collect and cross-check their data. This type of evaluation is an ongoing process that is an integral part of teaching and intervention.

As we discussed earlier, the focus of initial evaluation for eligibility is clearly a yes-or-no decision for special education and related services, whereas the primary concerns of ongoing evaluation are designing interventions and measuring progress. Evaluation for eligibility must be multidisciplinary, with an emphasis on ruling out as many causes of the problem as possible. Evaluation for instruction or other intervention, by contrast, focuses more on the teacher's assessment of the student's classroom behavior and school performance and what can be done to improve them.

EVALUATION FOR INSTRUCTION AND OTHER INTERVENTIONS

Adequate evaluation for the purpose of intervention requires careful attention to a wide range of factors that may be important in the origins and modification of problem behavior or academic deficits. Many educators consider the evaluation process to be synonymous with testing. However, testing is usually considered to be focused on the demonstration of a single behavior or skill under controlled circumstances, whereas assessment and evaluation are broader collections of techniques for collecting evidence to support decision making. All tests are assessments, but because assessment can include activities such as interviews, work samples, and observations of student behavior, not all assessments are tests. Whenever possible, information must be obtained from parents, teachers, peers, the student, and impartial observers.

Evaluation for special education interventions also requires focusing on the student's problems as they are manifested in school, meaning that assessment must focus on the skills and behaviors students need to be successful in school settings. Procedures for evaluating referred students should include at least standardized tests of intelligence and achievement, behavior ratings, assessment of peer relations, interviews, self-reports, and direct observations (Landrum, 2000, 2017), and we consider each briefly in subsequent sections. An important approach to evaluation that offers particular benefit to monitoring the effects of instruction is curriculum-based assessment (CBA; Espin, McMaster, Rose, & Wayman, 2012; Hosp, Hosp, & Howell, 2016). CBA may also be applied to social skills.

With regard to problem behavior specifically, a critical evaluation question to answer is this: What purpose or function does a particular behavior serve in the student's life? A **functional behavioral assessment** (FBA) is an approach to assessment designed to answer this question (Fox & Gable, 2004; McConnell, Cox, Thomas, & Hilvitz, 2001; O'Neill et al., 1997). The function of behavior is the critical issue to be addressed in an evaluation, and a well-designed functional behavioral assessment may draw on all of the types of assessment information we discuss in this section.

Finally, we might approach the assessment of behavior much the same as we do the assessment of academic skills. Social–emotional behavior can be analyzed as an instructional problem: How can we teach the student a better way of behaving? A clear focus on teaching helps educators tie assessment directly to instruction, prevent misbehavior from occurring, and keep a focus on a positive plan for intervention. Ultimately, the goal of assessment should be *precorrection*—guiding the student away from misbehavior and toward the desired response through skillful, carefully planned instruction linked directly to assessment (Colvin, Sugai, & Patching, 1993; Kauffman, Pullen et al., 2011; Walker et al., 2004).

Standardized, Norm-Referenced Tests of Intelligence and Achievement

Some assessments used with students with EBD will be standardized, **norm-referenced** assessments. In assessment, standardization means simply that the measure or procedure is carried out the same way with each individual with whom it's used. Standardization is necessary if we are to compare the results of one student's assessment to other students or to compare the results of a given assessment procedure on the same student from one administration to another.

Norm referencing refers to the way meaning is assigned to the scores a test yields. In a norm-referenced test, the student's performance is evaluated by the extent to which it's different from the mean score of the norm group for the test. Intelligence tests and most commercially available achievement tests are norm-referenced; the test manuals accompanying these tests contain tables of data indicating what the norms are for test-takers of various ages and grade levels. Better assessments will generally provide details as well on the composition of the normative group in terms of gender, ethnicity, and socioeconomic status. For many classroom tests, however, a national norm may not be particularly relevant; rather than compare an individual or group of students from a given classroom with national averages, it may be more important to compare results to last year's students, to all students in the same school or district, or even to scores from this same group earlier in the school year. In some cases, a norm isn't needed at all, as the only question a teacher is asking is whether a particular content or set of skills has been mastered (e.g., all the letters of the alphabet, multiplication facts, or the parts of an atom). In such cases, teachers may use a **criterion-referenced test**—one in which an individual's score is compared to some preset criterion for passing. In a criterion-referenced test, the number or percentage of items for which an individual provided the desired responses is important (e.g., 90 percent). In a norm-referenced test, the number of desired responses provided by an individual is important, but only relative to the number of desired responses provided by the comparison group for the student (e.g., a student may score at the 50th percentile, meaning that her score was the same or better than 50 percent of all students in the normative sample for the test or another comparison group). To be useful, comparison groups, or norm groups, must be composed of individuals who are like the test taker in some important and task-relevant way. Age and grade level are often used for academic and intellectual measures. For some measures, the gender, language, or culture of the participant may be important.

Whenever a teacher uses information from a norm-referenced measure, the extent to which the norm group is reasonable for making comparisons in evaluating a given student should be considered. If the reading abilities of young children were compared to older children, they probably wouldn't fare well. Conversely, students who have been retained and have repeated a given grade may benefit from that additional year of instruction, and they presumably would fare better than their classmates who had only one year of instruction. The point is simply that in order to make a meaningful comparison of students' reading performance to some other group, the comparison group should be composed of individuals at the same age or grade level who have been exposed to similar amounts of reading instruction. Whatever the case, specification of the comparison or norm group is necessary to properly interpret any scores on a norm-referenced test. A relatively recent development in this regard is the argument that cultural norms for different ethnic groups should be considered when evaluating an individual's behavior or performance. In addition, some researchers point to differences in the cognitive development of males and females at different points in their education. Selecting norm groups of only members of certain ethnicities or one gender may have advantages under some conditions but may also exacerbate perceptions of differences based on superficial characteristics alone.

With attention to issues regarding the comparability of norm groups, standardized tests can be used to estimate what a student has learned and to compare his or her performance to the norms of age-mates. They can provide a description of current abilities and point to general areas in need of instruction. A test of intelligence provides evidence of a student's learning in general skill areas that are predictive of performance in schooling; a test of academic achievement taps more specific skills. Neither type of test, however, provides much information about just what a student should be taught.

There are good reasons for using standardized intelligence and achievement tests (see Fuchs & Young, 2006; Kauffman, 2010c, 2011; Lindstrom, 2017). It's helpful, for example, to know how a student's progress in learning skills compares to other students' progress in a national sample. However, one must take care to avoid a number of potentially serious pitfalls, which include a) failure to consider the margin of error in the scores students achieve at a given testing, b) the limited ability of some measures to detect changes in scores over time or after instruction, c) failure to consider the match between an achievement test and the instructional expectations of a particular student's class, and d) failure of the scores to predict important outcomes.

As we mentioned earlier in this chapter, the results of any measure are composed of at least two parts: the true ability we are attempting to measure (resulting in a hypothetical true score) and measurement error. We describe the average error in a measure using the **standard error of measurement** (or SEM). When educators are considering whether scores represent meaningful growth (e.g., tests administered at the beginning and again at the end of the year), they must examine the extent to which the difference between scores exceeds the SEM. For example, if a given test has an SEM of ± 3, there is a good chance that a change of only three points in a student's score or a large group's average score at a subsequent testing may be due to measurement error and not actual improvement or deterioration in performance.

Measures used to evaluate student performance vary in their ability to detect changes in scores over time or after instruction. Norm-referenced tests often can't detect small changes in student behavior because such tests are purposefully designed to be general enough to be used across the entire nation. Consequently, variations in curriculum, activities, and teacher background tend to be averaged out of the test. In addition, norm-referenced, standardized measures usually cover a very large age span so that there are too few items on any scale (i.e., there may be only a few items for a given area of content for a given age or grade level) to accurately and reliably detect small changes in student performance. In contrast, because they include a larger sample of content of a particular domain at a specific level, classroom tests and curriculum-based measurement of student performance can help guide instruction and provide students with feedback about their progress far better than can standardized, norm-referenced tests, which are better suited to detecting larger changes in behavior across long time periods (Brigham, Tochterman, & Brigham, 2001).

Failure to consider the match between an achievement test and the instructional expectations of a particular student's class can lead to senseless interpretation of test results. Although general curriculum standards have been established in most states (and a move toward a national curriculum, or at least toward a common core of standards, has gained considerable traction in recent years), variability exists among teachers of the same course, the same content, and the same grade level, even within the same school. Teachers who want measures that reflect their own instruction should use curriculum-based measurement rather than norm-referenced, standardized tests. To be meaningful, measurement of the effects of instruction obviously must be tailored directly to actual instruction (e.g., Fuchs & Fuchs, 2011).

One of the largest problems in educational measurement is the failure of scores to predict important outcomes. For example, an IQ derived from a standardized test isn't a measure of intellectual potential, nor is it static or immutable; it's merely a measure of general learning in certain areas compared to the learning of other students of the same age who formed the normative sample. An IQ is only a moderately accurate predictor of what a student is likely to learn in the future if no special intervention is provided. Remember, too, that a student's performance on a given test on a given day can be influenced by many factors. Even under the best conditions, the score is an estimate of a range in which the student's true score is likely to fall.

Awareness of the pitfalls associated with standardized testing is particularly important in evaluating students with EBD. These disorders tend to interfere with learning and academic performance during both instruction and testing. Consequently, students with such disorders are likely to perform below their true abilities on standardized tests. As a group, they tend to score lower than average on intelligence and achievement tests. Careful evaluation of their abilities is warranted, therefore, to avoid mistakes in setting expectations for their performance.

Objections to well-known intelligence and achievement tests, as well as to other standardized measures, are often based on criticism of the inappropriate use and interpretation of test scores. Note that these criticisms are centered on uninformed or unprofessional assessment procedures on the part of educators rather than on the tests themselves; such misuse or misinterpretation can, of course, ruin the value of any evaluation procedure. The benefits and limitations of standardized and normative testing have been discussed in detail (see Salvia, Ysseldyke, & Witmer, 2012; Taylor, 2009). To summarize, despite their limitations, standardized tests of intelligence and achievement, used with appropriate caution, can be helpful in assessing important areas of strength, weakness, and progress in students with EBD (Kauffman, 2010c, 2011; Kauffman & Hallahan, 2005b; Kauffman & Konold, 2007).

Behavior Ratings

Behavior rating scales are commonly used in the evaluation of EBD and developing educational programs for students with EBD (Jones, Dohrn, & Dunn, 2004). Sometimes several individuals (parents and teachers, for instance) complete rating scales, and then the ranges are compared to assess the level of agreement about the student's behavior. When aggregated, ratings by several individuals also reduce the possibility of bias. In fact, one should be very wary of making judgments based on the ratings of a single observer, be it parent or teacher. As Pierangelo and Giuliani (2006) commented, "By getting various viewpoints, a more comprehensive evaluation of the child's daily functioning can be established" (p. 193) (see also Konold & Pianta, 2007). The scores obtained on rating scales can be compared to norms that are helpful in judging whether behavior demands intervention and in describing or classifying the types of problems a child or youth exhibits (Gresham, 2015); we discuss classification further at the end of this chapter.

In addition to their usefulness for description and classification, rating scales can be administered repeatedly and the scores used to evaluate progress in reaching intervention goals. However, behavior ratings aren't adequate for pinpointing specific behaviors as targets for change, something for which direct observation is required (Alberto & Troutman, 2017).

Rating scales are subject to the same dangers of misuse and misinterpretation as any other standardized assessment instrument regarding reliability, validity, inappropriate application, and bias (cf. Pierangelo & Giuliani, 2006; Reitman, Hummek, Franz, & Gross, 1998). Another possible misuse is to ask teachers or others who aren't sufficiently acquainted with a student to complete a behavior rating scale.

Direct Observation and Measurement

A large body of behavioral research supports the commonsense practice of observing students in the environments in which problems are reported (Alberto & Troutman, 2017; Greenwood, Carta, & Dawson, 2000; Kerr & Nelson, 2010). Direct observation means that an observer (e.g., teacher, psychologist, parent) sees the behavior as it occurs; direct measurement means that the occurrence of the behavior is recorded immediately. Thus, direct observation and measurement yield information on the frequency, rate, percentage of opportunities, and so on, with which a behavior occurs, rather than a rating.

Behavior observations have the benefit of sensitivity to small changes in behavior (Alberto & Troutman, 2017; Gresham, 2015; Walker et al., 2004). Thus, improvements or deteriorations in a student's behavioral functioning may be detected earlier by observational methods than by rating scales.

Direct observation and measurement involve not only recording the behavior of the student in question but also selecting a) the setting(s) or context(s) in which behavior will be measured, b) a systematic method of observing and recording, c) procedures designed to ensure reliability of observation, and d) means of accumulating, displaying, and interpreting the data. In addition to observation of the behavior itself, the immediate antecedents (what happens just before) and consequences (what happens just after) are typically observed and recorded in an initial assessment. The reason for recording antecedents and consequences is that these are often conditions or events that help to explain why the behavior occurs and that, if altered, may change the behavior (see Kauffman, Pullen et al., 2011).

An extensive technology of direct observation and measurement has been developed, much of which is directly applicable to teaching. However, observation and measurement systems can become very complex and costly, resulting in their being used only by specialists. Keeping observation and recording systems simple and inexpensive enough to be used in everyday teaching practice is a major goal. Such teacher-friendly systems are readily available for use in classroom intervention (see Alberto & Troutman, 2017; Kauffman, Pullen et al., 2011; Kerr & Nelson, 2010). Moreover, the use of computer-assisted observation systems (e.g., Tapp, Wehby, & Ellis, 1995) has evolved into tablet, smartphone, or other handheld-based observation tools that allow for highly accurate recording and summarizing of events that are critical to understanding behavior in classroom settings (e.g., Lewis, Scott, Wehby, & Wills, 2014).

An emerging approach, sometimes described as a hybrid or combination of direct observation and rating scale, is known as direct behavior rating, or DBR (Chafouleas, 2011; Volpe & Briesch, 2012). In such systems, a teacher rates a child's performance on a single item, or very small number of items following a short period of time. For example, a teacher may complete a daily card on which she marks 1, 2, or 3 to indicate a student's level of engagement (or absence of disruptions) during math class.

Direct observation is a particularly important approach to evaluating disorders that involve externalizing problems—those in which the student strikes out at and disturbs others. Regardless of the type of behavior involved, direct observation can address questions like these:

- In what settings (home, school, math class, or playground) is the problem behavior or behavioral deficit exhibited?
- With what frequency, duration, or force does the behavior occur in various settings?
- What happens immediately before the behavior occurs? What seems to set the occasion for it?
- What happens immediately after the behavior occurs that may serve to strengthen or weaken it?
- What other inappropriate responses are observed?
- What appropriate behavior could be taught or strengthened to lessen the problem?
- What does the student's behavior communicate to others?

Direct observation requires careful definition of observable target behaviors and frequent (usually daily) recording of occurrence. Some interventions and evaluation procedures depend on this methodology. A behavioral approach to teaching makes direct observation a central feature of intervention. Curriculum-based assessment depends on direct observation and recording of academic and social behavior, and direct observation is a required part of functional analysis. Direct observation is also an important aspect of many interventions derived from a social-cognitive model. Thus, of all the alternative means of evaluation for intervention, direct observation and measurement of behavior is perhaps the most central in importance (see Landrum & Kauffman, 2006).

Interviews

Interviews vary widely in structure and purpose. They can be freewheeling conversations or can follow a prescribed line of questioning for obtaining information about specific behaviors or developmental milestones (Orvaschel, 2006; Sharp et al., 2006). They can be conducted with verbal children as well as with adults, including school staff, parents, and others who may have contact with the target student (Scott, Liaupsin, Nelson, & Jolivette, 2003). They may be designed to assess a wide range of problems or to assess particular types of disorders such as depression or anxiety (Hodges & Zeman, 1993; Pierangelo & Giuliani, 2006; Taylor, 2009) or to help discriminate among skill acquisition, performance, and fluency deficits (Gresham, 2015). As we discuss in a later section, teacher interviews (and sometimes interviews with other relevant staff and parents, depending on the nature and context of a given behavioral concern) are a typical part of the process of functional behavioral assessment (FBA) (e.g., Hagan-Burke, Gilmour, Gerow, & Crowder, 2015).

Skillful interviewing is no simple matter. When troublesome behavior is the focus of the interview, it's common for the interviewee to become defensive. Differences in the cultural backgrounds of the interviewer and interviewee may foster miscommunication, and an interview in which answers represent half-truths, misleading information, avoidance, or misunderstandings won't be much help in evaluation. Furthermore, one must maintain a healthy skepticism about the accuracy of interview responses that require memory of long-past events.

It's also important to weigh carefully the interviewees' subjective opinions, especially when their responses are emotionally charged or seriously discrepant from other subjective reports or objective evidence. Finally, extracting and accurately recording the most relevant information from an interview requires keen judgment and excellent communication skills (Orvaschel, 2006).

Interviews should help the evaluator get an impression of how the student and significant others interact and feel about each other. They should also help members of the evaluation team decide what additional types of information they need. But interviews can accomplish these ends only to the extent that the interviewer has great interpersonal skills, the experience and sensitivity to make sound clinical judgments, and the ability to focus on information about the relevant behavior and its social contexts.

Descriptions of behavior, competencies, environmental conditions, and consequences obtained from interviews may be helpful but are often inaccurate and can't be relied on without verification from other sources. It's important to note discrepancies between reports given to interviewers and information obtained from direct observation because those discrepancies can sometimes be crucial in designing interventions. If, for example, teachers or parents report that they frequently praise appropriate behavior and ignore misconduct but direct observation shows the opposite, then the adults' misperceptions must be taken into account in designing an intervention plan.

Assessment of Peer Relations

Interaction with and acceptance by one's peer group are necessary for normal social development. Students with EBD often don't develop normal peer relations (Landrum, 2017; Walker et al., 2004). Some are socially withdrawn and maintain a low profile with their classmates by avoiding peer interaction. Others are aggressive toward peers. A disruptive influence in any group activity, they maintain a high profile with their classmates, though the attention they receive isn't positive; their peers often actively reject them (LeBlanc, Sautter, & Dore, 2006).

Researchers have noted that students with conduct problems may in fact have friendships, but the peers they affiliate with tend to be other deviant students (Card & Hodges, 2006; Estell, Farmer, Irvin, Crowther, Akos, & Boudah, 2009; Gest, Farmer, Cairns, & Xie, 2003; Olthof & Goossens, 2008; Parker, Rubin, Erath, Wojslawowicz, & Buskirk, 2006; Rubin, Coplan, & Bowker, 2009). In any case, a significant number of students with EBD often end up alone because they do not have the necessary social skills for the positive reciprocal exchanges that characterize friendships, or they only develop friendships with others who are a negative influence.

Assessment of peer relations is a critical aspect of research and practice, including the identification of subtypes of disorders, determining social status, selecting students for social skills training, judging the outcomes of intervention, and predicting long-term outcomes (Gresham, Robichaux, York, & O'Leary, 2012; Lane, Menzies, Oakes, & Germer, 2014). Peer relations may be evaluated by a variety of methods. Some screening instruments include rating scales that are completed by peers; some include sociometric questions for assessing acceptance or rejection among peers or patterns of peer affiliation. Sometimes interviews regarding social relationships are also employed. Sociometric techniques aren't necessarily part of a screening procedure but are often used in research and evaluation in which peer relations are a central concern (Mpofu, Carney, & Lambert, 2006). Direct observation is sometimes used to measure how often the student makes social initiations or responds appropriately to peers' initiations. Brown, Odom, and Buysse (2002) observed that differing methods of assessment of peer relations often provide different results. Consequently, they suggested that multiple strategies be used when assessing peer relations.

Self-Reports

Self-reports typically require students to respond to checklists, rating scales, or interviews in which they describe their behavior or feelings. How students perceive themselves and how they respond emotionally to various circumstances is an important part of the assessment. Self-reports are particularly important when evaluating disorders such as substance abuse, anxiety, fears, and depression—disorders that involve high levels of affect and often aren't open to direct observation. However, self-reports are of limited value for youngsters who are nonverbal or unable to organize their responses coherently. In addition, self-reports are susceptible to intentional over- or underreporting for a number of reasons, including the tendency of students to tell examiners what they think examiners want to know, or the desire to present themselves in a particular light. Therefore, self-report data should be corroborated by other sources of data.

Some behavior rating scales include self-reports, along with ratings by teachers and parents (e.g., *Behavior Assessment System for Children* (BASC-3), Reynolds & Kamphaus, 2015), and may yield scores on multiple dimensions of behavior. Other self-report scales are designed to tap particular self-perception, affective, or behavioral domains such as self-concept, loneliness, alcohol use, depression, and so on. Like all other assessment strategies, self-reports must be interpreted with caution regarding their reliability and validity, and always in the context of other sources of information.

Curriculum-Based Evaluation

An evaluation methodology involving frequent, direct measurement of students' performance using their typical curriculum materials emerged in the mid-1980s (Deno, 2003; Howell & Hyatt, 2004). It has been called *curriculum-based measurement* (CBM), *curriculum-based assessment* (CBA), and *curriculum-based evaluation* (Howell, Fox, & Morehead, 1993; Howell & Hyatt, 2004; Shapiro & Keller, 2006; see also Berkeley & Riccomini, 2017). More commonly, these constructs may be referred to generically as progress-monitoring, and as Shinn (2014) noted, frequent progress monitoring by whatever name is among the powerful tools teachers have to support the academic progress of students with EBD.

There are several key differences between CBA and the traditional forms of norm-referenced testing described earlier in this chapter (Deno, 2003). Most important is that in CBA the curriculum materials relevant to the assessed student are used as the sample from which test items are drawn. In traditional testing, items are constructed to create a general representation of the curriculum. However, the purpose of most norm-referenced procedures is to rank individuals relative to a group. Therefore, items in norm-referenced tests are selected for their ability to spread the performance of individuals out rather than to tap actual curricular goals. CBA, in contrast, tracks differences in progress within the individual rather than between individuals.

Curriculum-based assessment is a general term used to refer to any information-gathering procedure that obtains information about student performance in the curriculum. *Curriculum-based measurement* (CBM) is a specialized set of procedures within CBA that is used to measure student growth in basic skills (Deno, 2003; Hosp, Hosp, & Howell, 2007).

Curriculum-based measurements are typically short, frequently administered measures of performance on a single task (e.g., math, reading, writing, spelling). Because the measures are repeated, it is important that the tasks selected are appropriate for repeated measure. Tasks that require extended practice are usually the best candidates for repeated measures. Reading fluency and arithmetic computations are two such skills (see Berkeley & Riccomini, 2017; O'Connor, Sanchez, & Kimm, 2017). In secondary content classes, measures of content-related vocabulary have proven to be valid and reliable indicators of progress (Busch & Espin, 2003). Individual students' performances are compared to those of others in the same school using the same curriculum. For example, students might be asked to read aloud for one minute from a passage in their usual reader, perhaps three times per week. Their reading rates (words read correctly per minute, errors per minute, or both) are then recorded. To evaluate written language, students might be asked to provide a three-minute sample of their writing in response to a topic sentence. Math performance might be evaluated by asking students to complete as many computation problems as they can in two minutes, with the problems taken from their basal text. The results of these assessments are displayed on a graph, and progress is compared to a line of expected progress called an aim line. See Figure 15.1 for an example of a CBM chart. Teachers can intervene by altering the educational program when a student's performance falls below the aim line for a specified number of observations (usually three or four). Note that the aim line (dashed line) in Figure 15.1 is ascending from left to right. In this case, the goal is to increase the target behavior, and data points below the aim line indicate problematic performance. If the goal was to decrease the target behavior, the aim line would

Figure 15.1   Sample Curriculum-Based Measurement Graph

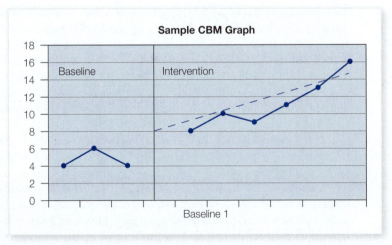

descend across the graph, and problematic performance would result in student data points above the aim line.

Many teachers are resistant to using CBM in their classrooms (Deno, 2003). Sometimes, teachers resist CBM because they believe that the focus on discrete units of measure (e.g., accuracy in oral reading) is somehow an illegitimate measure of progress. A great deal of accumulated research suggests that this fear is unfounded. According to one of the most comprehensive reviews of research on formative evaluation (another term for progress monitoring), frequent progress monitoring provides among the most powerful effects teachers can have on students' academic success (Hattie, 2008). This confirms an earlier analysis by Forness, Kavale, Blum, and Lloyd (1997). Other teachers express reluctance to use CBM because it is quite different from the measurement systems with which they are familiar. This reluctance is truly unfortunate because IEPs developed from CBM data are far more likely to be legally correct and beneficial to the students with disabilities for whom they are designed (Berkeley & Riccomini, 2017; Yell & Stecker, 2003).

Curriculum-based evaluation is important because most students who receive special education because of EBD have academic deficits (see Kauffman & Brigham, 2009; Kerr & Nelson, 2010; Landrum, 2017). Furthermore, proponents of curriculum-based methods include social skills among measurable performances (Howell & Hyatt, 2004; Kauffman et al., 2012). A student's and his or her classmates' specific behavioral problems or social skills (such as hitting classmates, making derogatory comments about self, making positive social initiations, and taking turns) can be recorded systematically for comparison. If the student's behavior is significantly different from that of other students, then he or she may be identified as needing a special teaching procedure to change the targeted behavior, and the results can be evaluated by noting changes in the student's behavior compared to the peer group.

The significant difference between this kind of curriculum-based evaluation and direct observation is this: A curriculum-based approach assumes that the school is using a coherent social skills curriculum—that is, that social skills are being taught systematically. Unfortunately, social skills curricula are not yet well developed, and many schools have not implemented existing curricula (Walker et al., 2004).

MANIFESTATION DETERMINATION

Manifestation determination assessment procedures are intended to ascertain whether or not a student's misbehavior and disability are related, which may be necessary when considering potential disciplinary action for students with EBD. This is often a very difficult task. Nevertheless, a manifestation determination (MD) is required when disciplinary procedures used by school officials result in a change in the student's placement or result in suspension from school for more than ten consecutive days or expulsion from school.

Yell (2016) and Yell and Drasgow (2000) discussed the importance of manifestation determination, and suggested that MD assessments should include a) examinations of school records to establish the student's educational history; b) interviews of parents, teachers, the target student, and other students; and c) observations of the student's behavior in different contexts (e.g., playground, different classrooms or classroom activities, cafeteria). Parents may also submit assessment data (e.g., evaluations by a private psychologist or a physician) to the

MD team. After collecting relevant data, the team must first determine whether or not the student's IEP was appropriate relative to the behavior of concern. That is, they must determine whether the behavior was adequately addressed in the IEP if the behavior had been noted as an aspect of the student's disability. If the IEP is appropriate, the team must then determine whether services are being provided in accordance with the IEP. If the answer to either of these questions is no, the team must redesign the IEP and institute services to prevent future episodes of the behavior. In such a case, the MD action ends because the behavior and disability are considered to be related by virtue of the inappropriate IEP or the failure to enact its services. If the answer to either of these questions is yes, the MD team must then consider whether or not the student's disability impaired his or her ability to a) understand the consequences of the action and b) control the target behavior. If the behavior is determined to be related to the disability, schools are required to address the behavior through the IEP rather than simply punishing it.

FUNCTIONAL BEHAVIORAL ASSESSMENT

Since at least the early 1990s, emphasis was placed on analyzing the *function* of students' behavior (Cipani, 1999; O'Neill et al., 1997). A functional behavioral assessment (FBA) is a systematic process of obtaining and analyzing assessment data to better understand what may be causing problem behavior in the first place, and what may be maintaining that behavior. The objective is not merely to better understand the nature and causes of problem behavior; rather, with these assessment data, educators should be able to develop more effective and positive interventions. The goal of an FBA is to improve the effectiveness and efficiency of behavioral supports for students by linking intervention directly to the function of the behavior (Sugai, Horner, & Gresham, 2002). Martens and Lambert (2014) described FBA as a set of procedures that help identify a) what might be maintaining (reinforcing) a given problem behavior, b) what elements in the environment currently serve to prompt the student to engage in problem behavior, c) whether the student is presently capable of engaging in a more appropriate alternative behavior to earn the same reinforcer, and d) what reinforcers might be preferred and useful for encouraging the replacement behavior.

The requirement for schools to conduct FBAs and develop positive behavior intervention plans for students with disabilities who display problem behavior was included in IDEA amendments of 1997. Although the promotion of functional analysis of behavior was generally welcomed, some wondered whether the professional capacity in schools was adequate to meet this demand on a widespread basis (e.g., Sasso, Conroy, Stichter, & Fox, 2001), especially given that FBAs can be complex and time-consuming (Alberto & Troutman, 2017; Kerr & Nelson, 2010).

The purposes of an FBA are straightforward, but the implementation in schools has been somewhat controversial (Fox & Gable, 2004; Sasso, Conroy, Stichter, & Fox, 2001). The 1997 amendments to IDEA included the requirement that schools conduct an FBA for students with disabilities whose behavior impacted their own or others' learning. This was welcomed by many professionals and advocates, but some questioned whether schools were adequately staffed and trained to implement these FBA requirements (Sasso et al., 2001). The way in which a functional assessment is conducted is not mysterious, but, done well, it is time-consuming and requires knowledge of a variety of assessment strategies (Alberto & Troutman, 2017; Kerr & Nelson, 2010). It usually begins with a structured teacher interview (or self-interview) in which the objective is to clarify the nature of the problem behavior (including its form, frequency, duration, and intensity) and the contexts (e.g., time, situations) in which it tends to occur. The responses of others to the student's behavior are assessed, including the responses of peers, teachers, and parents. The student's behavior is tracked throughout the day to see how, when, and where it occurs and what consequences it produces—what it gets for the student and what it allows the student to avoid. Then, in the light of all the assessment data, the teacher forms a hypothesis about why the behavior is occurring and what might be altered to resolve the problem.

An FBA may be more difficult for older students, those with greater cognitive abilities, and those students with more complex social–emotional problems. Sometimes it's very difficult to find an activity that the student prefers but is consistent with program goals. However, functional analyses provide the basis for arranging classroom conditions and instructional procedures that give students maximum freedom and self-control while resolving their behavior problems. Knowing the function served by a certain behavior can also increase the empathy of teachers toward their students (Rao, Hoyer, Meehan, Young, & Guerrera, 2003), but it's of little other use unless it leads to a behavioral intervention plan based on the function (Scott et al., 2003).

Positive Behavior Intervention Plan

By law (the IDEA), if a disabled student's behavior is interfering with his or her educational progress, then the IEP team must write a positive *behavior intervention plan* (BIP) as part of the IEP, and the BIP must be based on an FBA of the problem (see Bateman & Linden, 2012; Yell, 2016; Yell, Bradley, & Shriner, 1999). A positive BIP is one that is focused clearly on conditions that maximize the likelihood that the student will exhibit the desired, appropriate behavior rather than on eliminating behavioral problems. Behavioral problems may of course be reduced or eliminated in the process, but that desirable outcome is achieved indirectly through encouragement of desirable behavior.

Assessment as an Instructional Problem: Precorrection as a Positive BIP

Teachers often forget that the most effective strategies for teaching academic skills can be applied to teaching appropriate social–emotional behavior. Whether the instructional problem is academic or social–emotional, taking careful note of the situations or contexts in which a particular mistake is most likely to occur is the first step in resolving the problem. Having noted the likely context of a typical error, the teacher may then modify the context to make the error less likely to occur. Other techniques for decreasing the chances that the student will make an error include helping the student rehearse (practice) the correct response, reinforcing (rewarding) correct responses, prompting (reminding or assisting) the student to give the correct response when necessary, and monitoring the student's progress. This approach—combining assessment with proactive teaching strategies—may be used to prevent much misbehavior. Therefore, Colvin, Sugai, and Patching (1993) used the term *precorrection* to describe strategies for avoiding the need to correct behavior. Precorrection generally involves at least these steps: a) identifying the contexts that typically result in problem behaviors, b) defining desired alternative responses—replacement behaviors—that can replace anticipated problem behavior, c) reviewing the expected positive behaviors *before* the student encounters the problem context, d) prompting the student to engage in the desired behaviors in the problem context, and e) reinforcing the positive behaviors when they are observed (see Ennis, Schwab, & Jolivette, 2012; Hayden & Kroeger, 2016).

A simple example of precorrection described by Stetter (1995) may clarify the concept and procedures of precorrection. Stetter observed that second-grade students identified as at-risk frequently forgot necessary items (e.g., eating utensils, napkins) when going through the cafeteria serving line. Consequently, they often left the lunch table, returning to the serving line to retrieve these items. This may seem an insignificant matter to those uninitiated into teaching students who are at high risk of school failure. However, the experienced teacher knows that more serious problems often grow around such mundane, seemingly trivial behavior. Leaving one's place and food at the lunch table, returning to (and, likely, butting into) the serving line, and coming back to the table are events rife with possibilities for conflict (e.g., pushing, accusations, verbal confrontations, tussles that may escalate to more serious antisocial conduct). Stetter's approach to assessment focused on the question, How can I teach the desired behavior? rather than, How can I put a stop to the problem behavior? Her observations indicated that students tended to forget items in the context of preparing to leave the classroom for lunch and entering the cafeteria line; therefore, she decided to work on teaching students to remember all necessary items while going through the line so that they would not need to return. Her teaching procedures were straightforward:

- *Emphasize the expected behavior.* Remember all needed items while in the serving line.
- *Modify the context.* In the classroom before leaving for lunch, list all items needed (milk, fork, napkin, straw, etc.).
- *Conduct behavioral rehearsal.* Ask students to repeat the list of needed items.
- *Provide strong reinforcement.* Give students rewards such as small candies, points, or extra recess time for remembering everything.
- *Prompt desired behavior just before performance.* Just before entering the cafeteria, provide the reminder, "Now, be sure to remember everything you need."
- *Monitor performance.* Keep count of the number of times students return to the serving line.

Stetter's (1995) assessment of the problem and her teaching procedures related to the assessment—her precorrection plan—resulted in an immediate and dramatic drop in the number of students returning to the serving line. During the ten school days before she implemented her precorrection plan, she observed six or seven returns daily; during the ten days following her implementation of the plan, she observed two returns on the first day and one or zero returns thereafter. Furthermore, after she implemented her precorrection plan, she observed her students engaging in prosocial behavior, such as sharing items appropriately or reminding each other not to forget items. The advantages were that she didn't need to "fuss" at children or correct them. Neither did she need to cajole or discourage their behavior. The children made their own choices, and very often they made the "right" choices. It was a positive experience for both the teacher and her students.

ADAPTATIONS FOR INCLUSION IN GENERAL EDUCATION ASSESSMENTS

During the 1990s, federal and state authorities became very concerned about the perceived general decline in student achievement, and such concern continues in the twenty-first century. This resulted in emphasis on "standards-based" reforms or creating standards of academic achievement measured by standardized tests. Reformers feel that teachers' expectations have been too low and that all students should be held to higher standards of performance. Although the expectation that all students, regardless of disability, will achieve the same level of proficiency is patently absurd (Kauffman, 2010c; Kauffman & Konold, 2007; Rothstein, Jacobsen, & Wilder, 2006; Thurlow & Quenemoen, 2017), the No Child Left Behind Act (NCLB) of 2001 wrote such nonsense into law. Common Core State Standards (CCSS) are the most recent example of the standards-driven movement, and these standards too carry the message that all students—including those with disabilities—are capable of achieving proficiency on grade-level skills and content. Even though the CCSS have been adopted by nearly all states, it remains to be seen how students with disabilities will fare with these standards, and what, if any, consequences will result for states, districts, schools, teachers, and students should students with disabilities fail to meet these new standards.

Because special education is an integral part of our system of public education and special educators place such heavy emphasis on participation in general education, students with disabilities are included in the quest for higher standards. The expectations are judged to be too low for students in special education; reformers conclude that students with disabilities should not only be expected to learn the general curriculum but also be expected to perform at a level comparable to that of students without disabilities on assessments of progress (see Kauffman, 2005). Moreover, reformers argue, no school or state should be allowed to avoid responsibility for demonstrating that its students with disabilities are making acceptable progress in the general education curriculum. Failure to teach students with disabilities the same things that are taught in general education has been interpreted to mean that the expectations for these students are lower, resulting in their low achievement and failure to make a successful transition to adult life (see Hallahan, Kauffman, & Pullen, 2015).

Actually, we have little information about how students with disabilities have been progressing compared to general norms or how education reforms might affect them. We have evidence that more students with disabilities are participating in statewide testing and that the states are improving in their ability to document the participation and performance of students with disabilities in such assessments (Thompson & Thurlow, 2001; see also Thurlow & Quenemoen, 2017). Many controversies have been generated by the standards-based reform movement:

- What should the standards be?
- How high should they be?
- In what areas of the curriculum should they be set?
- Who should set them?
- How should progress toward them be measured?
- What should be the consequences for students—and for schools or states—if standards are not met?

For students with disabilities, additional questions arise:

- Should all standards apply to all students, regardless of their disability?
- Should state or district standards in age-appropriate academic disciplines take precedence over remedial or vocational education or education in self-care?
- What should be the consequences of failing to meet a given standard if the student has a disability?
- Under what circumstances are alternative standards appropriate?
- Under what circumstances should special accommodations be made in assessing progress toward a standard?

Answering questions like these requires professional judgment in the individual case (see Kauffman & Hallahan, 2005b).

The law recognizes that some students with disabilities have educational needs that are not addressed in the general education curriculum. However, each student's IEP must include a statement of measurable annual goals, including benchmarks or short-term objectives related to the following:

1. Meeting the child's needs that result from the child's disability to enable the child to be involved in and progress in the general curriculum

2. Meeting each of the child's other educational needs that result from the child's disability.

Thus, the IEP team for each child with a disability must make an individualized determination regarding how the child will participate in the general curriculum, and what, if any, educational needs that will not be met through involvement in the general curriculum should be addressed in the IEP. This includes children who are educated in separate classrooms or schools.

Accommodations for evaluation procedures might involve altering the time given for responding, changing the setting in which the assessment is done, or using an alternative format for either the presentation of tasks or the type of response required. Although such accommodations may make a significant difference in how students with some disabilities are able to perform on standardized tests, accommodations are often difficult to select and sometimes do not actually help students (e.g., Harrison, Bunford, Evans, & Owens, 2013; Kauffman, McGee, & Brigham, 2004; Lindstrom, 2017). Consider a student with problems maintaining on-task behavior for extended periods of time. For such a student, providing extended time to complete the test may actually be detrimental. A better approach might be to break the test up into smaller sections delivered at different times. Selection of appropriate test accommodations must always be based on the characteristics of the individual student and the nature and demands of the test (Kettler, 2012).

EVALUATION AND SOCIAL VALIDATION

Those who are responsible for assessing students must be concerned with the scientific or technical quality of their work, as well as the social validity of the outcomes. *Social validity* means that the clients (students, parents, and teachers) who are ostensibly being helped, as well as those who intervene, are convinced that a) a significant problem is being addressed, b) the intervention procedures are acceptable, and c) the outcome of intervention is satisfactory (cf. Luiselli & Reed, 2011). *Social validation* is the process of evaluating the clinical importance and personal, or social, meaningfulness of intervention. Social validation involves social comparison and subjective evaluation (i.e., comparison to peers who don't exhibit the disorder). It requires subjective judgments of specially trained or nonprofessional persons about the client's behavior.

To the extent that a student's behavior is markedly different from that of a valid comparison group before intervention but indistinguishable from the comparison group's behavior after intervention, social validity is established by social comparison. (This is consistent with curriculum-based methodology.) And to the extent that students and trained observers perceive that the quality of the student's behavior is unacceptable before intervention but markedly improved or desirable after intervention, social validity is indicated by subjective evaluation. Social validation is a particularly important issue for special educators as the lines between general and special education are blurred, and students with disabilities are increasingly educated in general education classrooms, and taught primarily by general education teachers.

USE OF EVALUATION DATA IN WRITING INDIVIDUAL EDUCATION PROGRAMS

Evaluation for special education carries legal as well as professional implications. Ultimately, evaluation data must be used to arrive at legitimate decisions about the student's identification, instruction, and placement. At the center of the federal law known as IDEA is the requirement that every student who has a disability and needs special education because of the disability will have a written individual education program (IEP) describing the appropriate education the student will receive (Bateman, 2017; Bateman & Linden, 2012; Huefner, 2006; Yell, 2016).

There has been much misunderstanding of the process of writing and using IEPs, and we cannot provide all the relevant information here (see Bateman, 2017; Bateman & Linden, 2012; Yell, 2016 for detailed discussion of IEPs). Writing IEPs demands not only knowledge of what an IEP is but also of the requirements regarding who writes the IEP and how the IEP team functions. Some of the basic questions about IEPs are answered in the following sections.

Notes on the IEP

An IEP is a written agreement between the parents and the school about what the student needs and what will be done to address those needs. It is, in effect, a contract specifying the services to be provided for the student, but not a contract to meet goals. By law, an IEP must include the following:

- The student's present levels of academic achievement and functional performance (sometimes denoted as the PLAAFP statement)
- Measurable annual goals for the student (note that the requirement for more specific short-term instructional objectives or benchmarks for annual goals was removed from the IDEA regulations in the 2004 reauthorization, though states may still require them)

- The special education and related services that will be provided
- The extent to which the student will participate in general state- or district-wide assessments of educational progress
- The extent to which the student will not participate in general classroom and school activities with nondisabled peers
- For students whose behavior impedes their learning or that of others, particularly if disciplinary action is contemplated, a positive behavior intervention plan (BIP) based on a functional behavioral assessment (FBA)
- For older students, specific plans for transition to work or further education
- Plans for starting the services and the anticipated duration of the services
- Appropriate plans for evaluating, at least annually, whether the objectives are being achieved

Who writes the IEP? For the student's first IEP, the law states that at least the following must be involved:

- The student's parent(s) or legal guardian
- The student's special education teacher
- The student's general education teacher(s)
- A representative of the public agency or school—other than the student's teacher—who is qualified to provide or supervise special education
- At least one person with the appropriate skills and knowledge needed to interpret assessment data
- The student, if appropriate

Teachers aren't legally liable for their students' reaching IEP goals. That is, federal law doesn't require that the stated goals be met. However, teachers and other school personnel are responsible for seeing that the IEP is written to include the required components, that the parents have an opportunity to review and participate in developing the IEP, that it's approved by the parents before placement, and that the services called for in it are actually provided. Teachers and other school personnel are responsible for making a good-faith effort to achieve the goals spelled out in the IEP.

All types of evaluation procedures may yield relevant information about a student's education. Several procedures are particularly important, however, for the IEPs of students with EBD. Although not every acceptable IEP includes them, direct observation, curriculum-based evaluation, and social validation procedures offer rich sources of information that should be the basis for instructional planning. Direct observational data allow the teacher to choose specific behavioral targets for intervention and to set quantitative goals and objectives for behavioral change. Curriculum-based procedures allow the teacher to be precise about academic goals and objectives in the student's everyday curriculum. A curriculum-based approach also encourages the teacher to select or devise a social skills curriculum, an essential area of learning for students with EBD. Both direct behavioral observation and curriculum-based evaluation encourage appropriate social comparisons and provide the basis for social validation. The legal mandates for involving a multidisciplinary team in the eligibility decision and encouraging parents to participate in development of the IEP require at least a minimal level of social validation.

IEPs differ greatly in format, level of detail, and conceptual orientation. This may be understandable, given the freedom of schools to choose their own formats, the slow progress toward a consensus on how to write so-called "standards-based" IEPs (see Caruana, 2015), the range of conceptual models in the field of EBD, and the differences in individual students' needs, as well as their parents' wishes and demands (see Bateman, 2017; Yell, 2016). However, according to Yell, Gatti, and Allday (2014), a legally correct and useful IEP should contain information that addresses at least these questions:

- What are the student's unique educational needs?
- What measurable goals would be associated with this individual student achieving meaningful educational benefit?
- What special education services will be provided to address each identified educational need?
- How will the student's progress in the instructional program be monitored?

It is often the case that teachers find writing IEP goals addressing academic performance to be easier to write, or at least more straightforward. Curriculum-based measures, and even standardized assessments, often provide clear indicators of current performance and allow for the establishment of clear goals (e.g., reading sixty correct words per minute in a fourth-grade text; solving two-digit multiplication problems with 90 percent accuracy). In contrast, establishing present levels of performance and establishing meaningful goals may prove more challenging.

A variety of publications offer help in writing IEPs (see Yell & Plotner, 2014). In our view, Bateman and Linden (2012) provide perhaps the most reliable and helpful guide. In their text, Bateman and Linden include specific examples of IEP development for students who display persistent challenging behavior. For example, one sample IEP in their text is for Curt, a student whose current performance in the social-behavioral realm includes ten to thirty instances per day of inappropriate talk or drawings about extremely violent acts or scenes. Services targeting this area of need then include a behavior contract, one hour weekly of targeted social skills instruction, and providing a space for Curt to display appropriate artwork in the classroom. Curt's goal in this example is to reach no instances of inappropriate talk or drawing about weapons, violence, or blood, with intermediate goals set at reaching no more than two instances per day within ten days, and no more than one instance per week within thirty days. Note that because the behavior occurs at such a high rate initially, intermediate goals are to *reduce* the behavior to more manageable levels, even though the ultimate goal is to reach zero instances.

The full sample IEPs for Curt and other students provided by Bateman and Linden (2012) include characteristics and instructional strategies for academic as well as behavioral problems, and while these are not perfect examples, they are excellent resources for teachers. They provide sample IEPs that address all of the critical questions required by law and are good illustrations of how behavioral problems and intervention plans can be presented in legally defensible and educationally useful ways.

The IEP and Placement

The educational placement of students with disabilities, especially those with EBD, is one of the most controversial issues in special education. According to Yell and colleagues (2014), confusion around the placement process for students with EBD may be evident in the volume of litigation that has arisen regarding IEP teams' procedural or substantive errors in placement decisions. The issues regarding placement are complex, and we can't explore all of them here (see Crockett & Kauffman, 1999; Dupre, 1996, 1997; Jakubecy, Mock, & Kauffman, 2003; Kauffman, Lloyd, Baker, & Riedel, 1995; Kauffman, Lloyd et al., 1995a, b). However, it's critically important that administrators and teachers understand the following requirements of federal law (IDEA) and regulations:

1. Schools must provide a full continuum of alternative placements, ranging from placement in general education with needed supports to placement in residential treatment centers and hospitals. It's illegal to place all students in a single type of setting regardless of their disabilities (e.g., to state that *all* students with EBD will receive their education in a self-contained classroom or that *all* students will receive special education in a mainstream or inclusionary setting) or to refuse to provide a particular alternative (e.g., a special self-contained class) that will meet the student's needs.

2. Students must be placed in the least-restrictive environment in which their appropriate education can be offered. Potential negative effects of a placement on the student and on regular classroom peers must be considered in making placement decisions.

3. Placement decisions must be individualized, be based on the student's IEP, and be made *after* appropriate education is described in the IEP. Placements must be chosen on the basis of the student's individual educational needs, not on the basis of a label or category.

CLASSIFICATION

In the preceding sections, we outlined the processes schools undertake in screening for behavior problems, determining whether individual students are eligible for special education services due to EBD, and evaluation for planning instruction and intervention. A separate purpose of evaluation involves classifying disorders—grouping together individuals with common behavioral characteristics so that we might better understand the origins, nature, course, and treatment of such disorders. We have stressed that students with EBD are unique individuals, and further, that their educational plans must by law be individualized. But a system of classification is basic to any science, and a valid system of classification provides a useful tool and a common language for professionals to communicate about EBD, with the goal of better understanding and ultimately better interventions (see Kauffman, 2011, 2012a, 2012b).

Classification should be based on reliably observed phenomena, and the classification of a given disorder should have a clear relationship to its nature, origin, course, and treatment. Ideally, a classification system should include *operationally defined categories*—categories defined in such a way that the behaviors forming them can be measured. The system should also be reliable: An individual should be classified consistently by different observers, and the assignment of someone to a category should be consistent over a reasonable period of time. The categories should be valid: Assignment to a category should be determinable in a variety of ways (by a variety of observational systems or rating scales), and it should be highly predictive of particular behaviors (recall our previous discussion of reliability and validity).

We shall briefly discuss two major types of classification: psychiatric and dimensional. Of the alternative systems available, psychiatric classification typically carries the greatest legal authority, but dimensional classification has the greatest relevance for educators and most closely approximates the ideal system.

Psychiatric Classification

Psychiatry, mimicking the empirical classification of diseases in physical medicine, has devised systems of classification based on demonstrated or presumed *mental diseases*. Historically, many psychiatric classifications have been unreliable and have had few or no implications for treatment, particularly educational interventions (Achenbach, 1985; Kratochwill & McGivern, 1996; Sinclair, Forness, & Alexson, 1985). However, psychiatric classifications are widely used, and educators will encounter psychiatric labels in working with students with EBD (e.g., *obsessive-compulsive disorder*), and teachers must understand these (Mattison, 2014). But these are not diagnoses made by school personnel. Students are eligible for special education services under the category of emotional disturbance (the term used in the federal regulations associated with IDEA, as we discussed extensively in Chapter 2) only when a school-based team determines that they meet the eligibility criteria as spelled out in the federal definition. Many students identified with EBD by their schools will have psychiatric diagnoses as well, presumably because they have had extensive contact with psychiatric professionals outside of school, but many will not. Much progress has been made in psychiatric classification in recent decades. Categories are now more objective and reliable than they were a quarter century ago. Nevertheless, psychiatric categories are not aligned with eligibility criteria for special education. Again, students are not identified for special education through psychiatric diagnosis.

The most widely accepted psychiatric system of classification is the one devised by the American Psychiatric Association. The standard psychiatric diagnoses are those included in the most recent edition of the American Psychiatric Association's *Diagnostic and Statistical Manual of Mental Disorders* (2013), or DSM, now in its fifth edition and usually referred to as *DSM 5*. The fifth edition represented a significant departure from the classification system— a multi-axial system—that had been used in previous editions since 1980. Prior to DSM V, axial classification meant that disorders were noted in the categories associated with Axes I, II, and III, while Axis IV was used to denote any psychosocial and environmental problems or factors (life circumstances) that might affect the diagnosis, treatment, or prognosis of disorders (things like an individual's primary support group, or economic situation). Axis V was the clinicians' estimate of the individual's overall level of functioning in everyday life. Besides the classifications it lists, *DSM 5* is designed to help professionals in psychiatry and other disciplines in planning treatment and predicting outcomes.

In *DSM 5*, clinical disorders, personality disorders, and general medical conditions or neurological disorders that might impact psychiatric problems (formerly Axes I, II, and III, respectively) are now merely listed as individual diagnoses, prioritized in terms of need for treatment. Clinicians using the DSM are encouraged to make separate notation of factors that formerly fell under Axes IV and V. Clinical disorders include such things as conduct disorder, anxiety disorders, ADHD, and major depressive disorder. Personality disorders include such things as antisocial personality disorder and obsessive-compulsive disorder (OCD). Medical conditions or neurological problems include things like traumatic brain injury or diseases that might impact the individual's functioning.

In *DSM 5*, most diagnostic categories that impact children and adolescents are included in a section entitled *neurodevelopmental disorders*. In previous editions of the DSM, the majority of these were included under the category "Disorders Usually First Diagnosed in Infancy, Childhood, or Adolescence." Neurodevelopmental disorders in *DSM 5* fall into the following categories:

- Intellectual disabilities
- Communication disorders
- Autism spectrum disorders
- Attention-deficit/hyperactivity disorder
- Specific learning disorder
- Motor disorder
- Other developmental disorders

Children and youth may certainly receive diagnoses from other categories as well; those listed under neurodevelopmental disorders are simply those that typically have their onset during childhood. These disorders may indeed accompany emotional or behavioral disorders of other types, but they are typically considered in detail in books or chapters devoted exclusively to them (e.g., Hallahan, Lloyd, Kauffman, Weiss, & Martinez, 2005).

A number of other disorders included under the category of "Disorders Usually First Diagnosed in Infancy, Childhood, or Adolescence" in previous editions of DSM have been moved to separate categories, in part in because of the focus of the new DSM on life-span development rather than distinguishing disorders solely by age-related criteria. These include more severe disorders, such as **pica** and **rumination**, moved to the broader category "Feeding and Eating Disorders," and **separation anxiety** and **selective mutism**, moved to the category "Anxiety Disorders." Probably most relevant for professionals in the area of EBD, oppositional defiant disorder and conduct disorder have been moved to the new category "Disruptive, Impulse-Control, and Conduct Disorders," which also includes **intermittent explosive disorder**, **antisocial personality disorder**, **pyromania** (associated with fire and fire-setting), and **kleptomania** (associated with stealing). For many diagnoses, age of onset remains a critical diagnostic notation (e.g., conduct disorder is diagnosed as either childhood onset, adolescent onset, or unspecified onset).

We don't attempt to define all these categories here; most have been discussed in previous chapters. In the *DSM 5*, each category and subcategory is associated with a number (e.g., autism spectrum disorder is 299.00), which we have not included.

The *DSM 5* is the result of more than a decade of work in revising the traditional categories and classification system used in previous versions of DSM, and these had been largely unchanged for many years. Moreover, this revision represents a fundamental change from the traditional multi-axial system of classification. For these reasons, it remains unknown as yet whether and how the use of *DSM 5* will impact diagnostic practice for children and youth with emotional and behavioral disorders. Of particular interest will be the extent to which the new DSM will address historical concerns about diagnostic reliability; the diagnostic guidelines provided with the previous version of the DSM (*DSM-IV-TR*) were thought to have improved the reliability of psychiatric diagnoses generally, but it is not known how the move away from the multi-axial system in *DSM 5* will impact this concern.

A child or youth doesn't qualify for special education simply because he or she carries a *DSM 5* diagnosis. Although many of those who carry psychiatric labels are eligible for special education, it's important to remember that identification for special education is independent of and uses criteria different from those in any *DSM* classification system.

Behavioral Dimensions

Psychiatric classification is focused primarily on differentiating among *kinds* of disorders. Dimensional classification indicates how much individuals differ in the degree to which they exhibit a type of behavior. Behavioral dimensions are descriptions of behavioral clusters (highly intercorrelated behaviors). Statistical procedures, such as factor analysis, are used to find behavioral dimensions based on behavior ratings. The statistical analyses reveal which behavior problems tend to occur together to form a dimension. In early studies (e.g., Ackerson, 1942; Hewitt & Jenkins, 1946), behavior traits were obtained from reports in children's case histories. The behaviors were listed and then clustered by visual inspection of the data. Current statistical analyses are much more precise.

Studies of behavioral dimensions or types have generally found two major classifications, or *broadband* problems. One of these is typically referred to as **externalizing** problems (sometimes also called *undercontrolled*). It's characterized by aggression, striking out against others, impulsive and disobedient behavior, and delinquency. The other is typically called **internalizing** problems (sometimes called *overcontrolled*). It's characterized by anxiety, social withdrawal, and depression. More specific problems, such as hyperactivity, delinquency, depression, conduct disorder, and so on are often referred to as *narrowband* problems.

Although the broadband types called *externalizing* and *internalizing* appeared in many early studies, they aren't mutually exclusive (see Achenbach, 1985, 1991; Achenbach & Edelbrock, 1981, 1989, 1991; Achenbach, Howell, Quay, & Conners, 1991; Waldman & Lilienfeld, 1995). That is, a given individual may have multiple types of problems, sometimes including multiple types of more narrowly defined disorders, some of the externalizing, and some of the internalizing type. Individuals may show more than one disorder simultaneously or alternate between types. For example, a student can have conduct disorder (an externalizing type) and also be depressed (an internalizing type). Of course, we can compare groups also, not just individuals, in the types of behavioral problems they exhibit. Emerging research, mostly based on twin studies, provides tentative support for a model in which genetic influences might produce a general risk for psychiatric disorders, and environmental influences contributing to the type—externalizing or internalizing—of disorder a child might develop (Rhee, Lahey, & Waldman, 2015).

Researchers have developed a number of instruments that have good evidence of reliability and validity for detecting students with or at risk for both externalizing and internalizing disorders. It has been assumed that many assessment approaches are likely to more readily identify those students who display externalizing disorders, as their behavior will be obvious to any adult with whom they spend time, but in fact use some type of dimensional classification. These include the *Behavioral and Emotional Screening System* (BASC-3 BESS) (Reynolds & Kamphaus, 2015), the *Systematic Screening for Behavioral Disorders* (SSBD) (Walker,

Severson, & Feil, 2014; the *Social Skills Improvement System* (SSIS) (Gresham & Elliott, 2008), and the *Student Risk Screening Scale* (SRSS) (Drummond, 1994).

The SRSS, which is available as a free-access screening tool, includes seven items which teachers rate on a 4-point scale: 0 = never, 1 = occasionally, 2 = sometimes, and 3 = frequently. The seven items rated are:

1. Steal

2. Lie, cheat, sneak

3. Behavior problem

4. Peer rejection

5. Low academic achievement

6. Negative attitude

7. Aggressive behavior

Although this scale was designed originally to detect risk for "antisocial behavior," the nature of the items makes clear that there was a focus on externalizing disorders. Despite this, researchers have shown that the use of this scale allows the detection of students with both externalizing and internalizing behavioral risk. Lane and her colleagues (Lane, Little et al., 2009) have recently undertaken efforts to add items to this scale specifically to improve the detection of students whose difficulties may be primarily of the internalizing type. Items added to the SRSS in their recent research include:

1. Emotionally flat

2. Shy, withdrawn

3. Sad, depressed

4. Anxious

5. Lonely

An important concept underlying the classification of behavioral dimensions is that all individuals exhibit the characteristics of all the dimensions but to varying degrees (Waldman & Lillenfeld, 1995). As we suggested earlier, an individual may be rated high on more than one dimension. Many students with EBD have multiple problems, and they may receive high ratings on several dimensions (Landrum, Wiley, Tankersley, & Kauffman, 2014; Tankersley & Landrum, 1997). Students' behavior is classified according to certain statistical clusters of items on the rating scale; *individuals* aren't classified. Although the same perspective is taken in some psychiatric classifications (that is, disorders are classified, not people), dimensional classification has the advantage of being based on more reliable, empirically derived categories.

These observations bring us back to a foundational concept related to the definition of *disorder*: EBD is not an all-or-nothing phenomenon. How different an individual's behavior must be from that of others before we invoke the label "disordered" is a matter of judgment, an arbitrary decision based on an explicit or implicit value system. The same concept applies to the subclassification of disorders within the general category. How high an individual's rating must be on a particular factor or dimension before his or her behavior is said to be problematic is a matter of judgment. That judgment may be guided by statistical analyses, but the statistics themselves aren't sufficient (see Kauffman & Lloyd, 2017). Classification using a dimensional system, like psychiatric classification, is not, by itself, sufficient to make a child or youth eligible for special education services.

Multiple Classifications and the Issue of Comorbidity

Regardless of whether psychiatric or dimensional classification systems are used, researchers and clinicians frequently find that children and youth exhibit more than one type of problem or disorder (see Landrum, 2017; Kessler, Berglund, Demler, Jin, & Walters, 2005; Kessler, Chiu, Demler, & Walters, 2005; Tankersley & Landrum, 1997). In fact, it is now generally accepted that co-morbidity is more the norm than the exception (Rhee, Lahey, & Waldman, 2015). Multiple classifications may be more common than single classifications. For example, a youngster who exhibits conduct disorder may also be depressed, one with schizophrenia may exhibit conduct disorder as well, a pervasive developmental disorder may be accompanied by an elimination disorder, or a child may be rated high on both externalizing and internalizing items because his or her behavior vacillates quickly from one extreme to the other. A word commonly used to describe the co-occurrence of disorders is *comorbidity*. The comorbidity of behavioral and learning problems makes effective treatment of one in the absence of treatment for the other extremely difficult, if not impossible.

Classification of Severe Disorders

Behavior along the different dimensions can vary from minor, even trivial, to extremely serious problems. In fact, many or most of the students who are said to have EBD, regardless of their diagnostic classification, have very serious problems (Mattison, 2011). Their problems are not mild; by analogy, their problems are more like pneumonia than the sniffles or a mild cold. In most cases, they have not been identified as having EBD because of some minor problem but because their problems are grave.

Some youngsters' behavior, though, is characterized by differences that appear to be qualitatively as well as quantitatively different. These children are frequently described as inaccessible to others, as unreachable or out of touch with reality, or as having intellectual disabilities. They are often unresponsive to other people, have bizarre language and speech patterns or no functional language at all, exhibit grossly inappropriate behavior, lack everyday living skills, or perform stereotypical, ritualistic behavior. There isn't much debate about whether children can exhibit the severe disorders that are often referred to in the general case as *psychosis*. Prior and Werry (1986) provided a nontechnical definition of psychotic behavior: "The interpretation of oneself, of the world, and of one's place in it, is so seriously at variance with the actual facts of the matter as to interfere with everyday adaptation and to strike the impartial observer as incomprehensible" (p. 156). Many of the children classified as having a pervasive developmental disorder fit such a description.

There is considerable debate about how to subdivide severe disorders in a reliable and helpful way. However, because autism spectrum disorders are now a separate category under IDEA, we do not discuss them further in this text. In Chapter 13, we focused instead on the severe disorder known as schizophrenia and the extremes of other EBD.

Confusion and disagreement regarding diagnostic classification persist. However, when the onset of symptoms of schizophrenia takes place during childhood or adolescence, the child's condition may be indistinguishable from schizophrenia as it occurs in adults (Asarnow, Thompson, & Goldstein, 1994; Gottesman, 1991), though as we noted, onset prior to age eighteen is unusual and onset prior to age thirteen is extremely rare. Nonetheless, the early signs of schizophrenia in very young children are sometimes indistinguishable from autism spectrum disorders, and children with autism or other disorders are sometimes diagnosed with schizophrenia as adolescents or adults. Moreover, other severe and disabling disorders may be mistaken for schizophrenia (Stayer et al., 2004).

Schizophrenia is fundamentally a disorder of thinking and perception. Children or youth with schizophrenia may exhibit bizarre behavior, delusions, and distorted perceptions, sometimes including hallucinations, and their affect is typically inappropriate in many social circumstances. They may believe they are being controlled by alien forces. Delusions and hallucinations are rare in preadolescents, but they are sometimes a part of severe disorders such as schizophrenia. The case of Erin (see the accompanying case book) illustrates the experience of hallucinations by a preadolescent with childhood-onset schizophrenia.

NECESSITY OF CLASSIFICATION

The search continues for reliable, valid classifications with relevance for intervention. Although classification of disordered behavior carries the risk that individuals will needlessly be stigmatized by labels for their differences, it would be foolish to abandon the task of classifying people's problems. Giving up all uses of classification is tantamount to abandoning the scientific study of social and behavioral difficulties. Indeed, we need labels for problems to communicate about them and to take preventive action (Kauffman, 2011, 2012a, 2012b, 2014a, 2014b, 2014c; Kauffman & Konold, 2007). Nevertheless, we must try to reduce the social stigma of the words that describe behavioral differences.

Complexity and Ambiguity

Classification is a complex undertaking, and scholars frequently disagree about how particular behavioral characteristics should be categorized. Furthermore, any set of categories yet devised leaves the categorical home of some behaviors in doubt. All comprehensive systems of classification produce a residual or miscellaneous category for behavioral odds and ends or they result in arbitrary assignment of certain behaviors to a category of questionable homogeneity. As we saw in Parts 2 and 3, both the disorders of behavior and their causes are usually multidimensional. Life seldom refines disorders or their causes into pure, unambiguous forms. Youngsters seldom show teachers or researchers a single disorder uncontaminated by elements of other problems, and the cause of a disorder is virtually never found to be a single factor. As a case in point, consider the interrelationships among *hyperactivity, conduct disorder*, and *delinquency*. Hyperactivity is a prominent feature of the behavior of many children who have a conduct disorder. Conduct disorder and delinquency are overlapping categories because conduct disorder is characterized by overt aggression or covert antisocial behavior, such as stealing, lying, and fire setting; delinquency is also often characterized by such behavior but involves breaking the law. The same factors that cause conduct disorder and delinquency may also contribute to hyperactivity. Thus, grouping specific types of disorders is necessarily somewhat subjective, and classifications always contain a certain amount of ambiguity.

SUMMARY

Evaluation for instruction should typically include standardized tests of intelligence and achievement, behavior ratings, assessment of peer relations, interviews, self-reports, and direct behavioral observations. An approach with high utility for educators is curriculum-based evaluation, in which students' performance is measured frequently using the curriculum materials in which they are working. Curriculum-based methods can be applied to social skills as well as to the traditional academic curriculum.

Whenever a student's behavior results in disciplinary actions that are likely to result in a change in placement or removal from school, teams are required to make a manifestation determination about the relation of the behavior to the student's disability and the adequacy of the IEP and the services provided through it.

Functional behavioral assessment may indicate how classroom conditions and instructional procedures may be arranged to give students maximum freedom and self-control while resolving their behavioral problems. An instructional approach to assessment, known as precorrection, helps integrate assessment and teaching procedures and allows teachers to prevent many behavioral problems. A positive behavior intervention plan is consistent with the idea of precorrection.

Students with disabilities must be included, with appropriate accommodations, in general assessments of educational progress that are administered state- or district-wide. Selections of effective and appropriate accommodations must be made in consideration of the characteristics of individual students and the requirements of specific tests.

Social validation is an evaluation strategy involving comparisons between behavior-disordered students and their peers as well as comparisons between the target student's behavior before and after intervention. It emphasizes obtaining objective evidence and consensus among the principal parties that a) the problem is important, b) the intervention is appropriate, and c) the outcome is satisfactory.

Evaluation data should be useful in writing the IEP for a student who is placed in special education. Direct observation, curriculum-based evaluation, and social validation are procedures with special relevance for the IEPs of students with EBD. IEPs vary greatly in format and content, but all must contain certain elements: unique characteristics or needs; special education, related services, or modifications; beginning date and duration of services; and present levels of performance and measureable annual goals. Schools must offer a full continuum of placement options. Students must be placed in the least-restrictive environment in which an appropriate education can be provided. Placement decisions must be individualized and must be made after, not before, appropriate education is described.

Classification is basic to any science, including the science of human behavior. Classifications should help us understand the nature, origin, and course of whatever is being classified. Psychiatric classification systems have not been especially useful to educators because they are not highly reliable or valid for teaching purposes. Teachers will probably encounter the most widely accepted psychiatric classification system, that of the American Psychiatric Association (various editions and revisions of the DSM, the official diagnostic and statistical manual).

Dimensional classifications more closely approximate the ideal system in terms of reliability, validity, and utility in education. An assumption underlying the dimensional approach is that all individuals exhibit behavior that is classifiable but to varying degrees; thus, we classify behavior, not individuals. The broadest categories in a quantitative, dimensional approach to disordered behavior are internalizing (withdrawal) and externalizing (acting out). Within these broad dimensions, more specific categories have been described. Students with EBD typically obtain higher ratings on all or most problem dimensions than do students in other special education categories. Boys usually obtain higher problem scores than girls. Differences between categories of students tend to be greatest for the conduct disorder dimension.

The most severe disabilities present particular difficulties for classification. A common category of severe disabilities is schizophrenia. The onset of schizophrenia is unusual in childhood. Schizophrenia includes disordered thought patterns and may also include hallucinations or delusions.

Classification can't be avoided because categories and labels are essential for human communication about disorders. All systems of classification include some miscellaneous categories and ambiguities. Many children and youth with EBD exhibit more than one type or dimension of disorder. Most students with EBD have severe problems. The co-occurrence of disorders is often referred to as comorbidity.

✔ ENHANCEDetext **END-OF-CHAPTER 15 QUIZ**

Click on the checkmark icon to access an end-of-chapter quiz. Answer the questions to gauge your understanding of chapter concepts and better prepare you for case discussion.

CASE FOR DISCUSSION (See case book for additional cases.)

A Special Challenge: Roger

Roger is brooding again. His brooding is typically followed by agitated behavior and a blowup or peak. He seems to be in the early stages of his typical pattern. Today, as usual, everyone in the special middle school for kids with disabilities is wondering what will happen, worried about whether Roger will make it through the day in school or have to be sent home. Everyone is cringing, realizing that today seems likely another in which the adults end up in a physical struggle with Roger or somebody gets hurt or property is destroyed. Physical struggles with seventh graders like Roger don't make people feel good, competent, or wise. They make the adults who are responsible for Roger and the rest of the school feel defeated and stupid. Roger seems to know that. He revels in taking the fight to others.

Roger's anger seems bottomless. Adults struggle to find what sets him off. Sometimes, it seems like academic work, sometimes it seems like something else. The first goal in trying to keep him in school is just to keep him from hurting himself or someone else in one of his frequent explosions. The staff of the school try to ready themselves for what they've come to see as the inevitable punch,

push, or flying chair that marks the beginning of one of Roger's seething, full-blown tantrums. In his tantrums he screams things like, "Fuck you!" "To hell with everybody!" "You'd better not try to stop me!" "I'll knock your fucking teeth down your throat, and that's not a threat, that's a PROMISE!" He tears up books, throws chairs—actually threw one through a supposedly shatter-proof window. Everyone hopes that nobody gets hurt in the process of restraining Roger. Everybody would like to find a way of reducing the frequency and severity of Roger's tantrums.

Some people call Roger's conduct "challenging behavior." Well, it's a challenge, for sure. But that euphemism doesn't help anyone address the problem. True, Roger's behavior is a challenge to the staff, who must figure out how to change it. And teaching Roger any academic or social skills is a challenge. Whatever academic task the teacher gives him, whatever academic or behavioral expectation a teacher sets, Roger seems to follow the same pattern: brooding, becoming more and more agitated, eventually engaging the teacher or other staff in an all-out physical struggle. Teachers have tried modifying his assignments, lowering their expectations, requiring only a minimum amount of work. But, so far Roger has been "winning" in that he doesn't conform to any expectations for doing actual school-work. The teachers are so frustrated that they'd just like to leave Roger alone, let him sit quietly (if he will) without doing anything.

Questions About the Case

1. If you were Roger's teacher, what assessment strategies would you use?

2. Suppose you were to write an IEP for Roger based on the information you have from this case. What would you write for him (see our description of IEPs and the examples for Curt and Aaron).

3. Imagine that you are interviewing Roger's parents and teachers. What questions would you ask of them that, if answered, might help you find a way of assessing his problems and teaching him more successfully?

Adjustment disorders Maladaptive reactions to an identifiable and stressful life event or circumstance. Includes impairment of social and/or occupational functioning. Maladaptive behavior is expected to change when stress is removed.

Affective disorders *See* Mood disorders.

Amnesia Chronic or severe inability to remember; loss of memory that is general or more than temporary.

Anorexia nervosa Severe self-starvation and marked weight loss that may be life threatening. Occurs most often in adolescent girls.

Anoxia; Hypoxia Deprivation of oxygen for a long enough time to result in brain trauma.

Anxiety disorders Disorders in which anxiety is the primary feature. Anxiety may focus on specific situations, such as separation or social contact with strangers, or it may be generalized and pervasive.

Anxiety withdrawal Behavior characterized by anxiety, feelings of inadequacy, embarrassment, shyness, and withdrawal from social contact.

Asperger's syndrome (AS) Impairment of social behavior (e.g., eye-to-eye gaze, facial expression, peer relationships, sharing of experience, social reciprocity) and restricted, repetitive, stereotyped patterns of behavior or interests but without significant delay in language or cognitive development.

Athetoid movement Involuntary, jerky, writhing movements (especially of the fingers and wrists) associated with athetoid cerebral palsy.

Attention deficit and disruptive behavior disorders Includes attention deficit–hyperactivity disorder (ADHD), conduct disorder (CD), oppositional defiant disorder (ODD), and disruptive behavior disorder.

Attention deficit–hyperactivity disorder (ADHD) A disorder that includes inattention, impulsivity, and hyperactivity, beginning before age seven and of sufficient severity and persistence to result in impairment in two or more settings (e.g., home and school) in social, academic, or occupational functioning. May be primarily hyperactive–impulsive type or primarily inattentive type.

Attentional strategies Use of verbal labeling, rehearsal, self-instruction, or other techniques to improve a child's ability to attend efficiently to appropriate stimuli.

Authoritative A style of parenting that is demanding but responsive (contrast with authoritarian).

Autism; Autistic *See* Autism spectrum disorder.

Autism spectrum disorder Autism is a pervasive developmental disorder with onset before age three in which there is qualitative impairment of social interaction and communication and restricted, repetitive, stereotyped patterns of behavior, interests, and activities. Autism spectrum disorder (ASD) includes the full range of autism symptoms, from classic autism as just defined, to a generally milder form known as Asperger's syndrome and autistic-like behavior.

Aversive conditioning A form of punishment; presenting an aversive (painful or unpleasant) consequence following a behavior to reduce the frequency or probability of its recurrence.

Behavior intervention plan (BIP) A plan for changing a problem behavior.

Behavioral model Assumptions that emotional or behavioral disorders result primarily from inappropriate learning and that the most effective preventive actions and therapeutic interventions involve controlling the child's environment to teach appropriate responses.

Behavior modification Systematic control of environmental events, especially of consequences, to produce specific changes in observable responses. May include reinforcement, punishment, modeling, self-instruction, desensitization, guided practice, or any other technique for strengthening or eliminating a particular response.

Behaviorally disordered A common term used in some states to refer to students identified with emotional disturbance (the term used in federal law) for special education purposes.

Biological model Assumptions that emotional or behavioral disorders result primarily from dysfunction of the central nervous system (because of brain lesions, neurochemical irregularities, or genetic defects) and that the most effective preventive actions and therapeutic interventions involve prevention or correction of such biological defects.

Bipolar disorder Major mood disorder characterized by both manic and depressive episodes. *See also* Depression, Manic.

Brain syndrome *See* Organic brain syndrome.

Bulimia Recurrent episodes of binge eating followed by purging (by vomiting or enemas) or other compensatory behavior (e.g., fasting or excessive exercise) intended to prevent weight gain, accompanied by preoccupation with body shape or weight.

Case An example. A story describing a problem and information relevant to understanding it.

Catatonic behavior Characterized by muscular rigidity and mental stupor, sometimes alternating with periods of extreme excitement; inability to move or interact normally; "frozen" posture or affect.

Catharsis In psychoanalytic theory, the notion that it is therapeutic to express one's feelings freely under certain conditions (e.g., that aggressive drive can be reduced by free expression of aggression in a safe way, such as hitting a punching bag or a doll).

Cerebral palsy A developmental disability resulting from brain damage before, during, or soon after birth and having as a primary feature weakness or paralysis of the extremities. Often accompanied by intellectual disabilities, sensory deficiencies, and/or behavioral disorders.

Cerebral trauma *See* Traumatic brain injury.

Character disorder Acting-out, aggressive behavior with little or no indication of associated anxiety or guilt.

357

Childhood disintegrative disorder Normal development followed by significant loss, after age two but before age ten, of previously acquired social, language, self-care, or play skills with qualitative impairment in social interaction or communication and stereotyped behavior.

Childhood psychosis Used to denote a wide range of severe and profound disorders of children, including autism, schizophrenia, and symbiotic psychosis.

Choreoathetoid movement Involuntary, purposeless, uncontrolled movement characteristic of some types of neurological disorders.

Comorbid condition A condition or disorder occurring simultaneously with another.

Comorbidity Two or more disorders occurring together, as in comorbidity of depression and conduct disorder.

Compulsion An overwhelming urge to engage in a certain behavior, often repetitively or ritualistically (e.g., locking a door three times).

Conceptual model A theory. In emotional or behavioral disorders, a set of assumptions regarding the origins and nature of the problem and the nature of therapeutic mechanisms; a set of assumptions guiding research and practice.

Conduct disorder; Conduct problem Repetitive, persistent pattern of behavior violating basic rights of others or age-appropriate social norms or rules, including aggression toward people and animals, destruction of property, deceitfulness or theft, and serious violation of family or school rules. Onset may be in childhood or adolescence, and severity may range from mild to severe.

Contingency contract In behavior modification, a written agreement between a child and an adult (or adults) specifying the consequences for specific behavior.

Counterconditioning Behavior therapy that teaches, by means of classical and operant conditioning, adaptive responses that are incompatible with maladaptive responses.

Countertheorists *See* Humanistic education.

Craniocerebral trauma *See* Traumatic brain injury.

Criterion-referenced test Assessment or test based on a standard or criterion that the student should be able to reach rather than an average or norm.

Curriculum-based evaluation; Curriculum-based assessment; Curriculum-based measurement Evaluation or assessment based on the student's performance in the actual curriculum with the materials (texts, problems) that the teacher is using for instruction. Requires frequent, brief measurement of the student's performance using regular instructional materials.

Cyclothymia; Cyclothymic disorder Fluctuation of mood alternating between depression and mania but with symptoms not severe enough to be considered bipolar disorder. *See also* Bipolar disorder; Depression; Manic.

Delinquency; Delinquent; Juvenile delinquent The illegal behavior of a minor.

Delusion Abnormal mental state in which something is falsely believed.

Delusional disorder Disorder characterized by nonbizarre (i.e., potentially true) delusions without schizophrenia.

Depression; Depressive episode Depressed mood and loss of interest or pleasure in nearly all normal activities; episode lasting for at least two weeks.

Desensitization; Systematic desensitization Elimination of fears or phobias by gradually subjecting the fearful individual to successively more anxiety-provoking stimuli (real or imagined) while the individual remains relaxed and free of fear.

Developmental disorders Disorders apparently caused by the child's failure to develop at a normal rate or according to the usual sequence.

Diagnostic and Statistical Manual of Mental Disorders (DSM) Editions designated by Roman numerals, as *DSM–IV* for the fourth edition. Revised third edition is referred to as *DSM–III–R*. The most recent edition released in 2000 involved a "text revision" and is often referred to as *DSM–IV–TR*. *DSM V* was published in 2013.

Distractibility Inability to direct and sustain attention to the appropriate or relevant stimuli in a given situation. *See also* Selective attention.

Down syndrome A genetic defect in which the child is born with an extra chromosome (number 21 in the 23 pairs; hence, trisomy 21) in each cell; a syndrome associated with intellectual disabilities.

Dynamic psychiatry The study of emotional processes, mental mechanisms, and their origins; study of evolution, progression, or regression in human behavior and its motivation. Distinguished from *descriptive psychiatry*, in which focus is on static clinical patterns, symptoms, and classification.

Dysphoria General feeling of unhappiness or unwellness, especially when disproportionate to its cause or inappropriate to one's life circumstances. Opposite of *euphoria*.

Dysthymia Feeling of depressed mood on most days for at least two years but not of the severity required for diagnosis of a major depressive episode or clinical depression.

Echolalia; Echolalic The parroting repetition of words or phrases either immediately after they are heard or later. Typical in very young children who are learning to talk. Among older children and adults, usually observed only in individuals with schizophrenia or autism.

Ecobehavioral analysis A procedure in which naturally occurring, functional events are identified and employed to improve instruction and behavior management.

Ecological model Assumptions that emotional or behavioral disorders result primarily from flaws in a complex social system in which various elements of the system (e.g., child, school, family, church, community) are highly interdependent and that the most effective preventive actions and therapeutic interventions involve changes in the entire social system.

Educateur An individual broadly trained to enhance social development of children and youth in various community contexts. Someone trained in education and related disciplines to intervene in the social ecology of troubled children and youth.

Ego The conscious mind. In Freudian psychology, the volitional aspect of behavior.

Ego psychology Psychological theories or models emphasizing the ego.

Elective mutism *See* Selective mutism.

Electroencephalogram (EEG) A graphic record of changes in the electrical potential of the brain. Used in neurological and psychiatric research.

Emotional disturbance The term used in federal special education law (IDEA) for the disability category referred to professionally as emotional and behavioral disorder (EBD).

Emotional intelligence Adeptness in assessing and managing emotions, including skills in awareness of one's own emotions, recognition of others' emotional states, regulation of one's own emotions and motivation, and management of interpersonal relationships.

Emotional lability Unstable or rapidly shifting emotional states.

Encephalitis Inflammation of the brain, usually as a result of infection and often accompanied by behavioral manifestations such as lethargy.

Encopresis Incontinence of feces, which may consist of passing feces into the clothing or bed at regular intervals or leaking mucus and feces into the clothing or bed almost continuously.

Endogenous depression Depression apparently precipitated by biological factors rather than adverse environmental circumstances.

Enuresis; Enuretic Incontinence of urine, which may be diurnal (wetting oneself during the day) or nocturnal (bed-wetting).

Epilepsy Recurrent abnormal electrical discharges in the brain that cause seizures. A person is not considered to have epilepsy unless repeated seizures occur.

Ethology Scientific comparative study of animal and human behavior, especially study of the development of human character.

Eugenics Belief that human qualities can be improved through selective mating. A science dealing with improving inherited characteristics of a race or breed.

Euphoria Feeling of elation. Extreme and unrealistic happiness.

Externalizing Describes behavior that involves acting out, such as fighting, or physical or verbal aggression. Sometimes used to describe conduct disorder.

Facilitated communication (FC) A procedure said to allow persons who are unable to communicate through speech to communicate by using a keyboard. A facilitator assists communication by giving emotional and physical support as the disabled person types. FC has not been supported by scientific research.

Feeding disorder of infancy or early childhood Feeding disturbance, occurring before age six, characterized by persistent failure to eat adequately and gain weight but not due to gastrointestinal or other general medical conditions.

Follow-back studies Studies in which adults with a given disorder are "followed back" in time in an attempt to find the antecedents of their condition in their medical, educational, or social histories.

Fragile X syndrome A genetic disorder, associated primarily with intellectual disabilities but also a variety of other mental or behavioral problems, in which part of the X chromosome shows variations, such as breaks or gaps.

Frustration–aggression hypothesis Hypothesis that frustration always produces aggression and that aggression is always the result of frustration.

Functional analysis Assessment of behavior to determine the purposes, goals, or function of behavior.

Functional behavioral assessment (FBA) Procedures designed to find out why a student exhibits problem behavior, including assessment of the antecedents and consequences of behavior and the apparent purpose of the problem behavior.

Gender dysphoria Feeling strongly that one is not the gender one appears to be or is biologically.

General intelligence The totality of skills and knowledge that enable a person to solve problems and meet social expectations. The theory that intelligence consists of general problem-solving abilities rather than abilities to perform specific tasks.

Heightened risk A higher chance or risk than is true for the general population that an individual will experience an event or condition (e.g., use drugs, acquire a traumatic head injury, become delinquent, fail in school, be diagnosed with schizophrenia, etc.).

Holistic education An approach emphasizing individuals' construction of their own realities based on personal experience and rejecting traditional analytic and quantitative views of reality.

Humanistic education Education suggested by countertheorists, who call for radical school reform and/or greater self-determination by the child. Education in which freedom, openness, innovation, self-direction, and self-evaluation by students and mutual sharing between students and teachers are practiced.

Hyperactivity; Hyperactive High level of motor activity accompanied by socially inappropriate behavior, often including conduct disorder, distractibility, and impulsivity.

Hyperkinesis Excessive motor activity.

Hyperthyroidism Enlargement of and excessive secretion of hormones from the thyroid gland that may result in nervousness, weakness, and restless overactivity.

Hypoglycemia Abnormally low level of blood sugar that may produce behavioral symptoms such as irritability, fretfulness, confusion, negativism, or aggression. May be associated with diabetes.

Hypomanic *See* Manic.

Hypoxia Severely reduced supply of oxygen. *See* Anoxia.

Immaturity–inadequacy Disorder characterized by social incompetence, passivity, daydreaming, and behavior typical of younger children.

Impulsivity Tendency to react quickly and inappropriately to a situation rather than take time to consider alternatives and choose carefully.

Incidence The rate of occurrence (as new cases) of a specific disorder in a given population during a given period of time (e.g., 25 per 1,000 per year).

Inclusion Philosophy that students should be educated alongside peers without disabilities, typically in general education settings.

Incontinence; Incontinent The release of urine or feces at inappropriate times or places. Lack of control of bladder or bowel function.

Index crime   An act that is illegal regardless of the person's age. Crimes for which the FBI keeps records, including the range from misdemeanors to murder.

Individualized Education Program (IEP)   Document required under IDEA for each student receiving special education services; IEP delineates services to be provided, and goals to be addressed.

Individuals with Disabilities Education Act (IDEA)   The federal special education law, enacted in 1990, that amended the Education for All Handicapped Children Act of 1975 (which was also known as Public Law 94–142), most recently reauthorized in 2004. The 2004 reauthorization changed the name of the law to the Individuals with Disabilities Education Improvement Act; sometimes referred to as IDEIA or IDEIA 2004, the original acronym IDEA is still more commonly used even when referring to the most recent reauthorization.

Induction approach   Use of reasoning, explanation, modeling, and expressions of love and concern in discipline, especially in teaching or enforcing moral standards.

Infantile autism   *See* Autistic spectrum disorder.

Interactional–transactional model   Assumptions that emotional or behavioral disorders result primarily from the mutual influence of the child and other people on each other and that the most effective preventive actions and therapeutic interventions involve changing the nature of interactions and transactions between the child and others.

Interim alternative educational setting (IAES)   A placement that may be used for students with disabilities when they commit disciplinary infractions resulting in temporary suspension or expulsion from school for more than ten days. Special education must be continued in the IAES.

Intermittent explosive disorder   Disorder characterized by recurrent outbursts in which the individual fails to control aggressive impulses.

Internalizing   Behavior typically associated with social withdrawal, such as shyness, anxiety, or depression.

Intervention   Method or strategy used in treatment of an emotional or behavioral disorder.

Intrapsychic; Intrapsychic causal factors   Having to do with the mind; in the mind itself. Conflict or disequilibrium between parts of the mind (in psychoanalytic theory, the id, the ego, and the superego), especially conflict in the unconscious.

Juvenile delinquency   *See* Delinquency.

Kanner's syndrome; Early infantile autism   Originally described by Leo Kanner in 1943. *See also* Autistic spectrum disorder.

Kleptomania   Disorder characterized by inability to resist urge to steal; the act of stealing itself—not the stolen item(s)—typically results in feelings of gratification, pleasure, or relief

Lability   *See* Emotional lability.

Life-impact curriculum   A special curriculum intended to change students' thinking about their experiences and choices. A curriculum based on humanistic or holistic philosophy.

Life space crisis intervention   Ways of talking with children based on psychoeducational theory to help them understand and change their behavior through reflection and planning. *See also* Life space interview.

Life space interview (LSI)   Therapeutic way of talking with disturbed children about their behavior. A set of techniques for managing behavior by means of therapeutic communication.

Locus of control   Belief that one's behavior is under internal or external control. Individuals have an internal locus to the extent that they believe they are responsible for their actions, an external locus to the extent that they believe chance or others' actions determine their behavior.

Macroculture   A nation or other large social entity with a shared culture.

Mania   Excessive excitement or enthusiasm, usually centered on a particular activity or object.

Manic; Manic episode   Persistently elevated, expansive, or irritable mood. Episode of such mood lasting at least one week.

Manifestation determination   A school-based process used to determine whether a student's misbehavior is due to his or her disability, usually in the process of determining appropriate disciplinary action for serious behavioral offenses.

Megavitamin therapy   Administration of extremely large doses of vitamins in the hope of improving or curing behavior disorders.

Metacognition; Metacognitive   Thinking about thinking. Awareness and analysis of one's thought processes. Controlling one's cognitive processes.

Microculture   A smaller group existing within a larger cultural group and having unique values, style, language, dialect, ways of communicating nonverbally, awareness, frame of reference, and identification.

Minimal brain dysfunction; Minimal brain damage   Term applied to children who exhibit behavioral characteristics (e.g., hyperactivity, distractibility) thought to be associated with brain damage, in the absence of other evidence that their brains have been damaged.

Minimal cerebral dysfunction   *See* Minimal brain dysfunction.

Mnemonics   Tools to help with memory.

Modeling   Providing an example to imitate. Behavior modification technique in which a clear model of the desired behavior is provided. (Typically, reinforcement is given for imitation of the model.)

Mood disorders   Disorders of emotion that color outlook on life. Usually characterized by either elation or depression. May be episodic or chronic, manic, or depressive.

Moral therapy; Moral treatment   Treatment provided in the late 18th and early 19th centuries characterized by humane and kindly care, therapeutic activity, and consistent consequences for behavior.

Multiaxial assessment   A system used in the *DSM–IV* in which the client is rated on five axes: clinical disorders, personality disorders or intellectual disabilities, general medical conditions, psychosocial and environmental problems, and global assessment of functioning.

Multiple intelligences   Highly specific types of problem-solving abilities (e.g., analytical, synthetic, and practical abilities) or intelligence in specific areas (e.g., linguistic, musical, spatial, interpersonal, intrapersonal, bodily–kinesthetic, or logical–mathematical). The theory that persons do not have a general intelligence but specific intelligences in various areas of performance.

Negative reinforcement Withdrawal or postponement of a negative reinforcer (aversive event or stimulus) contingent upon a behavior, which increases the probability that the behavior will be repeated.

Negative reinforcement trap Interaction pattern described first by Gerald Patterson, in which a teacher or parent may inadvertently negatively reinforce a child (by removing a demand or aversive) in response to an undesired behavior, which in turn negatively reinforces the teacher/parent, as the aversive the child created (e.g., crying, whining) is also avoided. Referred to as a *trap* because each party is then more likely to engage in the same negative pattern in the future.

Neologism A coined word that is meaningless to others. A meaningless word in the speech of a person with a psychotic disorder or a pervasive developmental disorder.

Neuroleptics Antipsychotic drugs. Drugs that suppress or prevent symptoms of psychosis. Major tranquilizers.

Neurosis; Neurotic behavior Emotional or behavioral disorder characterized by emotional conflict but not loss of contact with reality.

No Child Left Behind Act (NCLB) Major federal legislation enacted in 2001 with emphasis on increased accountability for schools; greater choice for parents of children attending schools that do not demonstrate "adequate yearly progress" (AYP); and increased flexibility for states and local schools in how they spend federal education money.

Nonsuicidal self-injury (NSSI) Self-injury that is not intended to be fatal and is typically compulsive, ritualistic, and episodic in nature (e.g., cutting or carving on the skin).

Normative Based on a norm, a sample assumed to provide a normal distribution of scores. Based on comparison to a statistical average for a representative sample of individuals.

Norm-referenced Based on a comparison to the average performance of a similar group of individuals.

Obesity Unhealthful, excessive accumulation of body fat.

Obsession Fixation on a specific object, event, or idea.

Obsessive-compulsive disorder (OCD) Disorder in which the individual has a level of *obsessions* (fixations on specific objects, events, or ideas) or *compulsions* (overwhelming desire to engage in a particular, often repetitive behavior) to a point that it interferes with daily functioning.

Operant conditioning Changing behavior by altering its consequences. Altering the future probability of a response by providing reinforcement or punishment as a consequence.

Oppositional defiant disorder (ODD) A pattern of negativistic, hostile, and defiant behavior that is unusual for the individual's age and developmental level, lasting at least six months and often characterized by fits of temper, arguing with adults, refusing to comply with adults' requests or rules, and deliberately annoying others and resulting in significant impairment of social, academic, or occupational functioning.

Organic brain syndrome; Organic psychosis Disorder caused by brain damage.

Organic mental disorders Disorders caused by transient or permanent brain dysfunction, often resulting from *anoxia*, ingestion of drugs or other toxic substances, or injury to brain tissue.

Organicity Behavioral indications of brain damage or organic defects.

Orthomolecular therapy Administration of chemical substances, vitamins, or drugs on the assumption that they will correct a basic chemical or molecular error that causes emotional or behavioral disorders.

Overcorrection Set of procedures designed to overcorrect behavioral errors. May be *positive practice* overcorrection (requiring the individual to practice a more adaptive or appropriate form of behavior) or *restitution* overcorrection (requiring the individual to restore the environment to a condition better than its status before the misbehavior occurred).

Overselective attention *See* Selective attention.

Parasuicide Attempted suicide.

Permissive approach to education Allowing children to behave as they wish within broad or loosely defined limits, on the assumption that it is therapeutic to allow them to act out their feelings (unless they endanger someone) and that the teacher must be permissive to build a sound relationship with children. Derived mostly from psychoanalytic theory.

Person variables Thoughts, feelings, and perceptions. Private events or states.

Personal agency The assumption, based on social learning theory, that a person is self-conscious and can make predictions and choices.

Personality disorders Deeply ingrained, inflexible, maladaptive patterns of relating to, perceiving, and thinking about the environment and oneself that impair adaptive functioning or cause subject distress.

Personality problem Disorder characterized by neurotic behavior, depression, and withdrawal.

Pervasive developmental disorder (PDD) Distortion of or lag in all or most areas of development, as in autism. *See also* Asperger's syndrome; Childhood disintegrative disorder; Rett's disorder.

Phenomenological model Assumptions that emotional or behavioral disorders result primarily from inadequate or distorted conscious experience with life events and that the most effective preventive actions and therapeutic interventions involve helping individuals examine their conscious experience of the world.

Phobia Irrational and debilitating fear.

Pica Persistent eating of nonnutritional substances (e.g., paint, plaster, cloth).

Play therapy Therapeutic treatment in which the child's play is used as the theme for communication between therapist and child.

Polydrug Using multiple drugs simultaneously, often intentionally to achieve some desired effect.

Positive behavior support (PBS)/Positive behavioral intervention and supports (PBIS) Interchangeable terms referring to a model of behavioral intervention that involves the systematic application of behavior analysis to solve behavior problems. Emphasis is on positive procedures and focus on environmental and contextual variables that influence behavior in different settings. Although the terms PBS and PBIS are often used interchangeably, PBS sometimes refers to a belief in behavior management without the use of punishment under any circumstances.

Positive practice *See* Overcorrection.

Positive reinforcement Presentation of a positive reinforcer (reward) contingent upon a behavior, which increases the probability that the behavior will be repeated.

Postencephalitic behavior syndrome Abnormal behavior following encephalitis (inflammation of the brain).

Posttraumatic stress disorder (PTSD) Disorder in which after experiencing a highly traumatic event the individual persistently reexperiences the event, avoids stimuli associated with the event, becomes generally unresponsive, or has persistent symptoms of arousal (e.g., hypervigilant, irritable, difficulty concentrating, difficulty sleeping), resulting in significant impairment of everyday functioning.

Pragmatics The practical use of language in social situations. The functional use rather than the mechanics of language.

Precorrection The strategy of anticipating and avoiding misbehavior by identifying and modifying the context in which it is likely to occur. Using proactive procedures to teach desired behavior rather than focusing on correction of misbehavior.

Premorbid; Premorbid personality Condition or personality characteristics predictive of later onset of illness or disorder.

Prevalence The total number or percent of individuals with a specific disorder in a given population (e.g., 2 percent). *Point prevalence* refers to the number or percentage at a particular point in time; *cumulative prevalence* to the number or percentage over a given period of time (e.g., the cumulative percentage of children who have a disorder before they complete high school).

Primary prevention Procedures designed to keep a disorder (or disease) from occurring.

Primary process thinking Psychoanalytic concept that disorganized or primitive thought or activity represents direct expression of unconscious mental processes. Distinguished from *secondary process* (rational, logical) thinking.

Prosocial behavior Behavior that facilitates or maintains positive social contacts. Desirable or appropriate social behavior.

Pseudoretardation Level of functioning associated with intellectual disabilities that increases to normal level of functioning when environmental factors are changed. Falsely diagnosed intellectual disabilities.

Psychoactive substance use disorders Disorders involving abuse of mood-altering substances (e.g., alcohol or other drugs).

Psychoanalytic model Assumptions that emotional or behavioral disorders result primarily from unconscious conflicts and that the most effective preventive actions and therapeutic interventions involve uncovering and understanding unconscious motivations.

Psychodynamic model *See* Psychoanalytic model.

Psychoeducational model Approach to education that takes into account psychodynamic concepts such as unconscious motivation but focuses intervention on the ego processes by which the child gains insight into his or her behavior.

Psychoneurosis; Psychoneurotic *See* Neurosis.

Psychopath; Psychopathic An individual who exhibits mostly amoral or antisocial behavior and is usually impulsive, irresponsible, and self-gratifying without consideration for others. Also called *sociopath* or *sociopathic*.

Psychopathology Mental illness. In psychiatry, the study of significant causes and development of mental illness. More generally, emotional or behavioral disorder.

Psychophysiological Physical disorder thought to be caused by psychological (emotional) conflict.

Psychosexual disorder Disorders involving sexual functioning or sex-typed behavior.

Psychosis A major mental illness in which thought processes are disordered (e.g., schizophrenia).

Psychosomatic; Psychosomaticization *See* Psychophysiological.

Psychotherapy Any type of treatment relying primarily on verbal and nonverbal communication between patient and therapist rather than on medical procedures. Not typically defined to include behavior modification. Typically administered by a psychiatrist or a clinical psychologist.

Psychotic disorder; Psychotic behavior Emotional or behavioral disorder characterized by major departure from normal patterns of acting, thinking, and feeling (e.g., schizophrenia). *See also* Schizophrenic disorder; Substance-induced psychotic disorder.

Punishment Consequences that reduce future probability of a behavior. May be *response cost* (removal of a valued object or commodity) or *aversive conditioning* (presentation of an aversive stimulus such as a slap or an electric shock).

Pyromania Disorder characterized by fascination with fire and repeated acts of intentional fire setting, typically for reasons of pleasure or gratification.

Rave An all-night dance party frequented by adolescents and young adults, generally involving electronic dance music and abuse of the drug ecstasy and other controlled substances.

Reactive attachment disorder of infancy or early childhood Markedly disturbed and developmentally inappropriate social behavior beginning before age five and assumed to be caused by neglect of the child's basic emotional and physical needs or by repeated changes in primary caregiver (e.g., frequent changes in foster placement).

Reactive depression Depression apparently precipitated by a specific event. Depression that is a reaction to adverse circumstances.

Reactive disorders Emotional or behavioral disorders apparently caused by reaction to stressful circumstances.

Recidivists *Recidivism* refers to repeat offending or law-breaking; recidivists are those who are known to have committed multiple offenses.

Reciprocal inhibition *See* Desensitization.

Reinforcement Presenting or removing stimuli following a behavior to increase its future probability. *Positive reinforcement* refers to presenting positive stimuli (rewards). *Negative reinforcement* refers to removing negative stimuli (punishers) contingent on a response. Both positive and negative reinforcement increase the rate or strength of the response.

Reliability The extent to which a measure would yield the same results if administered again.

Respondent behavior An elicited response. Reflexive behavior elicited automatically by presenting a stimulus (e.g., pupillary contraction elicited by shining a light in the eye).

Respondent conditioning Process by which a previously neutral stimulus comes to elicit a respondent behavior after the neutral stimulus has been paired with presentation of another stimulus (an unconditioned stimulus that already elicits a response) on one or more trials.

Response cost (RC) Punishment technique consisting of taking away a valued object or commodity contingent on a behavior. A fine. Making an inappropriate response "cost" something to the misbehaving child.

Response to intervention (RTI) A tiered model of service delivery; the term most often applies to academics but can also refer to tiered behavior supports. In an RTI framework, all students receive a universal tier of effective instruction (Tier I). Students who do not respond adequately to Tier I then received more targeted Tier II instruction, typically in small groups. Students not responsive to Tier II supports then receive Tier III intervention, often individualized instructional support.

Response topography The particular movements that comprise a response. How the response looks to an observer as opposed to the effect of the response on the environment.

Restitution *See* Overcorrection.

Rett's disorder Apparently normal development through at least age 5 months, followed by deceleration of head growth between ages 5 months and 48 months, loss of psychomotor skills, and severe impairment of expressive and receptive language. Usually associated with severe intellectual disabilities.

Risk The chance or probability that a specified outcome or set of outcomes will occur. A risk factor is an event or condition increasing the probability of a specified outcome.

Rumination; Mercyism Regurgitation with loss of weight or failure to thrive.

Schizoaffective disorder An episode of mood disorder concurrent with schizophrenia.

Schizoid; Schizophrenic spectrum behavior *See* Schizophreniform disorder.

Schizophrenia *See* Schizophrenic disorder.

Schizophrenic disorder Psychotic disorder characterized by distortion of thinking, abnormal perception, and bizarre behavior and emotions lasting at least six months.

Schizophreniform disorder Behavior like that seen in schizophrenia but not as long in duration or accompanied by decline in functioning. *See also* Schizophrenic disorder.

Schizophrenogenic Someone (in psychoanalytic theory, typically the mother) or something that causes schizophrenia.

School phobia Fear of going to school, usually accompanied by indications of anxiety about attendance, such as abdominal pain, nausea, or other physical complaints just before leaving for school in the morning.

Screening A quick, easy assessment process designed to capture a broad look at a group to determine who might warrant further, more in depth assessment in a given domain.

Secondary prevention Procedures implemented soon after a disorder (or disease) has been detected. Designed to reverse or correct a disorder or prevent it from becoming worse.

Selective attention Ability to direct and sustain one's attention to the appropriate and relevant stimuli in a given situation. Disorders of selective attention include *underselective attention* (inability to focus attention only on relevant stimuli or to disregard irrelevant stimuli) and *overselective attention* (inability to attend to all the relevant stimuli or tendency to focus on an irrelevant stimulus).

Selective mutism Consistent failure to speak in specific social circumstances in which speaking is expected, such as school (and despite speaking in other situations, e.g., home) but not due to lack of knowledge of or ability to use language.

Self-instruction Telling oneself what to do or how to perform. Technique for teaching children self-control or how to improve their performance by talking to themselves about what they are doing.

Self-stimulation Any repetitive, stereotyped activity that seems only to provide sensory feedback.

Sensitization approach Use of harsh punishment, threats, and overpowering force in discipline, especially in teaching or enforcing moral standards.

Separation anxiety disorder Developmentally inappropriate and excessive anxiety about separation from home or those to whom the individual is attached lasting at least four weeks, beginning before age eighteen, and causing significant distress or impairment of social or academic functioning.

Sequela Something that follows. A consequence. The lingering effect of an injury or disease (pl. *sequelae*).

Social-cognitive theory; social-cognitive model A model for behavior that draws on social-learning theory, which is based on a behavioral model, but also incorporates a cognitive influence. *See* Social learning theory.

Social learning theory Assumptions that antecedent or setting events (e.g., models, instructions), consequences (rewards and punishments), and cognitive processes (perceiving, thinking, feeling) influence behavior. Includes features of behavioral model or behavior modification with additional consideration of cognitive factors.

Social validity The acceptability and significance of a treatment procedure as judged by parents or other consumers.

Socialized delinquency; Subcultural delinquency Delinquent behavior in the context of an antisocial peer group.

Sociological model Approximate equivalent of *ecological model*.

Sociopath; Sociopathic *See* Psychopath.

Soft neurological signs Behavioral indications, such as uncoordination, distractibility, impulsivity, perceptual problems, and certain patterns of nerve reflexes, that may occur in individuals who are not brain damaged as well as in those who are. Signs that an individual may be brain damaged but that cannot be said to indicate the certainty of brain damage.

Somatic Physical. Of or relating to the body.

Somatoform disorders Physical symptoms suggesting a physical disorder, in the absence of demonstrable organic findings to explain the symptoms.

Standard error of measure (SEM) An estimate of how much a score obtained for an individual on a given assessment might vary from his or her true score.

Status offense An act that is illegal only if committed by a minor (e.g., buying or drinking alcohol).

Stereotype A simplified, standardized concept or image with particular meaning in describing a group. A routine or persistently repeated behavior.

Stereotypic behavior Persistent repetition of speech or motor activity.

Stereotypic movement disorder Repetitive, seemingly driven, nonfunctional motor behavior that markedly interferes with normal activities or results in self-inflicted injury requiring medical treatment.

Stereotypy A persistent, repetitive behavior or vocalization associated with self-stimulation, self-injury, or tic.

Strauss syndrome Group of emotional and behavioral characteristics, including hyperactivity, distractibility, impulsivity, perceptual disturbances, no family history of intellectual disabilities, and medical history suggestive of brain damage. Named after Alfred A. Strauss.

Structured approach to education Making the classroom environment highly predictable by providing clear directions for behavior, firm expectations that students will behave as directed, and consistent consequences for behavior. Assumes that children lack order and predictability in everyday life and will learn self-control in a highly structured (predictable) environment. Derives primarily from learning theory.

Substance-induced psychotic disorder Delusions or hallucinations caused by intoxication with or withdrawal from drugs or other substances.

Systematic desensitization *See* Desensitization.

Target assessment Definition and direct measurement (counting) of behaviors that are considered to be a problem (as opposed to administering psychological tests designed to measure behavioral traits or mental characteristics).

Temperament Inborn emotional or behavioral style, including general level of activity, regularity or predictability, approach or withdrawal, adaptability, intensity of reaction, responsiveness, mood, distractibility, and persistence.

Tertiary prevention Procedures designed to keep a severe or chronic disorder (or disease) from causing complications or overwhelming the individual or others.

Therapeutic milieu Total treatment setting that is therapeutic. Environment that includes attention to therapeutic value of both physical and social surroundings.

Tic Sudden, rapid, recurrent, nonrhythmic, stereotyped movement or vocalization.

Tic disorder Stereotyped movement disorder in which there is disregulation of gross motor movement. Recurrent, involuntary, repetitive, rapid, purposeless movement. May be transient or chronic.

Time-out Technically, time out from positive reinforcement. Interval during which reinforcement (rewards) cannot be earned. In classroom practice, usually a brief period of social isolation during which the child cannot receive attention or earn rewards.

Token economy; Token reinforcement; Token system System of behavior modification in which tangible or token reinforcers, such as points, plastic chips, metal washers, poker chips, or play money, are given as rewards and later exchanged for backup reinforcers that have value in themselves (e.g., food, trinkets, play time, books). A miniature economic system used to foster desirable behavior.

Topography *See* Response topography.

Tourette's disorder Multiple motor and vocal tics occurring many times daily (not necessarily together), with onset before age eighteen and causing marked distress or significant impairment of social or occupational functioning.

Tourette's syndrome (TS) *See* Tourette's disorder.

Transactions Exchanges.

Transference Unconscious redirection of feelings toward a different person (e.g., responding to teacher as if to parent). In psychoanalytic theory, responding to the therapist as if to another person, usually a parent.

Transition The movement from school to post-school environments; under IDEA, students receiving special education services are entitled to coordinated transition services to help them move on successfully to post-school employment, further schooling or training, and independent living.

Traumatic brain injury (TBI) Injury to the brain caused by an external force, not caused by a degenerative or congenital condition, and resulting in a diminished or altered state of consciousness and neurological or neurobehavioral dysfunction.

Traumatic head injury *See* Traumatic brain injury.

Triadic reciprocality The mutual influences of environment, person variables (thoughts, feelings), and behavior in social development.

Triennial evaluation Evaluation conducted every three years to determine whether a student identified as eligible for special education services continues to meet eligibility criteria (i.e., still has a disability under IDEA).

Underselective attention *See* Selective attention.

Unipolar In psychology, feelings characterized by mood swings in one direction (e.g., swings from normal feelings to feelings of depression without swings to manic behavior or feelings of euphoria).

Unsocialized aggression Unbridled aggressive behavior characterized by hostility, impulsivity, and alienation.

Validity The extent to which an assessment measures what it purports to measure.

Vicarious extinction Extinction of a fear response by watching someone else engage in an anxiety-provoking activity without apparent fear. Loss of fear (or other response) by observing others' behavior.

Vicarious reinforcement Reinforcement obtained by watching someone else obtain reinforcers (rewards) for a particular response.

Abidin, R. R., & Robinson, L. L. (2002). Stress, biases, or professionalism: What drives teachers' referral judgments of students with challenging behaviors? *Journal of Emotional and Behavioral Disorders, 10*, 204–212.

Achenbach, J. (2015, December 2). Faster, cheaper way to alter DNA points up ethics issues: Summit on gene editing examines technology that makes changes heritable. *Washington Post*, A7.

Achenbach, T. M. (1982). Assessment and taxonomy of children's behavior disorders. In B. B. Lahey & A. E. Kazdin (Eds.), *Advances in clinical child psychology* (Vol. 5, pp. 2–38). New York, NY: Plenum.

Achenbach, T. M. (1985). *Assessment and taxonomy of child and adolescent psychopathology*. Beverly Hills, CA: Sage.

Achenbach, T. M. (1991). *Manual for the Child Behavior Checklist/4–18 and 1991 profile*. Burlington, VT: University of Vermont, Department of Psychiatry.

Achenbach, T. M., & Edelbrock, C. S. (1981). Behavior problems and competencies reported by parents of normal and disturbed children aged four through sixteen. *Monographs of the Society for Research in Child Development, 46*(1, Serial No. 188).

Achenbach, T. M., & Edelbrock, C. S. (1989). Diagnostic, taxonomic, and assessment issues. In T. H. Ollendick & M. Hersen (Eds.), *Handbook of child psychopathology* (2nd ed., pp. 53–69). New York, NY: Plenum.

Achenbach, T. M., & Edelbrock, C. S. (1991). *Child behavior checklist—Teacher's report*. Burlington, VT: University Associates in Psychiatry.

Achenbach, T. M., Howell, C. T., Quay, H. C., & Conners, C. K. (1991). National survey of problems and competencies among four- to sixteen-year-olds. *Monographs of the Society for Research in Child Development, 56*(3, Serial No. 225).

Ackerson, L. (1942). *Children's behavior problems*. Chicago, IL: University of Chicago Press.

Adamczyk-Robinette, S. L., Fletcher, A. C., & Wright, K. (2002). Understanding the authoritative parenting—early adolescent tobacco use link: The mediating role of peer tobacco use. *Journal of Youth and Adolescence, 31*, 311–318.

Adams, P. J., Katz, R. C., Beauchamp, K., Cohen, E., & Zavis, D. (1993). Body dissatisfaction, eating disorders, and depression: A developmental perspective. *Journal of Child and Family Studies, 2*, 37–46.

Ahern, E. C., Lyon, T. D., & Quas, J. A. (2011). Young children's emerging ability to make false statements. *Developmental Psychology, 47*(1), 61–66.

Albano, A. M., Chorpita, B. F., & Barlow, D. H. (2003). Childhood anxiety disorders. In E. J. Mash & R. A. Barkley (Eds.), *Child psychopathology* (2nd ed., pp. 279–329). New York, NY: Guilford.

Alberto, P. A., & Troutman, A. C. (2017). *Applied behavior analysis for teachers* (9th ed.). Upper Saddle River, NJ: Pearson.

Algozzine, K., & Algozzine, B. (2014). Schoolwide prevention and proactive behavior. In P. Garner, J. M. Kauffman, & J. G. Elliott (Eds.), *The Sage handbook of emotional and behavioral difficulties* (2nd ed.) (pp. 363–372). London, U.K.: Sage.

Alter, P. J., Conroy, M. A., Mancil, G. R., & Haydon, T. (2008) A comparison of functional behavior assessment methodologies with young children: Descriptive methods and functional analysis. *Journal of Behavioral Education, 17*, 200–219.

American Educational Research Association, American Psychological Association, & National Council on Measurement in Education. (1999). *Standards for educational and psychological testing*. Washington, DC: Authors.

American Educational Research Association, American Psychological Association, & National Council on Measurement in Education (2014). *Standards for educational and psychological testing*. Washington, DC: AERA.

American Psychiatric Association. (2000). *Diagnostic and statistical manual of mental disorders* (4th text rev. ed.). Washington, D.C.: American Psychiatric Publishing.

American Psychiatric Association. (2013). *Diagnostic and statistical manual of mental Disorders* (5th ed.). Arlington, VA: American Psychiatric Publishing.

American Psychological Association. (1993). *Violence and youth: Psychology's response: Vol. 1. Summary report of the American Psychological Association Commission on Violence and Youth*. Washington, DC: Author.

Anastasiou, D. (Ed.). (2017). Section XIII. Cultural and international issues. In J. M. Kauffman, D. P. Hallahan, & P. C. Pullen (Eds.), *Handbook of special education* (2nd ed.). New York, NY: Taylor & Francis.

Anastasiou, D., Gardner, R., III, & Michail, D. (2011). Ethnicity and exceptionality. In J. M. Kauffman & D. P. Hallahan (Eds.), *Handbook of special education* (pp. 745–758). New York, NY: Taylor & Francis.

Anastasiou, D., & Kauffman, J. M. (2009). When special education goes to the marketplace: The case of vouchers. *Exceptionality, 17*, 205–222.

Anastasiou, D., & Kauffman, J. M. (2011). A social constructionist approach to disability: Implications for special education. *Exceptional Children, 77*, 367–384.

Anastasiou, D., & Kauffman, J. M. (2012). Disability as cultural difference: Implications for special education. *Remedial and Special Education, 33*, 139–149.

Anastasiou, D., & Kauffman, J. M. (2013). The social model of disability: Dichotomy between impairment and disability. *Journal of Medicine and Philosophy, 38*, 441–459.

Anastasiou, D., Kauffman, J. M., & Michail, D. (2016). Disability in multicultural theory: Conceptual and social justice issues. *Journal of Disability Policy Studies, 27*, 3–12.

Anastasiou, D., & Keller, C. D. (2017). Cross-national differences in special education: A typological approach.

In J. M. Kauffman, D. P. Hallahan, & P. C. Pullen (Eds.), *Handbook of special education* (2nd ed.). New York, NY: Taylor & Francis.

Anastasiou, D., Morgan, P. L., Farkas, G., & Wiley, A. (in press, 2017). Minority disproportionate representation in special education: Politics and evidence, issues and implications. In J. M. Kauffman & D. P. Hallahan (Eds.), *Handbook of special education* (2nd ed.). New York, NY: Routledge.

Anderson, J. C. (1994). Epidemiological issues. In T. H. Ollendick, N. J. King, & W. Yule (Eds.), *International handbook of phobic and anxiety disorders in children and adolescents* (pp. 43–65). New York: Plenum.

Anderson, J., & Werry, J. S. (1994). Emotional and behavioral problems. In I. B. Pless (Ed.), *The epidemiology of childhood disorders* (pp. 304–338). New York: Oxford University Press.

Armstrong, S. W., & Kauffman, J. M. (1999). Functional behavioral assessment: Introduction to the series. *Behavioral Disorders, 24*, 167–168.

Anonymous. (1994). First person account: Schizophrenia with childhood onset. *Schizophrenia Bulletin, 20*, 587–590.

Arthur, M. W., Hawkins, D. J., Pollard, J. A., Catalano, R. F., & Baglioni, A. J. (2002). Measuring risk and protective factors for substance use, delinquency, and other adolescent problem behaviors: The Communities That Care Youth Survey. *Evaluation Review, 26*, 575–601.

Arnold-Saritepe, A. M., Mudford, O. C. & Cullen, C. (2016). Gentle teaching. In R. M. Foxx & J. A. Mulick (Eds.), *Controversial therapies for autism and intellectual disabilities: Fad, fashion, and science in professional practice* (2nd ed.) (pp. 223–244). New York, NY: Francis & Taylor.

Asarnow, J. R., & Asarnow, R. F. (2003). Childhood-onset schizophrenia. In E. J. Mash & R. A. Barkley (Eds.), *Child psychopathology* (2nd ed., pp. 455–485). New York, NY: Guilford.

Asarnow, J. R., Thompson, M. C., & Goldstein, M. J. (1994). Childhood-onset schizophrenia: A follow-up study. *Schizophrenia Bulletin, 20*, 599–617.

Asarnow, R. F., Asamen, J., Granholm, E., Sherman, T., Watkins, J. M., & Williams, M. E. (1994). Cognitive/neuropsychological studies of children with schizophrenic disorders. *Schizophrenia Bulletin, 20*, 647–669.

Asarnow, R. F., & Asarnow, J. R. (1994). Childhood-onset schizophrenia: Editors' introduction. *Schizophrenia Bulletin, 20*, 591–597.

Azar, S. T., & Wolfe, D. A. (1998). Child physical abuse and neglect. In E. J. Mash & R. A. Barkley (Eds.), *Treatment of childhood disorders* (2nd ed., pp. 501–544). New York: Guilford.

Baer, J. S., MacLean, M. G., Marlatt, G. A. (1998). Linking etiology and treatment for adolescent substance abuse: Toward a better match. In R. Jessor (Ed.), *New perspectives on adolescent risk behavior* (pp. 182–220). New York: Cambridge University Press.

Bagner, D. M., Harwood, M. D., & Eyberg, S. M. (2006). Psychometric considerations. In M. Hersen (Ed.), *Clinician's handbook of child behavioral assessment* (pp. 63–79). Boston, MA: Academic Press.

Bagwell, C. L., & Coie, J. D. (2004). The best friendships of aggressive boys: Relationship quality, conflict management, and rule-breaking behavior. *Journal of Experimental Child Psychology, 88*(1), 5–24.

Bagwell, C. L., Molina, B. S. G., Kashdan, T. B., Pelham, W. E., & Hoza, B. (2006). Anxiety and mood disorders in adolescents with childhood attention-deficit/hyperactivity disorder. *Journal of Emotional and Behavioral Disorders, 14*, 178–187.

Baker, H. J. (1934). Common problems in the education of the normal and the handicapped. *Exceptional Children, 1*, 39–40.

Baker, P. (1996, January 16). Virginia joins movement to get tough on violent youths. *The Washington Post*, pp. B1, B4.

Bandura, A. (1977). *Social learning theory*. Upper Saddle River, NJ: Prentice Hall.

Bandura, A. (1978). The self-system in reciprocal determinism. *American Psychologist, 33*, 344–358.

Bandura, A. (1986). *Social foundations of thought and action: A social cognitive theory*. Upper Saddle River, NJ: Prentice Hall.

Bandura, A. (1995a). Comments on the crusade against the causal efficacy of human thought. *Journal of Behavior Therapy and Experimental Psychiatry, 26*, 179–190.

Bandura, A. (1995b). Exercise of personal and collective efficacy in changing societies. In A. Bandura (Ed.), *Self-efficacy in changing societies* (pp. 1–45). New York: Cambridge University Press.

Bandura A., & Locke, E. A. (2003). Negative self-efficacy and goal effects revisited. *Journal of Applied Psychology, 88*, 87–99.

Banks, J. A., & Banks, C. A. (2007). *Multicultural education: Issues and perspectives* (6th ed.). Hoboken, NJ: Wiley.

Barkley, R. A. (2003). Attention-deficit/hyperactivity disorder. In E. J. Mash & R. A. Barkley (Eds.), *Child psychopathology* (2nd ed., pp. 75–143). New York, NY: Guilford.

Barlow, Z. (2003, July 19). When gangs come to town: Small towns like Staunton are "virgin territory." *The Roanoke Times*, pp. A1, A6, A7.

Baron, A., & Galizio, M. (2005). Positive and negative reinforcement: Should the distinction be preserved? *The Behavior Analyst, 28*, 85–98.

Baron, A., & Galizio, M. (2006). The distinction between positive and negative reinforcement: Use with care. *The Behavior Analyst, 29*, 141–151.

Barrios, B. A., & O'Dell, S. L. (1998). Fears and anxieties. In E. J. Mash & R. A. Barkley (Eds.), *Treatment of childhood disorders* (2nd ed., pp. 249–337). New York: Guilford.

Bateman, B. D. (1992). Learning disabilities: The changing landscape. *Journal of Learning Disabilities, 25*, 29–36.

Bateman, B. D. (1994). Who, how, and where: Special education's issues in perpetuity. *Journal of Special Education, 27*, 509–520.

Bateman, B. D. (2004). *Elements of successful teaching: General and special education students*. Verona, WI: IEP Resources.

Bateman, B. D. (2007). Law and the conceptual foundations of special education practice. In J. B. Crockett, M. M., Gerber, & T. J. Landrum (Eds.), *Achieving the radical reform of special education: Essays in honor of James M. Kauffman* (pp. 95–114). Mahwah, NJ: Erlbaum.

Bateman, B. D. (2017). Individual education programs for children with disabilities. In J. M. Kauffman, D. P. Hallahan, & P. C. Pullen (Eds.), *Handbook of special education* (2nd ed.). New York, NY: Taylor & Francis.

Bateman, B. D., & Chard, D. J. (1995). Legal demands and constraints on placement decisions. In J. M. Kauffman, J. W. Lloyd, D. P. Hallahan, & T. A. Astuto (Eds.), *Issues in educational placement: Students with emotional and behavioral disorders* (pp. 285–316). Hillsdale, NJ: Erlbaum.

Bateman, B. D., & Linden, M. A. (2012). *Better IEPs: How to develop legally correct and educationally useful programs* (5th ed.). Verona, WI: Attainment.

Bateman, B. D., Lloyd, J. W., & Tankersley, M. (Eds.) (2015). *Enduring issues in special education: Personal perspectives.* New York, NY: Routledge.

Bateman, B. D., Lloyd, J. W., Tankersley, M., & Brown, T. S. (2015). What is special education? In B. D. Bateman, J. W. Lloyd, & M. Tankersley (Eds.), *Enduring issues in special education: Personal perspectives* (pp. 11–20). New York, NY: Routledge.

Batshaw, M. L. (2002b). Chromosomes and heredity: A toss of the dice. In M. L. Batshaw (Ed.), *Children with disabilities* (5th ed., pp. 3–26). Baltimore, MD: Brookes.

Batshaw, M. L. (Ed.). (2002a). *Children with disabilities* (5th ed.). Baltimore, MD: Brookes.

Baumeister, R. F., Campbell, J. D., Krueger, J. I., & Vohs, K. D. (2003). Does high self-esteem cause better performance, interpersonal success, happiness, or healthier lifestyles? *Psychological Science in the Public Interest, 4*(1), 1–44.

Baumrind, D. (1995). *Child maltreatment and optimal caregiving in social contexts.* New York: Garland.

Baumrind, D. (1996). The discipline controversy revisited. *Journal of Applied Family and Child Studies, 45*, 405–414.

Bayat, M. (2011). Clarifying issues regarding the use of praise with young children. *Topics in Early Childhood Special Education, 31*, 121–128.

Bear, G. G. (1998). School discipline in the United States: Prevention, correction, and long-term social development. *School Psychology Review, 27*, 14–32.

Beardslee, W. R., Versage, E. M., Van de Velde, P., Swatling, S., & Hoke, L. (2002). Preventing depression in children through resiliency promotion: The preventive intervention project. In R. J. McMahon & R. D. Peters (Eds.), *The effects of parental dysfunction on children* (pp. 71–86). New York, NY: Kluwer.

Beck, A. T. (1976). *Cognitive therapy and emotional disorders.* New York, NY: International Universities Press.

Becker, J. V., & Bonner, B. (1998). Sexual and other abuse of children. In R. J. Morris & T. R. Kratochwill (Eds.), *The practice of child therapy* (3rd ed., pp. 367–389). Boston: Allyn & Bacon.

Becker, W. C. (1964). Consequences of different kinds of parental discipline. In M. L. Hoffman & L. W. Hoffman (Eds.), *Review of child development research* (Vol. 1, pp. 169–208). New York, NY: Russell Sage Foundation.

Beer, D. A., Karitani, M., Leonard, H. L., March, J. S., & Sweda, S. E. (2002). Obsessive-compulsive disorder. In S. Kutcher (Ed.), *Practical child and adolescent psychopharmacology* (pp. 159–186). New York, NY: Cambridge University Press.

Beesdo, K., Knappe, S., & Pine, D. S. (2009). Anxiety and anxiety disorders in children and adolescents: Developmental issues and implications for DSM-V. *Psychiatric Clinics of North America, 32*, 483–524.

Beidel, D. C., & Turner, S. M. (1998). *Shy children, phobic adults: Nature and treatment of social phobia.* Washington, D.C.: American Psychological Association.

Belcher, T. L. (1995). Behavioral treatment vs. behavioral control: A case study. *Journal of Developmental and Physical Disabilities, 7*, 235–241.

Belia, S., Fidler, F., Williams, J., & Cumming, G. (2005). Researchers misunderstand confidence intervals and standard error bars. *Psychological Methods, 10*(4), 389.

Bell, R. Q. (1968). A reinterpretation of the direction of effects in studies of socialization. *Psychological Review, 75*, 81–95.

Bellack, A. S., Mueser, K. T., Gingerich, S., & Agresta, J. (2004). *Social skills training for schizophrenia: A step-by-step guide.* New York: Guilford.

Bellipanni, K. D., Tingstrom, D. H., Olmi, D. J., & Roberts, D. S. (2013). The sequential introduction of positive antecedent and consequent components in a compliance training package with elementary students. *Behavior modification, 37*(6), 768–789.

Bennett, D. E., Zentall, S. S., French, B. F., & Giorgetti-Borucki, K. (2006). The effects of computer-administered choice on students with and without characteristics of attention-deficit/hyperactivity disorder. *Behavioral Disorders, 31*, 189–203.

Bergman, R. L., Piacentini, J., & McCracken, J. T. (2002). Prevalence and description of selective mutism in a school-based sample. *Journal of the American Academy of Child and Adolescent Psychiatry, 41*, 938–946.

Berkeley, S., & Riccomini, P. J. (2017). Academic progress monitoring. In J. M. Kauffman, D. P. Hallahan, & P. C. Pullen (Eds.), *Handbook of special education* (2nd ed.). New York: Taylor & Francis.

Berliner, D. C. (2010). *Poverty and potential: Out-of-school factors and school success.* Boulder and Tempe: Education and the Public Interest Center & Education Policy Research Unit. Retrieved December 18, 2010 from http://epicpolicy.org/publication/poverty-and-potential.

Berry, C. S. (1936). The exceptional child in regular classes. *Exceptional Children, 3*, 15–16.

Best, S. J., Heller, K. W., & Bigge, J. L. (2005). *Teaching individuals with physical or multiple disabilities* (5th ed.). Upper Saddle River, NJ: Prentice Hall.

Best, S. J., Heller, K. W., & Bigge, J. L. (2010). *Teaching individuals with physical or multiple disabilities* (6th ed.). Upper Saddle River, NJ: Prentice Hall.

Beyers, J. M., & Loeber, R. (2003). Untangling developmental relations between depressed mood in male adolescents. *Journal of Abnormal Child Psychology, 31*, 247–266.

Bhatia, S., K., & Bhatia, S. C. (2007). Childhood and adolescent depression. *American Family Physician, 75*, 73–80.

Bicard, D. F., & Neef, N. A. (2002). Effects of strategic versus tactical instructions on adaptation to changing contingencies in children with ADHD. *Journal of Applied Behavior Analysis, 35,* 375–389.

Bielinski, J. (2001). Overview of test accommodations. *Assessment for Effective Intervention, 26*(2), 17–20.

Bierman, K. L., Coie, J. D., Dodge, K. A., Greenberg, M. T., Lochman, J. E., McMahon, R. J., et al. (2002). Using the Fast Track randomized prevention trial to test the early-starter model of the development of serious conduct problems. *Development and Psychopathology, 14,* 925–943.

Biglan, A. (1995). Translating what we know about the context of antisocial behavior into lower prevalence of such behavior. *Journal of Applied Behavior Analysis, 28,* 479–492.

Biklen, D. (1990). Communication unbound: Autism and praxis. *Harvard Educational Review, 60,* 291–314.

Biklen, D., & Schubert, A. (1991). New words: The communication of students with autism. *Remedial and Special Education, 12*(6), 46–57.

Billingsley, B. S., Fall, A., & Williams, T. O. (2006). Who is teaching students with emotional and behavioral disorders? A profile and comparison to other special educators. *Behavioral Disorders, 31,* 252–264.

Blackburn, R. (1993). *The psychology of criminal conduct: Theory, research, and practice.* New York, NY: Wiley.

Blackorby, J., Knokey, A., Wagner, M., Levine, P., Schiller, E., & Sumi, C. (2007, February). *SEELS: What makes a difference? Influences on outcomes for students with disabilities.* Project Report, U. S. Department of Education contract # ED-00-CO-0017.

Blake, C., Wang, W., Cartledge, G., & Gardner, R. (2000). Middle school students with serious emotional disturbances serve as social skills trainers and reinforcers for peers with SED. *Behavioral Disorders, 25,* 280–298.

Bloch, M. H., Peterson, B. S., Scahill, L., Otka, J., Katsovich, L., Zhang, H. J., Leckman, J. F. 2006). Adulthood outcome of tic and obsessive-compulsive symptom severity in children with Tourette syndrome. *Archives of Pediatrics and Adolescent Medicine, 160,* 65–69.

Bodfish, J. W. (2007). Stereotypy, self-injury, and related abnormal repetitive behaviors. In J. W. Jacobson, J. A. Mulick, & J. Rojahn (Eds.), *Handbook of intellectual and developmental disabilities* (pp. 481–505). New York, NY: Springer.

Boe, E. E., & Cook, L. H. (2006). The chronic and increasing shortage of fully certified teachers in special and general education. *Exceptional Children, 72,* 443–460.

Bolgar, R., Zweig-Frank, H., & Paris, J. (1995). Childhood antecedents of interpersonal problems in young adult children of divorce. *Journal of the American Academy of Child and Adolescent Psychiatry, 34,* 143–150.

Bower, E. M. (1960). *Early identification of emotionally handicapped children in school.* Springfield, IL: Thomas.

Bower, E. M. (1981). *Early identification of emotionally handicapped children in school* (3rd ed.). Springfield, IL: Thomas.

Bower, E. M. (1982). Defining emotional disturbance: Public policy and research. *Psychology in the Schools, 19,* 55–60.

Bracey, G. W. (2007, May 2). A test everyone will fail. *The Washington Post,* A25.

Bradley, R., Doolittle, J., & Bartolotta, R. (2008). Building on the data and adding to the discussion: The experiences and outcomes of students with emotional disturbance. *Journal of Behavioral Education, 17,* 4–23.

Brantlinger, E. A. (Ed.). (2006). *Who benefits from special education? Remediating (fixing) other people's children.* Mahwah, NJ: Erlbaum.

Bremner, R. H. (Ed.). (1970). *Children and youth in America: A documentary history: Vol. 1. 1600–1865.* Cambridge, MA: Harvard University Press.

Bremner, R. H. (Ed.). (1971). *Children and youth in America: A documentary history: Vol. 2. 1866–1932.* Cambridge, MA: Harvard University Press.

Briggs-Gowan, M. J., Carter, A. S., Bosson-Heenan, J., Guyer, A. E., & Horwitz, S. M. (2006). Are infant-toddler social-emotional and behavioral problems transient? *Journal of the American Academy of Child and Adolescent Psychiatry, 45,* 849–858.

Brigham, F. J., Ahn, S. Y., Stride, A. N., & McKenna, J. W. (2017). FAPE accompli: Misapplication of the principles of inclusion and students with EBD. In J. P. Bakken, F. E. Obiakor, & A. Rotatori (Eds.), *Advances in special education, Vol. 31a—General and special education in an age of change.* Bingley, UK: Emerald.

Brigham, F. J., Bakken, J. P., & Rotatori, A. F. (2012). Families and students with emotional and behavioral disorders. In J. P. Bakken, F. E. Obiakor, & A. Rotatori (Eds.), *Advances in special education, Vol. 23—Behavioral disorders: Current perspectives and issues* (pp. 205–228). Bingley, U.K.: Emerald.

Brigham, F. J., & Cole, J. E. (1999). Selective mutism: Developments in definition, etiology, assessment and treatment. In T. Scruggs & M. Mastropieri (Eds.), *Advances in learning and behavioral disabilities* (Vol. 13, pp. 183–216). Greenwich, CT: JAI.

Brigham, F. J., & Kauffman, J. M. (1998). Creating supportive environments for students with emotional or behavioral disorders. *Effective School Practices, 17*(2), 5–35.

Brigham, F. J., Tochterman, S., & Brigham, M. S. P. (2001). Students with emotional and behavioral disorders and their teachers in test-linked systems of accountability. *Assessment for Effective Intervention, 26*(1), 19–27.

Brigham, F. J., Weiss, M., & Jones, C. D. (1998, April). *Synthesis of follow-along and outcome studies of students with mild disabilities.* Paper presented at the annual meeting of the Council for Exceptional Children, Minneapolis, MN.

Brigham, M. M., Brigham, F. J., & Lloyd, J. W. (2002, November). *Accommodations and assessment: Supporting, distracting or enabling?* Paper presented at the annual conference of Teacher Educators of Children with Behavior Disorders, Scottsdale, AZ.

Brooks, D. (2011). *The social animal: The hidden sources of love, character, and achievement.* New York, NY: Random House.

Brooks, M. (2014). *At the edge of uncertainty: 11 discoveries taking science by surprise.* New York, NY: Overlook.

Brown, F. (1943). A practical program for early detection of atypical children. *Exceptional Children, 10,* 3–7.

Brown, W. H., Musick, K., Conroy, M., & Schaffer, E. H. (2001). A proactive approach for promoting young children's compliance. *Beyond Behavior, 11*(20), 3–8.

Brown, W. H., Odom, S. L., & Buysse, V. (2002). Assessment of preschool children's peer-related social competence. *Assessment for Effective Intervention, 27*(4), 61–71.

Bruhn, A., McDaniel, S., & Kreigh, C. (2015). Self-monitoring interventions for students with behavior problems: A systematic review of current research. *Behavioral Disorders, 40,* 102–121.

Bryant, E. S., Rivard, J. C, Addy, C. L., Hinkle, K. T., Cowan, T. M., & Wright, G. (1995). Correlates of major and minor offending among youth with severe emotional disturbance. *Journal of Emotional and Behavioral Disorders, 3,* 76–84.

Bukstein, O. G. (1995). *Adolescent substance abuse: Assessment, prevention, and treatment.* New York: Wiley.

Bullis, M., & Cheney, D. (1999). Vocational and transition interventions for adolescents and young adults with emotional or behavioral disorders. *Focus on Exceptional Children, 31*(7), 1–24.

Burke, J. D., Loeber, R., & Birmaher, B. (2002). Oppositional defiant disorder and conduct disorder: A review of the past 10 years, part II. *Journal of the Academy of Child and Adolescent Psychiatry, 41,* 1275–1293.

Burns, J. M., & Swerdlow, R. H. (2003). Right orbitofrontal tumor with pedophilia symptom and constructional apraxia sign. *Archives of Neurology, 60,* 437–440.

Burns, M. K., & Symington, T. (2002). A meta-analysis of pre-referral intervention teams: Student and systemic outcomes. *Journal of School Psychology, 40*(5), 437–447.

Busch, T. W., & Espin, C. A. (2003). Using curriculum-based measurement to prevent learning and assess learning in content areas. *Assessment for Effective Intervention, 28*(3/4), 49–58.

Butler, C. M., & Watkins, T. R. (2006). Effective social control measures in school and community programs: Implications for policy and practice. In B. Sims & P. Preston (Eds.), *Handbook of juvenile justice: Theory and practice* (pp. 145–167). Boca Raton, FL: Taylor & Francis.

Caeti, T. J., & Fritsch, E. J. (2006). Is it time to abolish the juvenile justice system? In B. Sims & P. Preston (Eds.), *Handbook of juvenile justice: Theory and practice* (pp. 653–673). Boca Raton, FL: Taylor & Francis.

Caldarella, P., Larsen, R. A., Williams, L., Wehby, J. H., Wills, H., & Kamps, D. (2016). Monitoring academic and social skills in elementary school: A psychometric evaluation of the classroom performance survey. *Journal of Positive Behavior Interventions,* published online before print, doi: 10.1177/1098300716665081.

Campbell, S. B. (1983). Developmental perspectives in child psychopathology. In T. H. Ollendick & M. Hersen (Eds.), *Handbook of child psychopathology* (pp. 13–40). New York: Plenum.

Cannon, Y., Gregory, M., & Waterstone, J. (2013). A solution hiding in plain sight: Special education and better outcomes for students with social, emotional, and behavioral challenges. *Fordham Urban Law Journal, 41,* 403–497.

Cantrell, R. P., & Cantrell, M. L. (Eds.). (2007). *Helping troubled children and youth: Continuing evidence for the Re-ED approach.* Nashville, TN: American Re-Education Association.

Caplan, R., Guthrie, D., Tang, B., Komo, S., & Asarnow, R. F. (2000). Thought disorder in childhood schizophrenia: Replication and update of concept. *Journal of the American Academy of Child and Adolescent Psychiatry, 39,* 771–778.

Caprara, G., Barbarnelli, C., Pastorelli, C., Bandura, A., & Zimbardo, P. (2000). Prosocial foundations of children's academic achievement. *Psychological Science, 11,* 302–326.

Capuzzi, D., & Gross, D. R. (2014). *Youth at risk: A prevention resource for counselors, teachers, and parents.* John Wiley & Sons.

Card, N. A., & Hodges, E. V. E. (2006). Shared targets for aggression by early adolescent friends. *Developmental Psychology, 42,* 1327–1338.

Card, N. A., Stucky, B. D., Sawalani, G. M. and Little, T. D. (2008), Direct and indirect aggression during childhood and adolescence: A meta-analytic review of gender differences, intercorrelations, and relations to maladjustment. *Child Development, 79,* 1185–1229.

Carey, G., & Goldman, D. (1997). The genetics of antisocial behavior. In D. M. Stoff, J. Breiling, & J. D. Maser (Eds.), *Handbook of antisocial behavior* (pp. 243–254). Hoboken, NJ: John Wiley & Sons.

Carlberg, C., & Kavale, K. (1980). The efficacy of special versus regular class placement for exceptional children: A meta-analysis. *Journal of Special Education, 29,* 155–162.

Carr, A. (2002). *Depression and attempted suicide in adolescence.* Malden, MA: BPS Blackwell.

Cartledge, G., Kea, C. D., & Ida, D. J. (2000). Anticipating differences—celebrating strengths: Providing culturally competent services for students with serious emotional disturbance. *Teaching Exceptional Children, 32*(3), 30–37.

Caruana, V. (2015). Accessing the common core standards for students with learning disabilities: Strategies for writing standards-based IEP goals. *Preventing School Failure: Alternative Education for Children and Youth, 59*(4), 237–243.

Caspi, A., Henry, B., McGee, R. O., Moffitt, T. E., & Silva, P. A. (1995). Temperamental origins of child and adolescent behavior problems: From age three to age fifteen. *Child Development, 66,* 55–68.

Center, D. B., & Kemp, D. (2003). Temperament and personality as potential factors in the development and treatment of conduct disorders. *Education and Treatment of Children, 26,* 75–88.

Cepeda, C. (2007). *Psychotic symptoms in children and adolescents: Assessment, differential diagnosis, and treatment.* New York, NY: Routledge.

Cha, C. B., & Nock, M. K. (2014). Suicidal and nonsuicidal self-injurious thoughts and behaviors. In E. J. Mash & R. A. Barkley (Eds.), *Child psychopathology* (2nd ed., pp. 317–342). New York, NY: Guilford.

Chafouleas, S. M. (2011). Direct behavior rating: A review of the issues and research in its development. *Education and Treatment of Children, 34*(4), 575–591.

Chan, D. W. (2006). Perceived multiple intelligences among male and female Chinese gifted students in Hong Kong: The structure of the Student Multiple Intelligences Profile. *Gifted Child Quarterly, 50*, 325–338.

Chang, J. J., Chen, J. J., & Brownson, R. C. (2003). The role of repeat victimization in adolescent delinquent behaviors and recidivism. *Journal of Adolescent Health, 32*, 272–280.

Chang, V. Y., Bendel, T. L., Koopman, C., McGarvey, E. L., & Canterbury, R. J. (2003). Delinquents' safe sex attitudes. *Criminal Justice and Behavior, 30*, 210–229.

Chase, P. N. (2006). Teaching the distinction between positive and negative reinforcement. *The Behavior Analyst, 29*, 113–115.

Chassin, L., Ritter, J., Trim, R. S., & King, K. M. (2003). Adolescent substance use disorders. In E. J. Mash & R. A. Barkley (Eds.), *Child psychopathology* (2nd ed., pp. 199–230). New York, NY: Guilford.

Cheney, D., & Bullis, M. (2004). Research findings and issues in the school-to-community transition of adolescents with emotional or behavioral disorders. In R. B. Rutherford, M. M. Quinn, & S. R. Mathur (Eds.), *Handbook of research in emotional and behavioral disorders*. New York, NY: Guilford.

Chess, S., & Thomas, A. T. (2003). Foreword. In B. K. Keogh, *Temperament in the classroom: Understanding individual differences* (pp. ix–xii). Baltimore, MD: Brookes.

Chow, J. C., & Wehby, J. H. (2016). Associations between language and problem behavior: A systematic review and correlational meta-analysis. *Educational Psychology Review*, 1–22. (Online first publication) doi:10.1007/s10648-016-9385-z.

Christakis, N. A., & Fowler, J. H. (2007). The spread of obesity in a large social network over 32 years. *New England Journal of Medicine, 357*, 370–379.

Cimpric, A. (2010, April). *Children accused of witchcraft: An anthropological study of contemporary practices in Africa*. Dakar: UNICEF.

Cipani, E. (1999). *A functional analysis of behavior (FAB) model for school settings*. Visalia, CA: Cipani & Associates.

Clark, H. G., & Mathur, S. R. (2010). Practices in transition for youth in the juvenile justice system. In D. Cheney (Ed.), *Transition of secondary students with emotional or behavioral disabilities: Current approaches for positive outcomes* (2nd ed., pp. 375–395). Arlington, VA: Council for Children with Behavioral Disorders/Division of Career Development and Transition.

Clark, H. G., & Unruh, D. (2010). Transition practices for adjudicated youth with E/BDs and related disabilities. *Behavioral Disorders, 36*, 43–51.

Clarkwest, A., Killewald, A. A., & Wood, R. G. (2015). Stepping up or stepping back: Highly disadvantaged parents' responses to the Building Strong Families program. In O. Patterson & E. Fosse (Eds.), *The cultural matrix: Understanding black youth* (pp. 444–470). Cambridge, MA: Harvard University Press.

Cline, D. H. (1990). A legal analysis of policy initiatives to exclude handicapped/disruptive students from special education. *Behavioral Disorders, 15*, 159–173.

Cluett, S. E., Forness, S. R., Ramey, S., Ramey, C., Hsu, C., Kavale, K. A., Gresham, F. M. (1998). Consequences of differential diagnostic criteria on identification rates of children with emotional or behavior disorders. *Journal of Emotional and Behavioral Disorders, 6*, 130–140.

Cohan, S. L., Chavira, D. A., & Stein, M. B. (2006). Practitioner review: Psychosocial interventions for children with selective mutism: A critical evaluation of the literature from 1990–2005. *Journal of Child Psychology and Psychiatry, 47*, 1085–1097.

Coleman, M., & Vaughn, S. (2000). Reading interventions for students with emotional/behavioral disorders. *Behavioral Disorders, 25*, 93–104.

Coles, E. K., Pelham, W. E., Gnagy, E. M., Burrows-MacLean, L., Fabiano, G. A., Chacko, A., et al. (2005). A controlled evaluation of behavioral treatment with children with ADHD attending a summer treatment program. *Journal of Emotional and Behavioral Disorders, 13*, 99–112.

Collins, F. (2003, April 22). A common thread. *The Washington Post*, p. A19.

Collins, F., Green, E. D., Guttmacher, A. E., & Guyer, E. S. (2003). A vision for the future of genomics research. *Nature, 422*, 835–847.

Colvin, G. (1992). *Managing acting-out behavior*. Eugene, OR: Behavior Associates.

Colvin, G., Sugai, G., & Patching, B. (1993). Precorrection: An instructional approach for managing predictable problem behaviors. *Intervention in School and Clinic, 28*, 143–150.

Comer, J. P. (1988). Is "parenting" essential to good teaching? *NEA Today, 6*(6), 34–40.

Conduct Problems Prevention Research Group. (1999). Initial impact of the Fast Track prevention trial for conduct problems: II Classroom effects. *Journal of Consulting and Clinical Psychology, 67*, 648–657.

Conduct Problems Prevention Research Group. (2011). The effects of the Fast Track preventive intervention on the development of conduct disorder across childhood. *Child Development, 82*, 331–345.

Connor, D. F., Boone, R. T., Steingard, R. J., Lopez, I. D., & Melloni, R. (2003). Psychopharmacology and aggression: II. A meta-analysis of nonstimulant medication effects on overt aggression-related behaviors in youth with SED. *Journal of Emotional and Behavioral Disorders, 11*, 157–168.

Connor, D. F., Glatt, S. J., Lopez, I. D., Jackson, D., & Melloni, R. H. (2002). Psychopharmacology and aggression. I: A meta-analysis of stimulant effects on overt/covert aggression-related behaviors in ADHD. *Journal of the American Academy of Child and Adolescent Psychiatry, 41*, 253–261.

Conroy, M. A. (2017). Section XII: Early identification and intervention in exceptionality. In J. M. Kauffman, D. P. Hallahan, & P. C. Pullen (Eds.), *Handbook of special education* (2nd ed.). New York, NY: Taylor & Francis.

Conroy, M. A., & Davis, C. A. (2000). Early elementary-aged children with challenging behaviors: Legal and educational issues related to IDEA and assessment. *Preventing School Failure, 44*(4), 163–168.

Conroy, M. A., Davis, C. A., Fox, J. J., & Brown, W. H. (2002). Functional assessment of behavior and effective supports for young children with challenging behaviors. *Assessment for Effective Intervention, 27*(4), 35–47.

Conroy, M. A., Hendrickson, J. M., & Hester, P. P. (2004). Early identification and prevention of emotional and behavioral disorders. In R. B. Rutherford, M. M. Quinn, & S. R. Mathur (Eds.). *Handbook of research in emotional and behavioral disorders* (pp. 199–215). New York: Guilford.

Conroy, M. A., Stichter, J. P., & Gage, N. (2017). Current issues and trends in the education of children and youth with autism spectrum disorders. In J. M. Kauffman, D. P. Hallahan, & P. C. Pullen (Eds.), *Handbook of special education* (2nd ed.). New York, NY: Taylor & Francis.

Cook, B. G., Landrum, T. J., Tankersley, M., & Kauffman, J. M. (2003). Bringing research to bear on practice: Effecting evidence-based instruction for students with emotional or behavioral disorders. *Education and Treatment of Children, 26*, 345–361.

Cook, B. G., & Ruhaak, A. E. (2014). Causality and emotional or behavioral disorders: An introduction. In P. Garner, J. M. Kauffman, & J. G. Elliott (Eds.), *The Sage handbook of emotional and behavioral difficulties* (2nd ed.) (pp. 97–108). London, U.K.: Sage.

Cook, B. G., & Schirmer, B. R. (2006). Conclusion: An overview and analysis of the role of evidence-based practices in special education. In B. G. Cook & B. R. Schirmer (Eds.), *What is special about special education? Examining the role of evidence-based practices* (pp. 175–185). Austin, TX: Pro-Ed.

Cooper, P. (2014) Biology, emotion and behavior: The value of a biopsychosocial perspective in understanding SEBD. In P. Garner, J. M. Kauffman, & J. G. Elliott (Eds.), *The Sage handbook of emotional and behavioral difficulties* (2nd ed.) (pp. 109–130). London, U.K.: Sage.

Copeland, W. E., Keeler, G., Angold, A., & Costello, E. J. (2007). Traumatic events and posttraumatic stress in childhood. *Archives of General Psychiatry, 64*, 577–584.

Costello, E. J., Egger, H., & Angold, A. (2005). 1-year research update review: The epidemiology of child and adolescent psychiatric disorders: I. Methods and public health burden. *Journal of the American Academy of Child and Adolescent Psychiatry, 44*, 972–986.

Costello, E. J., Foley, D. L., & Angold, A. (2006). Ten-year research update review: The epidemiology of child and adolescent psychiatric disorders: II. Developmental epidemiology. *Journal of the American Academy of Child and Adolescent Psychiatry, 45*, 8–25.

Costenbader, V., & Buntaine, R. (1999). Diagnostic discrimination between social maladjustment and emotional disturbance: An empirical study. *Journal of Emotional and Behavioral Disorders, 7*, 2–10.

Cottle, M. (2001, June 18). Reform school. *The New Republic, 224*, 14–15.

Council for Children with Behavioral Disorders. (1996). Guidelines for providing appropriate services to culturally diverse youngsters with emotional and/or behavioral disorders: Report of the Task Force of the CCBD Ad Hoc Committee on Ethnic and Multicultural Concerns. *Behavioral Disorders, 21*, 137–144.

Council for Children with Behavioral Disorders Executive Committee. (1987). Position paper on definition and identification of students with behavioral disorders. *Behavioral Disorders, 13*, 9–19.

Council for Exceptional Children. (1997–1999). *CEC standards for professional practice in special education.* Reston, VA: Council for Exceptional Children.

Crawford, L., & Tindal, G. (2002). Curriculum-based collaboration in secondary schools. In M. R. Shinn, H. M. Walker, & G. Stoner (Eds.), *Interventions for academic and behavior problems II: Preventive and remedial approaches* (pp. 825–853). Bethesda, MD: National Association of School Psychologists.

Crenshaw, T. M., Kavale, K. A., Forness, S. R., & Reeve, R. E. (1999). Attention deficit hyperactivity disorder and the efficacy of stimulant medication: A meta-analysis. In T. Scruggs & M. Mastropieri (Eds.), *Advances in learning and behavioral disabilities* (Vol. 13, pp. 135–165). Greenwich, CT: JAI.

Crews, G. A., Purvis, J. R., & Hjelm, M. (2006). The emerging problem of preppie gangs in America. In B. Sims & P. Preston (Eds.), *Handbook of juvenile justice: Theory and practice* (pp. 193–217). Boca Raton, FL: Taylor & Francis.

Crijnen, A. A. M., Achenbach, T. M., & Verhulst, F. C. (1997). Comparisons of problems reported by parents of children in 12 cultures: Total problems, externalizing, and internalizing. *Journal of the Academy of Child and Adolescent Psychiatry, 36*, 1269–1277.

Crockett, J. B. (Ed.). (2001). The meaning of science and empirical rigor in the social sciences [Special issue]. *Behavioral Disorders, 27*(1).

Crockett, J. B., & Kauffman, J. M. (1999). *The least restrictive environment: Its origins and interpretations in special education.* Mahwah, NJ: Erlbaum.

Cullinan, D. (2002). *Students with emotional and behavior disorders: An introduction for teachers and other helping professionals.* Upper Saddle River, NJ: Merrill/Prentice Hall.

Cullinan, D. (2004). Classification and definition of emotional and behavioral disorders. In R. B. Rutherford, M. M. Quinn, & S. R. Mathur (Eds.). *Handbook of research in emotional and behavioral disorders* (pp. 32–53). New York: Guilford.

Cullinan, D., Epstein, M. H., & Lloyd, J. W. (1991). Evaluation of conceptual models of behavior disorders. *Behavioral Disorders, 16*, 148–157.

Cullinan, D., & Kauffman, J. M. (2005). Do race of student and race of teacher influence ratings of emotional and behavioral problem characteristics of students with emotional disturbance? *Behavioral Disorders, 30*, 393–402.

Culp, A. M., Clyman, M. M., & Culp, R. E. (1995). Adolescent depressed mood, reports of suicide attempts, and asking for help. *Adolescence, 30*, 827–837.

Cummings, E. M., & Davies, P. (1999). Depressed parents and family functioning: Interpersonal effects and children's functioning and development. In T. Joiner & J. C. Coyne (Eds.), *The interactional nature of depression* (pp. 299–327). Washington, DC: American Psychological Association.

Curry, J. F., March, J. S., & Hervey, A. S. (2004). Comorbidity of childhood and adolescent anxiety disorders: Prevalence and implications. In T. S. Ollendick & J. S. March (Eds.), *Phobic and anxiety disorders in children and adolescents* (pp. 116–140). New York, NY: Oxford University Press.

Dadds, M. R. (2002). Learning and intimacy in the families of anxious children. In R. J. McMahon & R. D. Peters (Eds.), *The effects of parental dysfunction on children* (pp. 87–104). New York, NY: Kluwer.

Dean, A. J., Duke, S. G., George, M., & Scott, J. (2007). Behavioral management leads to reduction in aggression in a child and adolescent psychiatric inpatient unit. *Journal of the American Academy of Child and Adolescent Psychiatry, 46,* 711–720.

DeJong, S., & Frazier, J. A. (2003). Bipolar disorder in children with pervasive developmental disorder. In B. Geller & M. P. DelBello (Eds.), *Bipolar disorder in childhood and early adolescence* (pp. 51–75). New York, NY: Guilford.

Delaney, T. (2006). *American street gangs.* Upper Saddle River, NJ: Prentice Hall.

Dell Orto, A. E., & Power, P. W. (2000). *Brain injury and the family: A live and living perspective* (2nd ed.). Washington, DC: CRC.

DeLuca, S., Clampet-Lundquist, S., & Edin, K. (2016). *Coming of age in the other America.* New York, NY: Russel Sage Foundation.

Denham, S., Blair, K., Schmidt, M., & DeMulder, E. (2002). Compromised emotional competence: Seeds of violence sown early? *American Journal of Orthopsychiatry, 72,* 70–82.

Deno, S. L. (2003). Curriculum-based measures: Development and perspectives. *Assessment for Effective Intervention, 28*(3/4), 3–12.

DeVoe, J. F., & Bauer, L (2010). *Student victimization in U.S. schools: Results from the 2007 School Crime Supplement to the National Crime Victimization Survey* (NCES 2010-319). Washington, DC: National Center for Education Statistics, Institute of Education Sciences, U.S. Department of Education.

Dinitz, S., Scarpitti, F. R., & Reckless, W. C. (1962). Delinquency vulnerability: A cross group and longitudinal analysis. *American Sociological Review, 27,* 515–517.

Dodge, K. A., & Pettit, G. S. (2003). A biopsychosocial model of the development of chronic conduct problems in adolescence. *Developmental Psychology, 39,* 349–371.

Donenberg, G. R., Bryant, F. B., Emerson, E., Wilson, H. W., & Pasch, K. E. (2003). Tracing the roots of early sexual debut among adolescents in psychiatric care. *Journal of the American Academy of Child and Adolescents in Psychiatric Care, 42,* 594–608.

Donohue, B. C., Karmely, J., & Strada, M. J. (2006). Alcohol and drug abuse. In M. Hersen (Ed.), *Clinician's handbook of child behavioral assessment* (pp. 337–375). Boston MA: Academic Press.

Donovan, J., & Jessor, R. (1985). Structure of problem behavior in adolescence and young adulthood. *Journal of Consulting and Clinical Psychology, 53,* 890–904.

Dow, S. P., Sonies, B. C., Scheib, D., Moss, S. E., & Leonard, H. L. (1995). Practical guidelines for the assessment and treatment of selective mutism. *Journal of the American Academy of Child and Adolescent Psychiatry, 34,* 836–846.

Doyle, C. (2003). Child emotional abuse: The role of educational professionals. *Educational and Child Psychology, 20,* 8–21.

Drummond, T. (1994). *The Student Risk Screening Scale* (SRSS). Grants Pass, OR: Josephine County Mental Health Program.

Dulcan, M. (1997). Practice parameters for the assessment and treatment of children, adolescents, and adults with attention-deficit/hyperactivity disorder. *Journal of the American Academy of Child and Adolescent Psychiatry, {Suppl. 36}* (10), 85S–121S.

Duncan, B. B., Forness, S. R., & Hartsough, C. (1995). Students identified as seriously emotionally disturbed day treatment: Cognitive, psychiatric, and special education characteristics. *Behavioral Disorders, 20,* 238–252.

Dunlap, G., & Fox, L. (2014). Supportive interventions for young children with social, emotional, and behavioral delays and disorders. In H. M. Walker & F. M. Gresham (Eds.), *Handbook of evidence-based practices for emotional and behavioral disorders: Applications in schools* (pp. 503–517). New York, NY: Guilford.

Dunlap, G., Strain, P. S., Fox, L., Carta, J. J., Conroy, M., Smith, B. J., … Sowell, C. (2006). Prevention and intervention with young children's challenging behavior: Perspectives regarding current knowledge. *Behavioral Disorders, 32,* 29–45.

DuPaul, G. J., & Barkley, R. A. (1998). Attention-deficit hyperactivity disorder. In R. J. Morris & T. R. Kratochwill (Eds.), *The practice of child therapy* (3rd ed., pp. 132–166). Boston: Allyn & Bacon.

Dupre, A. P. (1996). Should students have constitutional rights? Keeping order in the public schools. *George Washington Law Review, 65*(1), 49–105.

Dupre, A. P. (1997). Disability and the public schools: The case against "inclusion." *Washington Law Review, 72,* 775–858.

Dwyer, R. G., & Laufersweiler-Dwyer, D. L. (2006). Juvenile sex offenders: An overview. In B. Sims & P. Preston (Eds.), *Handbook of juvenile justice: Theory and practice* (pp. 359–374). Boca Raton, FL: Taylor & Francis.

Earley, P. (2006). *Crazy: A father's search through America's mental health madness.* New York, NY: Penguin.

Eber, L., Malloy, J. M., Rose, J., & Flamini, A. (2014). School-based wraparound for adolescents: The RENEW model for transition-age youth with or at risk of emotional and behavior disorders. In H. M. Walker & F. M. Gresham (Eds.), *Handbook of evidence-based practices for emotional and behavioral disorders: Applications in schools* (pp. 1–5; 583–585). New York, NY: Guilford.

Eddy, J. M., Reid, J. B., & Curry, V. (2002). The etiology of youth antisocial behavior, delinquency, and violence and a public health approach to prevention. In M. R. Shinn, H. M. Walker, & G. Stoner (Eds.), *Interventions for academic and behavior problems II: Preventive and remedial approaches* (pp. 27–52). Bethesda, MD: National Association of School Psychologists.

Edgar, E., & Siegel, S. (1995). Postsecondary scenarios for troubled and troubling youth. In J. M. Kauffman, J. W. Lloyd,

D. P. Hallahan, & T. A. Astuto (Eds.), *Issues in educational placement: Students with emotional and behavioral disorders* (pp. 251–283). Hillsdale, NJ: Erlbaum.

Edgar, E. B. (1987). Secondary programs in special education: Are many of them justifiable? *Exceptional Children, 53,* 555–561.

Eggers, C., Bunk, D., & Drause, D. (2000). Schizophrenia with onset before the age of eleven: Clinical characteristics of onset and course. *Journal of Autism and Developmental Disorders, 30,* 29–38.

Egley, A., Jr., & Ritz, C. E. (2006). *Highlights of the 2004 National Youth Gang Survey.* Fact Sheet No. 2006-01. Washington, DC: U.S. Department of Justice, Office of Juvenile Justice and Delinquency Prevention.

Ehrensaft, M. K., Wasserman, G. A., Verdelli, L., Greenwald, S., Miller, L. S., & Davies, M. (2003). Maternal antisocial behavior, parent practices, and behavior problems in boys at risk for antisocial behavior. *Journal of Child and Family Studies, 12,* 27–40.

Eiduson, B. T., Eiduson, S., & Geller, E. (1962). Biochemistry, genetics, and the nature–nurture problem. *American Psychologist, 119,* 342–350.

Elliott, S. N., & Gresham, F. M. (2007). *Social Skills Improvement System: Classwide Intervention Program.* Bloomington, MN: Pearson Assessments.

Eme, R. F., & Danielak, M. H. (1995). Comparison of fathers of daughters with and without maladaptive eating attitudes. *Journal of Emotional and Behavioral Disorders, 3,* 40–45.

Engelmann, S. (1997). Theory of mastery and acceleration. In J. W. Lloyd, E. J. Kameenui, & D. Chard (Eds.), *Issues in educating students with disabilities* (pp. 177–195). Mahwah, NJ: Erlbaum.

Engelmann, S., & Carnine, D. (2011). *Could John Stuart Mill have saved our schools?* Verona, WI: Attainment.

Ennis, R. P., Schwab, J. R., & Jolivette, K. (2012). Using precorrection as a secondary-tier intervention for reducing problem behaviors in instructional and noninstructional settings. *Beyond Behavior, 22*(1), 40–47.

Ensminger, M. E., & Juon, H. S. (1998). Transition to adulthood among high-risk youth. In R. Jessor (Ed.), *New perspectives on adolescent risk behavior* (pp. 365–391). New York, NY: Cambridge University Press.

Epstein, M. H. (2004). *Behavioral and Emotional Rating Scale: A Strength-Based Approach to Assessment: Examiner's Manual.* Pro-Ed.

Epstein, M. H., & Cullinan, D. (1998). Scale for assessing emotional disturbance. Austin, TX: *Pro-Ed.*

Espin, C. A., McMaster, K. L., Rose, S., & Wayman, M. M. (Eds.). (2012). *A measure of success: The influence of curriculum-based measurement on education.* Minneapolis, MN: University of Minnesota Press.

Esposito, C., Johnson, B., Wolfsdorf, B. A., & Spirito, A. (2003). Cognitive factors: Hopelessness, coping, and problem solving. In A. Spirito, & J. C. Overholser (Eds.), *Evaluating and treating adolescent suicide attempters: From research to practice* (pp. 89–112). New York, NY: Academic Press.

Estell, D. B., Farmer, T. W., Irvin, M. J., Crowther, A., Akos, P., & Boudah, D. J. (2009). Students with exceptionalities and the peer group context of bullying and victimization in late elementary school. *Journal of Child and Family Studies, 18,* 136–150.

Evans, E. D., & Richardson, R. C. (1995). Corporal punishment: What teachers should know. *Teaching Exceptional Children, 27*(2), 33–36.

Evans, S. W., Rybak, T., Strickland, H., & Owens, J. S. (2014). The role of school mental health models in preventing and addressing children's emotional and behavioral problems. In H. M. Walker & F. M. Gresham (Eds.), *Handbook of evidence-based practices for emotional and behavioral disorders: Applications in schools* (pp. 394–409). New York, NY: Guilford.

Evertson, C., & Weinstein, C. (Eds.). (2006). *Handbook of classroom management: Research, practice, and contemporary issues.* Mahwah, NJ: Erlbaum.

Eyre, S. L., & Millstein, S. G. (1999). What leads to sex? Adolescents' preferred partners and reasons for sex. *Journal of Research on Adolescence, 9,* 277–307.

Fagan, J., & Wilkinson, D. L. (1998). Social contexts and functions of adolescent violence. In D. S. Elliott, B. A. Hamburg, & K. R. Williams (Eds.), *Violence in American schools* (pp. 31–54). New York: Cambridge University Press.

Fairbanks, S., Sugai, G., Guardino, D., & Lathrop, M. (2007). Response to intervention: Examining classroom behavior support in second grade. *Exceptional Children, 73,* 288–310.

Farmer, T. W. (2000). Misconceptions of peer rejection and problem behavior: A social interactional perspective of the adjustment of aggressive youth with mild disabilities. *Remedial and Special Education, 21,* 194–208.

Farmer, T. W., Leung, M-C., Pearl, R., Rodkin, P. C., Cadwallader, T. W., & Van Acker, R. (2002). Deviant or diverse peer groups? The peer affiliations of aggressive students. *Journal of Educational Psychology, 94,* 611–620.

Farmer, T. W., Rodkin, P. C., Pearl, R., & Van Acker, R. (1999). Teacher-assessed behavioral configurations, peer assessments, and self-concepts of elementary students with mild disabilities. *Journal of Special Education, 33*(3), 66–80.

Farrington, D. P. (2007). Introduction. In G. Sayre-McCord (Ed.), *Crime and family: Selected essays of Joan McCord* (pp. 1–10). Philadelphia, PA: Temple University Press.

Farrington, D. P., Loeber, R., Stallings, R., & Ttofi, M. M. (2011). Bullying perpetration and victimization as predictors of delinquency and depression in the Pittsburgh Youth Study. *Journal of Aggression, Conflict and Peach Research, 3,* 74–81.

Farson, M. R. (1940). Education of the handicapped child for social competency. *Exceptional Children, 6,* 138–144, 150.

Feil, E. G. (1999). Using the preschool-age as a developmental leverage to prevent behavior problems with early screening and intervention. *Effective School Practices, 17*(3): 50–55.

Feil, E. G., Frey, A. Walker, H. M., Small, J. W., Seeley, J. R., Golly, A., & Forness, S. R. (2014). The efficacy of a home-school intervention for pre-schoolers with challenging behaviors: A randomized controlled trial of preschool first step to success. *Journal of Early Intervention, 36,* 151–170.

Feil, E. G., Small, J. W., Forness, S. R., Serna, L. A., Kaiser, A. P., Hancock, T. B., et al. (2005). Using different measures, informants, and clinical cut-off points to estimate prevalence of emotional or behavioral disorders in preschoolers: Effects on age, gender, and ethnicity. *Behavioral Disorders, 30*, 375–391.

Fisher, M. (2003, April 6). Pass/fail. *The Washington Post Magazine*, 14–18, 37–48.

Fitzgerald, H. E., Davies, W. H., & Zucker, R. A. (2002). Growing up in an alcoholic family: Structuring pathways for risk aggregation and theory-driven intervention. In R. J. McMahon & R. D. Peters (Eds.), *The effects of parental dysfunction on children* (pp. 127–146). New York, NY: Kluwer.

Flannery, D. J., & Huff, C. R. (Eds.). (1999). *Youth violence: Prevention, intervention, and social policy*. Washington, DC: American Psychiatric Press.

Fletcher, K. E. (2003). Childhood posttraumatic stress disorder. In E. J. Mash & R. A. Barkley (Eds.), *Child psychopathology* (2nd ed., pp. 330–371). New York, NY: Guilford.

Flory, K., Milich, R., Lynam, D. R., Leukefeld, C., & Clayton, R. (2003). The relationship between disruptive behavior disorders and substance use and dependence symptoms in young adulthood: Individuals with symptoms of attention-deficit/hyperactivity disorder are uniquely at risk. *Psychology of Addictive Behaviors, 17*, 151–158.

Ford, A. D., Olmi, D. J., Edwards, R. P., & Tingstrom, D. H. (2001). The sequential introduction of compliance training components with elementary-aged children in general education classroom settings. *School Psychology Quarterly, 16*(2), 142–157.

Ford, M. C. (2006). The relationship between childhood maltreatment and delinquency. In B. Sims & P. Preston (Eds.), *Handbook of juvenile justice: Theory and practice* (pp. 127–143). Boca Raton, FL: Taylor & Francis.

Forness, S. R. (1988a). Planning for the needs of children with serious emotional disturbance: The national special education and mental health coalition. *Behavioral Disorders, 13*, 127–133.

Forness, S. R. (1988b). School characteristics of children and adolescents with depression. In R. B. Rutherford, C. M. Nelson, & S. R. Forness (Eds.), *Bases of severe behavioral disorders of children and youth* (pp. 177–203). Boston: Little, Brown.

Forness, S. R. (2005). The pursuit of evidence-based practice in special education for children with emotional or behavioral disorders. *Behavioral Disorders, 30*, 311–330.

Forness, S. R., & Beard, K. Y. (2007). Strengthening the research base in special education: Evidence-based practice and interdisciplinary collaboration. In J. Crockett, M. Gerber, & T. J. Landrum (Eds.), *Achieving the radical reform of special education: Essays in honor of James M. Kauffman* (pp. 169–188). Mahwah, NJ: Erlbaum.

Forness, S. R., Freeman, S. F. N., & Paparella, T. (2006). Recent randomized clinical trials comparing behavioral interventions and psychopharmacologic treatments for school children with EBD. *Behavioral Disorders, 31*, 284–296.

Forness, S. R., Freeman, S. F. N., Paparella, T., Kauffman, J. M., & Walker, H. M. (2012). Special education implications of point and cumulative prevalence for children with emotional or behavioral disorders. *Journal of Emotional and Behavioral Disorders, 20*, 1–14.

Forness, S. R., & Kavale, K. A. (1997). Defining emotional or behavioral disorders in school and related services. In J. W. Lloyd, E. J. Kameenui, & D. Chard (Eds.), *Issues in educating students with disabilities* (pp. 45–61). Mahwah, NJ: Erlbaum.

Forness, S. R., & Kavale, K. A. (2001). Ignoring the odds: Hazards of not adding the new medical model to special education decisions. *Behavioral Disorders, 26*, 269–281.

Forness, S. R., Kavale, K. A., Blum, I. M., & Lloyd, J. W. (1997). Mega-analysis of meta-analyses: What works in special education and related services. *Teaching Exceptional Children, 29*(6), 4–9.

Forness, S. R., Kavale, K. A., King, B. H., & Kasari, C. (1994). Simple versus complex conduct disorders: Identification and phenomenology. *Behavioral Disorders, 19*, 306–312.

Forness, S. R., Kavale, K. A., Sweeney, D. P., & Crenshaw, T. M. (1999). The future of research and practice in behavioral disorders: Psychopharmacology and its school implications. *Behavioral Disorders, 24*, 305–318.

Forness, S. R., & Knitzer, J. (1992). A new proposed definition and terminology to replace "serious emotional disturbance" in Individuals with Disabilities Education Act. *School Psychology Review, 21*, 12–20.

Forness, S. R., Walker, H. M., & Kavale, K. A. (2003). Psychiatric disorders and treatment. *Teaching Exceptional Children, 36*(2), 42–49.

Fosse, E. (2015). The values and beliefs of disconnected black youth. In O. Patterson & E. Fosse (Eds.), *The cultural matrix: Understanding black youth* (pp. 139–166). Cambridge, MA: Harvard University Press.

Fox, J., & Gable, R. A. (2004). Functional behavioral assessment. In R. B. Rutherford, M. M. Quinn, & S. R. Mathur (Eds.), *Handbook of research in emotional and behavioral disorders* (pp. 143–162). New York, NY: Guilford.

Foxx, R. M. (2016a). The perpetuation of the myth of the nonaversive treatment of severe behavior. In R. M. Foxx & J. A. Mulick (Eds.), *Controversial therapies for autism and intellectual disabilities: Fad, fashion, and science in professional practice* (2nd ed.) (pp. 223–244). New York, NY: Francis & Taylor.

Foxx, R. M. (2016b). Why ABA is not a fad, a pseudoscience, a dubious or controversial treatment, or politically correct. In R. M. Foxx & J. A. Mulick (Eds.), *Controversial therapies for autism and intellectual disabilities: Fad, fashion, and science in professional practice* (2nd ed.) (pp. 422–432). New York, NY: Francis & Taylor.

Foxx, R. M., & Mulick, J. A. (Eds.) (2016). *Controversial therapies for autism and intellectual disabilities*. New York. Routledge.

Freeman, K. A., & Hogansen, J. M. (2006). Conduct disorders. In M. Hersen (Ed.), *Clinician's handbook of child behavioral assessment* (pp. 477–501). Boston, MA: Academic Press.

Frey, A.J., Lingo, A., & Nelson, C.M. (2008). Positive Behavior Support. A call for leadership. *Children & Schools, 30*, 5–14.

Frey, A. J., Small, J., Feil, E., Seeley, J., Walker, H., & Golly, A. (2013). The feasibility of First Step to Success with preschoolers. *Children & Schools, 35*(3), 171–186.

Frick, P. J., & Loney, B. R. (2002). Understanding the association between parent and child antisocial behavior. In R. J. McMahon & R. D. Peters (Eds.), *The effects of parental dysfunction on children* (pp. 105–126). New York, NY: Kluwer Academic.

Fridrich, A. H., & Flannery, D. J. (1995). The effects of ethnicity and acculturation on early adolescent delinquency. *Journal of Child & Family Studies, 4*, 69–87.

Fuchs, D., & Young, C. L. (2006). On the irrelevance of intelligence in predicting responsiveness to reading instruction. *Exceptional Children, 73*, 8–30.

Fuchs, L. S., & Fuchs, D. (2001). Helping teachers formulate sound test accommodation decisions for students with learning disabilities. *Learning Disabilities Research & Practice, 16*(3), 174–181.

Fuchs, L. S., & Fuchs, D. (2011). Using CBM for Progress Monitoring in Reading. *National Center on Student Progress Monitoring*.

Fuchs, L. S., Fuchs, D., Eaton, S. B., Hamlett, C., Binkley, E., & Crouch, R. (2000). Using objective data sources to enhance teacher judgments about test accommodations. *Exceptional Children, 67*, 67–81.

Fujiura, G. T., & Yamaki, K. (2000). Trends in demography of childhood poverty and disability. *Exceptional Children, 66*, 187–199.

Furlong, M. J., Morrison, G. M., & Jimerson, S. (2004). Externalizing behaviors of aggression and violence and the school context. In R. B. Rutherford, M. M. Quinn, & S. R. Mathur (Eds.). *Handbook of research in emotional and behavioral disorders* (pp. 243–261). New York, NY: Guilford.

Gadow, K. D., & Sprafkin, J. (1993). Television "violence" and children with emotional and behavioral disorders. *Journal of Emotional and Behavioral Disorders, 1*, 54–63.

Gage, N., Adamson, R., Mitchell, B. S., Lierheimer, K., O'Connor, K. V., Bailey, N., … Jones, S. (2010). Promise and possibility in special education services for students with emotional or behavioral disorders: Peacock Hill revisited. *Behavioral Disorders, 35*(4), 294–307.

Gagnon, J. C. (2010). Characteristics of and services provided to youth in secure care facilities. *Behavioral Disorders, 36*, 7–19.

Gagnon, J. C., & Leone, P. E. (2005). Elementary day and residential schools for children with emotional and behavioral disorders: Characteristics and entrance and exit policies. *Remedial and Special Education, 26*, 141–150.

Gallagher, J. J. (2007). *Driving change in special education.* Baltimore, MD: Brookes.

Gardner, M. (2001, January/February). Facilitated communication: A cruel farce. *Skeptical Inquirer*, 17–19.

Garfinkel, L. (2010). Improving family involvement for juvenile offenders with emotional/behavioral disorders and related disabilities. *Behavioral Disorders, 36*, 52–60.

Garland, E. J. (2002). Anxiety disorders. In S. Kutcher (Ed.), *Practical child and adolescent psychopharmacology* (pp. 187–229). New York, NY: Cambridge University Press.

Garner, P. (2014). Curriculum, inclusion and EBD. In P. Garner, J. M. Kauffman, & J. Elliott (Eds), *The Sage handbook of emotional and behavioral difficulties* (2nd ed.) (pp. 291–302). London, U.K.: Sage.

Garner, P., Kauffman, J. M., & Elliott, J. G. (Eds.). (2014). *The Sage handbook of emotional and behavioral difficulties* (2nd ed.). London, U.K.: Sage.

Gavazzi, S. M., Wasserman, D., Partridge, C., & Sheridan, S. (2000). The Growing Up FAST Diversion Program: An example of juvenile justice program development for outcome evaluation. *Aggression and Violent Behavior, 5*, 159–175.

Gay, L. R, Mills, G. E., & Airasian, P. W. (2009). *Educational research: Competencies for analysis and applications* (9th ed.). Boston: Allyn & Bacon.

Geller, B., & DelBello, M. P. (Eds.). (2003). *Bipolar disorder in childhood and early adolescence.* New York, NY: Guilford.

Genaux, M., Morgan, D. P., & Friedman, S. G. (1995). Substance use and its prevention: A summary of classroom practices. *Behavioral Disorders, 20*, 279–289.

Gerber, M. M. (2005). Teachers are still the test: Limitations of response to instruction strategies for identifying children with learning disabilities. *Journal of Learning Disabilities, 38*, 516–524.

Gerber, M. M. (2014). Developing intervention and resilience strategies. In P. Garner, J. M. Kauffman, & J. G. Elliott (Eds.), *The Sage handbook of emotional and behavioral difficulties* (2nd ed.) (pp. 279–290). London, U.K.: Sage.

Gerber, M. M. (2017). A history of special education. In J. M. Kauffman, D. P. Hallahan, & P. C. Pullen (Eds.), *Handbook of special education* (2nd ed.). New York, NY: Taylor & Francis.

Gerber, M. M., & Semmel, M. I. (1984). Teacher as imperfect test: Reconceptualizing the referral process. *Educational Psychologist, 19*, 137–148.

Gerenser, J., & Forman, B. (2007). Speech and language deficits in children with developmental disabilities. In J. W. Jacobson, J. A. Mulick, & J. Rojahn (Eds.), *Handbook of intellectual and developmental disabilities* (pp. 563–579). New York, NY: Springer.

Germann, G., & Tindal, G. (1985). An application of curriculum-based assessment: The use of direct and repeated measurement. *Exceptional Children, 52*, 244–265.

Gershoff, E. T. (2002). Corporal punishment by parents and associated child behaviors and experiences: A meta-analytic and theoretical review. *Psychological Bulletin, 128*, 539–579.

Gershon, J. (2002). A meta-analytic review of gender differences in ADHD. *Journal of Attention Disorders, 5*, 143–154.

Gest, S. D., Farmer, T., Cairns, B., & Xie, H. (2003). Identifying children's peer social networks in school classrooms: Links between peer reports and observed interactions. *Social Development, 12*(4), 513–529.

Gibbs, J. T., & Huang, L. N. (Eds.) (1998). *Children of color: Psychological interventions with culturally diverse youth.* San Francisco: Jossey-Bass.

Ginsburg, C., & Demeranville, H. (1999). Sticks and stones: The jailing of mentally ill kids. *Nation, 269*(21), 17–20.

Goin, M. K. (2007, July 8). The wrong place to treat mental illness. *Washington Post*, B7.

Goldstein, A. P., Carr, E. G., Davidson, W. S., & Wehr, P. (Eds.) (1981). *In response to aggression.* New York, NY: Pergamon.

Goldstein, R. N. (2014). *Plato at the Googleplex: Why philosophy won't go away*. New York: Random House.

Goodman, R. (1997). The strengths and difficulties questionnaire: A research note. *Journal of Child Psychology and Psychiatry, 38*, 581–586.

Goodman, S. H., Gravitt, G. W., & Kaslow, N. J. (1995). Social problem solving: A moderator of the relation between negative life stress and depression symptoms in children. *Journal of Abnormal Child Psychology, 23*, 473–485.

Goldston, D. B. (2003). *Measuring suicidal behavior and risk in children and adolescents*. Washington, DC: American Psychological Association.

Goleman, D. (1995). *Emotional intelligence*. New York: Bantam.

Gordon, B. N., & Schroeder, C. S. (1995). *Sexuality: A developmental approach to problems*. New York: Plenum.

Gottesman, I. (1987). Schizophrenia: Irving Gottesman reveals the genetic factors. *University of Virginia Alumni News, 75*(5), 12–14.

Gottesman, I. I. (1991). *Schizophrenia genesis: The origins of madness*. New York, NY: Freeman.

Graber, J. A., Brooks-Gunn, J., & Galen, B. R. (1998). Betwixt and between: Sexuality in the context of adolescent transitions. In R. Jessor (Ed.), *New perspectives on adolescent risk behavior* (pp. 270–316). New York: Cambridge University Press.

Grapen, M., Cross, D., Ortigo, K., Graham, A., Johnson, E., Evces, M., … Bradley, B. (2011). Perceived neighborhood disorder, community cohesion, and PTSD symptoms among low-income African Americans in a urban health setting. *American Journal of Orthopsychiatry, 81*, 31–37.

Graziano, A. M., & Dorta, N. J. (1995). Behavioral treatment. In M. Hersen & R. T. Ammerman (Eds.), *Advanced abnormal child psychology* (pp. 171–187). Hillsdale, NJ: Erlbaum.

Greenwood, C. R., Carta, J. J., & Dawson, H. (2000). Ecobehavioral assessment system software (EBASS): A system for observation in education settings. In T. Thompson, D. Felce., & F. J. Symons (Eds.), *Behavioral observation: Technology and applications in developmental disabilities* (pp. 229–251). Baltimore, MD: Brookes.

Gregory, A., Cornell, D., Fan, X., Sheras, P. L, Shih, T., & Huang, F. (2010). Authoritative school discipline: High school practices associated with lower student bullying and victimization. *Journal of Educational Psychology, 102*, 483–496.

Gresham, F. M. (2014). Treatment integrity within a three-tiered model. In H. M. Walker & F. M. Gresham (Eds.), *Handbook of evidence-based practices for emotional and behavioral disorders: Applications in schools* (pp. 446–456). New York, NY: Guilford.

Gresham, F. M. (2015). *Disruptive behavior disorders: Evidence-based practice for assessment and intervention*. New York: Guilford.

Gresham, F. M., & Elliott, S. N. (1990). *Social Skills Rating System*. Circle Pines, MN: American Guidance Service.

Gresham, F. M., & Elliott, S. N. (2008). *Social Skills Improvement System (SSIS) Rating Scales*. Upper Saddle River, NJ: Pearson.

Gresham, F. M., & Elliott, S. N. (2014). Social skills assessment and training in emotional and behavioral disorders. In H. M. Walker & F. M. Gresham (Eds.), *Handbook of evidence-based practices for emotional and behavioral disorders: Applications in schools* (pp. 152–172). New York, NY: Guilford.

Gresham, F. M., Elliott, S. N., & Evans-Fernandez, S. E. (1993). *Student Self-Concept Scale*. Circle Pines, MN: American Guidance Service.

Gresham, F. M., & Kern, L. (2004). Internalizing behavior problems in children and adolescents. In R. B. Rutherford, M. M. Quinn, & S. R. Mathur (Eds.), *Handbook of research in emotional and behavioral disorders* (pp. 262–281). New York, NY: Guilford.

Gresham, F. M., MacMillan, D. L., & Bocian, K. (1996). "Behavioral Earthquakes": Low frequency, salient behavioral events that differentiate students at-risk for behavioral disorders. *Behavioral Disorders, 21*, 277–292.

Gresham, F. M., Robichaux, N., York, H., & O'Leary, K. (2012). Issues related to identifying and implementing evidence-based social skills interventions for students with high-incidence disabilities. In B. G. Cook, M. Tankersley, & T. J. Landrum (Eds.), *Classroom Behavior, Contexts, and Interventions: Advances in Learning and Behavioral Disabilities, Volume 25* (pp. 23–45). Bingley, UK: Emerald Group Publishing Limited.

Griffin-Shelley, E. (1994). *Adolescent sex and love addicts*. Westport, CT: Praeger.

Grigorenko, E. L. (2014). Genetic causes and correlates of EBD: A snapshot in time and space. In P. Garner, J. M. Kauffman, & J. G. Elliott (Eds.), *The Sage handbook of emotional and behavioral difficulties* (2nd ed.) (pp. 131–144). London, U.K.: Sage.

Groopman, J. (2007, April 9). What's normal? The difficulty of diagnosing bipolar disorder in children. *The New Yorker*, 28–33.

Grosenick, J. K., & Huntze, S. L. (1979). *National needs analysis in behavior disorders: A model for a comprehensive needs analysis in behavior disorders*. Columbia, MS: University of Missouri, Department of Special Education.

Gully, V., Northup, J., Hupp, S., Spera, S., LeVelle, J., & Ridgway, A. (2003). Sequential evaluation of behavioral treatments and methylphenidate dosage for children with attention deficit hyperactivity disorder. *Journal of Applied Behavior Analysis, 36*, 375–378.

Gumpel, T. P., Wiesenthal, V., & Söderberg, P. (2015). Narcissism, perceived social status, and social cognition and their influence on aggression. *Behavioral Disorders, 40*, 138–156.

Gunter, P. L., Hummel, J. H., & Conroy, M. A. (1998). Increasing correct academic responding: An effective intervention strategy to decrease behavior problems. *Effective School Practices, 17*(2), 36–54.

Haas, A. P., Eliason, M., Mays, V. M., Mathy, R. M., Cochran, S. D., D'Augelli, A. R., … Clayton, P. J. (2010). Suicide and suicide risk in lesbian, gay, bisexual, and transgender populations: Review and recommendations. *Journal of Homosexuality, 58*, 10–51.

Hagan-Burke, S., Gilmour, M. W., Gerow, S., & Crowder, W. C. (2015). Identifying academic demands that occasion problem behaviors for students with behavioral disorders: Illustrations at the elementary school level. *Behavior Modification, 39*(1), 215–241.

Hagedorn, J. M. (Ed.). (2007). *Gangs in the global city: Alternatives to traditional criminology.* Urbana, IL: University of Illinois Press.

Hallahan, D. P., & Kauffman, J. M. (1977). Categories, labels, behavioral characteristics: ED, LD, and EMR reconsidered. *Journal of Special Education, 11*, 139–149.

Hallahan, D. P., Kauffman, J. M., & Pullen, P. C. (2015). *Exceptional learners: An introduction to special education* (13th ed.). Upper Saddle River, NJ: Pearson Education.

Hallahan, D. P., Lloyd, J. W., Kauffman, J. M., Weiss, M., & Martinez, E. (2005). *Introduction to learning disabilities* (3rd ed.). Boston, MA: Allyn & Bacon.

Hallenbeck, B. A., & Kauffman, J. M. (1995). How does observational learning affect the behavior of students with emotional or behavioral disorders? A review of research. *Journal of Special Education, 29*, 45–71.

Hammen, C. L., & Rudolph, K. D. (2003). Childhood mood disorders. In E. J. Mash & R. A. Barkley (Eds.), *Child psychopathology* (2nd ed., pp. 233–278). New York: Guilford.

Hammen, C. L., Rudolph, K. D., & Abaied, J. L. (2014). Child and adolescent depression. In E. J. Mash & R. A. Barkley (Eds.), *Child psychopathology* (2nd ed., pp. 225–263). New York, NY: Guilford.

Hanson, M. J., & Carta, J. J. (1996). Addressing the challenges of families with multiple risks. *Exceptional Children, 62*, 201–212.

Harden, P. W., Pihl, R. O., Vitaro, F., Gendreau, P. L., & Tremblay, R. E. (1995). Stress response in anxious and nonanxious disruptive boys. *Journal of Emotional and Behavioral Disorders, 3*, 183–190.

Hare, E. H. (1962). Masturbatory insanity: The history of an idea. *Journal of Mental Science, 108*, 1–25.

Harrington, R. (2001). Cognitive behaviour therapy. In H. Remschmidt (Ed.), *Psychotherapy with children and adolescents* (pp. 113–123). New York: Cambridge University Press.

Harris, J. R. (1995). Where is the child's environment? A group socialization theory of development. *Psychological Review, 102*, 458–489.

Harrison, J. R., Bunford, N., Evans, S. W., & Owens, J. S. (2013). Educational accommodations for students with behavioral challenges: A systematic review of the literature. *Review of Educational Research, 83*(4), 551–597.

Harry, B., & Klingner, J. (2006). *Why are so many minority students in special education? Understanding race & disability in schools.* New York, NY: Teachers College Press.

Harry, B., & Klingner, J. (2007). Discarding the deficit model. *Educational Leadership, 64*(5), 16–21.

Harry, B., & Klingner, J. (2014). *Why are so many minority students in special education? Understanding race & disability in schools* (2nd ed.). New York: Teachers College Press.

Hart, B., & Risley, T. R. (1995). *Meaningful differences in the everyday experience of young American children.* Baltimore: Brookes.

Hartman, C., Hox, J., Mellenbergh, G. J., Boyle, M. H., Offord, D. R., Racine, Y., et al. (2001). DSM–IV internal construct validity: When a taxonomy meets data. *Journal of Child Psychology & Psychiatry & Allied Disciplines, 42*, 817–836.

Harvill, L. M. (1991). Standard error of measurement. *Educational Measurement: Issues and Practice, 10*, 33–41.

Hattie, J. (2008). *Visible learning: A synthesis of over 800 meta-analyses relating to achievement.* New York: Routledge.

Hattie, & Yates, (2013). *Visible learning and the science of how we learn.* New York, NY: Routledge.

Hawkins, S., & Radcliffe, J. (2006). Current measures of PTSD for children and adolescents. *Journal of Pediatric Psychology, 31* (4), 420–430.

Hay, D. A., & Levy, F. (2001). Implications of genetic studies of attentional problems for education and intervention. In F. Levy & D. A. Hay (Eds.), *Attention, genes and ADHD* (pp. 214–224). Philadelphia, PA: Taylor & Francis.

Hayden, E. P., & Mash, E. J. (2014). Child psychopathology: A developmental-systems perspective. In E. J. Mash & R. A. Barkley (Eds) *Child psychopathology* (3rd ed.) (pp. 3–72). New York, NY: Guilford.

Haydon, T., & Kroeger, S. D. (2016). Active supervision, precorrection, and explicit timing: a high school case study on classroom behavior. *Preventing School Failure: Alternative Education for Children and Youth, 60*(1), 70–78.

Hendershott, A. B. (2002). *The politics of deviance.* San Francisco, CA: Encounter.

Henderson, J., & MacKay, S. (2010). Retail availability of fire-starting materials and their misuse by children and adolescents. *Fire Safety Journal, 44*, 131–134.

Herbert, M. (1994). Etiological considerations. In T. H. Ollendick, N. J. King, & W. Yule (Eds.), *International handbook of phobic and anxiety disorders in children and adolescents* (pp. 3–20). New York: Plenum.

Heron, M. (2016). Deaths: Leading Causes for 2013. National vital statistics reports: from the Centers for Disease Control and Prevention, National Center for Health Statistics, National Vital Statistics System, 65(2), 1–14.

Hersen, M. (Ed.). (2006). *Clinician's handbook of child behavioral assessment.* Boston: Academic Press.

Heubeck, B., & Lauth, G. (2014). Parent training for behavioral difficulties during the transition to school: Promises and challenges for prevention and early intervention. In P. Garner, J. M. Kauffman, & J. G. Elliott (Eds.), *The Sage handbook of emotional and behavioral difficulties* (2nd ed.) (pp. 317–334). London, U.K.: Sage.

Heward, W. L. (2003). Ten faulty notions about teaching and learning that hinder the effectiveness of special education. *The Journal of Special Education, 36*, 186–205.

Hewitt, L. E., & Jenkins, R. L. (1946). *Fundamental patterns of maladjustment: The dynamics of their origin.* Springfield, IL: State of Illinois.

Higa-McMillan, C. K., Francis, S. E., & Chorpita, B. F. (2014). Anxiety disorders. In E. J. Mash & R. A. Barkley (Eds.), *Child psychopathology* (2nd ed., pp. 345–428). New York, NY: Guilford.

Hill, H. M., Soriano, F. I., Chen, S. A., & LaFromboise, T. D. (1994). Sociocultural factors in the etiology and prevention of violence among ethnic minority youth. In L. D. Eron, J. H. Gentry, & P. Schlegel (Eds.), *Reason to hope: A psychosocial perspective on violence and youth* (pp. 59–97). Washington, DC: American Psychological Association.

Hills, A., L., Afifi, T. O., Cox, B. J., Bienvenu, O. J., & Sareen, J. (2009). Externalizing psychopathology and risk for suicide attempt: Cross-sectional and longitudinal findings from the Baltimore Epidemiologic Catchment Area Study. *The Journal of Nervous and Mental Disease, 197*, 293–297.

Himle, M. B., Flessner, C. A., Bonow, J. T., & Woods, D. W. (2006). Habit disorders. In M. Hersen (Ed.), *Clinician's handbook of child behavioral assessment* (pp. 527–546). Boston, MA: Academic Press.

Hinshaw, S. P., & Lee, S. S. (2003). Conduct and oppositional defiant disorders. In E. J. Mash & R. A. Barkley (Eds.), *Child psychopathology* (2nd ed., pp. 144–198). New York, NY: Guilford.

Hintze, J. M. (2002). Interventions for fears and anxiety problems. In M. R. Shinn, H. M. Walker, & G. Stoner (Eds.), *Interventions for academic and behavior problems II: Preventive and remedial approaches* (pp. 939–960). Bethesda, MD: National Association of School Psychologists.

Hirsch, S. E., Lloyd, J. W., & Kennedy, M. J. (2014). Improving behavior through instructional practices for students with high incidence disabilities: EBD, ADHD, and LD. In P. Garner, J. M. Kauffman, & J. G. Elliott (Eds.), *The Sage handbook of emotional and behavioral difficulties* (2nd ed.) (pp. 205–220). London, U.K.: Sage.

Hobbs, N. (1966). Helping the disturbed child: Psychological and ecological strategies. *American Psychologist, 21*, 1105–1115.

Hobbs, N. (1974). Nicholas Hobbs. In J. M. Kauffman & C. D. Lewis (Eds.), *Teaching children with behavior disorders: Personal perspectives* (pp. 142–167). Upper Saddle River, NJ: Merrill/Prentice Hall.

Hodges, K., & Zeman, J. (1993). Interviewing. In T. H. Ollendick & M. Hersen (Eds.), *Handbook of child and adolescent assessment* (pp. 65–81). New York, NY: Pergamon.

Hodgkinson, H. L. (1995). What should we call people? Race, class, and the census for 2000. *Phi Delta Kappan, 77*, 173–179.

Hollo, A., Wehby, J. H., & Oliver, R. M. (2014). Unidentified language deficits in children with emotional and behavioral disorders: a meta-analysis. *Exceptional Children, 80*(2), 169–186.

Hooper, S. R., Roberts, J. E., Zeisel, S. A., & Poe, M. (2003). Core language predictors of behavioral functioning in early elementary school children: Concurrent and longitudinal findings. *Behavioral Disorders, 29*, 10–24.

Hops, H., Finch, M., & McConnell, S. (1985). Social skills deficits. In P. H. Bornstein & A. E. Kazdin (Eds.), *Handbook of clinical behavior therapy with children* (pp. 543–598). Homewood, IL: Dorsey.

Horn, W. F., & Tynan, D. (2001). Time to make special education "special" again. In C. E. Finn, A. J. Rotherham, & C. R.

Hokanson (Eds.), *Rethinking special education for a new century* (pp. 23–51). Washington, DC: Fordham Foundation.

Hosp, M. K., Hosp, J. L., & Howell, K. W. (2007). *The ABCs of CBM: A practical guide to curriculum-based measurement*. New York, NY: Guilford Press.

Hosp, M. K., Hosp, J. L., & Howell, K. W. (2016). *The ABCs of CBM: A practical guide to curriculum-based measurement*. New York: Guilford Publications.

Houchins, D. E., Shippen, M. E., & Lambert, R. (2010). Advancing high-quality literacy research in juvenile justice: Methodological and practical considerations. *Behavioral Disorders, 36*, 61–69.

Howell, K. W., Fox, S. L., & Morehead, M. K. (1993). *Curriculum-based evaluation for teaching and decision making* (2nd ed.). Pacific Grove, CA: Brooks/Cole.

Howell, K. W., & Hyatt, K. (2004). Curriculum-based measurement of students with EBD: Assessment for databased decision making. In R. B. Rutherford, M. M. Quinn, & S. R. Mathur (Eds.). *Handbook of research in emotional and behavioral disorders* (pp. 181–198). New York, NY: Guilford.

Hudley, C., & Graham, S. (1995). School-based interventions for aggressive African-American boys. *Applied and Preventive Psychology, 4*, 185–195.

Hudson, J. I., Hiripi, E., Pope, H. G., & Kessler, R. C. (2007). The prevalence and correlates of eating disorders in the National Comorbidity Survey Replication. *Biological Psychiatry, 61*, 348–358.

Huefner, D. S. (2006). *Getting comfortable with special education law: A framework for working with children with disabilities* (2nd ed.). Norwood, MA: Christopher Gordon.

Huesmann, L. R., Moise-Titus, J., Podolski, C., & Eron, L. (2003). Longitudinal relations between children's exposure to TV violence and their aggressive and violent behavior in young adulthood: 1977–1992. *Developmental Psychology, 39*, 201–221.

Hufner, D. S. (2015). Placements for special education students: The promise and the peril. In B. D. Bateman, J. W. Lloyd, & M. Tankersley (Eds.), *Enduring issues in special education: Personal perspectives* (pp. 215–230). New York, NY: Routledge.

Hultquist, A. M. (1995). Selective mutism: Causes and interventions. *Journal of Emotional and Behavioral Disorders, 3*, 100–107.

Hurley, K. D., Lambert, M. C., Epstein, M. H., & Stevens, A. (2015). Convergent validity of the strength-based Behavioral and Emotional Rating Scale with youth in a residential setting. *The Journal of Behavioral Health Services & Research, 42*, 346–354.

Hyman, I. A. (1995). Corporal punishment, psychological maltreatment, violence, and punitiveness in America: Research, advocacy, and public policy. *Applied and Preventive Psychology, 4*, 113–130.

Hyter, Y. D., Rogers-Adkinson, D. L., Self, T. L., & Jantz, J. (2002). Pragmatic language intervention for children with language and emotional/behavioral disorders. *Communication Disorders Quarterly, 23*(1), 4–16.

Insel, B. J., & Gould, M. S. (2008). Impact of modeling on adolescent suicidal behavior. *Psychiatric Clinics of North America, 31*, 293–316.

Ispa-Landa, S. (2015). Effects of affluent suburban schooling: Learning skilled ways of interacting with educational gatekeepers. In O. Patterson & E. Fosse (Eds.), *The cultural matrix: Understanding black youth* (pp. 393–414). Cambridge, MA: Harvard University Press.

Jakubecy, J. J., Mock, D. R., & Kauffman, J. M. (2003). Special education, current trends. In J. W. Guthrie (Ed.), *Encyclopedia of education* (2nd ed., pp. 2284–2290). New York, NY: Macmillan Reference.

Jenkins, J. M., Rasbash, J., & O'Connor, T. G. (2003). The role of the shared family context in differential parenting. *Developmental Psychology, 39*, 99–113.

Jensen, P. S., Hinshaw, S. P., Swanson, J. M., Greenhill, L. L., Conners, C., Arnold, L., … Wigal, T. (2001). Findings from the NIMH Multimodal Treatment Study of ADHD (MTA): Implications and applications for primary care providers. *Journal of Developmental & Behavioral Pediatrics, 22*, 60–73.

Jessor, R. (1998). New perspectives on adolescent risk behavior. In R. Jessor (Ed.), *New perspectives on adolescent risk behavior* (pp. 1–10). New York, NY: Cambridge University Press.

Jessor, R., & Jessor, S. L. (1977). *Problem behavior and psychosocial development: A longitudinal study of youth*. New York, NY: Academic Press.

Jessor, R., Van Den Bos, J., Vanderryn, J., Costa, F. M., & Turbin, M. S. (1995). Protective factors in adolescent problem behavior: Moderator effects and developmental change. *Developmental Psychology, 31*, 923–933.

Johns, B. J., Kauffman, J. M., & Martin, E. W. (2016). The concept of RTI: Billion dollar boondoggle. Available from http://SpedPro.org/documents/JohnsEtAl_ConceptRTI_2016.pdf.

Johnson, J. G., Cohen, P., Kasen S., & Brook, J. S. (2007). Extensive television viewing and the development of attention and learning difficulties during adolescence. *Archives of Pediatrics and Adolescent Medicine, 161*, 480–486.

Johnston, H. F., & March, J. S. (1992). Obsessive–compulsive disorders in children and adolescents. In W. R. Reynolds (Ed.), *Internalizing disorders in children and adolescents* (pp. 107–148). New York: Wiley.

Johnston, L. D., O'Malley, P. M., Bachman, J. G., & Schulenberg, J. E. (2009). *Monitoring the Future national survey results on drug use, 1975–2008: Volume I, Secondary school students* (NIH Publication No. 09-7402). Bethesda, MD: National Institute on Drug Abuse.

Jolivette, K., & Nelson, C. M. (2010a). Introduction to the special issue of behavioral disorders: Juvenile justice issues. *Behavioral Disorders, 36*, 4–6.

Jolivette, K., & Nelson, C. M. (2010b). Adapting positive behavioral interventions and supports for secure juvenile justice settings: Improving facility-wide behavior. *Behavioral Disorders, 36*, 28–42.

Jones, V., Dohrn, E., & Dunn, C. (2004). *Creating effective programs for students with emotional and behavior disorders: Interdisciplinary approaches for adding meaning and hope to behavior change interventions*. Boston, MA: Allyn & Bacon.

Judson, O. (2002). *Dr. Tatiana's sex advice to all creation*. New York, NY: Holt.

Justice, L. (2006). *Communication sciences and disorders: An introduction*. Upper Saddle River, NJ: Prentice Hall.

Kame'enui, E. J. (2015). Special education as "specially designed instruction": Ode to the architecture of information and the message. In B. D. Bateman, J. W. Lloyd, & M. Tankersley (Eds.), *Enduring issues in special education: Personal perspectives* (pp. 74–91). New York, NY: Routledge.

Kaminer, Y. (1994). *Adolescent substance abuse: A comprehensive guide to theory and practice*. New York: Plenum.

Kanner, L. (1960). Child psychiatry: Retrospect and prospect. *American Journal of Psychiatry, 117*, 15–22.

Kaplan, S. G., & Cornell, D. G. (2005). Threats of violence by students in special education. *Behavioral Disorders, 31*, 107–119.

Kashani, J. H., Dahlmeier, J. M., Borduin, C. M., Soltys, S., & Reid, J. C. (1995). Characteristics of anger expression in depressed children. *Journal of the American Academy of Child and Adolescent Psychiatry, 34*, 322–326.

Kaslow, N. J., Morris, M. K., & Rehm, L. P. (1998). Childhood depression. In R. J. Morris & T. R. Kratochwill (Eds.), *The practice of child therapy* (3rd ed., pp. 48–90). Boston, MA: Allyn & Bacon.

Katsiyannis, A. (1994). Pre-referral practices: Under Office of Civil Rights scrutiny. *Journal of Developmental and Physical Disabilities, 6*, 73–76.

Kauffman, J. M. (1976). Nineteenth century views of children's behavior disorders: Historical contributions and continuing issues. *Journal of Special Education, 10*, 335–349.

Kauffman, J. M. (1997). Conclusion: A little of everything, a lot of nothing is an agenda for failure. *Journal of Emotional and Behavioral Disorders, 5*, 76–81.

Kauffman, J. M. (1999a). Comments on social development research in emotional and behavioral disorders. *Journal of Emotional and Behavioral Disorders, 7*, 189–191.

Kauffman, J. M. (1999b). Educating students with emotional or behavioral disorders: What's over the horizon? In L. M. Bullock & R. A. Gable (Eds.), *Educating students with emotional and behavioral disorders: Historical perspective and future directions* (pp. 38–59). Reston, VA: Council for Children with Behavioral Disorders.

Kauffman, J. M. (1999c). How we prevent the prevention of emotional and behavioral disorders. *Exceptional Children, 65*, 448–468.

Kauffman, J. M. (1999d). The role of science in behavioral disorders. *Behavioral Disorders, 24*, 265–272.

Kauffman, J. M. (1999e). The special education story: Obituary, accident report, conversion experience, reincarnation, or none of the above? *Exceptionality, 8*(1), 3–11.

Kauffman, J. M. (1999f). Today's special education and its messages for tomorrow. *Journal of Special Education, 32*, 244–254.

Kauffman, J. M. (1999g). What we make of difference and the difference we make. Foreword in V. L. Schwean & D. H.

Saklofske (Eds.), *Handbook of psychosocial characteristics of exceptional children* (pp. ix–xii). New York: Plenum.

Kauffman, J. M. (2003a). Appearances, stigma, and prevention. *Remedial and Special Education, 24*, 195–198.

Kauffman, J. M. (2003b). Reflections on the field. *Behavioral Disorders, 28*, 205–208.

Kauffman, J. M. (2004). The president's commission and the devaluation of special education. *Education and Treatment of Children, 27*, 307–324.

Kauffman, J. M. (2005). Waving to Ray Charles: Missing the meaning of disability. *Phi Delta Kappan, 86*, 520–521, 524.

Kauffman, J. M. (2007a). Conceptual models and the future of special education. *Educatioin and Treatment of Children, 30*(4), 241–258.

Kauffman, J. M. (2007b). Would we recognize progress if we saw it? *Journal of Behavioral Education*.

Kauffman, J. M. (2007c). Labels and the nature of special education: We need to face realities. *Learning Disabilities: A Multidisciplinary Journal*.

Kauffman, J. M. (2008a). Emotional and behavioral disorders. In E. M. Anderman & L. H. Anderman (Eds.), *Psychology of classroom learning: An encyclopedia*, Vol. 1, (pp. 361–365). Farmington Hills, MI: Gale/Cengage Learning.

Kauffman, J. M. (2008b). Special education. In T. L. Good (Ed.), *21st Century education: A reference handbook*, Vol. 1, (pp. 405–413). Thousand Oaks, CA: Sage.

Kauffman, J. M. (2009). Attributions of malice to special education policy and practice. In T. E. Scruggs & M. A. Mastropieri (Eds.), *Advances in learning and behavioral disabilities: Vol. 22. Policy and practice* (pp. 33–66). Bingley, U.K.: Emerald.

Kauffman, J. M. (2010a). Commentary: Current status of the field and future directions. *Behavioral Disorders, 35*, 180–184.

Kauffman, J. M. (2010b). The problem of early identification. In H. Ricking & G. C. Schulze (Eds.), *Förderbedarf in der emotionalen und sozialen Entwicklung: Prävention, Interdisziplinarität, und Professionalisierung* (pp. 171–177). Bad Heilbrunn, Germany: Klinkhardt.

Kauffman, J. M. (2010c). *The tragicomedy of public education: Laughing and crying, thinking and fixing.* Verona, WI: Attainment.

Kauffman, J. M. (2011). *Toward a science of education: The battle between rogue and real science.* Verona, WI: Attainment.

Kauffman, J. M. (2012a). Labeling and categorizing children and youth with emotional and behavioral disorders in the USA: Current practices and conceptual problems. In T. Cole, H. Daniels, & J. Visser (Eds.), *International companion to emotional and behavioural difficulties*. London, U.K.: Taylor & Francis.

Kauffman, J. M. (2012b). Science and the education of teachers. In R. Detrich, R. Keyworth, & J. States (Eds.), *Advances in evidence-based education, Volume 2. Education at the crossroads: The state of teacher education* (pp. 47–64). Oakland, CA: Wing Institute. CA.

Kauffman, J. M. (2014a). How we prevent the prevention of emotional and behavioral difficulties in education. In P. Garner, J. M. Kauffman, & J. G. Elliott (Eds.), *The Sage handbook of emotional and behavioral difficulties* (2nd ed.) (pp. 505–516). London, U.K.: Sage.

Kauffman, J. M. (2014b). Past, present, and future in EBD and special education. In B. Cook, M. Tankersley, & T. Landrum (Eds.), *Advances in learning and behavioral disabilities, Vol. 27: Classroom behavior, contexts, and interventions* (pp. 63–87). Bingley, U.K.: Emerald.

Kauffman, J. M. (2014c). Prologue: On following the scientific evidence; Epilogue: Science, a harsh mistress. In H. M. Walker & F. M. Gresham (Eds.), *Handbook of evidence-based practices for emotional and behavioral disorders: Applications in schools* (pp. 1–5; 583–585). New York, NY: Guilford.

Kauffman, J. M. (2015a). Opinion on recent developments and the future of special education. *Remedial and Special Education, 36*, 9–13.

Kauffman, J. M. (2015b). The "B" in EBD is not just for bullying. *Journal of Research in Special Educational Needs, 15*, 167–175.

Kauffman, J. M. (2015c). Why exceptionality is more important for special education than exceptional children. *Exceptionality, 23*, 225–236.

Kauffman, J. M. (2015d). Why we should have special education. In B. Bateman, M. Tankersley, & J. Lloyd (Eds.), *Enduring issues in special education: Personal perspectives* (pp. 397–408). New York, NY: Routledge.

Kauffman, J. M. (2016). Anxiety about the future of special education for students with emotional and behavioral disorders. *Journal of Modern Education Review, 6*, 357–363.

Kauffman, J. M. (in preparation). Foreword. In C. Watkins, D. Carnine, J. Lloyd, & T. Slocum (Eds.), *Does Direct Instruction deserve status as an evidence-based practice?* Eugene, OR: Association for Direct Instruction.

Kauffman, J. M., & Anastasiou, D. (2017). On cultural politics in special education: Is much of it justifiable? *Journal of Disability Policy Studies*.

Kauffman, J. M., Anastasiou, D., Badar, J., Travers, J. C., & Wiley, A. L. (2016). Inclusive education moving forward. In J. P. Bakken, F. E. Obiakor, & A. Rotatori (Eds.), *Advances in special education, Vol. 31b—General and special education in an age of change: Roles of professionals involved* (pp. 153–177). Bingley, U.K.: Emerald.

Kauffman, J. M., Anastasiou, D., & Maag, J. W. (2016). Special education at the crossroad: An identity crisis and the need for a scientific reconstruction. *Exceptionality*, doi: 10.1080/09362835.2016.1238380.

Kauffman, J. M., & Badar, J. (2013). How we might make special education for students with emotional or behavioral disorders less stigmatizing. *Behavioral Disorders, 39*, 16–27.

Kauffman, J. M., & Badar, J. (2014a). Better thinking and clearer communication will help special education. *Exceptionality, 22*, 17–32. doi: 10.1080/09362835.2014.865953

Kauffman, J. M., & Badar, J. (2014b). Instruction, not inclusion, should be the central issue in special education: An alternative view from the USA. *Journal of International Special Needs Education, 17*, 13–20.

Kauffman, J. M., & Badar, J. (2016). It's instruction over place—not the other way around! *Phi Delta Kappan, 98*(4), 55–59.

Kauffman, J. M., & Badar, J. (2017). Extremism and disability chic. *Exceptionality*.

Kauffman, J. M., Badar, J., & Wiley, A. L. (in press). RtI: Controversies and solutions. In P. C. Pullen & M. M. Kennedy (Eds.), *Handbook of response to intervention and multi-tiered systems of support*. New York, NY: Routledge.

Kauffman, J. M., Bantz, J., & McCullough, J. (2002). Separate and better: A special public school class for students with emotional and behavioral disorders. *Exceptionality, 10*, 149–170.

Kauffman, J. M., & Brigham, F. J. (2009). *Working with troubled children*. Verona, WI: Attainment.

Kauffman, J. M., Brigham, F. J., & Mock, D. R. (2004). Historical to contemporary perspectives on the field of emotional and behavioral disorders. In R. B. Rutherford, M. M. Quinn, & S. R. Mathur (Eds.), *Handbook of research in emotional and behavioral disorders* (pp. 15–31). New York: Guilford.

Kauffman, J. M., Bruce, A., & Lloyd, J. W. (2012). Response to intervention (RtI) and students with EBD. In J. P. Bakken, F. E. Obiakor, & A. Rotatori (Eds), *Advances in special education: Vol. 22. Behavioral disorders: Current perspectives and issues*. Bingley, U.K.: Emerald.

Kauffman, J. M., Conroy, M., Gardner, R., & Oswald, D. (2008). Cultural sensitivity in the application of behavior principles to education. *Education and Treatment of Children, 31*, 239–262.

Kauffman, J. M., & Hallahan, D. P. (Eds.). (2005a). *The illusion of full inclusion: A comprehensive critique of a current special educational bandwagon* (2nd ed.). Austin, TX: Pro-Ed.

Kauffman, J. M., & Hallahan, D. P. (2005b). *What special education is and why we need it*. Boston, MA: Allyn & Bacon.

Kauffman, J. M., & Hallahan, D. P. (2009). Parental choices and ethical dilemmas involving disabilities: Special education and the problem of deliberately chosen disabilities. *Exceptionality, 17*, 45–62.

Kauffman, J. M., & Kneedler, R. D. (1981). Behavior disorders. In J. M. Kauffman & D. P. Hallahan (Eds.), *Handbook of special education* (pp. 165–194). Upper Saddle River, NJ: Prentice Hall.

Kauffman, J. M., & Konold, T. R. (2007). Making sense in education: Pretense (including NCLB) and realities in rhetoric and policy about schools and schooling. *Exceptionality, 15*, 75–96.

Kauffman, J. M., & Landrum, T. J. (2006). *Children and youth with emotional and behavioral disorders: A history of their education*. Austin, TX: Pro-Ed.

Kauffman, J. M., & Landrum, T. J. (2007). Educational service interventions and reforms. In J. W. Jacobson, J. A. Mulick, & J. Rojahn (Eds.), *Handbook of intellectual and developmental disabilities* (pp. 173–188). New York, NY: Springer.

Kauffman, J. M., & Landrum, T. J. (2009). Politics, civil rights, and disproportional identification of students with emotional and behavioral disorders. *Exceptionality, 17*, 177–188.

Kauffman, J. M., & Lewis, C. D. (Eds.). (1974). *Teaching children with behavior disorders: Personal perspectives*. Upper Saddle River, NJ: Merrill/Prentice Hall.

Kauffman, J. M., & Lloyd, J. W. (1995). A sense of place: The importance of placement issues in contemporary special education. In J. M. Kauffman, J. W. Lloyd, D. P. Hallahan, & T. A. Astuto (Eds.), *Issues in educational placement: Students with emotional and behavioral disorders* (pp. 3–19). Hillsdale, NJ: Erlbaum.

Kauffman, J. M., & Lloyd, J. W. (2017). Statistics, data, and special education decisions: Basic links to realities. In J. M. Kauffman, D. P. Hallahan, & P. C. Pullen (Eds.), *Handbook of special education* (2nd ed.). New York, NY: Taylor & Francis.

Kauffman, J. M., Lloyd, J. W., Baker, J., & Riedel, T. M. (1995). Inclusion of all students with emotional or behavioral disorders? Let's think again. *Phi Delta Kappan, 76*, 542–546.

Kauffman, J. M., Lloyd, J. W., Hallahan, D. P., & Astuto, T. A. (Eds.). (1995a). *Issues in educational placement: Students with emotional and behavioral disorders*. Hillsdale, NJ: Erlbaum.

Kauffman, J. M., Lloyd, J. W., Hallahan, D. P., & Astuto, T. A. (Eds.). (1995b). Toward a sense of place for special education in the 21st century. In J. M. Kauffman, J. W. Lloyd, D. P. Hallahan, & T. A. Astuto (Eds.), *Issues in educational placement: Students with emotional and behavioral disorders* (pp. 379–385). Hillsdale, NJ: Erlbaum.

Kauffman, J. M., McGee, K., & Brigham, M. (2004). Enabling or disabling? Observations on changes in the purposes and outcomes of special education. *Phi Delta Kappan, 85*, 618–620.

Kauffman, J. M., Mock, D. R., & Simpson, R. L. (2007). Problems related to underservice of students with emotional or behavioral disorders. *Behavioral Disorders, 33*, 43–57.

Kauffman, J. M., Mock, D. R., Tankersley, M., & Landrum, T. J. (2008). Effective service delivery models. In R. J. Morris & N. Mather (Eds.), *Evidence-based interventions for students with learning and behavioral challenges* (pp. 359–378). Mahwah, NJ: Lawrence Erlbaum Associates.

Kauffman, J. M., Nelson, C. M., Simpson, R. L., & Mock, D. R. (2017). Contemporary issues. In J. M. Kauffman, D. P. Hallahan, & P. C. Pullen (Eds.), *Handbook of special education* (2nd ed.). New York, NY: Taylor & Francis.

Kauffman, J. M., & Pullen, P. L. (1996). Eight myths about special education. *Focus on Exceptional Children, 28*(5), 1–12.

Kauffman, J. M., Pullen, P. L., Mostert, M. P., & Trent, S. C. (2011). *Managing classroom behavior: A reflective case-based approach* (5th ed.) Upper Saddle River, NJ: Pearson Education.

Kauffman, J. M., & Sasso, G. M. (2006a). Toward ending cultural and cognitive relativism in special education. *Exceptionality, 14*, 65–90.

Kauffman, J. M., & Sasso, G. M. (2006b). Certainty, doubt, and the reduction of uncertainty: A rejoinder. *Exceptionality, 14*, 109–120.

Kauffman, J. M., Simpson, R. L., & Mock, D. R. (2009). Problems related to underservice: A rejoinder. *Behavioral Disorders, 34*, 172–180.

Kauffman, J. M., & Smucker, K. (1995). The legacies of placement: A brief history of placement options and issues with commentary on their evolution. In J. M. Kauffman,

J. W. Lloyd, D. P. Hallahan, & T. A. Astuto (Eds.), *Issues in educational placement: Students with emotional and behavioral disorders* (pp. 21–44). Hillsdale, NJ: Erlbaum.

Kauffman, J. M., Ward, D. M., & Badar, J. (2016). The delusion of full inclusion. In R. M. Foxx & J. A. Mulick (Eds.), *Controversial therapies for autism and intellectual disabilities* (2nd ed.) (pp. 71–86). New York, NY: Taylor & Francis.

Kavale, K. A., & Forness, S. R. (2000). History, rhetoric and reality: An analysis of the inclusion debate. *Remedial and Special Education, 21*, 279–296.

Kavale, K. A., Kauffman, J. M., Bachmeier, R. J., & LeFever, G. G. (2008). Response-to-intervention: Separating the rhetoric of self-congratulation from the reality of specific learning disability identification. *Learning Disability Quarterly, 31*, 135–150.

Kavale, K. A., Mathur, S. R., & Mostert, M. P. (2004). Social skills training and teaching social behavior to students with EBD. In R. B. Rutherford, M. M. Quinn, & S. R. Mathur (Eds.), *Handbook of research in emotional and behavioral disorders* (pp. 446–461). New York, NY: Guilford.

Kavale, K. A., & Mostert, M. P. (2003). River of ideology, islands of evidence. *Exceptionality, 11*, 191–208.

Kazdin, A. E. (1993). Conduct disorder. In T. H. Ollendick & M. Hersen (Eds.), *Handbook of child and adolescent assessment* (pp. 292–310). New York: Pergamon.

Kazdin, A. E. (1994). Interventions for aggressive and antisocial children. In L. D. Eron, J. H. Gentry, & P. Schlegel (Eds.), *Reason to hope: A psychosocial perspective on violence and youth* (pp. 341–382). Washington, DC: American Psychological Association.

Kazdin, A. E. (1995). *Conduct disorders in childhood and adolescence* (2nd ed.). Thousand Oaks, CA: Sage.

Kazdin, A. E. (1998). Conduct disorder. In R. J. Morris & T. R. Kratochwill (Eds.), *The practice of child therapy* (3rd ed., pp. 199–230). Boston: Allyn & Bacon.

Kazdin, A. E. (2001). *Behavior modification in applied settings* (6th ed.). Belmont, CA: Wadsworth.

Kazdin, A. E. (2003). Problem-solving skills training and parent management training for conduct disorder. In A. E. Kazdin & J. R. Weisz (Eds.), *Evidence-based psychotherapies for children and adolescents* (pp. 241–262). New York: Guilford Press.

Kazdin, A. E. (2008). *The Kazdin method for parenting the defiant child*. Boston, MA: Houghton Mifflin.

Kazdin, A. E., & Marciano, P. L. (1998). Childhood and adolescent depression. In E. J. Mash & R. A. Barkley (Eds.), *Treatment of childhood disorders* (2nd ed., pp. 211–248). New York: Guilford.

Kearney, C., & Albano, A.M. (2007). *When children refuse school: A cognitive-behavioral therapy approach* (2nd ed.). New York, NY: Oxford University Press.

Kendall, P. C., & Gosch, E. A. (1994). Cognitive-behavioral interventions. In T. H. Ollendick, N. J. King, & W. Yule (Eds.), *International handbook of phobic and anxiety disorders in children and adolescents* (pp. 415–438). New York: Plenum.

Kendziora, K. T. (2004). Early intervention for emotional and behavioral disorders. In R. B. Rutherford, M. M. Quinn, & S. R. Mathur (Eds.), *Handbook of Research in Emotional and Behavioral Disorders* (pp. 327–351). New York, NY: Guilford Press.

Keogh, B. K. (2003). *Temperament in the classroom: Understanding individual differences*. Baltimore, MD: Brookes.

Kerr, M. M., & Nelson, C. M. (2010). *Strategies for addressing behavior problems in the classroom* (6th ed.). Upper Saddle River, NJ: Merrill/Prentice Hall.

Kerr, M. M., Nelson, C. M., & Lambert, D. L., (1987). *Helping adolescents with learning and behavior problems*. Upper Saddle River, NJ: Merrill/Prentice Hall.

Kessler, R. C., Berglund, P., Demler, O., Jin, R., & Walters, E. E. (2005). Lifetime prevalence and age-of-onset distributions of DSM-IV disorders in the national comorbidity survey replication. *Archives of General Psychiatry, 62*, 593–602.

Kessler, R. C., Chiu, W. T., Demler, O., & Walters, E. E. (2005). Prevalence, severity, and comorbidity of 12-month DSM-IV disorders in the national comorbidity survey replication. *Archives of General Psychiatry, 62*, 617–627.

Kettler, R. J. (2012). Testing accommodations: Theory and research to inform practice. *International Journal of Disability, Development and Education, 59*(1), 53–66.

Kimonis, E. R., Frick, P. J., & McMahon, R. G. (2014). Conduct and oppositional defiant disorders. In E. J. Mash & R. A. Barkley (Eds.) *Child psychopathology* (3rd ed.) (pp. 145–179). New York, NY: Guilford.

King, N. J., Hamilton, D. I., & Murphy, G. C. (1983). The prevention of children's maladaptive fears. *Child and Family Behavior Therapy, 5*(2), 43–57.

King, N. J., Heyne, D., & Ollendick, T. H. (2005). Cognitive-behavioral treatments for anxiety and phobic disorders in children and adolescents: A review. *Behavioral Disorders, 30*, 241–257.

Kingery, P. M., & Walker, H. M. (2002). What we know about school safety. In M. R. Shinn, H. M. Walker, & G. Stoner (Eds.), *Interventions for academic and behavior problems II: Preventive and remedial approaches* (pp. 71–88). Bethesda, MD: National Association of School Psychologists.

Klein, M. W. (1995). *The American street gang: Its nature, prevalence, and control*. New York, NY: Oxford University Press.

Klein, M. W. (2006). The value of comparisons in street gang research. In J. F. Short & L. A. Hughes (Eds.), *Studying youth gangs* (pp. 129–144). New York, NY: Rowman & Littlefield.

Klein, R. G., & Last, C. G. (1989). *Anxiety disorders in children*. Newbury Park, CA: Sage.

Kleinheksel, K. A., & Summy, S. E. (2003). Enhancing student learning and social behavior through mnemonic strategies. *Teaching Exceptional Children, 36*(2), 30–35.

Klinger, L. G., Dawson, G., Barnes, K., & Crisler, M. (2014). Autism spectrum disorder. In E. J. Mash & R. A. Barkley (Eds.), *Child psychopathology* (3rd ed., pp. 531–572). New York: Guilford.

Klingner, J., Moore, B., Davidson, A. O., Boele, A., Boardman, A., Figueroa, R., ... Sager, N. (2015). Cultural and linguistic diversity in special education. In B. D. Bateman, J. W. Lloyd, &

M. Tankersley (Eds.), *Enduring issues in special education: Personal perspectives* (pp. 110–131). New York, NY: Routledge.

Knitzer, J. (1982). *Unclaimed children: The failure of public responsibility to children and adolescents in need of mental health services.* Washington, DC: Children's Defense Fund.

Knoll, C., & Sickmund, M. (2010). *Delinquency cases in juvenile court, 2007.* Office of Juvenile Justice and Delinquency Prevention Fact Sheet. Washington, D.C.: U. S. Department of Justice.

Kohler, P. K., Manhart, L. E., & Lafferty, W. E. (2008). Abstinence-only and comprehensive sex education and the initiation of sexual activity and teen pregnancy. *Journal of Adolescent Health, 42*, 344–351.

Kohn, A. (1993). *Punished by rewards.* New York, NY: Houghton Mifflin.

Kolko, D. (2002). (Ed.). *Handbook on firesetting in children and youth.* New York, NY: Academic Press.

Kolko, D. J., Herschell, A. D., & Scharf, D. M. (2006). Education and treatment for boys who set fires: Specificity, moderators, and predictors of recidivism. *Journal of Emotional and Behavioral Disorders, 14*, 227–239.

Kolko, D. J., & Kazdin, A. E. (1986). A conceptualization of fire setting in children and adolescents. *Journal of Abnormal Child Psychology, 14*, 49–61.

Kolko, D. J., & Kazdin, A. E. (1989). The Children's Firesetting Interview with psychiatrically referred and nonreferred children. *Journal of Abnormal Child Psychology, 17*, 609–624.

Konold, T. R., & Pianta, R. C. (2007). The influence of informants on ratings of children's behavioral functioning: A latent variable approach. *Journal of Psychoeducational Assessment, 25*, 222–236.

Konopasek, D. E., & Forness, S. R. (2014). Issues and criteria for effective use of psychopharmacological interventions in schooling. In H. M. Walker & F. M. Gresham (Eds.), *Handbook of evidence-based practices for emotional and behavioral disorders: Applications in schools* (pp. 457–472). New York, NY: Guilford.

Kopelowicz, A., Liberman, R. P., & Zarate, R. (2006) Recent advances in social skills training for schizophrenia. *Schizophrenia Bulletin, 32* (suppl 1), S12–S23.

Kotchick, B. A., Shaffer, A., Miller, K. S., & Forehand, R. (2001). Adolescent sexual risk behavior: A multi-system perspective. *Clinical Psychology Review, 21*, 493–519.

Kotler, L. A., Devlin, M. J., & Walsh, B. T. (2002). Eating disorders and related disturbances. In S. Kutcher (Ed.), *Practical child and adolescent psychopharmacology* (pp. 410–430). New York: Cambridge University Press.

Kratochwill, T. R., & McGivern, J. E. (1996). Clinical diagnosis, behavioral assessment, and functional analysis: Examining the connection between assessment and intervention. *School Psychology Review, 25*, 342–355.

Kratzer, L., & Hodgins, S. (1999). A typology of offenders: A test of Moffitt's theory among males and females from childhood to age 30. *Criminal Behavior and Mental Health, 9*, 57–73.

Kroneman, L. M., Loeber, R., Hipwell, A. E., & Koot, H. M. (2009). Girls' disruptive behavior and its relationship to

family functioning: A review. *Journal of Child and Family Studies, 18*, 259–273.

Kuniyoshi, J., & McClellan, J. M. (2014). Early-onset schizophrenia. In E. J. Mash & R. A. Barkley (Eds). *Child psychopathology* (3rd ed.) (pp. 573–592). New York, NY: Guilford.

Kurlan, R. (2010). Tourette's syndrome. *New England Journal of Medicine, 363*, 2332–2338.

Kusumakar, V., Lazier, L., MacMaster, F. P., & Santor, D. (2002). Bipolar mood disorders: Diagnosis, etiology, and treatment. In S. Kutcher (Ed.), *Practical child and adolescent psychopharmacology* (pp. 106–133). New York, NY: Cambridge University Press.

Kutcher, S. (Ed.). (2002). *Practical child and adolescent psychopharmacology.* New York, NY: Cambridge University Press.

Kyger, M. M. (1999). *Fix it before it breaks: Training teachers to use precorrection procedures.* Unpublished doctoral dissertation, University of Virginia, Charlottesville.

Laird, R. D., Pettit, G. S., Bates, J. E., & Dodge, K. A. (2003). Parents' monitoring-relevant knowledge and adolescents' delinquent behavior: Evidence of correlated developmental changes and reciprocal influences. *Child Development, 74*, 752–768.

Lajiness-O'Neill, R., & Erdodi, L. A. (2017). Traumatic brain injury. In J. M. Kauffman, D. P. Hallahan, & P. C. Pullen (Eds.), *Handbook of special education* (2nd ed.). New York, NY: Taylor & Francis.

Lambros, K. M., Ward, S. L., Bocian, K. M., MacMillan, D. L., & Gresham, F. M. (1998). Behavioral profiles of children at-risk for emotional and behavioral disorders: Implications for assessment and classification. *Focus on Exceptional Children, 30*(5), 1–16.

Landrum, T. J., (1997). Why data don't matter. *Journal of Behavioral Education, 7*, 123–129.

Landrum, T. J. (2000). Assessment for eligibility: Issues in identifying students with emotional or behavioral disorders. *Assessment for Effective Intervention, 26*(1), 41–49.

Landrum, T. J. (2015). Science matters in special education. In B. Bateman, M. Tankersley, & J. Lloyd (Eds.), *Enduring issues in special education: Personal perspectives* (pp. 429–440). New York, NY: Routledge.

Landrum, T. J. (2017). Emotional and behavioral disorders. In J. M. Kauffman, D. P. Hallahan, & P. C. Pullen (Eds.), *Handbook of special education* (2nd ed.). New York, NY: Taylor & Francis.

Landrum, T. J., & Kauffman, J. M. (2003). Emotionally disturbed, education of. In J. W. Guthrie (Ed.), *Encyclopedia of education* (2nd ed., pp. 726–728). New York: Macmillan Reference.

Landrum, T. J., & Kauffman, J. M. (2006). Behavioral approaches to classroom management. In C. M. Evertson & C. S. Weinstein (Eds.), *Handbook of classroom management: Research, practice, and contemporary issues* (pp. 47–71). Mahwah, NJ: Erlbaum.

Landrum, T. J., Scott, T. M., & Lingo, A. S. (2011). Classroom misbehavior is predictable and preventable. *Phi Delta Kappan, 93*(2), 30–34.

Landrum, T. J., & Tankersley, M. T. (1999). Emotional and behavioral disorders in the new millennium: The future is now. *Behavioral Disorders, 24*, 319–330.

Landrum, T. J., & Tankersley, M. T. (2004). Science in the schoolhouse: An uninvited guest. *Journal of Learning Disabilities, 37*, 207–212.

Landrum, T. J., Tankersley, M., & Kauffman, J. M. (2006). What's special about special education for students with emotional or behavioral disorders. In B. Cook & B. Shirmer (Eds.), *What's special about special education? Examining the role of evidence-based practices* (pp. 12–25) Austin, TX: PRO-ED.

Landrum, T. J., Wiley, A. L., Tankersley, M., & Kauffman, J. M. (2014). Is EBD "special," and is "special education" an appropriate response? In P. Garner, J. M. Kauffman, & J. G. Elliott (Eds.), *The Sage handbook of emotional and behavioral difficulties* (2nd ed.) (pp. 69–81). London: Sage.

Lane, K. L. (2004). Academic instruction and tutoring interventions for students with emotional and behavioral disorders: 1990 to the present. In R. B. Rutherford, M. M. Quinn, & S. R. Mathur (Eds.), *Handbook of research in emotional and behavioral disorders* (pp. 462–486). New York, NY: Guilford.

Lane, K. L., & Menzies, H. M. (Eds.). (2010). Special issue: Reading and writing interventions for students with and at risk for emotional and behavioral disorders. *Behavioral Disorders, 35*(2).

Lane, K. L., Barton-Arwood, S. M., Rogers, L. A., & Robertson, E. J. (2007). Literacy interventions for students with and at-risk for emotional or behavioral disorders: 1997–present. In J. B. Crockett, M. M. Gerber, & T. J. Landrum (Eds.), *Achieving the radical reform of special education: Essays in honor of James M. Kauffman* (pp. 213–241). Mahwah, NJ: Erlbaum.

Lane, K. L., Carter, E. W., Pierson, M. R., & Glaeser, B. C. (2006). Academic, social, and behavioral characteristics of high school students with emotional disturbances or learning disabilities. *Journal of Emotional and Behavioral Disorders, 14*(2), 108–117.

Lane, K. L., Kalberg, J. R., Lambert, E. W., Crnobori, M., & Bruhn, A. L. (2010). A comparison of systematic screening tools for emotional and behavioral disorders: A replication. *Journal of Emotional and Behavioral Disorders, 18*, 100–112.

Lane, K. L., Kalberg, J. R., & Menzies, H. M. (2009). *Developing schoolwide programs to prevent and manage problem behaviors: A step-by-step approach*. New York, NY: Guilford.

Lane, K. L., Little, M. A., Casey, A. M., Lambert, W., Wehby, J. H., & Weisenbach, J. L., et al. (2009). A comparison of systematic screening tools for emotional and behavioral disorders: How do they compare? *Journal of Emotional and Behavioral Disorders, 17*, 93–105.

Lane, K. L., Menzies, H. M., Bruhn, A. L., & Crnobori, M. (2011). *Managing challenging behaviors in schools: Research-based strategies that work*. New York, NY: Guilford.

Lane, K, L., Menzies, H. M., Oakes, W. P., & Germer, K. A. (2014). Screening and identification approaches for detecting students at-risk. In H. M. Walker & F. M. Gresham (Eds.), *Handbook of evidence-based practices for students having emotional and behavioral disorders* (2nd ed.) (pp. 129–151). New York: Guilford.

Lane, K. L., Menzies, H. M., Oakes, W. P., & Kalberg, J. R. (2012). *Systematic screenings of behavior to support instruction: From preschool to high school*. New York, NY: Guilford.

Lane, K. L., & Walker, H. M. (2015). The connection between assessment and intervention: How can screening lead to better intervention? In B. Bateman, J. W. Lloyd, & M. Tankersley (Eds.), *Enduring issues in special education: Personal perspectives* (pp. 285–301). New York: Routledge.

Lattimore, P. K., Visher, C. A., & Linster, R. L. (1995). Predicting rearrest for violence among serious youthful offenders. *Journal of Research in Crime and Delinquency, 32*, 54–83.

Laub, J. H., & Lauritsen, J. L. (1998). The interdependence of school violence with neighborhood and family conditions. In D. S. Elliott, B. A. Hamburg, & K. R. Williams (Eds.), *Violence in American schools* (pp. 127–155). New York, NY: Cambridge University Press.

LaVigna, G. W., & Donnellan, A. M. (1986). *Alternatives to punishment: Solving behavior problems with nonaversive strategies*. New York: Irvington.

Lay, B., Blanz, B., Hartmann, M., & Schmidt, M. H. (2000). The psychosocial outcome of adolescent-onset schizophrenia: A 12-year followup. *Schizophrenia Bulletin, 26*, 801–816.

Learoyd-Smith, S., & Daniels, H. (2014). Social contexts, cultures and environments. In P. Garner, J. M. Kauffman, & J. G. Elliott (Eds.), *The Sage handbook of emotional and behavioral difficulties* (2nd ed.) (pp. 145–164). London, U.K.: Sage.

LeBlanc, L. A., Sautter, R. A., & Dore, D. J. (2006). In M. Hersen (Ed.), *Clinician's handbook of child behavioral assessment* (pp. 377–399). Boston, MA: Academic Press.

Lee, P., Moss, S., Friedlander, R., Donnelly, T., & Horner, W. (2003). Early-onset schizophrenia in children with mental retardation: Diagnostic reliability and stability of clinical features. *Journal of the American Academy of Child and Adolescent Psychiatry, 42*, 162–169.

Leech, S. L., Day, N. L., Richardson, G. A., & Goldschmidt, L. (2003). Predictors of self-reported delinquent behavior in a sample of young adolescents. *Journal of Early Adolescence, 23*, 78–106.

Leff, S. S., Waanders, C., Waasdorp, T. E., & Paskewich, B. S. (2014). Bullying and aggression in school settings. In H. M. Walker & F. M. Gresham (Eds.), *Handbook of evidence-based practices for emotional and behavioral disorders: Applications in schools* (pp. 277–291). New York, NY: Guilford.

Lembke, E. S. (2015). Who should receive special education services and how should educators identify which students are to receive special education services? In B. D. Bateman, J. W. Lloyd, & M. Tankersley (Eds.), *Enduring issues in special education: Personal perspectives* (pp. 133–153). New York, NY: Routledge.

Lemov, D. (2014). *Teach like a champion 2.0: 62 techniques that put students on the path to college*. San Francisco, CA: Jossey-Bass.

Lenzenweger, M. F., & Dworkin, R. H. (Eds.). (1998). *Origins and development of schizophrenia: Advances in experimental psychopathology*. Washington, DC: American Psychological Association.

Leone, P. E., Rutherford, R. B., & Nelson, C. M. (1991). *Special education in juvenile corrections*. Reston, VA: Council for Exceptional Children.

Lerman, D. C., & Vorndran, C. M. (2002). On the status of knowledge for using punishment: Implications for treating behavior disorders. *Journal of Applied Behavior Analysis, 35,* 431–464.

Lern, L. (2017, January 3). Detentions, suspension and expulsion do not curb violent behavior. The Hechinger Report. Retrieved January 7 from http://hechingerreport.org/detentions-suspension-expulsion-not-curb-violent-behavior.

Levy, F., & Hay, D. A. (Eds.). (2001). *Attention, genes and ADHD.* Philadelphia, PA: Taylor & Francis.

Lewinsohn, P. M., Gotlib, I. H., & Seeley, J. R. (1995). Adolescent psychopathology. IV: Specificity of psychosocial risk factors for depression and substance abuse in older adolescents. *Journal of the American Academy of Child and Adolescent Psychiatry, 34,* 1221–1229.

Lewis, C. D. (1974). Introduction: Landmarks. In J. M. Kauffman & C. D. Lewis (Eds.), *Teaching children with behavior disorders: Personal perspectives* (pp. 2–23). Upper Saddle River, NJ: Merrill/Prentice Hall.

Lewis, T. J., Lewis-Palmer, T., Stichter, J., & Newcomer, L. L. (2004). Applied behavior analysis and the education and treatment of students with emotional and behavioral disorders. In R. Rutherford, M. M. Quinn, & S. Mathur (Eds.), *Handbook of research in emotional and behavioral disorders* (pp. 523–545). New York, NY: Guilford.

Lewis, T. J., Mitchell, B. S., Johnson, N. W., & Richter, M. (2014). Supporting children and youth with emotional/behavioral disorders through school-wide systems of positive behavioral support. In P. Garner, J. M. Kauffman, & J. G. Elliott (Eds.), *The Sage handbook of emotional and behavioral difficulties* (2nd ed.) (pp. 373–384). London, U.K.: Sage.

Lewis, T. J., Scott, T. M., Wehby, J. H., & Wills, H. P. (2014). Direct observation of teacher and student behavior in school settings: Trends, issues and future directions. *Behavioral Disorders, 39,* 190–200.

Lewis, T. J., Sugai, G., & Colvin, G. (1998). Reducing problem behavior through a school-wide system of effective behavioral support: Investigation of a school-wide social skills training program and contextual interventions. *School Psychology Review, 27,* 446–459.

Leyba, E. G., & Massat, C. R. (2009). Attendance and truancy: Assessment, prevention, and intervention strategies for school social workers. In C. R. Massat, R. Constable, S. McDonald & J. P. Flynn (Eds.), *School social work: Practice, policy and research* (7th ed.) (pp. 692–712). Chicago, IL: Lyceum Books.

Liaupsin, C. J., Jolivette, K., & Scott, T. M. (2004). Schoolwide systems of behavior support: Maximizing student success in schools. In R. B. Rutherford, M. M. Quinn, & S. R. Mathur (Eds.), *Handbook of research in emotional and behavioral disorders* (pp. 487–501). New York, NY: Guilford.

Liddle, H. A., Dakof, G. A., Turner, R. M., Henderson, C. E., & Greenbaum, P. E. (2008). Treating adolescent drug abuse: A randomized trial comparing multidimensional family therapy and cognitive behavior therapy. *Addiction, 103,* 1660–1670.

Lien-Thorne, S., & Kamps, D. (2005). Replication of the First Step to Success intervention program. *Behavioral Disorders, 31,* 18–32.

Lindberg, L. D., & Maddow-Zimet, I. (2012). Consequences of sex education on teen and young adult sexual behaviors and outcomes. *Journal of Adolescent Health, 51*(4), 332–338.

Lindsay, R. (2016). California voters legalize recreational marijuana: Will federal law follow? Christian Science Monitor, retrieved from http://www.csmonitor.com/USA/2016/1109/California-voters-legalize-recreational-marijuana-Will-federal-law-follow.

Lindstrom, J. H. (2017). High stakes testing and accommodations. In J. M. Kauffman, D. P. Hallahan, & P. C. Pullen (Eds.), *Handbook of special education* (2nd ed.). New York: Taylor & Francis.

Lingo, A.S., Slaton, D.B., & Jolivette, K. (2006). Effects of corrective reading on the reading abilities and classroom behaviors of middle school students with reading deficits and challenging behaviors. *Behavioral Disorders, 31,* 265–283.

Linnoila, M. (1997). On the psychobiology of antisocial behavior. In D. M. Stoff, J. Breiling, & J. D. Maser (Eds.), *Handbook of antisocial behavior* (pp. 336–340). New York, NY: Wiley.

Lloyd, J. W., Forness, S. R., & Kavale, K. A. (1998). Some methods are more effective than others. *Intervention in School and Clinic, 33*(4), 195–200.

Lloyd, J. W., & Hallahan, D. P. (2007). Advocacy and reform of special education. In J. B. Crockett, M. M. Gerber, & T. J. Landrum (Eds.), *Achieving the radical reform of special education: Essays in honor of James M. Kauffman* (pp. 245–263). Mahwah, NJ: Erlbaum.

Lloyd, J. W., & Kauffman, J. M. (1995). What less restrictive placements require of teachers. In J. M. Kauffman, J. W. Lloyd, D. P. Hallahan, & T. A. Astuto (Eds.), *Issues in educational placement: Students with emotional and behavioral disorders* (pp. 317–334). Hillsdale, NJ: Erlbaum.

Lloyd, J. W., Kauffman, J. M., Landrum, T. J., & Roe, D. L. (1991). Why do teachers refer pupils for special education? An analysis of referral records. *Exceptionality, 2,* 115–126.

Lloyd, J. W., Tankersley, M., & Bateman, B. D. (2015). Introduction: Does special education have issues? In B. D. Bateman, J. W. Lloyd, & M. Tankersley (Eds.), *Enduring issues in special education: Personal perspectives.* New York, NY: Routledge.

Loeber, R. (1982). The stability of antisocial and delinquent child behavior: A review. *Child Development, 53,* 1431–1446.

Loeber, R., & Farrington, D. P. (2000). Young children who commit crime: Epidemiology, developmental origins, risk factors, early interventions, and policy implications. *Development and Psychopathology, 12,* 737–762.

Loeber, R., Farrington, D. P., & Petechuk, D. (2003). *Child delinquency: Early intervention and prevention.* US Department of Justice, Office of Justice Programs, Office of Juvenile Justice and Delinquency Prevention.

Loeber, R., Farrington, D. P., Stouthamer-Loeber, M., & Van Kammen, W. B. (1998a). *Antisocial behavior and mental health problems: Explanatory factors in childhood and adolescence.* Mahwah, NJ: Erlbaum.

Loeber, R., Farrington, D. P., Stouthamer-Loeber, M., & Van Kammen, W. B. (1998b). Multiple risk factors for multi-problem boys: Co-occurrence of delinquency, substance use, attention deficit, conduct problems, physical aggression, covert behavior, depressed mood, and shy/withdrawn behavior. In R. Jessor (Ed.), *New perspectives on adolescent risk behavior* (pp. 90–149). New York, NY: Cambridge University Press.

Loeber, R., Green, S. M., Keenan, K., & Lahey, B. B. (1995). Which boys will fare worse? Early predictors of the onset of conduct disorder in a six-year longitudinal study. *Journal of the American Academy of Child and Adolescent Psychiatry, 34,* 499–509.

Loeber, R., & Schmaling, K. B. (1985a). Empirical evidence for overt and covert patterns of antisocial conduct problems: A meta analysis. *Journal of Abnormal Child Psychology, 13,* 337–352.

Loeber, R., & Schmaling, K. B. (1985b). The utility of differentiating between mixed and pure forms of antisocial child behavior. *Journal of Abnormal Child Psychology, 13,* 315–336.

Loeber, R., & Stouthamer-Loeber, M. (1998). *Juvenile aggression at home and at school.* In D. S. Elliott, B. A. Hamburg, & K. R. Williams (Eds.), *Violence in American schools: A new perspective* (pp. 94–126). New York: Cambridge University Press.

Loeber, R., Wung, P., Keenan, K., Giroux, B., Stouthamer-Loeber, M., Van Kammen, W., & Maughan, B. (1993). Developmental pathways in disruptive child behavior. *Development and Psychopathology, 5,* 103–134.

Logan, S. (2009). *This is for the Mara Salvatrucha: Inside the MS-13, America's most violent gang.* New York, NY: Hyperion.

Long, N. J., Wood, M. M., & Fecser, F. A. (2001). *Life space crisis intervention: Talking with students with in conflict.* Austin, TX: Pro-Ed.

Lonke, P. T. (2017). Communication disorders. In J. M. Kauffman, D. P. Hallahan, & P. C. Pullen (Eds.), *Handbook of special education* (2nd ed.). New York, NY: Taylor & Francis.

Lous, A. M., de Wit, C. A. M., De Bruyn, E. E. J., & Riksen-Walraven, J. M. (2002). Depression markers in young children's play: A comparison between depressed and nondepressed 3- to 6-year-olds in various play situations. *Journal of Child Psychology and Psychiatry and Allied Disciplines, 43,* 1029–1038.

Louv, R. (2005). *The last child in the woods: Saving our children from nature-deficit disorder.* Chapel Hill, NC: Algonquin Press.

Luiselli, J. K., & Reed, D. D. (2011). Social validity. In S. Goldstein & J. Naglieri (Eds.), *Encyclopedia of Child Behavior and Development* (p. 1406). New York: Springer.

Lundman, R. J. (1993). *Prevention and control of juvenile delinquency* (2nd ed.). New York: Oxford University Press.

Lynn, D., & King, B. H. (2002). Aggressive behavior. In S. Kutcher (Ed.), *Practical child and adolescent psychopharmacology* (pp. 305–327). New York: Cambridge University Press.

Lyons-Ruth, K., Zeanah, C. H., Benoit, D., Madigan, S., & Mills-Koonce, R. (2014). Disorder and risk for disorder during infancy and toddlerhood. In E. J. Mash & R. A. Barkley (Eds.) *Child psychopathology* (3rd ed.) (pp. 673–736). New York, NY: Guilford.

Maag, J. W. (2001). Rewarded by punishment: Reflections on the disuse of positive reinforcement in schools. *Exceptional Children, 67,* 173–186.

Maag, J. W. (2006). Social skills training for students with emotional and behavioral disorders: A review of reviews. *Behavioral Disorders, 32,* 5–17.

Maag, J. W., & Swearer, S. M. (2005). Cognitive-behavioral interventions for depression: Review and implications for school personnel. *Behavioral Disorders, 30,* 250–276.

Macera, M. H., & Mizes, J. S. (2006). Eating disorders. In M. Hersen (Ed.), *Clinician's handbook of child behavioral assessment* (pp. 437–457). Boston, MA: Academic Press.

Madge, N., & Harvey, J. G. (1999). Suicide among the young—The size of the problem. *Journal of Adolescence, 22,* 145–155.

Mahfouz, N. (2001). *The Cairo trilogy* (W. M. Hutchins, O. E., Kenny, L. M. Kenny, & A. B. Samaan, Trans.). London, U.K.: Everyman.

Malecki, C. K., & Demaray, M. K. (2003). Carrying a weapon to school and perceptions of social support in an urban middle school. *Journal of Emotional and Behavioral Disorders, 11,* 169–178.

Malone, J. C. (2003). Advances in behaviorism: It's not what it used to be. *Journal of Behavioral Education, 12,* 85–89.

March, J. S. (1995). Cognitive-behavioral psychotherapy for children and adolescents with OCD: A review and recommendations for treatment. *Journal of the American Academy of Child and Adolescent Psychiatry, 34,* 7–18.

March, J. S., & Mulle, K. (1998). *OCD in children and adolescents: A cognitive-behavioral treatment manual.* New York: Guilford.

Mark Twain Foundation. (1966). *Mark Twain: Collected tales, sketches, speeches, & essays, 1891–1910.* New York: Library of America.

Marsh, R. L., & Patrick, S. B. (2006). Juvenile diversion programs. In B. Sims & P. Preston (Eds.), *Handbook of juvenile justice: Theory and practice* (pp. 473–430). Boca Raton, FL: Taylor & Francis.

Marshall, W. (2015). Hip-hop's irrepressible refashionability: Phases in the cultural production of black youth. In O. Patterson & E. Fosse (Eds.), *The cultural matrix: Understanding black youth* (pp. 167–197). Cambridge, MA: Harvard University Press.

Martella, R. C., Nelson, J. R., Marchand-Martella, N. E., & O'Reilly, M. (2012). *Comprehensive behavior management: Individualized, classroom, and schoolwide, approaches* (2nd ed.). London, U.K.: Sage.

Martens, B. K., & Lambert, T. L. (2014). Conducting functional behavior assessments for students with emotional/behavioral disorders. In H. M. Walker & F. M. Gresham (Eds.), *Handbook of evidence-based practices for emotional and behavioral disorders: Applications in schools* (pp. 243–257). New York, NY: Guilford.

Martens, E. H., & Russ, H. (1932). *Adjustment of behavior problems of school children: A description and evaluation of the clinical program in Berkeley, Calif.* Washington, DC: U.S. Government Printing Office.

Martin, E. W. (2013). *Breakthrough: Federal special education legislation 1965–1981.* Sarasota, FL: Bardolf.

Martin, J. A. (1981). A longitudinal study of the consequences of early mother–infant interaction: A microanalytic approach. *Monographs of the Society for Research in Child Development, 43*(3, Serial No. 190).

Mash, E. J., & Barkley. R. A. (Eds.) (2003). Child psychopathology (2nd ed). New York, NY: Guilford.

Mash, E. J., & Barkley, R. A. (Eds.). (2014). *Child psychopathology* (3rd ed.). New York, NY: Guilford.

Masi, G., Sbrana, B., Poli, P., Tomaiuolo, F., Favilla, L., & Marcheschi, M. (2000). Depression and school functioning in non-referred adolescents: A pilot study. *Child Psychiatry and Human Development, 30*, 161–171.

Mathur, S. R., & Schoenfeld, N. (2010). Effective instructional practices in juvenile justice facilities *Behavioral Disorders, 36*, 20–27.

Matson, J. L., & Laud, R. B. (2007). Assessment and treatment [of] psychopathology among people with developmental delays. In J. W. Jacobson, J. A. Mulick, & J. Rojahn (Eds.), *Handbook of intellectual and developmental disabilities* (pp. 507–539). New York, NY: Springer.

Mattai, A. K., Hill, J. L., & Lenroot, R. K. (2010). Treatment of early onset schizophrenia. *Current Opinion in Psychiatry, 23*, 304–310.

Mattison, R. E. (2004). Psychiatric and psychological assessment of EBD during school mental health consultation. In R. B. Rutherford, M. M. Quinn, & S. R. Mathur (Eds.), *Handbook of research in emotional and behavioral disorders* (pp. 163–180). New York: Guilford.

Mattison, R. E. (2011, October 29). *A psychiatric consultant/researcher's perspective on the future of the EBD field*. Presentation at the 35th Annual Conference of Teacher Educators for Children with Behavioral Disorders, Tempe, AZ.

Mattison, R. E. (2014). The interface between child psychiatry and special education in the treatment of students with emotional/behavioral disorders in school settings. In H. M. Walker & F. M. Gresham (Eds.), *Handbook of evidence-based practices for emotional and behavioral disorders: Applications in schools* (pp. 104–126). New York, NY: Guilford.

Mattison, R. E., Hooper, S. R., & Carlson, G. A. (2006). Neuropsychological characteristics of special education students with serious emotional/behavioral disorders. *Behavioral Disorders, 31*, 176–188.

Maxson, C. (2011). Street gangs. In J. Q. Wilson & J. Petersilia (Eds.), *Crime and public policy* (pp. 158–182). New York, NY: Oxford University Press.

Mayer, G. R., Nafpaktitis, M., Butterworth, T., & Hollingsworth, P. (1987). A search for the elusive setting events of school vandalism: A correlational study. *Education and Treatment of Children, 10*, 259–270.

Mayer, G. R., & Sulzer-Azaroff, B. (1991). Interventions for vandalism. In G. Stoner, M. R. Shinn, & H. M. Walker (Eds.), *Interventions for achievement and behavior problems* (pp. 559–580). Silver Spring, MD: National Association of School Psychologists.

Mayer, G. R., & Sulzer-Azaroff, B. (2002). Interventions for vandalism and aggression. In M. R. Shinn, H. M. Walker, & G. Stoner (Eds.), *Interventions for academic and behavior problems II: Preventive and remedial approaches* (pp. 853–884). Bethesda, MD: National Association of School Psychologists.

Mayer, M. J., & Furlong, M. J. (2010). How safe are our schools? *Educational Researcher, 39*(1), 16–26.

Mayer, M. J., & Leone, P. E. (2007). School violence and disruption revisited: Equity and safety in the school house. *Focus on Exceptional Children, 40*(1), 1–28.

McClelland, M. M., & Scalzo, C. (2006). Social skills deficits. In M. Hersen (Ed.), *Clinician's handbook of child behavioral assessment* (pp. 313–335). Boston, MA: Academic Press.

McConnell, M. E., Cox, C. J., Thomas, D. D., & Hilvitz, P. B. (2001). *Functional behavioral assessment*. Denver, CO: Love.

McGinnis, J. C., Friman, P. C., & Carlyon, W. D. (1999). The effect of token rewards on "intrinsic" motivation for doing math. *Journal of Applied Behavior Analysis, 32*, 375–379.

McGrath, H. (2014). Directions in teaching social skills to students. In P. Garner, J. M. Kauffman, & J. G. Elliott (Eds.), *The Sage handbook of emotional and behavioral difficulties* (2nd ed.) (pp. 303–316). London, U.K.: Sage.

McLean, M., Wolery, M., & Bailey, D. B. (2004). *Assessing infants and preschoolers with special needs* (3rd ed.). Upper Saddle River, NJ: Prentice Hall.

McLoughlin, J. A., & Nall, M. (1994). Allergies and learning/behavioral disorders. *Intervention in School and Clinic, 29*, 198–207.

McMahon, R. J., & Wells, K. C. (1998). Conduct problems. In E. J. Mash & R. A. Barkley (Eds.), *Treatment of childhood disorders* (2nd ed., pp. 111–207). New York: Guilford.

McMaster, K., Fuchs, D., Fuchs, L. S., & Compton, D. L. (2002). Monitoring the academic progress of children who are unresponsive to generally effective early reading intervention. *Assessment for Effective Intervention, 27*(4), 23–34.

McWhorter, J. H. (2000). Explaining the black education gap. *The Wilson Quarterly, 24*(3), 73–92.

Meadows, N. B., & Stevens, K. B. (2004). Teaching alternative behaviors to students with emotional and behavioral disorders. In R. B. Rutherford, M. M. Quinn, & S. R. Mathur (Eds.), *Handbook of research in emotional and behavioral disorders* (pp. 385–398). New York: Guilford.

Meese, R. L. (2005). A few new children: Postinstitutionalized children of intercountry adoption. *Journal of Special Education, 39*, 157–167.

Metropolitan Area Child Study Research Group (2002). A cognitive-ecological approach to preventing aggression in urban settings: initial outcomes for high-risk children. *Journal of Consulting and Clinical Psychology, 70*(1), 179–194.

Middleton, M. B., & Cartledge, G. (1995). The effects of social skills instruction and parental involvement on the aggressive behavior of African American males. *Behavior Modification, 19*, 192–210.

Milby, J. B., Robinson, S. L., & Daniel, S. (1998). Obsessive compulsive disorders. In R. J. Morris & T. R. Kratochwill (Eds.), *The practice of child therapy* (3rd ed., pp. 5–47). Boston: Allyn & Bacon.

Miller, G. E., & Prinz, R. J. (1991). Designing interventions for stealing. In G. Stoner, M. R. Shinn, & H. M. Walker (Eds.), *Interventions for achievement and behavior problems* (pp. 593–616). Silver Spring, MD: National Association of School Psychologists.

Miller, J. (2015). Culture, inequality, and gender relations among urban black youth. In O. Patterson & E. Fosse (Eds.), *The cultural matrix: Understanding black youth* (pp. 369–390). Cambridge, MA: Harvard University Press.

Miller, K. S., Potter, G. W., & Kappeler, V. E. (2006). The myth of the juvenile superpredator. In B. Sims & P. Preston (Eds.), *Handbook of juvenile justice: Theory and practice* (pp. 173–192). Boca Raton, FL: Taylor & Francis.

Miller-Johnson, S., Coie, J. D., Maumary-Gremaud, A., Lochman, J., & Terry, R. (1999). Peer rejection and aggression in childhood and severity and type of delinquency during adolescence among African-American youth. *Journal of Emotional and Behavioral Disorders, 7*, 137–146.

Mills, G. E., & Gay, L. R. (2016). *Educational research: Competencies for analysis and applications* (11th ed.). Boston: Pearson.

Mindell, J. A., & Owens, J. A. (2003). *A clinical guide to pediatric sleep: Diagnosis and management of sleep problems.* New York, NY: Lippincott Williams & Wilkins.

Miner, M. H. (2002). Factors associated with recidivism in juveniles: An analysis of serious juvenile sex offenders. *Journal of Research and Crime and Delinquency, 39*, 421–436.

Mirza, K. A. H. (2002). Adolescent substance use disorder. In S. Kutcher (Ed.), *Practical child and adolescent psychopharmacology* (pp. 328–381). New York: Cambridge University Press.

Mithaug, D. K., & Mithaug, D. E. (2003). Effects of teacher-directed versus student-directed instruction on self-management of young children with disabilities. *Journal of Applied Behavior Analysis, 36*, 133–136.

Mock, D., & Kauffman, J. M. (2002). Preparing teachers for full inclusion: Is it possible? *The Teacher Educator, 37*, 202–215.

Montague, M., & Dietz, S. (2009). Evaluating the evidence base for cognitive strategy instruction and mathematical problem solving. *Exceptional Children, 75*, 285–302.

Mooney, P., Epstein, M. H., Reid, R., & Nelson, J. R. (2003). Status and trends of academic research for students with emotional disturbance. *Remedial and Special Education, 24*, 273–287.

Moore, D. R., Chamberlain, P., & Mukai, L. H. (1979). Children at risk for delinquency: A follow-up comparison of aggressive children and children who steal. *Journal of Abnormal Child Psychology, 7*, 345–355.

Moore, J. W., & Edwards, R. P. (2003). An analysis of aversive stimuli in classroom demand contexts. *Journal of Applied Behavior Analysis, 36*, 339–348.

Morgan, P. L., Farkas, G., Cook, M., Strassfeld, N. M., Hillemeier, M. M., Pun, W. H., & Schussler, D. L. (2016). Are black children disproportionately overrepresented in special education? A best-evidence synthesis. *Exceptional Children, 83*, 1–18.

Morgan, P. L., Farkas, G., Hillemeier, M., Mattison, R., Maczuga, S., Li, H., & Cook, M. (2015). Minorities are disproportionately underrepresented in special education: Longitudinal evidence across five disability conditions. *Educational Researcher, 20*, 1-15.

Morris, R. J., & Kratochwill, T. R. (1983). *Treating children's fears and phobias.* New York: Pergamon.

Morris, R. J., & Kratochwill, T. R. (1998). Childhood fears and phobias. In R. J. Morris & T. R. Kratochwill (Eds.), *The practice of child therapy* (3rd ed., pp. 91–131). Boston: Allyn & Bacon.

Morris, R. J., & Mather, N. (Eds.). (2008). *Evidence-based interventions for students with learning and behavioral challenges.* Mahwah, NJ: Erlbaum.

Morse, W. C. (1985). *The education and treatment of socioemotionally impaired children and youth.* Syracuse, NY: Syracuse University Press.

Morse, W. C. (1994). Comments from a biased point of view. *Journal of Special Education, 27*, 531–542.

Mostert, M. P. (2001). Facilitated communication since 1995: A review of published studies. *Journal of Autism and Developmental Disorders, 31*, 287–313.

Mostert, M. P., Kauffman, J. M., & Kavale, K. R. (2003). Truth and consequences. *Behavioral Disorders, 28*, 333–347.

Mostert, M. P., Kavale, K. A., & Kauffman, J. M. (Eds.). (2008). *Challenging the refusal of reasoning in special education.* Denver, CO: Love.

Mountjoy, P. T., Ruben, D. H., & Bradford, T. S. (1984). Recent technological advancements in the treatment of enuresis. *Behavior Modification, 8*, 291–315.

Mowbray, C. T., & Mowbray, O. P. (2006). Psychosocial outcomes of adult children of mothers with depression and bipolar disorder. *Journal of Emotional and Behavioral Disorders, 14*, 130–142.

Mpofu, E., Carney, J., & Lambert, M. C. (2006). Peer sociometric assessment. In M. Hersen (Ed.), *Clinician's handbook of child behavioral assessment* (pp. 235–263). Boston, MA: Academic Press.

Mueller, C., Field, T., Yando, R., Harding, J., Gonzalez, K. P., Lasko, D., et al. (1995). Under-eating and over-eating concerns among adolescents. *Journal of Child Psychology and Psychiatry, 36*, 1019–1025.

Mukherjee, S. (2016, March 28). Annals of science. Runs in the family: New findings about schizophrenia rekindle old questions about genes and identity. *The New Yorker*, 26–32.

Mukhopadhyay, C., & Henze, R. C. (2003). How real is race? Using anthropology to make sense of human diversity. *Phi Delta Kappan, 84*, 669–678.

Mulick, J. A., & Butter, E. M. (2016). Positive behavior support: A paternalistic utopian delusion. In R. M. Foxx & J. A. Mulick (Eds.), *Controversial therapies for autism and intellectual disabilities: Fad, fashion, and science in professional practice* (2nd ed.) (pp. 303–321). New York, NY: Francis & Taylor.

Mundschenk, N. A., & Simpson, R. (2014). Defining emotional or behavioral disorders: The quest for affirmation. In P. Garner, J. M. Kauffman, & J. G. Elliott (Eds.), *The Sage handbook of emotional and behavioral difficulties* (2nd ed.) (pp. 43–54). London, U.K.: Sage.

Muris, P., Merckelbach, H., Mayer, B., & Snieder, N. (1998). The relationship between anxiety disorder symptoms and negative self-statements in normal children. *Social Behavior and Personality, 26*, 307–316.

Murphy, D. M. (1986). The prevalence of handicapping conditions among juvenile delinquents. *Remedial and Special Education, 7*(3), 7–17.

Nader, K., & Fletcher, K. E. (2014). Childhood posttraumatic stress disorder. In E. J. Mash & R. A. Barkley (Eds.). *Child psychopathology* (2nd ed., pp. 476–528). New York, NY: Guilford.

Nakamura, D. (2003, April 6). Fast times at Asakita High. *The Washington Post Magazine*, 28–31, 48–51.

Nanda, M. (1998). The epistemic charity of the social constructivist critics of science and why the third world should refuse the offer. In N. Koertge (Ed.), *A house built on sand: Exposing postmodernist myths about science* (pp. 286–311). New York: Oxford University Press.

National Mental Health Association. (1986). *Severely emotionally disturbed children: Improving services under Education of the Handicapped Act (P.L. 94–142)*. Washington, DC: Author.

National Research Council. (2002). *Minority students in special and gifted education*. (M. S. Donovan & C. T. Cross, Eds.), Committee on Minority Representation in Special Education. Washington, DC: National Academy Press, Division of Behavioral and Social Sciences Education.

Neighbors, H. W., Caldwell, C., Williams, D. R., Nesse, R., Taylor, R. J., Bullard, K. M., ... Jackson, J. S. (2007). Race, ethnicity, and the use of services for mental disorders: Results from a national survey of American life. *Archives of General Psychiatry, 64*, 485–494.

Nelson, C. M., Jolivette, K., Leone, P. E., & Mathur, S. R. (2010). Meeting the needs of at-risk and adjudicated youth with behavioral challenges: The promise of juvenile justice. *Behavioral Disorders, 36*, 70–80.

Nelson, C. M. & Kauffman, J. M. (2009). The past is prologue: Suggestions for moving forward in emotional and behavioral disorders. *Beyond Behavior, 18*(2), 36–41.

Nelson, C. M., Leone, P. E., & Rutherford, R. B. (2004). Youth delinquency: Prevention and intervention. In R. B. Rutherford, M. M. Quinn, & S. R. Mathur (Eds.), *Handbook of research in emotional and behavioral disorders* (pp. 282–301). New York, NY: Guilford.

Nelson, J. R., Benner, G. J., & Bohaty, J. (2014). Addressing the academic problems and challenges of EBD students. In H. M. Walker & F. M. Gresham (Eds.), *Handbook of evidence-based practices for emotional and behavioral disorders: Applications in schools* (pp. 363–377). New York, NY: Guilford.

Nelson, J. R., Benner, G. J., & Cheney, D. (2005). An investigation of the language skills of students with emotional disturbance served in public school settings. *Journal of Special Education, 39*, 97–105.

Nelson, J. R., Benner, G. J., & Rogers-Adkinson, D. L. (2003). An investigation of the characteristics of K–12 students with co-morbid emotional disturbance and significant language deficits served in public school settings. *Behavioral Disorders, 29*, 25–33.

Nelson, J. R., Roberts, M. L., Mathur, S R., & Rutherford, R. B. (1999). Has public policy exceeded our knowledge base? A review of the functional behavioral assessment literature. *Behavioral Disorders, 24*, 169–179.

Nelson, J. R., Stage, S., Duppong-Hurley, K., Synhorst, L., & Epstein, M. H. (2007). Risk factors predictive of the problem behavior of children at risk for emotional and behavioral disorders. *Exceptional Children, 73*, 367–379.

Newcomb, M. D., & Richardson, M. A. (1995). Substance use disorders. In M. Hersen & R. T. Ammerman (Eds.), *Advanced abnormal child psychology* (pp. 411–431). Hillsdale, NJ: Erlbaum.

Newcomer, P. L., Barenbaum, E., & Pearson, N. (1995). Depression and anxiety in children and adolescents with learning disabilities, conduct disorders, and no disabilities. *Journal of Emotional and Behavioral Disorders, 3*, 27–39.

Newsom, C., & Kroeger, K. A. (2016). Nonaversive treatment. In R. M. Foxx & J. A. Mulick (Eds.), *Controversial therapies for autism and intellectual disabilities: Fad, fashion, and science in professional practice* (2nd ed.) (pp. 322–338). New York, NY: Francis & Taylor.

Ng-Mak, D. S., Salzinger, S., Feldman, R., & Stueve, A. (2002). Normalization of violence among inner-city youth: A formulation for research. *American Journal of Orthopsychiatry, 72*, 92–101.

Nicholson, T. (2014). Academic achievement and behavior. In P. Garner, J. M. Kauffman, & J. Elliott (Eds), *The Sage handbook of emotional and behavioral difficulties* (2nd ed.) (pp. 177–188). London: Sage.

Nigg, J. T. (2006). *What causes ADHD? Understanding what goes wrong and why*. New York: Guilford.

Nigg, J. T., & Barkley, R. A. (2014). Attention-deficit/hyperactivity disorder. In E. J. Mash & R. A. Barkley (Eds.). *Child psychopathology* (2nd ed., pp. 75–143). New York, NY: Guilford.

Noble, K. G., Houston, S. M., Brito, N. H., Hauke, B, Kan, E. Kuperman, J. M... . Sowell, E. R. (2015). Family income, parental education and brain structure in children and adolescents. *Nature Neuroscience, 18*, 773–778.

Nock, M. K., Kazdin, A. E., Hiripi, E., & Kessler, R. C. (2006). Prevalence, subtypes, and correlates of DSM-IV conduct disorder in the National Comorbidity Survey Replication. *Psychological Medicine, 36*, 699–710.

Norton, M. I., & Ariely, D. (2011). Building a better America—One wealth quintile at a time. *Perspectives on Psychological Science, 6*, 9–12.

Nutt, A. E. (2016, March 22). Beyond the catchprase: OCD goes under the microscope so scientists can end the suffering it causes. *Washington Post*, A1, A12.

O'Brennan, L. M., Furlong, M. J., O'Malley, M. D., & Jones, C. N. (2014). The influence of school contexts and processes on violence and disruption. In P. Garner, J. M. Kauffman, & J. G. Elliott (Eds.), *The Sage handbook of emotional and behavioral difficulties* (2nd ed.) (pp. 165–176). London, U.K.: Sage.

O'Connell, K. A. (2015, May 19). Suddenly her pre-schooler stopped talking. A mom discovers what can make a child go silent. *Washington Post*, E1, E6.

O'Connell, M. E., Boat, T., & Warner, K. E. (Eds.) (2009). *Preventing mental, emotional, and behavioral disorders among young people: Progress and possibilities.* Washington, D.C.: The National Academies Press.

O'Connor, R. E., & Sanchez, V. (2017). Responsiveness to intervention models for reducing reading difficulties and identifying learning disabilities. In J. M. Kauffman, D. P. Hallahan, & P. C. Pullen (Eds.), *Handbook of special education* (2nd ed.). New York: Taylor & Francis.

O'Connor, R. E., Sanchez, V., & Kim, J. J. (2017). Responsiveness to intervention and multi-tiered systems of support for reducing reading difficulties and identifying learning disability. In J. M. Kauffman, D. P. Hallahan, & P. C. Pullen (Eds.), *Handbook of special education* (2nd ed.). New York: Taylor & Francis.

Odgers, C. L., Caspi, A., Broadbent, J. M., Dickson, N., Hancox, R . J., et al. (2007). Prediction of differential adult health burden by conduct problem subtypes in males. *Archives of General Psychiatry, 64,* 476–484.

Ohannessian, C. M., Hesslebrock, V. M., Kramer, J., Kuperman, S., Bucholz, M. A., Schuckit, M. A.,... Nurnberger, J. I. (2005). The relationship between parental psychopathology and adolescent psychopathology: An examination of gender patterns. *Journal of Emotional and Behavioral Disorders, 13,* 67–76.

O'Leary, K. D., & Wilson, G. T. (1975). *Behavior therapy: Applications and outcomes.* Upper Saddle River, NJ: Prentice Hall.

O'Leary, S. G. (1995). Parental discipline mistakes. *Current Directions in Psychological Science, 4,* 11–13.

Olfson, M., Druss, B. G., & Marcus, S. C. (2015). Trends in mental health care among children and adolescents. *New England Journal of Medicine, 372,* 2029–2038.

Oliver, C. (1995). Annotation: Self-injurious behaviour in children with learning disabilities: Recent advances in assessment and intervention. *Journal of Child Psychology and Psychiatry, 30,* 909–927.

Olsson, C. A., Bond, L., Burns, J. M., Vella-Brodrick, D. A., & Sawyer, S. M. (2003). Adolescent resilience: A concept analysis. *Journal of Adolescence, 26,* 1–11.

Olthof, T., & Goossens, F. A. (2008). Bullying and the need to belong: Early adolescents' bullying-related behavior and the acceptance they desire and receive from particular classmates. *Social Development, 17,* 24–46.

Olweus, D. (1979). Stability of aggressive reaction patterns in males: A review. *Psychological Bulletin, 86,* 852–875.

Olweus, D. (1991). Bully/victim problems among school children: Basic facts and effects of a school-based intervention program. In D. J. Pepler & K. H. Rubin (Eds.), *The development of childhood aggression* (pp. 411–446). Hillsdale, NJ: Erlbaum.

O'Mahony, P. (2014). Childhood emotional and behavioral problems and later criminality: Continuities and discontinuities. In P. Garner, J. M. Kauffman, & J. G. Elliott (Eds.), *The Sage handbook of emotional and behavioral difficulties* (2nd ed.) (pp. 189–204). London, U.K.: Sage.

O'Neill, R. E., Horner, R. H., Albin, R. W., Sprague, J. R., Storey, K., & Newton, J. S. (1997). *Functional assessment and program development for problem behavior.* Pacific Grove, CA: Brooks/Cole.

Orvaschel, H. (2006). Structured and semistructured interviews. In M. Hersen (Ed.), *Clinician's handbook of child behavioral assessment* (pp. 159–179). Boston, MA: Academic Press.

Osher, D., Cartledge, G., Oswald, D., Sutherland, K. S., Artiles, A. J., & Coutinho, M. (2004). Cultural and linguistic competency and disproportionate representation. In R. B. Rutherford, M. M. Quinn, & S. R. Mathur (Eds.), *Handbook of research in emotional and behavioral disorders* (pp. 54–77). New York, NY: Guilford.

Oswald, D. (2003). Response to Forness: Parting reflections on education of children with emotional or behavioral disorders. *Behavioral Disorders, 28,* 202–204.

Oswald, D. P., Best, A. M., Coutinho, M. J., & Nagle, H. A. L. (2003). Trends in the special education identification rates of boys and girls: A call for research and change. *Exceptionality, 11,* 223–237.

Oswald, D. P., Coutinho, M. J., Best, A. M., & Singh, N. N. (1999). Ethnic representation in special education: The influence of school-related economic and demographic variables. *Journal of Special Education, 32,* 194–206.

Overton, T. (2016). *Assessing learners with special needs: An applied approach* (8th ed.). Upper Saddle River, NJ: Pearson.

Palmer, D. S., Fuller, K., Arora, T., & Nelson, M. (2001). Taking sides: Parent views on inclusion for their children with severe disabilities. *Exceptional Children, 67,* 467–484.

Papolos, D. F. (2003). Bipolar disorder and comorbid disorders: The case for a dimensional nosology. In B. Geller & M. P. DelBello (Eds.), *Bipolar disorder in childhood and early adolescence* (pp. 76–106). New York, NY: Guilford.

Park, J., Turnbull, A. P., & Turnbull, H. R. (2002). Impacts of poverty on quality of life in families of children with disabilities. *Exceptional Children, 68,* 151–170.

Park, K. L., & Scott, T. M. (2009). Antecedent-based interventions for young children at risk for emotional and behavioral disorders. *Behavioral Disorders, 34,* 196–211.

Parker, J. G., Rubin, K. H., Erath, S., Wojslawowicz, J. C., & Buskirk, A. (2006). Peer relationships, child development, and adjustment: A developmental psychopathology perspective. In D. Cicchetti (Ed.), *Developmental psychopathology: Vol. 3: Risk, disorder, and adaptation* (pp. 419–493). New York, NY: Wiley.

Pascoe, J. M., Wood, D. L., Duffee, J. H., Kuo, A., & Committee on Psychosocial Aspects of Child and Family Health, Council on Community Pediatrics. American Academy of Pediatrics Technical Report (2016). *Pediatrics, 137*(4). Retrieved from http://pediatrics.aappublications.org/content/pediatrics/early/2016/03/07/peds.2016-0340.full.pdf. See also *Pediatrics,* 2016, *137*(4).

Patterson, G. R. (1973). Reprogramming the families of aggressive boys. In C. Thoresen (Ed.), *Behavior modification in education.* Chicago: University of Chicago Press.

Patterson, G. R. (1975). The aggressive child: Victim or architect of a coercive system? In L. A. Hammerlynck, L. C. Handy,

& E. J. Mash (Eds.), *Behavior modification and families* (pp. 267–316). New York: Brunner/Mazel.

Patterson, G. R. (1980). Mothers: The unacknowledged victims. *Monographs of the Society for Research in Child Development, 45*(5, Serial No. 186).

Patterson, G. R. (1982). *Coercive family process.* Eugene, OR: Castalia.

Patterson, G. R. (1986a). The contribution of siblings to training for fighting: A microsocial analysis. In D. Olweus, J. Block, & M. Radke-Yarrow (Eds.), *Development of antisocial and prosocial behavior: Research, theories, and issues* (pp. 235–262). New York: Academic Press.

Patterson, G. R. (1986b). Performance models for antisocial boys. *American Psychologist, 41,* 432–444.

Patterson, G. R., & Capaldi, D. M. (1990). A mediational model for boys' depressed mood. In J. Rolf, A. S. Masten, D. Cicchetti, K. H. Nuechterlein, & S. Weintraub (Eds.), *Risk and protective factors in the development of psychopathology* (pp. 141–163). New York: Cambridge University Press.

Patterson, G. R., Reid, J. B., & Dishion, T. J. (1992). *Antisocial boys.* Eugene, OR: Castalia.

Patterson, G. R., Reid, J. B., Jones, R. R., & Conger, R. E. (1975). *A social learning approach to family intervention: Vol. 1. Families with aggressive children.* Eugene, OR: Castalia.

Patterson, O. (2015a). The nature and dynamics of cultural processes. In O. Patterson & E. Fosse (Eds.), *The cultural matrix: Understanding black youth* (pp. 25–44). Cambridge, MA: Harvard University Press.

Patterson, O. (2015b). The social and cultural matrix of black youth. In O. Patterson & E. Fosse (Eds.), *The cultural matrix: Understanding black youth* (pp. 45–135). Cambridge, MA: Harvard University Press.

Patterson, O., & Fosse, E. (Eds.). (2015). *The cultural matrix: Understanding black youth.* Cambridge, MA: Harvard University Press.

Patterson, O., & Rivers, J. (2015). "Try on the outfit and just see how it works": The psychocultural responses of disconnected youth to work. In O. Patterson & E. Fosse (Eds.), *The cultural matrix: Understanding black youth* (pp. 415-443). Cambridge, MA: Harvard University Press.

Peacock Hill Working Group. (1991). Problems and promises in special education and related services for children and youth with emotional or behavioral disorders. *Behavioral Disorders, 16,* 299–313.

Pearl, R. (2002). Students with learning disabilities and their classroom companions. In B. Y. L. Wong & M. Donahue (Eds.), *The social dimensions of learning disabilities: Essays in honor of Tanis Bryan* (pp. 77–91). Mahwah, NJ: Erlbaum.

Penn, E. B., Greene, H. T., & Gabbidon, S. L. (Eds.). (2006). *Race and juvenile justice.* Durham, NC: Carolina Academic Press.

Perou, R., Bitsko, R., Blumberg, S. J., Pastor, P., Ghandour, R. M., Gfroerer, J. C., ... Huang, L. N. (2013, May 17). Mental health surveillance among children—United States, 2005–2011. *Supplements 62*(02), 1–35.

Peterson, L., Reach, K., & Grabe, S. (2003). Health-related disorders. In E. J. Mash & R. A. Barkley (Eds.). *Child psychopathology* (2nd ed., pp. 716–749). New York, NY: Guilford.

Peterson, R., & Ishii-Jordan, S. (Eds.). (1994). *Multicultural issues in the education of students with behavioral disorders.* Cambridge, MA: Brookline.

Petrosino A., Turpin-Petrosino, C., & Buehler J. (2002). "Scared Straight" and other juvenile awareness programs for preventing juvenile delinquency. *Cochrane Database of Systematic Reviews, Issue 2.* Art. No.: CD002796.

Pfiffner, L. J., & O'Leary, S. G. (1987). The efficacy of all-positive management as a function of the prior use of negative consequences. *Journal of Applied Behavior Analysis, 20,* 265–271.

Piacentini, J., Chang, S., Snorrason, I., & Woods, D. W. (2014). Obsessive-compulsive spectrum disorders. In E. J. Mash & R. A. Barkley (Eds.), *Child psychopathology* (2nd ed., pp. 429–475). New York, NY: Guilford.

Pierangelo, R., & Giuliani, G. A. (2006). *Assessment in special education* (2nd ed.). Boston, MA: Allyn & Bacon.

Pinker, S. (2002). *The blank slate: The modern denial of human nature.* New York, NY: Viking.

Pinsonneault, I. L., Richardson, J. P., & Pinsonneault, J. (2002). Three models of educational interventions for child and adolescent firesetters. In D. Kolko (Ed.), *Handbook on firesetting in children and youth* (pp. 261–278). New York, NY: Academic Press.

Pionek Stone, B., Kratochwill, T. R., Sladezcek, I., & Serlin, R. C. (2002). Treatment of selective mutism: A best-evidence synthesis. *School Psychology Quarterly, 17,* 168–190.

Place, M., Reynolds, J., Cousins, A., & O'Neill, S. (2002). Developing a resilience package for vulnerable children. *Child and Adolescent Mental Health, 7,* 162–167.

Plasencia-Peinado, J., & Alvarado, J. L. (2000). Assessing students with emotional and behavioral disorders using curriculum-based measurement. *Assessment for Effective Intervention, 26*(1), 59–66.

Plomin, R. (1995). Genetics and children's experiences in the family. *Journal of Child Psychology and Psychiatry, 36,* 33–68.

Polanczyk, G., Moffitt, T. E., Arsenault, L., Cannon, M., Ambler, A., Keefe, R. S. E., ... Caspi, A. (2010). Etiological and clinical features of childhood psychotic symptoms. *Archives of General Psychiatry, 67,* 328–338.

Polsgrove, L. (2003). Reflections on past and future. *Behavioral Disorders, 28,* 221–226.

Polsgrove, L., & Smith, S. W. (2004). Informed practice in teaching behavioral self-control to children with EBD. In R. B. Rutherford, M. M. Quinn, & S. R. Mathur (Eds.), *Handbook of research in emotional and behavioral disorders* (pp. 399–425). New York: Guilford.

Ponitz, C. C., Rimm-Kaufman, S. E., Grimm, K. J., & Curby, T. W. (2009). Kindergarten classroom quality, behavioral engagement, and reading achievement. *School Psychology Review, 38,* 102–120.

Popenhagen, M. P., & Qualley, R. M. (1998). Adolescent suicide: Detection, intervention, and prevention. *Professional School Counseling, 1*(4), 30–36.

Postel, H. H. (1937). The special school versus the special class. *Exceptional Children, 4*, 12–13, 18–19.

Poulin, F., & Boivin, M. (1999). Proactive and reactive aggression and boys' friendship quality in mainstream classrooms. *Journal of Emotional and Behavioral Disorders, 7*, 168–177.

Powell, S., & Nelson, B. (1997). Effects of choosing academic assignments on a student with attention deficit hyperactivity disorder. *Journal of Applied Behavior Analysis, 30*, 181–183.

Preston, P. (2006). The disabled juvenile offender. In B. Sims & P. Preston (Eds.), *Handbook of juvenile justice: Theory and practice* (pp. 347–358). Boca Raton, FL: Taylor & Francis.

Prior, M., & Werry, J. S. (1986). Autism, schizophrenia, and allied disorders. In H. C. Quay & J. S. Werry (Eds.), *Psychopathological disorders of childhood* (3rd ed., pp. 156–210). New York, NY: Wiley.

Pullen, P. C., & Hallahan, D. P. (2015). What is special education instruction? In B. D. Bateman, J. W. Lloyd, & M. Tankersley (Eds.), *Enduring issues in special education: Personal perspectives* (pp. 37–50). New York, NY: Routledge.

Pullen, P. C., Lane, H. B., Ashworth, K. E., & Lovelace, S. P. (2017). Learning disabilities. In J. M. Kauffman, D. P. Hallahan, & P. C. Pullen (Eds.), *Handbook of special education* (2nd ed.). New York, NY: Taylor & Francis.

Pullen, P. L. (2004). *Brighter beginnings for teachers*. Lanham, MD: Scarecrow Education.

Putnam, R. D. (2015). *Our kids: The American dream in crisis*. New York, NY: Simon & Schuster.

Qi, C. H., & Kaiser, A. P. (2003). Behavior problems of preschool children from low-income families: A review of the literature. *Topics in Early Childhood Education, 23*, 188–216.

Quay, H. C. (1986a). Classification. In H. C. Quay & J. S. Werry (Eds.), *Psychopathological disorders of childhood* (3rd ed., pp. 1–34). New York, NY: Wiley.

Quay, H. C. (1986b). Conduct disorders. In H. C. Quay & J. S. Werry (Eds.), *Psychopathological disorders of childhood* (3rd ed., pp. 35–72). New York: Wiley.

Quay, H. C., & La Greca, A. M. (1986). Disorders of anxiety, withdrawal, and dysphoria. In H. C. Quay & J. S. Werry (Eds.), *Psychopathological disorders of childhood* (3rd ed., pp.73–110). New York: Wiley.

Rabian, B., & Silverman, W. K. (1995). Anxiety disorders. In M. Hersen & R. T. Ammerman (Eds.), *Advanced abnormal child psychology* (pp. 235–252). Hillsdale, NJ: Erlbaum.

Rabiner, D. L., Coie, J. D., Miller-Johnson, S., Boykin, A. M., & Lochman, J. E. (2005). Predicting the persistence of aggressive offending of African-American males from adolescence into young adulthood: The importance of peer relations, aggressive behavior, and ADHD symptoms. *Journal of Emotional and Behavioral Disorders, 13*, 131–140.

Ramakrishnan, K. (2008). Evaluation and treatment of enuresis. *American Family Physician, 78*, 489–496.

Rao, S., Hoyer, L., Meehan, K., Young, L., & Guerrera, A. (2003). Using narrative logs: Understanding students' challenging behaviors. *Teaching Exceptional Children, 35*(5), 22–29.

Rapee, R. M., Schniering, C. A., & Hudson, J. L. (2009). Anxiety disorders during childhood and adolescence: Origins and treatment. *Annual Review of Clinical Psychology, 5*, 311–341.

Rapp, J. T., Miltenberger, R. G., Galensky, T. L., Ellingson, S. A., & Long, E. S. (1999). A functional analysis of hair pulling. *Journal of Applied Behavior Analysis, 32*, 329–337.

Rapport, M. D., Timko, T. M., & Wolfe, R. (2006). Attention-deficit/hyperactivity disorder. In M. Hersen (Ed.), *Clinician's handbook of child behavioral assessment* (pp. 401–435). Boston: Academic Press.

Ravitch, D. (2003). *The language police: How pressure groups restrict what students learn*. New York: Knopf.

Ravitch, D. (2010). *The death and life of the great American school system*. New York: Basic Books.

Reed, L., Gable, R. A., & Yanek, K. (2014). Hard times and an uncertain future: Issues that confront the field of emotional disabilities. In P. Garner, J. M. Kauffman, & J. G. Elliott (Eds.), *The Sage handbook of emotional and behavioral difficulties* (2nd ed.) (pp. 453–464). London, U.K.: Sage.

Reid, J. B., & Eddy, J. M. (1997). The prevention of antisocial behavior: Some considerations in the search for effective interventions. In D. M. Stoff, J. Breiling, & J. D. Maser (Eds.), *Handbook of antisocial behavior* (pp. 343–356). New York, NY: Wiley.

Reid, J. B., & Hendricks, A. (1973). Preliminary analysis of the effectiveness of direct home intervention for the treatment of predelinquent boys who steal. In L. A. Hammerlynck, L. C. Handy, & E. J. Mash (Eds.), *Behavior change: Methodology, concepts and practice* (pp. 209–219). Champaign, IL: Research Press.

Reid, J. B., & Patterson, G. R. (1976). The modification of aggression and stealing behavior of boys in the home setting. In A. Bandura & E. Ribes (Eds.), *Behavior modification: Experimental analyses of aggression and delinquency* (pp. 123–145). Hillsdale, NJ: Erlbaum.

Reid, R., Trout, A. L., & Schartz, M. (2005). Self-regulation interventions for children with attention deficit/hyperactivity disorder. *Exceptional Children, 71*, 361–377.

Reinke, W. M. Frey, A. J., Herman, K. C., & Thompson, C. V. (2014). Improving engagement and implementation of interventions for children with emotional and behavioral disorders in home and school settings. In H. M. Walker & F. M. Gresham (Eds.), *Handbook of evidence-based practices for emotional and behavioral disorders: Applications in schools* (pp. 432–445). New York, NY: Guilford.

Reitman, D., Hummek, R., Franz, D. Z., & Gross, A. M. (1998). A review of methods and instruments for assessing externalizing disorders: Theoretical and practical considerations in rendering a diagnosis. *Clinical Psychology Review, 18*, 555–584.

Reschly, D. J. (1997). Utility of individual ability measures and public policy choices for the 21st century. *School Psychology Review, 26*, 234–241.

Reynolds, C. R., & Kamphaus, R. W. (2004). *Behavior Assessment Scale for Children* (2nd ed.). Circle Pines, MN: AGS Publishing.

Reynolds, C., & Kamphaus, R. (2015). Behavioral Assessment System for Children—Third edition (BASC-3). Upper Saddler River, NJ: Pearson.

Reynolds, W. M. (1992). Depression in children and adolescents. In W. R. Reynolds (Ed.), *Internalizing disorders in children and adolescents* (pp. 149–253). New York: Wiley.

Reynolds, W. M. (2006). Depression. In M. Hersen (Ed.), *Clinician's handbook of child behavioral assessment* (pp. 291–312). Boston, MA: Academic Press.

Rhee S. H., Lahey B. B., Waldman I. D. (2015). Comorbidity among dimensions of childhood psychopathology: Converging evidence from behavior genetics. *Child Development Perspectives, 9,* 26–31.

Rhode, G., Jenson, W. R., & Reavis, H. K. (2010). *The tough kid book: Practical classroom management strategies* (2nd ed). Eugene, OR: Pacific Northwest Publishing.

Ricaurte, G. A., Yuan, J., Hatzidimitriou, G., Cord, B. J., & McCann, U. D. (2003). "MDMA ("Ecstasy") and neurotoxicity": Response. *Science, 300,* 1504–1505.

Richardson, B. G., & Shupe, M. J. (2003). The importance of teacher self-awareness in working with students with emotional and behavioral disorders. *Teaching Exceptional Children, 36*(2), 8–13.

Rimm-Kaufman, S. E., & Kagan, J. (2005). Infant predictors of kindergarten behavior: The contribution of inhibited and uninhibited temperament types. *Behavioral Disorders, 30,* 331–347.

Robb, A. S., & Dadson, M. J. (2002). Eating disorders in males. *Child and Adolescent Psychiatric Clinics of North America, 11,* 399–418.

Roberts, R. E., Roberts, C. R., & Xing, Y. (2006). Prevalence of youth-reported DSM-IV psychiatric disorders among African, European, and Mexican American adolescents. *Journal of the Academy of Child and Adolescent Psychiatry, 45,* 1329–1337.

Robins, L. N. (1966). *Deviant children grown up.* Baltimore: Williams & Wilkins.

Robins, L. N. (1986). The consequences of conduct disorder in girls. In D. Olweus, J. Block, & M. Radke-Yarrow (Eds.), *Development of antisocial and prosocial behavior: Research, theories, and issues* (pp. 385–414). New York: Academic Press.

Rock, M. L., & Billingsley, B. S. (2015). Who makes a difference! Next generation special education workforce renewal. In B. D. Bateman, J. W. Lloyd, & M. Tankersley (Eds.), *Enduring issues in special education: Personal perspectives* (pp. 168–185). New York, NY: Routledge.

Rodriguez, J. O., Montesinos, L., & Preciado, J. (2005). A 19th century predecessor of the token economy. *Journal of Applied Behavior Analysis, 38,* 427.

Roerig, J. L., Mitchell, J. E., Myers, T. C., & Glass, J. B. (2002). Pharmacotherapy and medical complications of eating disorders in children and adolescents. *Child and Adolescent Psychiatric Clinics of North America, 11,* 365–385.

Rogers-Adkinson, D. (1999). Psychiatric disorders in children. In D. Rogers-Adkinson & P. Griffith (Eds.), *Communication disorders and children with psychiatric and behavioral disorders* (pp. 39–68). San Diego, CA: Singular.

Rogers-Adkinson, D. L. (2003). Language processing in children with emotional disorders. *Behavioral Disorders, 29,* 43–47.

Rogers-Adkinson, D., & Griffith, P. (Eds.). (1999). *Communication disorders and children with psychiatric and behavioral disorders.* San Diego, CA: Singular.

Rojewski, J. W., & Gregg, N. (2017). Choice patterns and behaviors of work-bound youth with high incidence disabilities. In J. M. Kauffman, D. P. Hallahan, & P. C. Pullen (Eds.), *Handbook of special education* (2nd ed.). New York, NY: Taylor & Francis.

Roll, J. M. (2005). Assessing the feasibility of using contingency management to modify cigarette smoking by adolescents. *Journal of Applied Behavior Analysis, 38,* 463–467.

Romaniuk, C., Miltenberger, R., Conyers, C., Jenner, N., Jurgens, M., & Ringenberg, C. (2002). The influence of activity choice on problem behaviors maintained by escape versus attention. *Journal of Applied Behavior Analysis, 35,* 349–362.

Rooney, K. J. (2017). Attention-deficit/hyperactivity disorder. In J. M. Kauffman. D. P. Hallahan, & P. C. Pullen (Eds.), *Handbook of special education* (2nd ed.). New York, NY: Taylor & Francis.

Rosenberg, M. S., & Jackman, L. A. (2003). Development, implementation, and sustainability of comprehensive schoolwide behavior management systems. *Intervention in School and Clinic, 39,* 10–21.

Rosenblatt, P., Edin, K, & Zhu, Q. (2015). "I do me": Young black men and the struggle to resist the street. In O. Patterson & E. Fosse (Eds.), *The cultural matrix: Understanding black youth* (pp. 229–251). Cambridge, MA: Harvard University Press.

Rosenfield, R., Bray, T. M., & Egley, A. (1999). Facilitating violence: A comparison of gang-motivated, gang-affiliated and nongang youth homicides. *Journal of Quantitative Criminology, 15,* 495–516.

Rosenthal, P. A., & Rosenthal, S. (1984). Suicidal behavior by preschool children. *American Journal of Psychiatry, 141,* 520–525.

Rothman, E. P. (1970). *The angel inside went sour.* New York, NY: McKay.

Rothstein, R., Jacobsen, R., & Wilder, T. (2006, November). "*Proficiency for all*"—*An oxymoron.* Paper presented at a symposium on "Examining America's commitment to closing achievement gaps: NCLB and its alternatives." New York, NY: Teachers College, Columbia University.

Rubin, K. H., Burgess, K. B., Kennedy, A. E., & Stewart, S. L. (2003). Social withdrawal in childhood. In E. J. Mash & R. A. Barkley (Eds.), *Child psychopathology* (2nd ed., pp. 372–406). New York, NY: Guilford.

Rubin, K.H., Coplan, R.J., & Bowker, J.C. (2009). Social withdrawal and shyness in childhood and adolescence. *Annual Review of Psychology, 60,* 141–171.

Rupke, S. J., Blecke, D., & Renfro, M. (2006). Cognitive therapy for depression. *American Family Physician, 73,* 83–86.

Russell, A. T. (1994). The clinical presentation of childhood-onset schizophrenia. *Schizophrenia Bulletin, 20,* 631–646.

Rutter, M. (1995). Clinical implications of attachment concepts: Retrospect and prospect. *Journal of Child Psychology and Psychiatry, 36,* 549–571.

Ryan, J. B., Sanders, S., Katsiyannis, A., & Yell, M. (2007). Using time-out effectively in the classroom. *Teaching Exceptional Children, 39,* 60–67.

Ryan, N. D. (2002). Depression. In S. Kutcher (Ed.), *Practical child and adolescent psychopharmacology* (pp. 91–105). New York, NY: Cambridge University Press.

Sachs, B. (1905). *A treatise on the nervous diseases of children: For physicians and students.* New York, NY: William Wood.

Sacks, O. (1995). *An anthropologist on Mars.* New York, NY: Knopf.

Sacks, O. (2015). *On the move: A life.* New York: Knopf.

Sacks, P. (1999). *Standardized minds: The high price of America's testing culture and what we can do to change it.* Cambridge, MA: Perseus.

Saez, M. (2010, July 17). Striking it richer: The evolution of top incomes in the United States (update with 2008 estimates). Retrieved September 28, 2010 from http://elsa.berkeley.edu/~saez/saez-UStopincomes-2008.pdf.

Saigh, P. A. (1998). Posttraumatic stress disorder. In R. J. Morris & T. R. Kratochwill (Eds.), *The practice of child therapy* (3rd ed., pp. 390–418). Boston: Allyn & Bacon.

Salvia, J., Ysseldyke, J. E., & Witmer, S. (2017). *Assessment in special and inclusive education.* Boston, MA: Cengage Learning.

Sampson, R. T. (2015). Continuity and change in neighbourhood culture: Toward a structurally embedded theory of social altruism and moral cynicism. In O. Patterson & E. Fosse (Eds.), *The cultural matrix: Understanding black youth* (pp. 201–228). Cambridge, MA: Harvard University Press.

Sasso, G. M. (2001). The retreat from inquiry and knowledge in special education. *The Journal of Special Education, 34,* 178–193.

Sasso, G. M. (2007). Science and reason in special education: The legacy of Derrida and Foucault. In J. B. Crockett, M. M. Gerber, & T. J. Landrum (Eds.), *Achieving the radical reform of special education: Essays in honor of James M. Kauffman* (pp. 143–167). Mahwah, NJ: Erlbaum.

Sasso, G. M., Conroy, M. A., Stichter, J. P., & Fox, J. J. (2001). Slowing down the bandwagon: The misapplication of functional assessment for students with emotional and behavioral disorders. *Behavioral Disorders, 26,* 282–296.

Satterfield, J. H., Faller, K., Crinella, F. M., Schell, A. M., Swanson, J. M., & Homer, L. D. (2007). A 30-year prospective follow-up study of hyperactive boys with conduct problems: Adult criminality. *Journal of the American Academy of Child and Adolescent Psychiatry, 46,* 601–610.

Sayre-McCord, G. (Ed.). (2007). *Crime and family: Selected essays of Joan McCord.* Philadelphia, PA: Temple University Press.

Schaeffer, J. L., & Ross, R. G. (2002). Childhood-onset schizophrenia: Premorbid and prodromal diagnostic and treatment histories. *Journal of the American Academy of Child and Adolescent Psychiatry, 41,* 538–545.

Schaffner, L. (2006). *Girls in trouble with the law.* New Brunswick, NJ: Rutgers University Press.

Scheuermann, B., & Webber, J. (2002). *Autism: Teaching does make a difference.* Belmont, CA: Wadsworth.

Schnoes, C., Reid, R., Wagner, M., & Marder, C. (2006). ADHD among students receiving special education services: A national survey. *Exceptional Children, 72,* 483–496.

Schofield, H. T., Bierman, K. L., Heinrichs, B., Nix, R. L., & Conduct Problems Prevention Research Group (2008). Predicting early sexual activity with behavior problems exhibited at school entry and in early adolescence. *Journal of Abnormal Child Psychology, 36,* 1175–1188.

Schreibman, L. (1994). General principles of behavior management. In E. Schopler & G. B. Mesibov (Eds.), *Behavioral issues in autism* (pp. 11–38). New York: Plenum.

Schreibman, L., Stahmer, A. C., & Akshoomoff, N. (2006). Pervasive developmental disorders. In M. Hersen (Ed.), *Clinician's handbook of child behavioral assessment* (pp. 503–525). Boston: Academic Press.

Schwartz, I. S., & Baer, D. M. (1991). Social validity assessments: Is current practice state of the art? *Journal of Applied Behavior Analysis, 24,* 189–204.

Scott, T. M., & Alter, P. J. (2017). Examining the case for functional behavior assessment as an evidence-based practice for students with emotional and behavioral disorders in general education classrooms. *Preventing School Failure: Alternative Education for Children and Youth, 61*(1), 80–93.

Scott, T. M., Liaupsin, C. J., Nelson, C. M., & Jolivette, K. (2003). Ensuring student success through team-based functional behavioral assessment. *Teaching Exceptional Children, 35*(5), 16–21.

Scott, T. M., & Nelson, C. M. (1999). Functional behavioral assessment: Implications for training and staff development. *Behavioral Disorders, 24,* 249–252.

Scott, T. M. & Shearer-Lingo, A. (2002). The effects of reading fluency instruction on the academic and behavioral success of middle school students in a self-contained EBD classroom. *Preventing School Failure, 46,* 167–173.

Scruggs, T. E., & Mastropieri, M. A. (2015). What makes special education special? In B. D. Bateman, J. W. Lloyd, & M. Tankersley (Eds.), *Enduring issues in special education: Personal perspectives* (pp. 22–35). New York, NY: Routledge.

Scruggs, T., Mastropieri, M., Brigham, F. J., & Milman, L. (2017). Science and social studies. In J. M. Kauffman, D. P. Hallahan, & P. C. Pullen (Eds.), *Handbook of special education* (2nd ed.). New York, NY: Taylor & Francis.

Scull, A. (2015). *Madness in civilization: A cultural history of insanity from the Bible to Freud, from the madhouse to modern medicine.* Princeton, NJ: Princeton University Press.

Sedgwick, J. (2007). *In my blood: Six generations of madness and desire in an American family.* New York, NY: Harper Collins.

Seeley, J. R., Rohde, P., Lewinsohn, P. M., & Clarke, G. N. (2002). Depression in youth: Epidemiology, identification, and intervention. In M. R. Shinn, H. M. Walker, & G. Stoner (Eds.), *Interventions for academic and behavior problems II: Preventive and remedial approaches* (pp. 885–911). Bethesda, MD: National Association of School Psychologists.

Seeley, J. R., Severson, Hf. H., & Fixsen, A. A. M. (2014). Empirically based targeted prevention approaches for addressing externalizing and internalizing behavior disorders within school contexts. In H. M. Walker & F. M. Gresham (Eds.), *Handbook of evidence-based practices for emotional and behavioral disorders: Applications in schools* (pp. 307–323). New York, NY: Guilford.

Serbin, L. A., Stack, D. M., Schwartzman, J. C., Bentley, V., Saltaris, C., & Ledingham, J. E. (2002). A longitudinal study of aggressive and withdrawn children in adulthood: Patterns of parenting and risk to offspring. In R. J. McMahon & R. D. Peters (Eds.), *The effects of parental dysfunction on children* (pp. 43–69). New York, NY: Kluwer.

Serna, L. A., Lambros, K., Nielsen, E., & Forness, S. R. (2002). Head Start children at risk for emotional or behavioral disorders: Behavior profiles and clinical implications of a primary prevention program. *Behavioral Disorders, 27*, 137–141.

Serna, L., Nielsen, E., Lambros, K., & Forness, S. (2000). Primary prevention with children at risk for emotional or behavioral disorders: Data on a universal intervention for Head Start classrooms. *Behavioral Disorders, 26*, 70–84.

Severson, H., & James, L. (2002). Prevention and early interventions for addictive behaviors: Health promotion in the schools. In M. R. Shinn, H. M. Walker, & G. Stoner (Eds.), *Interventions for academic and behavior problems II: Preventive and remedial approaches* (pp. 681–702). Bethesda, MD: National Association of School Psychologists.

Shaffer, D., Gould, M., & Hicks, R. C. (1994). Worsening suicide rates in Black teenagers. *American Journal of Psychiatry, 151*, 1810–1812.

Shaffer, D., & Waslick, B. D. (Eds.). (2002). *The many faces of depression in children and adolescents*. Washington, DC: American Psychiatric Publishing.

Shane, H. C. (Ed.). (1994). *Facilitated communication: The clinical and social phenomenon*. San Diego: Singular.

Shapiro, E. S. (2011). *Academic skills problems: Direct assessment and intervention*. New York: Guilford Press.

Shapiro, E. S., Durnan, S. L., Post, E. E., & Levinson, T. S. (2002). Self-monitoring procedures for children and adolescents. In M. R. Shinn, H. M. Walker, & G. Stoner (Eds.), *Interventions for academic and behavior problems II: Preventive and remedial approaches* (pp. 433–454). Bethesda, MD: National Association of School Psychologists.

Shapiro, E. S., & Keller, M. A. (2006). Academic skills problems. In M. Hersen (Ed.), *Clinician's handbook of child behavioral assessment* (pp. 605–630). Boston, MA: Academic Press.

Sharp, W. G., Reeves, C. B., & Gross, A. M. (2006). Behavioral interviewing of parents. In M. Hersen (Ed.), *Clinician's handbook of child behavioral assessment* (pp. 103–124). Boston, MA: Academic Press.

Sheehan, S. (1993a, January 11). A lost childhood. *New Yorker*, pp. 54–85.

Sheehan, S. (1993b, January 18). A lost motherhood. *New Yorker*, pp. 52–79.

Sheras, P. (2002). *Your child: Bully or victim? Understanding and ending school yard tyranny*. New York, NY: Skylight.

Shermer, M. (2011). *The believing brain: From ghosts and gods to politics and conspiracies—How we construct beliefs and reinforce them as truths*. New York: Times Books.

Shiner, R. L., & Tackett, J. L. (2014). Personality disorders in children and adolescents. In E. J. Mash & R. A. Barkley (Eds.). *Child psychopathology* (2nd ed., pp. 848–896). New York, NY: Guilford.

Shinn, M. R. (2014). Progress monitoring methods and tools for academic performance. In H. M. Walker & F. M. Gresham (Eds.), *Handbook of evidence-based practices for emotional and behavioral disorders: Applications in schools* (pp. 104–126). New York, NY: Guilford.

Shinn, M. R., Shinn, M. M., Hamilton, C., & Clarke, B. (2002). Using curriculum-based measurement in general education classrooms to promote reading success. In M. R. Shinn, H. M. Walker, & G. Stoner (Eds.), *Interventions for academic and behavior problems II: Preventive and remedial approaches* (pp. 113–142). Bethesda, MD: National Association of School Psychologists.

Shinn, M. R., Walker, H. M., & Stoner, G. (Eds.). (2002). *Interventions for academic and behavior problems II: Preventive and remedial approaches*. Bethesda, MD: National Association of School Psychologists.

Shirk, S. R., Kaplinski, H., & Gudmundsen, G. (2009). School-based cognitive-behavioral therapy for adolescent depression. *Journal of Emotional and Behavioral Disorders, 17*, 106–117.

Shores, D., & Wehby, J. H. (1999). Analyzing the social behavior of students with emotional and behavioral disorders in classrooms. *Journal of Emotional and Behavioral Disorders, 7*, 194–199.

Short, J. F., & Hughes, L. A. (Eds.). (2006a). *Studying youth gangs*. New York, NY: Rowman & Littlefield.

Short, J. F., & Hughes, L. A. (2006b). Moving gang research forward. In J. F. Short & L. A. Hughes (Eds.), *Studying youth gangs* (pp. 225–238). New York, NY: Rowman & Littlefield.

Sidman, M. (2006). The distinction between positive and negative reinforcement: Some additional considerations. *The Behavior Analyst, 29*, 135–139.

Siegel, L. J. (1992). Somatic disorders of childhood and adolescence. In W. R. Reynolds (Ed.), *Internalizing disorders in children and adolescents* (pp. 283–310). New York: Wiley.

Siegel, L. J. (1998). Somatic disorders. In R. J. Morris & T. R. Kratochwill (Eds.), *The practice of child therapy* (3rd ed., pp. 231–302). Boston: Allyn & Bacon.

Siegel, L. J., & Ridley-Johnson, R. (1985). Anxiety disorders of childhood and adolescence. In P. H. Bornstein & A. E. Kazdin (Eds.), *Handbook of clinical behavior therapy with children* (pp. 266–308). Homewood, IL: Dorsey.

Siegel, L., & Welsh, B. (2011). *Juvenile delinquency: The core* (4th ed.). Belmont, CA: Wadsworth.

Siegel L., & Welsh, B. (2012). *Juvenile delinquency: Theory, practice, and law* (11th ed.). Belmont, CA: Cengage Learning/ Wadsworth.

Silbereisen, R. K. (1998). Lessons we learned—problems still to be solved. In R. Jessor (Ed.), *New perspectives on adolescent risk behavior* (pp. 518–543). New York, NY: Cambridge University Press.

Silvestri, S. M., & Heward, H. L. (2016). The neutralization of special education, revisited. In R. M. Foxx & J. A. Mulick (Eds.), *Controversial therapies for autism and itellectual disabilities: Fad, fashion, and science in professional practice* (2nd ed) (pp. 136–153). New York, NY: Routledge.

Sims, B., & Preston, P. (Eds.) (2006). *Handbook of juvenile justice: Theory and practice*. Boca Raton, FL: Taylor & Francis.

Sinclair, E., Forness, S. R., & Alexson, J. (1985). Psychiatric diagnosis: A study of its relationship to school needs. *Journal of Special Education, 19*, 333–344.

Singer, G. H. S., Maul, C., Wang, M., & Ethridge, B. L. (2017). Resilience in families of children with disabilities: Risk and protective factors. In J. M. Kauffman, D. P. Hallahan, & P. C. Pullen (Eds.), *Handbook of special education* (2nd ed.). New York, NY: Taylor & Francis.

Skiba, R. J., Middelberg, L V., & McClain, M. B. (2014). Multicultural issues for schools and students with emotional and behavioral disorders: Disproportionality in discipline and special education. In H. M. Walker & F. M. Gresham (Eds.), *Handbook of evidence-based practices for emotional and behavioral disorders: Applications in schools* (pp. 54–70). New York, NY: Guilford.

Smit, F., Monshouwer, K., & Verdurmen, J. (2002). Polydrug use among secondary school students: Combinations, prevalences and risk profiles. *Drug Education Prevention & Policy, 9*, 355–365.

Smith, K. (1992). Suicidal behavior in children and adolescents. In W. R. Reynolds (Ed.), *Internalizing disorders in children and adolescents* (pp. 255–282). New York: Wiley.

Smith, P. K., Mahdavi, J., Carvalho, M., Fisher, S., Russell, S., & Tippett, N. (2008), Cyberbullying: its nature and impact in secondary school pupils. *Journal of Child Psychology and Psychiatry, 49*, 376–385.

Smith, R. G., & Churchill, R. M. (2002). Identification of environmental determinants of behavior disorders through functional analysis of precursor behaviors. *Journal of Applied Behavior Analysis, 35*, 125–136.

Smith, T. B., McCullough, M. E., & Poll, J. (2003). Religiousness and depression: Evidence for a main effect and the moderating influence of stressful life events. *Psychological Bulletin, 129*, 614–636.

Smucker, K. S., Kauffman, J. M., & Ball, D. W. (1996). School-related problems of special education foster care students with emotional or behavioral disorders: Comparison to other groups. *Journal of Emotional and Behavioral Disorders, 4*, 30–39.

Snell, M. E., & Brown, F. (2006). *Instruction of students with severe disabilities* (6th ed.). Upper Saddle River, NJ: Prentice Hall.

Snider, V. E. (2006). *Myths and misconceptions about teaching: What really happens in the classroom*. Lanham, MD: Rowman & Littlefield.

Snyder, J. M. (2001). *AD/HD & driving. A guide for parents of teens with AD/HD*. Whitefish, MT: CHAAD. Also retrieved from www.whitefishconsultants.com

Specter, M. (2009). *Denialism: How irrational thinking hinders scientific progress, harms the planet, and threatens our lives*. New York, NY: Penguin.

Spencer, T., Biederman, J., & Wilens, T. (2002). Attention-deficit/hyperactivity disorder. In S. Kutcher (Ed.), *Practical child and adolescent psychopharmacology* (pp. 230–264). New York: Cambridge University Press.

Spergel, I. A. (1995). *The youth gang problem: A community approach*. New York: Oxford University Press.

Spergel, I. A. (2007). *Reducing youth gang violence*. New York, NY: Rowman & Littlefield.

Spergel, I. A., Wa, K. M., & Sosa, R. V. (2006). The comprehensive, community-wide, gang program model: Success and failure. In J. F. Short and L. A. Hughes (Eds.), *Studying youth gangs* (pp. 203–224). Lanham, MD: AltaMira Press.

Spirito, A., & Overholser, J. C. (Eds.). (2003). *Evaluating and treating adolescent suicide attempters: From research to practice*. New York, NY: Academic Press.

Sprafkin, J., Gadow, K. D., & Adelman, R. (1992). *Television and the exceptional child: A forgotten audience*. Hillsdale, NJ: Erlbaum.

Sprague, J. R., Jolivette, K., & Nelson, C. M. (2014). Applying positive behavioral interventions and supports. In H. M. Walker & F. M. Gresham (Eds.), *Handbook of evidence-based practices for emotional and behavioral disorders: Applications in schools* (pp. 261–276). New York, NY: Guilford.

Sprick, R. S., & Howard, L. M. (1995). *The teacher's encyclopedia of behavior management*. Longmont, CO: Sopris West.

Sridhar, D., & Vaughn, S. (2001). Social functioning of students with learning disabilities. In D. P. Hallahan & B. K. Keogh (Eds), *Research and global perspectives in learning disabilities: Essays in honor of William M. Cruickshank* (pp. 65–91). Mahwah, NJ: Erlbaum.

Sroufe, L. A., Steucher, H. U., & Stutzer, W. (1973). The functional significance of autistic behaviors for the psychotic child. *Journal of Abnormal Child Psychology, 1*, 225–240.

St. George, D. (2007, June 19). Getting lost in the great indoors: Many adults worry about children losing touch with nature. *The Washington Post*, A1, A10.

St. George, D. (2011, October 18). He wants kids in class—not in court. *Washington Post*, C1, C4.

Stage, S. A., & Quiroz, D. R. (1997). A meta-analysis of interventions to decrease disruptive classroom behavior in public education settings. *School Psychology Review, 26*, 333–368.

Stark, K. D., Ostrander, R., Kurowski, C. A., Swearer, S., & Bowen, B. (1995). Affective and mood disorders. In M. Hersen & R. T. Ammerman (Eds.), *Advanced abnormal child psychology* (pp. 253–282). Hillsdale, NJ: Erlbaum.

Stayer, C., Sporn, A., Gogtay, N., Tossell, J., Lenane, M., Gochman, P., & Rapoport, J. L. (2004). Looking for childhood schizophrenia: Case series of false positives. *Journal of the American Academy of Child and Adolescent Psychiatry, 43*, 1026–1029.

Steege, M. W., & Brown-Chidsey, R. (2005). Functional behavioral assessment: The cornerstone of effective problem solving.

In R. Brown-Chidsey (Ed.), *Assessment for intervention: A problem solving approach* (pp. 131–154). New York: Guilford.

Steele, R. G., Forehand, R., Armistead, L., & Brody, G. (1995). Predicting alcohol and drug use in early adulthood: The role of internalizing and externalizing behavior problems in early adolescence. *American Journal of Orthopsychiatry, 65,* 380–388.

Steinberg, L., & Avenevoli, S. (1998). Disengagement from school and problem behavior in adolescence: A developmental–contextual analysis of the influences of family and part-time work. In R. Jessor (Ed.), *New perspectives on adolescent risk behavior* (pp. 392–424). New York: Cambridge University Press.

Steiner, H. (1997). Practice parameters for the assessment and treatment of children and adolescents with conduct disorder. *Journal of the American Academy of Child and Adolescent Psychiatry, Supplement, 36*(10), 122S–139S.

Sternberg, R. J., & Grigorenko, E. L. (2002). Difference scores in the identification of children with learning disabilities: It's time to use a different method. *Journal of School Psychology, 40,* 65–83.

Stetter, G. M. T. (1995). *The effects of pre-correction on cafeteria behavior.* Unpublished manuscript, University of Virginia, Charlottesville.

Stevenson-Hinde, J., & Shouldice, A. (1995). 4.5 to 7 years: Fearful behaviour, fears and worries. *Journal of Child Psychology and Psychiatry, 36,* 1027–1038.

Stichter, J. P., Conroy, M. A., & Kauffman, J. M. (2008). *An introduction to students with high-incidence disabilities.* Upper Saddle River, NJ: Merrill/Prentice Hall.

Stokes, T. F., & Osnes, P. G. (1991). Honesty, lying, and cheating: Their elaboration and management. In G. Stoner, M. R. Shinn, & H. M. Walker (Eds.), *Interventions for achievement and behavior problems* (pp. 617–631). Silver Spring, MD: National Association of School Psychologists.

Stouthamer-Loeber, M., & Loeber, R. (1986). Boys who lie. *Journal of Abnormal Child Psychology, 14,* 551–564.

Strain, P. S., Odom, S. L., & McConnell, S. (1984). Promoting social reciprocity of exceptional children: Identification, target behavior selection, and intervention. *Remedial and Special Education, 5*(1), 21–28.

Strain, P. S., & Timm, M. A. (2001). Remediation and prevention of aggression: An evaluation of the Regional Intervention Program over a quarter century. *Behavioral Disorders, 26,* 297–313.

Strand, P. S., Barnes-Holmes, Y., & Barnes-Holmes, D. (2003). Educating the whole child: Implications of behaviorism as a science of meaning. *Behavioral Education, 12,* 103–117.

Stribling, F. T. (1842). Physician and superintendent's report. In *Annual Reports to the Court of Directors of the Western Lunatic Asylum to the Legislature of Virginia* (pp. 1–70). Richmond, VA: Shepherd & Conlin.

Striegel-Moore, R. H., Dohm, F. A., Kraemer, H. C., Taylor, C. B., Daniels, S., Crawford, P. B., et al. (2003). Eating disorders in white and black women. *American Journal of Psychiatry, 160,* 1326–1331.

Stubblefield, A. (2011). Sound and fury: When opposition to facilitated communication functions as hate speech. *Disability Studies Quarterly, 31*(4), accessed November 1, 2011 at http://dsq-sds.org/article/view/1729/1777.

Sturmey, P. (2007). Psychosocial and mental status assessment. In J. W. Jacobson, J. A. Mulick, & J. Rojahn (Eds.), *Handbook of intellectual and developmental disabilities* (pp. 295–315). New York, NY: Springer.

Substance Abuse and Mental Health Services Administration. (2010). *Results from the 2009 National Survey on Drug Use and Health: Volume I. Summary of National Findings.* Office of Applied Studies, NSDUH Series H-38A, HHS Publication No. SMA 10-4856Findings. Rockville, MD.

Sugai, G., & Colvin, G. (1997). Debriefing: A transition step for promoting acceptable behavior. *Education and Treatment of Children, 20,* 209–221.

Sugai, G., & Horner, R. (2006). A promising approach for expanding and sustaining school-wide positive behavior support. *School Psychology Review, 35,* 245–259.

Sugai, G., Horner, R. H., & Gresham, F. M. (2002). Behaviorally effective school environments. In M. R. Shinn, H. Walker, & G. Stoner (Eds.), *Interventions for achievement and behavior problems II: Preventative and remedial approaches* (pp. 315–350). Bethesda, MD: National Association of School Psychologists.

Sugai, G., Horner, R. H., & Sprague, J. R. (1999). Functional assessment-based behavior support planning: Research to practice. *Behavioral Disorders, 24,* 253–257.

Sugai, G., & Lewis, T. J. (2004). Social skills instruction in the classroom. In C. B. Darch & E. J. Kame'enui (Eds.), *Instructional classroom management: A positive approach to behavior management* (2nd ed., pp. 152–173). White Plains, NY: Longman.

Suhay, L. (2007, June 16). Va. Tech lesson: What families need to help. *Washington Post,* A15.

Sukhodolsky, D. G., & Butter, E. M. (2007). Social skills training for children with intellectual disabilities. In J. W. Jacobson, J. A. Mulick, & J. Rojahn (Eds.), *Handbook of intellectual and developmental disabilities* (pp. 601–618). New York: Springer.

Sutherland, K. S., & Conroy, M. (2010). Preventing problem behavior in young children: The role of teacher-child interactions. In H. Ricking & G. C. Schulze (Eds.), *Förderbedarf in der emotionalen und sozialen Entwicklung: Prävention, Interdisziplinarität, und Professionalisierung* (pp. 189–197). Bad Heilbrunn, Germany: Klinkhardt.

Sutphen, R. D., Ford, J. P., & Flaherty, C. (2010). Truancy interventions: A review of the research literature. *Research on Social Work Practice, 20,* 161–171.

Swan, A. J., Cummings, C. M., Caporino, N. E., & Kendall, P. C. (2014). Evidence-based intervention approaches for students with anxiety and related disorders. In H. M. Walker & F. M. Gresham (Eds.), *Handbook of evidence-based practices for emotional and behavioral disorders: Applications in schools* (pp. 324–344). New York, NY: Guilford.

Sweeney, D. P., & Hoffman, C. D. (2004). Research issues in autism spectrum disorders. In R. B. Rutherford, M. M. Quinn,

& S. R. Mathur (Eds.). *Handbook of research in emotional and behavioral disorders* (pp. 302–318). New York: Guilford.

Talbott, E., & Callahan, K. (1997). Antisocial girls and the development of disruptive behavior disorders. In J. W. Lloyd, E. J. Kame'enui, & D. Chard (Eds.), *Issues in educating students with disabilities* (pp. 305–322). Mahwah, NJ: Erlbaum.

Talbott, E., Celinska, D., Simpson, J., & Coe, M. G. (2002). "Somebody else making somebody else fight": Aggression and the social context among urban adolescent girls. *Exceptionality, 10*, 203–220.

Talbott, E., & Thiede, K. (1999). Pathways to antisocial behavior among adolescent girls. *Journal of Emotional and Behavioral Disorders, 7*, 31–39.

Tankersley, M., & Landrum, T. J. (1997). Comorbidity of emotional and behavioral disorders. In J. W. Lloyd, E. J. Kame'enui, & D. Chard (Eds.), *Issues in educating students with disabilities* (pp. 153–173). Mahwah, NJ: Erlbaum.

Tankersley, M., Landrum, T. J., & Cook, B. G. (2004). How research informs practice in the field of emotional and behavioral disorders. In R. B. Rutherford, M. M. Quinn, & S. R. Mathur (Eds.), *Handbook of research in emotional and behavioral disorders* (pp. 98–114). New York, NY: Guilford.

Tanner, E. M., & Finn-Stevenson, M. (2002). Nutrition and brain development: Social policy implications. *American Journal of Orthopsychiatry, 72*, 182–193.

Tapp, J., Wehby, J., & Ellis, D. (1995). A multiple option observation system for experimental studies: MOOSES. *Behavior Research Methods, Instruments, & Computers, 27*(1), 25–31.

Tapscott, M., Frick, P. J., Wootton, J. M., & Kruh, I. (1996). The intergenerational link to antisocial behavior: Effects of paternal contact. *Journal of Child and Family Studies, 5*, 229–240.

Tattum, D. P., & Lane, D. A. (Eds.). (1989). *Bullying in schools*. Stoke-on-Trent, England: Trentham.

Tavris, Carol (2003). The widening scientist-practitioner gap: A view from the bridge. In S. O. Lilienfeld, J. M. Lohr, & S. J. Lynn (Eds.), *Science and pseudoscience in contemporary clinical psychology*. New York: Guilford Press.

Taylor, C. A., Manganello, J. A., Lee, S. J., & Rice, J. C. (2010). Mothers' spanking of 3-year-old children and subsequent risk of children's aggressive behavior. *Pediatrics, 125*, 1057–1065.

Taylor, P. D., & Turner, R. K. (1975). A clinical trial of continuous, intermittent, and overlearning "bell and pad" treatments for nocturnal enuresis. *Behaviour Research and Therapy, 13*, 281–293.

Taylor, R. L. (2006). *Assessment of exceptional students: Educational and psychological procedures* (7th ed.). Boston: Allyn & Bacon.

Taylor, R. L. (2009). *Assessment of exceptional students: Educational and psychological procedures* (8th ed.). Upper Saddle River, NJ: Pearson.

Taylor-Richardson, K. D., Heflinger, C. A., & Brown, T. N. (2006). Experience of strain among different types of caregivers responsible for children with serious emotional and behavioral disorders. *Journal of Emotional and Behavioral Disorders, 14*, 157–168.

Terr, L. C. (1995). Childhood traumas: An outline and overview. In G. S. Everly & J. M. Lating (Eds.), *Psychotraumatology: Key papers and core concepts in post-traumatic stress* (pp. 301–320). New York: Plenum.

Thomas, A., & Chess, S. (1984). Genesis and evolution of behavioral disorders: From infancy to early adult life. *American Journal of Psychiatry, 141*, 1–9.

Thomas, A., Chess, S., & Birch, H. G. (1968). *Temperament and behavior disorders in children*. New York, NY: New York University Press.

Thompson, R. A., & Wilcox, B. L. (1995). Child maltreatment research: Federal support and policy issues. *American Psychologist, 50*, 789–793.

Thompson, S. J., & Thurlow, M. L. (2001). Participation of students with disabilities in statewide assessment systems. *Assessment for Effective Intervention, 26*(2), 5–8.

Thompson, S. J., Thurlow, M. L., Esler, A., & Whetsone, P. J. (2001). Addressing standards and assessments on the IEP. *Assessment for Effective Intervention, 26*(2), 77–84.

Thunfors, P., & Cornell, D. (2008). The popularity of middle school bullies. *Journal of School Violence, 7*, 65–82.

Thurlow, M. L., & Quenemoen, R. F. (2017). Standards-based reform and students with disabilities. In J. M. Kauffman, D. P. Hallahan, & P. C. Pullen (Eds.), *Handbook of special education* (2nd ed.). New York: Taylor & Francis.

Tobin, T. J., & Sugai, G. M. (1999). Using sixth-grade school records to predict school violence, chronic discipline problems, and high school outcomes. *Journal of Emotional and Behavioral Disorders, 7*, 40–53.

Tolan, P. H. (1987). Implications of age of onset for delinquency risk. *Journal of Abnormal Child Psychology, 15*, 47–65.

Tolan, P. H., & Thomas, P. (1995). The implications of age of onset for delinquency risk. II: Longitudinal data. *Journal of Abnormal Child Psychology, 23*, 157–181.

Torres, J. B., Solberg, V. S. H., & Carlstrom, A. M. (2002). The myth of sameness among Latino men and their machismo. *American Journal of Orthopsychiatry, 72*, 163–81.

Tournaki, N., & Criscitiello, E. (2003). Using peer tutoring as a successful part of behavior management. *Teaching Exceptional Children, 36*(2), 22–29.

Treasure, J., Claudino, A. M., & Zucker, N. (2010). Eating disorders. *The Lancet, 375*, 583–593.

Trenholm, C., Devaney, B., Fortson, K., Quay, L., Wheeler, J., & Clark, M. (2007). *Impacts of Four Title V, Section 510 Abstinence Education Programs: Final Report*. Trenton, NJ: Mathematica Policy Research.

Trout, A., Epstein, M. H., Mickelson, W. T., Nelson, J. R., & Lewis, L. M. (2003). Effects of a reading intervention for kindergarten students at-risk of emotional disturbance and reading deficits. *Behavioral Disorders, 28*, 313–321.

Trout, A. L., Nordness, P. D., Pierce, C. D., & Epstein, M. H. (2003). Research on the academic status of children and youth with emotional and behavioral disorders: A review of the literature from 1961–2000. *Journal of Emotional and Behavioral Disorders, 11*, 198–210.

Turner, S. M., Beidel, D. C., Roberson-Nay, R., & Tervo, K. (2003). Parenting behaviors in parents with anxiety disorders. *Behaviour Research and Therapy, 41*, 541–554.

Udry, F. R., & Bearman, P. S. (1998). New methods for new research on adolescent sexual behavior. In R. Jessor (Ed.), *New perspectives on adolescent risk behavior* (pp. 242–269). New York: Cambridge University Press.

Umbreit, M. S., Greenwood, J., & Coates, R. (2000). *Restorative justice and mediation series*. Washington, D.C.: U.S. Department of Justice, Office for Victims of Crime.

Ungar, M. (2011). The social ecology of resilience: Addressing contextual and cultural ambiguity of a nascent construct. *American Journal of Orthopsychiatry, 81*, 1–17.

Unruh, D., & Bullis, M. (2005). Female and male juvenile offenders with disabilities: Differences in the barriers to their transition to the community. *Behavioral Disorders, 30*, 105–117.

Unruh, D. K., & Murray, C. J. (2014). Improving the transition outcomes for students with emotional and behavioral disorders. In H. M. Walker & F. M. Gresham (Eds.), *Handbook of evidence-based practices for emotional and behavioral disorders: Applications in schools* (pp. 410–431). New York, NY: Guilford.

Upadhyaya, H. P., Brady, K. T., Wharton, M., & Liao, J. (2003). Psychiatric disorders and cigarette smoking among child and adolescent psychiatry inpatients. *American Journal of Addictions, 12*, 144–152.

Urbach, B. J., Reynolds, K. M., & Yacoubian, G. S., Jr. (2002). Exploring the relationship between race and ecstasy involvement among a sample of arrestees. *Journal of Ethnicity in Substance Abuse, 1*, 49–61.

U. S. Department of Education. (2009). 28th Annual report to Congress on the implementation of the *Individuals with Disabilities Education Act*, 2006. Washington, DC: Author.

U.S. Department of Health and Human Services. (2001). *Report of the Surgeon General's conference on children's mental health: A national action agenda*. Washington, DC: Author.

U.S. Department of Health and Human Services, Administration for Children and Families, Administration on Children, Youth and Families, Children's Bureau (2015). *Child maltreatment 2013*. Available from http://www.acf.hhs.gov/programs/cb/research-data-technology/statistics-research/child-maltre

Vance, T. D. (2016). *Hillbilly elegy: A memoir of a family and culture in crisis*. New York, NY: HarperCollins.

van Lier, P. A. C., Vitaro, F., Barker, E. D., Koot, H. M., & Tremblay, R. E. (2009). Developmental links between trajectories of physical violence, vandalism, theft, and alcohol-drug use from childhood to adolescence. *Journal of Abnormal Child Psychology, 37*, 481–492.

Vasquez, J. A. (1998, Winter). Dinstinctive traits of Hispanic students. *Prevention Researcher*, pp. 1–4.

Vaughn, M. G., Fu, Q., DeLisi, M., Wright, J. P., Beaver, K. M., Perron, B. E., & Howard, M. O. (2010). Prevalence and correlates of fire-setting in the United States: Results from the National Epidemiological Survey on Alcohol and Related Conditions. *Comprehensive Psychiatry, 51*, 217–223.

Vaughn, S., Kim, A., Sloan, C. V. M., Hughes, M. T., Elbaum, B., & Sridhar, D. (2003). Social skills interventions for young children with disabilities. *Remedial and Special Education, 24*, 2–15.

Vermeiren, R., Schwab-Stone, M., Ruchkin, V., De Clippele, A., & Deboutte, D. (2002). Predicting recidivism in delinquent adolescents from psychological and psychiatric assessment. *Comprehensive Psychiatry, 43*, 142–149.

Viana, A. G., Beidel, D. C., & Rabian, B. (2009). Selective mutism: A review and integration of the last 15 years. *Clinical Psychology Review, 29*, 59–67.

Vivian, D., Fischel, J. E., & Liebert, R. M. (1986). Effect of "wet nights" on daytime behavior during concurrent treatment of enuresis and conduct problems. *Journal of Behavior Therapy and Experimental Psychiatry, 17*, 301–303.

Volpe, R. J., & Briesch, A. M. (2012). Generalizability and dependability of single-item and multiple-item direct behavior rating scales for engagement and disruptive behavior. *School Psychology Review, 41*(3), 246.

Volz, C., & Heyman, I. (2007). Case series: Transformation obsession in young people with obsessive-compulsive disorder. *Journal of the Academy of Child and Adolescent Psychiatry, 46*, 766–772.

Von Ranson, K. M., & Wallace, L. M. (2014). Eating disorders. In E. J. Mash & R. A. Barkley (Eds.). *Child psychopathology* (2nd ed., pp. 801–847). New York, NY: Guilford.

Wagner, M., Friend, M., Bursuck, W. D., Kutash, K., Duchnowski, A. J., Sumi, W. C., et al. (2006). Educating students with emotional disturbances: A national perspective on school programs and services. *Journal of Emotional and Behavioral Disorders, 13*(2), 79–96.

Waldman, I. D., & Lillenfeld, S. O. (1995). Diagnosis and classification. In M. Hersen & R. T. Ammerman (Eds.), *Advanced abnormal child psychology* (pp. 21–36). Hillsdale, NJ: Erlbaum.

Walker, H. M. (1986). The Assessment for Integration into Mainstream Settings (AIMS) assessment system: Rationale, instruments, procedures, and outcomes. *Journal of Clinical Child Psychology, 15*, 55–63.

Walker, H. M. (1995). *The acting-out child: Coping with classroom disruption* (2nd ed.). Longmont, CO: Sopris West.

Walker, H. M. (2003, February 20). *Comments on accepting the Outstanding Leadership Award from the Midwest Symposium for Leadership in Behavior Disorders*. Kansas City, KS: Author.

Walker, H. M., Block-Pedego, A., Todis, B., & Severson, H. (1991). *School Archival Records Search (SARS)*. Longmont, CO: Sopris West.

Walker, H. M., Forness, S. R., Kauffman, J. M., Epstein, M. H., Gresham, F. M., Nelson, C. M., & Strain, P. S. (1998). Macrosocial validation: Referencing outcomes in behavioral disorders to societal issues and problems. *Behavioral Disorders, 24*, 7–18.

Walker, H. M., & Gresham, F. M. (Eds.). (2014). *Handbook of evidence-based practices for emotional and behavioral disorders: Applications in schools*. New York, NY: Guilford.

Walker, H. M., Kavanagh, K., Stiller, B., Golly, A., Severson, H., & Feil, E. G. (1998). First Step to Success: An early intervention approach for preventing school antisocial behavior. *Journal of Emotional and Behavioral Disorders, 6*, 66–80.

Walker, H. M., & McConnell, S. (1988). *The Walker–McConnell Scale of Social Competence and School Adjustment: A social skills rating scale for teachers.* Austin, TX: Pro-Ed.

Walker, H. M., McConnell, S., Holmes, D., Todis, B., Walker, J., & Golden, N. (1983). *The Walker social skills curriculum: The ACCEPTS program.* Austin, TX: Pro-Ed.

Walker, H. M., Nishioka, V. M., Zeller, R., Severson, H. H., & Feil, E. G. (2000). Causal factors and potential solutions for the persistent under-identification of students having emotional or behavioral disorders in the context of schooling. *Assessment for Effective Intervention, 26*(1), 29–39.

Walker, H. M., Ramsey, E., & Gresham, F. M. (2004). *Antisocial behavior in school: Strategies and best practices* (2nd ed.). Pacific Grove, CA: Brooks/Cole.

Walker, H. M., & Rankin, R. (1983). Assessing the behavioral expectations and demands of less restrictive settings. *School Psychology Review, 12*, 274–284.

Walker, H. M., Schwarz, I. E., Nippold, M. A., Irvin, L. K., & Noell, J. W. (1994). Social skills in school-age children and youth: Issues and best practices in assessment and intervention. *Topics in Language Disorders, 14*(3), 70–82.

Walker, H. M., & Severson, H. H. (1990). *Systematic Screening for Behavior Disorders (SSBD): A multiple gating procedure.* Longmont, CO: Sopris West.

Walker, H. M., Severson, H. H., & Feil, E. G. (1994). *The Early Screening Project: A proven child-find process.* Longmont, CO: Sopris West.

Walker, H. M., Severson, H. H., & Feil, E. G. (2014). *Systematic screening for behavior disorders (SSBD)* (2nd ed.). Eugene, OR: Pacific Northwest Publishing.

Walker, H. M., Severson, H. H., Naquin, G., D'Atrio, C., Feil, E., Hawken, L., & Sabey, C. (2010). Implementing universal screening systems within an RtI/PBS context (pp. 96–120). In B. Doll, W. Pfohl, & J. Yoon (Eds.), *Handbook of youth prevention science.* New York, NY: Routledge.

Walker, H. M., Severson, H. H., Nicholson, F., Kehle, T., Jenson, W. R., & Clark, E. (1994). Replication of the Systematic Screening for Behavior Disorders (SSBD) procedure for the identification of at-risk children. *Journal of Emotional and Behavioral Disorders, 2*, 66–77.

Walker, H. M., Severson, H. H., Seeley, J. R., Feil, E. G., Small, J., Golly, A. M., … Forness, S. R. (2014). The evidence base of the First Step Intervention for preventing emerging antisocial behavior patterns. In H. M. Walker & F. M. Gresham (Eds.), *Handbook of evidence-based practices for emotional and behavioral disorders: Applications in schools* (pp. 518–533). New York, NY: Guilford.

Walker, H. M., Severson, H., Stiller, B., Williams, G., Haring, N., Shinn, M., & Todis, B. (1988). Systematic screening of pupils in the elementary age range at risk for behavior disorders: Development and trial testing of a multiple gating model. *Remedial and Special Education, 9*(3), 8–20.

Walker, H. M., & Shinn, M. R. (2002). Structuring school-based interventions to achieve integrated primary, secondary and tertiary prevention goals for safe and effective schools. In M. R. Shinn, H. M. Walker, & G. Stoner (Eds.), *Interventions for academic and behavior problems II: Preventive and remedial approaches* (pp. 1–26). Bethesda, MD: National Association of School Psychologists.

Walker, H. M., Shinn, M. R., O'Neill, R. E., & Ramsey, E. (1987). A longitudinal assessment of the development of antisocial behavior in boys: Rationale, methodology, and first year results. *Remedial and Special Education, 8*(4), 7–16.

Walker, H. M., & Sprague, J. R. (1999). The path to school failure, delinquency, and violence: Causal factors and some potential solutions. *Interventions in School and Clinic, 35*, 67–73.

Walker, H. M., & Sprague, J. R. (2007). Early, evidence-based intervention with school-based behavior disorders: Key issues, continuing challenges, and promising practices. In J. B. Crockett, M. M. Gerber, & T. J. Landrum (Eds.), *Achieving the radical reform of special education: Essays in honor of James M. Kauffman* (pp. 37–58). Mahwah, NJ: Erlbaum.

Walker, H. M., Yell, M. L., & Murray, C. M. (2014). Identifying EBD students in the context of schooling using the Federal ED definition: Where we've been, and where we need to go. In P. Garner, J. M. Kauffman, & J. G. Elliott (Eds.), *The Sage handbook of emotional and behavioral difficulties* (2nd ed.) (pp. 55–68). London, U.K.: Sage.

Walker, H. M., Zeller, R. W., Close, D. W., Webber, J., & Gresham, F. (1999). The present unwrapped: Change and challenge in the field of behavior disorders. *Behavioral Disorders, 24*, 293–304.

Walkup, J. T. (2002). Tic disorders and Tourette's syndrome. In S. Kutcher (Ed.), *Practical child and adolescent psychopharmacology* (pp. 382–409). New York, NY: Cambridge University Press.

Wallerstein, J. S. (1987). Children of divorce: Report of a ten-year follow-up of early latency-age children. *American Journal of Orthopsychiatry, 57*, 199–211.

Wang, P. S., Berglund, P., Olfson, M., Pincus, H. A., Wells, K. B., & Kessler, R. C. (2005). Failure and delay in initial treatment contact after first onset of mental disorders in the national comorbidity survey replication. *Archives of General Psychiatry, 62*, 603–613.

Wang, P. S., Lane, M., Olfson, M., Pincus, H. A., Wells, K. B., & Kessler, R. C. (2005). Twelve-month use of mental health services in the United States. *Archives of General Psychiatry, 62*, 629–640.

Wang, S. (2007, July 24). Shock value. *The Washington Post*, F1, F5.

Warner, J. (2010). *We've got issues: Children and parents in the age of medication.* New York, NY: Riverhead Books.

Warren, J. S., Edmonson, H. M., Griggs, P., Lassen, S. R., McCart, A., Turnbull, A., & Sailor, W. (2003). Urban applications of school-wide positive behavior support: Critical issues and lessons learned. *Journal of Positive Behavior Interventions, 5*, 80–91.

Waslick, B. D., Kandel, R., & Kakouros, A. (2002). Depression in children and adolescents. In D. Shaffer, & B. D. Waslick, (Eds.), *The many faces of depression in children and adolescents* (pp. 1–36). Washington, D.C.: American Psychiatric Publishing.

Wasserstein, J., Wolf, L. E., & Lefever, F. F. (Eds.). (2001). *Adult attention deficit disorder: Brain mechanisms and life outcomes*. New York: New York Academy of Sciences.

Webb, M. W., II. (1983). A scale for evaluating standardized reading tests, with results for *Nelson-Denny, Iowa*, and *Stanford*. *Journal of Reading, 26*(5), 424–429.

Webber, J., & Scheuermann, B. (1991). Accentuate the positive. Eliminate the negative. *Teaching Exceptional Children, 24*, 13–19.

Webster-Stratton, C., & Dahl, R. W. (1995). Conduct disorder. In M. Hersen & R. T. Ammerman (Eds.), *Advanced abnormal child psychology* (pp. 333–352). Hillsdale, NJ: Erlbaum.

Wehby, J. H., & Lane, K. L. (Eds.). (2003). Special series: Academic status of children with emotional disturbance. *Journal of Emotional and Behavioral Disorders, 11*(4), Whole issue.

Wehby, J. H., Symons, F. J., & Canale, J. A. (1998). Teaching practices in classrooms for students with emotional and behavioral disorders: Discrepancies between recommendations and observations. *Behavioral Disorders, 24*, 51–56.

Wehmeyer, M. L. (2001). Assessment in self-determination: Guiding instruction and transition planning. *Assessment for Effective Intervention, 26*(4), 41–49.

Weiner, J. (1999). *Time, love, memory: A great biologist and his quest for the origins of behavior*. New York, NY: Knopf.

Weiss, R. (1995, June 13). Gene studies fuel the nature-nurture debate. *The Washington Post (Health section)*, pp. 11, 13.

Weiss, R. (1996, January 9). The perfect fat pill is still a long weigh off: As discoveries mount, so does evidence of the body's complexity. *The Washington Post (Health section)*, p. 11.

Wentzel, K. R., & Asher, S. R. (1995). The academic lives of neglected, rejected, and controversial children. *Child Development, 66*, 754–763.

Werner, E. E. (1999). Risk and protective factors in the lives of children with high-incidence disabilities. In R. Gallimore, L. P. Bernheimer, D. L. MacMillan, D. L. Speece, & S. Vaughn (Eds.), *Developmental perspectives on children with high-incidence disabilities* (pp. 15–31). Mahwah, NJ: Erlbaum.

Werry, J. S. (1986a). Biological factors. In H. C. Quay & J. S. Werry (Eds.), *Psychopathological disorders of childhood* (3rd ed., pp. 294–331). New York: Wiley.

Werry, J. S. (1986b). Organic and substance use disorders. In H. C. Quay & J. S. Werry (Eds.), *Psychopathological disorders of childhood* (3rd ed., pp. 211–230). New York: Wiley.

Werry, J. S. (1986c). Physical illness, symptoms and allied disorders. In H. C. Quay & J. S. Werry (Eds.), *Psychopathological disorders of childhood* (3rd ed., pp. 232–293). New York: Wiley.

West, B. A., Swahn, M. H., & McCarty, F. (2010). Children at risk for suicide attempt and attempt-related injuries: Findings from the 2007 Youth Risk Behavior Survey. *Western Journal of Emergency Medicine, 11*, 257–263.

Weyandt, L. L. (2007). *An ADHD primer* (2nd ed.). Mahwah, NJ: Erlbaum.

Whalen, C. K. (1983). Hyperactivity, learning problems, and the attention deficit disorders. In T. H. Ollendick & M. Hersen (Eds.), *Handbook of child psychopathology* (pp. 151–199). New York, NY: Plenum.

Whalen, C. K., & Henker, B. (1991). Social impact of stimulant treatment for hyperactive children. *Journal of Learning Disabilities, 24*, 231–241.

Wheeler, J. J., & Mayton, M. R. (2014). The integrity of interventions in social emotional skill development for students with emotional and behavioral disorders. In P. Garner, J. M. Kauffman, & J. G. Elliott (Eds.), *The Sage handbook of emotional and behavioral difficulties* (2nd ed.) (pp. 385–398). London, U.K.: Sage.

Whelan, R. J. (1999). Historical perspective. In L. M. Bullock & R. A. Gable (Eds.), *Educating students with emotional and behavioral disorders: Historical perspective and future directions* (pp. 3–36). Reston, VA: Council for Children with Behavioral Disorders.

Whelan, R. J. (Ed.). (1998). *Emotional and behavioral disorders: A 25-year focus*. Denver, CO: Love.

White, K. K. (2006). Restorative justice programming. In B. Sims & P. Preston (Eds.), *Handbook of juvenile justice: Theory and practice* (pp. 509–520). Boca Raton, FL: Taylor & Francis.

Whitlock, J. (2010) Self-injurious behavior in adolescents. *PLoS Med 7*(5): e1000240. doi:10.1371/journal.pmed.1000240.

Wickman, E. K. (1929). *Children's behavior and teachers' attitudes*. New York: Commonwealth Fund, Division of Publications.

Wilcox, B. (Ed.). (2010). *When marriage disappears*. Charlottesville, VA: National Marriage Project and the Institute for American Values.

Wilens, T. E., Biederman, J., & Spencer, T. J. (2002). Attention deficit/hyperactivity disorder across the lifespan. *Annual Review of Medicine, 53*, 113–131.

Wiley, A. L. (2015). Place values: What moral psychology can tell us about the full inclusion debate in special education. In B. D. Bateman, J. W. Lloyd, & M. Tankersley (Eds.), *Enduring issues in special education: Personal perspectives* (pp. 232–250). New York, NY: Routledge.

Wiley, A L., Brigham, F. J., Kauffman, J. M., & Bogan, J. E. (2013). Disproportionate poverty, conservatism, and the disproportionate identification of minority students with emotional and behavioral disorders. *Education and Treatment of Children, 36*(4), 29–50.

Wiley, A. L., Kauffman, J. M., & Plageman, K. (2015). Conservatism and the under-identification of students with emotional and behavioral disorders in special education. *Exceptionality, 22*, 237–251.

Wiley, A. L., & Siperstein, G. N. (2011). Seeing red, feeling blue: The impact of state political leaning on state identification rates for emotional disturbance. *Behavioral Disorders, 36*, 195–207.

Williams, K. E., & Foxx, R. M. (2016). The gluten-free, casein-free diet. In R. M. Foxx & J. A. Mulick (Eds.), *Controversial therapies for autism and intellectual disabilities: Fad, fashion, and science in professional practice* (2nd ed.) (pp. 410–421). New York, NY: Taylor & Francis.

Williams, R. L. M. (1985). Children's stealing: A review of theft-control procedures for parents and teachers. *Remedial and Special Education, 6*(2), 17–23.

Williams, T. C. (2007, May 28). Black culture beyond hip-hop. *The Washington Post,* A17.

Willingham, D. T. (2004, Summer). Reframing the mind. *Education Next.* Retrieved December 20, 2007, from http://www .hoover.org/publications/ednext/3398131.html.

Willingham, D. T. (2009). *Why don't students like school? A cognitive scientist answers questions about how the mind works and what it means for your classroom.* San Francisco, CA: Jossey-Bass.

Wilson, E. O. (1998). *Consilience: The unity of knowledge.* New York: Vintage.

Wilson, G. T., Becker, C. B., & Heffernan, K. (2003). Eating disorders. In E. J. Mash & R. A. Barkley (Eds.). *Child psychopathology* (2nd ed., pp. 687–715). New York, NY: Guilford.

Witt, J. C., VanDeHeyden, A. M., & Gilbertson, D. (2004). Instruction and classroom management: Prevention and intervention research. In R. B. Rutherford, M. M. Quinn, & S. R. Mathur (Eds.), *Handbook of research in emotional and behavioral disorders* (pp. 426–445). New York, NY: Guilford.

Wodarski, J. S., & Feit, M. D. (1995). *Adolescent substance abuse: An empirical-based group preventive health paradigm.* New York: Haworth.

Wolfe, V. V. (1998). Child sexual abuse. In E. J. Mash & R. A. Barkley (Eds.), *Treatment of childhood disorders* (2nd ed., pp. 545–597). New York: Guilford.

Wong, B. Y. L., & Donahue, M. (Eds.). (2002). *The social dimensions of learning disabilities: Essays in honor of Tanis Bryan.* Mahwah, NJ: Erlbaum.

Wooden, W. S., & Berkey, M. L. (1984). *Children and arson: America's middle class nightmare.* New York: Plenum.

Woodruff-Borden, J., & Leyfer, O. T. (2006). Anxiety and fear. In M. Hersen (Ed.), *Cinician's handbook of child behavioral assessment* (pp. 267–290). Burlington, MA: Elsevier Academic Press.

Xie, H., Cairns, R. B., & Cairns, B. D. (1999). Social networks and social configurations in inner-city schools: Aggression, popularity, and implications for students with EBD. *Journal of Emotional and Behavioral Disorders, 7,* 147–155.

Yacoubian, G. S. (2003). Correlates of ecstasy use among students surveyed through the 1997 College Alcohol Study. *Journal of Drug Education, 33,* 61–69.

Yamamoto, J., Silva, J. A., Ferrari, M., & Nukariya, K. (1997). Culture and psychopathology. In G. Johnson-Powell, J. Yamamoto, G. E. Wyatt, & W. Arroyo (Eds.), *Transcultural child development: Psychological assessment and treatment* (pp. 34–57). New York: Wiley.

Ybarra, M. L., Diener-West, M., Markow, D., Leaf, P. J., Hamburger, M., & Boxer, P. (2008). Linkages between internet and other media violence with seriously violent behavior by youth. *Pediatrics, 122:*5, 929–937.

Yell, M. L. (2012). *The law and special education* (3rd ed.). Upper Saddle River, NJ: Merrill/Pearson.

Yell, M. L. (2016). *The law and special education* (4th ed.). Upper Saddle River, NJ: Pearson.

Yell, M. L., Bradley, R., & Shriner, J. G. (1999). The IDEA amendments of 1997: A school-wide model for conducting functional behavioral assessments and developing behavior intervention plans. *Education and Treatment of Children, 22,* 244–266.

Yell, M. L., Crockett, J. B., Shriner, J. G., & Rozalski, M. (2017). Free appropriate public education. In J. M. Kauffman, D. P. Hallahan, & P. C. Pullen (Eds.), *Handbook of special education* (2nd ed.). New York, NY: Taylor & Francis.

Yell, M. L., & Drasgow, E. (2000). Legal requirements for assessing students with emotional and behavioral disorders. *Assessment for Effective Intervention, 26*(1), 5–17.

Yell, M. L., Gatti, S. N., & Allday, R. A. (2014). Legislation, regulation, litigation, and the delivery of support services to students with emotional and behavioral disorders in school settings. In H. M. Walker & F. M. Gresham (Eds.), *Handbook of evidence-based practices for emotional and behavioral disorders* (pp. 71–85). New York: Routledge.

Yell, M. L., Katsiyannis, A., & Bradley, M. R. (2017). The Individuals with Disabilities Education Act: The evolution of special education law. In J. M. Kauffman, D. P. Hallahan, & P. C. Pullen (Eds.), *Handbook of special education* (2nd ed.). New York: Taylor & Francis.

Yell, M. L., & Plotner, A. J. (2014). Developing educationally meaningful and legally sound individual education programs. In M. L. Yell, N. B. Meadows, E. Drasgow, & J. G. Shriner (Eds.), *Evidence-based practices for educating students with emotional and behavioral disorders* (2nd ed.) (pp. 190–214). Upper Saddle River, NJ: Pearson.

Yell, M. L., & Stecker, P. M. (2003). Developing legally correct and educationally meaningful IEPs using curriculum-based measurement. *Assessment for Effective Intervention, 28*(3/4), 73–88.

Young, E. L., Sabbah, H. Y., Young, B. J., Reiser, M. L., & Richardson, M. J. (2010). Gender differences and similarities in a screening process for emotional and behavioral risks in secondary schools. *Journal of Emotional and Behavioral Disorders, 18,* 225–235.

Youngstrom, E. A., & Algorta, G. P. (2014). Pediatric bipolar disorder. In E. J. Mash & R. A. Barkley (Eds). *Child psychopathology* (3rd ed.) (pp. 264–316). New York, NY: Guilford.

Zabel, R. H., & Nigro, F. A. (1999). Juvenile offenders with behavioral disorders, learning disabilities, and no disabilities: Self-reports of personal, family, and school characteristics. *Behavioral Disorders, 25,* 22–40.

Zack, I. (1995, October 11). UVA forums to focus on roles of black males. *Charlottesville Daily Progress,* pp. B1–B2.

Zahn-Waxler, C., Shirtcliff, E. A., & Marceau, K. (2008). Disorders of childhood and adolescence: Gender and psychopathology. *Annual Review of Clinical Psychology, 4,* 275–303.

Zigler, E. F., & Finn-Stevenson, M. (1997). Policy efforts to enhance child and family life: Goals for 2010. In R. P. Weissberg, T. P. Gullotta, R. L. Hampton, B. A. Ryan, & G. R. Adams (Eds.), *Establishing preventive services* (pp. 27–60). Thousand Oaks, CA: Sage.

Zigmond, N. (2003). Where should students with disabilities receive special education services? Is one place
better than another? *The Journal of Special Education, 37*,
193–199.

Zigmond, N. (2007). Delivering special education is a two-per-
son job: A call for unconventional thinking. In J. B. Crockett,
M. M. Gerber, & T. J. Landrum (Eds.), *Achieving the radical
reform of special education: Essays in honor of James M. Kauffman*
(pp. 115–137). Mahwah, NJ: Erlbaum.

Zigmond, N. (2015). Where should students with disabilities
receive their education? In B. D. Bateman, J. W. Lloyd, & M.
Tankersley (Eds.), *Enduring issues in special education: Personal
perspectives* (pp. 198–213). New York, NY: Routledge.

Zigmond, N., & Kloo, A. (2017). General and special education are (and should be) different. In J. M. Kauffman, D. P.
Hallahan, & P. C. Pullen (Eds.), *Handbook of special education*
(2nd ed.). New York, NY: Taylor & Francis.

Zigmond, N., Kloo, A., & Volonino, V. (2009). What, where,
and how? Special education in the climate of full inclusion.
Exceptionality, 17, 189–204.

Zimmerman, F. J., & Chistakis, D. A. (2005). Children's television viewing and cognitive outcomes. *Archives of Pediatrics and
Adolescent Medicine, 159*, 619–625.

Zirpoli, T. J., & Lloyd, J. W. (1987). Understanding and managing self-injurious behavior. *Remedial and Special Education,
8*(5), 46–57.

AUTHOR INDEX

SUBJECT INDEX